A Guide and Reference with Readings

 W9-AXI-374

ready to revise?

Revising & Editing *450*
38 Revising Your Own Work *452*
39 Peer Editing *458*

need research help?

Research & Sources *464*
40 Beginning Your Research *466*
41 Finding Print and Online Sources *472*
42 Doing Field Research *478*
43 Evaluating Sources *482*
44 Annotating Sources *487*
45 Summarizing Sources *491*
46 Paraphrasing Sources *494*
47 Integrating Sources into Your Work *497*
48 Documenting Sources *501*
49 MLA Documentation and Format *503*
50 APA Documentation and Format *540*

need design help?

Media & Design *566*
51 Understanding Digital Media *568*
52 Digital Elements *577*
53 Tables, Graphs, and Infographics *584*
54 Designing Print and Online Documents *592*

need proofreading help?

Common Errors *600*
55 Capitalization *602*
56 Apostrophes *605*
57 Commas *607*
58 Comma Splices, Run-ons, and Fragments *610*
59 Subject / Verb Agreement *614*
60 Irregular Verbs *618*
61 Pronoun / Antecedent Agreement *620*
62 Pronoun Reference *622*
63 Pronoun Case *624*
64 Misplaced and Dangling Modifiers *627*
65 Parallelism *629*

need more examples?

Readings *632*
66 Narratives *634*
67 Reports *686*
68 Arguments *735*
69 Evaluations *764*
70 Causal Analyses *799*
71 Proposals *858*
72 Literary Analyses *898*
73 Rhetorical Analyses *969*

reference

reader

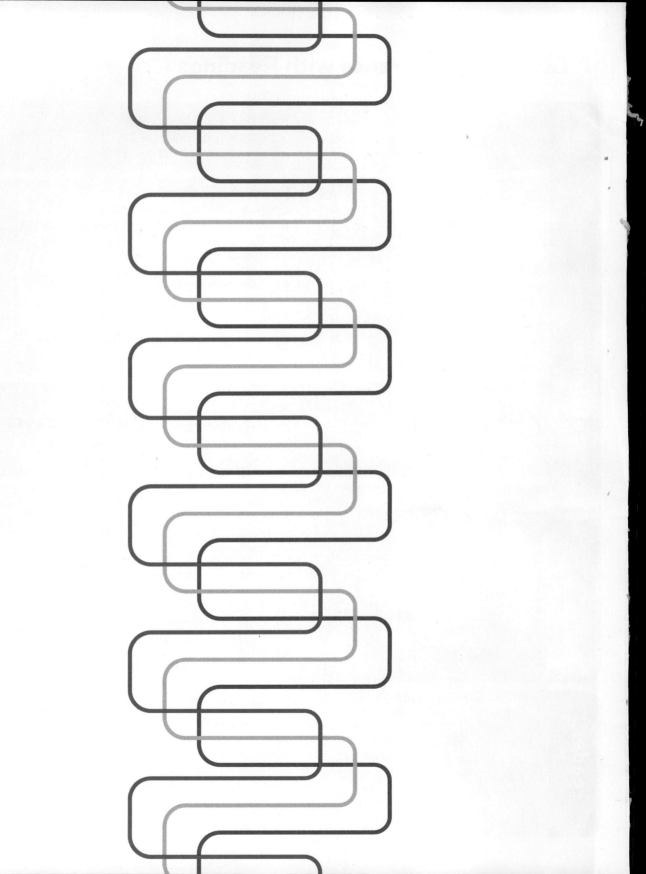

SECOND EDITION

HOW TO WRITE ANYTHING

A Guide and Reference
with Readings

John J. Ruszkiewicz

UNIVERSITY OF TEXAS AT AUSTIN

Jay T. Dolmage

UNIVERSITY OF WATERLOO

BEDFORD/ST. MARTIN'S
Boston ◆ New York

For Bedford/St. Martin's

Senior Executive Editor: Leasa Burton
Senior Development Editor: Ellen Darion
Senior Production Editor: Rosemary R. Jaffe
Assistant Production Manager: Joe Ford
Senior Marketing Manager: Molly Parke
Editorial Assistant: Alyssa Demirjian
Copyeditor: Jennifer Brett Greenstein
Indexer: Mary White
Permissions Manager: Kalina K. Ingham
Senior Art Director and Text Design: Anna Palchik
Cover Design: Marine Miller
Composition: Cenveo Publisher Services
Printing and Binding: RR Donnelley and Sons

President: Joan E. Feinberg
Editorial Director: Denise B. Wydra
Editor in Chief: Karen S. Henry
Director of Marketing: Karen R. Soeltz
Director of Production: Susan W. Brown
Associate Director, Editorial Production: Elise Kaiser
Managing Editor: Elizabeth M. Schaaf

Library of Congress Control Number: 2011934580

Manufactured in the United States of America.

6   5   4   3   2   1
f   e   d   c   b   a

For information, write: Bedford/St. Martin's, 75 Arlington Street, Boston, MA 02116 (617-399-4000)

ISBN: 978-0-312-67489-2

How to Write Anything: A Guide and Reference with Readings is not a humble title. You might wonder whether any book, especially one designed expressly as a guide for college writers, should promise so much. The simple answer is *no*; the more intriguing one is *maybe*.

What, after all, do writers do when they face an assignment? They try to grasp what the project requires; they look for examples of the genre; they wrestle with basic language and research skills. *How to Write Anything* guides college writers through these stages for their most common academic and professional assignments. In doing so, it lays out strategies to follow in any situation that requires purposeful writing.

But rarely do different writers work in the same order, and the same writer is likely to follow different paths for different projects. *How to Write Anything* doesn't define a single process of writing or imagine that all students using it will have the same skills and interests. Instead, a modular chapter organization and an innovative system of cross-references encourage students to navigate the book's materials to find exactly the information they want at the level of specificity they need—which pretty much sums up the rationale for the book. *How to Write Anything* is both focused and flexible, marrying the rich perspectives of a full rhetoric and reader to the efficiency of a brief handbook. Building on these principles, this second edition includes more genres, defines genres more precisely, and offers students more tools for exploring them.

A Guide, Reference, and Reader

The Guide, in Parts 1 and 2, covers the genres of writing that instructors frequently assign in composition classes or that students encounter in other undergraduate courses. Each chapter lays out the basics of a genre, such as narrative or argument, then presents the writing process as a flexible series of rhetorical choices—Exploring Purpose and Topic; Understanding Your Audience; Finding and Developing Materials; Creating a Structure; and Choosing a Style and Design. These choices provide students with a framework for writing in any situation and in any genre, and encourage writers to explore the range of possibilities within genres. The explanations here are direct, practical, and economical. If writers do need more help with a particular topic, targeted cross-references make it easy to find in the Reference section.

The Reference section (Parts 3 through 9) covers key aspects of the writing process—with separate parts devoted to Ideas; Shaping and Drafting; Style; Revising and Editing; Research and Sources; Media and Design; and Common Errors. While the topics will seem familiar to most writing instructors, the fresh and lively material here is designed to expand points introduced in the Guide. For instance, a writer might turn to these sections to find specific techniques for generating ideas or arguments or guidance for making a formal style feel more friendly. The organization of *How to Write Anything* lets students quickly find what they need without getting bogged down in other material.

Part 10, the Reader, is an anthology of forty-one additional contemporary selections organized by genres covered in the Guide. Drawn from a variety of sources such as print and online journals, books, scholarly and popular magazines, blogs, and graphic novels, the readings offer both solid models for writing as well as compelling topics for students to respond to. Some examples include Tricia Rose's exploration of the relationship between hip hop music and violence, Lynda Barry's graphic literacy narrative, Nicholas Carr on "what the Internet is doing to our brains," and evaluations of everything from force fields to shopping malls to reality television shows. The Reader includes fresh content from established authors such as Jonathan Franzen, Camille Paglia, Gish Jen, and Maureen Dowd, as well as from newer voices such as Adam Bradley, Ira Sukrungruang, and Molly Young. Headnotes provide context for all readings in the text, and selections in the Reader are followed by analysis questions and writing assignments, which feature cross-references from the questions back to the Guide and Reference sections of the book. These readings, and the questions that follow them, are intended to help students more deeply consider and use the major genres in *How to Write Anything*.

Key Features

A Flexible Writing Process

Writers get started, develop ideas, and revise in different ways. *How to Write Anything* acknowledges this by asking students to think about their *own* processes and what they need help with. At the beginning of each Guide chapter, "How to Start" questions anticipate where students get stuck when writing and direct them to specific materials within the chapter for help. For example, one writer might need advice about finding a topic, while another will already have a topic but need assistance with audience, or developing or organizing ideas.

In this hyperlinked era, it is important for information to be intuitive, easy to find, and, above all, relevant and useful. With this in mind, the cross-references between the Guide, Reference, and Reader sections target only the topics that students are most likely to need help with for the assignment at hand. The simple language and unobtrusive design of the cross-references make it easy for students to find the exact help they need and to stay focused on their own writing.

Professional and Student Writing

How to Write Anything: A Guide and Reference with Readings contains an ample selection of readings, more than thirty-eight in the Guide chapters and forty-one in the Reader. Selections illustrate key principles and show how genres change in response to different contexts and audiences. Every chapter in the Guide includes many complete examples of the genres under discussion, most of these texts annotated to show how they meet criteria set down in *How to Write Anything*. The assignments at the end of these chapters are closely tied to the chapter readings, so students can use the sample texts both as models and as springboards for discussion and exploration.

Just as important, the models in *How to Write Anything* are approachable. The readings—some by published professionals and others by student writers—reveal the diversity of contemporary writing being done in these genres. The student samples are especially inventive—chosen to motivate undergraduates to take comparable risks with their own writing. Together, the readings and exercises suggest to writers not just the rules for each genre, but also the many creative possibilities of working in these genres.

"How To" Visual Tutorials

Throughout the book, students will recognize a world they already live in, one which assumes that composing occurs in more than just words. But learning occurs in more than just words too. Savvy readers of telegraphic text messages, quick-cut visuals, and blogs will no doubt appreciate the direct yet context-rich advice in the book's "How To" Visual Tutorials. Through drawings, photographs, and screenshots, these tutorials offer step-by-step instructions for challenging topics, ranging from how to browse the Internet for ideas to how to cite a variety of materials in both MLA and APA formats.

New to This Edition

How to Write Anything remains a uniquely flexible text: It works with any writing process, any genre, anywhere. In this revision we added reference chapters at the heart of academic writing—critical thinking, genre, and strategies. And to give students more support for academic skills, there are new chapters on synthesis and annotated bibliography, along with a new emphasis on multimodal composing.

More Support for Academic Writing

Three brief new chapters focus on important academic skills. **"Synthesis Papers"** shows students how to summarize, compare, and assess materials from different sources. **"Critical Thinking"** lays out rhetorical appeals and logical fallacies, and an **"Annotated Bibliographies"** chapter provides guidelines for this popular research assignment.

Another new chapter, "Strategies," explores rhetorical tools that work across genres, including comparison and contrast, classification, description, definition, and division.

New Visual Tutorials show how to document a wider range of electronic sources.

New Genre Chapter and a Wider Range of Genres

The new reference chapter, "Genre," defines this key concept, discusses why it matters, and shows students how genres help writers accomplish the work they want to do. New genres covered in this edition of *How to Write Anything* include annotated bibliographies and synthesis papers. New model readings engage students with fresh topics, including Sasha Frere-Jones on the future of music broadcasting and Gish Jen on the legacy of Holden Caufield. Many more readings can be found in the e-library and the e-book (see pp. xiii and xiv for more information).

More Advice for Students Using Multimedia

Two new reference chapters, "Understanding Digital Media" and "Digital Elements," explore audio, video, blogs, and wikis.

All genre chapters now feature multimodal assignment options, for example, preparing an evaluation in which a visual comparison plays a major role.

New "Your Turn" Activities

The "Your Turn" activities encourage students to apply the advice in the book, letting them try out genres and strategies before tackling a complete assignment. For example, one prompt asks students to transform a popular song title (consider "Taxman," "Waiting on the World to Change," or "Concrete and Barbed Wire") into a thesis statement that would be suitable for an academic paper. Additional "Your Turn" activities are available both on the free student site and in the e-book. For more on the e-book, see page xiv.

Invitation to Write

How to Write Anything was designed and edited to be compact and readable. But it retains a personal voice, frank and occasionally humorous, on the grounds that a textbook without character won't convince students that their own prose should have a style adapted to real audiences. And if some chapters operate like reference materials, they still aren't written coldly or dispassionately—not even the section on Common Errors.

So if *How to Write Anything* seems like an ambitious title, maybe it's because learning to write should be a heady enterprise, undertaken with confidence and optimism. Our hope is that this book will encourage students to grasp the opportunities that the writing affords and gain the satisfaction that comes from setting ideas (and words) into motion.

Acknowledgments

The following reviewers were very helpful through several drafts of this book: Angela K. Albright, NorthWest Arkansas Community College; Ellen Arnold, Coastal Carolina University; Diann L. Baecker, Virginia State University; Lisa Baird, Flagler College; Sandie McGill Barnhouse, Rowan-Cabarrus Community College; Bethany Joy Bear, Baylor University; Andrea L. Beaudin, Southern Connecticut State University; Quinton Blackwell, Towson University; Glenn Blalock, Baylor University; Patricia Boyd, Arizona State University; Kevin F. Boyle, College of Southern Nevada; Bob Brown, Chippewa Valley Technical College; Jon Byrne, Itasca Community College; Giselle Muñoz Caro, University of Puerto Rico; Frankie Chadwick, University of Arkansas at Little Rock; Miriam Chirico, Eastern Connecticut State University; Ron Christiansen, Salt Lake Community College; Tara Cole, Oklahoma State University–Oklahoma City; Z. Katherine Combiths, Virginia Tech; Michelle Cox, Bridgewater State College; Mark Crane, Utah Valley State College; Linsey Cuti, Kankakee Community College; Tracy L. Dalton, Missouri State University; Cathy Decker, Chaffey College; Lauren DeGraffenreid, University of Nevada, Reno; Jim Dervin, Winston-Salem State University; Anthony Edgington, University of Toledo; Caroline L. Eisner, University of Michigan; Jennie Enger, North Dakota State University; Ruth Fair, Winston-Salem State University; Maureen Fitzpatrick, Johnson County Community College; Shawnee Fleenor, Asbury University; Amy Foley, Roberts Wesleyan College; Hank Galmish, Green River Community College; John Gides, California State University–Northridge; Maura Grady, University of Nevada, Reno; Christine Grossman, North Dakota State University; Steffen Guenzel, The University of Alabama; Mark Helm, The Art Institute of Tennessee–Nashville; Virginia Scott Hendrickson, Missouri State University; Kathryn Owen Hix,

Greenville Technical College; Jordynn Jack, University of North Carolina at Chapel Hill; Karen Jobe, Oklahoma State University–Oklahoma City; Judith Angelique Johnson, Minnesota State University, Mankato; Jessica Fordham Kidd, University of Alabama; Noreen Lace, California State University–Northridge; Mark Lanting, Kankakee Community College; Lynn Lewis, University of Oklahoma; Mary Libertin, Shippensburg University of Pennsylvania; Amy Locklear, Auburn University–Montgomery; Paula Makris, Wheeling Jesuit University; Cynthia K. Marshall, Wright State University; Leigh A. Martin, Community College of Rhode Island; Kit McChesney, University of Colorado at Boulder; Miles McCrimmon, J. Sargeant Reynolds Community College; Erica Messenger, Bowling Green State University; Mary Ellen Muesing, University of North Carolina–Charlotte; Bryan Peters, Jefferson College; Valarie Phelps, Western Kentucky University; Elizabeth Porto, University of Massachusetts–Amherst; Shay Rahm-Barnett, University of Central Oklahoma; Jennifer A. Rea, Rockford College; Rachel Reed, Auburn University–Montgomery; Juliann Reineke, Greenville Technical College; Mark Reynolds, Jefferson Davis Community College; Rob Roensch, Towson University; Abby Rotstein, College of Southern Nevada; Bridget F. Ruetenik, Penn State Altoona; Jim Schrantz, Tarrant County College; Wendy Sharer, Eastern Carolina University; Marti Singer, Georgia State University; Marian Smith, Chippewa Valley Technical College; David Sorrells, Lamar State College–Port Arthur; William H. Thelin, University of Akron; James G. Van Belle, Edmonds Community College; Carol Westcamp, University of Arkansas–Fort Smith; Darren Wieland, Minnesota State University, Mankato; Rita Wisdom, Tarrant County College–Northeast Campus; Kelli Wood, El Paso Community College; Mary K. Zacharias, San Jacinto College Central.

All books are collaborations, but we have never before worked on a project that more creatively drew upon the resources of an editorial team and publisher. *How to Write Anything* began with the confidence of Joan Feinberg, president of Bedford/St. Martin's, that we could develop a groundbreaking brief rhetoric. She had the patience to allow the idea to develop at its own pace and then assembled an incredible team to support it. We are grateful for the contributions of Denise Wydra, Editorial Director; Karen Henry, Editor in Chief; and Leasa Burton, Senior Executive Editor.

We are also indebted to Anna Palchik, Senior Art Director and designer of the text, and Rosemary Jaffe, Senior Production Editor. Special thanks to Sarah Macomber, who conceived the original Visual Tutorials, to Peter Arkle and Anna Veltfort for their drawings, Christian Wise for his photographs, and to Allie Goldstein, Sophia Snyder, and Shannon Walsh for their help with art research. They all deserve credit for the distinctive and accessible visual style of *How to Write Anything*.

For their marketing efforts, we are grateful to the guidance offered by Karen R. Soeltz, Karita dos Santos, and Molly Parke. And for all manner of tasks, including updating the Visual Tutorials, coordinating permissions and reviews, and manuscript preparation, we thank Alyssa Demirjian.

But our greatest debt is to Ellen Darion, who was our splendid editor on this lengthy project: always confident about what we could accomplish, patient when chapters went off-track, and perpetually good-humored. If *How to Write Anything* works, it is because Ellen never wavered from our original high aspirations for the book. Her hand is in every chapter, every choice of reading, and every assignment.

Finally, we are extraordinarily grateful to our former students whose papers or paragraphs appear in *How to Write Anything*. Their writing speaks for itself, but we have been inspired, too, by their personal dedication and character. These are the sort of students who motivate teachers, and so we are very proud to see their work published in *How to Write Anything*: Jordyn Brown, Marissa Dahlstrom, Manasi Deshpande, Micah T. Eades, Lynn Ehlers, Kyu-heong Kim, Wade Lamb, Cheryl Lovelady, Shane McNamee, Matthew Nance, Miles Pequeno, Heidi Rogers, Kanaka Sathasivan, Kelsi Stayart, J. Reagan Tankersley, Katelyn Vincent, and Annie Winsett.

John J. Ruszkiewicz
Jay T. Dolmage

Get More Digital Choices for *How to Write Anything*, Second Edition

How to Write Anything doesn't stop with a book. Online, you'll find both free and affordable premium resources to help students get even more out of the book and your course. To learn more about or order any of the products below, contact your Bedford/St. Martin's sales representative, e-mail sales support (sales_support@bfwpub.com), or visit the Web site at **bedfordstmartins.com/ howtowrite/catalog**.

Student Site for How to Write Anything
bedfordstmartins.com/howtowrite

Send students to free and open resources, choose flexible premium resources, or upgrade to an expanding collection of innovative digital content.

Free and open resources for *How to Write Anything* provide students with easy-to-access reference materials, visual tutorials, and support for working with sources.

- Checklists for writing different genres
- Links to more models
- Five free videos of real writers from *VideoCentral*
- Three free tutorials from *ix visualizing composition* by Cheryl Ball and Kristin Arola
- *Research and Documentation Online* by Diana Hacker

A free *E-Library for How to Write Anything*. Because there are some things you can't do in print, the second edition of *How to Write Anything* is available with a digital collection of multimodal readings, including a video featuring the writer Michael Pollan encouraging people to see the world from "a plant's-eye view" and an online newspaper's product review of the Rosetta Stone language instruction system. The e-library also includes student models, video tutorials about documenting sources, and assignment options, all packaged for free with the print book. This extra content is also integrated into the *How to Write Anything e-Book*. To order the *E-Library for How to Write Anything* packaged with the print book, use ISBN 978-1-4576-2264-9.

VideoCentral: English is a growing collection of videos for the writing class that captures real-world, academic, and student writers talking about how and why they write. Writer and teacher Peter Berkow interviewed hundreds of people—from Michael Moore to Cynthia Selfe—to produce fifty brief videos about topics such as revising and getting feedback. *VideoCentral* can be packaged for free with *How to Write Anything*. An activation code is required. To order *VideoCentral* packaged with the print book, use ISBN 978-1-4576-1121-6.

E-book Options
bedfordstmartins.com/howtowrite/catalog

With a Bedford e-book, you get the complete text in an interactive online version, plus additional content in the *E-Library for How to Write Anything* and more options for customizing the book to suit your course. **You can** move or hide chapters to match your syllabus and add notes and links that build on the text and engage students in conversation. **Students can** find the book online anytime, anywhere; highlight and add notes to make the text their own; and watch videos and complete practice exercises while they're online. An activation code is required. To order the *How to Write Anything e-Book,* use ISBN 978-0-312-62996-0. To order it packaged with the print book, use ISBN 978-1-4576-1123-0.

Students can also purchase *How to Write Anything* in other popular e-book formats for computers, tablets, and e-readers. For more details, visit **bedfordstmartins.com/ebooks**.

CompClass for How to Write Anything
yourcompclass.com

An easy-to-use online course space designed for composition, *CompClass for How to Write Anything* comes preloaded with the *How to Write Anything e-Book* and the *E-Library for How to Write Anything* as well as the complete Bedford e-library for composition, including *VideoCentral* and *i•cite visualizing research*. *CompClass for How to Write Anything* can be purchased separately at **yourcompclass.com** or packaged with the print book at a significant discount. An activation code is required. To order *CompClass for How to Write Anything* with the print book, use ISBN 978-1-4576-1120-9.

Instructor Resources
bedfordstmartins.com/howtowrite/catalog

You have a lot to do in your course. Bedford/St. Martin's wants to make it easy for you to find the support you need—and to get it quickly. Request a print copy of any of these resources through our online catalog or your sales representative.

Teaching with How To Write Anything is available both in print and as a PDF that can be downloaded from the Bedford/St. Martin's online catalog. In addition to chapter overviews and teaching tips, the Instructor's Manual includes sample syllabi, correlations to the Council of Writing Program Administrators' Outcomes Statement, and classroom activities.

Portfolio Teaching, **Second Edition, by Nedra Reynolds and Rich Rice** provides all the information instructors and writing program directors need to use portfolio assessment successfully in a writing course. *Portfolio Keeping,* Second Edition, is a companion guide for students. Bedford *Bits* at **bedfordbits.com** collects creative ideas for teaching a range of composition topics in an easily searchable blog format.

Free Bedford Coursepacks for the most common course management systems—Blackboard, WebCT, Angel, and Desire2Learn—allow you to easily download our most popular digital materials for your course. For details, visit **bedfordstmartins.com/coursepacks**.

Correlation to the Council of Writing Program Administrators' (WPA) Outcomes Statement

How to Write Anything helps students build proficiency in the five categories of learning that writing programs across the country use to assess their work: rhetorical knowledge; critical thinking, reading, and writing; writing processes; knowledge of conventions; and composing in electronic environments. A detailed correlation follows.

Features of *How to Write Anything, A Guide and Reference with Readings,* Second Edition, Correlated to the WPA Outcomes Statement

Desired Student Outcomes	Relevant Features of *How to Write Anything*
Rhetorical Knowledge	
Respond to the needs of different audiences.	Each assignment chapter in the Guide has a section called "Understanding Your Audience"; the need to consider one's audience is covered in the discussion of every genre. Chapter 3, "Arguments," includes a section on responding to opposing claims and points of view, and Chapters 2 and 4, "Reports" and "Evaluations," discuss writing for experts, general audiences, novices, or peers.
Respond appropriately to different kinds of rhetorical situations.	Each assignment chapter in the Guide offers detailed advice on responding to a particular rhetorical situation, from arguing a claim and proposing a solution to writing an e-mail or a résumé. Chapter 25, "Genre," explains how genres help writers accomplish the work they want to do.
Use conventions of format and structure appropriate to the rhetorical situation.	Each chapter in Part 1 includes sections on both "Creating a Structure" and "Choosing a Style and Design" appropriate for the genre covered there. See also "Getting the Details Right" sections in Part 2 chapters. Structure is also covered in Part 4, "Shaping and Drafting," in Chapters 25–34: "Genre," "Thesis," "Strategies," "Organization," "Outlines," "Paragraphs," "Transitions," "Introductions," "Conclusions," and "Titles." Document design is covered in Chapter 54, "Designing Print and Online Documents."
Adopt appropriate voice, tone, and level of formality.	See the "Choosing a Style and Design" sections in Part 1 chapters, and the "Getting the Details Right" sections in Part 2 chapters. Part 5 features chapters on "High, Middle, and Low Style" (35); "Inclusive and Culturally Sensitive Style" (36), and "Vigorous, Clear, and Economical Style" (37).
Understand how genres shape reading and writing.	Each chapter in Part 1 offers student and professional readings accompanied by annotations and commentary about the key features of the genre. Each chapter also begins with a list of examples of the genre that will be familiar to students, followed by a section on understanding the genre covered in that chapter. Chapter 25, "Genre," explains how genres help writers accomplish the work they want to do.

Desired Student Outcomes	Relevant Features of *How to Write Anything*
Rhetorical Knowledge (*continued*)	
Write in several genres.	Chapters 1–18 in the Guide (Parts 1 and 2) cover the following genres and assignments: Narratives, Reports, Arguments, Evaluations, Proposals, Causal, Literary, and Rhetorical Analyses, Essay Examinations, Annotated Bibliographies, Synthesis Papers, Position Papers, E-mails, Business Letters, Résumés, Personal Statements, Lab Reports, and Oral Reports. Chapter 25, "Genre," explains how genres help writers accomplish the work they want to do. Part 7 covers research strategies students will use while writing these genres, while Part 8 addresses digital media and strategies students will need for public writing such as brochures and newsletters.
Critical Thinking, Reading, and Writing	
Use writing and reading for inquiry, learning, thinking, and communicating.	The assignment chapters in the Guide emphasize the connection between reading and writing a particular genre: each chapter includes model readings whose annotations address the key features of the genre. Each Part 1 chapter shows students the rhetorical choices they need to consider when writing their own papers in these genres and offers assignments to actively engage them in these choices. Chapter 22, "Critical Thinking," explains rhetorical appeals and logical fallacies. Reference chapters in Parts 3 through 8 cover invention, reading, writing, research, and design strategies that work across all genres.
Understand a writing assignment as a series of tasks, including finding, evaluating, analyzing, and synthesizing appropriate primary and secondary sources.	Each chapter in Part 1 includes a section on "Finding and Developing Ideas." Chapter 12, "Synthesis Papers," shows students how to summarize, compare, and assess the views offered by different sources. Chapter 21 introduces close reading and logical fallacies, while Part 7, "Research and Sources," includes Chapters 41, "Finding Print and Online Sources"; 42, "Doing Field Research"; 43, "Evaluating Sources"; 44, "Annotating Sources"; 45, "Summarizing Sources"; and 46, "Paraphrasing Sources."
Integrate their own ideas with others.	Chapter 47, "Integrating Sources into Your Work," provides detailed advice on integrating and introducing quotations, paraphrasing, summarizing, and avoiding plagiarism.

Desired Student Outcomes	Relevant Features of *How to Write Anything*
Processes	
Be aware that it usually takes multiple drafts to create and complete a successful text.	Chapter 38, "Revising Your Own Work," discusses the importance of revising and gives detailed advice on how to approach different types of revision. Targeted cross-references throughout the text help students get the revision help they need when they need it.
Understand the collaborative and social aspects of writing processes.	Chapter 20 covers collaboration as a strategy of invention; Chapter 23 encourages students to consult experts such as an instructor, a librarian, or a tutor at the writing center. Chapter 39 teaches students to give constructive feedback to other writers. Chapter 42 provides thorough coverage of field research.
Learn to critique their own and others' work.	Chapter 38 focuses students on revising their own work, while Chapter 39 guides students to give useful feedback to other writers.
	Chapter 22 helps students uncover logical fallacies, while Chapter 44 shows them how to identify claims, assumptions, and evidence.
Use a variety of technologies to address a range of audiences.	Chapters 51 and 52 cover digital media, including blogs, Web sites, wikis, podcasts, videos, and remixes. Chapter 54 covers creating visuals on a computer and downloading them from the Web.
	Each assignment chapter includes at least one visual example of the genre that the chapter focuses on, and many of the reference chapters include Visual Tutorials featuring photographs and illustrations that provide students with step-by-step instructions for challenging topics, such as using the Web to browse for ideas. This emphasis on visuals, media, and design helps students develop visual literacy they can use in their own work.
	Chapter 13 covers e-mail; Chapter 18 addresses presentation software; Chapter 38 covers spelling and grammar checkers; and Chapters 41 and 43 cover finding, evaluating, and using print and electronic resources for research.
Knowledge of Conventions	
Learn common formats for different kinds of texts.	Each assignment chapter in the Guide covers a format specific to the genre covered there; see sections "Choosing a Style and Design" in the Part 1 chapters and "Getting the Details Right" in the Part 2 chapters.
	Sample e-mails, business letters, résumés, and lab reports all appear in Part 2; Chapters 49 and 50 include sample MLA and APA research paper pages. Chapter 51 covers general design principles; Chapter 52 addresses understanding and using images, and Chapter 53 focuses on tables, graphs, and infographics.

Desired Student Outcomes	Relevant Features of *How to Write Anything*
Knowledge of Conventions (*continued*)	
Develop knowledge of genre conventions ranging from structure and paragraphing to tone and mechanics.	Each assignment chapter in Part 1 presents key features of a specific genre, both in the introductory sections and via annotated models. Structure, paragraphing, tone, and mechanics are addressed in these chapters and in targeted cross-references integrated throughout the Guide. These cross-references neatly link the assignment chapters to the reference chapters, helping students choose their own best path through the material. Structure and paragraphing, for example, are covered in Part 4, "Shaping and Drafting"; tone is covered in Part 5, "Style"; and mechanics in Part 9, "Common Errors."
Control such surface features as syntax, grammar, punctuation, and spelling.	Chapters 38 and 39 provide editing and proofreading advice. Part 9, "Common Errors," includes chapters on grammar, punctuation, and mechanics. Targeted cross-references throughout the text send students to these chapters as needed.
Composing in Electronic Environments	
Use electronic environments for drafting, reviewing, revising, editing, and sharing texts.	Chapters 51 and 52 focus on digital media, including blogs, Web sites, wikis, podcasts, videos, and remixes. Chapter 13 covers e-mails; Chapter 18 covers presentation software, and Chapters 38 and 39 address word-processing programs.
Locate, evaluate, organize, and use research material collected from electronic sources, including scholarly library databases, other official databases (e.g., federal government databases), and informal electronic networks and Internet sources.	Part 7, "Research and Sources," includes thorough coverage of finding and using online sources in Chapters 40, 41, 43, and 48. Chapters 49 and 50 provide instruction and models for documenting online sources in both MLA and APA formats. Visual Tutorials also address these tasks; see How to Cite from a Web Site in MLA (pp. 526–27) and in APA (pp. 556–57) and How to Cite from a Database in MLA (pp. 528–29) and in APA (pp. 558–59).
Understand and exploit the differences in the rhetorical strategies and in the affordances available for both print and electronic composing processes and texts.	The text and e-book include a wide range of print and multimodal genres, from essays and scholarly articles to photographs, infographics, Web sites, and audio and video presentations. Rhetorical choices that students make in each genre are covered in the Guide chapters and appear in discussions of the writing context and in abundant models in the book.

Contents

Preface   v

guide

Part 1   Genres   2

1   Narratives   4

Deciding to write a narrative   5
   REFLECTION: **Mark Edmundson,** *The Pink Floyd Night School*   7

Exploring purpose and topic   10
   Brainstorm, freewrite, build lists, and use memory prompts to find a topic for a narrative   10
   Choose a manageable subject   10

Understanding your audience   11
   Select events that will keep readers engaged   12
   Pace the story effectively   12
   Tailor your writing to your intended readers   13

Finding and developing materials   14
   Consult documents   14
   Consult images   14
   Trust your experiences   14

Creating a structure   16
   Consider a simple sequence   16
   Build toward a climax   16

Choosing a style and design 18
  Don't hesitate to use first person—*I* 18
  Use figures of speech such as similes, metaphors, and analogies to make memorable comparisons 19
  In choosing verbs, favor active rather than passive voice 19
  Use powerful and precise modifiers 20
  Use dialogue to propel the narrative and to give life to your characters 20
  Develop major characters through language and action 21
  Develop the setting to set the context and mood 21
  Use images to tell a story 22

Examining models 23
  LITERACY NARRATIVE: Richard Rodriguez, *Strange Tools* 23
  STUDENT MEMOIR: Miles Pequeno, *Check. Mate?* 29
  GRAPHIC NARRATIVE (EXCERPT): Marjane Satrapi, from *Persepolis* 35

  ASSIGNMENTS 43

2 **Reports 44**

Deciding to write a report 45
  Present information 45
  Find reliable sources 46
  Aim for objectivity 46
  Present information clearly 46
  NEWS REPORT: Laura Layton, *Uranus's Second Ring-Moon System* 47

Exploring purpose and topic 49
  Answer questions 49
  Review what is already known about a subject 49
  Report new knowledge 50

Understanding your audience 51
  Suppose you are the expert 51
  Suppose you are the novice 51
  Suppose you are the peer 51

Finding and developing materials 52
  Base reports on the best available sources 52
  Base reports on multiple sources 53
  Fact-check your report 53

Creating a structure 54
  Organize by date, time, or sequence 54
  Organize by magnitude or order of importance 54
  Organize by division 55

Organize by classification   56
Organize by position, location, or space   56
Organize by definition   56
Organize by comparison/contrast   57
Organize by thesis statement   58

Choosing a style and design   59
Present the facts cleanly   59
Keep out of it   59
Avoid connotative language   59
Cover differing views fairly, especially those you don't like   60
Pay attention to elements of design   60

Examining models   61
INVESTIGATIVE REPORT: **Tyghe Trimble,** *The Running Shoe Debate: How Barefoot Runners Are Shaping the Shoe Industry*   61
ACADEMIC REPORT: **Annie Winsett,** *Inner* and *Outer Beauty*   66
FLOWCHART: **Mike Wirth and Suzanne Cooper-Guasco,** *How Our Laws Are Made*   70

ASSIGNMENTS   71

3 Arguments   72

Deciding to write an argument   73
Offer levelheaded and disputable claims   73
Offer good reasons to support a claim   74
Understand opposing claims and points of view   74
Use language strategically—and not words only   74
ARGUMENT TO ADVANCE A THESIS: **Scott Keyes,** *Stop Asking Me My Major*   75

Exploring purpose and topic   79
Learn much more about your subject   79
State a preliminary claim, if only for yourself   79
Qualify your claim to make it reasonable   80
Examine your core assumptions   80

Understanding your audience   82
Consider and control your ethos   82
Consider your own limits   83
Consider race and ethnicity   83
Consider gender and sexual orientation   83
Consider income and class   83
Consider religion and spirituality   84
Consider age   84

Finding and developing materials   85
  List your reasons   85
  Assemble your hard evidence   86
  Cull the best quotations   86
  Find counterarguments   87
  Consider emotional appeals   87
Creating a structure   88
  Spell out what's at stake   88
  Make a point or build toward one   89
  Address counterpoints when necessary, not in a separate section   89
  Hold your best arguments for the end   90
Choosing a style and design   91
  Invite readers with a strong opening   91
  Write vibrant sentences   92
  Ask rhetorical questions   93
  Use images and design to make a point   94
Examining models   95
  EXPLORATORY ARGUMENT: **Lynn Ehlers,** *"Play 'Free Bird'!"*   95
  REFUTATION ARGUMENT: **Cathy Young,** *Duke's Sexist Sexual
    Misconduct Policy*   101
  VISUAL ARGUMENT: **IfItWereMyHome.com,** *Visualizing the BP
    Oil Spill Disaster*   104

  ASSIGNMENTS   105

4   **Evaluations**   106

Deciding to write an evaluation   107
  Make value judgments   107
  Establish and defend criteria   108
  Offer convincing evidence   108
  Offer useful advice   108
  PRODUCT REVIEW: **David Pogue,** *Looking at the iPad from Two Angles*   109
Exploring purpose and topic   113
  Evaluate a subject you know well   113
  Evaluate a subject you need to investigate   113
  Evaluate a subject you'd like to know more about   113
  Evaluate a subject that's been on your mind   113
  Keep an open mind   114
Understanding your audience   115
  Write for experts   115
  Write for a general audience   115
  Write for novices   116

Finding and developing materials   117
    Decide on your criteria   117
    Look for hard criteria   117
    Argue for criteria that can't be measured   119
    Stand by your values   119
    Gather your evidence   120

Creating a structure   121
    Choose a simple structure when your criteria and categories are
        predictable   121
    Choose a focal point   122
    Compare and contrast   123

Choosing a style and design   124
    Use a high or formal style   124
    Use a middle style   124
    Use a low style   125
    Present evaluations visually   125

Examining models   127
    ARTS REVIEW: **Charles Isherwood,** *Stomping onto Broadway with a
        Punk Temper Tantrum*   127
    SOCIAL SATIRE: **Jordyn Brown,** *A Word from My Anti-Phone
        Soapbox*   131
    VISUAL COMPARISON: **Insurance Institute for Highway Safety,**
        Crash Test   136

    ASSIGNMENTS   137

5   **Causal Analyses**   138

Deciding to write a causal analysis   139
    Don't jump to conclusions   140
    Appreciate your limits   140
    Offer sufficient evidence for claims   140
    CAUSAL ANALYSIS: **Jonah Goldberg,** *Global Warming and the Sun*   141

Exploring purpose and topic   144
    Look again at a subject you know well   145
    Look for an issue new to you   145
    Examine a local issue   146
    Choose a subject with many dimensions   146
    Tackle an issue that seems settled   146

Understanding your audience   147
    Create an audience   147
    Write to an existing audience   147

Finding and developing materials 149
    Understand necessary causes 149
    Understand sufficient causes 149
    Understand precipitating causes 150
    Understand proximate causes 150
    Understand remote causes 150
    Understand reciprocal causes 150
    Understand contributing factors 151
    Come to conclusions thoughtfully 151
    Don't oversimplify situations or manipulate facts 151

Creating a structure 152
    Explain why something happened 152
    Explain the consequences of a phenomenon 153
    Suggest an alternative view of cause and effect 153
    Explain a chain of causes 154

Choosing a style and design 155
    Consider a middle style 155
    Adapt the style to the subject matter 155
    Use appropriate supporting media 156

Examining models 157
    RESEARCH STUDY: **Kyu-heong Kim,** *Bending the Rules for ESL Writers* 157
    EXPLORATORY ESSAY: **Liza Mundy,** *What's Really behind the Plunge in Teen Pregnancy?* 165
    CULTURAL ANALYSIS: **Charles Paul Freund,** *The Politics of Pants* 170

    ASSIGNMENTS 175

6   **Proposals** 176

Deciding to write a proposal 177
    Define a problem 178
    Target the proposal 178
    Consider reasonable options 178
    Make specific recommendations 178
    Make realistic recommendations 178
    TRIAL BALLOON: **Barrett Seaman,** *How Bingeing Became the New College Sport* 179

Exploring purpose and topic 182
    Look for a genuine issue 182
    Look for a challenging problem 182
    Look for a soluble problem 182
    Look for a local issue 182

Understanding your audience 184
    Write to people who can make a difference 184
    Rally people who represent public opinion 185

Finding and developing materials 187
    Define the problem 187
    Examine prior solutions 187
    Make a proposal 187
    Defend the proposal 188
    Figure out how to implement the proposal 188

Creating a structure 189

Choosing a style and design 190
    Use a formal style 190
    Use a middle style, when appropriate 190
    Pay attention to elements of design 191

Examining models 192
    FORMAL PROPOSAL: **Donald Lazere,** *A Core Curriculum for Civic Literacy* 192
    MANIFESTO: **Katelyn Vincent,** *Technology Time-out* 198
    VISUAL PROPOSAL: **Pallettruth.com,** *Asian Longhorned Beetles from Wood Pallets Invading NYC!* 204

    ASSIGNMENTS 205

7 | **Literary Analyses** 206

Deciding to write a literary analysis 207
    Begin with a close reading 208
    Make a claim or an observation 208
    Present works in context 208
    Draw on previous research 208
    Use texts for evidence 208
    LITERARY INTERPRETATION: **Kelsi Stayart,** *Authentic Beauty in Morrison's* The Bluest Eye 209

Exploring purpose and topic 217
    Choose a text you connect with 217
    Choose a text you want to learn more about 217
    Choose a text that you don't understand 217

Understanding your audience 218
    Clearly identify the author and works you are analyzing 218
    Define key terms 218
    Don't aim to please professional critics 219

Finding and developing materials 220
   Examine the text closely 221
   Focus on the text itself 221
   Focus on its meanings, themes, and interpretations 221
   Focus on its authorship and history 222
   Focus on its genre 222
   Focus on its influence 223
   Focus on its social connections 223
   Find good sources 223

Creating a structure 226
   Focus on a particular observation, claim, or point 226
   Imagine a structure 226
   Work on your opening 227

Choosing a style and design 228
   Use a formal style for most assignments 228
   Use a middle style for informal or personal papers 229
   Describe action in the present tense 229
   Provide dates for authors and literary works 229
   Use appropriate abbreviations 230
   Follow conventions for quotations 230
   Cite plays correctly 230
   Explore alternative media 230

Examining models 231
   CLOSE READING: **Emily Dickinson,** *I felt a Funeral, in my Brain* 231
      Kanaka Sathasivan, *Insanity: Two Women* 232
   CULTURAL ANALYSIS: **Kelli Marshall,** *Show Musical Good, Paired Segments Better: Glee's Unevenness Explained* 238
   PHOTOGRAPHS AS LITERARY TEXTS: **Dorothea Lange,** *Jobless on Edge of Pea Field, Imperial Valley, California* 246
      Walker Evans, *Burroughs Family Cabin, Hale County, Alabama* 247
      Gordon Parks, *American Gothic* 248

   ASSIGNMENTS 249

8 **Rhetorical Analyses** 250

Deciding to write a rhetorical analysis 251
   Take words and images seriously 252
   Make strong claims about texts 252
   Pay attention to audience 252
   Mine texts for evidence 252
      ANALYSIS OF AN ADVERTISEMENT: **Seth Stevenson,** *Ad Report Card: Can Cougars Sell Cough Drops?* 253

Exploring purpose and topic   256
> Make a difference   256
> Choose a text you can work with   256
> Choose a text you can learn more about   256
> Choose a text with handles   256
> Choose a text you know how to analyze   257

Understanding your audience   258

Finding and developing materials   259
> Consider the topic or subject matter of the text   259
> Consider the audiences of the text   259
> Consider its author   259
> Consider its medium or language   259
> Consider its occasion   260
> Consider its contexts   260
> Consider its use of rhetorical appeals   260

Creating a structure   262
> Develop a structure   262

Choosing a style and design   263
> Consider a high style   263
> Consider a middle style   263
> Make the text accessible to readers   263
> Annotate the text   263

Examining models   264
> **ANALYSIS OF AN ARGUMENT: Matthew James Nance,** *A Mockery of Justice*   264
> **CULTURAL ANALYSIS: J. Reagan Tankersley,** *Humankind's Ouroboros*   270
> **ANALYSIS OF A VISUAL TEXT: Beth Teitell,** *A Jacket of the People*   279
>
> **ASSIGNMENTS**   281

Part 2   Special Assignments   282

9   Essay Examinations   284

Understanding essay exams   285
> Anticipate the types of questions you might be asked   285
> Read exam questions carefully   285

Sketch out a plan for your essay(s)   285
Organize your answer strategically   285
Offer strong evidence for your claims   286
Come to a conclusion   286
Keep the tone serious   286
Don't panic   286

Wade Lamb, *Plato's* Phaedrus   287

Getting the details right   289
Use transition words and phrases   289
Do a quick check of grammar, mechanics, and spelling   289
Write legibly or print   289

10 **Position Papers** 290

Understanding position papers   291
Read the assignment carefully   292
Review assigned material carefully   292
Mine the texts for evidence   292
Organize the paper sensibly   292

Heidi Rogers, *Triumph of the Lens*   293

Getting the details right   295
Edit the final version   295
Identify key terms and concepts and use them correctly and often   295
Treat your sources appropriately   295
Spell names and concepts correctly   295
Respond to your colleagues' work   295

11 **Annotated Bibliographies** 296

Understanding annotated bibliographies   297
Begin with an accurate bibliography of research materials   297
Describe or summarize the content of each item in the
    bibliography   297
Assess the quality or importance of the work   298
Explain the role the work plays in your research   298

Getting the details right   299
Get the information on your sources right   299
Follow correct documentation style   299
Keep your summaries and assessments brief   299
Follow directions carefully   299

12   **Synthesis Papers** 300

Understanding synthesis papers 301
   Read reputable sources on your subject 301
   Summarize and paraphrase what you have read 301
   Examine the connections between your sources 302
   Acknowledge disagreements and rebuttals 302

Lauren Chiu, *Time to Adapt?* 305

Getting the details right 308
   Introduce materials that provide a context for your topic 308
   Cite materials that explain or complicate your thesis 308
   Don't rush to judgment 308
   Tell a story 308
   Cite materials that support your thesis 308
   Acknowledge materials that run counter to your thesis 309
   Pay attention to language 309
   Be sure to document your sources 309

13   **E-mails** 310

Understanding e-mail 311
   Explain your purpose clearly and logically 311
   Tell readers what you want them to do 311
   Write for intended and unintended audiences 312
   Minimize the clutter 312
   Keep your messages brief 312
   Distribute your messages sensibly 312

John Ruszkiewicz, *Annual Big Bend Trip* 313

Getting the details right 314
   Choose a sensible subject line 314
   Arrange your text sensibly 314
   Check the recipient list before you hit send 314
   Include an appropriate signature 314
   Use standard grammar 315
   Have a sensible e-mail address 315
   Don't be a pain 315

14   **Business Letters** 316

Understanding business letters 317
   Explain your purpose clearly and logically 317
   Tell your readers what you want them to do 317

Write for your audience   318
Keep the letter focused and brief   318
Use a conventional form   318
Distribute copies of your letter sensibly   319

Nancy Linn, *Cover Letter*   320

John Humbert, *To* Home Design *Magazine*   321

Getting the details right   322
Use consistent margins and spacing   322
Finesse the greeting   322
Spell everything right   322
Photocopy the letter as a record   322
Don't forget the promised enclosures   322
Fold the letter correctly and send it in a suitable envelope   323

15   **Résumés**   324

Understanding résumés   325
Gather the necessary information   326
Decide on appropriate categories   326
Arrange the information within categories in reverse chronological order   327
Design pages that are easy to read   327
Proofread every line in the résumé several times   327

Andrea Palladino, *Résumé*   328

Getting the details right   329
Don't leave unexplained gaps in your education or work career   329
Be consistent   329
Protect your personal data   329
Consider having your résumés designed and printed professionally   329

16   **Personal Statements**   330

Understanding personal statements   331
Read the essay prompt carefully   331
Be realistic about your audience   331
Gather your material   331
Decide on a focus or theme   332
Organize the piece conventionally   332
Try a high or middle style   332

Michael Villaverde, *Application Essay for Academic Service Partnership Foundation Internship*   333

Getting the details right   335
    Don't get too artsy   335
    Use common sense   335
    Write the essay yourself   335

17   Lab Reports   336

Understanding lab reports   337
    Follow instructions to the letter   338
    Look at model reports   338
    Be efficient   338
    Edit the final version   338

Shane McNamee, *Synthesis of Luminol*   339

Getting the details right   344
    Keep the lab report impersonal   344
    Keep the style clear   344
    Follow the conventions   344
    Label charts, tables, and graphs carefully   345
    Document the report correctly   345

18   Oral Reports   346

Understanding oral reports   347
    Know your stuff   347
    Organize your presentation   347
    Stay connected to your listeners   348
    Use your voice and body   348
    Adapt your material to the time available   348
    Practice your presentation   349
    Prepare for the occasion   349

Terri Sagastume, *Presentation on Edenlawn Estates*   350

Getting the details right   351
    Be certain you need presentation software   351
    Use slides to introduce points, not cover them   351
    Use a simple and consistent design   352
    Consider alternatives to slide-based presentations   352

reference

Part 3   Ideas 354

19 Brainstorming 356

Find routines that support thinking 357

Build lists 357

Map your ideas 358

Try freewriting 358

Use memory prompts 359

Search online for your ideas 359

VISUAL TUTORIAL: How to Browse for Ideas 360

20 Brainstorming with Others 362

Choose a leader 363

Begin with a goal and set an agenda 363

Set time limits 363

Encourage everyone to participate 363

Avoid premature criticism 363

Test all ideas 364

Keep good records 364

Agree on an end product 364

21 Smart Reading 365

Read to deepen what you already know 366

Read above your level of knowledge 366

Read what makes you uncomfortable 366

Read against the grain 367

Read slowly   367

Annotate what you read   367

Read visually   368

22   **Critical Thinking**   372

Think in terms of claims and reasons   372

Think in terms of premises and assumptions   373

Think in terms of evidence   375

Anticipate objections   375

Avoid logical fallacies   375

23   **Experts**   379

Talk with your instructor   379

Take your ideas to the writing center   379

Find local experts   380

Check with librarians   380

Chat with peers   380

VISUAL TUTORIAL: How to Use the Writing Center   382

24   **Writer's Block**   384

Break the project into parts   384

Set manageable goals   385

Create a calendar   385

Limit distractions   386

Do the parts you like first   386

Write a zero draft   386

Reward yourself   387

| Part 4 | **Shaping & Drafting** 388 |

25 | **Genre** 390

Recognize the variety of genres 391
Know how to use genres 392
Appreciate that genres change 392

26 | **Thesis** 393

Write a complete sentence 393
Make a significant claim or assertion 394
Write a declarative sentence, not a question 394
Expect your thesis to mature 394
Introduce a thesis early in a project 395
Or state a thesis late in a project 395
Write a thesis to fit your audience and purpose 396

27 | **Strategies** 398

Use description to set a scene 398
Use division to divide a subject 400
Use classification to sort objects or ideas by consistent principles 401
Use definition to clarify meaning 402
Use comparison and contrast to show similarity and difference 404

28 | **Organization** 406

Examine model documents 406
Sketch out a plan or sequence 406
Visualize structure when appropriate 407
Provide clear steps or signals for readers 407
Deliver on your commitments 407

29   **Outlines** 408

Begin with scratch outlines 408

List key ideas 409

Look for relationships 409

Subordinate ideas 409

Decide on a sequence 410

Move up to a formal outline 411

30   **Paragraphs** 412

Make sure paragraphs lead somewhere 412

Develop ideas adequately 413

Organize paragraphs logically 414

Design paragraphs for readability 415

Use paragraphs to manage transitions 415

31   **Transitions** 416

Use appropriate transitional words and phrases 417

Use the right word or phrase to show time or sequence 417

Use sentence structure to connect ideas 417

Pay attention to nouns and pronouns 418

Use synonyms 418

Use physical devices for transitions 419

Read a draft aloud to locate weak transitions 419

32   **Introductions** 420

Announce your project 421

Preview your project 421

Provide background information 422

Catch the attention of readers 423

Set a tone 423

Follow any required formulas 423

Write an introduction when you're ready 424

33 **Conclusions** 425

Summarize your points, then connect them 425

Reveal your point 426

Finish dramatically 427

34 **Titles** 428

Use titles to focus documents 428

Create searchable titles 429

Avoid whimsical or suggestive titles 429

Capitalize and punctuate titles carefully 429

Part 5 **Style** 430

35 **High, Middle, and Low Style** 432

Use high style for formal, scientific, and scholarly writing 433

Use middle style for personal, argumentative, and some academic writing 435

Use a low style for personal, informal, and even playful writing 437

MODEL: **Sid Jacobson and Ernie Colón,** *The 9/11 Report: A Graphic Adaptation* 439

36 **Inclusive and Culturally Sensitive Style** 440

Avoid expressions that stereotype genders 440

Avoid expressions that stereotype races, ethnic groups, or religious groups 441

Treat all people with respect 442

Avoid sensational language 442

37 **Vigorous, Clear, Economical Style** 444

Use strong, concrete subjects and objects 444

Avoid clumsy noun phrases 445

Avoid sentences with long windups 445

Use action verbs when possible   446

Avoid strings of prepositional phrases   446

Don't repeat key words close together   446

Avoid doublings   447

Turn clauses into more direct modifiers   447

Cut introductory expressions such as *it is* and
 there is/are when you can   448

Vary your sentence lengths and structures   448

Listen to what you have written   448

Cut a first draft by 25 percent—or more   448

Part 6   Revising & Editing   450

38   Revising Your Own Work   452

Revise to see the big picture   453

Edit to make the paper flow   453

Edit to get the details right   454

VISUAL TUTORIAL: How to Revise Your Work   456

39   Peer Editing   458

Peer edit the same way you revise your own work   459

Be specific in identifying problems or opportunities   459

Offer suggestions for improvement   459

Praise what is genuinely good in the paper   460

Use proofreading symbols   460

Keep comments tactful   461

VISUAL TUTORIAL: How to Insert a Comment in
 a Word Document   462

Part 7   Research & Sources   464

40   Beginning Your Research   466

Know your assignment   466

Come up with a plan   467

Find a manageable topic   467

Seek professional help   468

Distinguish between primary and secondary sources   469

Record every source you examine   470

Prepare a topic proposal   470

41   Finding Print and Online Sources   472

Learn to navigate the library catalog   473

Locate research guides   473

Identify the best reference tools for your needs   474

Use online sources intelligently   475

42   Doing Field Research   478

Interview people with unique knowledge of your subject   479

Make careful and verifiable observations   480

Learn more about fieldwork   481

43   Evaluating Sources   482

Preview source materials for their key features
and strategies   482

Check who published or produced the source   483

Check who wrote the work   483

Consider the audience for a source   483

Establish how current a source is   486

Check the source's documentation   486

44   **Annotating Sources** 487

Annotate sources to understand them   487

Read sources to identify claims   487

Read sources to understand assumptions   487

Read sources to find evidence   488

Record your personal reactions to source material   488

45   **Summarizing Sources** 491

Use a summary to recap what a writer has said   491

Be sure your summary is accurate and complete   492

Use a summary to record your take on a source   492

Prepare a summary to provide a useful record of a source   493

Use summaries to prepare an annotated bibliography   493

46   **Paraphrasing Sources** 494

Identify the key claims and structure of the source   494

Track the source faithfully   494

Record key pieces of evidence   495

Be certain your notes are entirely in your own words   495

Avoid misleading or inaccurate paraphrasing   495

Use your paraphrases to synthesize sources   496

47   **Integrating Sources into Your Work** 497

Cue the reader in some way whenever you introduce borrowed
        material, whether it is summarized, paraphrased, or quoted
        directly   497

Select an appropriate "verb of attribution" to frame borrowed
        material   498

Use ellipsis marks [. . .] to shorten a lengthy quotation   498

Use brackets [ ] to insert explanatory material
        into a quotation   499

Use ellipsis marks, brackets, and other devices to make quoted
  materials suit the grammar of your sentences   500
Use [sic] to signal an obvious error in quoted material   500

48 **Documenting Sources** 501
Understand the point of documentation   501
Understand what you accomplish through documentation   501

49 **MLA Documentation and Format**   503
Document sources according to convention   503
MLA in-text citation   505
MLA works cited entries   512
VISUAL TUTORIAL: How to Cite from a Book   516
VISUAL TUTORIAL: How to Cite from a Magazine   522
VISUAL TUTORIAL: How to Cite from a Web Site   526
VISUAL TUTORIAL: How to Cite from a Database   528
Sample MLA pages   538

50 **APA Documentation and Format**   540
APA in-text citation   543
APA reference entries   549
VISUAL TUTORIAL: How to Cite from a Web Site   556
VISUAL TUTORIAL: How to Cite from a Database   558
Sample APA pages   563

Part 8   Media & Design   566

51 **Understanding Digital Media**   568
Choose a media format based on what you hope
  to accomplish   569
Use blogs to create communities   570

Create Web sites to share information   570

Use wikis to collaborate with others   571

Make podcasts to share audio files   572

Use maps to position ideas   572

Make "movies" to show and tell   575

Try remixes and mashups to create something new   575

52   **Digital Elements**   577

VISUAL TUTORIAL: How to Insert an Image into a Word Document   578

Have good reasons for using new media   580

Download and save digital elements   580

Use tools to edit digital media   581

Use appropriate digital formats   582

Caption images correctly   583

Respect copyrights   583

53   **Tables, Graphs, and Infographics**   584

Use tables to present statistical data   585

Use line graphs to display changes or trends   586

Use bar and column graphs to plot relationships within
      sets of data   586

Use pie charts to display proportions   588

Use maps to display varying types of information   589

Explore the possibilities of infographics   589

54   **Designing Print and Online Documents**   592

Understand the power of images   592

Keep page designs simple and uncluttered   593

Keep the design logical and consistent   594

Keep the design balanced   595

Use templates sensibly   596

Coordinate your colors   598

Use headings if needed   598

Choose appropriate fonts   598

Part 9   Common Errors   600

55   Capitalization   602

Capitalize the names of ethnic, religious, and political groups   602

Capitalize modifiers formed from proper nouns   602

Capitalize all words in titles except prepositions, articles, or conjunctions   603

Take care with compass points, directions, and specific geographical areas   604

Understand academic conventions   604

Capitalize months, days, holidays, and historical periods   604

56   Apostrophes   605

Use apostrophes to form the possessive   605

Use apostrophes in contractions   606

Don't use apostrophes with possessive pronouns   606

57   Commas   607

Use a comma and a coordinating conjunction to join two independent clauses   607

Use a comma after an introductory word group   607

Use commas with transitional words and phrases   608

Put commas around nonrestrictive (that is, nonessential) elements   608

Use commas to separate items in a series   608

Do not use commas to separate compound verbs   609

Do not use a comma between subject and verb   609

Do not use commas to set off restrictive elements   609

58 Comma Splices, Run-ons, and Fragments 610

Identify comma splices and run-ons 610

Fix comma splices and run-ons 611

Identify sentence fragments 612

Fix sentence fragments in your work 612

Watch for fragments in the following situations 612

Use deliberate fragments only in appropriate situations 613

59 Subject/Verb Agreement 614

Be sure the verb agrees with its real subject 614

In most cases, treat multiple subjects joined by
   and as plural 615

When compound subjects are linked by *either . . . or* or
   neither . . . nor, make the verb agree with the nearer
   part of the subject 616

Confirm whether an indefinite pronoun is singular, plural,
   or variable 616

Be consistent with collective nouns 617

60 Irregular Verbs 618

61 Pronoun/Antecedent Agreement 620

Check the number of indefinite pronouns 621

Correct sexist pronoun usage 621

Treat collective nouns consistently 621

62 Pronoun Reference 622

Clarify confusing pronoun antecedents 622

Make sure a pronoun has a plausible antecedent 623

Be certain that the antecedent of *this, that,*
   or *which* isn't vague 623

63 **Pronoun Case** 624

Use the subjective case for pronouns that are subjects 624
Use the objective case for pronouns that are objects 625
Use *whom* when appropriate 625
Finish comparisons to determine the right case 626
Don't be misled by an appositive 626

64 **Misplaced and Dangling Modifiers** 627

Position modifiers close to the words they modify 627
Place adverbs such as *only, almost, especially,*
  and *even* carefully 627
Don't allow a modifier to dangle 628

65 **Parallelism** 629

When possible, make compound items parallel 629
Keep items in a series parallel 630
Keep headings and lists parallel 630

reader

Part 10 **Readings** 632

66 **Narratives: Readings** 634

LITERACY NARRATIVE: David Sedaris, *Me Talk Pretty One Day* 635
MEMOIR: Rob Sheffield, *Rumblefish* 642
GRAPHIC NARRATIVE (EXCERPT): Lynda Barry, *Lost and Found* 654
REFLECTION: Naomi Shihab Nye, *Mint Snowball* 661
MEMOIR: Ira Sukrungruang, *Chop Suey* 664
LITERACY NARRATIVE: Jonathan Franzen, *The Comfort Zone* 668

67 **Reports: Readings 686**

INFORMATIVE REPORT: **Sharon Begley,** *Learning to Love Climate "Adaptation"* 687

INFORMATIVE REPORT: **David Wolman,** *The Truth about Autism: Scientists Reconsider What They Think They Know* 691

INFORMATIVE REPORT: **Kathryn Miles,** *Dog Is Our Copilot* 703

LEGAL REPORT: **Philip Deloria,** *The Cherokee Nation Decision* 717

DESCRIPTIVE REPORT: **Molly Young,** *Sweatpants in Paradise* 726

68 **Arguments: Readings 735**

EDITORIAL: **Maureen Dowd,** *Don't Send in the Clones* 736

PROFILE: **Nancy Gibbs,** *Cool Running* 739

ARGUMENT FOR CHANGE: **Emily Bazelon,** *Hitting Bottom: Why America Should Outlaw Spanking* 743

ANALYSIS OF CULTURAL VALUES: **Poranee Natadecha-Sponsel,** *The Young, the Rich, and the Famous: Individualism as an American Cultural Value* 748

POLICY ARGUMENT: **Daniel Engber,** *Glutton Intolerance* 758

69 **Evaluations: Readings 764**

TELEVISION REVIEW: **Carrie Brownstein,** *So I Thought I Could Dance* 765

SCIENTIFIC EVALUATION: **Michio Kaku,** *Force Fields* 769

TECHNOLOGY REVIEW: **Sasha Frere-Jones,** *You, the D.J.* 783

TELEVISION REVIEW: **Nelle Engoron,** *Why Mad Men Is Bad for Women* 788

CONCERT REVIEW: **Ann Powers,** *Live Review: Lady Gaga at Staples Center* 795

70   **Causal Analyses: Readings**   799

TECHNOLOGY ANALYSIS: **Nicholas Carr,** *Is Google Making Us
Stupid?*   800

CULTURAL ANALYSIS: **Natalie Angier,** *Almost Before We Spoke,
We Swore*   811

CULTURAL ANALYSIS: **Alex Williams,** *Here I Am Taking My Own
Picture*   818

CAUSAL ANALYSIS: **Virginia Postrel,** *Pop Psychology*   823

EXPLORATORY ESSAY: **Tricia Rose,** *Hip Hop Causes
Violence*   829

71   **Proposals: Readings**   858

PROPOSAL FOR CHANGE: **Bill Gates and Melinda Gates,** *Educating
America's Young People for the Global Economy*   859

PROPOSAL FOR CHANGE: **Eileen McDonagh and Laura Pappano,** *Time
to Change the Rules*   872

PROPOSAL FOR CHANGE: **Thomas L. Friedman,** *Start-Ups,
Not Bailouts*   884

SATIRICAL PROPOSAL: **Kembrew McLeod,** *A Modest Free Market
Proposal for Education Reform*   887

PROPOSAL FOR CHANGE: **Peter Singer,** *"One Person, One Share" of the
Atmosphere*   892

72   **Literary Analyses: Readings**   898

FORMAL ANALYSIS: **Adam Bradley,** *Rap Poetry 101*   899

TEXTUAL ANALYSIS:

Charles Schulz, *Peanuts* (cartoon)   913

Geraldine DeLuca, *"I felt a Funeral, in my Brain": The Fragile Comedy of
Charles Schulz*   914

TEXTUAL ANALYSIS:

Joni Mitchell, *"Woodstock"* (song lyrics)   925

Camille Paglia, *"Woodstock"*   927

HISTORICAL ANALYSIS: **Sara Buttsworth,** *CinderBella: Twilight, Fairy
Tales, and the Twenty-First-Century American Dream*   935

CULTURAL ANALYSIS: **Gish Jen,** *Holden Raises Hell*   961

| 73 | **Rhetorical Analyses: Readings**   969 |

DISCOURSE ANALYSIS: Deborah Tannen, *Oh, Mom. Oh, Honey.: Why Do You Have to Say That?*   970

ANALYSIS OF AN ADVERTISEMENT: Stanley Fish, *The Other Car*   976

CULTURAL ANALYSIS: Laurie Fendrich, *The Beauty of the Platitude*   980

MEDIA ANALYSIS: John W. Jordan, *Sports Commentary and the Problem of Television Knowledge*   983

ANALYSIS OF AN ADVERTISEMENT: Caroline Leader, *Dudes Come Clean: Negotiating a Space for Men in Household Cleaner Commercials*   988

Index   I-1

guide

Genres

chronicle events in people's lives

1 **Narratives** 4

provide readers with reliable information

2 **Reports** 44

ask readers to consider debatable ideas

3 **Arguments** 72

make a claim about the merit of something

4 **Evaluations** 106

explain how, why, or what if something happens

5 **Causal Analyses** 138

define a problem and suggest a solution

6 **Proposals** 176

respond critically to cultural works

7 **Literary Analyses** 206

examine in detail the way texts work

8 **Rhetorical Analyses** 250

Need a form that you don't see here? Try "Special Assignments," p. 282.

How to start
- Need a **topic**? See page 10.
- Need to choose the right **details**? See page 14.
- Need to **organize the events** in your story? See page 16.

1 Narratives

chronicle events in people's lives

Chances are you've shared bits and pieces of your life story in writing many times. In doing so, you've written personal narratives. *Personal* does not necessarily mean that writers of personal narratives are always baring their souls. Instead, it implies that they are telling stories from a unique perspective, providing details only they could know and insights only they could have.

REFLECTION
For a scholarship application, you include a *personal reflection*, explaining how a summer job in a drugstore made you first consider a career in pharmacy.

LITERACY NARRATIVE
To work at the campus writing center, you must prepare a *literacy narrative* detailing your own experiences with writing and language.

STUDENT MEMOIR
You direct your grandparents to a community group that is collecting *memoirs* from local citizens so that they can describe their experiences as immigrants.

GRAPHIC NARRATIVE
You want more people to think about bicycling to work, so you create a *visual narrative* about your own experiences as an urban cyclist, posting both photographs and videos on a blog.

DECIDING TO WRITE A NARRATIVE.   Narratives may describe almost any human activity that writers want to share with readers: school, family, work experiences, personal tragedies, travel, sports, growing up, relationships, and so on. Stories can be told in words or through other media, including photographs, film, songs, cartoons, and more. ○ Expect a narrative you write to do the following.

Tell a story.   In a narrative, something usually happens. Maybe all you do in the piece is reflect on a single moment when something peculiar caught your attention. Or your story could follow a simple sequence of events—the classic road-trip script. Or you might spin a tale complicated enough to seem like an actual plot, with a connected beginning, middle, and end. In every case, though, you need to select specific events that serve your purpose in writing, whatever it may be. Otherwise you're just rambling.

StoryCorps Story-Booth   StoryCorps is a national project of Sound Portraits Productions meant to inspire people to record one another's stories in sound. And, yes, there's an iPhone app.

(Photo of the StoryCorps Story-Booth, courtesy of StoryCorps. Learn more at www.storycorps.net.)

choose a genre
p. 390

Make a point—usually.   Your point may depend on your specific reason for writing a narrative. If your insurance agent asks about your recent auto wreck, she probably just wants to know who hit whom and how you are involved in the incident. But most narratives will be less cut-and-dry and more reflective, enabling you to connect with audiences more subtly—to amuse, enlighten, and, perhaps, even to change them. ⚪ Some narratives are therapeutic too, enabling you to confront personal issues or to get a weight off your chest.

Observe details closely.   What makes a narrative memorable and brings it to life are its details—the colors, shapes, textures, sounds, and smells that you share with readers through language or other media. Those physical impressions go a long way toward convincing people that a story is credible and honest. They prove that you were close enough to an experience to have an insider's perspective. So share your sensory reactions with readers, conveying specific information as events unfurl. But don't fall back on clichés to make your points. Give readers evidence that the story really belongs to you.

Sara Smith, a college student, keeps a journal both to explore ideas that are important to her and so she'll have a reservoir of events and memories for writing assignments. Does this journal entry suggest any paper topics to you?

> My Dad friended me last night. How lame is that? Last month he didn't know how to send an e-mail and all of a sudden he has his own page on Facebook. It's really sad, it's worse than sad, it's pathetic. He's lonely. Has no friends. So he puts up a picture of us — a father and his very happy daughter, both with the Albert Einstein crazy hair except his is grey and mine is brown, both beaming — to show people what a good family guy he is. There should be an age limit or something, for Facebook.

develop a statement
p. 393

Reflection

Mark Edmundson, a professor of English at the University of Virginia, tells a lengthy tale about an odd job he had after graduating from college as a lesson to students today not to rush into their professional careers without first experiencing the world. The narrative is key to his argument—it engages readers with details about working on a concert for the band Pink Floyd, but then leads up to a splendid climax. The article may seem like a story, but it is tightly organized to make a point.

The Pink Floyd Night School

Mark Edmundson

May 2, 2010

"So, what are you doing after graduation?"

In the spring of my last year in college I posed that question to at least a dozen fellow graduates-to-be at my little out-of-the-way school in Vermont. The answers they gave me were satisfying in the extreme: not very much, just kick back, hang out, look things over, take it slow. It was 1974. That's what you were supposed to say.

My classmates weren't, strictly speaking, telling the truth. They were, one might even say, lying outrageously. By graduation day, it was clear that most of my contemporaries would be trotting off to law school and graduate school and to cool and unusual internships in New York and San Francisco.

But I did take it slow. After graduation, I spent five years wandering around doing nothing—or getting as close to it as I could manage. I was a cab driver, an obsessed moviegoer, a wanderer in the mountains of Colorado, a teacher at a crazy grand hippie school in Vermont, the manager of a movie house (who didn't do much managing), a crewman on a ship and a doorman at a disco.

The most memorable job of all, though, was a gig on the stage crew for a rock production company in Jersey City. We did our shows at Roosevelt Stadium, a grungy behemoth that could hold 60,000, counting seats on the grass. I humped amps out of the trucks and onto the stage; six or so hours later I humped them back. I did it for the Grateful Dead and Alice Cooper and the Allman Brothers and Crosby, Stills & Nash on

This opening question will be repeated again later in the narrative, giving a tight structure to the story.

The paragraph is full of authentic details about the 1970s. Note the word choices too: *gig, grungy, humped.*

the night that Richard Nixon resigned. But the most memorable night of that most memorable job was the night of Pink Floyd.

Pink Floyd demanded a certain quality of sound. They wanted their amps stacked high, not just on stage, where they were so broad and tall and forbidding that they looked like a barricade in the Paris Commune. They also wanted amp clusters at three highly elevated points around the stadium, and I spent the morning lugging huge blocks of wood and circuitry up and up and up the stairs of the decayed old bowl.

There was one other assignment: a parachute-like white silken canopy roof that Pink Floyd required over the stage. It took about six hours to get the thing up and in position. We were told that this was the first use of the canopy and Pink's guys were unsteady. They had some blueprints, but those turned out not to be of much use. Eventually the roof did rise and inflate, with American know-how applied. Such know-how involved a lot of spontaneous knot-tying and strategic rope tangling.

Pink Floyd went on at about 10 that night and the amp clusters that we'd expended all that servile sweat to build didn't work—people had sat on them, kicked them or cut the cords. So Pink made its noise, the towers stayed mute, the mob flicked on lighters at the end and then we spent three hours breaking the amps down and loading the truck. We refused to go after the speakers all the way up the stadium steps and, after some sharp words, Pink's guys had to scramble up and retrieve them.

There was, for the record, almost always tension between the roadies and the stage crew. One time, at a show by (if memory serves) Queen, their five roadies got into a brawl with a dozen of our stage crew guys; then the house security, mostly Jersey bikers and black-belt karate devotees, heard the noise and jumped in. The roadies held on for a while, but finally they saw it was a lost cause. One of them grabbed a case of champagne from the truck cab and opened a bottle and passed it around—all became drunk and happy. Pink's road manager wanted the inflatable canopy brought down gently, then folded and packed securely in its wooden boxes. The problem was that the thing was full of helium and no one knew where the release valve was; we'd also secured it to the stage with so many knots of such foolish intricacy that their disentanglement would have given a gang of sailors pause. Everyone was tired. Those once intoxicated were no longer. It was 4 a.m. and time to go home.

Edmundson must digress here to explain the tensions between roadies and stage crews so the key incident in his story makes sense.

The details here about Jimbo keep readers amused and engaged by the story.

An hour went into concocting strategies to get the floating billowy roof down. It became a regular seminar. Then came Jim—Jimbo—our crew chief, who looked like a good-natured Viking captain and who defended the integrity of his stage crew at every turn, even going so far as to have screamed at Stevie Nicks, who was yelling at me for having dropped a guitar case, that he was the only one who had the right to holler at Edmundson. Faced with the Pink Floyd roof crisis, Jimbo did what he always could be counted on to do in critical circumstances, which is to say, he did something.

Jimbo walked softly to a corner of the stage, reached into his pocket, removed a buck knife and with it began to saw one of the ropes attaching the holy celestial roof to the earth. Three or four of us, his minions, did the same. "Hey, what are you doing?" wailed Pink's head roadie. "I'll smash your—" Only then did he realize that Jimbo had a knife in his hand, and that some of the rest of us did, too. In the space of a few minutes, we sawed through the ropes.

There came a great sighing noise as the last thick cord broke apart. For a moment there was nothing; for another moment, more of the same.

Then the canopy rose into the air and began to float away, like a gorgeous cloud, white and soft. The sun at that moment burst above the horizon and the silk bloomed into a soft crimson tinge. Jimbo started to laugh his big bear-bellied laugh. We all joined. Even Pink's guys did. We were like little kids on the last day of school. We stood on the naked stage, watching the silk roof go up and out, wafting over the Atlantic. Some of us waved.

"So, what are you doing after graduation?" Thirty-five years later, a college teacher, I ask my students the old question. They aren't inclined to dissimulate now. The culture is on their side when they tell me about law school and med school and higher degrees in journalism and business; or when they talk about a research grant in China or a well-paying gig teaching English in Japan.

Here's the one major point of the story, the reason Edmundson has offered his personal experience to readers.

I'm impressed, sure, but I'm worried about them too. Aren't they deciding too soon? Shouldn't they hang out a little, learn to take it slow? I can't help it. I flash on that canopy of white silk floating out into the void. I can see it as though it were still there. I want to point up to it. I'd like for my students to see it, too.

The opening question is repeated, but note the difference now in the students' answers.

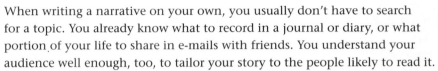

Exploring purpose and topic

▶ topic

When writing a narrative on your own, you usually don't have to search for a topic. You already know what to record in a journal or diary, or what portion of your life to share in e-mails with friends. You understand your audience well enough, too, to tailor your story to the people likely to read it.

Assigned to write a narrative in school, however, you face different choices. Typically, such an assignment asks you to describe an event that has changed or shaped you. Or perhaps an instructor requests a story that explores an aspect of your personality or reveals something about the communities to which you belong. But when no topic ideas present themselves, consider the following strategies.

For example, this picture of Niki de Saint Phalle's sculpture *Sun God* got one student writing about her very colorful trip to San Diego, California.

Brainstorm, freewrite, build lists, and use memory prompts to find a topic for a narrative. It might help, for example, to scroll through some old photographs on your computer or even to pick up your yearbook. Talk with others, too, about their choices of subjects or share ideas on a class Web site. Trading ideas might jog your own memory about an incident or moment worth retelling.

Choose a manageable subject. You may be tempted to write about life-changing events so dramatic that they can seem clichéd: deaths, graduations, car wrecks, winning hits, or first love. But understand that to make such topics work, you have to make them fresh for readers who've likely undergone similar experiences—or seen the movie. If you find an angle on such familiar events that belongs specifically to you and can express it originally, you might take the risk. ○

Alternatively, you can narrate a slice of life rather than the whole side of beef—your toast at a wedding rather than the three-hour reception, a single encounter on a road trip rather than the entire cross-country adventure, or the scariest part of the night you were home alone when the power went out, rather than a minute-by-minute description. Most big adventures contain within them dozens of more manageable tales.

get an idea
p. 356

Understanding your audience

People like to read other people's stories, so the audiences for narratives are large, diverse, and receptive. (Even many diarists secretly hope that someone someday will find and read the confidential story of their lives.) Most of these eager readers probably expect a narrative to make some point or reveal an insight. Typically, they hope to be moved by the piece, to learn something from it, or perhaps to be amused by it.

You can capitalize on those expectations, using stories to introduce ideas that readers might be less eager to entertain if presented more formally. Here's a writer for *Automobile* magazine using a brief anecdote to introduce a piece about electric cars:

> I took two semesters of physics in college. The first concerned the physical world — objects smashing into one another, mass, momentum — concepts that made intuitive sense. I got a B. The second focused on electromagnetic fields, which are invisible and have something to do with calculus. I got a D+. So it's perhaps understandable that I'm a bit apprehensive about the brave new world of the electric car.
>
> — Ezra Dyer, "On the Juice," July 2010

Sometimes, however, your audience is already attuned to a subject. For instance, people within well-defined social, political, ethnic, or religious groups are often eager to read and share their life experiences. Women and members of minority groups have used such narratives to document the adversities they face or to affirm their solidarity. Similarly, members of religious groups recall what it was like to grow up Jewish or Catholic or Baptist — and their readers appreciate when a story hits a familiar note. The best of these personal narratives, naturally, attract readers from outside the target audience too. O

Of course, you might decide that the target audience of a narrative is ultimately yourself: You write about personal experiences to understand them. Even then, be demanding. Think about how your story might sound ten or twenty years from now. Whatever the audience, you have choices to make.

respect your readers
p. 440

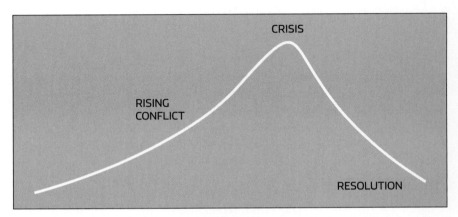

A Classic Narrative Arc   You'll need to decide where to start your story and where to stop. The plan shown in this illustration is effective because the action unfolds in a way that meets audience expectations.

Select events that will keep readers engaged.   Consider what parts of your topic will matter to readers. Which events represent high points in the action or moments that could not logically be omitted? Select those and consider cutting the others. Build toward a few major events in the story that support one or two key themes—in Edmundson's narrative (see p. 7) it's the canopy floating away.

Pace the story effectively.   Readers do want the story to move ahead, but not always at the same speed. Early on, they may want to learn about the characters involved in the action or to be introduced to the setting. You can slow the narrative to fill in these details and also to set up expectations for what will follow. For instance, if a person plays a role later in the story, introduce him or her briefly in the early paragraphs. If a cat matters, introduce the cat. But don't dwell on incidentals: Keep the story moving.

Tailor your writing to your intended readers. An informal story written for peers may need brisk action as well as slang and dialogue to sound convincing—though you shouldn't use rough language for cheap effects. In a narrative written for an academic audience, you might slow the pace and use more neutral language. But don't be too cautious. You still want the story to have enough texture to make your experiences seem authentic.

For instance, when writing a personal statement for an application to an academic program, keep a tight rein on the way you present yourself. ⦾ Here, for example, is a serious anecdote offered in an application to graduate school. You could easily imagine it told much more comically to friends.

> During my third year of Russian, I auditioned for the role of the evil stepsister Anna in a stage production of *Zolushka*. Although I welcomed the chance to act, I was terrified because I could not pronounce a Russian *r*. I had tried but was only able to produce an embarrassing sputter. Leading up to the play, I practiced daily with my professor, repeating "ryba" with a pencil in my mouth. When the play opened, I was able to say "*Kakoe urodstvo!*" with confidence. This experience gave me tremendous pride, because through it I discovered the power to isolate a problem, seek the necessary help, and ultimately solve it. I want to pass this power along to others by becoming a Russian language instructor.
>
> —Melissa Miller

refine your tone
p. 432

Finding and developing materials

▶ develop details

Photographs such as this one taken at a Fourth of July parade may recall not only the scene but also the moment the photo was taken, who was there, and so on.

When you write about an event soon after it occurs—for instance, an accident report for an insurance claim—you might have the facts fresh in your mind. Yet even in such cases, evidence helps back up your recollections. That's why insurance companies encourage drivers to carry a disposable camera in their cars in case they have a collision. The photo freezes details that human memory, especially under pressure, could ignore or forget. Needless to say, when writing about events in the more distant past, other aids to memory will help.

Consult documents. A journal, if you keep one, provides a handy record for personal narratives such as a job history or family chronicle. Even a daily planner or electronic calendar might hold the necessary facts to reconstruct a series of events: Just knowing when important meetings occurred may refresh your memory.

Consult images. Photographs and videos provide material for personal narratives of all sorts. Not only do they document people and places, but they may also generate ideas, calling to mind far more than just what appears in the images. In writing a personal narrative, such prompts may stimulate your recall of past events and, just as important, the feelings those events generated. Visual images also remind you of physical details—shapes, colors, and textures—that can add authenticity to a narrative and assure readers you're a sharp observer.

Trust your experiences. In gathering material for a narrative (or looking for a subject), you might doubt your credentials: "What have I done worth writing about"? ○ Most people underestimate the quality of their own experience. First-year college students, for example, are usually knowledgeable about high school or certain kinds of music or working minimum-wage jobs or dealing with difficult parents. You don't have to be an expert to observe life or have something to say about it.

Here's humorist David Sedaris—who has made a career writing about his very middle-class life from his unique personal perspective—describing the insecurity of many writers:

> When I was teaching—I taught for a while—my students would write as if they were raised by wolves. Or raised on the streets. They were middle-class kids and they were ashamed of their background. They felt like unless they grew up in poverty, they had nothing to write about. Which was interesting because I had always thought that poor people were the ones who were ashamed. But it's not. It's middle-class people who are ashamed of their lives. And it doesn't really matter what your life was like, you can write about anything. It's just the writing of it that is the challenge. I felt sorry for these kids, that they thought that their whole past was absolutely worthless because it was less than remarkable.
>
> —David Sedaris, interviewed in *January Magazine*, June 2000

Your Turn   Where might you search for ideas if you were writing a tale about some slice of your life? Obviously, relatives and friends might be good resources, as would photo albums and memory books. But how about some off-the-wall resources—your list of bookmarked Web sites, for example, or a hometown map, or maybe your clothes closet? List other offbeat memory prompts and compare your ideas with those your classmates suggest.

find a topic
p. 356

Creating a structure

▶ organize events

Don't be intimidated by the idea of organizing a narrative. ⭘ You know a great deal about narrative structure from watching films or TV. All the complex plot devices you see in dramas or comedies—from foreshadowing to flashback—can be adapted to narratives you create in prose. But you need to plan ahead, know how many words or pages you have to tell your story, and then be sure you connect your incidents with effective transitional words and phrases.

Consider a simple sequence.   In a simple sequence, one event follows another chronologically. This structure has its complications, but it's a natural choice for narrative. Journals and diaries probably have the simplest sequential structures, with writers just recording one event after another without connecting them by anything much more than a date.

> **First event**
> **Next event**
> **Next event**
> **Final event**

Build toward a climax.   Narratives become more complex if you want to present a set of incidents that lead to a *climax* or an *epiphany*. A climax is the moment when the action of a story peaks, takes an important turn, or is resolved. An epiphany is a moment of revelation when a writer or character suddenly sees events in a new light.

> **First event**
> **Next event**
> **Next event**
>
> **Climax and/or epiphany**
>
> **Final event**

connect ideas
p. 416

Narratives can have both structural features and often do—it's only logical that a major event in life would trigger heightened awareness or new understanding. In creating a structure for this kind of narrative, you can begin by deciding what that important event will be and then choosing other elements and incidents that lead up to or explain it. Omit everything not connected to that moment from the story. O

Similarly, when you want a narrative to make a specific point, include only events and incidents that reinforce your theme, directly or indirectly. Delete any actions that don't contribute to that point, however much you love them. Or refocus your narrative on a moment that you do love.

If every picture tells a story, what narrative does this image suggest? Consider the missing windmill blade, the worker's posture, the quiet sky, and any other details that seem important.

revise and edit
p. 452

Choosing a style and design

Narratives are usually written in middle or low styles. That's because both styles nicely mimic the human voice through devices such as contractions and colloquialisms. Both styles are also comfortable with *I*, the point of view of many stories. A middle style may be safe for reaching academic or professional audiences. But a low style, dipping into slang and unconventional speech, can more accurately capture many moments in life and thus feel more authentic. It's your choice.

Style is important because narratives get their energy and textures from sentence structures and vocabulary choices. In general, narratives require tight but expressive language—*tight* to keep the action moving, *expressive* to capture the gist of events. In a first draft, run with your ideas and don't do much editing. Flesh out the skeleton as you have designed it and then go back to see if the story works technically: Characters should be introduced and developed, locations identified and colored, events clearly explained and sequenced, key points made memorably and emphatically. You'll likely need several drafts to get these major items into shape.

Then look at your language and allow plenty of time for it. Begin with Chapter 37, "Vigorous, Clear, Economical Style." When the language is right, your readers get the impression that you have observed events closely. Here are some options for your narrative.

Don't hesitate to use first person—*I*.   Most personal narratives are about the writer, so first-person pronouns are used without apology. O (Third-person perspective tends to be used by essayists and humorists.)

A narrative often must take readers where the *I* has been, and using the first-person pronoun helps make writing authentic. Consider online journalist Michael Yon's explanation of why he reported on the Iraq War using *I* rather than a more objective third-person perspective:

> I write in first person because I am actually there at the events I write about. When I write about the bombs exploding, or the smell of blood, or the bullets snapping by, and I say *I*, it's because I was there. Yesterday a sniper shot at us, and seven of my neighbors were injured by a large bomb. These are my neighbors. These are soldiers. . . . I feel the fire from the explosions, and am lucky, very lucky, still to be alive. Everything here is first person.
>
> —Glenn Reynolds, *An Army of Davids*

define your style
p. 432

Use figures of speech such as similes, metaphors, and analogies to make memorable comparisons.   *Similes* make comparisons by using *like* or *as*: *He used his camera* like *a rifle. Metaphors* drop the *like* or *as* to gain even more power: *His camera was a rifle aimed at enemies.* An *analogy* extends the comparison: *His camera became a rifle aimed at his imaginary enemies, their private lives in his crosshairs.*

People use comparisons eagerly. Some are so common they've been reduced to invisible clichés: *hit me like a ton of bricks; dumb as an ox; clear as a bell.* You want to use similes and metaphors in your narratives that are fresher than these and yet not contrived or strained. Here's science writer Michael Chorost effortlessly deploying both a metaphor (*spins up*) and a simile (*like riding a roller coaster*) to describe what he experiences as he awaits surgery.

> I can feel the bustle and clatter around me as the surgical team spins up to take-off speed. It is like riding a roller coaster upward to the first great plunge, strapped in and committed.
>
> — *Rebuilt: How Becoming Part Computer Made Me More Human*

In choosing verbs, favor active rather than passive voice.   Active verbs propel the action (*Estela signed the petition*), while passive verbs slow it down by an unneeded word or two (*The petition was signed by Estela*). ○

Since narratives are all about movement, build sentences around strong and unpretentious verbs. Edit until you get down to the bone of the action and produce sentences as effortless as these from Joseph Epstein, describing the pleasures of catching plagiarists. ○ Verbs are highlighted in this passage; you'll find only one passive verb (*is followed*) in the mix.

> In thirty years of teaching university students I never encountered a case of plagiarism, or even one that I suspected. Teachers I've known who have caught students in this sad act report that the capture gives one an odd sense of power. The power derives from the authority that resides behind the word *gotcha*. This is followed by that awful moment — a veritable sadist's Mardi Gras — when one calls the student into one's office and points out the odd coincidence that he seems to have written about existentialism in precisely the same words Jean-Paul Sartre used fifty-two years earlier.
>
> — "Plagiary, It's Crawling All Over Me," *Weekly Standard*, March 6, 2006

> Need help seeing the big picture? See "How to Revise Your Work" on pp. 456–57.

improve your sentences
p. 444

avoid plagiarism
p. 497

> The difference between the almost right word and the right word is really a large matter — it's the difference between the lightning bug and the lightning.

—Mark Twain

Use powerful and precise modifiers.   In most cases, one strong word is better than several weaker ones (*freezing* rather than *very cold; doltish* rather than *not very bright*). Done right, proper modifiers can even make you hungry.

> My friend Barbara got the final stretch of the trip, a southwestern route of burritos and more burritos: with and without rice, with and without sour cream, planned burritos and serendipitous burritos.
>
> We pulled off the highway near Odessa, Texas, to hunt down a Taco Villa and, across the street, espied something called JumBurrito, an even smaller Texas chain. Taco Villa's grilled chicken burrito had a profusion of chicken that indeed tasted grilled, while JumBurrito's combination burrito redeemed dull beef with vibrant avocado.
>
> Neither approximated the majesty of the burrito I loved most, which I ate in Dallas, at a Taco Cabana. A great burrito is a balancing act, and the proportions of ground beef, beans, sour cream, and diced tomatoes in Taco Cabana's plump, heavy Burrito Ultimo (three Wet Naps) were spot on.
>
> —Frank Bruni, "Life in the Fast-Food Lane," *New York Times*, May 24, 2006

Use dialogue to propel the narrative and to give life to your characters.   What people say and how they say it can reveal a great deal about them without much commentary from you. But be sure the words your characters speak sound natural: *No* dialogue is better than awkward dialogue. Dialogue ordinarily requires quotation marks and new paragraphs for each change of speaker. But keep the tags simple: You don't have to vary much from *he said* or *she said*.

> "My dear Mr. Bennet," said his lady to him one day, "have you heard that Netherfield Park is let at last?"
>
> Mr. Bennet replied that he had not. "But it is," returned she; "for Mrs. Long has just been here, and she told me all about it."
>
> Mr. Bennet made no answer.
>
> "Do not you want to know who has taken it?" cried his wife, impatiently.
>
> "*You* want to tell me, and I have no objection to hearing it." This was invitation enough.
>
> —Jane Austen, *Pride and Prejudice*

Your Turn Good dialogue is hard to write. So practice. Write a one-page story mostly in dialogue, like the brief excerpt from *Pride and Prejudice*. Tell readers what you must about your characters, but let most of the action occur within their words. Then read your story aloud over and over and revise it until the dialogue sounds authentic. Get feedback from your classmates, and give them suggestions on their stories as well.

Develop major characters through language and action.   Search for the precise adjectives and adverbs to describe your characters' looks (*cheery, greedily*) and manners (*tight, conceitedly, smarmy*) or, even better, have them reveal their natures by their actions (*glancing in every mirror; ignoring the staff to fawn over the bigwigs*). In fact, you'll probably need to do both. Here's how one writer describes a classmate (ouch!) with whom she is partnered on a group project:

> Jane dragged me to her dorm one weekend to help her crunch the numbers. Her phone started ringing, but she told me to ignore it. The answering machine clicked on as a whiny, southern voice pleaded, "Jane, Honey, where *are* yew? Daddy and I have been trying to reach you for three days, but you haven't answered your dorm or cell phones. Please, call us so we'll know that you're okay. We love you very much, Sweetie."
>
> Jane's annoyance rivaled the desperation in her mother's voice. She had always claimed to love her family, but she barely batted an eye at her mom's concern for her well-being. "I don't have time for her right now," Jane stated coldly as she continued typing.
>
> —Bettina Ramon, "Ambition Incarnate"

If you are using dialogue—say it aloud as you write it. Only then will it have the sound of speech.

—John Steinbeck

Develop the setting to set the context and mood.   Show readers where and when events are occurring if the setting makes a difference—and that will be most of the time. Location (Times Square; dusty street in Gallup, New Mexico; your bedroom), as well as climate and time of day (cool dawn, exotic dusk, broiling afternoon), will help readers get a fix on the story. But don't churn out paragraphs of description ○ just for their own sake; readers will skate right over them.

develop a draft
p. 398

Use images to tell a story.   Consider whether photographs attached
to the narrative might help readers grasp the setting and situation. Or
use images simply to brighten your narrative or to illustrate a sequence of
events. An illustrated timeline is a simple form of this kind of narrative, as
are scrapbooks or high school yearbooks. More complex stories about your
life or community can be told by combining your words and pictures in
photo-essays or other media environments. **O**

Don't, however, use images as an excuse to avoid descriptive writing;
rather, consider how they complement your text, and so may have a legitimate place in your story.

Fisherman with His Catch, a 32-inch, 18-pound Striped Bass   Note how the
photograph conveys far more than the statistics alone would.

think visually
p. 592

Examining models

Such a piece typically narrates the processes by which a person learns to read or write or acquires an intellectual skill or ability. In "Strange Tools," author Richard Rodriguez explains how he developed his habits of reading. The selection is from *Hunger of Memory* (1981), in which Rodriguez explains how his life has followed the pattern of "the scholarship boy," described by Richard Hoggart as a youth from a lower-class background whose pursuit of education separates him from his community.

Strange Tools

RICHARD RODRIGUEZ

Sets the scene.

From an early age I knew that my mother and father could read and write both Spanish and English. I had observed my father making his way through what, I now suppose, must have been income tax forms. On other occasions I waited apprehensively while my mother read onion-paper letters airmailed from Mexico with news of a relative's illness or death. For both my parents, however, reading was something done out of necessity and as quickly as possible. Never did I see either of them read an entire book. Nor did I see them read for pleasure. Their reading consisted of work manuals, prayer books, newspapers, recipes.

Richard Hoggart imagines how, at home,

> . . . [The scholarship boy] sees strewn around, and reads regularly himself, magazines which are never mentioned at school, which seem not to belong to the world to which the school introduces him; at school he hears about and reads books never mentioned at home. When he brings those books into the house they do not take their place with other books which the family are reading, for often there are none or almost none; his books look, rather, like strange tools.

Hoggart's "scholarship boy" is a key theme in Rodriguez's work.

In our house each school year would begin with my mother's careful instruction: "Don't write in your books so we can sell them at the end of

23

the year." The remark was echoed in public by my teachers, but only in part: "Boys and girls, don't write in your books. You must learn to treat them with great care and respect."

Narrates early experiences as a reader.

OPEN THE DOORS OF YOUR MIND WITH BOOKS, read the red and white poster over the nun's desk in early September. It soon was apparent to me that reading was the classroom's central activity. Each course had its own book. And the information gathered from a book was unquestioned. READ TO LEARN, the sign on the wall advised in December. I privately wondered: What was the connection between reading and learning? Did one learn something only by reading it? Was an idea only an idea if it could be written down? In June, CONSIDER BOOKS YOUR BEST FRIENDS. Friends? Reading was, at best, only a chore. I needed to look up whole paragraphs of words in a dictionary. Lines of type were dizzying, the eye having to move slowly across the page, then down, and across. . . .The sentences of the first books I read were coolly impersonal. Toned hard. What most bothered me, however, was the isolation reading required. To console myself for the loneliness I'd feel when I read, I tried reading in a very soft voice. Until: "Who is doing all that talking to his neighbor?" Shortly after, remedial reading classes were arranged for me with a very old nun.

At the end of each school day, for nearly six months, I would meet with her in the tiny room that served as the school's library but was actually only a storeroom for used textbooks and a vast collection of *National Geographics*. Everything about our sessions pleased me: the smallness of the room; the noise of the janitor's broom hitting the edge of the long hallway outside the door; the green of the sun, lighting the wall; and the old woman's face blurred white with a beard. Most of the time we took turns. I began with my elementary text. Sentences of astonishing simplicity seemed to me lifeless and drab: "The boys ran from the rain. . . . She wanted to sing. . . . The kite rose in the blue." Then the old nun would read from her favorite books, usually biographies of early American presidents. Playfully she ran through complex sentences, calling the words alive with her voice, making it seem that the author somehow was

Details give Rodriguez's experiences impact.

speaking directly to me. I smiled just to listen to her. I sat there and sensed for the very first time some possibility of fellowship between a reader and a writer, a communication, never *intimate* like that I heard spoken words at home convey, but one nonetheless *personal*.

Most action occurs in Rodriguez's thoughts.

One day the nun concluded a session by asking me why I was so reluctant to read by myself. I tried to explain; said something about the way written words made me feel all alone—almost, I wanted to add but didn't, as when I spoke to myself in a room just emptied of furniture. She studied my face as I spoke; she seemed to be watching more than listening. In an uneventful voice she replied that I had nothing to fear. Didn't I realize that reading would open up whole new worlds? A book could open doors for me. It could introduce me to people and show me places I never imagined existed. She gestured toward the bookshelves. (Bare-breasted African women danced, and the shiny hubcaps of automobiles on the back covers of the *Geographic* gleamed in my mind.) I listened with respect. But her words were not very influential. I was thinking then of another consequence of literacy, one I was too shy to admit but nonetheless trusted. Books were going to make me "educated." *That* confidence enabled me, several months later, to overcome my fear of the silence.

In fourth grade I embarked upon a grandiose reading program. "Give me the names of important books," I would say to startled teachers. They soon found out that I had in mind "adult books." I ignored their suggestion of anything I suspected was written for children. (Not until I was in college, as a result, did I read *Huckleberry Finn* or *Alice's Adventures in Wonderland*.) Instead, I read *The Scarlet Letter* and Franklin's *Autobiography*. And whatever I read I read for extra credit. Each time I finished a book, I reported the achievement to a teacher and basked in the praise my effort earned. Despite my best efforts, however, there seemed to be more and more books I needed to read. At the library I would literally tremble as I came upon whole shelves of books I hadn't read. So I read and I read and I read: *Great Expectations*; all the short stories of Kipling; *The Babe Ruth Story*; the entire first volume of the

Encyclopaedia Britannica (A–ANSTEY); the *Iliad; Moby-Dick; Gone with the Wind; The Good Earth; Remond; Forever Amber; The Lives of the Saints; Crime and Punishment; The Pearl. . . .* Librarians who initially frowned when I checked out the maximum ten books at a time started saving books they thought I might like. Teachers would say to the rest of the class, "I only wish the rest of you took reading as seriously as Richard obviously does."

But at home I would hear my mother wondering, "What do you see in your books?" (Was reading a hobby like her knitting? Was so much reading even healthy for a boy? Was it the sign of "brains"? Or was it just a convenient excuse for not helping around the house on Saturday mornings?) Always, "What do you see . . . ?"

What *did* I see in my books? I had the idea that they were crucial for my academic success, though I couldn't have said exactly how or why. In the sixth grade I simply concluded that what gave a book its value was some major idea or theme it contained. If that core essence could be mined and memorized, I would become learned like my teachers. I decided to record in a notebook the themes of the books that I read. After reading *Robinson Crusoe,* I wrote that its theme was "the value of learning to live by oneself." When I completed *Wuthering Heights,* I noted the danger of "letting emotions get out of control." Rereading these brief moralistic appraisals usually left me disheartened. I couldn't believe that they were really the source of reading's value. But for many more years, they constituted the only means I had of describing to myself the educational value of books.

In spite of my earnestness, I found reading a pleasurable activity. I came to enjoy the lonely good company of books. Early on weekday mornings, I'd read in my bed. I'd feel a mysterious comfort then, reading in the dawn quiet—the bluegray silence interrupted by the occasional churning of the refrigerator motor a few rooms away or the more distant sound of a city bus beginning its run. On weekends I'd go to the public library to read, surrounded by old men and women. Or, if the weather was fine, I would take my books to the park and read in the shade of a

> Getting older, Rodriguez examines why he reads.

> Growing skill as a reader causes conflict for Rodriguez.

tree. A warm summer evening was my favorite reading time. Neighbors would leave for vacation and I would water their lawns. I would sit through the twilight on the front porches or in backyards, reading to the cool, whirling sounds of the sprinklers.

I also had favorite writers. But often those writers I enjoyed most I was least able to value. When I read William Saroyan's *The Human Comedy*, I was immediately pleased by the narrator's warmth and the charm of his story. But as quickly I became suspicious. A book so enjoyable to read couldn't be very "important." Another summer I determined to read all the novels of Dickens. Reading his fat novels, I loved the feeling I got—after the first hundred pages—of being at home in a fictional world where I knew the names of the characters and cared about what was going to happen to them. And it bothered me that I was forced away at the conclusion, when the fiction closed tight, like a fortune-teller's fist—the futures of all the major characters neatly resolved. I never knew how to take such feelings of a novel's meaning. Still, there were pleasures to sustain me after I'd finish my books. Carrying a volume back to the library, I would be pleased by its weight. I'd run my fingers along the edge of the pages and marvel at the breadth of my achievement. Around my room, growing stacks of paperback books reinforced my assurance.

I entered high school having read hundreds of books. My habit of reading made me a confident speaker and writer of English. Reading also enabled me to sense something of the shape, the major concerns, of Western thought. (I was able to say something about Dante and Descartes and Engels and James Baldwin in my high school term papers.) In these various ways, books brought me academic success as I hoped that they would. But I was not a good reader. Merely bookish, I lacked a point of view when I read. Rather, I read in order to acquire a point of view. I vacuumed books for epigrams, scraps of information, ideas, themes—anything to fill the hollow within me and make me feel educated. When one of my teachers suggested to his drowsy tenth-grade English class that a person could not have a "complicated idea" until he

Rodriguez concludes by raising doubts about the skills he has acquired.

had read at least two thousand books, I heard the remark without detecting either its irony or its very complicated truth. I merely determined to compile a list of all the books I had ever read. Harsh with myself, I included only once a title I might have read several times. (How, after all, could one read a book more than once?) And I included only those books over a hundred pages in length. (Could anything shorter be a book?)

There was yet another high school list I compiled. One day I came across a newspaper article about the retirement of an English professor at a nearby state college. The article was accompanied by a list of the "hundred most important books of Western Civilization." "More than anything else in my life," the professor told the reporter with finality, "these books have made me all that I am." That was the kind of remark I couldn't ignore. I clipped out the list and kept it for the several months it took me to read all of the titles. Most books, of course, I barely understood. While reading Plato's *Republic*, for instance, I needed to keep looking at the book jacket comments to remind myself what the text was about. Nevertheless, with the special patience and superstition of a scholarship boy, I looked at every word of the text. And by the time I reached the last word, relieved, I convinced myself that I had read *The Republic*. In a ceremony of great pride, I solemnly crossed Plato off my list.

STUDENT MEMOIR   In the following essay, Miles Pequeno uses a narrative about a chess match to describe a changing relationship with his father and preserve an important memory. The paper was written in response to an assignment in an upper-division college writing class.

Pequeno 1

Miles Pequeno

Professor Mitchell

English 102

May 12, 20--

Check. Mate?

"Checkmate! Right? You can't move him anywhere, right? I got you again!" I couldn't control my glee. For good measure, I even grabbed my rook, which stood next to his king, and gave him a posthumous beating. The deposed king tumbled from the round table and onto the hardwood floor with a thud. The sound of sure victory. Being eight, it was easy to get excited about chess. It gave me not only at least a few minutes of Dad's attention and approval, but the comfort of knowing I'd taste victory every time. Either Dad was letting me always win, or I was the prodigy he wanted me to be. I always liked to believe it was the latter.

The relationship I had with my father was always complicated. I loved him and he loved me; that much was understood. But his idea of fatherhood was a little unorthodox (or maybe too orthodox, I'm not sure which). We didn't play catch in the yard, but he did make flash cards to teach me my multiplication tables when I was still in kindergarten. He didn't take me to

Narrative opens with dialogue and action.

Uses particular details to explain relationship with father.

Pequeno 2

Astros games, but he made sure I knew lots of big words from the newspaper. We were close, but only on his terms.

Save for the ever-graying hair near his temples, he looks much the same now as he did when I was little: round belly, round face, and big brown eyes that pierced while they silently observed and inwardly critiqued. His black hair, coarse and thick, and day-or-two-old beard usually gave away his heritage. He came to our suburb of Houston from Mexico when he was a toddler, learned English watching Spider-Man cartoons, and has since spent his life catching up, constantly working at moving up in the world. Even more was expected of me, the extension of his hard work and dreams for the future. I had no idea at the time, but back when I was beating him at chess as a kid, I myself was a pawn. He was planning something.

Then a funny thing happened. After winning every game since age eight, the five-year winning streak ended. I lost. This time, Dad had decided to take off the training wheels. Just as he was thrust into the real world unceremoniously with my birth when he was but eighteen years old, I was forced to grow up a little early too. The message was clear: Nothing is being handed to you anymore, Son.

This abrupt lesson changed my outlook. I no longer wanted to make Dad proud; I wanted to equal or better him. I'd been conditioned to seek his attention and approval, and then the rug was pulled from beneath my feet. I awoke to the

Using first person, Pequeno draws on personal experience to describe and characterize his father.

Notice how a metaphor here (training wheels) blossoms into an analogy about growing up.

Pequeno 3

realization that it was now my job to prove that the student could become the teacher.

I spent time after school every day playing chess against the artificial intelligence of my little Windows 95 computer. I knew what problems I had to correct because Dad was sure to point them out in the days after forcing that first loss. I had trouble using my queen. Dad always either knocked her out early or made me too afraid to put her in play. The result was my king slaughtered time and time again as his bride, the queen, sat idle on the far side of the board.

Our chess set was made of marble, with green and white hand-carved pieces sitting atop the thick, round board. Dad kept the set next to the TV and, most nights, we'd take it down from the entertainment center and put it on the coffee table in front of the sofa, where we sat side by side and played chess while halfway paying attention to the television. One night after Mom's spaghetti dinner, I casually walked into the living room to find Dad sitting sipping a Corona and watching the Rockets game. Hakeem Olajuwon was having a great night. Usually, if Dad was really into something on TV, we'd go our separate ways and maybe play later. This night, I picked up the remote control from the coffee table. Off.

"Let's play," I said resolutely. I grabbed the marble chess set, with all the pieces exactly where I had put them in anticipation of this game. The board seemed heavier than usual as I carried it to the coffee table. I sat down next to him

Provides background information that is important later in story.

Paragraph sets the physical scene for climactic chess match.

First dialogue since opening signals rising action.

Pequeno 4

on the sofa and stared at the pieces, suddenly going blank.
The bishops might as well have been knights. I froze as Dad
asked me what color I wanted. Traditionally, this had been
merely a formality. I'd always picked white before because I
wanted to have the first move. That was the rule: *White moves
first, green next*.

"Green."

Then it all came back to me. The certainty of my
declaration surprised him. He furrowed his brows slightly
and leaned back just enough to show good-natured
condescension.

"You sure? That means I go first."

"I'm sure. Take white."

So he began his attack. He started off controlling one
side of the board, slowly advancing. The knights led the
charge, with the pawns waiting in the wings to form an
impenetrable wall around the royal family, who remained in
their little castle of two adjacent spaces.

Every move was made with painful precision. Now and
then after my moves, he'd sigh and sink a little into the sofa.
He'd furrow those big black brows, his eyes darting quickly
from one side of the board to the other, thinking two or three
moves ahead. Some of his mannerisms this time were
completely new, like the hesitation of his hand as he'd reach
for a piece and then jerk it back quickly, realizing that my
strategy had shut more than a few doors for him.

"Combat"
metaphor
in next few
paragraphs
moves story
forward.

Pequeno 5

Eventually I worked up the courage to thrust the queen into action. She moved with great trepidation at first, never attacking, merely sneaking down the board. In the meantime, Dad's advancing rooks and knights were taking out my line of pawns, which I'd foolishly put too far into play. Every risk either of us took was clearly calculated. Sometimes he'd mutter to himself, slowly realizing this game wasn't as usual.

Things were looking good. Even if I didn't win, I'd already won a victory by challenging him. But that wasn't what I had practiced for. It wasn't why I'd turned off the television, and it certainly wasn't why I was concentrating so hard on these white and green figurines.

I was locked in. This was more than father and son. This was an epic battle between generals who knew each other well enough to keep the other at bay. But I was advancing. Sure, there were losses, but that was the cost of war. I had a mission.

My queen finally reached his king unharmed.

"Check."

I uttered the word silently. As the game had progressed, gaining intensity and meaning, there was no conversation. In its place were sporadic comments, muttered with deference. So when I said "check," I made sure not to make a big deal of it. I said it quietly, softly. I didn't want to jinx myself with bragging, and I certainly didn't want to get too excited and break my own concentration. As his king scrambled for a safe hiding place, my knights continued their advance. I had

Another extended analogy.

Pequeno 6

planned for this stage of the game several moves before, which was apparently at least one move more than Dad was thinking ahead. Check again. More scrambling, and another check. It seemed I had him cornered. Then . . .

"Check." It wasn't the first time I had him in check, and I didn't expect it to be the last in this game.

"Mate," he whispered, faint hints of a smile beginning to show on the corners of his mouth, pushing his cheeks up slightly. I hadn't realized that I had won until he conceded defeat with that word. Raising his eyebrows, he leaned back into the cushion of the sofa. He looked a little tired.

"Mate?" I wasn't sure he was right. I didn't let myself believe it until I stared at these little marble men. Sure enough, his desperate king was cornered.

"Good game, Son."

And that was it. There was his approval right there, manifesting itself in that smile that said "I love you" and "you sneaky son of a bitch" at the same time. But I didn't feel like any more of a man than I had an hour before. In fact, I felt a little hollow. So I just kept my seat next to him, picked up the remote control again, and watched the Rockets finish off the Mavericks. Business as usual after that. I went back to my room and did some homework, but kept the chess game at the forefront of my mind.

Wait a second. Had he let me win? Damn it, I'd worked so hard just for him to toy with me again, even worse than

Note that story climax occurs mostly through dialogue.

Father's smile signals change in father-son relationship.

Pequeno 7

when he'd let me beat him before. No, there's no way he let
me win. Or maybe he did. I don't know.

I walked back into the living room.

"Rematch?"

So we played again, and I lost. It didn't hurt, though. It
didn't feel nearly as bad as when he first took off the training
wheels. This was a different kind of defeat, and it didn't
bother me one bit. I had nothing left to prove. If I'd lost, so
what? I'd already shown what I could do.

But what if he'd let me win?

Again, so what? I had made myself a better player than I
was before. I didn't need him to pass me a torch. I'd taken
the flame myself, like a thirteen-year-old Prometheus. After
that night, I was my own man, ready for everything: high
school, my first girlfriend, my parents' divorce, my first job,
moving away to college, starting a career. I never lost the
feeling that I could make everything work if I just chose the
right moves. I still live by that principle.

> Initial doubts about follow-up match lead to epiphany in final paragraph — sudden moment of insight.

GRAPHIC NARRATIVE (EXCERPT)   In *Persepolis* (2003), Marjane Satrapi uses the medium of
the graphic novel to narrate the story of her girlhood in Iran. As she grew up, she witnessed the overthrow
of the shah and the Islamic Revolution, and the subsequent war with Iraq. The selection on the following
pages describes life under the shah.

HE TOOK PHOTOS EVERY DAY. IT WAS STRICTLY FORBIDDEN. HE HAD EVEN BEEN ARRESTED ONCE BUT ESCAPED AT THE LAST MINUTE.

TODAY I WENT TO REY HOSPITAL WITH MY CAMERA.

PEOPLE CAME OUT CARRYING THE BODY OF A YOUNG MAN KILLED BY THE ARMY. HE WAS HONORED LIKE A MARTYR. A CROWD GATHERED TO TAKE HIM TO THE BAHESHTE ZAHRA CEMETERY.

THEN THERE WAS ANOTHER CADAVER, AN OLD MAN CARRIED OUT ON A STRETCHER. THOSE WHO DIDN'T FOLLOW THE FIRST ONE WENT OVER TO THE OLD MAN, SHOUTING REVOLUTIONARY SLOGANS AND CALLING HIM A HERO.

HERE IS ANOTHER MARTYR.

WELL, I WAS TAKING MY PHOTOS WHEN I NOTICED AN OLD WOMAN NEXT TO ME. I UNDERSTOOD THAT SHE WAS THE WIDOW OF THE VICTIM. I HAD SEEN HER LEAVE THE HOSPITAL WITH THE BODY.

PLEASE! STOP IT! STOP IT!

WHAT? WHAT IS IT?

STOP IT!

WHO ARE YOU?

HIS WIDOW!

ARE YOU A ROYALIST?

NO, BUT MY HUSBAND DIED OF CANCER...

Assignments

1. **Reflection:** Using Mark Edmundson's "The Pink Floyd Night School" as your model (p. 7), write a narrative about an event in your life that changed you and that might make some readers reconsider their choices in life too. While Edmundson is happy with the decision he made (to put off professional school for a while), your narrative might move in a different direction. If appropriate, supplement your story with photographs. (Wouldn't you like to see the canopy described in "The Pink Floyd Night School" as it floats away?)

2. **Literacy Narrative:** After reading Richard Rodriguez's "Strange Tools" (p. 23), write a literacy narrative of your own, recalling teachers or assignments that helped (or hindered) you in learning to read or write. Describe books that changed you or ambitions you might have to pursue a writing or media career. However, you don't have to be an aspiring writer to make sense of this assignment. Remember that there are many kinds of literacy. The narrative you write may be about your encounters with paintings, films, music, fashion, architecture, or maybe even video games.

3. **Student Memoir:** Using Miles Pequeno's "Check. Mate?" as a model (p. 29), compose a short narrative describing how an individual (like Pequeno's father) changed your life or made you see the world differently. Give readers a strong sense both of this person and your relationship to him or her. Make this a paper you might want to keep.

4. **Graphic Narrative:** *Persepolis* (p. 35) demonstrates that a story can be told in various media: This graphic novel even became an animated film in 2007. Using a medium other than words alone, tell a story from your own life or from your community. Draw it, use photographs, craft a collage, create a video, record interviews, or combine other media suited to your nonfiction tale.

5. **Your Choice:** Compose a personal narrative about a subject and for an audience of your choosing, perhaps using the assignment to serve some other purpose. Perhaps you have to prepare a personal statement for a scholarship application or you'd like to turn some blog entries you wrote while traveling in South America into a more coherent tale. You may experiment with media too, combining prose and images in a Web project or trying your hand at creating a photo narrative.

How to start

- Need a **topic**? See page 49.
- Need to **find information**? See page 52.
- Need to **organize that information**? See page 54.

2 Reports

provide readers with reliable information

You've been preparing reports since the second grade when you probably used an encyclopedia to explain why volcanoes erupt or who Franklin Roosevelt was. Today, the reports you write may be more ambitious.

NEWS REPORT — You write a *news report* for a stargazers' Web site, describing the discovery of a Martian cave by amateur astronomers at a high school.

INVESTIGATIVE REPORT — You write an *investigative report* to compare the case for and against allowing more oil drilling in shallow waters near American coastlines.

ACADEMIC REPORT — You research an *academic report* on countries that are competing for international attention by building skyscrapers or other signature buildings.

FLOWCHART — You draw a *flowchart* to highlight the tangled process street merchants in your community must endure to get a vendor's permit.

INFOGRAPHIC — You design an *infographic* to present recent data on the gender and ethnic makeup of students graduating from local high schools.

DECIDING TO WRITE A REPORT.   As you might guess, reports make up one of the broadest genres of writing. If you use Google to search the term online, you will turn up an unwieldy 1.5 billion items, beginning with the *Drudge Report* and moving on to sites that cover everything from financial news to morbidity studies. Such sites may not resemble the term papers, presentations, and lab reports you'll typically prepare for school. But they'll share at least some of the goals you'll have when drafting academic reports. ⭘

Present information.   Obviously, people read reports to discover what they don't already know or confirm what they do. They expect what they read to be timely and accurate. And sometimes, the information or data you present *will* be new (as in *news*), built from recent events or the latest

 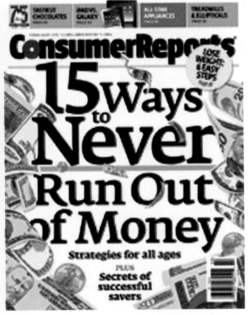

Stephen Colbert parodies the concept of the news report in his nightly putdown of cable-TV pundits, *The Colbert Report*. Treating the genre more conventionally is *Consumer Reports*, which offers objective assessments of consumer products and services in its widely read monthly magazine.

choose a genre
p. 390

research. But just as often, your reports will repackage data from existing sources. *Are dogs really color-blind?* The answer to such a question is already out there for you to find — if you know where to look.

Find reliable sources.   The heart and soul of any report will be reliable sources that provide or confirm information — whether they are "high government officials" quoted anonymously in news stories or scholarly articles listed in the bibliographies of college term papers. If asked to write a report about a topic new to you, immediately plan to do library and online research. ○

Just as often, the information in reports is generated by careful experiments and observations — as you acknowledge whenever you prepare a lab report for a biology or chemistry course. But even personal experience may sometimes provide material for reports, though anecdotes usually need corroboration to be convincing.

Aim for objectivity.   Writers and institutions (such as newspapers or government agencies) know that they'll lose credibility if their factual presentations seem incomplete or biased. Of course, smart readers understand that reports on contentious subjects — global warming, stem cell research, or health-care reform, for example — may lean one way or another. In fact, you may develop strong opinions based on the research you've done and be inclined to favor certain ideas. But readers of reports usually prefer to draw their own conclusions.

Present information clearly.   Readers expect material in reports and reference material to be arranged (and perhaps illustrated) for their benefit. ○ So when you put forward information, state your claims quickly and support them with data. You'll gain no points for surprises, twists, or suspense in a report. In fact, you'll usually give away the game on the first page of most reports by announcing not only your thesis but also perhaps your conclusions.

find a topic p. 356   think visually p. 592

This very brief report — actually a news item — from *Astronomy* magazine explains an astronomical discovery. Brief as it is, it shows how reports work.

Uranus's Second Ring-Moon System

LAURA LAYTON

Saturn isn't the only planet to harbor a complex ring structure. In 1986, NASA's *Voyager 2* spacecraft sent back images of a family of ten moons and a system of rings orbiting Uranus. New images from the Hubble Space Telescope (HST) increase those numbers.

On December 22, planetary astronomer Mark Showalter of the SETI Institute and Jack Lissauer of the NASA Ames Research Center announced the discovery of two additional moons and two large outer rings. HST's Advanced Camera for Surveys (ACS) imaged new moons Cupid and Mab as well as two faint, dusty rings from July 2003 through August 2005.

Newly discovered moon Cupid orbits in the midst of a swarm of inner moons known as the Portia group, so named after the group's largest moon. The Portia group lies just outside Uranus's inner ring system and inside the

Uranus
Hubble Space Telescope • ACS/HRC
NASA, ESA, and M. Showalter (SETI Institute)   STScI-PRC05-33

The Hubble telescope imaged Uranus's two newly discovered rings in 2003 and 2005. *(NASA, ESA, and M. Showalter of the SETI Institute.)*

Title is simple, factual.

Opening paragraphs present new information and sources.

Facts are presented clearly and objectively.

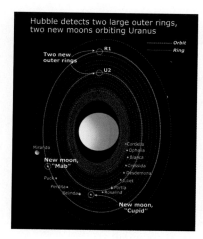

Hubble detects two large outer rings, two new moons orbiting Uranus

The features and locations of Uranus's known moons and rings.   (*NASA, ESA, and A. Field of STScI.*)

planet's larger, classical moon group of Belinda, Perdita, Puck, and Miranda. Mab, the smaller of the two newly detected moons, orbits outside the inner moon group and Cupid, but interior to Uranus's four outer moons.

A second ring system was also detected around Uranus and imaged by Hubble. Rings R/2003 U 1 and R/2003 U 2 (R1 and R2, respectively) both lie outside the orbit of the inner ring system. Researchers believe micron-size dust is a main constituent of these rings.

What is not clear is how these rings formed. Meteoroid impacts on Uranus's moons that eject fine dust may feed the rings or collisions among existing rings may produce new ones. Either way, the moons' small sizes and surface areas keep any ejected material from falling back to their surfaces and reaccreting. According to Showalter, "Dust material is coming off of Mab and spreading out to make this [R1] ring." It's not apparent what body provides the material for the inner (R2) ring. Lissauer theorizes that a disrupted moon may have been a source.

Showalter believes Uranus's ring-moon system is unstable and exhibits chaotic evolution. Since the last observations were made, Uranus's moons changed orbit. This has long-term implications for Uranus's ring-moon system. "Long-term changes to the system include collisions and crossing ring systems," adds Lissauer.

One thing is for sure, says Lissauer — "Our solar system is a dynamic place."

—*Astronomy*, December 28, 2005

Images and captions illustrate discovery.

Authorities are quoted.

Exploring purpose and topic

topic ◀

When assigned a report, think about the kinds of information you need to present and the subgenre of report you are preparing. Will your report merely answer a factual question about a topic and deliver basic information? Or are you expected to do a more in-depth study or compare different points of view, as you would in an investigative report? Or might the report deliver new information based on your own recent research or experiments? Consider your various options as you select a topic.

Answer questions.   For this kind of report, include basic facts and, perhaps, an overview of key features, issues, or problems. Think of an encyclopedia as a model: When you look up an article there, you usually aren't interested in an exhaustive treatment of a subject.

Assigned a report intended to answer basic questions, you can choose topics that would otherwise seem overly ambitious. So long as all that readers expect is an overview, not expertise, you could easily write two or three fact-filled pages on "Memphis and the Blues" or "The Battle of Marathon" by focusing on just a few key figures, events, and concepts. Given this opportunity, select a topic that introduces you to new ideas or perspectives — this could, in fact, be an instructor's rationale for this type of assignment.

Review what is already known about a subject.   Instructors who ask you to write five- or ten-page reports on specific subjects in a field — for example, to compare banking practices in Japan and the European Union or to describe current trends in museum architecture — doubtless know plenty about those subjects already. They want you to look at the topic in some depth to increase what *you* know. But the subject may also be evolving rapidly because of current events, technological changes, or ongoing research.

So consider updating an idea introduced in a lecture or textbook: You might be surprised by how much you can add to what an instructor has presented. If workers are striking in Greece again, make that a focal point of your general report on European Union economic policies; if your course covers globalism, consider how a world community made smaller by jet travel complicates the response to epidemic diseases. In considering topics for in-depth reports, you'll find "research guides" especially helpful. ○ You may also want to consult librarians or experts in the field you're writing about. ○

plan a project p. 466   ask for help p. 379

Field research is one way to acquire new information.

Report new knowledge.   Many schools encourage undergraduates to conduct original research in college. In most cases, this work is done under the supervision of an instructor in your major field, and you'll likely choose a topic only after developing expertise in some area. For a look at the types of research topics students from different schools have explored, search "undergraduate research journal" on the Web.

If you have trouble finding a subject for a report, try the brainstorming techniques suggested in Chapter 19, both to identify topic ideas and to narrow them to manageable size.

> **Your Turn**   Having trouble finding a fresh topic for a report? Let your own curiosity guide you. Make a list of things you'd simply like to know more about within the general area of your topic. If you need prompts, check out HowStuffWorks.com, especially its blogs and podcasts, such as "Stuff You Missed in History Class." You'll see that almost any subject or topic area is filled with interesting nooks and crannies.

Understanding your audience

You probably know that you should tailor any report to its potential readers. Well-informed audiences expect detailed reports that use technical language, but if your potential audience includes a range of readers, from experts to amateurs, design your work to suit them all. Perhaps you can use headings to ease novices through your report while simultaneously signaling to more knowledgeable readers what sections they might skip. O Make audience-sensitive moves like this routinely, whenever you are composing.

However, sometimes it's not the content that you must tailor for potential readers, but their perceptions of *you*. They'll look at you differently, according to the expertise you bring to the project. What are the options?

Suppose you are the expert.   This may be the typical stance of most writers of professional reports, who smoothly present material they know well enough to teach. But knowledgeable people still often make two common mistakes in presenting information. Either they assume an audience is as informed as they are, and so omit the very details and helpful transitions that many readers need, or they underestimate the intelligence of their readers and consequently bore them with trivial and unnecessary explanations. O Readers want a confident guide but also one who knows when — *and when not* — to define a term, provide a graph, or supply some context.

Suppose you are the novice.   In a typical report for school, you're likely dealing with material relatively new to you. Your expertise on language acquisition in childhood may be only a book chapter and two journal articles thick, but you may still have to write ten pages on the topic to pass a psychology course. Moreover, you not only have to provide information in a report, but you also have to convince an expert reader — your instructor — that you have earned the credentials to write about this subject.

Suppose you are the peer.   For some reports, your peers may be your primary audience. That's especially true of oral presentations in class. You know that an instructor is watching and likely grading the content — including your topic, organization, and sources. But that instructor may also be watching how well you adapt that material to the interests and capabilities of your classmates. O

Tips for Writing Credible Reports

- Choose a serious subject you know you can research.
- Model the project on professional reports in that area.
- Select sources recognized in the field.
- Document those sources correctly.
- Use the discipline's technical vocabulary and conventions.

think visually
p. 592

respect your
readers p. 440

understand oral
reports p. 346

Finding and developing materials

▶ find information

Once you have settled on a research topic and thesis, plan to spend time online, in a library, or in the field gathering the data you need for your report. Look beyond reference works such as dictionaries and encyclopedias toward resources used or created by experts in the field, including scholarly books published by university presses, articles in professional journals, government reports (also known as white papers), oral histories, and so on. Deliberately seek out materials that push you well beyond what you knew at the outset of the project. The level of the works you read may intimidate you at first, but that's a signal that you are learning something new — an outcome your instructor probably intended.

Sometimes, you will write reports based on information you discover yourself, either under the controlled conditions of a scientific experiment or through interviews, fieldwork, polling, or news gathering. ○ It's not easy to summarize all the rules that govern such work. They vary from field to field and major to major, and some you will learn in courses devoted to research methods. But even informal field research requires systematic procedures and detailed record keeping so that you can provide readers with data they can verify. To get reports right, follow these basic principles.

Base reports on the best available sources. You can't just do an online search on a topic and hope for the best. The quality of material on Web sites (and in libraries, for that matter) varies widely. You will embarrass yourself quickly if you don't develop procedures and instincts for evaluating sources. Look for materials — including data such as statistics and photographic reproductions — presented by reliable authors and experts and supported by major institutions in government, business, and the media. For academic papers, take your information whenever possible from journals and books published by university presses and professional organizations. ○

With Web materials, track them back to their original sources. Use the Google search engine for "Korean War," for instance, and you might find an item that seems generic — except that its URL indicates a military location (.mil). Opening the URL, however, you discover that a government institution — the Naval Historical Center — supports the site. So its

Need help finding relevant sources? See "How to Browse for Ideas" on pp. 360–61.

interview and observe
p. 478

find reliable sources
p. 482

information is likely to be credible but will reflect the perspectives of the Department of the Navy. That's information you need to know as you read material from the site.

Base reports on multiple sources.   Don't rely on a limited or narrow selection of material. Not all ideas or points of view deserve equal coverage, but neither should you take any particular set of claims for granted. Above all, avoid the temptation to base a report on a single source, even one that *is* genuinely excellent. You may find yourself merely paraphrasing the material, not writing a report of your own. ○

Fact-check your report.   It's a shame to get the big picture in focus in a report and then lose credibility because you slip up on a few easily verifiable facts. In a lengthy project, these errors might seem inevitable or just a nuisance. But misstatements can take on a life of their own and become lore — like the initial and exaggerated reports of crime and mayhem during Hurricane Katrina. So take the extra few minutes required to get the details right.

Some Online Sites for Locating Facts and Information

- **Alcove 9: An Annotated List of Reference Sites** A collection of online reference sites maintained by the Library of Congress.
- **Bartleby.com: Great Books Online** Includes online versions of key reference and literary works, from *Gray's Anatomy* to the *Oxford Shakespeare.*
- **Biography.com** A collection of twenty-five thousand brief biographies, from Julius Caesar to Miley Cyrus.
- **FedStats** *The* site for finding information gathered by the federal government. Also check out USA.gov.
- **Internet Public Library** Provides links to material on most major academic fields and subjects. Includes reference collections as well.
- **The World Factbook** Check here for data about any country — compiled by the CIA.

restate ideas
p. 494

Creating a structure

▶ organize
information

How does a report work? Not like a shopping mall — where the escalators and aisles are designed to keep you wandering and buying, deliberately confused. Not like a mystery novel that leads up to an unexpected climax, or even like an argument, which steadily builds in power to a memorable conclusion. Instead, reports lay all their cards on the table right at the start and hold no secrets. They announce what they intend to do and then do it, providing clear markers all along the way.

Clarity doesn't come easily; it only seems that way when a writer has been successful. You have to know a topic intimately to explain it to others. Then you need to choose a pattern that supports what you want to say. Among structures you might choose for drafting a report are the following, some of which overlap. O

Organize by date, time, or sequence.   Drafting a history report, you may not think twice about arranging your material chronologically: In 1958, the USSR launched *Sputnik*, the first Earth satellite; in 1961, the USSR launched a cosmonaut into Earth orbit; in 1969, the United States put two men on the moon. This structure puts information into a relationship readers understand immediately as a competition. You'd still have blanks to fill in with facts and details to tell the story of the race to the moon, but a chronological structure helps readers keep complicated events in perspective.

By presenting a simple sequence of events, you can use time to organize reports involving many kinds of information, from the scores in football games to the movement of stock markets to the flow of blood through the human heart. O

Organize by magnitude or order of importance.   Many reports present their subjects in sequence, ranked from biggest to smallest (or vice versa), most important to least important, most common/frequent to least, and so on. Such structures assume, naturally, that you have already done the research to position the items you expect to present. At first glance, reports of this kind might seem tailored to the popular media: "Ten Best Restaurants in Seattle," "One Hundred Fattest American Cities." But you might also use such a structure to report on the disputed causes of a war, the multiple effects of a stock market crash, or even the factors responsible for a disease.

develop a draft
p. 398

shape your work
p. 406

Organize by division.   It's natural to organize some reports by division — that is, by breaking a subject into its major parts. A report on the federal government, for example, might be organized by treating each of its three branches in turn: executive, legislative, and judicial. A report on the Elizabethan stage might examine the separate parts of a typical theater: the heavens, the balcony, the stage wall, the stage, the pit, and so on. Of course, you'd then

The Swan Theatre
The architectural layout of this Elizabethan theater, shown in this 1596 sketch by Johannes de Witt, might suggest the structure of a report describing the theater.

have to decide in what order to present the items, perhaps spatially or in order of importance. You might even use an illustration to clarify your report.

Organize by classification.   Classification is the division of a group of concepts or items according to specified and consistent principles. Reports organized by classification are easy to set up when you borrow a structure that is already well established — such as those below. A project becomes more difficult when you try to create a new system — perhaps to classify the various political groups on your campus or to describe the behavior of participants in a psychology experiment.

- **Psychology** (by type of study): abnormal, clinical, comparative, developmental, educational, industrial, social
- **Plays** (by type): tragedy, comedy, tragicomedy, epic, pastoral, musical
- **Nations** (by form of government): monarchy, oligarchy, democracy, dictatorship
- **Passenger cars** (by engine placement): front engine, mid engine, rear engine
- **Dogs** (by breed group): sporting, hound, working, terrier, toy, nonsporting, herding

Organize by position, location, or space.   Organizing a report spatially is a powerful device for arranging ideas — even more so today, given the ease with which material can be illustrated. O A map, for example, is a report organized by position and location. But it is only one type of spatial structure.

You use spatial organization in describing a painting from left to right, a building from top to bottom, a cell from nucleus to membrane. A report on medical conditions might be presented most effectively via cutaways that expose different layers of tissues and organs. Or a report on an art exhibition might follow a viewer through a virtual 3-D gallery.

Organize by definition.   Typically, definitions begin by identifying an object by its "genus" and "species" and then listing its distinguishing

think visually p. 592

features, functions, or variations. This useful structure is the pattern behind most entries in dictionaries, encyclopedias, and other reference works. It can be readily expanded too, once the genus and species have been established: *Ontario* is a *province of Canada* between Hudson Bay and the Great Lakes. That's a good start, but what are its geographical features, history, products, and major cities — all the things that distinguish it from other provinces? You could write a book, let alone a report, based on this simple structure.

Organize by comparison/contrast. You've probably been comparing and contrasting since the fourth grade, but that doesn't make this principle of organization any less potent for college-level reports. ○ You compare and contrast to highlight distinctions that might otherwise not be readily apparent. Big differences are usually uninteresting: That's why *Consumer Reports* doesn't

If you're looking for transportation, you're unlikely to opt for a horse. But you might compare a small car to a pickup.

understand evaluation p. 106

test Nikon SLRs against disposable cameras. But the differences between Nikons and Canons? That might be worth exploring.

Organize by thesis statement.   Obviously, you have many options for organizing a report; moreover, a single report might use several structural patterns. So it helps if you explain early in a report what its method of organization will be. That idea may be announced in a single thesis sentence, a full paragraph (or section), or even a PowerPoint slide. ○

SENTENCE ANNOUNCES STRUCTURE

In the late thirteenth century, Native Puebloans may have abandoned their cliff dwellings for several related reasons, including an exhaustion of natural resources, political disintegration, and, most likely, a prolonged drought.

—Kendrick Frazier, *People of Chaco: A Canyon and Its Culture*

PARAGRAPH EXPLAINS STRUCTURE

In order to detect a problem in the beginning of life, medical professionals and caregivers must be knowledgeable about normal development and potential warning signs. Research provides this knowledge. In most cases, research also allows for accurate diagnosis and effective intervention. Such is the case with cri du chat syndrome (CDCS), also commonly known as cat cry syndrome.

—Marissa Dahlstrom, "Developmental Disorders: Cri Du Chat Syndrome"

develop a statement p. 393

Choosing a style and design

Reports are typically written in a formal or *high* style—free of emotional language that might make them sound like arguments. ○ To separate fact from opinion, scientific and professional reports usually avoid personal references as well as devices such as contractions and dialogue. Reports in newspapers, magazines, and even encyclopedias may be less formal: You might detect a person behind the prose. But the style will still strive for impartiality, signaling that the writer's opinions are (or, at least, *should* be) less important than the facts reported.

Why tone down the emotional, personal, or argumentative temper of the language in reports? It's a matter of audience. The moment readers suspect that you are twisting language to advocate an agenda or moving away from a sober recital of facts, they will question the accuracy of your report. So review your drafts to see if a word or phrase might be sending the wrong signals to readers. Give your language the appearance of neutrality, balance, and perspective.

Present the facts cleanly. Get right to the point and answer key questions directly: *Who? What? Where? When? How? Why?* Organize paragraphs around topic sentences so readers know what will follow. Don't go off on tangents. Keep the exposition controlled and focus on data. When you do, the prose will seem coolly efficient and trustworthy.

Keep out of it. Write from a neutral, third-person perspective, avoiding the pronouns *I* and *you*. Like all guidelines, this one has exceptions, and it certainly doesn't apply across the board to other genres of writing. But when perusing a report, readers don't usually care about the writer's personal opinion unless that writer's individual experiences are part of the story.

Avoid connotative language. Maintaining objectivity is not easy because language is rife with *connotations*—the powerful cultural associations that may surround words, enlarging their meanings and sometimes imposing value judgments. Connotations make *shadowy* and *gloomy* differ from *dark*; *porcine* and *tubby*, from *overweight*. What's more, the connotations of individual words are not the same for every reader. One person may have no problem with a term like *slums*, but another person living in *low-income*

define your style p. 432

housing may beg to differ. Given the minefield of potential offenses that writing can be, don't use loaded words when more neutral terms are available and just as accurate. Choose *confident*, not *overweening* or *pompous*; try *corporate official* rather than *robber baron*—unless, of course, the more colorful term fits the context. **O**

Cover differing views fairly, especially those you don't like.   The neutrality of reports is often a fiction. You need only look at the white papers or fact sheets on the Web sites of various groups to appreciate how data presentation can sometimes be biased. But a report you prepare for a course or a professional situation should represent a good-faith effort to run the bases on a subject, touching all its major points. An upbeat report on growth in minority enrollment on your campus might also have to acknowledge areas where achievements have been lagging. A report on the economic boom that occurred during Bill Clinton's presidency (1993–2001) might also have to cover the dot-com bust and slide into recession at the end of his term.

Pay attention to elements of design.   Clear and effective design is particularly important in reports. **O** If your paper runs more than a few pages and can be readily divided into parts, consider using headings or section markers to help readers follow its structure and locate information. Documents such as term papers and lab reports may follow specific formulas, patterns, and templates that you will need to learn.

Many types of factual information are best presented graphically. This is especially the case with numbers and statistics. So learn to create or incorporate charts, graphs, photos, and illustrations, and also captions, into your work. Software such as Microsoft Word can create modest tables and simple graphics; generate more complex tables and graphs with software such as Excel, OmniGraffle or VectorDesigner. And remember that any visual items should be purposeful, not ornamental.

Many reports these days are, in fact, oral presentations that rely on presentation software such as PowerPoint, Keynote, or Prezi. You'll want to learn how to use these tools effectively.

improve your
sentences p. 444

think visually p. 592

Examining models

In "The Running Shoe Debate: How Barefoot Runners Are Shaping the Shoe Industry," an article published in *Popular Mechanics* (April 22, 2009), writer Tyghe Trimble looks into claims by some runners that they actually perform better without shoes because human beings were designed to run barefoot.

The Running Shoe Debate: How Barefoot Runners Are Shaping the Shoe Industry

TYGHE TRIMBLE

The Boston Marathon, one of the world's most competitive 26.2-mile races, had the best runners from Kenya, Ethiopia, the U.S. and around the globe churning out 5-minute miles on Monday for over two hours. While all eyes were on the front-runners—notably the United States' Ryan Hall (third) and Kara Goucher (third among female racers)—way back in the pack there was one person, Rick Roeber, who stole headlines with his unique running style. One glance at Roeber's feet and you can see what all the fuss is about: he isn't wearing shoes. And a number of people—ultra-marathoners, biomechanics experts and doctors included—think that's probably the best way to run. Some go so far as to say running shoes are in fact causing injuries.

While entry into the Boston Marathon is a feat in itself—Roeber needed to have about an 8-minute-mile pace over 26 miles to qualify—attempting the race barefoot is something most runners would find an absurd, even obscene, gesture. Runners are hooked on shoes. For good reason, it would appear: Ranging from 5 mm to 22 mm thick and made mostly of polymer, running shoes are engineered to support feet for mile after mile of rough asphalt and rocky terrain. They protect vulnerable soles from glass and debris, provide padding and, shoe companies claim, help correct problematic twists and turns of our ankles and legs caused by excessive pronation.

> Opening paragraph grabs readers' attention by getting right to the point.

> The rationale for running shoes is explained.

But to barefoot advocates such as Chris McDougall, author of *Born to Run*, Knopf, . . . Roeber is one of the few in Monday's race not drinking the shoe industry's Kool-Aid. In his book, McDougall follows the Tahumara, a Mexican tribe of ultrarunners who race from 50 to 200 miles straight without shoes, yet remain healthy and injury-free. Science doesn't support the shoe industry's claim that "humans are born broken," McDougall tells *PM*, [*Popular Mechanics*] and that running shoes exist to fix our stride. Humans have been barefoot for nearly 2 million years, but have had running shoes for only a little more than 40—when Nike-founder Bill Bowerman cobbled together the modern-day running shoe with glues, plastic and a waffle iron in his basement. Shoes cause runners to lose musculature in their feet, McDougall argues, and take away the natural cushion in their stride.

Trimble provides a brief history of running shoes.

Could shoes—and shoe companies—be part of a $25 billion snake oil industry, covering hundreds of thousands of perfectly able bare feet? Or is barefoot running dangerous for marathoners and weekend joggers alike? That's the debate now brewing in the running community. The answer depends in part on a classic chicken and egg question: Do we run the way we do because of running shoes, or do running shoes support the way we now run?

This brief paragraph identifies the questions the report will examine.

Taking It in Stride

In a back room at the $2 million New Balance running shoe research and development lab in Lawrence, Mass., the MTS 858 Mini Bionix II—a giant hydraulic piston with the cast of a foot attached—loudly pounds into the heel of a light blue, cushioned running shoe. This stress-testing machine, made by the same company that builds earthquake simulators, can apply 5620 pounds of force to a shoe 30 times every second (although researchers at New Balance tend to be gentler on the footwear). Down the hall, a glass plate sitting in the middle of a polished wooden floor conceals a camera that measures the impact of the shoe on the ground. Cameras also capture the light reflected by tiny silver dots worn by a runner on a treadmill, tracking hundreds of points on the body during each stride. Across the room, an outline of feet projected onto the wall conveys the treadmill runner's footstrike in real time.

Meanwhile, a computer records streams of data relaying angle and force, to be interpreted and analyzed by researchers later. This is high-tech bio-mechanics, all in the service of designing the perfect running shoe.

Some researchers and runners think this ideal shoe will be cushioned and wide, with high-tech gels, plastics and perhaps even moving parts to better absorb shock. To others, the perfect shoe looks more like a sock, with only a thin cover to protect feet from glass and other ground hazards. The two design camps split cleanly between catering to different strides: While the barefoot runner's gait tends to strike on the forefoot, a significant amount of shoe technology is aimed toward a heel-to-toe motion. A study from 1980, which was repeatedly cited by shoe experts at the New Balance labs, reveals how much more prevalent heel-to-toe running is. Analyzing the form of 753 runners, biomechanical researcher Benno Nigg found that 80 percent of runners (videotaped in two races) ran with a heel-to-toe motion; 45 percent of the faster runners (those with a 5-minute, 18-second-mile pace or better) ran heel-to-toe-step; the rest ran with what he calls a midfoot strike, in which the heel and forefoot strike the ground simultaneously.

Shoe companies design shoes for the vast majority—the 80 percent of heel-to-toe runners—and their goal is to prevent excessive rolling movement of the foot. "There are people who will pronate a lot but will not get injured," says Keith Williams, a senior lecturer at the University of California, Davis, who has consulted in the footwear industry for 30 years. "Then there are those who will pronate a little and get injured." To play it safe, shoe companies bulk up the heel, the arch and extend the sides of shoes, which stabilizes the foot as it rolls from heel to toe.

While there are as many ways to do this as there are shoes for sale, Sean Murphy, manager of advanced product engineering at New Balance, says shoe companies often fall back on what he calls the 22-12 solution—placing 22 millimeters of material under the heel of the shoe and 12 millimeters under the forefoot. "Shoe companies have been stuck in the paradigm of the 22-12 for years," Murphy says, and people buy them in part because it's the feel they've grown accustomed to. "We're just now building products for people who tend to run more on their forefoot, like many ultramarathoners."

> Trimble provides detailed information about the design of running shoes, but does not bury readers in technical language.

> Here and elsewhere, Trimble carefully identifies the credentials of any authority he quotes.

But according to McDougall, all shoes with cushioned heels, however spare, encourage heel-to-toe running, which he says leads to excessive pronation. "Take the heel off the shoe and those problems will be solved," McDougall says. In other words: Run barefoot. He points to a 2008 paper in the *British Journal of Sports Medicine*, in which the author, a researcher at the University of Newcastle in Australia, "revealed that there are no evidence-based studies—not one—that demonstrate that running shoes make you less prone to injury."

Murphy agrees. "The studies on injuries just aren't there," he says. However, there is also a dearth of studies demonstrating that running shoes make runners more prone to injury.

An important research question remains unresolved: Do shoes help runners?

The More Perfect Shoe

With or without shoes, humans are evolved to run. In a 2004 study published in *Nature*, Dennis Bramble and Daniel Lieberman provide clear physiological evidence of this: Humans are efficient sweaters, for one. We also have tall bodies with ample surface area to cool ourselves, large buttocks with muscles critical for stabilization in running, and long legs that include Achilles tendons—ideal for storing and releasing mechanical energy. These features, the authors argue, allowed us to be superior scavengers and even hunters (by tracking sprinting animals).

Trimble gets to the crux of the issues: Humans probably need shoes to run on man-made surfaces.

The problem modern-day runners face, according to Hugh Herr, *Popular Mechanics* 2005 Breakthrough Award winner and head of the biomechatronics group at MIT, isn't presented by our bodies but by the evolution of running surfaces. Humans that ran to scavenge or hunt for their food weren't pounding concrete. Herr is in a unique position to weigh in on shoe technology. He defended the double-prosthetic sprinter, Oscar Pistorius, in his appeal to the International Association of Athletics Federations board last year against charges that his Cheetah prosthetics provided a mechanical advantage. Herr also invented the iWalk Power-foot One, the most advanced robotic ankle in existence.

Bare feet just aren't meant to support running on modern day hard-top surfaces, Herr says. In his research, Herr focused on two problems with both shod and barefoot running—pronation angle and impact force. While barefoot running is best for a natural, stress-free

Trimble uses a middle style, its informal tone making the technical language easier to absorb.

pronation angle, Herr says, it is not ideal for coping with roads and sidewalks that can lead to stress-impact injuries. Shoes, on the other hand, excel at diminishing the force of impact on hard ground. But they do so at the cost of the natural stride—all the padding added to the shoe exaggerates the foot's rotation. "It's hard to design a shoe with pronation as small as what exists naturally," Herr says. "When you're barefoot, you have the advantage of the heel being very thin [and thus diminishing rotation]."

Herr's solution to the problem of shoe design is to start from scratch and fundamentally redesign the running shoe. His first-stage prototype looks nothing like any shoe for sale today. Called the SpringBuck, Herr's shoe is form fitting, taking advantage of the barefoot runner's naturally low pronation, while a spring-like heel diminishes the impact of feet on hard surfaces. This shoe even shows a metabolic reduction for the runner, Herr says, thanks to the optimized stride. Though no doubt radical to barefoot advocates and shoe labs alike, a running shoe that rethinks humans' relationship with their environment may fill the vacuum of science on the great shoe debate and finally provide a one-size-fits-all solution.

Trimble is careful not to take sides, though he sees the potential in new running shoe designs.

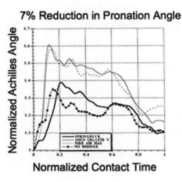
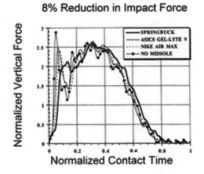

Pronation angle and force for bare feet, two supportive pairs of industry shoes, and Hugh Herr's SpringBuck design.

Charts compare the performance of Herr's new shoe design to that of more conventional ones.

ACADEMIC REPORT   Academic reports often support clear and straightforward thesis statements. The following short report does that in explaining the dual mission of Frank Gehry's celebrated Guggenheim Museum Bilbao. The paper below is based not only on sources but also on information gathered at the museum, in Spain's Basque Country.

Winsett 1

Annie Winsett

Professor Sidor

Writing 200

December 5, 20--

Inner and Outer Beauty

The Guggenheim Bilbao, designed by North American architect Frank Gehry (b. 1929), is a recent addition to the Solomon R. Guggenheim Foundation, a conglomeration of museums dedicated to modern American and European art. Home to several permanent works and host to visiting expositions, the Guggenheim Bilbao is itself an artistic wonder, perhaps more acclaimed than any of the art it houses. In design, the building meets the requirements of a proper museum, but it also signifies the rejuvenation of Spain's Basque Country.

> Thesis suggests a paper with two parts.

Like any museum, the Guggenheim Bilbao is dedicated to preserving and presenting works of art. Paintings and sculptures are here to be protected. So the thick glass panes of the Bilbao serve not only to let in natural light, but also to provide escape for the heat generated by the titanium

Winsett 2

outsides of the structure. The unconventional metal plating of the Guggenheim, guaranteed to last up to one hundred years, actually ensures its survival as well. Similarly, the floor material will be able to withstand the many visitors to come.

Even though the outside of the Guggenheim Bilbao appears to be composed of irregular forms only, the interior houses nineteen functional galleries. The alternating rooms and curving walkways around a central atrium provide an extensive journey through the world of art. So the unusual exterior structure actually allots a vast amount of wall and floor display space and serves the wide variety of art it houses more than adequately.

First section of paper explains how the avant-garde building functions as a museum.

Fig. 1. The Guggenheim Museum Bilbao

Winsett offers a photograph to convey Bilbao's extraordinary design.

Winsett 3

"But" at beginning of paragraph signals that report is moving into its second section.

But the Guggenheim Bilbao was created to do more. In 1991, having noted the economic depression facing one of its main industrial cities, the Basque Country government proposed that the Solomon R. Guggenheim Foundation locate its next museum in Bilbao ("History" 1). As part of a massive revitalization involving the city's port, railways, and airport, the new museum would enhance the cultural identity of the city. Perhaps a conventional structure would have met the need for societal enrichment.

Yet the Basque government achieved much more by selecting a design by Frank Gehry. Designed with computers, the museum presents an original and striking three-dimensional form not possible using conventional design methods. From above, it appears that its metal-coated solids extend from a central skylight in the shape of a flower ("Guggenheim"). The building also suggests a ship on the river's shore with edges that swoop upward in a hull-like fashion. The "scales" of metal that surround the structure's steel frame are like those of a fish. Undoubtedly, the design references the museum's coastal and riverside environment.

Report explains how museum represents city of Bilbao.

Whatever its intended form, Gehry's building captures the spirit of a renewed Bilbao in the twenty-first century. For instance, Gehry managed to incorporate the city's mining industries in the structural materials. The titanium plates reflect both the beautiful Basque sky and the core of the

Winsett 4

Basque economy. Also crucial is the tourism such an
incomparable structure might generate. Though most of
Gehry's works incorporate the unique materials and forms
seen in Bilbao, the Guggenheim is individual and original.
And travelers have flocked here to experience the futuristic
titanium masterpiece. As hoped, Bilbao and the Basque
Country have earned a revived place in the international
community. At the 2004 Venice Biennial, the Basque Country
was recognized for the most successful urban regeneration
project in the world, at the heart of which was the
Guggenheim museum ("Culture").

Winsett 5

Works Cited

"Culture." *Euskadi.net.* Eusko Jaurlaritza-Gobierno Vasco
(Basque Govt.), 17 Mar. 2005. Web. 7 Nov. 2006.

"Guggenheim Bilbao Museum." *Bilbao Metropoli-30.* Assn.
for the Revitalization of Metropolitan Bilbao, 2006. Web.
30 Oct. 2006.

"History of the Guggenheim Museum Bilbao." *Guggenheim
Bilbao.* Solomon R. Guggenheim Foundation, 26 Oct.
2006. Web. 29 Oct. 2006.

Paper uses
several online
sources.

FLOWCHART   This flowchart, created by Mike Wirth and Suzanne Cooper-Guasco, was a winner of the Sunlight Foundation's 2010 Design for America contest. The Foundation's goal with the contest was "to inspire the design community to tell great stories about how our government works, what our government does, and what it could do." The chart faithfully depicts the difficulty of moving bills through the U.S. Congress, but makes the process seem at least thought-provoking. The sequence, presented in bright—perhaps optimistic—colors, seems dynamic and plausible. To see this flowchart at full size, go to http://www.mikewirthart.com/wp-content/uploads/2010/05/howlawsmadeWIRTH2.jpg.

Passing a bill is complicated and so is the visual text.

Bill passage is pictured as a thick arc with a few smaller pathways. Key stages are marked by color.

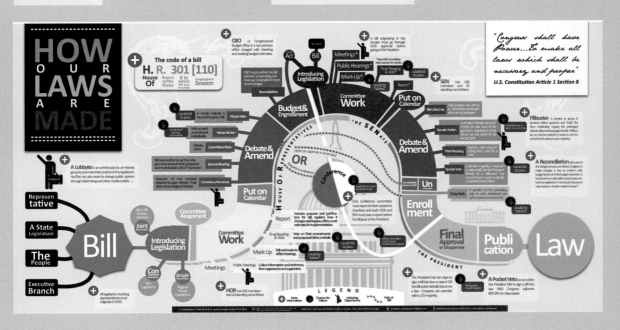

A legend explains how to interpret elements of the infographic.

Impediments are highlighted in red, including the critical budget stage.

Assignments

1. **News Report:** Imagine that you've been asked to prepare a factual report on some natural phenomena (like the rings of Uranus, see p. 47) to a group of ninth graders — one of the toughest audiences in the world. In a brief article, engage them with a topic of your choosing, perhaps reflecting your own interest in an offbeat subject. You might design the report as a paper, oral presentation, or Web site. Be sure to base it on reliable sources, which you should cite in some form within the report.

2. **Investigative Report:** In "The Running Shoe Debate" (p. 61), Tyghe Trimble presents both sides of a controversy without taking a position himself. Prepare a similar report, preferably on a subject you already know something about. Draw upon your own experience to correct false impressions readers less knowledgeable than you might have about the topic. But be certain to look for new information to keep the report fresh, and to base all claims you make on reputable sources and authorities, which you should acknowledge in the paper itself (as Trimble does) or cite in the proper academic style. (For MLA style, see p. 503; for APA style, see p. 540.)

3. **Academic Report:** Write a factual report based on a topic from a course outside your major — in other words, on a subject generally new to you. Like Annie Winsett in "Inner *and* Outer Beauty" (p. 66), narrow your subject to a specific claim you can explore in several pages. Use trustworthy sources and document them correctly.

4. **Flowchart:** "How Our Laws Are Made" (see p. 70) is a schematic example of an important genre of report that explains how things work or get done. Sometimes called "process analyses," such reports include instruction manuals, handbooks, guidebooks, cookbooks, technical schematics, and so on. Choose a process you know well or want to learn more about, break it into stages, and then describe it accurately in a flowchart, a traditional paper, or some combination of these media.

5. **Your Choice:** Begin a project with a topic you would love to know more about. Do the necessary research to find out much more about your subject, narrowing it down to manageable size for a paper or oral presentation. Then either prepare a written version of the report to submit to your instructor or an oral version to share with a wider audience, perhaps your classmates if you can have the opportunity.

How to start
- Need a **topic**? See page 79.
- Need **support for your argument**? See page 85.
- Need to **organize your ideas**? See page 88.

3 Arguments

ask readers
to consider
debatable
ideas

It doesn't take much to spark an argument these days—a casual remark, a political observation, a dumb joke that hurts someone's feelings. Loud voices and angry gestures may follow, leaving observers upset and frustrated. But arguments aren't polarizing or hostile by nature, not when people more interested in generating light than heat offer them. Arguments should make us smarter and better able to deal with problems in the world. In fact, you probably make such constructive arguments all the time without raising blood pressures, at least not too much.

ARGUMENT TO ADVANCE A THESIS

In an op-ed for the local paper, you *argue the thesis* that people who talk on cell phones while driving are a greater hazard than drunk drivers because they are more numerous and more callous.

EXPLORATORY ARGUMENT

At a conference, you *explore the argument* that high school officials have adopted "zero tolerance" disciplinary policies to avoid the tough decisions that administrators are paid to make. You decide that they have.

REFUTATION ARGUMENT

In a term paper, you use facts and logic to *refute the argument* that students with college degrees will likely earn more in their lifetimes than students with only a high school diploma.

VISUAL ARGUMENT

Rather than write a letter to the editor about out-of-control salaries for NCAA football coaches, you create a *visual argument*—an editorial cartoon—suggesting that a local coach is paid more than the entire faculty.

DECIDING TO WRITE AN ARGUMENT.   Arguments come in many shapes to serve different purposes. Subsequent chapters in this section cover some genres often assigned in the classroom, including *evaluations, proposals,* and *literary analyses*. ○ But even less specialized arguments have distinctive features. In your projects, you'll aim to do the following.

Offer levelheaded and disputable claims.   You won't influence audiences by making points no one cares about. Something clear and specific ought to be at stake in any argument. Maybe you want to change readers' minds about an issue or shore up what they already believe. In either case, you'll need a well-defined and carefully qualified point, either stated or implied, if you hope to influence levelheaded people. ○

Poster by Ben Shahn, 1968
This poster illustrates the words of British pacifist and parliamentarian John Morley (1838–1923). Note how the style of Shahn's typography and crayon figure complement each other to make a memorable argument out of Morley's sober observation.

(Ben Shahn, "You have not converted a man because you have silenced him." 1968. Copyright © Estate of Ben Shahn / Licensed by VAGA, New York, NY. Photo copyright ©: Smithsonian American Art Museum, Washington, D.C. / Art Resource, NY.)

choose a genre
p. 390

develop a statement
p. 393

Offer good reasons to support a claim.   Without evidence and supporting reasons, a claim is just an assertion—and little better than a shout or a slogan. Slogans do have their appeal in advertising and politics. But they don't become arguments until they are developed through full-bodied thinking and supported by a paper trail of evidence.

Understand opposing claims and points of view.   You won't be able to make a strong case until you can *honestly* paraphrase ○ the logic of those who see matters differently. And, in your own arguments, you will seem smarter and more fair when you acknowledge these other *reasonable* opinions even as you refute them. Also be prepared to address less rational claims calmly, but firmly.

Use language strategically—and not words only.   Sensible opinions still have to dress for the occasion: You need to find the right words and images to carry a case forward. Fortunately, there are many ways to make words memorable. Design is increasingly important too. You may want to use images to influence readers or choose various media for your thoughts to reach different audiences. ○

It goes without saying that many appeals you encounter daily do not measure up to the criteria of serious argument. We've all been seduced by claims just because they are stylish, hip, or repeated so often that they begin to seem true. But if much persuasion doesn't seem fair or sensible, that's all the more reason to reach for a higher standard.

CARS HAVE BUMPERS.
BIKERS HAVE BONES.

DRIVE AWARE. RIDE AWARE.

UTAH DEPARTMENT OF PUBLIC SAFETY

What claim does this ad from the Utah Department of Public Safety actually make? Might anyone dispute it? Do you find the ad effective visually?

restate ideas
p. 494

think visually
p. 592

Here's a *Chronicle of Higher Education* article by Scott Keyes, a 2009 Stanford University graduate, who offers good reasons in support of a clear thesis—that parents and others should allow students to choose their own careers. Like the familiar five-paragraph essay you may have learned in high school, Keyes's essay offers the conventional three points to back up its claim. But "Stop Asking Me My Major" doesn't read like an article just going through the motions thanks to its fully developed introduction, careful attention to opposing arguments, and agreeable style.

The Chronicle of Higher Education

Commentary: January 10, 2010
Scott Keyes

Stop Asking Me My Major

Introductory section lays out the problem of choosing a major systematically, adding to Keyes's credibility.

One of my best friends from high school, Andrew, changed majors during his first semester at college. He and I had been fascinated by politics for years, sharing every news story we could find and participating in the Internet activism that was exploding into a new political force. Even though he was still passionate about politics, that was no longer enough. "I have to get practical," he messaged me one day, "think about getting a job after graduation. I mean, it's like my mom keeps asking me: What can you do with a degree in political science anyway?"

I heard the same question from my friend Jesse when students across campus were agonizing about which major was right for them. He wasn't quite sure what he wanted to study, but every time a field sparked his interest, his father would pepper him with questions about what jobs were available for people in that discipline. Before long, Jesse's dad had convinced him that the only way he could get a job and be successful after college was to major in pre-med.

My friends' experiences were not atypical.

Choosing a major is one of the most difficult things students face in college. There are two main factors that most students consider when making this decision. First is their desire to study what interests them. Second is the fear that a particular major will render them penniless after graduation and result in that dreaded postcollege possibility: moving back in with their parents.

All too often, the concern about a major's practical prospects are pushed upon students by well-intentioned parents. If our goal is to cultivate students who are happy and successful, both in college as well as in the job market, I have this piece of advice for parents: Stop asking, "What can you do with a degree in (fill in the blank)?" You're doing your children no favors by asking them to focus on the job prospects of different academic disciplines, rather than studying what interests them.

It is my experience, both through picking a major myself and witnessing many others endure the process, that there are three reasons why parents (and everyone else) should be encouraging students to focus on what they enjoy studying most, rather than questioning what jobs are supposedly available for different academic concentrations.

The first is psychological. For his first two years of college, Jesse followed his dad's wishes and remained a pre-med student. The only problem was that he hated it. With no passion for the subject, his grades slipped, hindering his chances of getting into medical school. As a result his employability, the supposed reason he was studying medicine in the first place, suffered.

The second reason to stop asking students what they can do with a major is that it perpetuates the false notion that certain majors don't prepare students for the workplace. The belief that technical majors such as computer science are more likely to lead to a job than a major such as sociology or English is certainly understandable. It's also questionable. "The problem," as my friend José explained to me, "is that even as a computer-science major, what I learned in the classroom was outdated by the time I hit the

Keyes spends five paragraphs developing his subject before offering his thesis.

job market." He thought instead that the main benefit of his education, rather than learning specific skills, was gaining a better way of thinking about the challenges he faced. "What's more," he told me, "no amount of education could match the specific on-the-job training I've received working different positions."

Finally, it is counterproductive to demand that students justify their choice of study with potential job prospects because that ignores the lesson we were all taught in kindergarten (and shouldn't ignore the closer we get to employment): You can grow up to be whatever you want to be. The jobs people work at often fall within the realm of their studies, but they don't have to. One need look no further than some of the most prominent figures in our society to see illustrations. The TV chef Julia Child studied English in college. Author Michael Lewis, whose best sellers focus on sports and the financial industry, majored in art history. Matt Groening, creator of *The Simpsons*, got his degree in philosophy, as did the former Hewlett-Packard chief executive Carly Fiorina. Jeff Immelt, chief executive of General Electric, focused on mathematics. Indeed, with the Department of Labor estimating that on average people switch careers (not just jobs) two or three times in their lives, relying on a college major as career preparation is misguided.

I'm not saying any applicant can get any job. Job seekers still need marketable skills if they hope to be hired. However, in a rapidly changing economy, which majors lead to what jobs is not so clear cut. Many employers look for applicants from a diverse background — including my friend who has a degree in biochemistry but was just hired at an investment consulting firm.

That doesn't mean that majors no longer matter. It is still an important decision, and students are right to seek outside counsel when figuring out what they want to study. But questioning how a particular major will affect their employability is not necessarily the best approach. Although parents' intentions may be pure — after all, who

Three reasons are offered to support the thesis, each more complex and fully developed.

The specific examples here illustrate Keyes's point.

An informal style, using "I" and even "you" when necessary, reaches out to audiences.

doesn't want to see their children succeed after graduation? — that question can hold tremendous power over impressionable freshmen. Far too many of my classmates let it steer them away from what they enjoyed studying to a major they believed would help them get a job after graduation.

One of those friends was Andrew. He opted against pursuing a degree in political science, choosing instead to study finance because "that's where the jobs are." Following graduation, Andrew landed at a consulting firm. I recently learned with little surprise that he hates his job and has no passion for the work.

Jesse, on the other hand, realized that if he stayed on the pre-med track, he would burn out before ever getting his degree. During his junior year he changed tracks and began to study engineering. Not only did Jesse's grades improve markedly, but his enthusiasm for the subject recently earned him a lucrative job offer and admission to a top engineering master's program.

Andrew and Jesse both got jobs. But who do you think feels more successful?

Objections are anticipated and treated as reasonable. But they are answered sensibly too.

Jesse and Andrew appear in the opening paragraphs as well, tying the argument together structurally.

Exploring purpose and topic

topic ◀

In a college assignment, you could be asked to write an argument about a general topic area related to a course, but you likely won't be told what your claim should be. That decision has to come from you, drawing on your knowledge, experiences, and inclinations. So choose subjects about which you genuinely care—not issues the media or someone else defines as controversial. You'll do a more credible job defending your defiant choice *not* to wear a helmet when cycling than explaining, one more time, why the environment should concern us all. And if environmental matters do roil you, stake your claim on a well-defined ecological problem—perhaps from within your community—that you might actually influence by the power of your rhetoric. O

If you really are stumped, the Yahoo Directory's list of "Issues and Causes"—with topics from *abortion* to *zoos*—offers problems enough to keep both Janeane Garofalo *and* Ann Coulter busy to the end of the century. To find it, search "Society and Culture" or "Issues and Causes" on the site's main Web directory. ("Society and Culture" itself offers a menu of intriguing topic areas.) Once you have an issue or even a specific claim, your real work begins.

Learn much more about your subject. Your first task is to do basic library and online research to get a better handle on your topic—*especially* when you think you already have all the answers. Chances are, you don't.

State a preliminary claim, if only for yourself. Some arguments fail because writers never focus their thinking. Instead, they wander around their potential subjects, throwing out ideas or making contradictory assertions, and leaving it to readers to assemble the random parts. To avoid this misdi- rection, begin with a *claim*—a *complete* sentence that states a position you will then have to defend. Though you will likely change this initial claim, such a statement will keep you on track as you explore a topic. Even a simple sentence helps:

> The college rankings published annually by *U.S. News & World Report* do more harm than good.
>
> Westerners should be less defensive about their cultures.
>
> People who oppose gay marriage don't know what they are talking about.

get an idea
p. 356

Arguments take many different forms, but finger-pointing is rarely a good persuasive tool.

Qualify your claim to make it reasonable. As you learn more about a subject, revise your topic idea to reflect the complications you encounter. ○ Your tentative thesis will likely grow longer, but the topic will actually narrow because of the issues and conditions you've specified. You'll also have less work to do, thanks to qualifying expressions such as *some, most, a few, often, under certain conditions, occasionally, when necessary*, and so on. Other qualifying expressions are highlighted below.

> The **statistically unreliable** college ratings published by *U.S. News & World Report* **usually** do more harm than good to students **because** some claim that they lead admissions officers to award scholarships on the basis of merit rather than need.
>
> Westerners should be **more** willing to defend their **cultural** values and **intellectual** achievements **if** they hope to **defend freedom** against its enemies.
>
> **Many conservative critics** who oppose gay marriage **unwittingly** undermine their own core principles, **especially monogamy and honesty.**

Examine your core assumptions. Claims may be supported by reasons and evidence, but they are based on assumptions. *Assumptions* are the principles and values on which we ground our beliefs and actions. Sometimes these assumptions are controversial and stand right out. At other times, they're so close to us, they seem invisible—they are part of the air we breathe. Expect to spend a paragraph defending any assumptions your readers might find controversial. ○

think critically
p. 372

develop ideas
p. 412

CLAIM

The statistically unreliable college ratings published by *U.S. News & World Report* usually do more harm than good to students because some people claim that they lead admissions officers to award scholarships on the basis of merit rather than need.

ASSUMPTION

Alleviating need in our society is more important than rewarding merit.
[Probably controversial]

CLAIM

Westerners should be more willing to defend their cultural values and intellectual achievements if they hope to defend freedom against its enemies.

ASSUMPTION

Freedom needs to be defended at all costs.
[Possibly controversial for some audiences]

CLAIM

Many conservative critics who oppose gay marriage unwittingly undermine their own core principles, especially monogamy and honesty.

ASSUMPTION

People should be consistent about their principles.
[Probably noncontroversial]

Your Turn   Many writers have a tough time expressing their topic in a complete sentence. They will offer a tentative word or phrase or sentence fragment instead of making the commitment that a full sentence demands, especially one with subordinators and qualifiers that begin to tie their ideas together. So give it a try. Take a topic you might write about and turn it into a full-bore sentence that tells readers what your claim is and how you intend to support it. Scott Keyes's topic sentence has fifty-one words (see p. 76); aim for at least twenty.

Understanding your audience

Retailers know audiences. In fact, they go to great lengths to pinpoint the groups most likely to buy their fried chicken or video games. They then tailor their images and advertising pitches to those specific customers. You'll play to audiences the same way when you write arguments—if maybe a little less cynically.

Understand that you won't ever please everyone in a general audience, even if you write bland, colorless mush—because some readers will then regard you as craven and spineless. In fact, how readers imagine you, *as the person presenting an argument*, may determine their willingness to consider your claims at all.

Readers do react differently to specific topics, so you will need to consider a variety of approaches when imagining the audiences for your arguments.

Consider and control your ethos.   People who study persuasion describe the character that writers create for themselves within an argument as their *ethos*—the voice and attitude they choose to give their appeal. It is a powerful concept, worth remembering. Surely you recognize when writers are coming across as, let's say, ingratiatingly confident or stupidly obnoxious. And don't you respond in kind, giving ear to the likable voice and dismissing the malicious one? A few audiences—like those for political blogs—may actually prefer a writer with a snarky ethos. But most readers respond better when writers seem reasonable, knowledgeable, and fair—neither insulting those who disagree with them nor making those who share their views embarrassed to have them on their side.

Control your ethos by adjusting the style, tone, and vocabulary of your argument: For instance, contractions can make you seem friendly (or too casual); an impressive vocabulary suggests that you are smart (or maybe just pompous); lots of name-dropping makes you seem hip (or perhaps pretentious). You may have to write several drafts to find a suitable ethos for a particular argument. ○ And, yes, your ethos may change from paper to paper, audience to audience.

revise and edit
p. 452

> **Your Turn**   Chances are you have some favorite Web sites or blogs you consult daily. Choose one of those sites, find an entry in it that expresses the *ethos* of the contributor(s) or the site itself, and then analyze that ethos. Is the character of the site friendly and down-to-earth? Arrogant and authoritative? Serious and politically concerned? Point to specific features of the site that help to create its ethos. If you don't consult blogs or Web sites, apply your analysis to a printed or oral text, perhaps an op-ed by a favorite columnist or a political speech by a public figure.

Consider your own limits.   If you read newspapers and magazines that mostly confirm your own political views, you might be in for a wake-up call when you venture an opinion beyond your small circle of friends. Tread softly. There are good reasons why people don't talk politics at parties. When you do argue about social, political, or religious issues, be respectful of those who work from premises different from your own.

Consider race and ethnicity.   The different lives people live as a result of their heritage play a role in many claims you might make about education, politics, art, religion, or even athletics. Be sensitive without being gutless. ○

Consider gender and sexual orientation.   These issues almost always matter, often in unexpected ways. Men and women, whether straight or gay, don't inhabit quite the same worlds. But, even so, you shouldn't argue, either, as if all men and all women think the same way—or should. False assumptions about gender can lead you into a minefield.

Consider income and class.   People's lives are often defined by the realities of their economic situations—and the assumptions that follow from privilege, poverty, or something in between. Think it would be just dandy to have an outdoor pool on campus or a convenient new parking garage? You may find that not everyone is as eager or as able as you to absorb the costs of such proposals to improve campus life. And if you intend to complain about

> Need help supporting your argument? See "How to Use the Writing Center" on pp. 382–83.

fat cats, ridicule soccer moms, or poke fun at rednecks, is it because you can't imagine them among your readers?

Consider religion and spirituality.   Members of different organized religions manage to insult each other almost without trying, more so now perhaps as religion routinely takes center stage in the political and diplomatic arena. People within the same denomination often hold incompatible views. And the word *atheist* can engender negative reactions in certain audiences. It takes skill and good sense to keep the differences in mind when your topic demands it.

Consider age.   Obviously, you'd write differently for children than for their parents on almost any subject, changing your style, vocabulary, and allusions. But consider that people at different ages really have lived different lives. The so-called Greatest Generation never forgot the Great Depression; teens today will remember the destruction of the World Trade Center towers on September 11, 2001, and perhaps the school shootings in Columbine, Colorado. They'll grow up with different attitudes, values, heroes, and villains. A writer has to be savvy enough to account for such differences when constructing an argument.

Gender attitudes develop early, along with some argument strategies.

Finding and developing materials

develop support ◄

You could write a book from the materials you'll collect researching some arguments. Material is out there on every imaginable subject, and the research techniques you use to prepare a report or term paper should work for arguments too. Since arguments often deal with current events and topics, start with a resource such as the Yahoo "Issues and Causes" directory mentioned earlier. Explore your subject, too, in *LexisNexis,* if your library gives you access to this huge database of newspaper articles. ○

As you gather materials, though, consider how much space you have to make your argument. Sometimes a claim has to fit within the confines of a letter to the editor, an op-ed column in a local paper, or a fifteen-minute PowerPoint lecture. Aristotle, still one of the best theorists on persuasion, thought arguments *should* be brief, with speakers limiting examples to the *minimum* necessary to make a case—no extra points for piling on. So gather big, and then select only the best stuff for your argument.

List your reasons.   You'll come up with reasons to support your claim almost as soon as you choose a subject. Write those down. Then start reading and continue to list new reasons as they arise, not being too fussy at this point. Be careful to paraphrase these ideas so that you don't inadvertently plagiarize them later.

Then, when your reading and research are complete, review your notes and try to group the arguments that support your position. It's likely you'll detect patterns and relationships among these reasons, and an unwieldy initial list of potential arguments may be streamlined into just three or four—which could become the key reasons behind your claim. Study these points and look for logical connections or sequences. Readers will expect your ideas to converge on a claim or lead logically toward it. ○

The whole is greater than the sum of its parts.

— Aristotle

ORIGINAL

Why ethanol won't solve our energy problems

- Using ethanol in cars actually increases NO_x emissions.
- Ethanol requires more energy to make than it produces.
- Ethanol reduces range: You can't drive as far on a gallon.
- Ethanol can plug up fuel systems of older cars.
- Ethanol produces much less energy per gallon than gas.
- Creating ethanol contributes to global warming.
- Ethanol is cheaper than gas only because of massive government subsidies.
- Ethanol harms performance in cars.

refine your search
p. 472

shape your work
p. 406

- Ethanol damages engines.
- Everyone's just on another eco bandwagon.
- Ethanol drives up crop prices, and thus food prices.

STREAMLINED

Why ethanol won't solve our energy problems

- Ethanol hurts performance of vehicles significantly.
- Ethanol is expensive to produce.
- Ethanol harms the environment.

Assemble your hard evidence.   Gather examples, illustrations, testimony, and numbers to support each main point. Record these items as you read, photocopying the data or downloading it carefully into labeled files. Take this evidence from the most reputable sources and keep track of all bibliographical information (author, title, publication info, URL) just as you would when preparing a term paper—even if you aren't expected to document your argument. You want that data on hand in case your credibility is later challenged.

If you borrow facts from a Web site, do your best to track the information down to its actual source. For example, if a blogger quotes statistics from the U.S. Department of Agriculture, take a few minutes to find the table or graph on the USDA Web site itself and make sure the numbers are reported accurately. ○

Think of hard evidence as a broad category that might also include photographs, video clips, or physical objects. Audiences do have a fondness for smoking guns—those pieces of indisputable evidence that clinch an argument. If you find one, use it.

Cull the best quotations.   You've done your homework for an assignment, reading the best available sources. So prove it in your argument by quoting from them intelligently. Choose quotations that do one or more of the following:

- Put your issue in focus or context.
- Make a point with exceptional power and economy.
- Support a claim or piece of evidence that readers might doubt.
- State an opposing point well.

analyze claims and
evidence p. 487

Copy passages that appeal to you, but don't plan on using all of them. An argument that is a patchwork of quotations reads like a patchwork of quotations—which is to say, *boring*.

Be scrupulous about getting the quotations right. That's easier now than in the past because files can be copied and downloaded electronically. But you still need to use such passages fairly and be prepared to cite and document them. ○

Find counterarguments.   If you study your subject thoroughly, you'll come across plenty of honest disagreement. List all the reasonable objections that you can find to your claim, either to your basic argument or to any controversial evidence you expect to cite. When possible, cluster these objections to reduce them to a manageable few. Decide which you must refute in detail, which you might handle briefly, and which you can afford to dismiss. ○

Ethanol counterarguments

- Ethanol is made from corn, a renewable resource.
- Ethanol is available today.
- Ethanol is locally made, not imported.
- Using ethanol decreases CO emissions.

Consider emotional appeals.   Nuclear power plants produce electricity without contributing significantly to global warming. But don't expect Americans who watched the Japanese deal with a nuclear crisis in 2011 following a tsunami to put aside their fears about atomic power readily, even to preserve the environment. Emotions play a powerful role in many arguments, a fact you cannot afford to ignore when a claim you make stirs up strong feelings. Questions to answer include the following:

Well-chosen visuals add power to an argument.   A writer trying to persuade readers not to buy fur might include this photo in an article. How would this image influence you, as a reader?

- What emotions might be raised to support my point?
- How might I responsibly introduce such feelings: through words, images, color, sound?
- How might any feelings my subject arouses work contrary to my claims or reasons?

understand citation styles p. 501

develop ideas p. 412

Creating a structure

▶ organize ideas

It's easy to sketch a standard structure for arguments: one that leads from claim to supporting reasons to evidence and even accommodates a counter-argument or two.

Introduction leading to a claim or thesis statement

First reason and supporting evidence (stronger)
Second reason and supporting evidence (strong)
Third reason and supporting evidence (strongest)

Counterarguments

Conclusions

The problem is that you won't read many effective arguments, either in or out of school, that follow this template. The structure isn't defective, just too simple to describe the way arguments really move when ideas matter. Some controversies need lots of background to get rolling, some require detours to resolve other issues first, and a great many arguments work best when writers simply lay out the facts and allow readers to draw their own conclusions—or be nudged toward them.

You won't write a horrible paper if you use the traditional model because all the parts will be in place. Thesis? Check. Three supporting reasons? Check. Counterarguments? Check. But you will sound exactly like what you are: A writer going through the motions instead of engaging with ideas. Here's how to get your ideas to breathe in an argument—while still hitting all the marks.

Spell out what's at stake.   When you write an argument, you start a disagreement, so you'd better explain why—as Scott Keyes does in "Stop Asking Me My Major" earlier in this chapter. Do you hope to fix a looming problem? Then describe what your concern is and make readers share it. Do you intend to correct a false notion or bad reporting? Then be sure to tell readers what setting the record straight accomplishes. Appalled by the apathy of voters, the dangers of global warming, the infringements of free speech on campus? Then explain what makes such issues matter today and why readers should pay attention. **O**

Don't just jump into a claim: Take a few sentences or paragraphs to set up the situation. Quote a nasty politician or tell an eye-popping story or two. Get readers invested in what's to come.

Make a point or build toward one.   Arguments can unfurl just as reports do, with unmistakable claims followed by reams of supporting evidence. But they can also work like crime dramas, in which the evidence in a case builds toward a compelling conclusion—your thesis perhaps. Consider the ethanol issue. You could argue straight up that this fuel causes more problems than it solves. Or you could open by wondering if ethanol really is the miracle fuel some claim it to be and then offer evidence that contradicts the media hype. In both cases, readers get the same claim and reasons. But the first approach might work better for readers already interested in environmental issues, while the second might grab those who aren't by arousing their curiosity. This is your call. **O**

Address counterpoints when necessary, not in a separate section.   *Necessary* is when your readers start thinking to themselves, "Yeah, but what about . . . ?" Such doubts likely surface approximately where your own do—and, admit it, you have *some* misgivings about your argument. So take them on. Strategically, it rarely makes sense to consign major objections to a lengthy section near the end of a paper. That's asking for trouble. Do you really want to offer a case for the opposition just when your readers are finishing up?

On the plus side, dealing with opposing arguments (or writing a refutation itself—see p. 101) can be like caffeine for your prose, sharpening your attention and reflexes. Here's Ann Hulbert, for example, eager to take on those who now argue that it's boys who are being shortchanged in schools by curriculums and modes of teaching that favor girls:

> Other complaints about boy-averse pedagogy also don't quite add up—in part because they contradict one another. Sommers blamed a touchy-feely, progressive ethos for alienating boys in the classroom; males, she argued,

develop a statement
p. 393

order ideas
p. 408

thrive on no-nonsense authority, accountability, clarity, and peer rivalry. But now *Newsweek* blames roughly the opposite atmosphere for boy trouble: the competitive, cut-and-dried, standardized-test-obsessed (and recess-less) pedagogical emphasis of the last decade. So much speculative certainty doesn't really shed much light on the puzzle of what's deterring young men from college.

– "Will Boys Be Boys?" *Slate.com*, February 1, 2006

Hold your best arguments for the end.   Of course, you want strong points throughout the paper. But you need a high note early on to get readers interested and then another choral moment as you finish to send them out the door humming. If you must summarize an argument, don't let a dull recap of your main points squander an important opportunity to influence readers. End with a rhetorical flourish that reminds readers how compelling your arguments are. ○

A pithy phrase, an ironic twist, and a question to contemplate can also lock down your case. Here's Maureen Dowd, bleakly—and memorably—concluding an argument defending the job journalists had done covering the Iraq War:

Journalists die and we know who they are. We know they liked to cook and play Scrabble. But we don't know who killed them, and their killers will never be brought to justice. The enemy has no face, just a finger on a detonator.

– "Live from Baghdad: More Dying," *New York Times*, May 31, 2006

Journalists undergo training to prepare for the dangers they are likely to face in conflict zones.

○
shape an ending
p. 425

Choosing a style and design

Arguments vary widely in style. An unsigned editorial you write to represent the opinion of a newspaper might sound formal and serious. Composing an op-ed under your own name, you'd likely ease up on the dramatic metaphors and allow yourself more personal pronouns. Arguing a point in an alternative newsletter, you might even slip into the lingo of its vegan or survivalist subscribers. Routine adjustments like these really matter when you need to attract and hold readers.

You should also write with sensitivity since some people reading arguments may well be wavering, defensive, or spoiling for a fight. There's no reason to distract them with fighting words if you want to offer a serious argument. Here's how political commentator Ann Coulter described a politically active group of 9/11 widows who she believed were using their status to shield their anti–Iraq War opinions from criticism:

> These broads are millionaires, lionized on TV and in articles about them, reveling in their status as celebrities and stalked by grief-arazzis. I have never seen people enjoying their husbands' death so much.
>
> – *Godless: The Church of Liberalism* (2006)

Any point Coulter might make simply gets lost in her breathtaking idiom of attack.

There are many powerful and aggressive ways to frame an argument without resorting to provocative language or fallacies of argument. ⭘ Some of these strategies follow.

Invite readers with a strong opening.   Arguments—like advertisements— are usually discretionary reading. People can turn away the moment they grow irritated or bored. So you have to work hard to keep them engrossed by your ideas. You may need to open with a little surprise or drama. Try a blunt statement, an anecdote, or a striking illustration if it helps—maybe an image too. Or consider personalizing the lead-in, giving readers a stake in the claim you are about to make. The following is a remarkable opening paragraph from an argument by Malcolm Gladwell on the wisdom of banning dogs by breed. When you finish, ask yourself whether Gladwell has earned your attention. Would you read the remainder of the piece?

avoid fallacies
p. 372

One afternoon last February, Guy Clairoux picked up his two-and-a-half-
year-old son, Jayden, from day care and walked him back to their house in
the west end of Ottawa, Ontario. They were almost home. Jayden was
straggling behind, and, as his father's back was turned, a pit bull jumped
over a backyard fence and lunged at Jayden. "The dog had his head in its
mouth and started to do this shake," Clairoux's wife, JoAnn Hartley, said
later. As she watched in horror, two more pit bulls jumped over the fence,
joining in the assault. She and Clairoux came running, and he punched the
first of the dogs in the head, until it dropped Jayden, and then he threw the
boy toward his mother. Hartley fell on her son, protecting him with her
body. "JoAnn!" Clairoux cried out, as all three dogs descended on his wife.
"Cover your neck, cover your neck." A neighbor, sitting by her window,
screamed for help. Her partner and a friend, Mario Gauthier, ran outside.
A neighborhood boy grabbed his hockey stick and threw it to Gauthier.
He began hitting one of the dogs over the head, until the stick broke. "They
wouldn't stop," Gauthier said. "As soon as you'd stop, they'd attack again.
I've never seen a dog go so crazy. They were like Tasmanian devils." The
police came. The dogs were pulled away, and the Clairouxes and one of
the rescuers were taken to the hospital. Five days later, the Ontario
legislature banned the ownership of pit bulls. "Just as we wouldn't let a
great white shark in a swimming pool," the province's attorney general,
Michael Bryant, had said, "maybe we shouldn't have these animals on the
civilized streets."

– "Troublemakers," *New Yorker*, February 6, 2006

Write vibrant sentences.   You can write arguments full throttle, using a
complete range of rhetorical devices, from deliberate repetition and parallelism to dialogue and quotation. Metaphors, similes, and analogies fit right
in too. The trick is to create sentences with a texture rich enough to keep
readers hooked, yet lean enough to advance an argument. In the following
three paragraphs, follow the highlighting to see how Thomas L. Friedman
uses parallelism and one intriguing metaphor after another to argue in favor
of immigration legislation after witnessing the diversity in a high school
graduation class in Maryland. **O**

improve your
sentences p. 444

There is a lot to be worried about in America today: a war in Iraq that is getting worse not better, an administration whose fiscal irresponsibility we will be paying for for a long time, an education system that is not producing enough young Americans skilled in math and science, and inner cities where way too many black males are failing. We must work harder and get smarter if we want to maintain our standard of living.

But if there is one reason to still be optimistic about America it is represented by the stunning diversity of the Montgomery Blair class of 2006. America is still the world's greatest human magnet. We are not the only country that embraces diversity, but there is something about our free society and free market that still attracts people like no other. Our greatest asset is our ability to still cream off not only the first-round intellectual draft choices from around the world but the low-skilled–high-aspiring ones as well, and that is the main reason that I am not yet ready to cede the twenty-first century to China. Our Chinese will still beat their Chinese.

This influx of brainy and brawny immigrants is our oil well – one that never runs dry. It is an endless source of renewable human energy and creativity. Congress ought to stop debating gay marriage and finally give us a framework to maintain a free flow of legal immigration.

– "A Well of Smiths and Xias," *New York Times*, June 7, 2006

Ask rhetorical questions.   The danger of rhetorical questions is that they can seem stagy and readers might not answer them the way you want. But the device can be very powerful in hammering a point home. Good questions also invite readers to think about an issue in exactly the terms that a writer prefers. Here's George Will using rhetorical questions to conclude a piece on global warming.

In fact, the earth is always experiencing either warming or cooling. But suppose the scientists and their journalistic conduits, who today say they were so spectacularly wrong so recently, are now correct. Suppose the earth is warming and suppose the warming is caused by human activity. Are we sure there will be proportionate benefits from whatever climate change can be purchased at the cost of slowing economic growth and spending trillions? Are we sure the consequences of climate change – remember, a thick sheet of ice once covered the Midwest – must be bad? Or has the science-journalism complex decided that debate about these questions, too, is "over"?

– "Let Cooler Heads Prevail," *Washington Post*, April 2, 2006

Use images and design to make a point. If we didn't know it already (and we did), the video and photographic images from 9/11, Hurricane Katrina, and the oil spill in the Gulf of Mexico clearly prove that persuasion doesn't occur by words only. We react powerfully to what we see with our own eyes. Consider, for example, this mug shot of Jared Loughner, the man charged in the January 2011 shooting of U.S. Representative Gabrielle Giffords. Claims that the attack was motivated by political rhetoric receded once the public got a look at the picture.

And yet words still play a part because most images become *focused* arguments only when accompanied by commentary—as commentators routinely prove when they put a spin on news photographs or video. And because digital technology now makes it so easy to incorporate nonverbal media into texts, whether on a page, screen, or Prezi whiteboard, you should always consider how just the right image might enhance the case you want to make. And now you don't always have to start with words. A series of photographs might be shaped into a photo-essay every bit as powerful as a conventional op-ed piece.

In fact, you already have the tools on your computer to create posters, advertisements, slides, and brochures, all of which may be instruments of persuasion. **O**

think visually
p. 592

Examining models

EXPLORATORY ARGUMENT   In "Play 'Free Bird'!" Lynn Ehlers draws on her personal feelings and experiences to question whether musicians in concert have an ethical obligation to play their fans' favorite songs. Although most of her classmates disagreed with her claim when she first offered it as a topic proposal, Ehlers learned from their objections how to strengthen her case. Watch as she builds up toward her claim, which isn't made explicitly until the final paragraph. See if you agree with the conclusion she comes to in this argument.

Ehlers 1

Lynn Ehlers

Prof. John Ruszkiewicz

Advanced Expository Writing

May 8, 20--

"Play 'Free Bird'!"

There aren't a lot of reasons I'd choose to be here, melting in the unsympathetic humidity of Austin in mid-July, gliding around an airtight snake pit of sweating high schoolers and their smearing punk rock makeup. Not a single inch of my shirt is *not* sticking to my body, and I can't move without adhering to three other people. It smells like a farm and I don't have enough cash for a beer.

And yet, here I am, about to pass out from dehydration at a Jimmy Eat World concert at Emo's outdoor stage with a few hundred other troopers. Why? Because I've loved this band for years—long after those mysterious artistry watchdogs exposed them for "selling out." And if it meant hearing "Bleed American" live, I'd have put up with twice as

> Opening sets the scene, but only the title hints at what the issue may be.

> The argument assumes an audience reasonably familiar with the music of Jimmy Eat World.

95

Ehlers 2

many drunks and a few more degrees of heat. But, as it turned out, it didn't mean hearing "Bleed American"; it meant sweltering through an hour-long set of boring acoustic versions of songs off *Futures* and crappy filler off *Clarity*. "Bleed American" is one of Jimmy Eat World's big singles, written in a minor key with an unlikely upbeat chorus and the band's trademark curious lyrics; the confidence in Jimmy Eat World's music was first established in this single, breaking away from the fuzzy, wandering sound of prior work. While I already knew that the true gems were not concert material, the fact that "Bleed American" didn't land in the set list seemed—in the words of my roommate and fellow attendee—"f-cking lame." The urge to throw a preteenesque fit was almost uncontrollable, but I reminded myself that it's their show, their band, and their damn song, and they can do what they want.

But can they really? In our entertainment-loving, rockstar-glorifying culture, we have created an interesting debate: Who owes whom? Are musicians indebted to their fans for their livelihoods, or are fans indebted to musicians for their talent? Was I obligated to appreciate the trash Jimmy Eat World played that clammy evening, or should the band have sucked it up and played their hits for yet another worshipful crowd? Concerts fall into a funny gray area between art and commodity—and, admittedly, our free market economy seems to put emphasis on the latter.

Ehlers's argument is finally raised by the exploratory question, "But can they really?"

Ehlers 3

Musicians are largely granted the blameless freedom to do as they please because concerts are products; if consumers don't like them, they can stop buying them.

But there is a difference between putting out an album and putting on a show—the dynamics between musician and fan are altered. An album is a finite product, which musicians craft privately, release for profit, and hope will be successful. Do fans participate in the studio? No. Do they dictate what songs go on an album, demand subtle nuances, produce the general sound? No. They can buy it, steal it, or ignore it—but they certainly can't contribute to the album's production.

And whereas musicians undeniably possess full creative license over albums, concerts take on an element of customer service. In putting on shows, musicians assume two kinds of obligation to their fans: first, the professional obligation to make good on services *explicitly* promised (meaning that the band will show up and do something resembling a music performance); and second, the more important *ethical* obligation to make good on services *implicitly* promised (such as the understood assumption that a band will play its hits at the show). Musicians know what fans want to hear because they know what songs pay their Los Angeles mortgages—but the decision to actually perform their top-selling singles is the ethical prerogative of the musician.

Ehlers examines the relationship between artists and audiences to clarify the matter for herself and her readers.

She draws an important and impressive distinction between albums and live performances.

Ehlers 4

The details here help to establish Ehlers's ethos: She is reasonably knowledge-able about music and musicians, not just blowing off steam.

Some musicians decide to completely scrap hits from their set lists—especially singles from previous albums. Radiohead periodically refuses to play their 1992 hit "Creep" off *Pablo Honey*, often for years at a stretch. In 2002, Beck announced to a Dallas crowd, "I just want to let you know now, I'm not going to play 'Loser.' It's not going to happen." Do Thome York and Beck know that "Creep" and "Loser" sold a significant portion of their tickets? Of course. But they've played those songs thousands of times—albums, practices, and especially those relentless tour schedules. And, as musicians, they have taken the liberty to shelve "Creep" and "Loser" until a time when playing them no longer causes physical pain. Yorke and Beck are under no explicit obligation to play their hits (or even to put on a quality show), and that's *why* it's a matter of ethics: the fact that musicians don't *have* to indulge fans with their implicit purchases, but still *should.*

But it's not just a matter of musicians providing implicit services; more importantly, it's a matter of musicians fulfilling ethical obligations as *artists*, by gratefully responding to the patronage that their artistry receives. Musicians create art that becomes significant and personal to individuals—and ultimately, the personal attachment fans forge with music is what sells tickets. The majority of fans who go to concerts—particularly, those who go to concerts frequently—truly do show up as patrons and revere music as inseparable from life.

Ehlers 5

Note how Ehlers makes playing songs fans want to hear an ethical, not a contractual, issue, upping the ante for artists.

These are the people who find the discussion of favorite albums to be more sensitive than politics or religion. These are the people who will never part with their CD (or vinyl) collections, regardless of the digital technology available, and despite having several albums in all three forms. These are the people who lean on music to get through life: who depend on Beck when they'd rather die than clean their apartment, and who depend on Radiohead in the face of failure and loneliness.

The repetition in this paragraph gives the argument a powerful emotional turn, emphasizing the artists' obligations to fans.

I was at the Jimmy Eat World show because I'd listened to *Futures* three times in a row on a summer road trip with my dad. I skipped seventh period choir in high school to listen to *Bleed American* in a car parked behind the school, wondering about the future with my feet out the window. I listened to "My Sundown" on repeat for days after my mom passed away, and "She's Perfect" the entire first week of college when I found myself on a campus without friends or food money. I've made Jimmy Eat World's music a part of my life, and, in return, at the concert in Austin they played the music they weren't tired of playing yet.

Now the argument becomes personal.

There's a strategic nod here to the *other* side of the argument.

Of course, musicians aren't contractually required to show gratitude for (or even acknowledge) the genuine relationship that fans develop with the band's music; in fact, it's easier and socially acceptable not to. The musicians' decision not to play the songs that they know people have fallen in love with— relying on them for comfort when things become unbearable,

Ehlers 6

dancing to them on a coffee table with a sloshing wine glass in one hand—is neither a professional nor legal infraction. But again, this is what makes it an ethical matter: It's the musicians' *ethical* obligation to reciprocate fan support with equivalent appreciation, even though they simply don't have to. And yes, it means playing the songs that fans continue to yell for and buy tickets for and spend their last dollar on to see live—despite the dread it breathes into musicians the second they wake up, hung over on a multithousand-dollar tour bus, surrounded by vintage guitars and their per diem allowance of top-shelf liquor. Musicians owe at least half of their success to the people who gave their product a chance and who connected with their art. Putting on a killer show—and playing the songs that matter to their fans—is the least they can do.

But with all her evidence in place, Ehlers finally makes an unequivocal claim: "It's the musicians' *ethical* obligation to reciprocate fan support. . . ."

Hey, guys, play "Bleed American," why don't ya?

REFUTATION ARGUMENT   Cathy Young, a Russian immigrant and writer for the *Boston Globe* and the Libertarian magazine *Reason*, takes issue with new sexual harassment guidelines. In this argument, which appeared in the *Boston Globe*, she explains why she believes they are deeply flawed and insulting to women and men alike.

Duke's Sexist Sexual Misconduct Policy

Cathy Young

April 14, 2010

Four years ago, Duke University became the center of a national controversy about sexual assault, wrongful accusations, and campus politics when four lacrosse players were falsely accused of raping an exotic dancer at a party. Now, Duke is back in the news with a campus policy that ostensibly seeks to prevent sexual assault—but, in fact, infantilizes women, redefines much consensual sex as potentially criminal, and does a grave disservice to both sexes.

The policy, introduced last fall but recently challenged by the Foundation for Individual Rights in Education, co-founded by Boston attorney Harvey Silverglate, targets "sexual misconduct"—everything from improper touching to forced sex. Some of the examples given in the text of the policy, such as groping an unwilling woman's breasts, are clearly sexual offenses not just under university regulations but under the law.

But the policy's far-reaching definition of sex without "affirmative consent" covers much more. Unlike the notorious Antioch College rules of the 1990s that required verbal consent to every new level of intimacy, Duke's policy recognizes non-verbal expressions of consent. However, it stresses that "consent may not be inferred from silence [or] passivity"—even in an ongoing sexual relationship.

> The thesis of the article comes at the end of the first paragraph, a common location.

> Young acknowledges some good sense in the Duke harassment policy.

Then the article begins to enumerate flaws in the school's new rules — the meat of the article.

What's more, consent can be invalidated by various circumstances — not just obvious ones such as being threatened or unconscious, but also being intoxicated to any degree, or "psychologically pressured," or "coerced." The latter is an extremely broad term, particularly since the policy warns that "real or perceived power differentials . . . may create an unintentional atmosphere of coercion." As FIRE has noted, a popular varsity athlete may face a presumption of coercion in any relationship with a fellow student.

Supporting her thesis, Young explains why she believes that the policy demeans women.

Meanwhile, women, the default victims in the Duke policy, are presumed passive and weak-minded: Goddess forbid they should take more than minimal responsibility for refusing unwanted sex. In one of the policy's hypothetical scenarios, a woman tells her long-term boyfriend she's not in the mood, but then "is silent" in response to his continued non-forcible advances; if he takes this as consent and they have sex, that is "sexual misconduct." Why she doesn't tell him to stop remains a mystery.

The man's behavior may be inconsiderate. However, adult college students have no more of a right to be protected from such ordinary pressures in relationships than, say, from being cajoled into buying expensive gifts for their significant other.

The refutation requires that readers agree that the harassment policy goes too far. So Young uses specific, though hypothetical, examples.

Most insidiously, under the new Duke policy the "offender" may face sanctions even if the "victim" doesn't think she is one. If a woman has a sexual encounter she regrets and tells a friend who decides she was coerced, the friend's third-party report can trigger an investigation. And if she tells a dorm adviser or a women's center staffer, they are obligated to report the incident.

About 15 years ago, as an undergraduate, a friend of mine was talked into a one-night stand in a situation some would call coercive: the man was a graduate student, and she felt somewhat intimidated by his intellectual brilliance. She went to a campus counselor hoping for advice on developing her assertiveness skills — only to be told that she had been assaulted and should not blame herself. My friend was frustrated and angry: in her view, the counselor was not only being unhelpful but telling her how to interpret her own experience. Imagine how much

Language of the conclusion is tough and heavily connotative: *pseudo-feminist, sex police, criminals, victims.*

more betrayed she would have felt if the counselor had been compelled to initiate proceedings on her behalf.

The policy has other questionable aspects. While such offenses as theft or assault are judged by a panel of three students and two faculty/staff members, sexual misconduct charges are to be heard by two faculty/staff members and one student; perhaps a jury of one's peers cannot be relied upon to enforce the party line.

Sexual violence and abuse is a real problem on college campuses; so are attitudes that, sometimes, still condone such behavior. But a pseudo-feminist sex police that turns a large percentage of students into either criminals or victims—and, in the process, trivializes real sexual violence—is hardly the solution.

Use of "the party line" aligns Duke's policy with that of authoritarian states.

VISUAL ARGUMENT   "Visualizing the BP Oil ~~Spill~~ Disaster" appeared on the Web site IfItWereMy-
Home.com in the aftermath of the collapse of the *Deepwater Horizon* oil rig on April 20, 2010. A graphic
on the site enabled viewers to visualize just how large the resulting oil spill was by entering their own location into a box on the site. In the screenshot here, the spill is centered over New York City and stretches
from Philadelphia almost to Boston. Without offering any explicit claim (except perhaps the deliberate
strike-through of the word "spill"), the IfItWereMyHome.com Web site makes a sobering argument about
the extent of the crisis and those responsible for it.

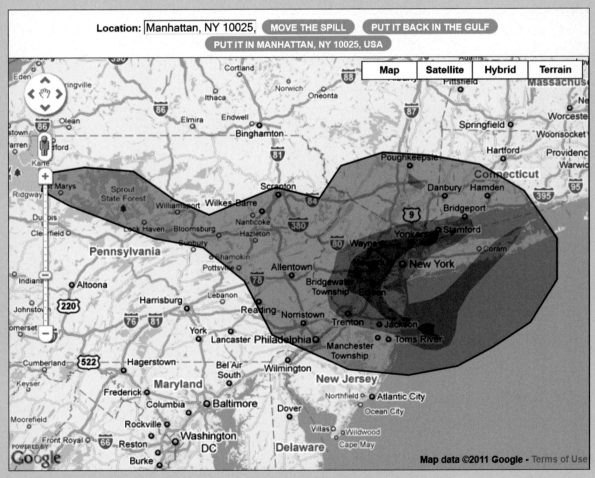

Courtesy IfItWereMyHome.com. Copyright © 2011 Google, Europa Technologies, INEGI.

Assignments

1. **Argument to Advance a Thesis:** Review the way Scott Keyes supports a clearly stated thesis in "Stop Asking Me My Major" (p. 75). Then write an argument that similarly provides direct support for a controversial claim in the public sphere—one that has implications for other people. Like Keyes, take the time to explain the issue you are addressing and then try to offer multiple reasons to support your thesis.

2. **Exploratory Argument:** Write an argument that works its way toward a thesis rather than stating it outright in the opening section. Share with readers the process of your thinking the way Lynn Ehlers does in "Play 'Free Bird'!" (p. 95), encouraging them, perhaps, to come to the same conclusion, as you carefully lay out and explain your evidence. The paper will probably work best if you choose a topic about which you have strong feelings or opinions.

3. **Refutation Argument:** Find a text with which you strongly disagree and then systematically refute it, as Cathy Young does with the Duke University sexual harassment policy (p. 101). The text can be a position or policy promoted by a politician or public or corporate official, or it can be an argument in itself—a column, editorial, even a section in a textbook. Make your opposition clear, but also be fair to the position you are attempting to refute. It is especially important that your readers be able to understand whatever you are analyzing, even if they aren't familiar with it. That's a real challenge, so don't hesitate to summarize, paraphrase, or quote from the material.

4. **Visual Argument:** Although "Visualizing the BP Oil ~~Spill~~ Disaster" (p. 104) presents an issue dramatically and cleverly, the text allows readers to draw their own conclusions. But other visual arguments—such as advertisements or editorial cartoons—are typically more aggressive about stating a message, combining images and words to make a point. Create a visual argument of your own using whatever medium you believe will convey your message most successfully. Start with a clear point in mind. Then figure out how to present your claim powerfully and memorably.

5. **Your Choice:** These days, most serious arguments explode across interactive and networked environments, where they can take on a life of their own. Working with a group, design a media project (blog, Web site, mash-up, video, etc.) to focus on an issue that members of your group believe deserves more attention. Pool your talents to develop the site technically, rhetorically, and visually. Be sure your project introduces the subject, explains its purpose, encourages interaction, and includes relevant images and, if possible, links.

How to start

- Need a **topic**? See page 113.
- Need **criteria for your evaluation**? See page 117.
- Need to **organize your criteria and evidence**? See page 121.

4 Evaluations

make a claim about the merit of something

Evaluations and reviews are so much a part of our lives that you might notice them only when they are specifically assigned. Commentary and criticism of all sorts just happen.

PRODUCT REVIEW   Given your work experience at a camera store, you are invited to write a *product review* for a co-op newsletter about a new 15.1-megapixel digital SLR for photographers on tight budgets.

ARTS REVIEW   You're never shy about sharing your opinions of movies, films, and restaurants, but find it painful when you have to write an *arts review* of *Götterdämmerung* for a music appreciation course. The opera lasts longer than a football game!

SOCIAL SATIRE   Tired of self-righteous cyclists who preach eco-fundamentalism and then clog traffic with monthly Critical Mass rides, you do what any irate citizen would — you mock them in a *social satire*.

VISUAL COMPARISON   You decide that the best way to document the work of a neighborhood group is to post *before* and *after* shots of the restorations it has done on several local buildings. Your *visual comparison* wins the group a grant from the city.

DECIDING TO WRITE AN EVALUATION.   It's one thing to offer an opinion, an entirely different matter to back up a claim with reasons and evidence. Only when you do will readers (or listeners) take you seriously. But you'll also have to convince them that you know *how* to evaluate a book, a social policy, a cultural trend, or even a cup of coffee by reasonable criteria. It helps when you use objective standards to make judgments, counting and measuring the road to excellence. But evaluations frequently involve people debating matters of taste — which draws good sense and wit into the mix. Here's how to frame this kind of argument. ○

Make value judgments.   You'll either judge something as good, bad, or indifferent when you write an evaluation or challenge an opinion someone else has offered. Of course, fair judgments can be quite complex: Even movie critics who do thumbs-up-or-down routines don't offer those verdicts until after they first talk about their subjects in detail.

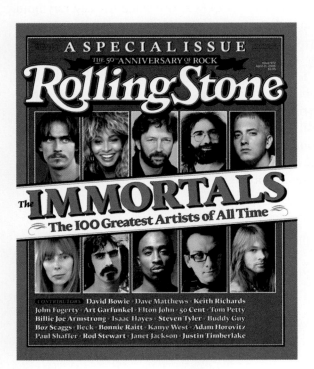

Popular magazines frequently evaluate or rank artists and celebrities, and their work.

(Cover photo from *Rolling Stone*, April 21, 2005. Copyright © Rolling Stone LLC 2005. All rights reserved. Reprinted by permission.)

choose a genre
p. 390

Establish and defend criteria.   *Criteria* are the standards by which objects are measured: *A good furnace should heat a home quickly and efficiently. Successful presidents leave office with the country in better shape than when they entered.* When readers will generally agree with your criteria, you need to explain little about them. When readers might disagree, you have to defend your criteria. ○ And sometimes you'll break new ground — as happened when critics first asked, *What is good Web design?* and *Which are the most significant social networks?* In such cases, new criteria of evaluation had to be invented and rationalized.

Offer convincing evidence.   Evidence in the form of facts, statistics, testimony, examples, good reasons, and keen observations provides the link between an evaluative claim and the criteria used to make it. If good furnaces heat homes quickly and efficiently, then you'd have to supply data to show that a product you judged faulty didn't meet those minimal standards. (It might be noisy and unreliable to boot.) Evidence will obviously vary from subject to subject; it could include anything from hard numbers to harrowing tales of personal woe. ○

Offer useful advice.   Some evaluations are just for fun: Consider all the hoopla that arguments about sports rankings generate. But most evaluations and reviews, when done right, also provide usable information, beneficial criticism, or even practical alternatives — sometimes offered in clever ways (charts, graphs, comparisons) to make it easy for readers to find and consult. So whether they examine humidifiers, restaurants, or candidates in a city council race, evaluations do important work.

develop ideas
p. 412

interview and
observe p. 478

Product Review

In a world mesmerized by technology, product reviews like this one by David Pogue examining the just-released Apple iPad are both instructive and entertaining. What makes Pogue's review notable is his frank recognition that techies and ordinary consumers will judge the iPad by entirely different standards. Accordingly, he writes two reviews. The article appeared in the *New York Times*.

Looking at the iPad from Two Angles

David Pogue

March 31, 2010

In 10 years of reviewing tech products for the *New York Times*, I've never seen a product as polarizing as Apple's iPad, which arrives in stores on Saturday.

"This device is laughably absurd," goes a typical remark on a tech blog's comments board. "How can they expect anyone to get serious computer work done without a mouse?"

"This truly is a magical revolution," goes another. "I can't imagine why anyone will want to go back to using a mouse and keyboard once they've experienced Apple's visionary user interface!"

Those are some pretty confident critiques of the iPad—considering that their authors have never even tried it.

In any case, there's a pattern to these assessments.

The haters tend to be techies; the fans tend to be regular people. Therefore, no single write-up can serve both readerships adequately. There's but one solution: Write separate reviews for these two audiences.

Read the first one if you're a techie. (How do you know? Take this simple test. Do you use BitTorrent? Do you run Linux? Do you have more e-mail addresses than pants? You're a techie.)

Read the second review if you're anyone else.

Think about the two quotations here: within them Pogue finds criteria of evaluation different enough to justify two reviews.

Pogue's test is a "stipulative definition" of techies created just for this essay. Does it help you understand his use of the term?

Review for Techies

The Apple iPad is basically a gigantic iPod Touch.

It's a half-inch-thick slab, all glass on top, aluminum on the back. Hardly any buttons at all—just a big Home button below the screen. It takes you to the Home screen full of apps, just as on an iPhone.

One model gets online only in Wi-Fi hot spots ($500 to $700, for storage capacities from 16 to 64 gigabytes). The other model can get online either using Wi-Fi or, when you're out and about, using AT&T's cellular network; that feature adds $130 to each price.

You operate the iPad by tapping and dragging on the glass with your fingers, just as on the iPhone. When the very glossy 9.7-inch screen is off, every fingerprint is grossly apparent.

There's an e-book reader app, but it's not going to rescue the newspaper and book industries (sorry, media pundits). The selection is puny (60,000 titles for now). You can't read well in direct sunlight. At 1.5 pounds, the iPad gets heavy in your hand after awhile (the Kindle is 10 ounces). And you can't read books from the Apple bookstore on any other machine—not even a Mac or iPhone.

When the iPad is upright, typing on the on-screen keyboard is a horrible experience; when the iPad is turned 90 degrees, the keyboard is just barely usable (because it's bigger). A $70 keyboard dock will be available in April, but then you're carting around two pieces.

At least Apple had the decency to give the iPad a really fast processor. Things open fast, scroll fast, load fast. Surfing the Web is a heck of a lot better than on the tiny iPhone screen—first, because it's so fast, and second, because you don't have to do nearly as much zooming and panning.

But as any Slashdot reader can tell you, the iPad can't play Flash video. Apple has this thing against Flash, the Web's most popular video format; says it's buggy, it's not secure and depletes the battery. Well, fine, but meanwhile, thousands of Web sites show up with empty white squares on the iPad—places where videos or animations are supposed to play.

YouTube, Vimeo, TED.com, CBS.com and some other sites are converting their videos to iPad/iPhone/Touch-compatible formats. But all the news sites and game sites still use Flash. It will probably be years before the rest of the Web's videos become iPad-viewable.

The "techie" review is factual, practical, and critical. Techies want a tool.

Techies do acknowledge some merits in the product.

There's no multitasking, either. It's one app at a time, just like on the iPhone. Plus no U.S.B. jacks and no camera. Bye-bye, Skype video chats. You know Apple is just leaving stuff out for next year's model.

The bottom line is that you can get a laptop for much less money—with a full keyboard, DVD drive, U.S.B. jacks, camera-card slot, camera, the works. Besides: If you've already got a laptop and a smartphone, who's going to carry around a third machine?

This first conclusion sums up the techie case against the iPad: Cheaper, more practical alternatives already exist.

Review for Everyone Else

The Apple iPad is basically a gigantic iPod Touch.

The simple act of making the multitouch screen bigger changes the whole experience. Maps become real maps, like the paper ones. You see your e-mail inbox and the open message simultaneously. Driving simulators fill more of your field of view, closer to a windshield than a keyhole.

The review for "everyone else" is yearning and appreciative. Non-techies want a relationship with their device.

The new iBook e-reader app is filled with endearing grace notes. For example, when you turn a page, the animated page edge actually follows your finger's position and speed as it curls, just like a paper page. Font, size and brightness controls appear when you tap. Tap a word to get a dictionary definition, bookmark your spot or look it up on Google or Wikipedia. There's even a rotation-lock switch on the edge of the iPad so you can read in bed on your side without fear that the image will rotate.

If you have the cellular model, you can buy AT&T service so you can get online anywhere. (Cellular iPads aren't available until next month; I tested a Wi-Fi-only model.)

(The great contract offer didn't last long.)

But how's this for a rare deal from a cell company: there's no contract. By tapping a button in Settings, you can order up a month of unlimited cellular Internet service for $30. Or pay $15 for 250 megabytes of Internet data; when it runs out, you can either buy another 250 megs, or just upgrade to the unlimited plan for the month. Either way, you can cancel and rejoin as often as you want—just March, July and November, for example—without penalty. The other carriers are probably cursing AT&T's name for setting this precedent.

The iPad's killer app, though, is killer apps. Apple says that 150,000 existing iPhone apps run on the iPad. They either appear actual size—small and dead center on the screen—or, with a tap, doubled to fill the screen, a little blurry. Still, all the greats work this way: Dragon Dictation, Skype (even voice calls, through its speaker and microphone) and those gazillion games.

But the real fun begins when you try the apps that were specially designed for the iPad's bigger screen. (When the iPad section of the App Store opens Saturday, it will start with 1,000 of them.)

That Scrabble app shows the whole board without your zooming or panning: a free companion app for your iPhone or Touch is called Tile Rack; it lets you fiddle with your letters in private, then flick them wirelessly onto the iPad's screen. Newspaper apps will reproduce the layout, photos and colors of a real newspaper. The Marvel comic-book app is brilliant in its vividness and panel-by-panel navigation. (Oops, maybe that app belongs in the review for techies.)

Hulu.com, the Web's headquarters for free hit TV shows, won't confirm the talk that it's working on an iPad app, but wow—can you imagine? A thin, flat, cordless, bottomless source of free, great TV shows, in your bag or on the bedside table?

Speaking of video: Apple asserts that the iPad runs 10 hours on a charge of its nonremovable battery—but we all know you can't trust the manufacturer. And sure enough, in my own test, the iPad played movies continuously from 7:30 a.m. to 7:53 p.m.—more than 12 hours. That's four times as long as a typical laptop or portable DVD player.

The iPad is so fast and light, the multitouch screen so bright and responsive, the software so easy to navigate, that it really does qualify as a new category of gadget. Some have suggested that it might make a good goof-proof computer for technophobes, the aged and the young; they're absolutely right.

And the techies are right about another thing: the iPad is not a laptop. It's not nearly as good for creating stuff. On the other hand, it's infinitely more convenient for consuming it—books, music, video, photos, Web, e-mail and so on. For most people, manipulating these digital materials directly by touching them is a completely new experience—and a deeply satisfying one.

The bottom line is that the iPad has been designed and built by a bunch of perfectionists. If you like the concept, you'll love the machine.

The only question is: Do you like the concept?

An important insight: "Real fun" explains what many consumers want from their handheld devices.

Both reviews are detailed, providing useful information and advice.

The conclusion draws a thoughtful distinction between devices that create and consume stuff: Is it also a difference between the two audiences of the review?

Exploring purpose and topic

Most evaluations you're required to prepare for school or work come with assigned topics. But to choose an object to evaluate, follow different strategies, depending on what you hope to accomplish. ○

topic ◀

Evaluate a subject you know well.   This is the safest option, built on the assumption that everyone is an expert on something. Years of reading *Cooks Illustrated* magazine or playing tennis might make it natural for you to review restaurants or tennis rackets. You've accumulated not only basic facts but also lots of hands-on knowledge—the sort that gives you confidence when you make a claim. So go ahead and demonstrate your expertise.

Evaluate a subject you need to investigate.   Perhaps you are considering graduate schools to apply to, looking for family-friendly companies to work for, or thinking about purchasing an HDTV. To make such choices, you'll need more information. So kill two birds with a single assignment: Use the school project to explore the issues you face, find the necessary facts and data, and make a case for (or against) Michigan State, Whole Foods, or Sony.

Evaluate a subject you'd like to know more about.   How do wine connoisseurs tell one cabernet from another and rank them so confidently? How would a college football championship team from the fifties match up against more recent winning teams? Use an assignment to settle questions like these that you and your friends may have debated late into the evening.

Evaluate a subject that's been on your mind.   Not all evaluations are driven by a need to make particular decisions. Instead, you may feel an obligation to make a critical point about social, cultural, and political issues: You believe a particular piece of health-care or immigration legislation is bad policy or find yourself disturbed by political trends or changes in society. An evaluation is the appropriate genre for giving voice to those criticisms, whether you compose a conventional piece or venture into the realms of satire or parody.

find a topic
p. 356

Keep an open mind.   Whatever your topic, you probably shouldn't begin most academic evaluations already knowing the outcome — hating a book before you read it or dead set against any chilies not grown in Hatch, New Mexico. Follow your criteria and data to the reasonable choice — even if it's one you don't prefer. Obvious exceptions to these guidelines might include subjects of the kind described under the previous heading: social, cultural, or political issues already settled in your mind. But, even then, don't review what you can't treat fairly.

Your Turn   Brainstorm to create a list of items or subjects that you know enough about, even without much research, to write a credible review. Some subjects will be obvious. If you make pottery, run track, or paint houses, you probably know enough about these subjects to judge pots, assess track shoes, or choose a good lacquer. But don't ignore other paths to expertise you may not even notice. Perhaps you have lived in several states long enough to write knowledgeably about their educational systems or arts communities. Or maybe you can write compellingly about local health-care facilities because of personal experiences with them. When you've compiled your list, compare it with ones that your classmates have drawn up. Their lists will probably suggest more topics for your own.

Understanding your audience

Your job as a reviewer is made easier when you can assume readers might be interested in your opinions. Fortunately, most people consult evaluations and reviews willingly, often hoping to find specific information: *Is the latest Stephen L. Carter novel up to snuff? Who's the most important American architect working today? Phillies or Braves in the NL East this year?* But you'll still have to gauge the level of potential readers and make appropriate adjustments — as David Pogue does explicitly in "Looking at the iPad from Two Angles" (p. 109).

Write for experts.   Knowledgeable readers can be a tough audience because they may bring strong, maybe inflexible, opinions to a topic. But if you know your stuff, you can take on the experts because they know their stuff too: You don't have to provide tedious background information or discuss criteria of evaluation in detail. You can use the technical vocabulary experts share and make allusions to people and concepts they'd recognize. ○ Here are a few in-crowd sentences from a review of the football video game *Backbreaker* from an online gaming site:

> *Backbreaker* joins the sports design trend of placing emphasis on the right analog stick. It's everything from your swim/rip move on defense, to your bonecrunching hit or tackle, to juking, spinning, selecting receivers and passing. You use the right trigger as an action modifier ("aggressive mode") to go into other areas of your player's toolset. Everything is contextual to the type of player you control and it's pick-up-and-play intuitive after one trip through the tutorial.
>
> –Kotaku, "*Backbreaker* Review: The Challenger Crashes"

Write for a general audience.   You have to explain more to general audiences than to specialists, clarifying your criteria of evaluation, providing background information, and defining key terms. But general readers usually are willing to learn more about a topic. Here's noted film critic Roger Ebert doing exactly that:

> *The Lake House* tells the story of a romance that spans years but involves only a few kisses. It succeeds despite being based on two paradoxes: time travel and the ability of two people to have conversations that are, under the terms established by the film, impossible. Neither one of these problems

> **Need help thinking about your audience?** See "How to Revise Your Work" on pp. 456–57.

bothered me in the slightest. Take time travel: I used to get distracted by its logical flaws and contradictory time lines. Now in my wisdom I have decided to simply accept it as a premise, no questions asked. A time-travel story works on emotional, not temporal, logic.

—rogerebert.com, June 16, 2006

Write for novices.   You have a lot of explaining to do when readers are absolutely fresh to a subject and need lots of background information. For instance, because *Consumer Reports* reviews a range of products well beyond the expertise of any individual, the editors always take care to explain how they make their judgments, whether the subject is washing machines, waffles, or Web sites. Do the same yourself. Take special care to define technical terms for your readers.

For example, at Digital Photography Review, a Web site that examines photographic equipment in detail, you will find the following warning attached to all its camera reviews: "If you're new to digital photography you may wish to read the Digital Photography *Glossary* before diving into this article (it may help you understand some of the terms used)." Clicking the link leads to a fully illustrated dictionary of terms meant to help amateurs understand the qualities of a good digital camera.

Are buffalo dangerous?
For some audiences, you have to explain everything.

Finding and developing materials

develop criteria ◀

When you are assigned to write a review, it makes sense to research your subject thoroughly, even one you think you know pretty well. Online research is inevitable: Do a quick Web search to see if your notions are still current in a world where opinions change rapidly. ○

For many subjects (and products especially), it's easy to discover what others have already had to offer, particularly when a topic has a distinctive name. Just type that name followed by the word *review* into an online search window and see what pops up. But don't merely parrot opinions you find in sources: Take issue with conventional views whenever you can offer smarter ones. (At one time, most critics thought good poetry should rhyme — until some poets and critics argued otherwise.) Make a fresh case of your own. To do that, focus on criteria and evidence.

Decide on your criteria.   Clarify your criteria, even if you're just evaluating pizza. Should the crust be hard or soft? Should the sauce be red and spicy, or white and creamy? How thick should the pizza be? How salty? And, for all these opinions — *why*?

Didn't expect the *why*? You really don't have a criterion until you attach a plausible reason to it. ○ The rationale should be clear in your own mind even if you don't expect to explain it in the review or evaluation itself: *Great pizza comes with a soft crust that wraps each bite and topping in a floury texture that merges the contrasting flavors.* More important, any criterion you use will have to make sense to readers either on its own (*Public art should be beautiful*) or after you've explained and defended it (*Public art should be scandalous because people need to be jolted out of conformist thinking*).

Look for hard criteria.   It helps when criteria are countable or observable. You'll seem objective when your criteria at least *seem* grounded in numbers. Think, for example, of how instructors set numerical standards for your performance in their courses, translating all sorts of activities, from papers to class participation, into numbers. Teachers aren't alone in deferring to numbers. CNET Reviews, for instance, uses a numerical rating system to evaluate televisions, as explained on its Web site:

refine your search
p. 472

develop a statement
p. 393

Design (30 percent of the total rating): We look at not only the overall aesthetics of the product but also its interface and included remote. An uninspiring but functional design will rate a 5. Higher scores will be given for a well-designed remote with backlit buttons, a clear onscreen navigation system, and particularly sleek cosmetics.

Features (30 percent of the total rating): The range of features is considered in determining this portion of the rating. From picture-in-picture (PIP) and 2:3 pull-down to the appropriate number of A/V inputs, we consider everything this product delivers to the consumer. A set that comes armed with a suitable number of inputs and basic features will earn a 5. Products with more inputs, individual input memories, or other extras will earn a better rating.

Performance (40 percent of the total rating): We consider picture quality to be the most important criteria for displays, so we give it the most weight. A score of 5 represents a television that can produce a serviceable picture with only a reasonable amount of adjustment. Sets with a particularly sharp picture; rich, accurate color; deep black levels; and good video processing will earn a higher score.

"Gentlemen, I've decided to retire. The new chairman will be the first one to throw a six."

Argue for criteria that can't be measured.   How do you measure the success or failure of something that can't be objectively calculated — a student dance recital, Jay-Z's latest recording, or the new abstract sculpture just hauled onto the campus? Do some research to find out how such topics are customarily evaluated and discussed. Get familiar with what sensible critics have to say about whatever you're evaluating — contemporary art, fine saddles, good teaching, effective foreign policy. If you read carefully, you'll find values and criteria embedded in all your sources. O

In the following excerpt, for example, James Morris explains why he believes American television is often better than Hollywood films. Morris's criteria are highlighted.

> What I admire most about these shows, and most deplore about contemporary movies, is the quality of the scripts. The TV series are devised and written by smart people who seem to be allowed to let their intelligence show. Yes, the individual and ensemble performances on several of the series are superb, but would the actors be as good as they are if they were miming the action? TV shows are designed for the small screen and cannot rely, as movies do, on visual and aural effects to distract audiences. If what's being said on TV isn't interesting, why bother to watch? Television is rigorous, right down to the confinement of hour or half-hour time slots, further reduced by commercials. There's no room for the narrative bloat that inflates so many Hollywood movies from their natural party-balloon size to Thanksgiving-parade dimensions.
>
> —"My Favorite Wasteland," *Wilson Quarterly*, Autumn 2005

Stand by your values.   Make sure you define criteria that apply to more than just the individual case you are examining at the moment. Think about what makes socially conscious rap music, world-class sculpture, a great president. For instance, you may have a special fondness for Jimmy Carter, but should criteria for great presidents be measured by what they do *after* they leave office? Similarly, you might admire artists or actors who overcome great personal tragedies on their paths to stardom. But to make such heroics a *necessary* criterion for artistic achievement might look like special pleading.

read closely
p. 365

Gather your evidence.   Some of the evidence for your evaluation will come from secondary sources, especially if you are assessing something like a government program or historical event. Before offering an opinion on the merits of Social Security or the wisdom of Truman's decision to drop atomic bombs to end World War II, expect to do critical reading. Weigh the evidence and arguments you find in these sources before you offer your own judgment — and then cite some of these sources for evidence and support. ○

Other evidence will come from careful observation. Sometimes, you'll just need to be attuned to the world around you — as Jordyn Brown is in cataloging the behavior of cell phone users (see p. 131). When reviewing a book, a movie, a restaurant, or a similar item, take careful notes not only of your initial impressions but also of the details that support or explain them. When appropriate, take the time to measure, weigh, photograph, or interview your subjects. If it makes sense to survey what others think about an issue (a campus political flap, for example), keep a record of such opinions. Finally, be willing to alter your opinion when the evidence you gather in support of a hypothesis heads in a direction you hadn't expected.

analyze claims and
evidence p. 487

Creating a structure

As with other arguments, evaluations have distinct parts that can be built into a pattern or structure.

organize criteria ◀

Choose a simple structure when your criteria and categories are predictable. A basic review might announce a subject and make a claim, list the criteria of evaluation, present evidence to show whether the subject meets those standards, and draw conclusions. Here's one version of that pattern with the criteria discussed all at once, at the opening of the piece.

> Introduction leading to an evaluative claim
>
> Criteria of evaluation stated and, if necessary, defended
>
> Subject measured by first criterion + evidence
> Subject measured by second criterion + evidence
> Subject measured by additional criteria + evidence
>
> Conclusion

And here's a template with the criteria of evaluation introduced one at a time.

> Introduction leading to an evaluative claim
>
> First criterion of evaluation stated and, if necessary, defended
>
> Subject measured by first criterion + evidence
>
> Second criterion stated/defended
>
> Subject measured by second criterion + evidence
>
> Additional criteria stated/defended
>
> Subject measured by additional criteria + evidence
>
> Conclusion

You might find structures this tight and predictable, for instance, in job-performance reviews at work or in consumer magazines. Once a pattern is established for measuring TVs, computers, paint sprayers, or even teachers (consider those forms you fill in at the end of the term), it can be repeated for each new subject and results can be compared.

Yet what works for hardware and tech products is not quite so convincing when applied to music, books, political policies, or societal behaviors that are more than the sum of their parts. Imagine a film critic whose *every* review marched through the same predictable set of criteria: acting, directing, writing, cinematography, and special effects. When a subject can't (or shouldn't) be reviewed via simple categories, you will need to decide which of its many possible aspects deserve attention. ○

Choose a focal point.   Look for features that you and your readers will surely notice, that is, what makes you react strongly and intellectually to the subject. You could, in fact, organize an entire review around one or more shrewd insights, and many reviewers do. The trick is to make connections

Do political pundits like Chris Matthews and Michelle Malkin lose their clout when they become predictable? Maybe they're exceptions.

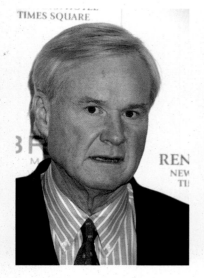

shape your work
p. 406

between key or controlling ideas and various aspects of your subject. Look carefully at Jordyn Brown's scathing satire of cell phone users (p. 131) and you'll discover that what holds it together is the complaint that people are missing important aspects of their life. Brown dramatizes that problem by beginning and ending the paper at a birthday party that she and a dozen friends are just barely attending:

> This dinner was supposed to be a festive gathering to celebrate our good friend Stacey's birthday. But no one mingled or celebrated, not even Stacey. Everyone seemed to be somewhere else. They had all wandered off to Google-town, Twitter-ville, and Texting-My-Boyfriend City; and I was left there alone at the Cheesecake Factory. . . . Twelve people preferred phone activities to talking to each other and *me* over three-tiered red velvet cheesecake. Seriously, people. Put those phones down. You're not thinking clearly.

Compare and contrast.   Another obvious way to organize an evaluation is to examine differences. ○ Strengths and weaknesses stand out especially well when similar subjects are examined critically, as in the following concluding paragraph of a road-test competition in *Popular Mechanics*:

> So was the Camaro worth the wait? Yes. The newest pony car delivers an undeniable mix of performance and value. It's the quickest and likely has the highest handling limits of the three coupes. The Mustang is the rough and tumble sports car. It's the most involving car to drive—it feels more organic than the other two. The Challenger R/T provides more comfort and practicality at the expense of all-out performance. Yet, to our eye, the Dodge just may be the best looking of the group. But these are muscle cars. And the Camaro's mix of power, poise and refinement just edges out the others—this time.
>
> —Ben Stewart, "Muscle Car Competition," March 23, 2009

use comparison and
contrast p. 404

Choosing a style and design

Depending on the aim of the review you are composing and your stance within it, evaluations can be written in any style, from high to low. ○ You should also look for opportunities to present evaluations visually.

Use a high or formal style.   Technical reviews tend to be the most formal and impersonal: They may be almost indistinguishable from reports, describing their findings in plain, unemotional language. Such a style gives the impression of scientific objectivity, even though the work may reflect someone's agenda. For instance, here's a paragraph in formal style from the National Assessment of Educational Progress summarizing the performance of American students in science.

> At grade 8, there was no overall improvement. In 2005, 59 percent of students scored at or above the *Basic* level. An example of the knowledge and skills at the *Basic* level is being able to compare changes in heart rate during and after exercise. Twenty-nine percent performed at or above the *Proficient* level. Identifying the energy conversions that occur in an electric fan is an example of the knowledge and skills at the *Proficient* level.
>
> —*Nation's Report Card*, 2005 Science Assessment (http://nationsreportcard.gov/science_2005)

Use a middle style.   When the writer has a more direct stake in the work — as is typical in restaurant or movie reviews, for example — the style moves more decisively toward the middle. Even though a reviewer may never use *I*, you still sense a person behind the writing, making judgments and offering opinions. That's certainly the case in these two paragraphs by Clive Crook, written shortly after the death of noted economist John Kenneth Galbraith: Words, phrases, even sentence fragments that humanize the assessment are highlighted, while a contrast to economist Milton Friedman also sharpens the portrait.

> Galbraith, despite the Harvard professorship, was never really an economist in the ordinary sense in the first place. In one of countless well-turned pronouncements, he said, "Economics is extremely useful as

define your style
p. 432

a form of employment for economists." He disdained the scientific
pretensions and formal apparatus of modern economics—all that math
and number crunching—believing that it missed the point. This view did
not spring from mastery of the techniques: Galbraith disdained them from
the outset, which saved time.

Friedman, in contrast, devoted his career to grinding out top-quality
scholarly work, while publishing the occasional best seller as a sideline. He
too was no math whiz, but he was painstakingly scientific in his methods
(when engaged in scholarly research) and devoted to data. All that was
rather beneath Galbraith. Brilliant, yes; productive, certainly. But he was a
bureaucrat, a diplomat, a political pundit, and a popular economics writer of
commanding presence more than a serious economic thinker, let alone a
great one.

—"John Kenneth Galbraith, Revisited," *National Journal*, May 15, 2006

Use a low style.   Many reviews get personal with readers, and some get
so chummy that they verge on rudeness. You probably want evaluations you
write for academic or work assignments to be relatively polite and low-key
in style, focused more on the subject than on you as the reviewer. But you
do have an enormous range of options — especially when writing social
and political commentary. Then, if your evaluations turn into satire, all the
gloves come off. In such situations, humor or sarcasm can be powerful tools,
but no style is more difficult to manage. Humor requires great precision and
economy, or the jokes fall flat, which is a good reason to look at models of
the kinds of evaluation you will be composing. Study the ones you admire
for lessons in style.

Present evaluations visually.   Evaluations work especially well when
claims can be supported by tables, charts, graphs, or other visual elements.
Readers see relationships that could not be conveyed quite as efficiently
in words alone. **O** And sometimes the images simply have more impact.
Consider your response to images of real fast-food items posted on an offbeat

display data
p. 425

Web site called the West Virginia Surf Report. Here's the description of the feature that appeared on the site:

> **Fast Food: Ads vs. Reality**   Each item was purchased, taken home, and photographed immediately. Nothing was tampered with, run over by a car, or anything of the sort. It is an accurate representation in every case. Shiny, neon-orange, liquefied pump-cheese, and all.

Here are several of the images the site presented of products purchased from well-known national chains:

  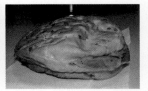

All you need to do is recall the photographs of these items you've seen posted in the fast-food restaurants and you can draw your own conclusion: *Caveat emptor!*

Your Turn   Almost everyone reads at least one critic or type of review regularly—of restaurants, movies, TV shows, sports teams, gizmos, video games, and so on. Pick a review by your favorite critic or, alternatively, a review you have read recently and noted. Then examine its style closely. Is it formal, informal, or casual? Technical or general? Serious or humorous? Full of allusions to stuff regular readers would get? What features of the style do you like? Do you have any reservations about the style? In a detailed paragraph, evaluate only the style of the reviewer or review (not the substance), organizing your work to support a clear thesis.

Examining models

People rely on critics of every kind of art and entertainment to help them decide what to read, watch, see, or hear. Charles Isherwood is an influential critic of the theater. In "Stomping onto Broadway with a Punk Temper Tantrum," he reviews an unusual item for the *New York Times*: the punk rock album *American Idiot* turned into a Broadway musical.

Stomping onto Broadway with a Punk Temper Tantrum

Charles Isherwood

April 21, 2010

Opening sentence states a thesis: The musical is emotional, thrilling, and gorgeous.

Rage and love, those consuming emotions felt with a particularly acute pang in youth, all but burn up the stage in "American Idiot," the thrillingly raucous and gorgeously wrought Broadway musical adapted from the blockbuster pop-punk album by Green Day.

Pop on Broadway, sure. But punk? Yes, indeed, and served straight up, with each sneering lyric and snarling riff in place. A stately old pile steps from the tourist-clogged Times Square might seem a strange place for the music of Green Day, and for theater this blunt, bold and aggressive in its attitude. Not to mention loud. But from the moment the curtain rises on

American Idiot: John Gallagher Jr., left, as Johnny, and Tony Vincent as St. Jimmy in the musical *American Idiot* at the St. James Theater. (Sara Krulwich/*The New York Times*.)

Isherwood sets the scene: a punk musical by a young cast in a stately old theater.

a panorama of baleful youngsters at the venerable St. James Theater, where the show opened on Tuesday night, it's clear that these kids are going to make themselves at home, even if it means tearing up the place in the process.

Which they do, figuratively speaking. "American Idiot," directed by Michael Mayer and performed with galvanizing intensity by a terrific cast, detonates a fierce aesthetic charge in this ho-hum Broadway season. A pulsating portrait of wasted youth that invokes all the standard genre conventions—bring on the sex, drugs and rock 'n' roll, please!—only to transcend them through the power of its music and the artistry of its execution, the show is as invigorating and ultimately as moving as anything I've seen on Broadway this season. Or maybe for a few seasons past.

Formal style employs complex sentence structures and a spirited vocabulary to characterize the show: *galvanizing, pulsating, invigorating, moving.*

Burning with rage and love, and knowing how and when to express them, are two different things, of course. The young men we meet in the first minutes of "American Idiot" are too callow and sullen and restless—too young, basically—to channel their emotions constructively. The show opens with a glorious 20-minute temper tantrum kicked off by the title song.

Ample, almost lush, descriptions help readers imagine the show. Performers are carefully credited.

"Don't want to be an American idiot!" shouts one of the gang. The song's signature electric guitar riff slashes through the air, echoing the testy challenge of the cry. A sharp eight-piece band, led by the conductor Carmel Dean, is arrayed around the stage, providing a sonic frame for the action. The simple but spectacular set, designed by Christine Jones, suggests an epically scaled dive club, its looming walls papered in punk posters and pimpled by television screens, on which frenzied video collages flicker throughout the show. (They're the witty work of Darrel Maloney.)

Who's the American idiot being referred to? Well, as that curtain slowly rose, we heard the familiar voice of George W. Bush break through a haze of television chatter: "Either you are with us, or with the terrorists." That kind of talk could bring out the heedless rebel in any kid, particularly one who is already feeling itchy at the lack of prospects in his dreary suburban burg.

Isherwood here introduces an important criterion: timelessness.

But while "American Idiot" is nominally a portrait of youthful malaise of a particular era—the album dates from 2004, the midpoint of the Bush years, and the show is set in "the recent past"—its depiction of the crisis of post-adolescence is essentially timeless. Teenagers eager for their lives to begin, desperate to slough off their old selves and escape boredom through pure sensation, will probably always be making the same kinds of mistakes, taking the same wrong turns on the road to self-discovery.

"American Idiot" is a true rock opera, almost exclusively using the music of Green Day and the lyrics of its kohl-eyed frontman, Billie Joe Armstrong, to tell its story. (The score comprises the whole of the title album as well as several songs from the band's most recent release, "21st Century Breakdown.") The book, by Mr. Armstrong and Mr. Mayer, consists only of a series of brief, snarky dispatches sent home by the central character, Johnny, played with squirmy intensity by the immensely gifted John Gallagher Jr. ("Spring Awakening," "Rabbit Hole").

> Rather than rehash the meager plot of the rock opera, Isherwood explains it through a string of telling incidents.

"I held up my local convenience store to get a bus ticket," Johnny says with a smirk as he and a pal head out of town.

"Actually I stole the money from my mom's dresser."

Beat.

"Actually she lent me the cash."

Such is the sheepish fate of a would-be rebel today. But at least Johnny and his buddy Tunny (Stark Sands) do manage to escape deadly suburbia for the lively city, bringing along just their guitars and the anomie and apathy that are the bread and butter of teenage attitudinizing the world over. ("I don't care if you don't care," a telling lyric, could be their motto.)

The friend they meant to bring along, Will (Michael Esper), was forced to stay home when he discovered that his girlfriend (Mary Faber) was pregnant. Lost and lonely, and far from ready for the responsibilities of fatherhood, he sinks into the couch, beer in one hand and bong in the other, as his friends set off for adventure.

Beneath the swagger of indifference, of course, are anxiety, fear and insecurity, which Mr. Gallagher, Mr. Esper and Mr. Sands transmit with aching clarity in the show's more reflective songs, like the hit "Boulevard of Broken Dreams" or the lilting anthem "Are We the Waiting." The city turns out to be just a bigger version of the place Johnny and Tunny left behind, a "land of make believe that don't believe in me." The boys discover that while a fractious 21st-century America may not offer any easy paths to fulfillment, the deeper problem is that they don't know how to believe in themselves.

> The style is given texture by song lyrics, characters' names, and crisp descriptions: "the swagger of indifference," "an androgynous goth drug pusher."

Johnny strolls the lonely streets with his guitar, vaguely yearning for love and achievement. He eventually hooks up with a girl (a vivid Rebecca

Naomi Jones) but falls more powerfully under the spell of an androgynous goth drug pusher, St. Jimmy, played with mesmerizing vitality and piercing vocalism by Tony Vincent. Tunny mostly stays in bed, clicker affixed to his right hand, dangerously susceptible to a pageant of propaganda about military heroism on the tube, set to the song "Favorite Son." By the time the song's over, he's enlisted and off to Iraq.

In both plotting and its emotional palette, "American Idiot" is drawn in brash, primary-colored strokes, maybe too crudely for those looking for specifics of character rather than cultural archetypes. But operas — rock or classical—often trade in archetypes, and the actors flesh out their characters' journeys through their heartfelt interpretations of the songs, with the help of Mr. Mayer's poetic direction and the restless, convulsive choreography of Steven Hoggett ("Black Watch"), which exults in both the grace and the awkwardness of energy-generating young metabolisms.

Line by line, a skeptic could fault Mr. Armstrong's lyrics for their occasional glibness or grandiosity. That's to be expected, too: rock music exploits heightened emotion and truisms that can fit neatly into a memorable chorus. The songs are precisely as articulate—and inarticulate—as the characters are, reflecting the moment in youth when many of us feel that pop music has more to say about us than we have to say for ourselves. (And, really, have you ever worked your way through a canonical Italian opera libretto, line by line?)

In any case the music is thrilling: charged with urgency, rich in memorable melody and propulsive rhythms that sometimes evolve midsong. The orchestrations by Tom Kitt (the composer of "Next to Normal") move from lean and mean to lush, befitting the tone of each number. Even if you are unfamiliar with Green Day's music, you are more likely to emerge from this show humming one of the guitar riffs than you are to find a tune from "The Addams Family" tickling your memory.

But the emotion charge that the show generates is as memorable as the music. "American Idiot" jolts you right back to the dizzying roller coaster of young adulthood, that turbulent time when ecstasy and misery almost seem interchangeable states, flip sides of the coin of exaltation. It captures with a piercing intensity that moment in life when everything seems possible, and nothing seems worth doing, or maybe it's the other way around.

Marginal notes:

In explaining what operas do, Isherwood offers another criterion of evaluation. Then he applies it to *American Idiot*.

Predictably, Isherwood also evaluates the show's music by standards he defines for rock/pop music.

Another criterion? A good musical sends patrons home humming a tune.

The conclusion leaves no doubt about the reasons for Isherwood's rave review.

SOCIAL SATIRE   Satires, which poke fun at the foibles of society in order to correct them, often require writers to draw exaggerated but recognizable portraits of people and situations. That's what Jordyn Brown attempts to do in a paper aimed at getting her friends to shut off their cell phones and pay more attention to life. If readers laugh too, that's all to the good.

Brown 1

Jordyn Brown

Professor Ruszkiewicz

Rhetoric 325M

May 5, 20--

A Word from My Anti-Phone Soapbox

I sat for at least five minutes staring at the tops of the other dinner guests' heads. All twenty-four eyes (that's twelve pairs) were unwaveringly fixed on their respective laps. I didn't understand why my friends held their phones under the table. We weren't in class. Perhaps it was a subconscious admittance of shame for their inattentiveness. I sat at the dinner table confused. This dinner was supposed to be a festive gathering to celebrate our good friend Stacey's birthday. But no one mingled or celebrated, not even Stacey. Everyone seemed to be somewhere else. They had all wandered off to Google-town, Twitter-ville, and Texting-My-Boyfriend City; and I was left there alone at the Cheesecake Factory.

Bitter frustration grew inside me because (a) my party's behavior was ridiculous and (b) I'd left my own phone in the car. Luckily, my thoughts occupied me and kept me from mounting

Opening paragraph, especially its final sentence, sets the scene and the tone.

Brown 2

my chair and giving my friends a stern and passionate tongue-lashing right in the middle of the restaurant. My peers disgusted me with their technological dependency. So I packaged the lecture I felt coming on at the dinner table neatly in my brain and will now recite it for you, minus the expletives.

In classical terms, the paper is an invective.

Maybe I'm just bitter because my phone is only capable of Stone Age maneuvers like making calls and texting. But having the whole World Wide Web in your hands has ruined all of you tech fiends. Look at yourselves. You can't bear to face that terrible affliction people had to endure years ago called *boredom*. So you fill up your fancy little devices with applications, games, movies, and music to ensure that you'll never have an unoccupied moment. What a shame that would be! America's greatest pastime used to be baseball. The magic of a triple play or an out-of-the-park home run made the hours spent watching inning after inning well worth it. But now you need constant stimulation. You want to see a home run every at-bat. Your movies need to be 90 percent car chase. Your telephones are full-on pocket-sized entertainment centers. You've bastardized thrill and excitement; you can't be pleased. The movie you saw last night wasn't too slow; your world is just too fast.

First attack focuses on the obsessive need for stimulation: "your world is just too fast."

Information just shouldn't be this readily available. You people can't handle it. You Urbanspoon one tasty restaurant

Brown 3

and think you're A. A. Gill, famous British food critic. This
constant tech stream has even ruined good arguments.
Before, you would argue fervently for hours.

"*Top Gun* came out in '84!"

"No man, it came out in '86!"

And then you'd go round and round and, at the end
of the night, no one really knew the right answer because
both debaters argued so well. But, oh no, these beautiful
moments are nearly extinct because some cocky know-it-all's
going to whip out his iPhone, always conveniently connected
to Google. And with a few strokes of his touch screen he'll
find a source, take the other guy down, and crush his spirit.
Braggarts today strut around like they know everything.
No, it's Google that knows everything; you just have a
cool phone.

And it's not just the search engines that give you
phone-tech junkies balloon heads. Twitter and Facebook have
you believing that people really want to know every minute
detail of your life. Now, I hate to be the bearer of bad news,
but unless you're Ashton Kutcher or Kim Kardashian, no one
is tracking your every move every second of the day. So cut
out all the Facebook statuses about your disposable-ware
crisis at Target. Don't waste the space on my news feed
with "Should I get paper or Styrofoam plates?" Annoying.

Second point is that technology makes us think we're smarter than we are.

Throughout, the casual style mimics speech: "what a shame that would be"; "but, oh no"; "pitiful."

Technology also makes us think we are the center of the universe.

Brown 4

And I don't care what you had for lunch. Don't TwitPic a picture of your meal, because it makes no sense. What if you'd done that ten years ago? If you had skipped into school with a picture you had gotten developed at the drugstore and gone around showing it to people, saying, "Hey guys, look what I had for dinner!" the whole fifth-grade class would have looked at you like you were insane. Twitter has made nonsense commonplace. No thought is too base to fill a tweet's 140 characters. Pitiful.

> The examples throughout work if readers recognize some truth under the exaggerations.

> The paragraph shows how smartphones are leading to breakdowns in social relations.

Sad to say, these handheld devices have turned you into technologically overindulged brats. You break into temper tantrums, stomping around, pouting, throwing your Blackberries at soft surfaces, and crossing your arms in agitation whenever you hit a dead zone and can't access your precious Internet. And you have even less patience for your friends when you text or call them. After all, everything you have to say — spoken or in text — is infinitely more important than anything else in their lives. The meaning of the word *urgent* has evolved since the earliest days of portable and instant communication devices. Once only physicians routinely received urgent messages: "Hurry, we need you, Dr. Cardiologist, to fix this man's horrible heart." But now *urgent* can mean, "911! What do you feel like eating for dinner? I'm at the grocery store now. Hurry and call me

Brown 5

back!!!" And I wouldn't dare let a text message from you sit in my in-box for more than an hour or I'd be in for a scolding the next time I see you.

So, Earth to you, the people who never part from their cell phones. I'm sure you've taken several breaks while reading this rant to check your e-mail and respond to a few texts. You probably missed most of the points of my argument too, much like you're missing what's going on in the world around you. Cell phones were initially meant to connect us, broadening the time frame during which people could communicate with one another. But with all the new apps being incorporated into these devices, isolation only grows, shrinking your world and perspective. You're all constantly talking and thinking about how *you* feel and what *you* think. You don't talk to Rachel or Stephen but to the "Twitter-verse" or to Facebook at large. You communicate without any idea of who's really listening.

Twelve people preferred phone activities to talking to each other and *me* over three-tiered red velvet cheesecake. Seriously, people. Put those phones down. You're not thinking clearly.

Like most satires, this one turns serious and offers a simple solution: Turn off the phone.

VISUAL COMPARISON How might the Insurance Institute for Highway Safety memorably celebrate its fiftieth anniversary? By crashing two cars fifty years apart in age to show how much crash safety has improved, thanks in part to the efforts of the group. The visual evidence represents a startling and memorable evaluation of their work.

Crash Test

Insurance Institute for Highway Safety

50 years
INSURANCE INSTITUTE FOR HIGHWAY SAFETY of research & communications

In the 50 years since US insurers organized the Insurance Institute for Highway Safety, car crashworthiness has improved. Demonstrating this was a crash test conducted on Sept. 9 between a 1959 Chevrolet Bel Air and a 2009 Chevrolet Malibu. In a real-world collision similar to this test, occupants of the new model would fare much better than in the vintage Chevy.

"It was night and day, the difference in occupant protection," says Institute president Adrian Lund. "What this test shows is that automakers don't build cars like they used to. They build them better."

The crash test was conducted at an event to celebrate the contributions of auto insurers to highway safety progress over 50 years. Beginning with the Institute's 1959 founding, insurers have maintained the resolve, articulated in the 1950s, to "conduct, sponsor, and encourage programs designed to aid in the conservation and preservation of life and property from the hazards of highway accidents."

Test compares crashworthiness then and now: 1959 Chevrolet Bel Air and 2009 Chevrolet Malibu in 40 mph frontal offset test (click on photos to see larger images).

Watch a video of the crash test

2009 Chevrolet Malibu   1959 Chevrolet Bel Air

Malibu post-crash   Bel Air post-crash

In the crash test involving the two Chevrolets, the 2009 Malibu's occupant compartment remained intact (above left) while the one in the 1959 Bel Air (right) collapsed.

Top photo testifies to the violence of the 40-mph crash.

The collision demolishes the front ends of both vehicles.

But the passenger compartments tell a different story, providing clear evidence of fifty years of progress in structural design and safety.

1. **Product Review:** Choose a product that you own or buy regularly, anything from a Coleman lantern to Dunkin' Donuts coffee. Then write a fully developed review modeled after David Pogue's "Looking at the iPad from Two Angles" (p. 109). Like Pogue, you should be attentive to your audience and specific about details, but you need not write separate reviews for different audiences. Use graphics if appropriate.

2. **Arts Review:** Drawing on your expertise as a consumer of popular culture (the way Charles Isherwood does in his *New York Times* review of *American Idiot*—see p. 127), explain why you admire a book, movie, television series, musical piece, artist, or performer that most people do not. For instance, you might argue that *Gilligan's Island* is as sophisticated a situation comedy as *Seinfeld*. Or, taking the opposite tack, explain why you don't share the public's enthusiasm for some widely admired artist or entertainment. Write a review strong enough to change someone's mind.

3. **Social Satire:** Using the techniques of social satire modeled in "A Word from My Anti-Phone Soapbox" (p. 131), assess a public policy, social movement, or cultural trend you believe deserves serious and detailed criticism. But don't write a paper simply describing your target as dangerous, pathetic, or unsuccessful. Instead, make people laugh at your target while also offering a plausible alternative.

4. **Visual Comparison or Review:** Construct an evaluation in which a visual comparison or some other sensory evidence plays a major role. You might use photographs the way the Insurance Institute for Highway Safety does (see p. 136). Or perhaps you can work in another medium to show, for example, how good or bad the instructions in a technical manual are, how much the brownies you baked differ from the ones on the box, or how ineffective the design of your school's Web site is. Be creative.

5. **Your Choice:** Evaluate a program or facility in some institution you know well (school, business, church, recreation center) that you believe works especially well or poorly. Prepare a presentation in the medium of your choice and imagine that your audience is an administrator with the power to reward or shut down the operation.

How to start ▶

- Need a **topic**? See page 144.
- Need to identify **possible causes**? See page 149.
- Need to **organize your analysis**? See page 152.

5 Causal Analyses

explain how,
why, or what
if something
happens

We all analyze and explain things daily. Someone asks, "Why?" We reply, "Because . . ." and then offer reasons and rationales. Such a response comes naturally.

CAUSAL ANALYSIS
: An instructor asks for a ten-page *causal analysis* examining the root causes of a major armed conflict during the twentieth century. You choose to write about the Korean War because you know almost nothing about it.

RESEARCH STUDY
: You notice that most students now walk across campus chatting on cell phones or listening to music. You develop a *research study* to examine whether this phenomenon has any relationship to a recent drop in the numbers of students joining campus clubs and activities across the country.

EXPLORATORY ESSAY
: To keep student enrollments from crashing, the provost of your school has proposed to tie future fee and tuition increases to the rate of inflation. In an *exploratory essay*, you respond that this move might actually have the opposite effect if student services and the development of new programs are curtailed.

CULTURAL ANALYSIS
: Why, you wonder, in a fully illustrated *cultural analysis*, does the mullet survive, decade after decade? What explains its enduring popularity?

DECIDING TO WRITE A CAUSAL ANALYSIS.   From climate change to childhood obesity to high school students performing poorly on standardized tests, the daily news is full of problems framed by *how*, *why*, and *what if* questions. These are often described as issues of *cause and effect*, terms we'll use frequently in this chapter. Take childhood obesity. The public wants to know why we have a generation of overweight kids. Too many cheeseburgers? Not enough dodgeball? People worry, too, about the consequences of the trend. Will these portly children grow into obese adults? Will they develop medical problems?

   We're interested in such questions because they really do matter, and we're often simply curious to find answers. But successful analyses of this sort call for more than a passing interest. They demand persistence, precision, and research. ○ Even then, you'll have to deal with a world that seems complicated or contradictory. Not every problem or issue can—or should—be explained simply. ○

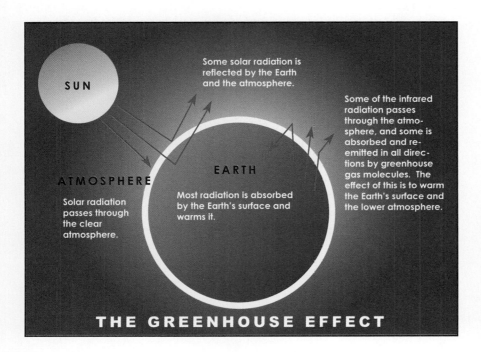

The Greenhouse Effect
Most scientists agree that the greenhouse effect, an increase in the concentration of certain atmospheric gases, is leading to climate change that will have dangerous consequences for us and our environment. (Other scientists have their doubts.)

choose a genre
p. 390

analyze claims and
evidence p. 487

Don't jump to conclusions.   It's just plain hard to say precisely which factors, past or present, account for a particular event, activity, or behavior. And it is even tougher to project how events or actions occurring today might affect the future. So qualify your claims and explanations sensibly or offer them tentatively. O

Trying to explain things to other people will quickly teach you humility—even if you *don't* jump to hasty conclusions. In fact, many explanations of cause and effect begin by undercutting or correcting someone else's prior claims, dutifully researched and sensibly presented.

Appreciate your limits.   There are rarely easy answers when investigating why things happen the way they do. The space shuttle *Columbia* burned up on reentry in 2003 because a 1.67-pound piece of foam hit the wing of the 240,000-pound craft on liftoff. Who could have imagined such an unlikely sequence of events? Yet investigators had to follow the evidence relentlessly to its conclusion, in this case tracing backwards from effect to cause.

But even when you intend to find correct explanations, the fact remains that you'll often have to settle for answers that are merely plausible or probable. That's because explanations—especially outside the hard sciences—typically deal with imprecise and unpredictable forces (including *people*) and sometimes require a leap of imagination.

Offer sufficient evidence for claims.   Your academic and professional analyses will be held to a high standard of proof—particularly in the sciences. O The evidence you provide may be a little looser when you write for popular media, where readers usually allow more anecdotal and casual examples. But even there, back up your claims with a preponderance of plausible evidence, not hearsay, and then be sure to qualify your conclusions carefully, making it clear when you are stepping into the realm of speculation.

develop a statement
p. 393

understand lab reports
p. 336

Whether the issue is the economy, health care, or climate change, public figures from presidents to pundits find themselves having to rely on expert opinion that is itself subject to interpretation. So do individual citizens. This short piece by Jonah Goldberg, a political commentator and global warming skeptic, typifies the dilemma. Not a scientist himself, Goldberg is in no position to make authoritative claims about the cause of global warming itself. But he can—and does—raise questions about how the studies are being reported to the public.

National Review Online

Posted: September 2, 2009
From: Jonah Goldberg

→ # Global Warming and the Sun

The style of the analysis is colloquial, as might be expected in a blog.

On the last day of August, scientists spotted a teeny-weeny sunspot, breaking a 51-day streak of blemish-free days for the sun. If it had gone just a bit longer, it would have broken a 96-year record of 53 days without any of the magnetic disruptions that cause solar flares. That record was nearly broken last year as well.

Wait, it gets even more exciting.

During what scientists call the Maunder Minimum — a period of solar inactivity from 1645 to 1715 — the world experienced the worst of the cold streak dubbed the Little Ice Age. At Christmastime, Londoners ice-skated on the Thames, and New Yorkers (then New Amsterdamers) sometimes walked over the Hudson from Manhattan to Staten Island.

Identifies the "Maunder Minimum" and acknowledges that its relationship to the "Little Ice Age" is controversial.

Of course, it could have been a coincidence. The Little Ice Age began before the onset of the Maunder Minimum. Many scientists think volcanic activity was a more likely, or at least a more significant, culprit. Or perhaps the big chill was, in the words of scientist Alan Cutler, writing in the *Washington Post* in 1997, a "one-two punch from a dimmer sun and a dustier atmosphere."

Well, we just might find out. A new study in the American Geophysical Union's journal, *Eos*, suggests that we may be heading into another quiet phase similar to the Maunder Minimum.

Goldberg is careful to cite what will look like credible sources: *Eos, Science.*

Meanwhile, the journal *Science* reports that a study led by the National Center for Atmospheric Research, or NCAR, has finally figured out why increased sunspots have a dramatic effect on the weather, increasing temperatures more than the increase in solar energy should explain. Apparently, sunspots heat the stratosphere, which in turn amplifies the warming of the climate.

Scientists have known for centuries that sunspots affect the climate; they just never understood how. Now, allegedly, the mystery has been solved.

Last month, in another study, also released in *Science,* Oregon State University researchers claimed to settle the debate over what caused and ended the last Ice Age. Increased solar radiation coming from slight changes in the Earth's rotation, not greenhouse-gas levels, were to blame.

What is the significance of all this? To say I have no idea is quite an understatement, but it will have to do.

Nonetheless, what I find interesting is the eagerness of the authors and the media to make it clear that this doesn't have any particular significance for the debate over climate change. "For those wondering how the (NCAR) study bears on global warming, Gerald Meehl, lead author on the study, says that it doesn't — at least not directly," writes Moises Velasquez-Manoff of the *Christian Science Monitor.* "Global warming is a long-term trend, Dr. Meehl says. . . . This study attempts to explain the processes behind a periodic occurrence."

This overlooks the fact that solar cycles are permanent "periodic occurrences," a.k.a. a very long-term trend. Yet Meehl insists the only significance for the debate is that his study proves climate modeling is steadily improving.

I applaud Meehl's reluctance to go beyond where the science takes him. For all I know, he's right. But such humility and skepticism seem to manifest themselves only when the data point to

Though not competent to critique the science itself, Goldberg is willing to comment on how scientific results are reported.

Goldberg complains that causal claims about climate are reported inconsistently.

something other than the mainstream narrative about global warming. For instance, when we have terribly hot weather, or bad hurricanes, the media see portentous proof of climate change. When we don't, it's a moment to teach the masses how weather and climate are very different things.

No, I'm not denying that man-made pollution and other activity have played a role in planetary warming since the Industrial Revolution.

But we live in a moment when we are told, nay lectured and harangued, that if we use the wrong toilet paper or eat the wrong cereal, we are frying the planet. But the sun? Well, that's a distraction. Don't you dare forget your reusable shopping bags, but pay no attention to that burning ball of gas in the sky — it's just the only thing that prevents the planet from being a lifeless ball of ice engulfed in darkness. Never mind that sunspot activity doubled during the 20th century, when the bulk of global warming has taken place.

What does it say that the modeling that guaranteed disastrous increases in global temperatures never predicted the halt in planetary warming since the late 1990s? (MIT's Richard Lindzen says that "there has been no warming since 1997 and no statistically significant warming since 1995.") What does it say that the modelers have only just now discovered how sunspots make the Earth warmer?

I don't know what it tells you, but it tells me that maybe we should study a bit more before we spend billions to "solve" a problem we don't understand so well.

The analysis grows highly rhetorical here to underscore what Goldberg sees as hypocrisy in climate change explanations.

Note that this analysis ends up with more questions than answers.

Exploring purpose and topic

▶ topic

To find a topic for an explanatory paper or causal analysis, begin a sentence with *why*, *how*, or *what if* and then finish it, drawing on what you may already know about an issue, trend, or problem. ○

This graph from *The Onion* (December 16, 2008) offers some explanations for the Great Recession.

(Reprinted with permission of THE ONION. Copyright © 2010, by ONION, INC. www.theonion.com.)

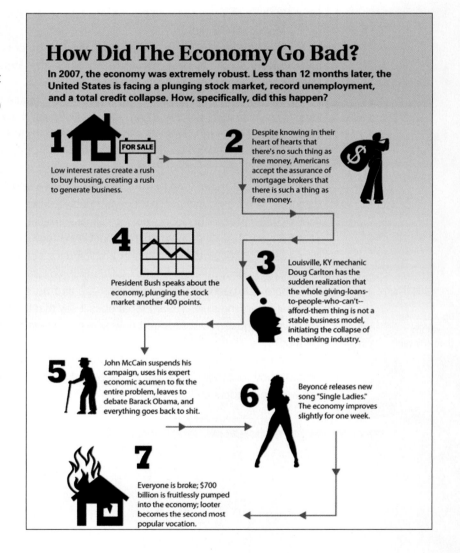

How Did The Economy Go Bad?

In 2007, the economy was extremely robust. Less than 12 months later, the United States is facing a plunging stock market, record unemployment, and a total credit collapse. How, specifically, did this happen?

1 Low interest rates create a rush to buy housing, creating a rush to generate business.

2 Despite knowing in their heart of hearts that there's no such thing as free money, Americans accept the assurance of mortgage brokers that there is such a thing as free money.

4 President Bush speaks about the economy, plunging the stock market another 400 points.

3 Louisville, KY mechanic Doug Carlton has the sudden realization that the whole giving-loans-to-people-who-can't-afford-them thing is not a stable business model, initiating the collapse of the banking industry.

5 John McCain suspends his campaign, uses his expert economic acumen to fix the entire problem, leaves to debate Barack Obama, and everything goes back to shit.

6 Beyoncé releases new song "Single Ladies." The economy improves slightly for one week.

7 Everyone is broke; $700 billion is fruitlessly pumped into the economy; looter becomes the second most popular vocation.

144

find a topic
p. 356

Why are American high schools producing fewer students interested in science?

Why is the occurrence of juvenile asthma spiking?

Why do so few men study nursing or so few women study petroleum engineering?

There are, of course, many other ways to phrase questions about cause and effect in order to attach important conditions and qualifications.

What if scientists figure out how to stop the human aging process—as now seems plausible within twenty years? What are the consequences for society?

How likely is it that a successful third political party might develop in the United States to end the deadlock between Republicans and Democrats?

As you can see, none of these topics would just drop from a tree—like the apocryphal apple that supposedly inspired Isaac Newton to ponder gravity. They require knowledge and thinking. So look for potential cause-and-effect issues in your academic courses or professional life. Or search for them in the culture and media—though you should probably shy away from worn-out subjects—college drinking, plagiarism, credit card debt—unless you can offer a fresh insight.

To find a subject, try the following approaches.

Look again at a subject you know well.   It may be one that has affected you personally or might in the future. Or a topic you think is ripe for rethinking because of insights you can offer. For instance, you may have experienced firsthand the effects of high-stakes testing in high school or have theories about why people your age still smoke despite the risks. Offer a hypothesis.

Look for an issue new to you.   Given a choice of topics for an academic paper, choose a subject you've always wanted to know more about (for example, the cultural effects of the Cold War). You probably won't be able to offer a thesis or hypothesis until after you've done some research, but that's the appeal of this strategy. The material is fresh and you are energized. ⭘

find a topic
p. 356

Examine a local issue. Is there an issue you can explore or test with personal research or observation? ○ Look for recent changes and examine why these changes happened or what the consequences may be. With a community issue, talk to the people responsible or affected. Tuition raised? Admissions standards lowered? Speech code modified? Why, or what if?

Choose a subject with many dimensions. An issue that is complicated and challenging will simply push you harder and sharpen your thinking. Don't rush to judgment; remain open-minded about contrary evidence, conflicting motives, and different points of view.

Tackle an issue that seems settled. If you really have guts, look for a phenomenon that most people assume has been adequately explained. Tired of the way Republicans, feminists, Wall Street economists, vegans, fundamentalists, or the women on *The View* smugly explain the way things are? Pick one sore point and offer a different—and better—analysis.

> **Your Turn**   After Richard Nixon won forty-nine states in the 1972 presidential election, the distinguished film critic Pauline Kael is reported to have said, "How can he have won? I don't know anyone who voted for him." Can you think of any times when you have similarly misread a situation because you did not have a perspective broad enough to understand all the forces in play? Identify such a situation and consider whether it might provide you with a topic for an explanatory paper. Alternatively, consider some of the times—maybe even beginning in childhood—when you have heard explanations for phenomena that you recognized as wildly implausible because they were superstitions, stereotypes, or simply errors. Again, consider whether you can turn one of these misconceptions into a topic for an explanatory paper.

interview and observe
p. 478

Understanding your audience

Audiences for cause-and-effect analyses and explanations are diverse, but it may help to distinguish between a readership you create by drawing attention to a subject and readers who come to your work because it deals with a topic they already care about.

Create an audience.   In some situations, you must set the stage for your causal analysis by telling readers why they should be concerned by the phenomenon you intend to explore. ○ Assume they are smart enough to become engaged by a topic once they appreciate its significance—and how it might affect them. But you first have to make that case. That's exactly what the editors of the *Wall Street Journal* do in an editorial noting the sustained *decrease* in traffic deaths that followed a congressional decision ten years earlier to do away with a national 55-mph speed limit.

> This may seem noncontroversial now, but at the time the debate was shrill and filled with predictions of doom. Ralph Nader claimed that "history will never forgive Congress for this assault on the sanctity of human life." Judith Stone, president of the Advocates for Highway and Auto Safety, predicted to Katie Couric on NBC's *Today Show* that there would be "6,400 added highway fatalities a year and millions of more injuries." Federico Peña, the Clinton administration's secretary of transportation, declared: "Allowing speed limits to rise above 55 simply means that more Americans will die and be injured on our highways."
>
> —"Safe at Any Speed," July 7, 2006

Anticipates readers who might ask, *Why does this issue matter?*

Write to an existing audience.   In many cases, you'll enter a cause-and-effect debate on topics already on the public agenda. You may intend to reaffirm what people now believe or, more controversially, ask them to rethink their positions. But in either case, you'll likely be dealing with readers as knowledgeable (and opinionated) as you are. In the following opening paragraphs, for example, from an article exploring the decline of sensuality in America, notice how culture critic Camille Paglia presumes an intelligent audience already engaged by her topic.

develop a statement
p. 393

Paglia guesses that readers understand the impetus for the new drug.

Will women soon have a Viagra of their own? Although a Food and Drug Administration advisory panel recently rejected an application to market the drug flibanserin in the United States for women with low libido, it endorsed the potential benefits and urged further research. Several pharmaceutical companies are reported to be well along in the search for such a drug.

Presumes readers who agree that "white upper middle class" means "anxious" and "overachieving."

The implication is that a new pill, despite its unforeseen side effects, is necessary to cure the sexual malaise that appears to have sunk over the country. But to what extent do these complaints about sexual apathy reflect a medical reality, and how much do they actually emanate from the anxious, overachieving, white upper middle class?

More concepts assumed: *1950s, frigidity, puritanism, media environment.*

In the 1950s, female "frigidity" was attributed to social conformism and religious puritanism. But since the sexual revolution of the 1960s, American society has become increasingly secular, with a media environment drenched in sex.

The real culprit, originating in the 19th century, is bourgeois propriety. As respectability became the central middle-class value, censorship and repression became the norm. Victorian prudery ended the humorous sexual candor of both men and women during the agrarian era, a ribaldry chronicled from Shakespeare's plays to the 18th-century novel. The priggish

Readers better know Western history too.

1950s, which erased the liberated flappers of the Jazz Age from cultural memory, were simply a return to the norm.

—"No Sex Please, We're Middle Class," *New York Times*, June 25, 2010

In the same article, Paglia describes Lady Gaga as "a high-concept fabrication without an ounce of genuine eroticism."

Finding and developing materials

Expect to do as much research for a causal analysis as for any fact-based report or argument. Even when you speculate about popular culture, as Charles Paul Freund does in "The Politics of Pants" (see p. 170), you need to show that you have considered what others have written on the subject. ○

Be careful, however, not to ascribe the wrong cause to an event just because two actions might have occurred close in time or have some other fragile connection. Does job growth really grow following tax rebates? Do children in fact do better in school if they have participated in Head Start programs? Exposing faulty causality in situations like these can make for powerful arguments. ○ You can avoid faulty analyses by appreciating the various kinds of valid causal relationships outlined below.

Understand necessary causes.   A *necessary cause* is any factor that must be in place for something to occur. For example, sunlight, chlorophyll, and water are all necessary for photosynthesis to happen. Remove one of these elements from the equation and the natural process simply doesn't take place. But since none of them could cause photosynthesis on their own, they are necessary causes, but not sufficient (see *sufficient cause* below).

consider causes ◀

On a less scientific level, necessary causes are those that seem so important that we can't imagine something happening without them. You might argue, for example, that a team could not win a World Series without a specific pitcher on the roster: Remove him and the team doesn't get to the play-offs. Or you might claim that, while fanaticism doesn't itself cause terrorism, terrorism doesn't exist without fanaticism. In any such analysis, it helps to separate necessary causes from those that may be merely *contributing* (see *contributing factors* on p. 151).

Understand sufficient causes.   A *sufficient cause*, in itself, is enough to bring on a particular effect. Not being eighteen would be a sufficient cause for being arrested for drinking alcohol in the United States. But there are many other potential sufficient causes for getting arrested. In a causal argument, you might need to establish which of several possible sufficient causes is the one actually responsible for a specific event or phenomenon—assuming that a single explanation exists. A plane might have crashed because it was overloaded, ran out of fuel, had a structural failure, encountered severe wind shear, and so on.

Understand precipitating causes.   Think of a *precipitating cause* as the proverbial straw that finally breaks the camel's back. In itself, the factor may seem trivial. But it becomes the spark that sets a field gone dry for months ablaze. By refusing to give up her bus seat to a white passenger in Montgomery, Alabama, Rosa Parks triggered a civil rights movement in 1955, but she didn't actually cause it: The necessary conditions had been accumulating for generations.

Understand proximate causes.   A *proximate cause* is nearby and often easy to spot. A corporation declares bankruptcy when it can no longer meet its massive debt obligations; a minivan crashes because a front tire explodes; a student fails a course because she plagiarizes a paper. But in an analysis, getting the facts right about such proximate causes may just be your starting point as you work toward a deeper understanding of a situation. As you might guess, proximate causes may sometimes also be sufficient causes.

Need help assessing your own work? See "How to Use the Writing Center" on pp. 382–83.

Understand remote causes.   A *remote cause*, as the term suggests, may act at some distance from an event but is intimately related to it. That bankrupt corporation may have defaulted on its loans because of a decade of bad management decisions; the tire exploded because it was underinflated and its tread worn; the student resorted to plagiarism *because* she ran out of time *because* she was working two jobs to pay for a Hawaiian vacation *because* she wanted a memorable spring break to impress her friends—a string of remote causes. Remote causes—which are usually contributing factors as well (see p. 151)—are what make many causal analyses challenging and interesting: Figuring them out is like detective work.

Understand reciprocal causes.   You have a *reciprocal* situation when a cause leads to an effect which, in turn, strengthens the cause. Consider how creating science internships for college women might encourage more women to become scientists who then sponsor more internships, creating yet more female scientists. Many analyses of global warming describe reciprocal

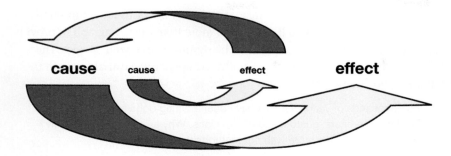

relationships, with CO_2 emissions supposedly leading to warming, which increases plant growth or alters ocean currents, which in turn releases more CO_2 or heat and so on.

Understand contributing factors.   When analyzing social or cultural issues, you'll often spend time assessing factors too general or ambiguous to be called necessary, sufficient, or even remote causes but which, nonetheless, might play a role in explaining an event. To account for an outbreak of high school violence in the late 1990s, social critics quickly identified a host of potential factors: divorce, guns, video games, goth culture, bullying, cliques, movies, psychosis, and so on. Though none of these explanations was entirely convincing, they couldn't simply be dismissed either. Many factors that might contribute to violence were (and remain) in play within the culture of American high schools.

Come to conclusions thoughtfully.   Explanations do often require some imagination: You are playing detective with the complexities of life, so you may need to think outside the box. But you also have to give your notions the same tough scrutiny that you would give any smart idea. Just because a causal explanation is clever or novel doesn't mean it's right. O

Don't oversimplify situations or manipulate facts.   By acknowledging any weaknesses in your own explanations and analyses, you may actually enhance your credibility or lead a reader toward a better conclusion than what you've come up with. Sometimes, you may have to be content with solving only part of a problem.

think critically
p. 372

Creating a structure

▶ organize ideas

Take introductions seriously. In explanations, they are unusually important and often quite lengthy; you'll often need more than one paragraph to provide enough detail for readers to appreciate the significance of your subject. The following brief paragraph might seem like the opener of a causal essay on the failures of dog training. ○

> For thousands of years, humans have been training dogs to be hunters, herders, searchers, guards, and companions. Why are we doing so badly? The problem may lie more with our methods than with us.
>
> —Jon Katz, "Train in Vain," *Slate.com*, January 14, 2005

In fact, *seven* paragraphs precede this one to set up the causal claim. Those paragraphs help readers (especially dog owners) recognize a problem many will find familiar. The actual first paragraph has Katz narrating a dog owner's dilemma.

> Sam was distressed. His West Highland terrier, aptly named Lightning, was constantly darting out of doors and dashing into busy suburban Connecticut streets. Sam owned three acres behind his house, and he was afraid to let the dog roam any of it.

By paragraph seven, Katz has offered enough corroborating situations to provoke a crisis in dogdom, a problem that leaves readers hoping for an explanation.

> The results of this failure are everywhere: Neurotic and compulsive dog behaviors like barking, biting, chasing cars, and chewing furniture—sometimes severe enough to warrant antidepressants—are growing. Lesser training problems—an inability to sit, stop begging, come, or stay—are epidemic.

Like Katz, you'll want to take the time necessary to introduce your subject and get readers interested. Then you have a number of options for developing your explanation or causal analysis.

Explain why something happened.   If you are simply offering plausible causes to explain a phenomenon, your structure will be quite simple. You'll move from an introduction that explains the phenomenon to a thesis

shape a beginning
p. 420

or hypothesis. Then you will work through your list of factors toward a conclusion. In a persuasive paper, you'd build toward the most convincing explanation supported by the best evidence.

> **Introduction leading to an explanatory or causal claim**
>
> **First cause explored + reasons/evidence**
> **Next cause explored + reasons/evidence . . .**
> **Best cause explored + reasons/evidence**
>
> **Conclusion**

Explain the consequences of a phenomenon.   A structure similar to the one just given lends itself to exploring the effects that follow from some action, event, policy, or change in the status quo. Once again, begin with an introduction that fully describes a situation you believe will have consequences, and then work through those consequences, connecting them as you need to. The conclusion could then draw out the implications of your paper.

> **Introduction focusing on a change or cause**
>
> **First effect proposed + reasons**
> **Other effect(s) proposed + reasons . . .**
>
> **Assessment and conclusion**

Suggest an alternative view of cause and effect.   A natural strategy is to open a causal analysis by refuting someone else's faulty claim and then offering a better one of your own. After all, we often think about causality when someone makes a claim we disagree with. It's a structure used in this chapter by Liza Mundy (p. 165).

> Introduction questioning a causal claim
>
> Reasons to doubt claim offered + evidence
> Alternative cause(s) explored . . .
> Best cause examined + reasons/evidence
>
> Conclusion

Explain a chain of causes.   Quite often, causes occur simultaneously, so in presenting them you have to make judgments about their relative importance. But maybe just as often, you'll be describing causes that operate in sequence: A causes B, B leads to C, C trips D, and so on. In such a case, you might use a sequential pattern of organization, giving special attention to the links (or transitions) in the chain. ○

> Introduction suggesting a chain of causes/consequences
>
> First link presented + reasons/evidence
> Next link(s) presented + reasons/evidence . . .
> Final link presented + reasons/evidence
>
> Conclusion

People have been writing causal analysis for centuries. Here is the title page of Edward Jenner's 1798 publication, *An Inquiry into the Causes and Effects of the Variolae Vaccinae.* Jenner's research led to a vaccine that protected human beings from smallpox.

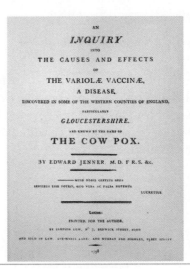

AN

INQUIRY

INTO

THE CAUSES AND EFFECTS

OF

THE VARIOLÆ VACCINÆ,

A DISEASE

DISCOVERED IN SOME OF THE WESTERN COUNTIES OF ENGLAND,

PARTICULARLY

GLOUCESTERSHIRE,

AND KNOWN BY THE NAME OF

THE COW POX.

BY EDWARD JENNER, M. D. F. R. S. &c.

—— QUID NOBIS CERTIUS IPSIS
SENSIBUS ESSE POTEST, QUO VERA AC FALSA NOTEMUS.
LUCRETIUS.

London:
PRINTED, FOR THE AUTHOR,
BY SAMPSON LOW, N°. 7, BERWICK STREET, SOHO:
AND SOLD BY LAW, AVE-MARIA LANE; AND MURRAY AND HIGHLEY, FLEET STREET.

1798

shape your work
p. 406

Choosing a style and design

When you analyze cause and effect, you'll often be offering an argument or exploring an idea for an audience you need to interest. You can do that through both style and design.

Consider a middle style.   Even causal analyses written for fairly academic audiences incline toward the middle style because of its flexibility: It can be both familiar and serious. ⭕ Here Robert Bruegmann, discussing the causes of urban sprawl, uses language that is simple, clear, and colloquial—and almost entirely free of technical jargon.

> When asked, most Americans declare themselves to be against sprawl, just as they say they are against pollution or the destruction of historic buildings. But the very development that one individual targets as sprawl is often another family's much-loved community. Very few people believe that they themselves live in sprawl or contribute to sprawl. Sprawl is where other people live, particularly people with less good taste. Much antisprawl activism is based on a desire to reform these other people's lives.
>
> —"How Sprawl Got a Bad Name," *American Enterprise*, June 2006

Adapt the style to the subject matter.   Friendly as it is, a middle style can still make demands of readers, as the following passage from an essay by Malcolm Gladwell demonstrates. To explain author Steve Johnson's theory that pop culture is making people smarter, Gladwell uses extremely intricate sentences filled with pop-culture allusions and cultural details. Yet he maintains a sense of voice too: Notice how he uses italics to signal how a word should be read. This is middle style at its complex best, making claims and proving them in a way that keeps readers interested.

> As Johnson points out, television is very different now from what it was thirty years ago. It's *harder.* A typical episode of *Starsky and Hutch*, in the 1970s, followed an essentially linear path: two characters, engaged in a single story line, moving toward a decisive conclusion. To watch an episode of *Dallas* today is to be stunned by its glacial pace—by the arduous attempts to establish social relationships, by the excruciating simplicity of the plotline, by how *obvious* it was. A single episode of *The Sopranos*, by contrast, might follow five narrative threads, involving a dozen characters

define your style
p. 432

who weave in and out of the plot. Modern television also requires the viewer to do a lot of what Johnson calls "filling in," as in a *Seinfeld* episode that subtly parodies the Kennedy assassination conspiracists, or a typical *Simpsons* episode, which may contain numerous allusions to politics or cinema or pop culture. The extraordinary amount of money now being made in the television aftermarket—DVD sales and syndication—means that the creators of television shows now have an incentive to make programming that can sustain two or three or four viewings.

—"Brain Candy," *The New Yorker*, May 16, 2005

Use appropriate supporting media.   Causal analyses have no special design features. But, like reports and arguments, they can employ charts that summarize information and graphics that illustrate ideas. *USA Today*, for instance, uses its daily "snapshots" to present causal data culled from surveys. Because causal analyses usually have distinct sections or parts (see "Creating a structure," p. 152), they do fit nicely into PowerPoint presentations. **O**

USA TODAY Snapshot

06/30/2006 - Updated 12:37 AM ET

Among students ages 12-17 who say they shun school restrooms, 62% say the smells bother them the most.

Why students avoid school restrooms

Odors   62%

Lack of toilet paper/soap   48%

Clogged toilets   30%

By Anne R. Carey and Gia Kereselidze, USA TODAY
Source: Kimberly-Clark Professional

A graphic like this one reflects a statistical approach to causality; its creators polled people to find out why they do what they do.

think visually
p. 592

Examining models

RESEARCH STUDY In a college paper, Kyu-heong Kim explains why the methods typically employed in writing centers to help students don't always work for some Asian students whose native language is not English. Like many causal analyses, his paper becomes an argument for change. But its most interesting parts are those that detail why best intentions sometimes go wrong.

Kim 1

Kyu-heong Kim

Professor Ruszkiewicz

English 300

April 26, 20--

Bending the Rules for ESL Writers

At most writing centers, the fundamental approaches and goals when tutoring ESL [English as a second language] students are essentially the same as those applied to native English writers. For example, at the University of Texas at Austin's Undergraduate Writing Center, writing consultants are trained to interact with ESL students just as they do "when working with native speakers, [being] nonevaluative, nondirective, and sensitive to writers' emotional investment in their writing" (Undergraduate 32). However, certain cultural barriers may prevent such nondirective and nonevaluative methods from being the most efficient or effective in improving the writing of ESL students from many backgrounds. Academic theorists fall on both sides of the issue regarding the merit of nondirectiveness and student empowerment, and this essay will examine both viewpoints.

The opening paragraph explains the issue to be addressed and the methodology of the paper.

Kim 2

It also includes interviews with two foreign writers as they get help with their papers, experiencing both the strengths and shortcomings of the nondirective approach used in most writing centers.

Since writing centers first became common in the United States in the mid-twentieth century, much has changed in the landscape of university enrollment. Specifically, the number of international students entering American universities has risen dramatically. Since the National Center for Education Statistics (NCES) began to collect data, the number of international students in postsecondary institutions in the United States has steadily increased from around 135,000 in 1970 to the current level of more than 620,000 (Planty et al. 96). International students now make up nearly 2 percent of total undergraduate enrollment, and at many writing centers, roughly a quarter of all consultations involve students from foreign cultures. Is it prudent then to apply the same techniques of writing center mentorship to this growing class of international students as those used upon native English speakers? This paper will focus on international students from the relatively culturally homogeneous nations of the Far East—China, Korea, Japan, and Taiwan—from which nearly 35 percent of all international students hail (Planty et al. 96).

Current writing center doctrine promotes a nondirective approach to tutoring. Philosophically, this stance is intended

Background information and statistics explain why the issues the paper raises are important.

Style of the paper is academic: formal and impersonal.

Kim 3

to "help writers to move away from a passive position" to "an active position . . . making their own decisions about a piece of writing that is truly their own" (Undergraduate 20). When applied to ESL writers, however, there are legitimate questions about the efficacy of this nondirective process. One camp argues that, due to the fundamental linguistic shortcomings of foreign writers, the nondirective approach presents pressures and situations that do little to improve the writing of these students. According to Ferris and Hedgcock, "in empowering students to retain ownership of their writing, we force them into roles for which they are not prepared and with which they are not comfortable" (142).

A Korean student working on a research application paper for a human development and family science course reported exactly this kind of problem with the nondirective approach. "When I go to the writing center with my paper, I often don't get the specific help that I want," she said. "It depends on who my tutor is, but they often ask me a lot of questions that I don't know the answers for. So, a lot of times, I will just ask my friends to edit my papers for me" (Cho). This writer's experience may indicate the frustrations of many ESL writers during their consultations at writing centers—an obstacle perhaps attributable to an incompatibility between Eastern Asian education and the current nondirective philosophy at most centers.

Kim cites a critic who argues that nondirective tutoring may have unanticipated consequences for ESL students.

Kim 4

The overarching educational structure of East Asian nations is top-down, with instruction going from the teacher to the student. As William Cummings explains, "Whereas Western educators lean toward a cognitive reasoning approach to values education, Eastern Asian educators favor a directive approach involving explicit teaching and consistent reinforcement" (286). There tends to be very little feedback from the student to the instructor, and discussion is kept at a minimum in favor of conveying information. Some believe that the fundamental difference in learning style originates from "Confucius and other Eastern Chou dynasty philosophers [who] established scholarly traditions and sociopolitical patterns that are still significant culturally" (Lee 3). International students from such nations may feel an inherent need to "[balance] the hierarchical, social orientation of Confucian ethics, heavy on loyalty, obedience, and learnedness" (3). So students who come from this culture may naturally feel uncomfortable in situations where they are encouraged to respond to and even disagree with their tutors—who, in their eyes, are authority figures in the situation. Ferris and Hedgcock suggest that "a nondirective approach can be confusing, frustrating, and even threatening to some ESL students depending on their cultural expectations and language ability" (144).

Because writers view tutors as teachers, students may take suggestions offered during the session as truth—

> ESL students face problems because of their attitudes toward authority.

Kim 5

incorporating them word-for-word into their writing. In turn, Feuerbacher notes that "writing instructors and tutors alike are often tempted to change the writer's text so much that it no longer reflects the voice and linguistic abilities of the writer but rather that of the instructor or tutor." But perhaps this fear forces many tutors to overcompensate and become even more nondirective in their approach when working with ESL students.

ESL students also have difficulty describing the problems they wish to address.

Many ESL sessions in writing centers also suffer from the effects of another common policy—student empowerment. Consultants at writing centers are usually trained to focus on issues the students want to work on. This approach may be beneficial when students enter the consultation clearly understanding the weaknesses of their papers, but may be insufficient if they do not. For example, ESL students from East Asia may hesitate to ask questions about higher-order concerns in their papers or be unable to formulate their concerns into questions. An ESL student who went to a writing center for help on his internal transfer application described this problem exactly:

> I always check the box for grammar [when I go to the writing center] because I don't know what else I should check. When the consultant asks me what I want to work on, I say "grammar" by default. That's what I did for this paper. (Chae)

The paper draws on printed sources as well as several interviews.

The student received plenty of grammatical feedback and was able to correct many of his mistakes; however, because of his

Kim 6

request to focus on grammar, several bigger problems in the paper were not addressed. As a result, the finished product lacked some key components of an internal transfer essay, such as a personal statement, a rationale for attending the school, and an explanation of the candidate's goals. "We didn't really talk about what makes a good transfer essay, because I told him [the tutor] I wanted to work on grammar," the writer said. "I didn't really know how to ask" (Chae).

The issue of formulating the right questions could indicate a greater cultural divide. According to Ki-joong Kim, a professor who has taught in both Korea and the United States, "Students in America often come with challenging questions regarding topics we have never covered, whereas Asian students' questions tend to be limited to the scope of material covered in classes" (Kim). Similarly, ESL expert Joy Reid attributes the inability of some foreign students to steer the consultation according to their concerns to inexperience, and offers expanded planning as a solution. "Because ESL student writers have probably had little or no experience with conferencing or with the responsibility of planning a conference, it is necessary to provide them with planning materials" (Reid 220).

Several solutions can be offered to address the issues stated above. When dealing with clarity and grammatical issues, it may be helpful if writing center tutors were given the freedom to be more directive with ESL students. ESL students would be

Kim makes it clear that cultural differences account for problems Asian students face in writing centers.

Kim 7

less discouraged if they saw progress in their papers through the session. To encourage ESL students to become more active in their consultations, steps might be taken to break down the perceived student-teacher barrier between the writer and the tutor. This might begin with an emphasis on peer tutoring, where writing center tutors introduce themselves as peers rather than as consultants. Before actual work begins on the paper, the consultant might take a few minutes to introduce himself or herself to help the writer feel more equal to the consultant. With a sense of equality, ESL writers might feel free to become a part of the discussion rather than remain listeners.

Similarly, consultants might also be given the freedom to go beyond addressing merely the concerns writers themselves identify and to address other problems that occur through the paper. Expanded pretutoring "planning materials" might also help ESL writers express thoughts and concerns they might find difficult to bring up during consultations (220).

The growing number of international students at American postsecondary institutions calls for adaptations in the methodology of writing centers. Understanding the differences in culture may enable providers of writing services at universities to better grasp techniques to service this growing clientele—techniques that often require modifications in traditional approaches.

Kim offers specific suggestions to improve writing center services for ESL students.

Kim 8

Works Cited

Chae, Seung-jun. Personal interview. 8 Mar. 2010.

Cho, Eun-saem. Personal interview. 7 Mar. 2010.

Cummings, William K. "Human Resource Development: The
    J-Model." *The Challenge of Eastern Asian Education:
    Implications for America*. Ed. William K. Cummings and
    Philip G. Altbach. Albany: State U of New York P, 1997. Print.

Ferris, Dana, and John S. Hedgcock. *Teaching ESL Composition:
    Purpose, Process, and Practice*. Mahwah: Erlbaum, 1998.
    Print.

Feuerbacher, Kellie, et al. "The ESL Experience in the Writing
    Center." *Praxis: A Writing Center Journal* 2 (2005). Web.
    10 Mar. 2010.

Kim, Ki-joong. Personal communication. 14 Apr. 2010.

Lee, Albert H. *East Asian Higher Education: Traditions and
    Transformations*. Oxford: IAU P, 1995. Print.

Planty, M., et al. *The Condition of Education 2009*. National
    Center for Education Statistics, Institute of Education
    Sciences, U.S. Department of Education, June 2009.
    Web. 10 Mar. 2010.

Reid, Joy M. *Teaching ESL Writing*. Englewood Cliffs:
    Regents-Prentice Hall, 1993. Print.

Undergraduate Writing Center. *UWC Consultant Handbook
    2009-2010*. Austin: U of Texas at Austin. Dept. of
    Rhetoric and Writing, 2009. Print.

Documentation style used is MLA.

EXPLORATORY ESSAY   Liza Mundy, a writer for the *Washington Post*, offers a classic kind of causal analysis—one in which readers are asked to consider a subject from an entirely different point of view. That shift in perspective illuminates her subject and raises unexpected and scary consequences.

Slate.com

Posted: Wednesday, May 3, 2006, at 10:20 AM ET
From: Liza Mundy

What's Really behind the Plunge in Teen Pregnancy?

Identifies a trend that needs a causal explanation.

May 3 — in case you didn't know it — was "National Day to Prevent Teen Pregnancy." In the past decade, possibly no social program has been as dramatically effective as the effort to reduce teen pregnancy, and no results so uniformly celebrated. Between 1990 and 2000, the U.S. teen pregnancy rate plummeted by 28 percent, dropping from 117 to 84 pregnancies per 1,000 women aged 15–19. Births to teenagers are also down, as are teen abortion rates. It's an achievement so profound and so heartening that left and right are eager to take credit for it, and both can probably do so. Child-health advocates generally acknowledge that liberal sex education and conservative abstinence initiatives are both to thank for the fact that fewer teenagers are ending up in school bathroom stalls sobbing over the results of a home pregnancy test.

Poses a question about causality.

What, though, if the drop in teen pregnancy isn't a good thing, or not entirely? What if there's a third explanation, one that has nothing to do with just-say-no campaigns or safe-sex educational posters? What if teenagers are less fertile than they used to be?

Not the girls — the boys?

Offers a startling hypothesis.

It's a conversation that's taking place among a different and somewhat less vocal interest group: scientists who study human and animal reproduction. Like many scientific inquiries, this one is hotly contested and not likely to be resolved anytime soon. Still, the fact that it's going on provides a useful reminder that not every social trend is the sole result of partisan policy initiatives and think-tank-generated outreach efforts. It reminds us that a drop in something as profound as fertility, in human creatures of any age, might also have something to do with health, perhaps even the future of the species.

The great sperm-count debate began in 1992, when a group of Danish scientists published a study suggesting that sperm counts declined globally by about 1 percent a year between 1938 and 1990. This study postulated that "environmental influences," particularly widely used chemical compounds with an impact like that of the female hormone estrogen, might be contributing to a drop in fertility among males. If true, this was obviously an alarming development, particularly given that human sperm counts are already strikingly low compared to almost any other species. "Humans have the worst sperm except for gorillas and ganders of any animal on the planet," points out Sherman Silber, a high-profile urologist who attributes this in part to short-term female monogamy. Since one man's sperm rarely has to race that of another man to the finish, things like speed and volume are less important in human sperm than in other animals, permitting a certain amount of atrophy among humans.

The Danish study set an argument in motion. Other studies were published showing that sperm counts were staying the same; still others showed them going up. In the late 1990s, however, an American reproductive epidemiologist named Shanna Swan published work confirming the Danish findings. In a well-respected study published in *Environmental Health Perspectives*, Swan, now at the University of Rochester Medical Center, found that sperm counts are dropping by about 1.5 percent a year in the United States and 3 percent in Europe and Australia, though they do not

---

Reminds readers how contentious studies of causality can be.

New causal factor is presented and explored.

Detailed paragraphs present evidence that sperm counts are dropping.

appear to be falling in the less-developed world. This may not sound like a lot, but cumulatively — like compound interest — a drop of 1 percent has a big effect. Swan showed, further, that in the United States there appears to be a regional variation in sperm counts: They tend to be lower in rural sectors and higher in cities, suggesting the possible impact of chemicals (such as pesticides) particular to one locality.

Swan is part of a group of scientists whose work suggests that environmental changes are indeed having a reproductive impact. Under the auspices of a women's health group at Stanford University and an alliance called the Collaborative on Health and the Environment, some of these scientists met in February 2005 at a retreat in Menlo Park, California, to discuss their findings. Among the evidence presented are several trends that seem to point to a subtle feminization of male babies: a worldwide rise in hypospadias, a birth defect in which the urethral opening is located on the shaft of the penis rather than at the tip; a rise in crypt-orchidism, or unde-scended testicles; and experiments Swan has done showing that in male babies with high exposure to compounds called phthal-ates, something called the anogenital distance is decreasing. If you measure the distance from a baby's anus to the genitals, the distance in these males is shorter, more like that of . . . girls.

Wildlife biologists also talked about the fact that alligators living in one contaminated Florida lake were found to have small phalli and low testosterone levels, while females in the same lake had problems associated with abnormally high levels of estrogen. In 1980, the alligators' mothers had been exposed to a major pesticide dump, which, some believe, was working like an estrogen on their young, disrupting their natural hormones. A report later published by this group pointed out that similar disruptions have been found in a "wide range of species from seagulls to polar bears, seals to salmon, mollusks to frogs." As evidence that a parent's exposure to toxicants

Analysis assumes a knowledge-able, not expert, audience.

can powerfully affect the development of offspring, the example of DES, or diethylstilbestrol, was also, of course, offered. Widely given to pregnant women beginning in the late 1930s under the mistaken assumption that it would prevent miscarriage, DES left the women unaffected but profoundly affected their female fetuses, some of whom would die of cancer, others of whom would find their reproductive capacity compromised. The consensus was that the so-called chemical revolution may well be disrupting the development of reproductive organs in young males, among others. This research is controversial, certainly, but accepted enough, as a hypothesis, that it appears in developmental-biology textbooks.

Tellingly, the U.S. government is also taking this conversation seriously. Together, the National Institutes of Health and the U.S. Centers for Disease Control are sponsoring a longitudinal effort to study the effect of environment on fertility. This study will track couples living in Texas and Michigan, following their efforts to become pregnant. The aim is to determine whether toxicants are affecting the reproductive potential of female and male alike.

It will be welcome information. In the United States, good statistics about infertility are strikingly hard to come by. There is no government-sponsored effort to track male fertility rates, even though male-factor problems account for half of all infertility. Even among women, who are regularly interrogated about reproductive details, it's difficult to get a good handle on developments. For years, government researchers included only married women in the category of "infertility," creating a real problem for demographers and epidemiologists looking for trends. The National Center for Health Statistics created a second category called "impaired fecundity," which includes any woman, of any marital category, who is trying to get pregnant and not having luck.

And the "impaired fecundity" category contains findings that may have a bearing on the are-young-men-more-infertile-than-

> Explains what other causal studies are needed.

> Puts qualifications and limits on available statistics.

their-fathers question. In the United States, "impaired fecundity" among women has seen, over several decades, a steady rise. And while much attention has focused on older women, the most striking rise between 1982 and 1995 took place among women under twenty-five. In that period, impaired fecundity in women under twenty-five rose by 42 percent, from 4.3 percent of women to 6.1 percent. Recently published data from 2002 show a continued rise in impaired fecundity among the youngest age cohort.

In a 1999 letter to *Family Planning Perspectives*, Swan sensibly proposed "that the role of the male be considered in this equation." If sperm counts drop each year, then the youngest men will be most acutely affected, and these will be the men who are having trouble impregnating their partners. In 2002, Danish researchers published an opinion piece in *Human Reproduction* noting that teen pregnancy rates (already much lower than in the United States) fell steadily in Denmark between 1985 and 1999. Unlike in the United States, in Denmark there have been no changes in outreach efforts to encourage responsible behavior in teens: no abstinence campaigns, no big new push for condom distribution. Wider social trends notwithstanding, they note that "it seems reasonable also to consider widespread poor semen quality among men as a potential contributing factor to low fertility rates among teenagers."

Among other things, the sperm-count debate reminds us that we should not be smug about the success of teen-pregnancy prevention efforts. We may not want today's teenagers to become pregnant now, but we certainly want them to become pregnant in the future, providing they want to be. If nothing else, the sperm-count hypothesis shows that when it comes to teenagers and sexual behavior, there's always something new to worry about.

Last paragraph warns against jumping to conclusions too quickly.

CULTURAL ANALYSIS   Charles Paul Freund's "The Politics of Pants," a summary of James Sullivan's book *Jeans: A Cultural History of an American Icon,* argues that consumers, not manufacturers or marketers, determine the cultural significance of products—such as jeans. In fact, Levi Strauss, the original manufacturer of blue jeans, had a hard time understanding why young people in the middle of the twentieth century adopted jeans as a symbol of freedom and protest. Maybe the pictures say it all?

The Politics of Pants

CHARLES PAUL FREUND

In the 1950s, Levi Strauss & Co. decided to update the image of its denim clothes. Until then, the company had been depending for sales on the romantic appeal of the gold rush and the rugged image of the cowboy. Hell, it was still calling its signature pants, the ones with the copper rivets, "waist overalls." It didn't want to abandon the evocative gold-rush connection, but the postwar world was filling with consumption-minded creatures called "teenagers," and it seemed time to rethink the company's pitch.

So in 1956 Levi Strauss tried an experiment, releasing a line of black denim pants it called Elvis Presley Jeans. It was the perfect endorsement. On the branding level, it was a successful marriage of an old product and its developing new character. People had long worn denim for work, or to "westernize" themselves; now a new set of customers was wearing it to identify themselves with the postwar scene of rebellious urban (and suburban) outliers. Upon the release of Elvis's 1956 hit movie *Jailhouse Rock,* writes James Sullivan in *Jeans: A Cultural History of an American Icon* (Gotham Books), "black jeans became the rage of the season." That transition would eventually make undreamed-of profits for Levi Strauss and its many competitors.

Elvis Presley made jeans hip, but he didn't like them.

Jeans were once for cowboys or actors who played them.

The endorsement was wonderfully revealing from within too. Elvis actually disliked denim. To him, as to most people from real working-class backgrounds, it was just a reminder of working hard and being poor. The less denim Elvis wore, the happier he was. As for the company suits at Levi Strauss, they had no idea where their new customers would take them. The company was a lot more comfortable dealing with a safe, midcult crooner like Bing Crosby. In 1951 Levi Strauss had presented Crosby with a custom-made denim tuxedo jacket, just the kind of empty PR stunt the company bosses understood. The eroticizing Presley was unknown territory to them, and they nearly fumbled the whole bad boy connection—one that had already emerged via Presley, Brando, James Dean, and even the Beats[1]—that would help put their product on nearly every pair of hips in the Western world (and on plenty of hips every-where else too).

---

[1]**Brando, James Dean, and even the Beats:** In the early 1950s, actors Marlon Brando and James Dean were known for their roles in disaffected-youth films such as *The Wild One* and *Rebel Without a Cause*. The "Beat Generation" of young poets came to prominence in the late 1950s and early 1960s, subsequently affecting the wider youth culture.

In fact, as Sullivan, a former critic for the *San Francisco Chronicle*, tells the story, the denim industry worked hard to undermine its own success. When jeans started making a transition from working clothes to something darker—the preferred style of the dreaded "juvenile delinquent"—the industry got worried. When school districts started promulgating antidungaree "dress codes," it panicked. Suddenly a Denim Council sprang up to persuade adults that jeans were "Right for School." Young people who wore denim, the industry group argued, were exemplary citizens who studied hard and who honored their fathers and mothers. Happily for Levi's, Wrangler, and Lee (and for Jordache, Guess, Lucky, and the wave of designers to come) nobody paid much attention to the Denim Council.

It was civil libertarians who took care of the dress codes, with a legal strategy the industry never would have dreamed of. Groups challenged the codes as, in Sullivan's words, "an imposition on freedom of expression."

Cool personified: James Dean, as Jett Rink in *Giant*.

In fact, the industry old-timers still don't get it. Looking back on the emergence of jeans wearing as an issue of "expression," one such old-timer can still tell Sullivan, "Amazing . . . Just for a pair of pants."

This series of events takes up just a few pages in one chapter of Sullivan's 303-page book. But I've focused on it because it is a stellar example of a primary market issue that many people—not only markets' critics but some of their defenders too—have failed to acknowledge. It's neither makers nor marketers who successfully attach meaning to the products they want to sell. It's the consumers who impute meaning to those products they choose to buy.

The anthropologist Grant McCracken has done a lot of scholarly work to elucidate this distinction, and the *New Yorker*'s Malcolm Gladwell has been a pioneer in reporting it. His famous 1997 piece "The Coolhunt" focused on consultants who attempt to monitor "coolness" as it is attached to—and detached from—consumer goods by a hierarchy of influential buyers. Gladwell offered case studies of brands, such as Hush Puppies shoes, that had become cool (for a while, anyway) without the manufacturer or its ad people ever having a clue. Jeans conquered the world—Levi's 501s are the single most successful garment ever designed—not because of the denim industry's efforts to give them meaning but in spite of them.

How to scare parents, in the 1950s: Brando in leather and denim.

The rest of Sullivan's book is addressed to the culture, the fashion, and of course the business of jeans. The last of these threads is the most valuable, since it is probably the least known and the most revealing. Who knew, for example, that leisure suits were introduced by Lee? (And what does *that* episode say about the marketers' conception, let alone control, of a product's meaning?) Sullivan's book is as comprehensive on its subject as you are likely to want, if not more so. Jeans and Jack Kerouac.[2] Jeans and the dude ranch. Jeans and the advent of the zipper. Jeans and punk. Jeans and disco. Jeans and the indigo trade. Thousand-dollar Jeans. Collectible jeans. Even pants (not jeans) and Brigham Young,[3] who in 1830 charged that trousers with buttons in front were "fornication pants."

There's even jeans and the color blue. Sullivan has penned an ode to blueness that goes on for four pages. ("The deeper blue becomes," he quotes the artist Wassily Kandinsky as saying, "the more urgently it summons man toward the infinite.") Best of all, though, is jeans and Vladimir Nabokov,[4] despite the fact that Nabokov has nothing much to say about jeans.

Sullivan uses Nabokov inventively, quoting from his 1955 novel, *Lolita*, to demonstrate how the narrator's "refined" sensibility is transformed by a whole world of low-end culture that has become — for him — eroticized. The novel's motels and shopping strips, writes Sullivan, "are the consummate low-culture backdrops for Lolita's jeans, sneakers, and lollipops." It's not just Lolita that Nabokov's intellectual narrator has fallen for. And if you don't see what eroticized low-end culture has to do with the triumph of American jeans, then Elvis really has left the building, and you've gone with him.

---

[2]**Jack Kerouac:** "Beat" writer; his novel *On the Road* was one of the best-known works to come out of the Beat Generation.

[3]**Brigham Young:** Influential nineteenth-century leader of the Church of Jesus Christ of Latter-day Saints (better known as the Mormon Church).

[4]**Vladimir Nabokov:** Russian writer of fiction; best known for his novel *Lolita*.

Assignments

1. **Causal Analysis:** Like Jonah Goldberg in "Global Warming and the Sun" (p. 141), you've probably been curious about or even skeptical of some causal claims made routinely. It might just be college faculty complaining about why students browse the Web during their classes. Or, more seriously, maybe you belong to a group that has been the subject of causal analyses verging on prejudicial. If so, refute what you regard as some faulty analysis of cause and effect by offering a more plausible explanation.

2. **Research Study:** Using Kyu-heong Kim's research essay "Bending the Rules for ESL Writers" as a model (p. 157), write a paper based on sources that examines an issue or problem in your major or in some area of special concern to you. The issue should be one that involves questions of how, why, or what if. Base your analysis on a variety of academic or public sources, fully documented. Like Kim, you may also draw on interviews if appropriate to your subject.

3. **Exploratory Essay:** Liza Mundy's analysis of cause and effect in "What's Really behind the Plunge in Teen Pregnancy?" (p. 165) has both cultural and political implications. Locate a similarly challenging analysis in a national newspaper or news magazine. Then write a detailed response to the causal issues it raises, suggesting, for instance, why you find it convincing, or speculating about how society might respond to its conclusions. You'll find many analyses covering topics such as the environment, terrorism, education, sports, religion, culture, and so on.

4. **Cultural Analysis:** After examining the way Charles Paul Freund deals with jeans (p. 170), identify a comparable trend you have noticed or a change in society or culture that deserves scrutiny. It might relate to technology, entertainment, political preferences, fashion, popularity of careers, or other areas. Write an analysis of the phenomenon, considering either causes or potential consequences of this new mania. Then illustrate the trend with images that suggest its cultural reach or significance. Spend some time in the opening of your paper describing the trend and establishing that it is consequential.

5. **Your Choice:** Politicians and pundits alike are fond of offering predictions, some hopeful, but many dire. The economy, they might suggest, is about to boom or slide into depression; sports dynasties are destined to blossom or collapse; printed books to disappear; American teens to grow fond of musicals. Identify one such prediction about which you have some doubts and develop a cause-and-effect analysis to suggest why it is likely to go awry. Be sure to explain in detail what factors you expect will make the prediction go wrong. If you are brave, offer an alternative vision of the future.

How to start

- Need a **topic**? See page 182.
- Need to come up with a **solution**? See page 187.
- Need to **organize your ideas**? See page 189.

6 Proposals

define a
problem and
suggest a
solution

Proposals are written to try to solve problems. Typically, you'll make a proposal to initiate an action or change. At a minimum, you hope to alter someone's thinking—even if only to recommend leaving things as they are.

TRIAL BALLOON
Degree programs at your school have so many complicated requirements that most students take far more time to graduate than they expect—adding thousands of dollars to their loans. As a *trial balloon*, you suggest that the catalog include accurate "time-to-degree" estimates for all degree programs and certificates.

FORMAL PROPOSAL
Noticing the difficulty people with disabilities have navigating government offices, a member of the city council for whom you are interning asks you to look into the problem. You prepare a *formal proposal* that assesses the situation, offers three specific improvements, and estimates the costs of the improvements.

MANIFESTO
Packaging is getting out of hand, and you've had enough. People can barely open the products they buy because everything is zipped up, shrink-wrapped, blister-packed, containerized, or child-protected. So you write a *manifesto* calling for saner and more eco-friendly approaches to product protection.

VISUAL PROPOSAL
You create a PowerPoint so members of your co-op can visualize how much better your building's study area would look with a few inexpensive tweaks in furniture, paint, and lighting. Your *visual proposal* gets you the job of implementing the changes.

DECIDING TO WRITE A PROPOSAL.   *Got an issue or a problem?
Good—let's deal with it.* That's the logic driving most proposals, both the
professional types that pursue grant money and the less formal propositions
that are part of everyday life, academic or otherwise. Like evaluations and
some explanations, proposals are another form of argument. ○

Although grant writing shares some of the elements of informal proposals, it is driven by rigid formulas set by foundations and government
agencies, usually covering things like budgets, personnel, evaluation,
outcomes, and so on. Informal proposals are much easier. Though they may
not funnel large sums of cash your way, they're still important tools for
addressing problems. A sensible proposal can make a difference in any
situation—be it academic, personal, or political.

You'll need to make the following moves in framing a proposal. Not
every proposal needs to do each of these things. In a first-round pitch, you
might launch a trial balloon to test whether an idea will work at all; a more
serious plan headed for public scrutiny would have to punch the ticket on
more of the items.

**Use Only What You
Need**   How do you
persuade people in a
community to save water?
Denver Water created an
innovative multimedia
ad campaign to sell its
proposal cleverly to its
community.

○
choose a genre
p. 390

Define a problem.   Set the stage for a proposal by describing the specific situation, problem, or opportunity in enough detail that readers *get it*: They see a compelling need for action. In many cases, a proposal needs to explain what's wrong with the status quo.

Target the proposal.   To make a difference, you have to reach people with the power to change a situation. That means first identifying such individuals (or groups) and then tailoring your proposal to their expectations. Use the Web or library, for example, to get the names and contact information of government or corporate officials. ○ When the people in power *are* the problem, go over their heads to more general audiences with clout of their own: voters, consumers, women, fellow citizens, the elderly, and so on.

Consider reasonable options.   Your proposal won't be taken seriously unless you have weighed all the workable possibilities, explaining their advantages and downsides. Only then will you be prepared to make a case for your own ideas.

Make specific recommendations.   Explain what you propose to do about the situation or problem; don't just complain that someone else has gotten it wrong. The more detailed your solution is, the better.

Make realistic recommendations.   You need to address two related issues: *feasibility* and *implementation*. A proposal is feasible if it can be achieved with available resources and is acceptable to the parties involved. And, of course, a feasible plan still needs a plausible pathway to implementation: *First we do this; then we do this*.

plan a project
p. 466

The following proposal originally appeared in *Time* (August 21, 2005). Its author, Barrett Seaman, doesn't have the space to do much more than alert the general public (or, more likely, parents of college students) to the need for action to end alcohol abuse on campuses. Still, he does offer a surprising suggestion—a trial balloon for dealing with bingeing. Although many readers might reject his idea initially, the proposal does what it must: It makes a plausible case and gets people thinking.

How Bingeing Became the New College Sport

BARRETT SEAMAN

In the coming weeks, millions of students will begin their fall semester of college, with all the attendant rituals of campus life: freshman orientation, registering for classes, rushing by fraternities and sororities, and, in a more recent nocturnal college tradition, "pregaming" in their rooms.

Pregaming is probably unfamiliar to people who went to college before the 1990s. But it is now a common practice among eighteen-, nineteen- and twenty-year-old students who cannot legally buy or consume alcohol. It usually involves sitting in a dorm room or an off-campus apartment and drinking as much hard liquor as possible before heading out for the evening's parties. While reporting for my book *Binge*, I witnessed the hospitalization of several students for acute alcohol poisoning. Among them was a Hamilton College freshman who had consumed twenty-two shots of vodka while sitting in a dorm room with her friends. Such hospitalizations are routine on campuses across the nation. By the Thanksgiving break of the year I visited Harvard, the university's health center had admitted nearly seventy students for alcohol poisoning.

When students are hospitalized—or worse yet, die from alcohol poisoning, which happens about 300 times each year—college presidents tend to react by declaring their campuses dry or shutting down fraternity houses. But tighter enforcement of the minimum drinking age of twenty-one is not the solution. It's part of the problem.

Defines problem he intends to address: bingeing known as pregaming.

Points out that current solutions to college drinking don't work.

Proposal draws on research the author has done.

Over the past forty years, the United States has taken a confusing approach to the age-appropriateness of various rights, privileges, and behaviors. It used to be that twenty-one was the age that legally defined adulthood. On the heels of the student revolution of the late '60s, however, came sweeping changes: The voting age was reduced to eighteen; privacy laws were enacted that protected college students' academic, health, and disciplinary records from outsiders, including parents; and the drinking age, which had varied from state to state, was lowered to eighteen.

Then, thanks in large measure to intense lobbying by Mothers Against Drunk Driving, Congress in 1984 effectively blackmailed states into hiking the minimum drinking age to twenty-one by passing a law that tied compliance to the distribution of federal-aid highway funds—an amount that will average $690 million per state this year. There is no doubt that the law, which achieved full fifty-state compliance in 1988, saved lives, but it had the unintended consequence of creating a covert culture around alcohol as the young adult's forbidden fruit.

Drinking has been an aspect of college life since the first Western universities in the fourteenth century. My friends and I drank in college in the 1960s—sometimes a lot but not so much that we had to be hospitalized. Veteran college administrators cite a sea change in campus culture that began, not without coincidence, in the 1990s. It was marked by a shift from beer to hard liquor, consumed not in large social settings, since that is now illegal, but furtively and dangerously in students' residences.

In my reporting at colleges around the country, I did not meet any presidents or deans who felt that the twenty-one-year age minimum helps their efforts to curb the abuse of alcohol on their campuses. Quite the opposite. They thought the law impeded their efforts since it takes away the ability to monitor and supervise drinking activity.

What would happen if the drinking age was rolled back to eighteen or nineteen? Initially, there would be a surge in binge drinking as young adults savored their newfound freedom. But over time, I predict, U.S. college students would settle into the saner approach to alcohol I saw on the one

Explains factors responsible for the spike in alcohol abuse.

Points out that current law makes it harder to deal with bingeing.

Offers specific proposal tentatively, posed as question.

Proposal
stands up
to tests of
feasibility,
acceptability,
and
practicality.

campus I visited where the legal drinking age is eighteen: Montreal's McGill University, which enrolls about two thousand American undergraduates a year. Many, when they first arrive, go overboard, exploiting their ability to drink legally. But by midterms, when McGill's demanding academic standards must be met, the vast majority have put drinking into its practical place among their priorities.

A culture like that is achievable at U.S. colleges if Congress can muster the fortitude to reverse a bad policy. If lawmakers want to reduce drunk driving, they should do what the Norwegians do: Throw the book at offenders no matter what their age. Meanwhile, we should let the pregamers come out of their dorm rooms so that they can learn to handle alcohol like the adults we hope and expect them to be.

States his
thesis and
then offers
precedents
for students
behaving
more
responsibly
with lower
drinking age.

Do current strict
drinking laws in the
United States actually
encourage students
to abuse alcohol?
In 2008, a coalition
of presidents from
one hundred colleges
recommended
lowering the drinking
age to eighteen.

Exploring purpose and topic

► topic

Most people will agree to a reasonable proposal—as long as it doesn't cost them anything. But moving audiences from *I agree* to *I'll actually do something about it* usually takes a powerful act of persuasion. And for that reason, proposals are typically structured as arguments, requiring all the strategies used in that genre. ○

Occasionally, you'll be asked to solve a particular problem in school or on the job. Having a topic assigned makes your task a little easier, but you can bet that any such problem will be complex and open to multiple solutions. Otherwise, there would be no challenge to it.

When choosing a proposal topic on your own, keep the following concerns in mind. ○

Look for a genuine issue. Spend the first part of your project defining a problem readers will care about. You may think it's a shame no one retails Prada close to campus, but your classmates could plausibly be more concerned with outrageous student fees or the high price of gasoline. Go beyond your own concerns in settling on a problem.

Look for a challenging problem. It helps if others have tried to fix it in the past, but failed—and for reasons you can identify. Times change, attitudes shift, technology improves: All of these can be factors that make what seemed like an insoluble problem in the past more manageable now. Choose a serious topic to which you can bring fresh perspectives.

Need help deciding what to write about? See "How to Browse for Ideas" on pp. 360–61.

Look for a soluble problem. Challenges *are* good, but impossible dreams are for Broadway musicals. Parking on campus is the classic impasse—always present, always frustrating. Steer clear of problems no one has ever solved, unless you have a *really* good idea.

Look for a local issue. It's best to leave "world peace" to celebrity activists like Bono. You can investigate a problem in your community more credibly, talking with people involved or searching local archives for material. ○ Doing so makes it easier to find an audience you can influence, including people potentially able to change the situation. It's more likely you'll get the attention of your dean of students than the secretary of state.

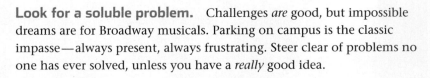

understand argument
p. 72

find a topic
p. 356

interview and observe
p. 478

In an editorial cartoon, Michael Ramirez uses a familiar biblical story to suggest that President Obama may have made too challenging a proposal when he asked Israeli leaders to "take risks for peace" in the Middle East. This cartoon originally appeared in *Investor's Business Daily* on July 9, 2010. (By permission of Michael Ramirez and Creators Syndicate, Inc.)

Your Turn   In 46 BCE, Julius Caesar used his authority as dictator to impose a new calendar on Rome because the old one had fallen five months out of synch with the seasons. Play Caesar today by imagining what problems you would fix if you could simply impose your will. Make a list. Narrow your more grandiose schemes (world peace) to more plausible ones (less rowdiness in the student section at football games), and then consider which items on your roster could be argued rationally and compellingly in a short paper. Compare your list with those of other students and discuss workable proposal topics.

Understanding your audience

While preparing a proposal, keep two audiences in mind—one fairly narrow and the other more broad. The first group includes people who could possibly do something about a problem; the second consists of general readers who could influence those in the first group by bringing the weight of public opinion down on them. And public opinion makes a difference.

Writers adjust for audience all the time in offering proposals. Grant writers, especially, make it a point to learn what agencies and institutions expect in applications. Quite often, it takes two or three tries to figure out how to present a winning grant submission. You won't have that luxury with most academic or political pieces, but you can certainly study models of successful proposals, noting how the writers raise an issue with readers, provide them with information and options, and then argue for a particular solution.

Write to people who can make a difference. For example, a personal letter you might prepare for the dean of students to protest her policies against displaying political posters in university buildings (including offices and dormitories) would likely have a respectful and perhaps legalistic tone, pointing to case law on the subject and university policies on freedom of speech. You'd also want to assure the dean of your good sense and provide her with sound reasons to consider your case.

You'd be in good company adopting such a strategy. Listen to how matter-of-factly environmentalist David R. Brower argues—in a famous proposal—that the gates of the massive Glen Canyon Dam should be opened and the waters of Lake Powell drained. Radical stuff, but his strategy was sensible. For one thing, he argued, the artificial reservoir leaked.

> One of the strongest selling points [for removing the dam] comes from the Bureau of Reclamation itself. In 1996, the bureau found that almost a million acre-feet, or 8 percent of the river's flow, disappeared between the stations recording the reservoir's inflow and outflow. Almost 600,000 acre-feet were presumed lost to evaporation. Nobody knows for sure about the rest. The bureau said some of the loss was a gain—being stored in the

banks of the reservoir—but it has no idea how much of that gain it will ever get back. Some bank storage is recoverable, but all too likely the region's downward-slanting geological strata are leading some of Powell's waters into the dark unknown. It takes only one drain to empty a bathtub, and we don't know where, when, or how the Powell tub leaks. A million acre-feet could meet the annual domestic needs of 4 million people and at today's prices are worth $435 million in the Salt Lake City area—more than a billion on my hill in Berkeley, California.

—"Let the River Run Through It," *Sierra*, March/April 1997

Rally people who represent public opinion.

Imagine you've had no response from the dean of students on the political poster proposal you made. Time to take the issue to the public, perhaps via an op-ed or letter sent to the student paper. Though still keeping the dean firmly in mind, you'd now also write to stir up student and community opinion. Your new piece could be more emotional than your letter and less burdened by legal points—though still citing facts and presenting solid reasons for allowing students more leeway in expressing their political beliefs on campus. ⚪

The fact is that people often need a spur to move them—that is, a persuasive strategy that helps them to imagine their role in solving a problem. Again, you'd be in good company in leading an audience to your position. As shown on page 186, when President John F. Kennedy proposed a mission to the moon in 1962, he did it in language that stirred a public reasonably skeptical about the cost and challenges of such an implausible undertaking.

Proposals to very small groups can be as simple as this unadorned but clear and direct leaflet.

refine your tone
p. 432

JFK Aims High   In 1962, the president challenged Americans to go to the moon; today American astronauts ride to the International Space Station on a Russian *Soyuz*.

There is no strife, no prejudice, no national conflict in outer space as yet. Its hazards are hostile to us all. Its conquest deserves the best of all mankind, and its opportunity for peaceful cooperation may never come again. But why, some say, the moon? Why choose this as our goal? And they may well ask why climb the highest mountain? Why, thirty-five years ago, fly the Atlantic? Why does Rice play Texas?

We choose to go to the moon. We choose to go to the moon in this decade and do the other things, not because they are easy, but because they are hard, because that goal will serve to organize and measure the best of our energies and skills, because that challenge is one that we are willing to accept, one we are unwilling to postpone, and one which we intend to win, and the others, too.

−Rice Stadium "Moon Speech," September 12, 1962

Finding and developing materials

Proposals might begin with whining and complaining (*I want easier parking!*), but they can't stay in that mode for long. Like any serious work, proposals must be grounded in solid thinking and research.

consider solutions ◀

What makes them distinctive, however, is the sheer variety of strategies you might use in a single document. To write a convincing proposal, you may have to narrate, report, argue, evaluate, and explore cause and effect. A proposal can be a little like old-time TV variety shows, with one act following another, displaying a surprising range of talent. Here's how you might develop those various parts.

Define the problem.   First, research the existing problem fully enough to explain it to your readers. Run through the traditional journalist's questions—*Who? What? Where? When? Why? How?*—to be sure you've got the basics of your topic down cold. When appropriate, interview experts or people involved with an issue; for instance, in college communities, the best repositories of institutional memory will usually be staff. ○

> *The Journalist's Questions*
>
> Who?   What?
> Where?   When?
> Why?   How?

Even when you think you know the topic well, spend time locating any documents that might provide hard facts to cite for skeptical readers. For instance, if you propose to change a long-standing policy, find out when it was imposed, by whom, and for what reasons.

Examine prior solutions.   If a problem is persistent, other people have certainly tried to solve it—or perhaps they caused it. In either case, do the research necessary to figure out, as best you can, what happened in these earlier efforts. But expect controversy. Your sources may provide different and contradictory accounts that you will have to sort out in a plausible narrative.

Once you know the history of an issue, shift into an evaluative mode to explain why earlier solutions or strategies did not work. ○ Provide reliable information so that readers can later make comparisons with your own proposal and appreciate its ingenuity.

Make a proposal.   Coming up with a proposal may take all the creativity you can muster, to the point where a strong case can be made for working collaboratively when that's an option. ○ You'll benefit from the additional

interview and observe p. 478

understand evaluation p. 106

collaborate p. 362

feedback. Be sure to write down your ideas as they emerge, so you can see what exactly you are recommending. Be specific about numbers and costs.

For instance, if you propose that high school students in your district take a course in practical economics (balancing a checkbook, credit card use, and so on) to better prepare them for adult responsibilities, do the research necessary to figure out who might teach such classes and how many new instructors the school district would have to hire. Your findings could preempt an implausibly expensive proposal or suggest more feasible alternatives for handling the problem that you see.

Defend the proposal.   Any ideas that threaten the status quo will surely provoke arguments. That's half the fun of offering proposals. So prove your position, using all the tools of argument available to you, from the logical and factual to the emotional. It is particularly important to anticipate objections, because readers invested in the status quo will have them in spades. Take time to define a successful solution to a problem, and point out every way your solution meets that definition. Above all, you've got to show that your idea will work.

Be prepared, too, to show that your plan is feasible—that is to say, that it can be achieved with existing or new resources. For example, you might actually solve your school's traffic problems by proposing a monorail linking the central campus to huge new parking garages. But who would pay for the multimillion-dollar system? Still, don't be put off too easily by the objection that *we can't possibly do that*. A little ingenuity goes a long way—it's part of the problem-solving process.

Figure out how to implement the proposal.   Readers will want assurances that your ideas can be implemented: Show them how. ○ Figure out what has to happen to meet your goals: where new resources will come from, how personnel can be recruited and hired, where brochures or manuals will be printed, and so on. Provide a timetable if you can.

think critically
p. 372

Creating a structure

Proposals follow the mental processes many people go through in dealing with issues and problems, and some of these problems have more history and complications than others. ○ Generally, the less formal the proposal, the fewer structural elements it will have. So you should adapt the proposal paradigm below to your purposes, using it as a checklist of *possible* issues to consider in your own project.

organize ideas ◄

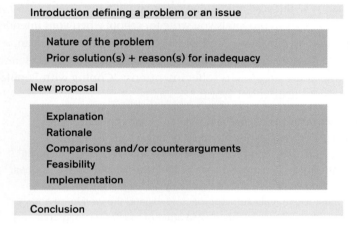

Introduction defining a problem or an issue

> **Nature of the problem**
> **Prior solution(s) + reason(s) for inadequacy**

New proposal

> **Explanation**
> **Rationale**
> **Comparisons and/or counterarguments**
> **Feasibility**
> **Implementation**

Conclusion

You might use a similar structure when you intend to explore the effects that follow from some action, event, policy, or change in the status quo. Once again, you'd begin with an introduction that fully describes the situation you believe will have consequences; then you would work through those consequences, connecting them as necessary. Your conclusion could then draw out the implications of your paper.

shape your work
p. 406

Choosing a style and design

Proposals do come in many forms and, occasionally, they may be frivolous or comic. But whenever you suggest upending the status quo or spending someone else's money, you probably need to show a little respect and humility.

Use a formal style.   Professional proposals—especially those seeking grant money—are typically written in a formal and impersonal high style, as if the project would be jeopardized by reviewers detecting the slightest hint of enthusiasm or personality. ○ But academic audiences are usually just as serious. So you might use a formal style in proposals you write for school when your intended readers are specific and official—a professor, a government agency, a dean.

Observe the no-nonsense tone Thao Tran adopts early in an academic essay whose title alone suggests its sober intentions: "Coping with Population Aging in the Industrialized World."

Point of view is impersonal: *This report* rather than *I*.

Purpose of proposal is clearly explained.

Premises and assumptions of proposal are offered in abstract language.

Leaders of industrialized nations and children of baby boomers must understand the consequences of population aging and minimize its economic effects. This report will recommend steps for coping with aging in the industrialized world and will assess counterarguments to those steps. With a dwindling workforce and rising elderly population, industrialized countries must take a multi-step approach to expand the workforce and support the elderly. Governments should attempt to attract immigrants, women, and elderly people into the workforce. Supporting an increasing elderly population will require reforming pension systems and raising indirect taxes. It will also require developing pronatalist policies, in which governments subsidize child rearing costs to encourage births. Many of these strategies will challenge traditional cultural notions and require a change in cultural attitudes. While change will not be easy, industrialized nations must recognize and address this trend quickly in order to reduce its effects.

Use a middle style, when appropriate.   You might shift toward a middle style whenever establishing a personal relationship could help your proposal or when you need to persuade a wider, more general audience.

It is possible, too, for styles to vary within a document. Your language might be coldly efficient as you scrutinize previous failures or tick off the advantages of your specific proposal. But as you near the end of the piece, you might decide another style would better reflect your vision for the future or your enthusiasm for an idea. Earlier in this chapter, environmentalist David R. Brower supplied an example of technical prose in explaining why

define your style
p. 432

draining Lake Powell would make commercial sense. Here is a far more emotional paragraph from the conclusion of his proposal:

> The sooner we begin, the sooner lost paradises will begin to recover – Cathedral in the Desert, Music Temple, Hidden Passage, Dove Canyon, Little Arch, Dungeon, and a hundred others. Glen Canyon itself can probably lose its ugly white sidewalls in two or three decades. The tapestries can reemerge, along with the desert varnish, the exiled species of plants and animals, the pictographs and other mementos of people long gone. The canyon's music will be known again, and "the sudden poetry of springs," Wallace Stegner's beautiful phrase, will be revealed again below the sculptured walls of Navajo sandstone. The phrase, "as long as the rivers shall run and the grasses grow," will regain its meaning.

Place names listed have poetic effect.

Lush details add to emotional appeal of proposal.

Final quotation summarizes mission of proposal.

Pay attention to elements of design.   Writers often incorporate images, charts, tables, graphs, and flowcharts to illustrate what is at stake in a proposal or to make comparisons easy. Images also help readers imagine solutions or proposals and make those ideas attractive. The SmartArt Graphics icon in the Microsoft Word Gallery opens up a range of templates you might use to help readers visualize a project. ○

form   structure   movement   color

You may have seen photographs of the new Dallas Cowboys Stadium that opened in Arlington, Texas, in 2009. But here's an early sketch of the HKS design, posted on the ArchDaily Web site, exploring various possibilities for the new building.

Your Turn   The style of proposals varies dramatically, depending on audience and purpose. Review the proposals in this chapter offered as models—including the visual proposals. Then explain in some detail exactly how the language (or the visual details) of one item works to make its case. You can focus on a whole essay, but you may find it more interesting just to explicate a few sentences or paragraphs or one or two visual details. For example, when does Barrett Seaman (p. 179), Michael Ramirez (p. 183), or Katelyn Vincent (p. 198) score style points with you? Be ready to explain your observation orally.

○
think visually
p. 592

Examining models

FORMAL PROPOSAL If democracy is to thrive, Donald Lazere believes that Americans need to know more about citizenship. So writing for the academic audience of *The Chronicle Review*, he makes a specific proposal for course work in civic education. Lazere is a professor emeritus at California Polytechnic State University at San Luis Obispo.

A Core Curriculum for Civic Literacy

Donald Lazere

January 31, 2010

Lazere defines a problem and surveys the ample literature on the subject.

The past few years have seen an outpouring of books and reports deploring Americans' civic ignorance, with titles like *Just How Stupid Are We?*, *The Dumbest Generation, The Age of American Unreason,* and *Tuned Out: Why Americans Under 40 Don't Follow the News.* This is a problem that everyone seems to complain about but no one tries to solve through any coordinated, nationwide effort.

National organizations have recently been formed, including the Campaign for the Civic Mission of Schools, the Carnegie Foundation for the Advancement of Teaching's Political Engagement Project, and Campus Compact and its Research University Civic Engagement Network. These organizations have published important interdisciplinary books, such as *Educating for Democracy*, by Anne Colby et al. (Jossey-Bass, 2007), and *Civic Engagement in Higher Education*, by Barbara Jacoby et al. (Jossey-Bass, 2009).

Many campus programs have also been exemplary, as surveyed in Charles Muscatine's *Fixing College Education* (University of Virginia Press, 2009). In *The Assault on Reason* (Penguin Press, 2007), Al Gore praised the American Political Science Association for starting a Task Force on Civic Education. That should prompt similar task forces in the Modern Language Association (my discipline) and other professional associations, along with a unifying interdisciplinary organization for

The proposal argues for a commission to create "a core curriculum for civic literacy."

secondary and postsecondary education, a National Commission on Civic Education. Liberal and conservative educators and politicians should collaborate in hammering out their differences on what should constitute a core curriculum for civic literacy. We can hope for sponsorship in this effort by both conservative and liberal foundations, as well as for support from the U.S. Department of Education and National Endowment for the Humanities.

One way to prompt deliberation here is to spin E. D. Hirsch's much-debated agenda for what every American needs to know to be culturally literate: What does every American need to know to be a civically literate, critically conscious, responsible citizen? And, as a corollary, what role should the humanities play in a renewal of education for civic literacy?

Two questions help to focus on the civic literacy problem as Lazere sees it.

My agenda would give priority to the factual knowledge and analytic skills that students need to make reasoned judgments about the partisan screaming matches and special-interest propaganda that permeate political disputes. One source for such knowledge and skills can be the disciplines of critical thinking and argumentative rhetoric. Unfortunately, few high schools or colleges require courses with that focus, which was also shamefully ignored by No Child Left Behind.

We have all by necessity been thinking a lot lately about one particular branch of civic literacy: economic knowledge. How many among us understand how or why our personal economic fates—mortgages, retirement pensions, and our colleges' financing and endowments—are captive to booms and busts in the stock market and the occult realm of national and international high finance? In the prophetic words of the "corporate cosmology" revealed by the arch-capitalist Arthur Jensen in Paddy Chayefsky's 1976 film, *Network*, "The totality of life on this planet" is now determined by "one vast and immane, interwoven, interacting, multivariate, multinational dominion of dollars."

Lazere uses a current issue to dramatize the need for better civic education.

What a tragic gulf lies between most citizens' understanding of economic forces and their power over each of our daily lives and livelihoods. And what an enormous hole there is, in both K–12 and college curricula, in teaching about those forces as an integral part of general education. I am not talking about courses in formal economics, but in thinking critically about the rhetoric of economic issues at the everyday level of political debates and news and opinion—although those studies would identify oversimplifications at that level that could certainly be pursued in economics classes.

The term "core curriculum" has sadly become a culture-war wedge issue, with conservatives pre-empting it in the cause of Eurocentric tradition and American patriotism, thus provoking intransigent opposition from progressive champions of cultural pluralism and identity politics. Surely, however, we should urge the opposing sides to seek common ground in a core curriculum for critical citizenship that transcends—or encompasses—ideological partisanship.

My own immodest proposal models a core curriculum that centrally includes critical thinking about, and analysis and practice of, public rhetoric, at the local, national, and international levels. Far from being a radical proposal, it is a conservative one in returning to something like the 18th-century rhetoric-based curriculum in American education.

That curriculum, as the historian of rhetoric S. Michael Halloran describes it, "address[ed] students as political beings, as members of a body politic in which they have a responsibility to form judgments and influence the judgments of others on public issues." Halloran and other historians have lamented the modern diffusion of studies in forensics, literature, composition, and other humanistic fields, as a result of the hegemony of disciplines and departments oriented toward specialized faculty research, which have become the tail that wags the curricular dog. Those forces and a depressing array of others have caused the study of political rhetoric to fall between the cracks of most current curricula, almost to the disappearing point.

So let's envision how a revived curriculum for civic literacy might be embodied in a sequence of undergraduate courses that would supplement, not supplant, basic courses in history, government, literature, and other humanist staples. These could be interdisciplinary offerings, with at least a partial component of English studies. Within English, they would follow, not replace, first-year writing—which in recent decades has focused on generating students' personal writing rather than critical analyses of readings or public rhetoric—and a second term in critical thinking and written and oral argumentative rhetoric.

To win wide support for civic education, the proposal stakes out a middle ground between warring political factions.

Style here reflects the intended academic audience: formal and technical.

The groundwork laid, Lazere now offers detailed course recommendations.

The following headings correspond to chapters in my textbook for such a second-term course, but my own and other instructors' experience in using the book is that for any single course or textbook to "cover" what really demands a full curriculum is an impossible expectation. So I will break that material down, more appropriately, into four courses:

Course 1: Thinking Critically About Political and Economic Rhetoric

This would begin with a survey of semantic issues in defining terms like left wing, right wing, liberal, conservative, radical, moderate, freedom, democracy, patriotism, capitalism, socialism, communism, Marxism, fascism, and plutocracy. It would explore their denotative complexity and the ways in which they are oversimplified or connotatively slanted in public usage.

Study would then focus on defining ideological differences between and within the left and right, nationally and internationally, and on understanding the relativity of political viewpoints on the spectrum from left to right. For example, *The New York Times* is liberal in relation to Fox News but conservative in relation to *The Nation*; the Democratic Party is liberal in relation to the Republicans but conservative in relation to European social-democratic parties. Principles of argumentative rhetoric would then be applied to "reading the news" on political and economic issues in a range of journalistic and scholarly sources and from a variety of ideological viewpoints, with emphasis on identifying the predictable patterns of partisan rhetoric in opposing sources.

Course 2: Thinking Critically About Mass Media

Key questions would include: Do the media give people what they want, or condition what they want? Are news media objective and neutral, and should they be? The debate over liberal versus conservative bias in media would be approached through weighing the diverse influences of employees (editors, producers, writers, newscasters, performers); owners, executives, and advertisers; external pressure groups; and audiences. Research on the cognitive effects of mass culture would be applied to such issues as the impact of electronic media on reading, writing, and political consciousness. Implicit political ideology in news and entertainment media would be studied through images of corporations, workers, and unions; the rich, poor, and middle class; gender roles, ethnic minorities, and gays; military forces and war; and immigrants, foreigners, other parts of the world, and Americans' international presence. A final topic of study would be how the Internet has altered all of those issues.

Course 3: Propaganda Analysis and Deception Detection

Study here would begin with problems in defining and evaluating propaganda. A survey of its sources would include government and the military, political parties, lobbies, advertising, public relations, foundations, and sponsored research in think tanks and elsewhere. The role of special interests, conflicts of interest, and special pleading in political and economic rhetoric would be examined, along with propagators' frequent resort to deceptive modes of argument or outright lying—especially with statistics. This course (or another entire one) would include topics in critical consumer education: reading the fine print in contracts, like those for student loans, credit cards, rental agreements, and mortgages; examining health and environmental issues in consumer products; and seeking out the often hidden facts of the production and marketing of food and pharmaceuticals.

Course 4: Civic Literacy in Practice

This would connect these academic studies with service learning, community or national activism, or work in government or community organizations, journalism, and elsewhere.

Two possible objections:

"What you are proposing is that English and other humanities courses take on the impossible burden of remediation for the failures of the entire American education system in civic literacy."

You betcha. It's a dirty job, but someone has to do it, and I don't see any likelier disciplines jumping into the breach, especially ones with

The proposal concludes by addressing feasibility issues and anticipating potential objections.

courses that are conventionally general education and breadth requirements. (Some communication and speech departments are in schools of liberal arts, but others are not; many offer courses in political rhetoric and media criticism, but those are mostly advanced ones for majors.) An ideal solution would be for these to be offered as interdisciplinary core courses, in which humanities faculty members would collaborate with those in the social sciences, communication, and so on. If civic education at the secondary level ever picks up the slack that it should, the college humanities involvement in such instruction can be phased out.

"Mightn't your proposals just be a Trojan horse for dragging in the academic left's same old agenda and biases?"

The courses could be conceived in their specifics and taught by instructors with varying ideological viewpoints—or best of all, through team teaching by liberal and conservative instructors. In principle, this framework would "teach the conflicts," on Gerald Graff's model, not through advocacy or the monologic perspective of any teacher's own beliefs, but through enabling students to identify and compare a full range of opposing ideological perspectives (including those of the instructor and the students), their points of opposition, and the partisan patterns and biases of their rhetoric. I have found it easy to grade students on the basis of their skill in articulating those points, without regard to my political viewpoints or theirs.

To be sure, this conception runs up against the near impossibility of anyone's even defining terms and points of opposition between, say, the left and right with complete objectivity and without injecting value judgments. That problem itself, however, can become a subject of study within these courses and in advanced scholarly inquiry. Indeed, the courses could prompt a wealth of related research and theoretical explorations, creating a fruitful arena for bridging the gap between advanced scholarship and undergraduate teaching.

MANIFESTO   Proposals often arise from a critical look at contemporary culture. Here, Katelyn Vincent draws upon her own experiences to argue, finally, that technology is taking up too much of our lives. She draws attention to the issue by dramatizing her own struggle to survive for twelve hours without the Internet.

Vincent 1

Katelyn Vincent

Professor Ruszkiewicz

Composition 2

November 11, 20--

Technology Time-out

"Are you sure you want to shut down?" A gray box has popped up and is waiting for my answer. No, I think to myself, I'm really not—and it's true. I have become so reliant on my computer that the thought of willingly turning it off during the day feels strange, almost wrong. And these days, it seems that everyone else shares the same addiction. The other day, when my roommate's Internet was down for a few hours, she had a mild panic attack. I thought it was silly—until I realized I would have had the same reaction if something similar had happened to me. Now, I consider myself to be a reasonably independent person, and the thought of being so dependent on something—especially a *machine*—horrified me. So I made a resolution—to avoid the Internet for twelve hours.

The gray box still waits. A blue button flashes on the screen in front on me, and the words "Shut Down" pulsate

The problem of Web addiction is identified, connecting the essay to a wide audience.

Vincent 2

before my eyes, daring me to make my decision. Giving in
to my curiosity, I click and watch as the luminous rectangle
in front of me fades slowly to black. That was easy enough,
I think to myself. Maybe I can handle this after all.

Vincent shifts
to present
tense to
intensify
the action.

Looking for something to do now that my primary
source of entertainment (and procrastination) has dissolved
into nothingness, I realize that it is eight o'clock and I have
not eaten anything since breakfast. In the kitchen, I reach
for the Fruity Cheerios on the top shelf of the pantry—a
food staple since I started college—and am this close to
pouring when I realize that *making* dinner might actually be
fun. Heck, I haven't made myself a real dinner in several
weeks, and since I usually spend this time Facebook-stalking
casual acquaintances from third grade and reading random
health articles on a too-familiar 9 × 13 glowing screen,
today I have the time to spare. Eagerly, I pull out the pasta
box that has been sleeping on my shelf for the past four
months and get to work. You know what would be great
with this, I think—some chicken. Mmm, I know, they have
an amazing chicken pasta recipe on Allrecipes.com, I'll just
go and . . . dammit. Never mind, I'll improvise. Surprisingly,
the chicken doesn't turn out horribly. My dinner is no
"Nicole's Tailgate Party Chicken Salad," but an alarmingly
strong lemon taste gives me a zesty kick in the mouth. And
to be honest, the fact that dinner is warm and homemade
makes it infinitely better than Fruity Cheerios.

The details are
homey and
believable.

Vincent 3

After dinner I again find myself bored—and wondering how many people have commented on my Facebook status. Wait a minute—why am I so concerned about this? Am I really so lame that my happiness depends on what people comment on my Facebook posts? God, I hope not. Trying to distract myself from this disturbing thought, I pull out my textbook to study—and once again, something doesn't feel right. I realize it has been over an hour since I checked Hotmail, Facebook, or MSN. My hand itches to press the power button and start clicking and clacking away—my prestudy ritual. Who knows how many e-mails, Facebook notifications, and important articles are popping up without my knowledge? What if I am missing something hugely important? Still, determined to stick it out, I dig in my backpack and stare into *Corporate Finance*, Second Edition. After three minutes, all I can think about is how much I would love to put in my headphones and crank up Pandora.com and my Michael Bublé playlist. This is going to be a long night.

> The strategy is to describe symptoms of Internet addiction that readers will recognize.

I guess, not surprisingly, I am more focused on *Corporate Finance* than I have ever been, which isn't saying much, but still—I'm impressed. I have turned off my cell phone and iPod as well, and before I know it I have read two whole sections of the book and done a chapter's worth of questions. Not bad for two hours of studying. Afterwards, I delve into marketing and manage to read an entire chapter from that book as well. I have to say, it feels good to accomplish something and not have to stress about it. And I actually think I learned

> Without getting technical, a full paragraph examines the limits of multitasking and the potential consequences for college students.

Vincent 4

something—a feeling I don't always get from studying, which for me is usually marked more by frantic memorization than any real retention of information. I guess part of the reason for my inability to recall is that studying for me usually means multitasking between chapter skimming, shopping for new boots on Amazon.com, and watching online clips from the latest episode of *Glee*. I usually switch back and forth between book and computer, spending about five minutes (max) on the book before some arbitrary whim or want enters my head and I have to go online and check it out before I can resume studying. It's gratifying to do something well for a change.

The paragraph ends with a clever but important insight, driving home a key theme of the paper.

It's also kind of nice not to be in continuous contact with the rest of the world, I think to myself. What with e-mail, Facebook, calling, and texting, I feel as if I am constantly communicating with everyone I know. I can text my mom, talk on the phone with my sister, Facebook-chat with my friend, and e-mail my professor—all at the same time! While establishing relationships with other people is fine, it is also enjoyable to spend some time alone once in a while: I feel as though I haven't been truly alone in ages. Even while studying finance, I realize I am calmer than I have been in weeks. For a change, I get the chance to recharge *my* batteries instead of just my Mac's.

The next morning I am back to Fruity Cheerios and instinctively reach for the power button on my Mac as soon as I wake up. Still moving around in the foggy space of sleepiness, it takes me a moment to realize that my self-imposed

Vincent 5

sentence is not up. So much for checking my e-mail and Weather.com before I head out. Then again, I realize, I go to bed so late that it doesn't really make sense that I would have gotten any new e-mails since the last time I checked— most normal people are in bed between the hours of 2 and 6 AM, after all. Why do I have to check everything in the morning again? I have done it for so long that I guess it's just habit by now. I could be using those twenty minutes to spend more time getting ready, or even better, sleeping. I guess the only Web site it really makes sense to check in the morning is Weather.com, and even that's not a complete necessity.

The extra moments give me more time to get ready, and those seemingly insignificant twenty minutes turn my usually hectic morning routine into a much calmer transition between sleep and class. For the first time this semester, I am *not* lathering myself into a frenzy, *not* frantically applying lip gloss on my way out, and *not* running to catch the bus that's about to leave (there goes my exercise). In fact, my entire morning is pretty mellow, and I don't even think about getting online again until lunchtime. By then, the twelve hours is up—but the only reason I get online is to register for classes. Why mess with a good thing?

As it turns out, the "hugely important" somethings I was missing during my online off-time consisted of one offer for a free colon cleanse, two "Take this quiz!" pop-ups on Facebook, a new MSN article on the latest *Dancing with the Stars*

Vincent realizes that technology has complicated her life and, by implication, the lives of her readers.

The humor here is yet another gesture to win over readers, who have likely received similar e-mails.

Vincent 6

results, and only one actual, legitimate e-mail—from my mother. Granted, I do get some important e-mails from time to time, but when I think about it, how many of them actually require that I respond immediately? Most likely, none.

So what did I learn from all this? That I *am* addicted to technology and our online world—and I have a feeling I am not too different from the rest of society. I couldn't go twelve hours Internet free without driving myself a little crazy. But at the same time, this addiction of ours is one that we, to some degree, have been forced into. While Amazon and Pandora are, admittedly, somewhat superfluous, the use of e-mail as the primary means of communication and Facebook as the major place of social interaction nowadays means that those who ignore them are left behind. We can't just decide to ignore technology completely; it has become a part of our world and something that we have to deal with daily, whether we want to or not.

But at the same time, it shouldn't be our *whole* world. After all, if our online world becomes our entire universe— what happens when the computer crashes? We crash with it. The only way to ensure that doesn't happen is to distance ourselves, when possible, from that which is slowly sucking us into dependency. We need to take some time to learn how to do things on our own, take time to do things well again, take time for ourselves, and, ultimately, just take time to learn that easier doesn't always mean better.

The essay concedes that most of us can't ignore technology: Turning off the Web entirely is not feasible.

In highly rhetorical language, Vincent makes a call for independence and change.

VISUAL PROPOSAL   Pallettruth.com is a site "dedicated to providing straight talk about wood pallets" in order to lobby for using plastic pallets to ship goods from country to country. In a graphic warning against bugs from wood pallets infesting trees in the New York City area, the group uses a poster to present alarming data from various government sites and to suggest how the trees might be saved.

Highly charged headline identifies a problem.

A map displays the growth of the beetle infestation.

Three specific solutions are offered.

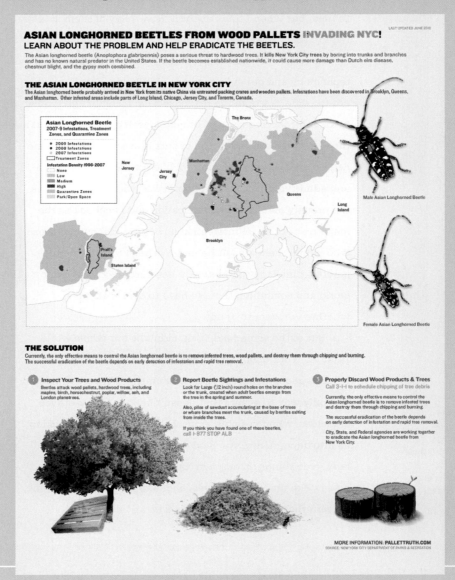

1. **Trial Balloon:** In calling for reducing the drinking age, Barrett Seaman's "How Bingeing Became the New College Sport" (p. 179) offers a solution to alcohol abuse that some might call "politically incorrect" — lowering the drinking age. Indeed, many politicians or school officials would likely be reluctant to support such a proposal — even if it might make people more responsible. Choose an issue that you think needs as radical a rethinking as college-age drinking, and write a research-based proposal of your own. Like Seaman, be sure to offer your ideas in language calm and persuasive enough to make responsible adults at least consider them.

2. **Formal Proposal:** Although Donald Lazere cites many studies to support his proposal for a formal curriculum in civic literacy, he likely was prompted to write "A Core Curriculum for Civic Literacy" (p. 192) by his experiences as a teacher for many years. Drawing on your own observations and experiences, identify a specific problem on your campus or in the local community. Research the issue thoroughly, using both human resources and materials such as college manuals and policies, campus newspapers, official records, reports, and so on. Come up with a plausible approach to the problem, and then write a proposal directed to a person or group with the power to deal with it. Use the formal, academic style of Lazere's essay as a model. Be sure to document your sources.

3. **Manifesto:** You likely identify with at least some of the issues Katelyn Vincent presents in "Technology Time-out" (p. 198) and with the manifesto she enunciates in her final paragraphs. Look for a problem that others might similarly recognize, describe the issue in enough detail to explain why adjustments may be necessary or desirable, and then make a compelling call for change.

4. **Visual Proposal:** The designers of "Asian Longhorned Beetles from Wood Pallets Invading NYC!" (p. 204) may have an agenda (selling plastic pallets), but their visual proposal provides useful information and a plan of action. Create a visual proposal of your own that does the same.

5. **Your Choice:** Proposals are usually practical documents, serving a specific need. Identify such a need in your life and address it through a clear, fact-based proposal. For example, you might write to your academic advisor or dean suggesting that a service-learning experience would be a better senior project for you than writing a traditional thesis — given your talents and interests. Or perhaps you might write to a banker (or wealthy relative) explaining why loaning you money to open a barbecue restaurant would make sound fiscal sense, especially since no one else in town serves decent brisket and ribs. In other words, write a paper to make your life better.

How to start
- Need to **find a text to analyze**? See page 217.
- Need to come up with **ideas**? See page 220.
- Need to **organize your ideas**? See page 226.

7 Literary Analyses

respond critically to cultural works

Unless you're an English major, the papers you write for Literature 101 may seem as mechanical as chemistry lab reports—something done just to get a degree. But hardly a day goes by when you don't respond strongly to some literary or cultural experience, sharing your insights and opinions about the books, music, and entertainment you love. It's worth learning to do this well.

LITERARY INTERPRETATION	After discussing Rudolfo Anaya's novel *Bless Me, Ultima* with classmates in a contemporary novels course, you write a *literary interpretation* of the work, arguing that it fits into the category of mythic coming-of-age story.
CLOSE READING	Unconvinced by a teacher's casual suggestion that the Anglo-Saxon author of "The Wanderer" (c. tenth century CE) was experiencing what we now call "alienation," you write a *close reading* of the poem to show why the modern concept doesn't suit the poem.
CULTURAL ANALYSIS	You've probably spent too many seasons watching the evolution of TV crime dramas that focus on detailed forensic analysis of victims—from *CSI* to *Bones*. But you use your knowledge to prepare a *cultural analysis* of these shows for a rhetoric class, suggesting that the programs subtly reinforce the public's faith in technology and science.
PHOTOGRAPHS AS LITERARY TEXTS	Rather than roll your eyes like your companions, you take abstract art seriously. So you study Kayla Mohammadi's painting (on p. 207), and then write a *visual analysis* to explain what you see in the work to someone who "doesn't get it."

DECIDING TO WRITE A LITERARY ANALYSIS.   In a traditional literary analysis, you respond to a poem, novel, play, or short story. That response can be analytical, looking at theme, plot, structure, characters, genre, style, and so on. Or it can be critical, theoretical, or evaluative—locating works within their social, political, historic, and even philosophic neighborhoods. Or you might approach a literary work expressively, describing how you connect with it intellectually and emotionally. Or you can combine these approaches or imagine alternative ones—perhaps reflecting new attitudes and assumptions about media.

Other potential genres for analysis include films, TV offerings, popular music, comic books, and games. ○ Distinctions between high and popular culture have not so much dissolved as ceased to be interesting. After all, you can say dumb things about *Hamlet* and smart things about *Mad Men*. Moreover, every genre of artistic expression—from sonnets to opera to graphic novels—at some point struggled for respectability. What matters is the quality of a literary analysis and whether you help readers appreciate

Red Tide—Maine by Kayla Mohammadi
The artist explains that "the intention is not literal portrayal, but rather a visual translation. A translation based on color, value, and space."

choose a genre
p. 390

the novel *Pride and Prejudice* or, maybe, the video game *Red Dead Redemption*. Expect your literary or cultural analyses to do *some* of the following.

Begin with a close reading.   In an analysis, you slow the pace at which people in a 24/7 world typically operate to look deliberately and closely at a text. You might study the way individual words and images connect in a poem, how plot evolves in a novel, or how complex editing defines the character of a movie. In short, you think about the *calculated* choices writers and artists make in creating their work. O

Make a claim or an observation.   Your encounter with a text will ordinarily lead to a thesis. The claim won't always be argumentative or controversial: You may be amazed at the simplicity of Wordsworth's Lucy poems or blown away by Jimi Hendrix's take on "All Along the Watchtower." But more typically, you'll make a statement or an observation that you believe is worth proving either by research or, just as often in college papers, by evidence from within the work itself.

Present works in context.   Works of art exist in our real world; that's what we like about them and why they sometimes change our lives. Your analysis can explore these relationships among texts, people, and society.

Draw on previous research.   Your response to a work need not agree with what others have written. But you should be willing to learn from previous scholarship and criticism—readily available in libraries or online. O

Use texts for evidence.   A compelling analysis unwraps the complexities of a book, movie, poem, drama, or song, explaining it so that readers might better appreciate what they did not notice before. In short, direct them to the neat stuff. For that reason, the well-chosen quotation is the mighty tool of successful literary papers. In your reading, mark any passages that strike you as memorable or important and keep track of them for later use.

read closely
p. 365

plan a project
p. 466

In "Authentic Beauty in Morrison's *The Bluest Eye*," Kelsi Stayart assembles ample evidence both from the text of a novel and from library research to show that the book affirms a new definition of beauty for African American women. Notice, too, that she places Toni Morrison's first novel within the context of its time — an era of important social change.

Stayart 1

Kelsi Stayart

Professor Samuels

E314L Reading Women Writers

May 8, 20--

Authentic Beauty in Morrison's *The Bluest Eye*

In *The Bluest Eye* (1970), novelist Toni Morrison critiques the ideals of beauty that cause racial self-loathing and, in the case of lead-character Pecola Breedlove, mental ruin. Beauty, as Morrison states, is "Probably the most destructive [of] ideas in the history of human thought" (122). However, within Morrison's scathing denunciation of conventional ideals of beauty is a subtle counterdiscourse; she suggests a new concept of beauty that goes beyond white skin, straight hair, and blue eyes. Through her diction, Toni Morrison embraces an authentically African American aesthetic in *The Bluest Eye* by creating a positive connotation for traditionally negative black characteristics.[1]

Morrison suggests an authentic and natural notion of beauty through her word choice in the description of her own

[1] I use the term "black" interchangeably with "African American" throughout this paper. However, my use of the term "black" reflects its usage in my historical research on the Black Power movement of the 1960s, as well as the text.

In a clear thesis sentence, Stayart makes the claim that the rest of the paper will develop.

Stayart 2

body given by Claudia MacTeer, who narrates parts of the
story. When Claudia remarks, "We felt comfortable in our skins,
enjoyed the news that our senses released to us, admired our
dirt, cultivated our scars," the reader notices Claudia's
contentment with her natural, African American characteristics
(Morrison 74). Words like "dirt" and "cultivated" carry an
earthy, natural connotation that stresses Claudia's real and
authentic beauty. The verbs in this passage give a positive tone
to characteristics usually considered unappealing: "admired
our dirt" and "cultivated our scars." Critic Mermann-Jozwiak
comments that "Claudia experiences pleasure in her body," as
is evident in words like "comfortable" and "admired" (199).
Claudia's contentment with her body exemplifies an
appreciation of black physical attributes; this attitude reflects
that of the Black Power movement of the 1960s, in which
African Americans were attempting to "embrace their African
heritage and challenge white domination by reversing notions
of beauty" (Spencer 970). This cultural return to an authentic
black aesthetic resembles Claudia's pride in her natural
characteristics. Morrison expands on this idea of appreciating
the natural by her depictions of dirtiness as a desirable and
down-to-earth characteristic.

In *The Bluest Eye*, Morrison embraces *dirtiness* as
authentic and natural by altering the standard connotation of
cleanliness. After establishing the typical associations between

Important characters are identified, even though the audience for the paper would be familiar with the novel.

Sources are cited to add more evidence and back up claims.

Transition at the end of this paragraph introduces the theme of the paragraph that follows.

Stayart 3

African Americans and dirt, she portrays cleanliness as synthetic and dirtiness as natural. For example, when Geraldine, a socially self-conscious black woman, encounters Pecola, she criticizes the girl's dirty appearance, "the dirty torn dress . . . the muddy shoes . . . the soiled socks . . . hair uncombed . . . shoes untied and caked with dirt" (Morrison 91-92). The reader understands that this idea of dirtiness is associated with African Americans when Geraldine thinks, "She had seen this girl all her life. . . . They were everywhere" (91-92). The word choice of this passage emphasizes dirtiness as a physical characteristic of Pecola and, by extension, African Americans. However, Morrison combats this derogatory stereotype by embracing dirtiness and devaluing cleanliness as sterile and undesirable. For example, Claudia describes, "a hateful bath in a galvanized zinc tub . . . the scratchy towels and the dreadful and humiliating absence of dirt. The irritable, unimaginative cleanliness. Gone the ink marks from legs and face, all my creations and accumulations of the day gone" (22). Morrison's diction here is ironic because she criticizes cleanliness as "scratchy," "hateful," "irritable," and "unimaginative" and the lack of dirt as "humiliating." Claudia describes her dirtiness as "creations and accumulations," which emphasizes the relationship of dirtiness to real life. Moreover, the use of "irritable" directly contrasts with the earlier phrase, "comfortable in our skins."

Throughout the paper, Stayart supports her claims with quotations from the novel.

The paper carefully examines the diction of the novel.

Stayart 4

Morrison embraces dirtiness as a natural physical attribute to uplift a stereotypically negative black characteristic. By devaluing cleanliness, Morrison portrays this supposed ideal as sterile and artificial. Similarly, she negatively depicts a white baby doll given to Claudia as synthetic and lifeless to reflect her preference for the authentic.

A second major point contrasts synthetic and real beauty in the novel.

By describing the blue-eyed baby doll as synthetic and artificial, Morrison is also able to devalue the ideal and uplift the real, living child of Pecola. Claudia imagines Pecola's baby with a "flared nose, kissing-thick lips, and the living, breathing silk of black skin" (Morrison 190). Racist exaggerations of African American features are countered here by the adjective "kissing-thick," which embraces the beauty of "black lips" (Spencer 969). "Living" and "breathing" similarly emphasize the lifelike authenticity of the black baby's skin. The positive connotations of "silk" reclaim the dark skin tone ordinarily used to subjugate and oppress African Americans. Claudia's description of Pecola's baby directly contrasts to her earlier, positive thoughts about her white doll. Comparing Pecola's infant to the doll, she notes, "No synthetic yellow bangs suspended over marble-blue eyes" (Morrison 190). She also notes that the doll's "hard unyielding limbs resisted my flesh . . . irritated any embrace" (20). Her depiction of the doll stresses that the blonde-haired, blue-eyed ideal of beauty is actually sterile, lifeless, and cold. In contrast, the black baby is a living body.

Stayart 5

A third major point follows carefully from the preceding one, helping to connect the argument.

Morrison extends this idea of a lifelike aesthetic by her sensual descriptions in the novel of African American females, showing appreciation for a realistic beauty that incorporates more than just the visual. Likewise, Mermann-Jozwiak notes that Morrison argues for a sensual beauty by "dislodging vision from its dominant position and emphasizing the role of the whole sensorium" (199-200). Morrison develops the idea of sensual beauty with her description of the youth of Cholly's elderly aunts:

> The odor of their armpits and haunches had mingled into a lovely musk; their eyes had been furtive, their lips relaxed, and the delicate turn of their heads on those slim black necks had been like nothing other than a doe's. Their laughter had been more touch than sound. (138)

In MLA style, quotations longer than three lines are indented.

The description of their odor as "a lovely musk" exemplifies an appreciation for physical characteristics that are natural, authentic, and atypically used to describe beauty. The comparison to a doe allows Morrison to highlight the grace and beauty in the women's mannerisms. Moreover, her description of their laughter as a "touch" builds upon this idea of defining beauty beyond visual terms. In this passage, Morrison creates an idea of beauty that stresses pride in black attributes that sets them apart from the "European standard of beauty" (Spencer 969).

Stayart 6

In the novel, Morrison also harshly critiques those who, like her character Geraldine, have denied their black authenticity and conformed to white standards. In Geraldine, Morrison creates a woman who represents the antisensual, her diction emphasizing the sterility of those who reject the authentic. The characterization of Geraldine moves from the general to the specific, stressing what she fears about her racial character:

> Wherever it erupts, this Funk, they wipe it away; where it crusts, they dissolve it; where it drips, flowers or clings, they find it and fight it until it dies. They fight this battle all the way to the grave. The laugh that is a little too loud; the enunciation a little too round; the gesture a little too generous. They hold their behind in for fear of a sway too free; when they wear lipstick, they never cover the entire mouth for fear of lips too thick, and they worry, worry, worry about the edges of their hair. (Morrison 83)

The words "wipe it away" and "dissolve" emphasize the cleansing of racial characteristics. The laugh, gestures, and lips of women like Geraldine are carefully controlled to avoid any hint of racial authenticity; in "worry, worry, worry" about their hair, Morrison references the practice of hair relaxation to mimic the standard white straight hair (Spencer 970). Morrison's move

The focus shifts to a character who resists the standard of beauty Morrison has defined in the novel. By undercutting Geraldine, Morrison also undercuts the ideas the character represents.

Stayart 7

against conforming to white standards again reflects the Black Power movement of the time, which called for racial pride and embraced "black culture as something unique, different and compelling" (Kuryla 115). During the 1960s, black models began to sport natural hairstyles and women were urged to "reject all white-oriented styles and to appreciate that 'black is beautiful'" (Wilson). Stokely Carmichael, a Black Power activist, stated, "We have to stop being ashamed of being black. A broad nose, a thick lip and nappy hair is us, and we are going to call that beautiful . . . we are not going to fry our hair anymore" (Spencer 971). Clearly, Morrison's criticism in *The Bluest Eye* reflects a general discourse during the 1960s that focused on a newfound appreciation for uniquely black qualities. Morrison's condemnation of Geraldine reflects the movement that called for African American women to "throw away their straightening combs" (Wilson). Through Geraldine, Morrison argues for black women to stop taming their natural appearances and appreciate the features that make them unique.

In *The Bluest Eye*, Morrison critiques white ideals of beauty by her celebration of African American features that had long been condemned as ugly. Her language and diction carefully argue for ethnic authenticity and an appreciation for one's natural characteristics. Morrison dares to imagine, in her novel, an authentic beauty that embraces the unique, distinctive, and genuine aspects of a woman.

Stayart sets her observations about the novel into a historical context.

The concluding paragraph efficiently summarizes the theme of the paper.

Stayart 8

Works Cited

Kuryla, Peter. "Black Consciousness." *Encyclopedia of African
American Society*. Ed. Gerald D. Jaynes. Vol. 1. Thousand
Oaks: Sage, 2005. 114-16. *Gale Virtual Reference Library*.
Gale. Web. 23 Apr. 2009.

Mermann-Jozwiak, Elisabeth. "Re-Membering the Body:
Body Politics in Toni Morrison's *The Bluest Eye*." *Lit:
Literature Interpretation Theory* 12.2 (June 2001):
189-203. *MLA International Bibliography*. EBSCO. Web.
22 Apr. 2009.

Morrison, Toni. *The Bluest Eye*. New York: Vintage, 2007.
Print.

Spencer, Robyn. "Hair and Beauty Culture in the United
States." *Encyclopedia of African-American Culture and
History*. Ed. Colin A. Palmer. 2nd ed. Vol. 3. Detroit:
Macmillan, 2006. 969-73. *Gale Virtual Reference Library*.
Gale. Web. 27 Apr. 2009.

Wilson, Jean Sprain. "Negro Models Capitalize on Their
African Heritage." *Los Angeles Times (1886-Current File)*.
20 Aug. 1968, f4. *ProQuest Historical Newspapers Los
Angeles Times (1881-1986)*.ProQuest. Web. 27 Apr. 2009.

Exploring purpose and topic

In most cases, you write a literary analysis to meet a course requirement, a paper usually designed to improve your skills as a reader of literature and art. Such a lofty goal, however, doesn't mean you can't enjoy the project or put your own spin on it.

find a text ◄

Your first priority is to read any assignment sheet closely to find out exactly what you are supposed to do. Underline any key words in the project description and take them seriously. Typically you will see terms such as *compare and contrast, classify, analyze,* or *interpret*. They mean different things.

Once you know your purpose in writing an analysis, you may have to choose a subject. ○ It's not unusual to have a work assigned (*Three pages on* The House on Mango Street *by Friday*), but more typically, you'll be able to select works to study from within a range defined by a course title or unit: British sci-fi; Puritan sermons; Native American literature since 1920. Which should you choose?

Choose a text you connect with.   It makes sense to spend time writing about works that move you, perhaps by touching on an aspect of your life or identity. You may feel more confident commenting on them because of who you are and what you've experienced.

Choose a text you want to learn more about.   In the back of their minds, most people have lists of works and artists they've always wanted to read or explore. So use an assignment as an opportunity to sample one of them: *Beowulf; The Chronicles of Narnia*; or the work of William Gibson, Leslie Marmon Silko, or the Clash. Or use an assignment to venture beyond works within your comfort zone: Examine writers and artists from different cultures and with challenging points of view.

Choose a text that you don't understand.   Most writers tend to write about works that are immediately accessible and relatively new: Why struggle with a hoary epic poem when you can just watch *The Lord of the Rings* on DVD? One obvious reason may be to figure out how works from different eras can still be powerfully connected to our own; the very strangeness of older and more difficult texts may even prompt you to ask more provocative questions. In short, you'll pay more attention to literary texts that place demands on you.

Stills from *Smoke Signals* (1998) and *Bury My Heart at Wounded Knee* (2007)   How much do you know about Native American fiction or film? Use an assignment as an opportunity to learn more.

get an idea
p. 356

217

Understanding your audience

Unless you write book reviews or essays for a campus literary magazine, the people reading your analyses of works of art and culture are likely a professor and other students in your course. But in either situation, assume a degree of expertise among your readers. Moreover, many people will examine a literary analysis simply because they're interested—a tremendous advantage. So be sure to respect the needs of your audience.

Clearly identify the author and works you are analyzing.   Seems like common sense, but this courtesy is often neglected in academic papers precisely because writers assume that *the teacher must know what I'm doing.* Don't make this mistake. Also briefly recap what happens in the works you are analyzing—especially with texts not everyone has read recently. ○ Follow the model of good reviewers, who typically summarize key elements before commenting on them. Such summaries give readers their bearings at the beginning of a paper. Here's James Wood introducing a novel by Marilynne Robinson that he will be reviewing for the *New York Times.*

> *Gilead* is set in 1956 in the small town of Gilead, Iowa, and is narrated by a seventy-six-year-old pastor named John Ames, who has recently been told he has angina pectoris and believes he is facing imminent death. In this terminal spirit, he decides to write a long letter to his seven-year-old son, the fruit of a recent marriage to a much younger woman. This novel is that letter, set down in the easy, discontinuous form of a diary, mixing long and short entries, reminiscences, moral advice, and so on.

Define key terms.   Many specialized and technical expressions are used in a literary analysis. Your instructor will know what an *epithet, peripeteia,* or *rondel* might be, but you may still have to define terms like these for a wider audience—your classmates, for instance. Alternatively, you can look for more familiar synonyms and expressions.

sum up ideas
p. 491

Don't aim to please professional critics.   Are you tempted to imitate the style of serious academic theorists you've encountered while researching your paper? No need—your instructor probably won't expect you to write in that way, at least not until graduate school.

Your Turn   In "Authentic Beauty in Morrison's *The Bluest Eye*" (p. 209), Kelsi Stayart summarizes the novel only minimally. What issues of audience might explain the exclusion of plot details from her paper, written for a college course in a sophomore-level class? Would *you* have appreciated more details about story and character—as a member of an audience Stayart could *not* have anticipated when she wrote her piece? Why or why not? Use your analysis of her paper and her original audience to guide your own choices in writing a literary analysis.

Finding and developing materials

▶ develop ideas

With an assignment in hand and works to analyze, the next step—and it's a necessary one—is to establish that you have a reliable "text" of whatever you'll be studying. In a course, a professor may assign a particular edition or literary anthology for you to use, making your job easier.

This Bedford/St. Martin's edition of *Frankenstein* provides important textual information and background. Look for texts with such material when studying classic novels, poems, and plays.

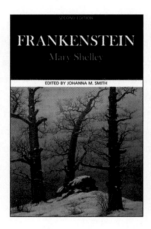

Be aware that many texts are available in multiple editions. (For instance, the novel *Frankenstein* first appeared in 1818, but the revised third edition of 1831 is the one most widely read today.) For classical works, such as the plays of Shakespeare, choose an edition from a major publisher, preferably one that includes thorough notes and perhaps some essays and criticism. When in doubt, ask your professor which texts to use. Don't just browse the library shelves.

Other kinds of media pose interesting problems as well. For instance, you may have to decide which version of a movie to study—the one seen by audiences in theaters or the "director's cut" on a DVD. Similarly, you might find multiple recordings of musical works: Look for widely respected performances. Even popular music may come in several versions: studio (*American Idiot*), live (*Bullet in a Bible*), alternative recording (*American Idiot: The Original Broadway Cast Recording*). Then there is the question of drama: Do you read a play on the page, watch a video when one is available, or see it in a theater? Perhaps you do all three. But whatever versions of a text you choose for study, be sure to identify them in your project, either in the text itself or on the works cited page. ○

understand citation styles p. 501

Establishing a text is the easy part. How then do you find something specific to write about, an angle on the subject? ○ Try the following strategies and approaches.

Examine the text closely.   Guided by your assignment, begin your project by closely reading, watching, or examining the selected work(s) and taking notes. Obviously, you'll treat some works differently than others. You can read a Seamus Heaney sonnet a dozen times to absorb its nuances, but it's unlikely you'd push through Rudolfo Anaya's novel *Bless Me, Ultima* more than once or twice for a paper. But, in either case, you'll need a suitable way to take notes or to annotate what you're analyzing.

Honestly, you should count on a minimum of two readings or viewings of any text, the first to get familiar with the work and find a potential approach, the second and subsequent readings to confirm your thesis and to find supporting evidence for it.

Focus on the text itself.   Your earliest literature papers probably tackled basic questions about plot, character, setting, theme, and language. But these are not simple matters—just the kinds of issues that fascinate most readers. You might, for example, look for moments when the plot of the novel you're examining reinforces its theme or study how characters change in response to specific events. Even the setting of a short story or film might be worth writing about when it becomes a factor in the story: Can you imagine the film *Casablanca* taking place in any other location? In how many books, TV shows, and films is New York City a virtual character?

Questions about language loom large in many analyses. How does word choice work with or against the subject of a poem? Does the style of a novel reinforce its story? How does a writer create irony through diction or dialogue? Indeed, any feature of a work might be researched and studied, from the narrators in novels to the rhyme schemes in poetry.

Focus on its meanings, themes, and interpretations.   Although finding themes or meanings in literary works seems like an occupation mostly for English majors, the tendency is actually universal and irresistible. If you take any work seriously, you'll discover angles and ideas worth sharing with readers.

find a topic
p. 356

Maybe *Seinfeld* is a modern version of *Everyman*, or *O Brother, Where Art Thou?* is a retelling of the *Odyssey* by Homer, or maybe not. Open your mind to possible connections: What have you seen like this before? What patterns do you detect? What images recur in the text or what ideas are supported or undercut?

Focus on its authorship and history.   Some artists stand apart from their creations, while others cannot be separated from them. So you might explore in what ways a work reflects the life, education, and attitudes of its author. What psychological forces or religious perspectives might be detected in particular characters or themes? Is the author writing to represent his or her gender, race, ethnicity, or class? Or does the work repudiate its author's identity, class, or religion?

Similarly, consider how a text embodies the assumptions, attitudes, politics, fashions, and even technology of the times during which it was composed. A work as familiar as Jonathan Swift's "A Modest Proposal" still requires readers to know at least a *little* about Irish and English politics in the eighteenth century. How does Swift's satire open up when you learn even more about its world?

Focus on its genre.   Literary genres are formulas. Take a noble hero, give him a catastrophic flaw, have him make a bad choice, and then kill him off: That's tragedy—or, in the wrong hands, melodrama. With a little brainstorming, you could identify dozens of genres and subcategories: epics, sonnets, historical novels, superhero comics, grand opera, soap opera, and so on. Artists' works often fall between genres, sometimes creating new ones. Readers, too, bring clear-cut expectations to a text: Try to turn a 007 action-spy thriller into a three-hankie chick flick, and you've got trouble in River City.

You can analyze genre in various ways. For instance, track a text backward to discover its literary forebears—the works that influenced its author. Even texts that revolt against previous genres bear traces of what they have rejected. It's also possible to study the way artists combine different genres or play with or against the expectations of audiences. Needless to say, you can also explore the relationships of works within a genre. In fact, it's often a shared genre that makes comparisons interesting or provocative. For example, what do twentieth-century coming-of-age stories such as *A Separate Peace*, *The Catcher in the Rye*, and *Lord of the Flies* have in common?

Focus on its influence.   Some works have an obvious impact on life or society, changing how people think or behave: *Uncle Tom's Cabin*, *To Kill a Mockingbird*, *Roots*, *Schindler's List*. TV shows have broadened people's notions of family; musical genres such as jazz and gospel have created and sustained entire communities.

But impact doesn't always occur on such a grand scale or express itself through social movements. Books influence other books, films other films, and so on—with not a few texts crossing genres. Who could have foreseen all the ties between comic books in the 1930s, TV shows in the 1950s, superhero films in the 1980s, and video games in the new century? And, for better or worse, books, movies, and other cultural productions influence styles, fashions, and even the way people speak. Consider *Clueless*, *High School Musical*, or *Glee*. You may have to think outside the box, but projects that trace and study influence can shake things up.

Focus on its social connections.   In recent decades, many texts have been studied for what they reveal about relationships between genders, races, ethnicities, and social classes. Works by new writers are now more widely read in schools, and hard questions are asked about texts traditionally taught: What do they reveal about the treatment of women or minorities? Whose lives have been ignored in dominant texts, or how are minorities or working classes represented? What responsibility do cultural texts have for maintaining repressive political or social arrangements? These critical approaches have changed how many people view literature and art, and you can follow up on such studies and extend them to texts you think deserve more attention. Such inquiries themselves, however, are as driven by political and social agendas as other kinds of analysis and so should also be subjected to the same critical scrutiny.

Find good sources.   Developing a literary paper provides you with many opportunities and choices. Fortunately, you needn't make all your decisions on your own. Ample commentary and research is available on almost any literary subject or method, both in print and online. ○ Your instructor and local librarians can help you focus on the best resources for your project, but the following boxes list some possibilities.

refine your search
p. 472

Literary Resources in Print

Abrams, M. H., and Geoffrey Harpham. *A Glossary of Literary Terms*. 9th ed. New York: Wadsworth, 2008.

Beacham, Walton, ed. *Research Guide to Biography and Criticism*. Washington: Research, 1986.

Birch, Dinah, ed. *The Oxford Companion to English Literature*. 7th ed. Oxford: Oxford UP, 2009.

Crystal, David. *The Cambridge Encyclopedia of Language*. 3rd ed. New York: Cambridge UP, 2010.

Encyclopedia of World Literature in the 20th Century. 3rd ed. Farmington Hills: St. James, 1999.

Gates, Henry Louis, Jr., et al. *The Norton Anthology of African American Literature*. 2nd ed. New York: Norton, 2003.

Gilbert, Sandra M., and Susan Gubar. *The Norton Anthology of Literature by Women: The Traditions in English*. 3rd ed. New York: Norton, 2007.

Harmon, William, and Hugh Holman. *A Handbook to Literature*. 11th ed. New York: Prentice, 2008.

Harner, James L. *Literary Research Guide: A Guide to Reference Sources for the Study of Literature in English and Related Topics*. 5th ed. New York: MLA, 2008.

Hart, James D. *The Oxford Companion to American Literature*. 6th ed. New York: Oxford UP, 1995.

Howatson, M. C. *The Oxford Companion to Classical Literature*. 2nd ed. New York: Oxford UP, 2006.

Leitch, Vincent, et al. *The Norton Anthology of Theory and Criticism*. 2nd ed. New York: Norton, 2010.

Preminger, Alex, and T. V. F. Brogan, eds. *The New Princeton Encyclopedia of Poetry and Poetics*. Princeton: Princeton UP, 1993.

Sage, Lorna. *The Cambridge Guide to Women's Writing in English*. Cambridge: Cambridge UP, 1999.

Literary Resources Online

Annual Bibliography of English Language and Literature (ABELL) (subscription)

Atlantic Unbound (http://www.theatlantic.com) (for culture and reviews)

Browne Popular Culture Library (http://www.bgsu.edu/colleges/library/pcl)

The Complete Works of William Shakespeare (http://thetech.mit.edu/Shakespeare)

Eserver.org: Accessible Writing (http://eserver.org)

A Handbook of Rhetorical Devices (http://www.virtualsalt.com/rhetoric.htm)

Images: A Journal of Film and Popular Culture (http://www.imagesjournal.com/)

Internet Public Library: Literary Criticism (http://www.ipl.org/div/litcrit/)

Literary Resources on the Net (http://andromeda.rutgers.edu/~jlynch/Lit)

Literature Resource Center (Gale Group – subscription)

MIT Libraries: Literature Resources (http://libraries.mit.edu/guides/subjects/literature/)

MLA on the Web (http://www.mla.org)

New York Review of Books (http://www.nybooks.com/)

New York Times Book Review (http://www.nytimes.com/pages/books)

The Online Books Page (http://onlinebooks.library.upenn.edu)

VoS: Voice of the Shuttle (http://vos.ucsb.edu/)

Yahoo! Arts: Humanities: Literature (http://dir.yahoo.com/arts/humanities/literature/)

Creating a structure

▶ organize ideas

The shape of your literary analysis evolves as you learn more about your topic and decide how to treat it. Your project takes on the character of a report if you're interested in sharing information or demonstrating a case. Or it becomes an argument if your thesis veers toward a controversial position. ○ Whatever its trajectory, give attention to certain features.

Focus on a particular observation, claim, or point.   Always have a point firmly in mind as you draft a project, whether you work with individual literary texts or more general cultural questions. Consider the following examples of claims or points that literary analyses might explore.

STUDY OF THEME

In *Bless Me, Ultima*, the youngster Antonio has to find a way to reconcile his traditional values and mystical beliefs with Ultima's prediction that he will become a "man of learning."

CONTRAST OF GENRES

The movie version of Annie Proulx's short story "Brokeback Mountain" actually improves on the original work, making it more powerful, specific, and believable.

CULTURAL ANALYSIS

One likely impact of digital technology will be to eliminate the barriers between art, entertainment, and commerce—with books becoming films, films morphing into games, and games inspiring graphic art.

Imagine a structure.   Here are three simple forms a literary analysis might take, the first developing from a thesis stated early on, the second comparing two works to make a point, and the third building toward a conclusion rather than opening with a thesis. ○

> **Introduction leading to a claim**
>
> > **First supporting reason + textual evidence**
> > **Second supporting reason + textual evidence**
> > **Additional supporting reasons + textual evidence**
>
> **Conclusion**

understand argument
p. 72

develop a statement
p. 393

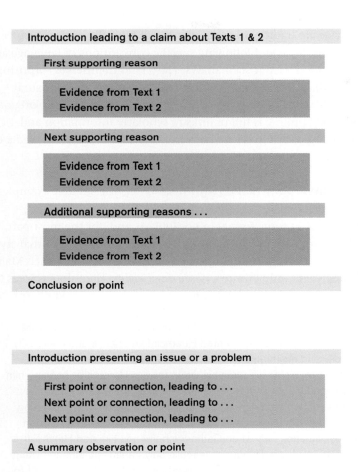

Introduction leading to a claim about Texts 1 & 2

First supporting reason

Evidence from Text 1
Evidence from Text 2

Next supporting reason

Evidence from Text 1
Evidence from Text 2

Additional supporting reasons . . .

Evidence from Text 1
Evidence from Text 2

Conclusion or point

Introduction presenting an issue or a problem

First point or connection, leading to . . .
Next point or connection, leading to . . .
Next point or connection, leading to . . .

A summary observation or point

Work on your opening. Be certain that your introductory sections
provide background for your analysis and identify what works you may be
examining, and what you hope to accomplish. ○ Provide enough context so
that the project stands on its own and would make sense to someone other
than the instructor who assigned it.

shape a beginning
p. 420

Choosing a style and design

Literary analyses are traditional assignments still typically done on paper using an academic style and following specific conventions of language and MLA documentation. ○ But such analyses also lend themselves surprisingly well to new media, especially when their topics focus on video or aural texts—as Kelli Marshall's essay on *Glee* (p. 238) demonstrates. The original version, published online, is full of links to scholarly information and, probably more important, to video clips from the show. Style and media can be relevant issues in literary and cultural projects.

Use a formal style for most assignments. As the student examples in this chapter suggest, the literary analyses you write for courses will typically be serious in tone, formal in vocabulary, and, for the most part, impersonal—all markers of a formal or high style. ○ Elements of that style can be identified in this paragraph from an academic paper in which Manasi Deshpande analyzes Emily Brontë's *Wuthering Heights*. Here she explores the character of its Byronic hero, Heathcliff:

Examines Heathcliff from the perspective of a potential reader, not from her own.

Complex sentences smoothly incorporate quotations and documentation.

Related points are expressed in parallel clauses.

Vocabulary throughout is accessible, but formal. No contractions are used.

In witnessing Heathcliff's blatantly violent behavior, the reader is caught between sympathy for the tormented Heathcliff and shock at the intensity of his cruelty and mistreatment of others. Intent on avenging Hindley's treatment of him, Heathcliff turns his wrath toward Hareton by keeping him in such an uneducated and dependent state that young Cathy becomes "upset at the bare notion of relationship with such a clown" (193). Living first under Hindley's neglect and later under Heathcliff's wrath, Hareton escapes his situation only when Catherine befriends him and Heathcliff dies. In addition, Heathcliff marries Isabella only because Catherine wants to "'torture [him] to death for [her] amusement'" and must "'allow [him] to amuse [himself] a little in the same style'" (111). Heathcliff's sole objective in seducing and running away with Isabella is to take revenge on Catherine for abandoning him. Heathcliff's sadism is so strong that he is willing to harm innocent third parties in order to punish those who have caused his misery. He even forces young Cathy and Linton to marry by locking them in Wuthering Heights and keeping Cathy from her dying father until she has married Linton, further illustrating his willingness to torture others out of spite and vengeance.

cite in MLA
p. 503

define your style
p. 432

Use a middle style for informal or personal papers.   Occasionally, for example, you may be asked to write brief essays called *position papers*, in which you record your immediate reactions to poems, short stories, or other readings. In these assignments, an instructor may expect to hear your voice and even encourage exploratory responses. Here is Cheryl Lovelady responding somewhat personally to a cultural text in a proposal to revive the Broadway musical *Fiddler on the Roof*:

> How can a play set in a small, tradition-bound Jewish village during the Russian Revolution be modernized? I would argue that *Fiddler on the Roof* is actually an apt portrayal of our own time. Throughout the show, the conflicted main character, Tevye, is on the brink of pivotal decisions. Perplexed by his daughters' increasingly modern choices, Tevye prays aloud, "Where do they think they are, America?" Tevye identifies America as a symbol of personal freedom — the antithesis of the tradition which keeps his life from being "as shaky as a fiddler on the roof." Forty years after the play's debut, America has become startlingly more like the Anatevka Tevye knows than the America he envisions. Post-9/11 America parallels Anatevka in a multitude of ways: political agendas ideologically separate the United States from most of the world; public safety and conventional wisdom are valued over individual freedoms; Americans have felt the shock of violence brought onto their own soil; minority groups are isolated or isolate themselves in closed communities; and societal taboos dictate whom people may marry.

Question focuses paragraph. Reply suggests strong personal opinion.

Basic style remains serious and quite formal: Note series of roughly parallel clauses that follow colon.

Describe action in the present tense.   Literary papers usually follow any number of stylistic conventions. In writing literary analyses, for example, you'll be doing plenty of summarizing and paraphrasing. In most cases, when you narrate the events in a story or poem, set the action in the present tense.

Provide dates for authors and literary works.   The first time you name authors or artists in a paper, give their dates of birth and death in parentheses. Similarly, provide a year of publication or release date for any major work you mention in your analysis.

> Joan Didion (b. 1934) is the author of *Play It as It Lays* (1970), *Slouching Towards Bethlehem* (1968), and *The Year of Magical Thinking* (2005).

A 1964 production of the musical *Fiddler on the Roof*.

Use appropriate abbreviations. An English or rhetoric major may want to own a copy of the *MLA Handbook for Writers of Research Papers* if for nothing more than its full chapter on abbreviations common in literary papers. Some of the abbreviations appear chiefly in notes and documentation; others make it easier to refer to very familiar texts; still others identify various parts and sections of literary works.

Follow conventions for quotations. In a literary paper, you'll be frequently citing passages from novels, short stories, and poems as well as quoting the comments of critics. All of these items need to be appropriately introduced and, if necessary, modified to fit smoothly into your sentences and paragraphs. O

Cite plays correctly. Plays are cited by act, scene, and line number. In the past, passages from Shakespeare were routinely identified using a combination of roman and arabic numerals. But more recently, MLA recommends arabic numerals only for such references.

FORMER STYLE

Hamlet's final words are "The rest is silence" (*Ham.* V.ii.358).

CURRENT STYLE

Hamlet's final words are "The rest is silence" (*Ham.* 5.2.358).

Explore alternative media. You can be creative with literary and cultural projects, depending on the tools and media available to you. O An oral presentation on a literary text can be handled impressively using presentation software such as PowerPoint or Prezi. When you want to show complex relationships between plot and character, you may find mind-mapping software of various kinds useful. And students have even used Google Maps to trace the physical locations or journeys in literary works as different as *The Aeneid* of Virgil and Cormac McCarthy's *The Road*. If your project is to be submitted in electronic form, you can, of course, incorporate photographs, images, or the spoken word into your project, as appropriate. "Appropriate" means that the media elements genuinely enrich your analysis.

use quotations
p. 497

go multimodal
p. 568

Examining models

In "Insanity: Two Women," Kanaka Sathasivan examines a poem (Emily Dickinson's "I felt a Funeral, in my Brain") and a short story (Charlotte Perkins Gilman's "The Yellow Wallpaper") to discover a disturbing common theme in the work of these two American women writers. The essay, written in a formal academic style, uses a structure that examines the works individually, drawing comparisons in a final paragraph. Note, in particular, how Sathasivan manages the close reading of the poem by Emily Dickinson, moving through it almost line by line to draw out its themes and meanings. Here's the text of "I felt a Funeral, in my Brain."

I felt a Funeral, in my Brain,
And Mourners to and fro
Kept treading – treading – till it seemed
That Sense was breaking through –

And when they all were seated,
A Service, like a Drum –
Kept beating – beating – till I thought
My Mind was going numb –

And then I heard them lift a Box
And creak across my Soul
With those same Boots of Lead, again,
Then Space – began to toll,

As all the Heavens were a Bell,
And Being, but an Ear,
And I, and Silence, some strange Race
Wrecked, solitary, here –

And then a Plank in Reason, broke,
And I dropped down, and down –
And hit a World, at every plunge,
And Finished knowing – then –

You can find the full text of "The Yellow Wallpaper" by searching online by the title. One such text is available at the University of Virginia Library Electronic Text Center: http://etext.virginia.edu/toc/modeng/public/GilYell.html.

Sathasivan 1

Kanaka Sathasivan

Professor Glotzer

English 102

March 3, 20--

Insanity: Two Women

The societal expectations of women in the late nineteenth century served to keep women demure, submissive, and dumb. Although women's rights had begun to improve as more people rejected these stereotypes, many women remained trapped in their roles because of the pressures placed on them by men. Their suppression had deep impacts not only on their lives but also on their art. At a time when women writers often published under male aliases to gain respect, two of America's well-known authors, Emily Dickinson (1830-1886) and Charlotte Perkins Gilman (1860-1935), both wrote disturbing pieces describing the spiritual and mental imprisonment of women. In verse, Dickinson uses a funeral as a metaphor for the silencing of women and the insanity it subsequently causes. Gilman's prose piece "The Yellow Wallpaper" (1899) gives us a firsthand look into the mental degradation of a suppressed woman. These two works use vivid sensory images and rhythmic narration to describe sequential declines into madness.

Works to be analyzed are set in context: late nineteenth century.

Identifies authors and sets works in thematic relationship.

States thesis for the comparison.

Sathasivan 2

In "I felt a Funeral, in my Brain" (first published in 1896), Dickinson outlines the stages of a burial ceremony, using them as metaphors for a silenced woman's departure from sanity. The first verse, the arrival of Mourners, symbolizes the imposition of men and society on her mind. They are "treading" "to and fro," breaking down her thoughts and principles, until even she is convinced of their ideas (Dickinson 3, 2). The Service comes next, representing the closure—the acceptance of fate. Her "Mind was going numb" as the sounds of the service force her to stop thinking and begin accepting her doomed life. These first two verses use repetition at parallel points as they describe the Mourners as "treading—treading" and the service as a drum "beating—beating" (Dickinson 3, 7). The repetition emphasizes the incessant insistence of men; they try to control threatening women with such vigor and persistence that eventually even the women themselves begin to believe men's ideas and allow their minds to be silenced.

As the funeral progresses, the Mourners carry her casket from the service. Here Dickinson describes how they scar her very Soul using the "same Boots of Lead" which destroyed her mind (Dickinson 11). From the rest of the poem, one can infer that the service took place inside a church, and the act of parting from a house of God places another level of finality on the loss of her spirituality. While the figures in the poem transport her, the church's chimes begin to ring, and, as if

> Offers close reading of Dickinson's poem.

Sathasivan 3

"all the Heavens were a Bell / And Being, but an Ear," the noise consumes her (Dickinson 13). In this tremendous sound, her voice finally dissolves forever; her race with Silence has ended, "Wrecked," and Silence has won (Dickinson 16). Finally, after the loss of her mind, her soul, and her voice, she loses her sanity as they lower her casket into the grave and bury her. She "hit a World, at every plunge, / And Finished knowing" (Dickinson 20). The worlds she hits represent further stages of psychosis, and she plunges deeper until she hits the bottom, completely broken.

With simple transition, turns to Gilman's short story.

Like Dickinson, Gilman in "The Yellow Wallpaper" also segments her character's descent into madness. The narrator of the story expresses her thoughts in a diary written while she takes a vacation for her health. Each journal entry represents another step toward insanity, and Gilman reveals the woman's psychosis with subtle hints and clues placed discreetly within the entries. These often take the form of new information about the yellow room the woman has been confined to, such as the peeled wallpaper or bite marks on the bedpost. The inconspicuous presentation of such details leads the reader to think that these artifacts have long existed, created by someone else, and only now does the narrator share them with us. "I wonder how it was done and who did it, and what they did it for," she says, speaking of a groove that follows the perimeter of the walls. Here, Gilman reuses specific words at

Sathasivan 4

crucial points in the narration to allude to the state of her character's mental health. In this particular example, both the narrator and the maid use the word "smooch" to describe, respectively, the groove in the wall and yellow smudges on the narrator's clothes. This repetition indicates that she created the groove in the room, a fact affirmed at the end of the story.

Gilman's narrator not only seems to believe other people have caused the damage she sees but also imagines a woman lives trapped within the paper, shaking the pattern in her attempts to escape. "I think that woman gets out in the daytime!" the narrator exclaims, recounting her memories of a woman "creeping" about the garden (Gilman 400, 401). Again, Gilman uses repetition to make associations for the reader as the narrator uses "creeping" to describe her own exploits. As in the previous example, the end of the story reveals that the woman in the paper is none other than the narrator, tricked by her insanity. This connection also symbolizes the narrator's oppression. The design of the wallpaper trapping the woman represents the spiritual bars placed on the narrator by her husband and doctor, who prescribes mental rest, forbidding her from working or thinking. Even the description of the room lends itself to the image of a dungeon or cell, with "barred" windows and "rings and things in the walls" (Gilman 392). Just as the woman escapes during the daytime, so too does the narrator, giving in to her sickness and disobeying her

Uses present tense to describe action in "The Yellow Wallpaper."

Sathasivan 5

husband by writing. Finally, like the woman in the paper breaking free, the narrator succumbs to her insanity.

Both Dickinson's and Gilman's works explore society's influence on a woman's mental health. Like Dickinson's character, Gilman's narrator has also been compelled into silence by a man. Although she knows she is sick, her husband insists it isn't so and that she, a fragile woman, simply needs to avoid intellectual stimulation. Like a Mourner, "treading—treading," he continually assures her he knows best and that she shouldn't socialize or work. This advice, however, only leads to further degradation as her solitude allows her to indulge her mental delusions. When the narrator attempts to argue with her husband, she is silenced, losing the same race as Dickinson's character.

In both these pieces, the characters remain mildly aware of their declining mental health, but neither tries to fight it. In Dickinson's poem, the woman passively observes her funeral, commenting objectively on her suppression and burial. Dickinson uses sound to describe every step, creating the feel of secondary sensory images—images that cannot create a picture alone and require interpretation to do so. Gilman's narrator also talks of her sickness passively, showing her decline only by describing mental fatigue. In these moments she often comments that her husband "loves [her] very dearly" and she usually accepts the advice he offers (Gilman

Draws attention to common themes and strategies in the two works.

Notes difference in technique between authors.

Sathasivan 6

396). Even on those rare occasions when she disagrees, she remains submissive and allows her suppression to continue. In contrast to Dickinson, Gilman uses visual images to create this portrait, describing most of all how the narrator sees the yellow wallpaper, an approach that allows insight into the narrator's mental state.

Both Dickinson and Gilman used their writing to make profound statements about the painful lives led by many women in the nineteenth century. Through repetition, metaphor, symbolism, and sensory images, both "I felt a Funeral, in my Brain" and "The Yellow Wallpaper" describe a woman's mental breakdown, as caused by societal expectations and oppression. The poetry and prose parallel one another and together give insight into a horrific picture of insanity.

Concludes that writers use similar techniques to explore a common theme in two very different works.

Sathasivan 7

Works Cited

Dickinson, Emily. "I felt a Funeral, in my Brain." *Concise Anthology of American Literature*. 5th ed. Ed. George McMichael. Upper Saddle River: Prentice, 2001. 1129. Print.

Gilman, Charlotte Perkins. "The Yellow Wallpaper." *The American Short Story and Its Writer, An Anthology*. Ed. Ann Charters. Boston: Bedford, 2000. 391-403. Print.

MLA documentation style used for in-text notes and works cited.

CULTURAL ANALYSIS   In "Show Musical Good, Paired Segments Better: *Glee*'s Unevenness Explained," Kelli Marshall uses the online academic forum FlowTV to present a detailed analysis of a problem she identifies in a popular television series. Her article includes traditional academic footnotes and documentation as well as images and charts in color and fully functioning links. Someone reading the item online can immediately access the various episodes of *Glee* that Marshall discusses in her argument.

FlowTV

Posted: January 16, 2010
From: Kelli Marshall, University of Toledo

Show Musical Good, Paired Segments Better: *Glee*'s Unevenness Explained

Opening paragraph provides background information on *Glee* necessary to understand its musical structure.

Before I explain why Fox's musical comedy-drama *Glee* often feels uneven, I'd like to point out what the show gets right. Principally, *Glee*'s creator, Ryan Murphy (*Nip/Tuck*), has adopted the most suitable musical subgenre for his project: the show musical.[1] Of the subgenres — fairy tale, folk, and show — the show musical, whose

Hey kids, let's put on a show (musical)!

numbers typically perform a purpose (e.g., auditions, rehearsals, performances), best caters to Murphy's objective that the cast doesn't "suddenly burst into song."[2] When the characters sing, Murphy claims, they will do so only when they are on stage practicing or performing, in the rehearsal classroom, or in a fantasy state (i.e., a performance in their head). Limiting the numbers to these situations, he believes, will make *Glee* "more accessible to people."[3]

 Glee may have assumed the best musical subgenre for its purpose, but the show doesn't always thrive within said subgenre. And people notice. For example, reviews of the first season swing frantically back and forth, from the show is "so funny, so bulging with vibrant characters" and "these performances are wonderful, . . . shaping a fully realized world" to this is "wildly incoherent" and "simply a mess." Much of this unevenness, I believe, boils down to Murphy's refusal to implement consistently one of the most important structural conventions of the musical genre: paired segments, evenly spaced thematic and/or sexual comparisons/oppositions underscored via setting, shot selection, music, dance, and personal style.[4] As Rick Altman explains, with musicals the viewer must "forget familiar notions of plot, psychological motivation, and causal relationships" and surrender instead to "simultaneity and similarity" (e.g., male/female, talented/inept, teacher/student, gay/straight, popular/ostracized).[5]

 At least three episodes of *Glee* feature uniform parallel segments: "Pilot," "Wheels," and "Journey." Significantly, these episodes are also the most highly praised of the season.[6] Unlike those which critics have panned or are divided over (e.g., "Hairography," "Once Upon A Mattress," "Home," "Funk"), these three carefully and consistently juxtapose individual characters and groups. For example, "Wheels" begins and ends with Artie (Kevin McHale) dancing in the school's auditorium, first by himself and then with his friends in

A footnote directs readers to evidence that critics prefer episodes of *Glee* with the structure that Marshall examines in this paper.

Marshall makes a clear and specific claim about the show to explain its perceived "unevenness."

Episodes with Paired Segments

<u>"Pilot"</u>

Rachel	"On My Own"	10m
Finn	"I Can't Fight This Feeling" / "Lovin', Touchin', Squeezin'"	20m
Rachel (et al)	"You're the One That I Want"	30m
Finn (et al)	"You're the One That I Want"	30m
Vocal Adrenaline	"Rehab"	40m
New Directions	"Don't Stop Believin'"	50m

<u>"Wheels"</u>

Artie	"Dancin' with Myself"	5m
Kurt	"Defying Gravity"	30m
Rachel	"Defying Gravity"	30m
Artie (et al)	"Proud Mary"	55m

<u>"Journey"</u>

New Directions	"Journey Mash-up"	12m
Vocal Adrenaline	"Bohemian Rhapsody"	20m
New Directions	"To Sir with Love" [to Schuester]	35m
Schuester	"Somewhere Over the Rainbow" [to New Directions]	55m

Not all that colorful, but at least consistent.

the glee club. Likewise, "Journey" contrasts the vocal and dance abilities of New Directions with that of its show-choir nemesis, Vocal Adrenaline, and then closes with another parallel segment: New Directions singing to their teacher/mentor, Mr. Schuester (Matthew Morrison) and Schuester returning the favor to his students (see table above). Through these parallel numbers, the characters develop and the viewer understands their growth.[7]

The first chart helps readers visualize the "paired segments" discussed in the previous paragraph.

What's more, the musical numbers in these three episodes are limited (unlike those in "The Power of Madonna," for instance) and spread evenly throughout. For example, like its show-musical predecessors *Singin' in the Rain* (Stanley Donen and Gene Kelly, 1952) and *The Band Wagon* (Vincente Minnelli, 1953), *Glee*'s "Pilot" features a song about every 10 minutes; moreover, "Wheels" positions its songs in a nearly perfect arc: one at the beginning, middle, and end. Finally, each of the numbers in these episodes serves a convincing purpose. For instance, in "Pilot," Rachel (Lea Michele) auditions for glee club with "On My Own," effectively informing the viewer she is both passionate about Broadway musicals and isolated in high school. Echoing this number, Finn (Cory Monteith) sings REO Speedwagon's "I Can't Fight This Feeling," conveying to us that although glee club isn't traditionally for football players, he won't be able to "fight the feeling" to join.

While "Pilot," "Wheels," and "Journey" achieve narrative and stylistic continuity via paired segments and purposeful performances, a large number of *Glee*'s episodes do not. As a result, the entire series can feel unbalanced, schizophrenic even. For example, the majority of the musical numbers in "Showmance," "Acafellas," "The Power of Madonna," and "Funk" may individually charm and/or entertain the viewer, but because they are detached from one another, they fail to form a coherent whole (see table p. 242). Admittedly, Sue Sylvester's (Jane Lynch) copycat performance of Madonna's "Vogue" is interesting and ambitious, but it has no corresponding number; hence, we do not fully understand what purpose it serves. The same goes for Schuester's weird flirtation with Sue ("Tell Me Something Good"), Rachel's cries over her love for Finn ("Take a Bow"), and Mercedes's (Amber Riley) fiery reaction to Kurt's (Chris Colfer) rejection of her ("Bust Your Windows"). Had Ryan Murphy et al. created musical numbers through which Sue, Finn, and Kurt

Marshall presents examples to explain why unpaired musical numbers don't work well.

Episodes without Paired Segments

"Showmance"

New Directions	"Gold Digger"
New Directions	"Push It"
Quinn (et al)	"Say a Little Prayer for Me"
Rachel	"It's Over Now"

"Acafellas"

Schuester (et al)	"Poison"
Vocal Adrenaline	"Mercy"
Mercedes	"Bust Your Windows"
Schuester (et al)	"I Wanna Sex You Up"

"The Power of Madonna"

Cheerios	"Ray of Light"
New Directions (girls)	"Express Yourself"
Rachel/Finn	"Borderline"/"Open Your Heart"
Sue Sylvester	"Vogue"
Couples (3)	"Like a Virgin"
Cheerios (Kurt/Mercedes)	"4 Minutes"
New Directions (guys)	"What It Feels Like for a Girl"
New Directions	"Like a Prayer"

"Funk"

Vocal Adrenaline	"Another One Bites the Dust"
Quinn	"It's a Man's Man's Man's World"
Puck/Mercedes	"Good Vibrations"
Will Schuester	"Tell Me Something Good"
Puck (et al)	"Loser"
New Directions	"Give Up the Funk"

More colors, more erratic.

The second chart helps readers visualize the contrast between *Glee* episodes with and without paired musical segments.

could reciprocate their feelings, rather than using snippets of dialogue or in some cases silence, these episodes would likely feel more complete. In this genre, reacting to such emotional performances via dialogue alone generally doesn't cut it.[8]

In interviews, Murphy claims that with *Glee* he is creating a "post-modern musical" in the vein of *Chicago* (Rob Marshall, 2002) or *Moulin Rouge* (Baz Luhrmann, 2001). But what he ostensibly fails to realize is that these two films — while perhaps modern in look, themes, and style (editing in particular) — still conform to the structure of classical musicals, operating almost exclusively through doubling or paired segments.[9] Furthermore, Murphy admits that he bases *Glee*'s musical numbers on "stuff that I like and that I think fits the characters and moves the story along." On its surface this is perhaps fine, but since musical narratives — like all genres, television shows included — necessitate structure, that "stuff that Murphy likes" needs to be framed more consistently within matched scenes and sequences. Perhaps then *Glee* wouldn't feel so uneven.

> Marshall points to other successful musicals to reinforce her claim that *Glee* succeeds when it uses a traditional structure.

Notes

1. The show musical is also known as the backstage musical and the self-reflective musical. On the latter, see Jane Feuer, "The Self-reflective Musical and the Myth of Entertainment," *Genre: The Musical*. Ed. Rick Altman (London: Routledge, 1981), 159-74.

2. Well-known examples of the fairy tale musical are *Top Hat* (Mark Sandrich, 1935) and *An American in Paris* (Vincent Minnelli, 1951), of the folk musical, *Oklahoma!* (Fred Zinnemann, 1955) and *Meet Me in St. Louis* (Vincent Minnelli, 1944), and of the show musical, *Singin' in the Rain* (Stanley Donen and Gene Kelly, 1952) and *Cabaret* (Bob Fosse, 1972). For a detailed explanation of the three musical subgenres, see Rick Altman, *The American Film Musical* (Bloomington: Indiana University Press, 1987).

> These are explanatory notes, with books and articles documented per the *Chicago Manual of Style*.

3. There are other reasons the show musical is the best option for *Glee* and Murphy's aims: first, it is the subgenre most closely tied to the music industry (Altman 271); second, its performances (like those in the folk musical) emphasize "the integration of the individual into a community or group" (Feuer 166); and third, it employs clichéd stereotypical characters but mainly to "restore meaning to the atmosphere that seems devoid of it" (Altman 252).

4. Altman, 33-45. While I'm arguing that *Glee* feels uneven because it consistently rejects paired segments, I'm also aware that the show likely feels this way because it juxtaposes ridiculous storylines (e.g., Terri Schuester's fake pregnancy, Sue Sylvester's outlandish attempts to sabotage Schuester and the glee club) with rather poignant ones (e.g., Kurt's conversations with his father, Quinn's parents disowning her). Moreover, as Todd VanDerWerff points out, some of *Glee*'s unpredictability may also have to do with its three-writer problem, i.e., *Glee*'s three writers — Ryan Murphy, Brad Falchuk, and Ian Brennan — "seem to have wildly different ideas of what the show is."

5. Altman, 28. In his work, Altman mostly considers heterosexual romantic couples; however, musicals also create parallel segments for groups of characters like those found in *Glee,* for instance, Sharks/Jets in *West Side Story* (Robert Wise and Jerome Robbins, 1961), Pink Ladies/T-Birds in *Grease!* (Randal Kleiser, 1978), and children/parents in *Mary Poppins* (Robert Stevenson, 1964), *The Sound of Music* (Robert Wise, 1965), and *Annie* (John Huston, 1982).

6. For critical reception, see *The Onion*'s AV Club, *Time*'s Tuned In, Metacritic, as well as *Wikipedia*'s summaries of "Pilot," "Wheels," and "Journey." I should note, however, that while "Wheels" was widely praised, it was not without controversy; some performers

with disabilities claimed it was inappropriate to cast an able-bodied actor (Kevin McHale) as a disabled student. Still, this criticism, while perhaps warranted, has little to do with the show's narrative structure.

7. One of the other relatively highly praised episodes, "Dream On," also includes paired segments. First, Schuester and his old show-choir nemesis, Bryan Ryan (Neil Patrick Harris), reunite by singing "Piano Man" and then compete with "Dream On." Second, Rachel and her mother, Shelby (Idina Menzel), pair up for "I Dreamed a Dream" (this also recalls Rachel's *Les Miserables* song from the "Pilot"). Third, an idealistic Artie performs "Safety Dance," and then later, a more rational Artie leads New Directions in "Dream a Little Dream of Me."

8. Musical numbers in these "unpaired-segment" episodes are also unevenly timed. For example, "Showmance" features songs at 10m, 35m, 50m, and 55m; "Acafellas" at 17m, 22m, 40m, and 50m; and "The Power of Madonna" at 10m, 14m, 22m, 38m, 41m, 52m, 58m, and 62m. Moreover, unlike "On My Own," "I Can't Fight This Feeling," and "To Sir with Love," many songs in these episodes fail to serve a convincing purpose. For instance, Finn and Rachel's "Borderline"/"Open Your Heart" duet takes the characters nowhere; at the end of the episode, neither character's heart is truly opened to the other. Likewise, "Gold Digger" does little more than showcase Mr. Schuester's rap/dance abilities.

9. Marsha Kinder, "Moulin Rouge," *Film Quarterly* (55.3): 52-59; Karen Perlman, "Cutting Rhythms in Chicago and Cabaret," *Cineaste* (Spring 2009): 28-32.

PHOTOGRAPHS AS LITERARY TEXTS   Photography attained its status as art in the twentieth century. Even documentary photographs not originally conceived as works of art became prized for their striking depictions of the human condition. Three artists recognized for such work are Dorothea Lange (1895–1965), Walker Evans (1903–1975), and Gordon Parks (1912–2006). During the Great Depression and subsequent years, they produced photographs for the Farm Security Administration (FSA) intended to record all aspects of American life. But their best portraits of people and places often reach beyond the immediate historical context, as the three images below and on pages 247–48 demonstrate. Note how these photographs present and frame their subjects, encouraging viewers to expand and interpret their meanings.

Dorothea Lange, "Jobless on Edge of Pea Field, Imperial Valley, California" (1937)

Walker Evans, "Burroughs Family Cabin, Hale County, Alabama" (1936)

Gordon Parks, "American Gothic" (1942)

Assignments

1. **Literary Interpretation:** Review Kelsi Stayart's "Authentic Beauty in Morrison's *The Bluest Eye*" (p. 209). Then examine how a favorite author or filmmaker treats a specific gender, ethnic, religious, political, sexual, or age group in a short story, novel, or film. Look in particular for themes or patterns that most readers (or you) may not have noticed before and which you can help readers better appreciate — reverse sexism in a summer superhero film, bigotry by exclusion in a children's novel, and so on. When readers would benefit, put these ideas in their specific cultural or historical contexts, as Stayart does with Toni Morrison's novel. If you can (as with poems or episodes of TV shows), consider examining several works by a single artist.

2. **Close Reading:** In "Insanity: Two Women" (p. 231), Kanaka Sathasivan does a close, almost line-by-line analysis of Emily Dickinson's "I felt a Funeral, in my Brain"; then she compares the themes and strategies of the poem to those she finds in Charlotte Gilman's "The Yellow Wallpaper." For a project of your own, do *either* a close reading of a favorite short poem or song *or* a comparison of two works from different genres or media.

   For the close reading, tease out all the meanings and strategies you can uncover and show readers how the text works. For the comparison, be sure to begin with works that interest you because of some important similarity: They may share a theme or plot, or even be the *same* work in two different media — *The Prince of Persia* video game and movie, for instance.

3. **Cultural Analysis:** In "Show Musical Good, Paired Segments Better: *Glee*'s Unevenness Explained" (p. 238), Kelli Marshall writes about the structure of a TV show that became a cultural phenomenon. Examine any work of literature, art, or popular culture that similarly reflects what you find to be an important trend or attitude in society. You may write about that trend itself or, like Marshall, examine some aspect of the work in detail: its meaning, theme, authorship, genre, and so on.

4. **Photographs as Literary Texts:** Photographers Dorothea Lange, Walker Evans, and Gordon Parks (pp. 246–48) recorded images documenting the long-term effects of the Great Depression. In a short paper, describe the specific scenes you would photograph today if you hoped to leave as important a documentary legacy as Lange, Evans, and Parks. To make the project manageable, focus on your local community. Showcase your own images in a photo-essay.

5. **Your Choice:** Write a paper about any work of poetry or fiction that you wish more people would read. Use your essay to explain (or, if necessary, defend) the qualities of the work that make it worth someone's serious attention.

How to start ● Need to **find a text to analyze**? See page 256.
● Need to come up with **ideas**? See page 259.
● Need to **organize your ideas**? See page 262.

8 Rhetorical Analyses

examine in detail the way texts work

Rhetorical analyses foster the kind of close reading that makes writers better thinkers. Moreover, they're everywhere in daily life, especially in politics and law. In fact, they're hard to avoid, especially if you spend much time reading new media.

ANALYSIS OF AN ADVERTISEMENT

You've seen too many slick TV spots touting smart phones that do everything but wash dishes. Your own new phone doesn't work quite so well. You consider writing an *analysis of an advertisement* as an op-ed piece for a local paper that would explore why consumers fall so readily for questionable claims.

ANALYSIS OF AN ARGUMENT

You find yourself impressed by a politician's authority and good sense, so you choose one of his speeches as the subject of an *analysis of an argument* you must write for a composition course. You want to discover exactly how and why he manages to sound so much more persuasive than most Washington pols.

CULTURAL ANALYSIS

You hear your great-grandmother reminiscing about an old neighborhood where every house had a front porch and swing where friends gathered in the evening. You realize that the porch embodies a great many lost values to her and could easily be the subject of a *cultural analysis* for a history class.

ANALYSIS OF A VISUAL TEXT

When your boss at a clothing store reports that upper management isn't happy with the company's online sales, you offer to do an *analysis of a visual text*: the retailer's Web site. Out-of-focus photographs and cluttered graphics make the site look downscale. You argue for a new look and masthead for the store's site.

DECIDING TO WRITE A RHETORICAL ANALYSIS.   You react to what others say or write all the time. Sometimes an advertisement, speech, or maybe a cultural image grabs you so hard that you want to take it apart to see how it works. Put those discoveries into words and you've composed a *rhetorical analysis.* ○

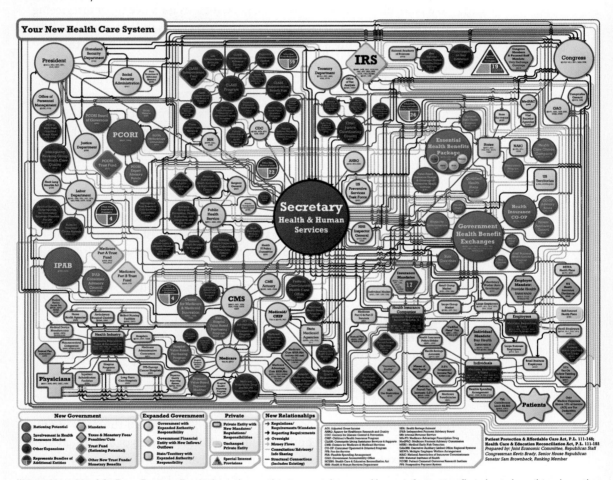

"Your New Health Care System"   At first glance, this item might seem like an informative flowchart describing how the health-care system works in the United States. But a rhetorical analysis of its details, especially its headings (for example, *New Government, Expanded Government, Special Interest Provisions*) and its authorship, might lead you to read it as a political argument.

choose a genre
p. 390

Rhetoric is the art of using language and media to achieve particular goals. A rhetorical analysis is an argument that takes a close look at the strategies of persuasion within a text; it lists and describes specific techniques that a writer, speaker, editor, artist, or advertiser has employed and then assesses their effectiveness. ○ You can take a rhetorical analysis one step further and respond to a particular argument by offering good reasons for agreeing or disagreeing with it. Such a detailed critique of a text is sometimes called a *critical analysis*.

When you write a rhetorical analysis, you'll do the following things.

Take words and images seriously.   When you compose an analysis, whether admiring or critical, hold writers to a high standard because their ideas may have consequences. Good notions deserve to be identified and applauded. And bad ones should be ferreted out, exposed, and sent packing. Learning to discern one from the other takes practice — which is what rhetorical analyses provide.

Make strong claims about texts.   Of course, you cannot make claims about texts until you know them inside out. The need for close examination may seem self-evident, but we blow through most of what we read (and see) without much thought. Serious critical or rhetorical analysis does just the opposite: It makes texts move like bullets in the movie *The Matrix*, their trajectories slowed and every motion magnified for careful study. ○

Pay attention to audience.   When doing a rhetorical analysis, understanding for *whom* a text is written can be as important as *what* it says. In fact, audiences drive the content, shape, and language of most arguments.

Mine texts for evidence.   Not only should you read texts closely in preparing a rhetorical analysis, but you should also use their words (and any other elements) as evidence for your claims. That's one of the goals of critical work of this kind: to find and cite what other readers of a text may have missed. Expect to quote often in a rhetorical analysis. ○

understand
argument p. 72

read closely
p. 365

use quotations
p. 497

This polished and highly entertaining rhetorical analysis is from the "Ad Report Card" series on *Slate.com*. Frequent contributor Seth Stevenson finds a highly suggestive TV ad for Hall's Refresh cough drops so puzzling that he does an in-depth examination of its potential target audiences to figure out what may be going on. His essay demonstrates the importance of audience analysis in understanding a rhetorical situation.

Slate.com

Posted: Monday, November 9, 2009, at 3:11 PM ET
From: Seth Stevenson

Ad Report Card: Can Cougars Sell Cough Drops?

Articles in this series always open with a description of the ad for readers who haven't seen it.

The Spot: *It's move-in day at a college dorm. A student asks his new roommate's mom whether she'd care for a Halls Refresh. The young man and the middle-aged mom suck on their lozenges, staring lasciviously into each other's eyes. We hear their thoughts. "So juicy!" thinks the mom. "Yeah, she likes it," thinks the student. The woman's husband and son walk in on this intimate moment. "Mom!" shouts the horrified son as the dad recoils. "New Halls Refresh with moisture action," says the announcer. "Surprisingly mouthwatering."*

This ad has been catching flak for its mildly disturbing visual of a frumpy mom making bedroom eyes at a college-age nerd. The American Decency Association posted a breathless, run-on rant on its Web site, sounding particularly distressed about the fact that the ad shows "mouths moving in sexually suggestive ways." A *Slate* colleague is also grossed out by the ad's use of the evocative phrase "moisture action."

Stevenson uses a key question to focus and structure his analysis.

True, the ad is a wee bit icky. But I'm having trouble working up much outrage. I'm more interested in a fundamental marketing question: Who, exactly, is this ad supposed to reach?

A personal and informal style works well in an online magazine like *Slate.com*.

I generally expect ads to use actors matching the product's target audience. Thus ads for Viagra feature older men, while ads for Barbie dolls star little girls. But in this ad, the characters shown enjoying Halls Refresh represent two different demographic categories with starkly different buying habits. Is Halls hoping to tempt fortysomething women with this new line of lozenges? Or college-age guys?

Let's first examine the evidence suggesting that the ad is meant to charm young dudes:

Cadbury, which owns Halls, is for the most part a candy company. Its offerings include Bubblicious, Sour Patch Kids, Swedish Fish, and countless chocolaty goodies. Unlike other Halls products, Halls Refresh is being pitched on the basis of its "mouthwatering," candylike qualities — not as a medicinal remedy for a sore throat.

Candy ads these days tend to rely on surreal, absurdist humor. There's the Starburst ad in which a guy communes with a llama and the Skittles ad that shows a man with a prehensile beard. Cadbury actually owns another confectionary brand that uses nonsensical, dude-focused advertising: Check out the Stride gum spot in which a team of lederhosen-clad dancers assaults a young man in a parking garage.

This Halls Refresh spot seems like a close cousin to those crazy candy ads. It's easy to imagine the mom and the student chewing on Skittles instead of sucking on Halls. And, through prior reporting, I happen to know that the target demographic for Skittles is 15-17 year-olds. Because that's who buys candy. Young guys — not middle-aged women.

Case closed, yes? Not quite. Let's consider the evidence on the other side of the ledger:

First, Halls Refresh is sugarless. This is an attribute not traditionally prized by young fellas, who like to guzzle down sugary colas and munch on 500-calorie burgers. The young man shown in the ad surely wouldn't be watching his weight. But the mom might be.

Looking up Halls Refresh on a search engine, I found a bunch of blogs that had been given samples of the lozenge to review. These samples were handed out by people trying to promote Halls Refresh. What sort of blogs were the samples given to? Almost exclusively blogs written by professional women and stay-at-home moms.

A press release introducing Halls Refresh also suggests that the product was designed to meet the needs not of carefree young

First part of the analysis looks in detail at the case for "dudes" as the target audience.

Second part presents evidence that older women may be the intended audience.

men but of harried adults. Its first paragraph declares that Halls Refresh is the perfect antidote whenever you get "the feeling that your mouth needs a refresher just as your presentation begins, when meeting the in-laws, when running errands under a tight schedule . . ." Not a lot of 18-year-old guys spend their time worrying about meeting in-laws. Or running errands, for that matter.

The clincher? Cadbury aired this ad during the premiere episode of *Cougar Town*, the Courteney-Cox-starring ABC show about an older woman who is forever scheming to date younger men. Referring back to my cast-your-target-demographic rule, I have to assume that a show with Courteney Cox in the lead role is meant to appeal to Courteney-Cox-age women. Though it's not totally clear to me why portrayals of cougardom are fun for middle-age women to watch. Is it an affirmation that they are still sexual beings? Or do they relate to Cox's foibles and take comfort in the show's sympathetic humor?

I have similar questions about the Halls Refresh spot, if it is, indeed, aimed at middle-age ladies. Do women fantasize about sharing a naughty moment over a lozenge with a scrawny dweeb? Being caught by their husband and child mid-suck?

Perhaps Cadbury — which has for the past several years been diversifying out of chocolate and into sugar-free chewing gum and cough drops — wants to reach a new category of consumer but doesn't yet know how to market effectively to anyone over 19. Or perhaps it hopes to split the difference, by pitching Halls Refresh to young men as a candy while telling grown-up women it's a functional cure for dry-mouthed moments.

Grade: C−. The ad's goals seem muddled. Worse, it's not funny. Cadbury didn't respond to my inquiries by press time, so I can't be sure about their intentions. But what do you think? Who, if anyone, does this ad appeal to?

> Best evidence comes last, but it raises more questions.

> The conclusion and C− grade suggest that Stevenson finds the ad ineffective in reaching *any* viewers.

Exploring purpose and topic

▶ find a text

Make a difference.   Done right, rhetorical analyses can be as important as the texts they examine. They may change readers' opinions, open their eyes to new ideas, or keep an important argument going. They may also draw attention to rhetorical strategies and techniques worth imitating or avoiding.

When you write an angry letter to the editor complaining about bias in the news coverage, you won't fret much about defining your purpose or topic—they are given. But when responding to a course assignment, particularly when you can choose a text on your own to analyze rhetorically, you've got to establish the boundaries. Given a choice, select a text to analyze with the following characteristics.

Choose a text you can work with.   Find a gutsy piece that makes a claim you or someone else might actually disagree with. It helps if you have a stake in the issue and already know something about it. The text should also be of a manageable length that you can explore coherently within the limits of the assignment.

Choose a text you can learn more about.   Some items won't make much sense out of context. So choose a text or series of texts that you can study and research. ○ It will obviously help to know when it was written, presented or produced, by whom, and where it first appeared. This information is as important for visual texts, such as advertisements, posters, and films, as for traditional speeches or articles.

Choose a text with handles.   Investigate arguments that do interesting things. Maybe a speech uses lots of anecdotes or repetition to generate emotional appeals; perhaps a photo-essay's commentary is more provocative than the images; a print ad may arrest attention by its simplicity but still be full of cultural significance. You've got to write about the piece. Make sure it offers you interesting things to say.

> **Need help deciding what to write about? See "How to Browse for Ideas" on pp. 360–61.**

find a topic
p. 356

Choose a text you know how to analyze.   Stick to printed texts if you aren't sure how to write about ads or films or even speeches. But don't sell yourself short. You can pick up the necessary vocabulary by reading models of rhetorical and critical analysis. Moreover, you don't always need highly technical terms to describe poor logic, inept design, or offensive strategies, wherever they appear. Nor do you need special expertise to describe cultural trends or detect political implications.

Your Turn   You don't need a highbrow or sophisticated topic for a successful rhetorical analysis, as Stevenson's essay on cough drops demonstrates (p. 253). It's a much better strategy to dissect a text that genuinely intrigues you and then make an audience as intrigued by it as you are. If you take an item seriously (zombies, for example: see p. 264), chances are that your readers will too. So begin an open-ended assignment by listing the sorts of texts you engage with regularly. Even text messages and tweets can be studied rhetorically if you find an angle on them.

Understanding your audience

Some published rhetorical analyses are written for ready-made audiences already inclined to agree with the authors. Riled up by an offensive editorial or a political campaign, people these days may even seek out and enjoy mean-spirited, over-the-top criticism, especially on the Web. But the rhetorical and critical analyses you write for class should be relatively restrained because you can't predict how your readers might feel about the arguments you are critiquing. So assume that you are writing for a diverse and thoughtful audience, full of readers who prefer reflective analysis to clever put-downs. You don't have to be dull or passionless. Just avoid the easy slide into rudeness. O

"got milk?" Advertisements in this famous series lend themselves to rhetorical analysis because they are so carefully designed for specific audiences, in this case fans of tennis superstar Serena Williams.

respect your readers
p. 440

Finding and developing materials

Before you analyze a text of any kind, do some background research. ○
Discover what you can about its author, creator, publisher, sponsor, and so
on. For example, it may be important to know that the TV commercial you
want to understand better has aired only on sports networks or lifestyle
programs on cable. Become familiar, too, with the contexts in which an
argument occurs. If you reply to a *Wall Street Journal* editorial, know what
news or events sparked that item and investigate the paper's editorial slant.

Read the piece carefully just for information first, highlighting names or
allusions you don't recognize. Then look them up: There's very little you can't
uncover quickly these days via a Web search. When you think you understand
the basics, you are prepared to approach the text rhetorically. Pay attention to any
standout aspects of the text you're analyzing—perhaps how it wins over wary
readers through conciliatory language or draws on the life experiences of its
author to frame its subject. ○ You might look at any of the following elements.

Consider the topic or subject matter of the text.   What is novel or
striking about the topic? How well defined is it? Could it be clearer? Is it
important? Relevant? Controversial? Is the subject covered comprehensively
or selectively? What is the level of detail? Does the piece make a point?

Consider the audiences of the text.   To whom is the piece addressed?
How is the text adapted to its audience? Who is excluded from the audience
and how can you tell? What does the text offer its audience: information,
controversy, entertainment? What does it expect from its audience?

Consider its author.   What is the author's relationship to the material? Is
the writer or creator personally invested or distant? Is the author an expert,
a knowledgeable amateur, or something else? What does the author hope to
accomplish?

Consider its medium or language.   What is the medium or genre of
the text: essay, article, editorial, advertisement, book excerpt, poster, video,
podcast, or other format? How well does the medium suit the subject? How
might the material look different in another medium? What is the level
of the language: formal, informal, colloquial? ○ What is the tone of the

find reliable
resources p. 482

read closely
p. 365

define your style
p. 432

text—logical, sarcastic, humorous, angry, condescending? How do the various elements of design—such as arrangement, color, fonts, images, white space, audio, video, and so on—work in the text?

Consider its occasion.   Why was the text created? To what circumstances or situations does it respond, and what might the reactions to it be? What problems does it solve or create? What pleasure might it give? Who benefits from the text?

Consider its contexts.   What purposes do texts of this type serve? Do texts of this sort have a history? Do they serve the interests of specific groups or classes? Have they evolved over time? Does the text represent a new genre?

Consider its use of rhetorical appeals.   Persuasive texts are often analyzed according to how they use three types of rhetorical appeal. Typically, a text may establish the character and credibility of its author (*ethos*), generate emotions in order to move audiences (*pathos*), and use evidence and logic to make its case (*logos*).

Ethos—the appeal to character—may be the toughest argumentative strategy to understand. Every text and argument is presented by someone or something, whether an individual, a group, or an institution. Audiences are usually influenced and swayed by writers or speakers who present themselves as knowledgeable, honest, fair-minded, and believable. Here Michael Ruse describes a witness whose frank words established his ethos at a 1981 court case dealing with requiring creation science in Arkansas schools.

> The assistant attorney general was trying to tie him into knots over some technical point in evolutionary biology. Finally, the man blurted out, "Mr. Williams, I'm not a scientist. . . . I am an educator, and I have my pride and professional responsibilities. And I just can't teach that stuff [meaning creationism] to my kids."
>
> —"Science for Science Teachers," *The Chronicle of Higher Education*, January 13, 2010

Pathos—the emotional appeal—is usually easy to detect. Look for ways that a text generates strong feelings to support its points, win over readers, or

This poster appears on the Web site of the Navy Environmental Health Center. Does that fact about its context change its message in any way?

influence them in other ways. The strategy is legitimate so long as an emotion fits the situation and doesn't manipulate audiences. For example, columnist Peggy Noonan routinely uses emotions to make her political points.

> We fought a war to free slaves. We sent millions of white men to battle and destroyed a portion of our nation to free millions of black men. What kind of nation does this? We went to Europe, fought, died, and won, and then taxed ourselves to save our enemies with the Marshall Plan. What kind of nation does this? Soviet communism stalked the world and we were the ones who steeled ourselves and taxed ourselves to stop it. Again: What kind of nation does this?
>   Only a very great one.
>
> —"Patriots, Then and Now," *Wall Street Journal*, March 30, 2006

Logos—the appeal to reason and evidence—is most favored in academic texts. Look carefully at the claims a text offers and whether they are supported by facts, data, testimony, and good reasons. What assumptions lie beneath the argument? Ask questions about evidence too. Does it come from reliable sources or valid research? Is it up-to-date? Has it been reported accurately and fully? Has due attention been given to alternative points of view and explanations? Has enough evidence been offered to make a valid point? You might ask such questions, for example, when a political commentator like George Will runs the numbers to prove a point, as in this excerpt from a column that appeared after Michelle and Barack Obama failed to win the 2016 Olympics for the city of Chicago.

> Both Obamas gave heartfelt speeches about . . . themselves. Although the working of the [International Olympic] committee's mind is murky, it could reasonably have rejected Chicago's bid for the 2016 Games on aesthetic grounds — unless narcissism has suddenly become an Olympic sport.
>   In the 41 sentences of her remarks, Michelle Obama used some form of the personal pronouns "I" or "me" 44 times. Her husband was, comparatively, a shrinking violet, using those pronouns only 26 times in 48 sentences. Still, 70 times in 89 sentences conveyed the message that somehow their fascinating selves were what made, or should have made, Chicago's case compelling.
>
> —"An Olympic Ego Trip," *Washington Post*, October 6, 2009

Creating a structure

▶ organize ideas

In a rhetorical analysis, you'll make a statement about how well the argumentative strategy of a piece works. Don't expect to come up with a thesis immediately or easily: You need to study a text closely to figure out how it works and then think about its strengths and weaknesses. Draft a tentative thesis (or hypothesis) and then refine your words throughout the process of writing until they assert a claim you can prove. ○

Look for a complex thesis. Don't just list some rhetorical features: *This ad has good logical arguments and uses emotions and rhetorical questions.* Why would someone want to read (or write) a paper with such an empty claim? The following thesis yields a far more interesting rhetorical analysis:

> The latest government antidrug posters offer good reasons for avoiding steroids but do it in a visual style so closely resembling bland health posters that most students will just ignore them.

Develop a structure.   Once you have a thesis or hypothesis, try sketching a design based on a thesis/supporting reason/evidence plan. Focus on those features of the text that illustrate the points you wish to make. You don't have to discuss every facet of the text.

Introduction leading to a claim
First supporting reason + textual evidence Second supporting reason + textual evidence Additional supporting reasons + textual evidence
Conclusion

In some cases, you might perform a line-by-line or paragraph-by-paragraph deconstruction of a text. This structure shows up frequently online. Such analyses practically organize themselves, but your commentary must be smart, accurate, and stylish to keep readers onboard.

Introduction leading to a claim
First section/paragraph + detailed analysis Next section/paragraph + detailed analysis Additional section/paragraph + detailed analysis
Conclusion

develop a statement
p. 393

Choosing a style and design

The style of your textual analyses will vary depending on audience, but you always face one problem that can sometimes be helped by design: making the text you are analyzing more accessible to readers.

Consider a high style.   Rhetorical and critical analyses you write in school will usually be formal and use a "high" style. ○ Your tone should be respectful, your vocabulary as technical as the material requires, and your perspective impersonal—avoiding *I* and *you*. Such a style gives the impression of objectivity and seriousness. Unless an instructor gives you more leeway, use a formal style for critical analyses.

Consider a middle style.   Oddly, rhetorical and critical analyses appearing in the public arena—rather than in the classroom—will usually be less formal and exploit the connection with readers that a middle style encourages. While still serious, such a style gives writers more options for expressing strong opinions and feelings (sometimes including anger, outrage, and contempt). In much public writing, you can detect a personal voice offering an opinion or advancing an agenda.

Make the text accessible to readers.   A special challenge in any rhetorical analysis is to help readers understand the texts you are scrutinizing. When possible with printed texts, attach a photocopy of the material directly to your analysis or include a link to it if you are working online. Also be sure to provide basic information about the author, title, place of publication, and date, and briefly explain the context of the work. With other types of subjects—such as movies, advertising campaigns, and so on—your task is more complicated. You'll often have to describe or summarize what you are describing in considerable detail.

As you can see, your rhetorical analysis should typically be written *as if readers do not have that text in hand or in front of them*. One way to achieve that clarity is to summarize and quote selectively from the text as you examine it, or to provide visual images. You can see examples of this technique in Matthew James Nance's essay on pages 264–69 and in J. Reagan Tankersley's analysis on pages 270–78.

Annotate the text.   When analyzing an image or a text available in digital form, consider attaching your comments directly to the item. Do this by simply inserting a copy of the image or article directly into your project and then using the design tools of your word processor to create annotations.

define your style
p. 432

Examining models

For a class assignment on rhetorical analysis, Matthew James Nance chose as his subject the award-winning feature article "Can't Die for Trying" by journalist Laura Miller—who later would serve as mayor of Dallas. In the essay, Nance explains in detail how Miller manages to present the story of a convicted killer who wants to be executed to readers who might have contrary views about capital punishment. Nance's analysis is both technical and objective. He does an especially good job of helping readers follow the argument of "Can't Die for Trying," a fairly long and complicated article.

Nance 1

Matthew James Nance

Professor Norcia

English 2

June 14, 20--

A Mockery of Justice

In 1987, David Martin Long was convicted of double homicide and sentenced to death. He made no attempt to appeal this sentence, and surprisingly, did everything he could to expedite his execution. Nonetheless, due to an automatic appeals process, Long remained on Texas's Death Row for twelve years before he was finally executed. For various reasons, including investigations into whether he was mentally ill, the state of Texas had continued to postpone his execution date. In 1994, when David Long was still in the middle of his appeals process, *Dallas Observer* columnist Laura Miller took up his case in the award-winning article "Can't Die for Trying." In this article, Miller explores the enigma of a legal

Sets scene carefully and provides necessary background information.

Nance 2

system in which a sociopath willing to die continues to be mired in the legal process. The article is no typical plea on behalf of a death-row inmate, and Miller manages to avoid a facile political stance on capital punishment. Instead, Miller uses an effective combination of logical reasoning and emotional appeal to evoke from readers a sense of frustration at the system's absurdity.

Miller defies expectations and Nance explains why in his thesis.

To show that David Martin Long's execution should be carried out as soon as possible, Miller offers a reasoned argument based on two premises: that he wants death and that he deserves it. Miller cites Long's statement from the day he was arrested: "I realize what I did was wrong. I don't belong in this society. I never have. . . . I'd just wish they'd hurry up and get this over with" (5). She emphasizes that this desire has not changed, by quoting Long's correspondence from 1988, 1991, and 1992. In this way, Miller makes Long's argument seem reasoned and well thought out, not simply a temporary gesture of desperation. "Yes, there are innocent men here, retarded men, insane men, and men who just plain deserve another chance," Long wrote [State District Judge Larry] Baraka in April 1992, "But I am none of these!" (5). Miller also points out his guilty plea, and the jury's remarkably short deliberation: "The jury took only an hour to find Long guilty of capital murder—and 45 minutes to give him the death penalty" (5). Miller does not stop there, however. She

Long paragraph furnishes detailed evidence for Miller's two premises.

Nance 3

gives a grisly description of the murders themselves, followed
by Long's calculated behavior in the aftermath:

> He hacked away at Laura twenty-one times before
> going back inside where he gave Donna fourteen
> chops. The blind woman, who lay in bed screaming
> while he savaged Donna, got five chops. Long washed
> the hatchet, stuck it in the kitchen sink, and headed
> out of town in Donna's brown station wagon. (5)

Miller's juxtaposition of reasoned deliberation with the
bloody narrative of the murders allows her to show that
Long, in refusing to appeal, is reacting justly to his own
sociopathy. Not only is it right that he die; it is also right that
he does not object to his death.

In the midst of this reasoned argument, Miller expresses
frustration at the bureaucratic inefficiency that is at odds
with her logic. She offers a pragmatic, resource-based view of
the situation:

> Of course, in the handful of instances where a person
> is wrongly accused . . . this [death-penalty activism] is
> noble, important work. But I would argue that in
> others—David Martin Long in particular—it is a sheer
> waste of taxpayer dollars. And a mockery of justice. (6)

Miller portrays the system as being practically
incompatible with her brand of pragmatism. The figures
involved in Long's case are painted as invisible, equivocal, or

---

Provides both summaries and quotations from article so that readers can follow Miller's argument.

To clarify Miller's point, Nance adds a phrase in brackets to the quotation.

Nance 4

both. For instance, in spite of Long's plea, Judge Baraka was forced to appoint one of Long's attorneys to start the appeals process. "The judge didn't have a choice. Texas law requires that a death-penalty verdict be automatically appealed. . . . [This] is supposed to expedite the process. But the court sat on Long's case for four long years" (5). Miller also mentions Danny Burn, a Fort Worth lawyer in association with the Texas Resource Center, one of the "do-good . . . organizations whose sole feverish purpose is to get people off Death Row. . . . No matter how airtight the cases" (6). Burn filed on Long's behalf, though he never met Long in person. This fact underscores Miller's notion of the death-row bureaucracy as being inaccessible, and by extension, incomprehensible.

> Notice how smoothly quotations merge into Nance's sentences.

This parade of equivocal incompetence culminates in Miller's interview with John Blume, another activist who argued on Long's behalf. Miller paints Blume as so equivocal that he comes across as a straw man. "As a general rule," says Blume, "I tend to think most people who are telling you that are telling you something else, and that's their way of expressing it. There's something else they're depressed or upset about" (6). The article ends with Miller's rejoinder: "Well, I'd wager, Mr. Blume, that something is a lawyer like you" (6). Whereas the article up to this point has maintained a balance between reason and frustration, here Miller seems to let gradually building frustration get the best of her. She

> Nance makes a clear judgment about Miller's objectivity — then offers evidence for his claim.

Nance 5

does not adequately address whether Blume might be correct in implying that Long is insane, mentally ill, or otherwise misguided. She attempts to dismiss this idea by repeatedly pointing out Long's consistency in his stance and his own statements that he is not retarded, but her fallacy is obvious: Consistency does not imply sanity. Clearly, Miller would have benefited from citing Long's medical history and comparing his case with those of other death-row inmates, both mentally ill and well. Then her frustrated attack on Blume would seem more justified.

Miller also evokes frustration through her empathetic portrayal of Long. Although the article is essentially a plea for Long to get what he wants, this fact itself prevents Miller from portraying Long sympathetically. Miller is stuck in a rhetorical bind; if her readers become sympathetic toward Long, they won't want him to die. However, the audience needs an emotional connection with Long to accept the argument on his behalf. Miller gets around this problem by abandoning sympathy altogether, portraying Long as a cold-blooded killer. The quotation "I've never seen a more cold-blooded, steel-eyed sociopath ever" (5) is set apart from the text in a large font, and Miller notes, "This is a case of a really bad dude, plain and simple. . . . Use any cliché you want. It fits" (5). Miller here opts for a weak appeal, evoking from the audience the same negative emotion that Long feels. She gives voice to Long's

> Nance examines the way Miller deals with the problem she has portraying a cold-blooded killer to readers.

Nance 6

frustration over his interminable appeals: "Long stewed. . . .
Long steamed. . . . Long fumes. . . ." (6). She also points out
Long's fear of himself: "I fear I'll kill again" (6). Clearly, the
audience is meant to echo these feelings of frustration and fear.
This may seem like a weak emotional connection with Long,
but perhaps it is the best Miller could do, given that a primary
goal of hers was to show that Long deserves death.

Laura Miller won the H. L. Mencken Award for this
article, which raises important questions about the legal
process. Part of its appeal is that it approaches capital
punishment without taking a simplistic position. It can
appeal to people on both sides of the capital punishment
debate. The argument is logically valid, and for the most
part, the emotional appeal is effective. Its deficiencies,
including the weak emotional appeal for Long, are ultimately
outweighed by Miller's overarching rationale, which calls for
pragmatism in the face of absurdity.

Nance 7

Work Cited

Miller, Laura. "Can't Die for Trying." *Dallas Observer*
    12 Jan. 1994: 5-6. Print.

CULTURAL ANALYSIS   J. Reagan Tankersley argues that zombies in movies and TV represent what people fear most at any given time. They become the image of our fears.

Tankersley 1

J. Reagan Tankersley

Professor Wilkes

Composition 1

November 24, 20--

Humankind's Ouroboros

Arguably, what we fear is perhaps the greatest indicator of how we behave as human animals. Fear is the emotion with the greatest impact on our fight or flight instincts; our animal brain is exposed when we decide to cover our eyes or keep on watching. It is why both lanes of traffic slow when there's been an accident: One lane brakes due to the obstruction; drivers in the other lane linger because everyone wants to see what happened, knowing it could've been us.

Horror films act in the same way. The monster movie of the Golden Age of Hollywood was the first sign that people can't always look away from what scares them. And it was lucrative. The horror genre remains one of the most prolific and profitable of the eleven classic genres of film, beginning with such titles as *Frankenstein* and *Dracula*. Within this body of works, none seems more prevalent today than the zombie movie, with the possible exception of highly sexualized vampire and werewolf dramas. Yet, despite a singular ability

Tankersley 2

to scare audiences, the zombie movie has never been a solid form in itself. The zombies of classical Hollywood are strikingly different from those seen in the summer blockbusters of the past few years. More than any other monster, the zombie is able to evolve according to what will scare us the most, depending on where we stand in our own history. So the ever-evolving design of the zombie is an arguably strong tether to our fears, to how we react as humans.

The first film considered to be a zombie movie was released in 1932, in the heart of the Classical Hollywood era, and starred the master of the monster film, Bela Lugosi. While *White Zombie* is a long stretch from the zombie films of today, it broke ground on the very concept of "zombification." The plot involves a plantation owner from Haiti who, using

A scene from *Dracula*.

Tankersley introduces his thesis: that zombies in films embody the current fears of our society.

Tankersley 3

witchcraft to win his love interest, accidentally turns her into a zombie obeying his every command. This plot hints at the roots of the zombie concept, which lie in voodoo legends, the word *zombie* originating in West Africa. The film was also the first to present on screen something akin to our modern image of the zombie: After she becomes a zombie, the love interest of the film is pale white, with the look of a corpse.

The film of that era that best predicted the future of the zombie film was the aptly named *Things to Come*, released in 1936. This adaptation of H. G. Wells's novel of the same name does not directly focus on zombies; however, its epic storyline includes a viral plague, which causes the infected to wander aimlessly, spreading the contagion on contact—an essential plot point in the large-scale zombie films to come. Both of these films reflect the concerns of the horror audience of the 1930s: fear of the mystical and fear of the future. *White Zombie* played to an uneasiness with voodoo magic, which some people associated with post-slavery African American culture. *Things to Come* captured the signature pessimism of H. G. Wells during an era of economic recession in the troubled period between two great wars.

Zombies took a backseat in the horror genre following the fall of Classical Hollywood. Moreover, the new medium of television did not allow for such sensational and scary subject matter. Things changed, however, with the rise of the New American Cinema in the 1960s, a school of filmmaking

The analysis explores the historical roots of today's zombie films.

Tankersley 4

that promoted noncontinuous editing and deliberately explicit images. George A. Romero, considered the father of the modern zombie, released *Night of the Living Dead* to horrify audiences in 1968. Romero is given this lofty title simply because he introduced what is considered the paradigmatic zombie, that is, the walking corpse who exists only to eat the flesh of the living. The film broke many cinematic taboos of the time, especially with a sequence involving a zombified child eating her parents. The shocking imagery from this scene sent tremors through the film community. This reimagining of the zombie played to an audience perhaps changed by the televised violence of the Vietnam War era; certainly, the explicit images of cannibalistic corpses brought the horror genre to a much higher level than the monster films of the previous age.

Romero's cult masterpiece was followed by a slew of mediocre-to-downright-horrible zombie films, all produced in the wake of *Night*'s success. These cheap imitations were quelled only briefly by Romero's next project, *Dawn of the Dead*, which debuted in 1978. Although it was released just ten years after the original, the film altered the nature of the zombie to again depict the current fears of the audience. With the demoralizing end of the Vietnam War, Americans adopted a more critical view of their national values. Romero's film, which takes place primarily in a shopping mall, became a direct commentary on growing levels of consumerism in

Tankersley focuses on the visual imagery of modern zombie films.

Tankersley 5

A scene from *Night of the Living Dead.*

America. Romero heightened his societal critique by increasing the scale of the zombie outbreak, presenting images of zombies—once people themselves—mindlessly consuming other people in a shopping mall, of all places. This level of rebuke represents a paradigm shift in the zombie film: It shows that the fear we experience from zombies comes not just from the gore and frightening images. Rather, it is from the fact that zombies *are* society, without its rules or adornments. Zombies became mindless consumers, a description increasingly given to society itself.

Romero's cinematic shift to a larger-scale zombie drama with social commentary failed to have much impact until recently. Between the original *Dawn of the Dead* and Zack Snyder's remake in 2004, there was again a very long train of awful zombie films. It wasn't until 2002, with the release of *28 Days Later*, that the zombie film again became a genre to be

Presents the post–Vietnam War zombie as a metaphor for consumerism.

Tankersley 6

reckoned with. Danny Boyle's foray into the zombie film is most notable for its sweeping views of an abandoned London, providing a postmortem view of society destroyed by an infection. Not only did Boyle manage to make the catastrophe seem brutally real through such heart-wrenching images as a notice board plastered with missing persons reports, he also revolutionized the zombie as a species. His ghouls—the result of animal testing gone horribly wrong—were more realistic and more frightening, leaving their infected victims with something similar to rabies. The defining differences between Boyle's zombies and those of the past, however, were their ability to run and their virus's aggressive capacity to infect on contact, transforming a victim into the undead in a matter of seconds. This gave the zombie genre a much-needed boost, especially since previous films were often criticized for featuring antagonists who could barely walk. Boyle's new zombies could sprint for longer periods than normal humans, due to a lack of physical pain, leaving the protagonists with no safe place to hide for long.

Boyle's film made another point: that zombie films can be constructed around more than just spooky lighting, token characters, cheap scares, and nauseating images. He achieved this goal by focusing on the living characters: Their personal fears and their realization that all the people they loved were gone, raising the question of what there was to survive for. This approach made the fear of zombies

Tankersley analyzes the physical details of *28 Days Later*.

A scene from *28 Days Later.*

as much internal as external; the fear becomes personal to
each individual audience member. A scene in which the
protagonist finds his parents — who committed suicide
before the infection spread to them — is all one needs to
understand the real terror that an event as widespread as
a zombie infection would create.

Numerous films after *28 Days Later* have approached
the human dimension of the zombie film similarly, ensuring

Tankersley 8

that audiences would effectively place themselves in
dire emotional situations. Of course, there remain the
blood-filled blockbusters, such as the *Resident Evil*
franchise, but Boyle's film, and some that followed, gave a
film buff something to appreciate in a zombie movie. This
greater sophistication is evident in what is currently the
zombie production to see, *The Walking Dead*, a television
series on AMC (American Movie Classics). The story has
its origin in a popular comic book series, but the television
show, directed by Frank Darabont (*The Shawshank
Redemption*), follows in Boyle's footsteps, exploring the
internal dramas of the characters as much as the physical
threat of the zombies. The series, still in release, has so
far been lauded by zombie enthusiasts, primarily because
it pulls back to the traditional zombies of Romero's age,
the aimlessly hobbling, sunken-eyed corpses. Thus far,
the show appears to have found a place in the zombie
canon.

The zombie began as a mysterious creature of mystical
origin, with no will of its own. It quickly evolved into the
flesh-eating monster that many associate with the term
today. And, although it has recently become the product of
viral testing and chemical warfare, the textbook zombie
remains unwavering in its basic mission—to scare people.
At the beginning of the twentieth century, audiences feared
the unknown, whether that was mysticism or troubling

Tankersley explains how zombie films are currently evolving.

Tankersley 9

political events. In the post-Vietnam War era, they began to question themselves, doubting their values and wondering if they were still the good guys that American leaders made them out to be. And finally, with the increasing threat of terrorism, people have returned to fearing the possibilities the future might bring. Now, *The Walking Dead* has moved beyond even this horror, with the source of its zombie infection completely unnamed. In the zombie films of the past ten years, it is clear that what we fear most is ourselves. We fear what people next to us may be capable of if their reason is taken from them by some man-made virus, unknown pathogen, or something else entirely. We all know that deep down, people are capable of heinous acts, and it is only reason that can stop them. But when reason is lost, human society has every faculty to consume itself.

The conclusion finally explains the visual image offered in the title of the paper: the serpent that devours itself.

Tankersley 10

Works Consulted

The Internet Movie Database (IMDb). Web. 15 Nov. 2010.

"List of Zombie Films." *Wikipedia.* Wikimedia Foundation,
     13 Nov. 2010. Web. 15 Nov. 2010.

"Main Film Genres." *Greatest Films — The Best Movies in
     Cinematic History*. Ed. Tim Dirks. 2010. Web. 15 Nov. 2010.

ANALYSIS OF A VISUAL TEXT   Can a jacket be read rhetorically? Beth Teitell gives it a try in this Web report posted on *Boston.com* after Republican candidate Scott Brown won the U.S. Senate seat held for decades by Ted Kennedy. A folksy, man-of-the-people image helped Brown to upset the much-favored Democratic candidate. But, as Teitell discovers, sometimes a jacket is just a jacket. Or is it?

Boston.com

Posted: January 28, 2010
From: Beth Teitell, *Globe* Correspondent

A Jacket of the People

Scott Brown's pickup truck got almost as much attention as the Senate candidate, but somehow his equally ubiquitous, equally everyman barn jacket cruised below the pundits' radar.

And yet, there it was, starring in his now-famous truck ad. There it was again, waving to motorists. And voting in the election.

But what do we know about that brown jacket, really? We spent more time talking about what Brown *wasn't* wearing than what he was. Is the slightly worn leather jacket what it appears to be — just something Brown had lying around the house? Or did the campaign hire a stylist to find Brown a jacket that said "Joe the Plumber," but cost $850, like the Burberry canvas barn jacket Saks is selling this season?

With the Senator-elect poised to start making national policy, a call to one of his campaign masterminds was in order. "It was made by an American company Golden Bear Sportswear," Brown senior adviser Eric Fehrnstrom told us. "He loves it because it fits and his daughter bought it for him, and he only has two jackets." (The other is a blue puffer snow jacket.)

Beyond providing warmth, Fehrnstrom said, the jacket did indeed send a message, just like the truck: Brown's a regular guy. "Scott is the Rocky Balboa of Massachusetts politics, and his barn coat may be as famous as Rocky's leather jacket. Maybe someday it will hang in the Smithsonian next to the *Spirit of St. Louis*."

Longtime Democratic consultant Michael Goldman, a senior consultant with the Government Insight Group, had a slightly different take. "There is no question that jacket was supposed to say, I'm not some wealthy lawyer from the suburbs, I'm just like you, a plain old truck-driving guy."

> Teitell intends to probe how deliberately Brown's jacket was used as a symbol in his campaign.

> Teitell first establishes the facts: The made-in-the-USA jacket was a gift.

> Two political professionals read the jacket as symbolic.

So does a fashion consultant, who offers a useful contrast.

Mary Lou Andre, a Needham-based wardrobe and corporate image consultant, says the jacket sent a rugged message that an "elitist" trench coat would not have.

"Most politicians, when you see them, don't have outerwear on," Andre said. "That jacket signified that he was out and about meeting people, that he was on the road, not in secret meetings trying to be made over."

Sadly, there's no exit polling showing how the election would have gone had he not worn the barn jacket, but history shows that garments as billboards don't always work. And John Kerry's barn jacket couldn't erase his man-of-only-certain-people image in 2004.

So what kind of guy wears a Golden Bear Sportswear leather barn jacket?

"We sell to everyone," said Everett LaRose, a salesman at the Andover Shop's Andover location, where a similar-looking Golden Bear Sportswear barn jacket goes for $675. Guess that depends on what your definition of "everyone" is.

Teitell confirms that the jacket was a gift from the candidate's daughter.

Brown himself didn't buy the jacket, it turns out. It was a gift from Arianna (the daughter who's "definitely not available"). Taking a break from studying pre-calculus over the weekend at Syracuse University, she reported that she bought it at the Wrentham Village Premium Outlets as a birthday present about five years ago.

"I like to make him look nice," Arianna said, adding that she also bought him a pea coat for Christmas, which he wore a few times on the campaign trail before "reverting" back to the barn jacket.

"I like buying clothes for him," she said. That's in contrast to her sister and her mother, she added, who are afraid to buy him clothes. "He never really wears them." But he does wear clothes from his own mother, she said, including that blue snow jacket.

"She seems to know what he likes to wear, which is good I guess," she said.

Arianna doesn't recall the barn jacket's price, but she says she can't imagine she spent more than $200 on the gift. What she does know is this: Before the campaign, the jacket didn't get quite as much use. "Until this election he probably only wore it to nice things. It's funny to see it all the time."

While the jacket may not have been purchased with prior intentions, it could still have become part of a deliberate campaign strategy.

Assignments

1. **Analysis of an Advertisement:** Using Seth Stevenson's "Ad Report Card: Can Cougars Sell Cough Drops?" on p. 253 as a model, write your own critical analysis of a single ad or full ad campaign you find worthy of attention. Choose a fresh campaign, one that hasn't yet received much commentary.

2. **Analysis of an Argument:** Browse recent news or popular-interest magazines (such as *Time, The Atlantic, GQ, The New Yorker,* and so on) to locate a serious article you find especially well argued and persuasive. Like Matthew James Nance in "A Mockery of Justice" (p. 264), study the piece carefully enough to understand the techniques it uses to influence readers. Then write a rhetorical analysis in which you make and support a specific claim about the rhetorical strategies of the piece.

3. **Cultural Analysis:** Identify a cultural phenomenon (TV talent shows), theme (men who won't grow up), trend (divorce parties) or image (disaster photos) and examine the way it either influences society or reflects the way that people are thinking or behaving. Make the analysis rhetorical by focusing on questions related to audience, social context, techniques of persuasion, or language. Help readers to see your subject in a new light or from a fresh perspective. Use J. Reagan Tankersley's "Humankind's Ouroboros" (p. 270) as a starting point.

4. **Analysis of a Visual Text:** Identify a physical object that has taken on a special symbolic or persuasive value not connected with its original purpose or use. Then examine it the way Beth Teitell looks into Scott Brown's jacket in "A Jacket of the People" (p. 279)—though your paper might move beyond reporting facts to become an argument with a specific claim. The trick will be to find an iconic object to write about: They can become so deeply embedded in our culture that we cease to notice their symbolic importance. Consider Mickey Mouse, Air Force One, a Yankee's baseball cap, the Starbucks logo, throwaway plastic shopping bags, Darth Vader's mask, the Duke's Dodge Charger, and so on.

    Alternatively, study the home page of an important institutional Web site to determine what signals its design sends to users. Examine all of its elements carefully, from the content on the page to its structure, design elements, images, colors, links, usability, and so on. Decide upon the qualities the site conveys, such as authority, credibility, power, competence, friendliness, danger, welcome, or warning. Then compose a piece in which you support a thesis about the rhetoric of the site design.

5. **Your Choice:** Fed up by the blustering of a talk-show host, political figure, op-ed columnist, local editorialist, or stupid advertiser? Try an item-by-item or paragraph-by-paragraph refutation of such a target, taking on his or her poorly reasoned claims, inadequate evidence, emotional excesses, or lack of credibility. Try to find a transcript or reproduction of the text you want to refute so that you can work from the facts just as they have been offered. If you are examining a visual text you can reproduce electronically, experiment with using callouts to annotate the problems as you find them.

Special Assignments

2

part two

require answers written within a time limit | **9** | **Essay Examinations** 284

require a brief critical response | **10** | **Position Papers** 290

summarize and assess sources | **11** | **Annotated Bibliographies** 296

require a response to multiple sources | **12** | **Synthesis Papers** 300

communicate electronically | **13** | **E-mails** 310

communicate formally | **14** | **Business Letters** 316

record professional achievements | **15** | **Résumés** 324

explain a person's experiences and goals | **16** | **Personal Statements** 330

record a scientific experiment | **17** | **Lab Reports** 336

present information to a live audience | **18** | **Oral Reports** 346

Need a form you don't see here? Try "Genres," p. 2.

How to start ▶ ● **Got a test tomorrow?**
Read exam questions carefully. See page 285.

9 Essay Examinations

require answers written within a time limit

Essay examinations test not only your knowledge of a subject but also your ability to write about it coherently and professionally.

- For a class in nursing, you must write a short essay about the role health-care providers play in dealing with patients who have been victims of domestic abuse.

- For an examination in a literature class, you must offer a close reading of a sonnet, explicating its argument and poetic images line by line.

- For a standardized test, you must read a passage by a critic of globalization and respond to the case made and evidence presented.

- For a psychology exam, you must explore the ethical issues raised by two research articles on brain research and the nature of consciousness.

UNDERSTANDING ESSAY EXAMS. You've probably taken enough essay exams to know that there are no magic bullets to slay this dragon, and that the best approach is to know your material well enough to make several credible points in an hour or so. You must also write—*under pressure*—coherent sentences and paragraphs. ○ Here are some specific strategies to increase your odds of doing well.

got a test ◄ tomorrow?

Anticipate the types of questions you might be asked. What happens in class—the concepts presented, the issues raised, the assignments given—is like a coming-attractions trailer for an exam. If you attend class regularly and do the required readings, you'll figure out at least some of an instructor's habitual moves and learn something to boot. Review any sample essay exams too—they may even be available on a course Web site.

Read exam questions carefully. Underscore key words such as *divide*, *classify*, *evaluate*, *compare*, *compare and contrast*, and *analyze* and then respect the differences between these strategies. ○ Exam questions may be short essays themselves, setting out background information or offering a passage to read before the actual query appears. Respond to that specific question and not to your own take on any preliminary materials.

Sketch out a plan for your essay(s). The first part of the plan should deal with *time*. Read all the exam questions carefully and then estimate how many minutes to spend on each—understanding that some will take more effort than others. (Pay attention to point totals too: Focus on essay questions that count more, but don't ignore any. Five points is five points.) Allow time for planning and editing each answer. Sketch outlines and come up with a thesis for each question. ○ Then stick to your time limits.

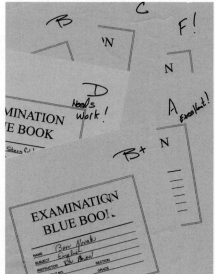

Organize your answer strategically. If any form of writing benefits from a pattern of development worn like an exoskeleton, it's a response to an essay question. In your first paragraph, state your main point and preview the structure of the whole essay. That way, even if you cannot finish, a reader will know where you were heading and possibly give you partial credit for incomplete work.

improve your
sentences p. 444

develop a draft
p. 398

develop a statement
p. 393

Offer strong evidence for your claims.   The overall structure of the essay should convey your grasp of concepts—your ability to see the big picture. Within that structure, arrange details and evidence to show your command of the subject. Use memorable examples culled from class reading to make your points: Cite important names, concepts, and dates; mention critical issues and terms; rattle off the accurate titles of books and articles.

Come to a conclusion.   Even if you run short on time, find a moment to write a paragraph that brings your ideas together. Don't just repeat the topic sentences of your paragraphs. A reader will already have those ideas firmly in mind as he or she judges your work. So add something new—an implication or extrapolation—to chew on. ○

Keep the tone serious.   Write essay examinations in a high or middle style. ○ Avoid a personal point of view unless the question invites you to enter your opinion on a controversy. Given the press of time, you can probably get away with contractions and some standard abbreviations. But make sure the essay reads like prose, not a text message.

Don't panic.   Keep your eye on the clock, but *don't panic*. Everyone else is working under the same constraints and will be able to produce only so much prose in an hour or two. If you've prepared for the exam and start with a plan, you may find first-rate ideas materializing in the process of writing. Even if they don't, keep writing. You'll get no credit for blank pages.

> **Your Turn**   Preparing for an examination now? Take a moment to list *from memory* as many of the key names, titles, and concepts likely to appear on that exam as you can—terms you are certain to need when you compose your essays. Then check these terms as you have written them down against the way they appear in your notes or textbooks, or on the course Web site. Have you gotten the names and titles right? Have you phrased the concepts correctly, and can you explain what they mean? Just as important, as you review your course materials, do you notice any important ideas that should have made your list, but didn't?

shape an ending
p. 425

refine your tone
p. 432

Wade Lamb offered the following response to this essay question on a midterm essay examination in a course entitled Classical to Modern Rhetoric:

> The structure of Plato's *Phaedrus* is dominated by three speeches about the lover and non-lover—one by Lysias and two by Socrates. How do these speeches differ in their themes and strategies, and what point do they make about rhetoric and truth?

Lamb 1

Wade Lamb

Professor Karishky

Rhetoric 101

September 19, 20--

Plato's *Phaedrus* is unique among Platonic dialogues because it takes place in a rural setting between only two characters—Socrates and the youth Phaedrus. It is, however, like Plato's *Gorgias* in that it is "based on a distinction between knowledge and belief" and focuses on some of the ways we can use rhetoric to seek the truth.

The first speech presented in *Phaedrus*, written by Lysias and read aloud by Phaedrus, is the simplest of the three. Composed by Lysias to demonstrate the power of rhetoric to persuade an audience, it claims perversely that it is better to have a sexual relationship with someone who doesn't love you than someone who does.

Socrates responds with a speech of his own making the same point, which he composes on the spot, but which he describes as "a greater lie than Lysias's." Unlike Lysias,

Opening focuses directly on issues posed in question.

Short quotation functions as piece of evidence.

Sensibly organized around three speeches to be examined: one paragraph per speech.

Lamb 2

however, Socrates begins by carefully defining his terms and organizes his speech more effectively. He does so to teach Phaedrus that in order to persuade an audience, an orator must first understand the subject and divide it into its appropriate parts. However, Socrates delivers this speech with a veil over his head because he knows that what he and Lysias have claimed about love is false.

The third speech—again composed by Socrates—is the most important. In it, Socrates demonstrates that persuasion that leads merely to belief (not truth) damages both the orator and the audience. He compares rhetoric such as that used by Lysias to the unconcerned and harmful lust of a non-lover. Good rhetoric, on the other hand—which Socrates says is persuasion that leads to knowledge—is like the true lover who seeks to lead his beloved to transcendent truth. Socrates shows that he believes good rhetoric should ultimately be concerned with finding and teaching truth, not just with making a clever argument someone might falsely believe, as Lysias's speech does.

By comparing the three speeches in *Phaedrus*, Plato shows that he gives some value to rhetoric, but not in the form practiced by orators such as Lysias. Plato emphasizes the importance of the distinction between belief and knowledge and argues that rhetoric should search for and communicate the truth.

Most important speech gets lengthiest and most detailed treatment.

Conclusion states Lamb's thesis, describing the point he believes Plato wished to make about rhetoric in *Phaedrus*.

Getting the details right

Allow a few minutes near the end of the exam period to reread what you
have written and insert corrections and emendations. You won't have time
to fix large-scale issues: If you've confused the Spanish Armada with Torque-
mada, you're toast. But a quick edit may catch embarrassing gaffes or
omissions. When you write quickly, you probably leave out or transpose
some words or simply use the wrong expression. Take a moment to edit
these fixable errors. In the process, you may also amplify or repair an idea or
two. Here are some other useful strategies to follow.

Use transition words and phrases.   Essay examinations are the perfect
place to employ such transparent transitional devices as *first, second,* and
third, or *next, even more important, nonetheless, in summary, in conclusion,*
and so on. Don't be subtle: The transitions guide you as you write and help
keep your instructor on track later. O You will seem to be in control of your
material.

Do a quick check of grammar, mechanics, and spelling.   Some
instructors take great offense at mechanical slips, even minor ones. At a
minimum, avoid the common errors covered in Part 9 of this book. Also be
sure to spell correctly any names and concepts that you've been reviewing in
preparation for the examination. O It's *Macbeth,* not *McBeth.*

Write legibly or print.   Few people do much handwriting anymore. But
essay examinations still often use paper or blue books. If you are out of practice or your handwriting is just flat-out illegible, print. Printing takes more
time, but instructors appreciate the effort. Write in ink, as pencil can be faint
and hard to read. Also consider double-spacing your essay to allow room
for corrections and additions. But be careful not to spread your words too
far apart. A blue book with just a few sentences per page undermines your
ethos: It looks juvenile.

revise and edit
p. 452

help with common
errors p. 600

How to start

Confused?
Read the assignment carefully. See page 292.

10 Position Papers

require a brief critical response

A course instructor may ask you to respond to an assigned reading, lecture, film, or other activity with a position paper in which you record your reactions to the material—such as your impressions or observations. Such a paper is usually brief—often not much longer than a page or two—and due the next class session. Typically, you won't have time for more than a draft and quick revision.

- You summarize and assess the findings of a journal article studying the relationship between a full night's sleep and student success on college exams.

- You speculate about how a feminist philosopher of science, whose work you have read for a class, might react to recent developments in genetics.

- You respond to ideas raised by a panel of your classmates discussing a proposition to restore the military draft or require an alternative form of national service.

- You offer a gut reaction to your first-ever viewing of *Triumph of the Will*, a notorious propaganda film made by director Leni Riefenstahl for Germany's National Socialist (Nazi) Party in 1935.

UNDERSTANDING POSITION PAPERS. Instructors usually have several goals in assigning position papers: to focus your attention on a particular reading or class presentation; to measure how well you've understood course materials; to push you to connect one concept or reading with another. Because they may want you to take some risks, instructors often mark position papers less completely than full essays and grade them by different standards.

You might be tempted to blow off these assignments because they can seem like quick, low-stakes items. That would be an error. Position papers give you practice in writing about a subject and so prepare you for other papers and exams. The assignments *may* even preview the types of essay questions an instructor favors. Position papers also help to establish your ethos in a course, marking you as a careful reader and thinker or, alternatively, someone just along for the ride.

Use a few simple strategies to write a strong position paper.

Protesters Taking a Position While some feel that security cameras ensure safety, others believe them to be an invasion of privacy.

▶ confused?

Read the assignment carefully.   Understand exactly what your instructor wants: Look for key words such as *summarize, describe, classify, evaluate, compare, compare and contrast,* and *analyze* and then respect the differences between them. ⚪

Review assigned material carefully.   Consider photocopying readings so that you can annotate their margins or underscore key claims and evidence. Practice smart reading: Always look for conflicts, points of difference, or issues raised in class or in the public arena—what some writers call *hooks*. Then use the most provocative material to jump-start your own thinking, using whatever brainstorming techniques work best for you. ⚪

Mine the texts for evidence.   Identify key passages worth quoting or features worth describing in detail. ⚪ Anchor your position paper around such strong passages. For instance, you may find some facts in the piece startling enough to mention, a claim or two you resist fiercely and want to dispute, or concise summaries of complicated positions you admire. Be sure, too, you know how to merge quoted material smoothly with your own writing.

Organize the paper sensibly.   Unless the assignment specifically states otherwise, don't write the position paper off the top of your head. Take the time to offer a thesis or to set up a comparison, an evaluation, or another structure of organization. Give a position paper the same structural integrity you would a longer and more consequential assignment.

Here's a position paper written by Heidi Rogers as an early assignment in a lower-level course on visual rhetoric. Rogers's assignment was to offer an honest response to director Leni Riefenstahl's infamous documentary, *Triumph of the Will,* which showcases the National Socialist Party rallies in Munich in 1934. In the film, we see the German people embracing Hitler and his Nazi regime as they consolidate their power.

develop a draft
p. 398

get an idea
p. 356

use quotations
p. 497

Rogers 1

Heidi Rogers

Professor Wachtel

Writing 203

September 22, 20--

Triumph of the Lens

The 1935 film *Triumph of the Will*, directed by Leni
Riefenstahl, masterfully shows how visuals can be a powerful
form of rhetoric. In the documentary we see Adolf Hitler, one
of the greatest mass murderers in history, portrayed as an
inspirational leader who could be the savior of Germany.
Watching the film, I was taken aback. I am supposed to detest
Hitler for his brutal crimes against humanity, and yet I found
myself liking him, even smiling as he greets his fellow
Germans on the streets of Munich. How did Riefenstahl
accomplish this, drawing viewers into her film and giving
Germans such pride in their leader?

Riefenstahl's technique is to layer selected visuals so as
to evoke the emotions she wants her audience to feel toward
Hitler and his regime. Her first step is to introduce images of
nature and locations that are peaceful and soothing. Next, she
inserts images of the German people themselves: children
playing, women blowing kisses to Hitler, men in uniform
proudly united under the Nazi flag. The next step is to weave
images of Hitler himself among these German people, so that
even when he isn't smiling or showing any emotions, it seems
as if he is conveying the happiness, pride, or strength evoked

Offers a thesis to explain
how film makes Hitler
attractive.

To explain how film works,
describes pattern she sees
in Riefenstahl's editing
technique.

Triumph of the Will features
numerous imposing shots of
crowds cheering for Hitler.

Rogers 2

by the images edited around him. The final piece of the puzzle is always to put Hitler front and center, usually giving a rousing speech, which makes him seem larger than life.

Provides extended example to support claim about how *Triumph of the Will* was edited.

A good example of this technique comes during the youth rally sequence. First, Riefenstahl presents peaceful images of the area around the Munich stadium, including beautiful trees with the sun streaming between the branches. We then see the vastness of the city stadium, designed by Hitler himself. Then we watch thousands of young boys and girls smiling and cheering in the stands. These masses erupt when Hitler enters the arena and Riefenstahl artfully juxtaposes images of him, usually with a cold, emotionless face, with enthusiastic youth looking up to him as if he were a god. Hitler then delivers an intoxicating speech about the future of Germany and the greatness that the people will achieve under his leadership. The crowd goes wild as he leaves the stage and we see an audience filled with awe and purpose.

Explores implications of claim—that clever editing enabled Riefenstahl to reach many audiences.

What Riefenstahl did in *Triumph of the Will* is a common technique in film editing. When you have to reach a massive audience, you want to cover all of your bases and appeal to all of them at once. Therefore, the more kinds of *ethos*, *pathos*, and *logos* you can layer onto a piece of film, the better your chances will be of convincing the greatest number of people of your cause. As hard as this is to admit, if I had lived in a devastated 1935 Germany and I had seen this film, I might have wanted this guy to lead my country too.

Getting the details right

Edit the final version.   Edit and proofread your text carefully before you turn it in. ○ Think of a position paper as a trial run for a longer paper. As such, it should follow the conventions of any given field or major. Even when an instructor seems casual about the assignment, don't ease up.

Identify key terms and concepts and use them correctly and often. The instructor may be checking to see how carefully you read. So, in your paper, make a point of referring to the new concepts or terms you've found in your reading, as Rogers does with *ethos*, *pathos*, and *logos* in her essay.

Treat your sources appropriately.   Either identify them by author and title within the paper or list them at the end in the correct documentation form (e.g., MLA or APA). Make sure quotations are set up accurately, properly intro-duced, and documented. Offer page numbers for any direct quotations. ○

Spell names and concepts correctly.   You lose credibility if you misspell technical terms or proper nouns that appear throughout the course readings. In literary papers especially, get characters' names and book titles right.

Respond to your colleagues' work.   Position papers are often posted to electronic discussion boards to jump-start conversations. So take the opportunity to reply substantively to what your classmates have written. Don't just say "I agree" or "You're kidding!" Add good reasons and evidence to your remarks. Remember, too, that your instructor may review these com-ments, looking for evidence of engagement with the course material. ○

Your Turn   Many blogs encourage readers to comment on their postings. You can use such sites to practice your skill at responding to what you read. On a news or cul-tural blog you scan regularly, locate a fairly lengthy and serious article to which some readers have already offered substantive responses, more than a line or two. After reading the article, think about what you might post in response. Then read through the actual postings. How does your brief response compare with what others have said? What strategies have they used that you admire? How did the best responders establish their credibility? And which responders did you take less seriously *and* why?

Chances are you'll be disappointed in much of what you read in online commentary. People may respond from prejudiced positions, focus on irrel-evant points, or take personal potshots at the original author. But from such respondents, you may learn what *not* to do in a serious academic paper.

---

revise and edit
p. 452

understand citation
styles p. 501

comment
p. 458

How to start

● **Need to write a summary?**
Check Chapter 45 for more details. See page 491.

11 Annotated Bibliographies

summarize and assess sources

When preparing a term paper, senior thesis, or other lengthy research project, an instructor may expect you to submit an annotated bibliography. The bibliography may be due weeks before you turn in the paper, or it may be turned in with the finished project.

- A sociology instructor asks that your topic proposal for a midterm paper on rural poverty include an annotated bibliography that demonstrates a range of perspectives in your reading.

- Your senior history thesis is based upon letters and archival materials found only in a local museum. So you attach an annotated bibliography to your completed project to give readers a clearer sense of what some of the handwritten documents cover.

- In writing a term paper on the cultural roots and connections of gangsta/reality rap, you decide to annotate your works cited items to let readers know what sources you found most authoritative and useful for future research.

UNDERSTANDING ANNOTATED BIBLIOGRAPHIES.   An annotated bibliography is an alphabetical list of the sources and documents you have used in developing a research project, with each item in the list summarized and, very often, evaluated.

Instructors usually ask you to attach an annotated bibliography to the final version of a project, enabling them to determine at a glance how well you've researched your subject. But some may ask you to submit an annotated bibliography earlier in the writing process—sometimes even as part of the topic proposal—to be sure you're on track, poring over good materials, and getting the most out of them. ○

Begin with an accurate bibliography of research materials.   Items in the alphabetical list should follow the guidelines of some documentation system, typically MLA or APA. In a paper using MLA documentation, the list is labeled "Works Cited" and includes only books, articles, and other materials actually mentioned in the project; it is labeled "Works Consulted" if you also want to include works you've read, but not actually cited. In APA-style projects, the list is called "References." ○

need to write ◀
a summary?

Describe or summarize the content of each item in the bibliography.   These summaries should be *very* brief, often just one or two sentences. Begin with a brief description of the work if it isn't self-evident (*a review of; an interview with; a CIA report on*). Then, in your own words, describe its contents, scope, audience, perspective, or other features relevant to your project. Your language should be descriptive and neutral. Be sure to follow any special guidelines offered by your instructor. For more about summarizing, see Chapter 45, "Summarizing Sources." ○

plan a project
p. 466

cite in APA
p. 540

understand citation
styles p. 501

Assess the quality or importance of the work.   Immediately follow-ing the summary, offer a brief appraisal of the item, responding to its quality, authority, thoroughness, length, relevance, usefulness, age (e.g., *up-to-date/ dated*), reputation in field (if known), and so on. Your remarks should be professional and academic: You aren't writing a movie review.

Explain the role the work plays in your research.   When an anno-tated bibliography is part of a topic proposal, assess the preliminary materi-als you have found and describe how you expect to use them in your project. Highlight works that seem to provide creative or fresh ideas, authoritative coverage, up-to-date research, diverse perspectives, or ample bibliographies.

The following three items are from an annotated bibliography offered as part of a topic proposal on the cultural impact of the iPod.

Full bibliographical citation in MLA style.

Summary of Stephenson's argument.

Potential role source might play in paper.

Stephenson, Seth. "You and Your Shadow." *Slate.com* 2 Mar. 2004. Web. 3 Mar. 2007. This article from *Slate.com*'s "Ad Report Card" series argues that the original iPod ads featuring silhouetted dancers may alienate viewers by suggesting that the product is cooler than the people who buy it. Stephenson explains why some people may resent the advertisements. The piece may be useful for explaining early reactions to the iPod as a cultural phenomenon.

Sullivan, Andrew. "Society Is Dead: We Have Retreated into the iWorld." *Sunday Times* 20 Feb. 2005. Web. 27 Feb. 2007. In this opinion piece, Sullivan examines how people in cities use iPods to isolate themselves from their surroundings. The author makes a highly personal, but plausible case for turning off the machines. The column demonstrates how quickly the iPod has changed society and culture.

Evaluation of Sullivan's opinion piece.

Citation demonstrates how to cite an article from a database — in this case, *OneFile*.

Walker, Rob. "The Guts of a New Machine." *New York Times Magazine* 30 Nov. 2003. *OneFile*. Web. 1 Mar. 2007. This lengthy report describes in detail how Apple developed the concept and technology of the iPod. Walker not only provides a detailed early look at the product, but also shows how badly Apple's competitors underestimated its market strength. May help to explain Apple's later dominance in smartphones as well.

Getting the details right

Annotated bibliographies can be informative and time-saving documents, as you'll discover if you happen to find a reliable one that covers a subject you are researching. As you prepare such a list, think about how your work might benefit other readers.

Get the information on your sources right.   As you format the items in your list, be sure that the titles, authors, page numbers, and dates are correct so that users can quickly locate the materials you have used.

Follow correct documentation style.   Documentation systems like MLA and APA can seem fussy, but they make life easier for researchers by standardizing the way all the identifying features of a source are treated. So if you get an entry right in your annotated bibliography, you make life easier for the next person who needs to cite that source. ○

Keep your summaries and assessments brief.   Don't get carried away. In most cases, instructors and other readers will want an annotated bibliography that they can scan. They'll appreciate writing that is both precise and succinct.

Follow directions carefully.   Some instructors may provide specific directions for annotated bibliographies, depending on the field or subject of your research. For example, they may ask you to supply the volume numbers, locations, and physical dimensions of books; describe illustrations; and so on.

> **Your Turn**   For a quick exercise in preparing an annotated bibliography, choose a film that has opened very recently, locate five or six reviews or news articles about it, and then prepare an annotated bibliography using these items. Imagine that you'll be writing a research paper about the public and critical reception the film received when it debuted. (Public and critical reaction may be quite different.) Be sure to choose a documentation system for your bibliography and to use it appropriately.

understand citation
styles p. 501

How to start ▶ ● **Need to write a synthesis paper?**
Summarize and paraphrase what you have read.
See page 301.

12 Synthesis Papers

require a response to multiple sources

In some classes, you may be asked to write a synthesis paper—in which you summarize, compare, or assess the views offered by different sources covering a specific topic. (This assignment is sometimes called a "literature review," but here "literature" is used as a general term to describe scholarship in a field; it does not mean you will work only with fiction, poetry, or drama.) A synthesis exercise or literature review prepares you to write on a topic by requiring you to stake out the claims already made by reputable writers, thus enabling you to move the argument forward. It also gives you important practice in using sources.

- In an English class, you review several new claims by writers challenging the authorship of the plays generally ascribed to William Shakespeare.

- For an engineering course, you are asked to prepare a literature review covering the most recently published research on lithium-ion polymer batteries.

- For a first-year writing course, you write a detailed synthesis examining the positions of authors who both support and challenge your view that we must learn to adapt to new media.

- In preparing a prospectus for a senior thesis, you prove your topic is viable by including a section in which you summarize the sources you expect to use and explain the different positions they represent.

UNDERSTANDING SYNTHESIS PAPERS.   In a synthesis, you weigh and consider the full range of responsible, fact-based opinion on a subject. For an assignment designed to teach how to use sources, you will ordinarily summarize and analyze a range of reputable authorities. In doing such an exercise, note what types of sources you must review, how to document them, ○ whether you may quote from them, and whether you are expected to develop a thesis derived from the materials you have read.

Need to write a ◄
synthesis paper?

If your assignment is to prepare a review of literature, you will identify and report on the most important books and articles on a subject, usually over a specified period of time: *currently, from the last five years, over the past three decades.*

The topic of the review may be assigned to you or be one you are considering for a thesis, term paper, or capstone project. Check whether your synthesis must follow a specific pattern of organization: Most literature reviews are chronological, though some are thematic, and still others are arranged by comparison and contrast. ○

Read reputable sources on your subject.   Synthesis papers almost always involve examining multiple articles, books, and research studies and then describing the relationships between them: *similarity, difference, congruence, divergence, consistency, inconsistency,* and so on. Consult with your instructor or a research librarian to separate mainstream and essential works on your topic from outliers, which may or may not deserve a closer look. Don't offer a thesis until you have carefully weighed the claims, reasons, and evidence in the sources you have examined. ○

In 1993, artists Tibor Kalman and Scott Stowell erected this yellow billboard in New York City's heavily trafficked Times Square perhaps to suggest a world of limitless choices. Exploring a new topic, you face similar possibilities and need to sort them out.

Summarize and paraphrase what you have read.   A typical synthesis assignment moves one step beyond summaries and paraphrases, but you will still need them to provide material for the judgments you make about various sources. (Review these skills, as necessary, in Chapters 45–46.) Summarize the sources you expect to mention briefly and paraphrase those materials you will refer to more extensively or quote from directly.

○
understand citation
styles p. 501

○
develop a draft
p. 398

○
read closely
p. 365

Examine the connections between your sources.   Read the sources you have collected *in relationship to each other* to determine precisely where they stand on a subject or how they affect the development of your own thesis. In particular, identify any sources that help readers understand how an issue is defined or how your own claims and reasons develop logically from ideas and information reported by other writers. Introduce such materials with verbs of attribution such as *describes, reports, points out, asserts, argues, claims, agrees, concurs*.

Acknowledge disagreements and rebuttals.   Your synthesis should summarize and paraphrase any reputable sources that challenge your thesis or, in a review of literature, represent a full range of opinions. Describe all the opinions you encounter accurately, introducing them with verbs of attribution such as *questions, denies, disagrees, contradicts, undermines, disputes, calls into question, takes issue with.*

If you have done an effective synthesis, your review of sources should enrich and complicate your understanding of a subject and prepare you to join an academic discussion already in progress. To give you an idea of how to bring sources into a conversation, we'll build a brief essay from a set of paragraphs drawn from sources focusing on one topic: whether new media technologies like the Web pose a threat to literacy and culture. Ideas that play a role in the essay are highlighted. The sources are presented alphabetically by author:

> I ask my students about their reading habits, and though I'm not surprised to find that few read newspapers or print magazines, many check in with online news sources, aggregate sites, incessantly. They are seldom away from their screens for long, but that's true of us, their parents, as well.
>
> — Sven Birkerts, "Reading in a Digital Age"

> The picture emerging from the research is deeply troubling, at least to anyone who values the depth, rather than just the velocity, of human thought. People who read text studded with links, the studies show, comprehend less than those who read traditional linear text. People who watch busy multimedia presentations remember less than those who take in information in a more sedate and focused manner. People who are continually distracted by emails, alerts and other messages understand less than those who are able to

restate ideas
p. 494

concentrate. And people who juggle many tasks are less creative and less productive than those who do one thing at a time.

It is this control, this mental discipline, that we are at risk of losing as we spend ever more time scanning and skimming online. If the slow progression of words across printed pages damped our craving to be inundated by mental stimulation, the Internet indulges it. It returns us to our native state of distractedness, while presenting us with far more distractions than our ancestors ever had to contend with.

— Nicholas Carr, "Does the Internet Make You Dumber?"

Today some 4.5 billion digital screens illuminate our lives. Words have migrated from wood pulp to pixels on computers, phones, laptops, game consoles, televisions, billboards and tablets. Letters are no longer fixed in black ink on paper, but flitter on a glass surface in a rainbow of colors as fast as our eyes can blink. Screens fill our pockets, briefcases, dashboards, living room walls and the sides of buildings. They sit in front of us when we work— regardless of what we do. We are now people of the screen. And of course, these newly ubiquitous screens have changed how we read and write.

— Kevin Kelly, "Reading in a Whole New Way"

I have been reading a lot on my iPad recently, and I have some complaints—not about the iPad but about the state of digital reading generally. Reading is a subtle thing, and its subtleties are artifacts of a venerable medium: words printed in ink on paper. Glass and pixels aren't the same.

— Verlyn Klinkenborg, "Further Thoughts of a Novice E-Reader"

The new media have caught on for a reason. Knowledge is increasing exponentially; human brainpower and waking hours are not. Fortunately, the Internet and information technologies are helping us manage, search and retrieve our collective intellectual output at different scales, from Twitter and previews to e-books and online encyclopedias. Far from making us stupid, these technologies are the only things that will keep us smart.

— Steven Pinker, "Mind over Mass Media"

No teenager that I know of regularly reads a newspaper, as most do not have the time and cannot be bothered to read pages and pages of text while they could watch the news summarized on the Internet or on TV.

— Matthew Robson, "How Teenagers Consume Media"

Then again, perhaps we will simply adjust and come to accept what James called "acquired inattention." E-mails pouring in, cell phones ringing, televisions blaring, podcasts streaming—all this may become background noise, like the "din of a foundry or factory" that James observed workers could scarcely avoid at first, but which eventually became just another part of their daily routine. For the younger generation of multitaskers, the great electronic din is an expected part of everyday life. And given what neuroscience and anecdotal evidence have shown us, this state of constant intentional self-distraction could well be of profound detriment to individual and cultural well-being. When people do their work only in the "interstices of their mind-wandering," with crumbs of attention rationed out among many competing tasks, their culture may gain in information, but it will surely weaken in wisdom.

—Christine Rosen, "The Myth of Multitasking"

The past was not as golden, nor is the present as tawdry, as the pessimists suggest, but the only thing really worth arguing about is the future. It is our misfortune, as a historical generation, to live through the largest expansion in expressive capability in human history, a misfortune because abundance breaks more things than scarcity. We are now witnessing the rapid stress of older institutions accompanied by the slow and fitful development of cultural alternatives. Just as required education was a response to print, using the Internet well will require new cultural institutions as well, not just new technologies.

—Clay Shirky, "Does the Internet Make You Smarter?"

Both Carr and Rosen are right about one thing: The changeover to digital reading brings challenges and changes, requiring a reconsideration of what books are and what they're supposed to do. That doesn't mean the shift won't be worth it. The change will also bring innovations impossible on Gutenberg's printed page, from text mixed with multimedia to components that allow readers to interact with the author and fellow consumers.

—Peter Suderman, "Don't Fear the E-Reader"

Here is a brief paper that synthesizes the positions represented in the preceding sources, quoting extensively from them and leading up to a thesis. We have boldfaced the authors' names the first time they appear, to emphasize the number of sources used in this short example.

Chiu 1

Lauren Chiu

Professor Larondo

Writing 203

March 19, 20--

Time to Adapt?

There is considerable agreement that the Internet and other electronic media are changing the way people read, write, think, and behave. Scholars such as **Sven Birkerts** report that their students do not seem to read printed materials anymore, a fact confirmed by fifteen-year-old intern **Matthew Robson**, when asked by his employer Morgan Stanley to describe the media habits of teenagers in England: "No teenager that I know of regularly reads a newspaper, as most do not have the time and cannot be bothered to read pages and pages of text."

But the changes we are experiencing may be more significant than just students abandoning the printed word. Working with an iPad, for instance, makes **Verlyn Klinkenborg** wonder whether reading on a screen may actually be a different and less perceptive experience than reading on paper. More worrisome, **Nicholas Carr** points to a growing body of research suggesting that the cognitive abilities of those who use media frequently may actually be degraded, weakening their comprehension and concentration. Yet, according to **Clay Shirky**, the Internet is increasing our ability to communicate immeasurably, and so we simply have to deal with whatever consequences follow from such a major shift in technology.

Two sources are cited to support a general claim about the media.

Other authorities amplify and complicate the issue.

Carr and Shirky are well-known authors with opposing views of the Web.

Chiu 2

Thinkers like Shirky argue that we do not, in fact, have any choice but to adapt to such changes.

Even **Christine Rosen**, a critic of technology, acknowledges that people will likely have to adjust to their diminished attention spans (110). After all, are there really any alternatives to the speed, convenience, and power of the new technologies when we have become what **Kevin Kelly** describes as "people of the screen" and are no more likely to return to paper for reading than we are to vinyl for music recordings? Fears of the Internet may be overblown too. **Peter Suderman** observes that changes in media allow us to do vastly more than we can with print alone. Moreover, because the sheer amount of knowledge is increasing so quickly, **Steven Pinker** argues that we absolutely need the new ways of communicating: "these technologies are the only things that will keep us smart."

We cannot, however, ignore voices of caution. The differences Carr describes between habits of deep reading and skimming are especially troubling because so many users of the Web have experienced them. And who can doubt the loss of seriousness in our public and political discussions these days? Maybe Rosen *is* right when she worries that our culture is trading wisdom for a glut of information. But it seems more likely that society will be better off trying to fix the problems electronic media are causing than imagining that we can return to simpler technologies that have already just about vanished.

In a full-length essay, this section would be much longer and quote more sources.

Concerns about the Web are portrayed as reasonable.

The writer states a thesis that might guide a longer analysis.

Chiu 3

Works Cited

Birkerts, Sven. "Reading in a Digital Age." *The American Scholar*. Phi Beta Kappa, Spring 2010. Web. 10 Sept. 2010.

Carr, Nicholas. "Does the Internet Make You Dumber?" *Wall Street Journal*. Wall Street Journal, 5 June 2010. Web. 9 Sept. 2010.

Kelly, Kevin. "Reading in a Whole New Way." *Smithsonian .com*. Smithsonian, Aug. 2010. Web. 13 Sept. 2010.

Klinkenborg, Verlyn. "Further Thoughts of a Novice E-Reader." *New York Times*. New York Times, 28 May 2010. Web. 12 Sept. 2010.

Pinker, Steven. "Mind over Mass Media." *New York Times*. New York Times, 10 June 2010. Web. 12 Sept. 2010.

Robson, Matthew. "How Teenagers Consume Media." *Guardian .co.uk*. Guardian News and Media, 13 July 2009. Web. 14 Sept. 2010.

Rosen, Christine. "The Myth of Multitasking." *The New Atlantis* 20 (Spring 2008): 105–110. Print.

Shirky, Clay. "Does the Internet Make You Smarter?" *Wall Street Journal*. Wall Street Journal, 4 June 2010. Web. 9 Sept. 2010.

Suderman, Peter. "Don't Fear the E-Reader." *Reason.com*. Reason Magazine, 23 Mar. 2010. Web. 11 Sept. 2010.

Getting the details right

Although synthesis assignments vary enormously, certain fine points are worth remembering.

Introduce materials that provide a context for your topic.   Open a synthesis paper by mentioning sources that help to shape your topic, place the subject in its historical or cultural contexts, and provide a rationale for your project. Look for authors or materials that help readers understand why an issue is important.

Cite materials that explain or complicate your thesis.   Introduce any writers whose ideas amplify or expand an issue you want to explore. In particular, look for authors who grab your attention or get cited as authorities in other materials. Summarize these materials adequately, yet concisely. In the preceding example, we are limited to only a sentence or two of discussion, but in a full essay your presentation would offer much more detail.

Don't rush to judgment.   In synthesizing, writers sometimes divide their sources too conveniently between those that support a claim and those that oppose it, ignoring complications and subtleties. Quite often, the most interesting relationships are to be found in places where belligerent authors unexpectedly agree or orthodox research generates unexpected results. When synthesizing sources for an assignment or a research project, don't precook the results or try to fit your materials into an existing framework.

Tell a story.   Whether your synthesis merely summarizes varying points of view or defends a thesis statement, create a narrative readers can follow. O Help them to understand the issues as you have come to appreciate them yourself. Separate major issues from minor ones, and use transitions as necessary to establish connections (*consequently*), highlight contrasts (*on the other hand*), show parallels (*similarly*), and so on.

Cite materials that support your thesis.   If you've done your job well, any thesis you derive from reading sources should do more than just echo opinions you have found in your research. But be sure to cite those writers who support or amplify your ideas.

understand narratives
p. 4

Acknowledge materials that run counter to your thesis.   The voices hardest to bring into your work may be those that disagree with you. Yet in academic and professional writing, you must not only acknowledge these dissenters, but also outline their ideas objectively and introduce any quotations from them fairly (Rosen *says*, not Rosen *whines*). ○

Pay attention to language.   Remember that the summaries of materials you cite should be in your own words; some synthesis assignments may even preclude direct quotations. If you do quote from sources, choose statements that cogently represent the positions of your sources.

Keep the style of your synthesis objective, neutral, and fairly formal. In most cases, avoid *I* when summarizing and paraphrasing. ○

Be sure to document your sources.   Keep track of all the materials you consult and be prepared to document them fully in an academic paper.

Your Turn   All the sources from which the paragraphs in this section come are available online. Choose two or three of them and write a detailed synthesis of their full positions, being sure to highlight the similarities and/or differences. For this exercise, you need not state a position of your own, nor should you criticize or slant your presentation of the source material. Keep your analysis as neutral and objective as you can, *especially* if you find yourself taking sides. When you are done, a reader should have some sense of the overall media controversy that these pieces address, but have no idea where you might stand.

---

use quotations
p. 497

refine your tone
p. 432

How to start ▶ ● **Want to get the reader's attention?**
Choose a sensible subject line. See page 314.

13

communicate electronically

E-mails

E-mail has quickly become the preferred method for most business (and personal) communication because it is quick, efficient, easy to archive, and easy to search.

- You write to the coordinator of the writing center to apply for a job as a tutor, courtesy copying the message to a professor who has agreed to serve as a reference.

- You send an e-mail to classmates in a writing class, looking for someone to collaborate on a Web project.

- You e-mail the entire College of Liberal Arts faculty to invite them to attend a student production of Chekhov's *Uncle Vanya*.

- You e-mail a complaint to your cable supplier because a premium sports channel you subscribe to has been unavailable for a week.

UNDERSTANDING E-MAIL.   E-mail is now so common and informal that writers take it for granted, forgetting the role e-mail can play when transacting business. Though usually composed quickly, e-mails have a long shelf life once they're archived. They can also spread well beyond their original audiences. Remember, too, that e-mails can be printed and filed as hard copy.

You probably know how to handle personal e-mails well enough. But you may not be as savvy about the more specialized messages you send to organizations, businesses, professors, groups of classmates, and so on. The following strategies will help.

Explain your purpose clearly and logically.   Use both the subject line and first paragraph of an e-mail to explain your reason for writing: Be specific about names, titles, dates, places, and so on, especially when your message opens a discussion. Write your message so that it will still make sense a year or more later, specifying references and pronouns (*we, it, them*). ○

Tell readers what you want them to do.   Lay out a clear agenda for accomplishing one task: Ask for a document, a response, or a reply by a specific date. If you have multiple requests to make of a single person or group, consider writing separate e-mails. It's easier to track short, single-purpose e-mails than to deal with complex documents requiring several different actions.

(DILBERT Copyright © 2010 by Scott Adams. Used by permission of UNIVERSAL UCLICK. All rights reserved.)

help with common
errors p. 600

Write for intended and unintended audiences.   The specific audience in the "To" line is usually the only audience for your message. But e-mail is more public than traditional surface mail, easily duplicated and sent to whole networks of recipients with just a click. So compose your business e-mails as if they *might* be read by everyone in a unit or even published in a local paper. Assume that nothing in business e-mail is private.

Minimize the clutter.   When e-mails run through a series of replies, they grow so thick with headers, copied messages, and signatures that any new message can be hard to find. Make the latest message stand out, perhaps separating it slightly from the headers and transmission data.

Keep your messages brief.   Lengthy blocks of e-mail prose without paragraph breaks irritate readers. Indeed, meandering or chatty e-mails in business situations can make a writer seem disorganized and out of control. Try to limit your e-mail messages to what fits on a single screen. If you can't, use headings, spacing, and color to create visual pauses—but remember that many people now view e-mail on mobile devices. Keep messages simple. **O**

Distribute your messages sensibly.   Send a copy of an e-mail to anyone directly involved in the message, as well as to those who might need to be informed. For example, if filing a grade complaint with an instructor, you may also copy the chair of his or her academic department or the dean of students. But don't let the copy (Cc) and blind copy (Bcc) lines in the e-mail header tempt you to send messages beyond the essential audience.

Here's a fairly informal e-mail announcing a weekend trip, written to members of a department. Despite the relaxed event it describes, the e-mail still provides clear and direct information, gets to the point quickly, and offers an agenda for action.

think visually
p. 592

Sent: September 7, 2011
To: DRW Faculty
From: John Ruszkiewicz
Subject: Annual Big Bend Trip
Cc: Alumni in Rhetoric
Bcc:
Attachments:

Dear Colleagues—

The Division of Rhetoric and Writing's eighth annual Big Bend trip is scheduled for October 7–10, 2011, at Big Bend National Park in West Texas. If you are considering making the trip this year, please let me know by e-mail and I will put you on the mailing list.

You should know that the trip is neither an official DRW event, nor highly organized—just a group of colleagues enjoying the best natural environment Texas has to offer for a few days. If you've been to Big Bend, you know what to expect. If you haven't, see <http://www.nps.gov/bibe/index.htm>.

The weather at Big Bend in October is usually splendid. I say "usually" because we had heavy rains a few years ago and even an ice storm once. But such precipitation is rare: It is a desert park.

In the past, most people have camped at the campground, which is first come, first serve. Lodging may be available in the park itself, but rooms are hard to get throughout the fall season. Also available are hotels in nearby Study Butte, Terlingua, and Lajitas.

I'll contact those interested in the trip in a few weeks. We can begin then to plan sharing rides and equipment. And please let other friends of the DRW know about the trip.

Best,
JR

John Ruszkiewicz, Professor
The University of Texas at Austin
Department of Rhetoric and Writing
Austin, TX
Phone: (512) 555-1234

Clear, specific subject line makes message easy to find and search: Key search term would be "Big Bend."

Business letters use colon after greeting, but e-mails are often less formal.

Opening paragraph explains point of e-mail and what colleagues should do.

Second paragraph provides background information for readers who haven't been on trip before—including helpful Web link.

Tone is professional, but casual, and language is tight and correct. No emoticons.

Final paragraph outlines subsequent actions, letting readers know what to expect.

Signature is complete, opening various routes for communication.

Getting the details right

▶ want to get the
reader's attention?

Because most people receive e-mail messages frequently, make any you send easy to process.

Choose a sensible subject line.   The subject line should clearly identify the topic and include helpful keywords that might later be searched. If your e-mail is specifically about a grading policy, your student loan, or mold in your gym locker, make sure a word you'll recall afterward—like *policy, loan,* or *mold*—gets in the subject line. In professional e-mails, subjects such as *A question, Hi!* or *Meeting* are useless.

Arrange your text sensibly.   You can do almost as much visually in e-mail as you can in a word-processing program, including choosing fonts, inserting lines, and adding color, images, and videos. But because so many people now read their messages on mobile devices, a simple block style with spaces between single-spaced paragraphs probably works best for most messages.

Check the recipient list before you hit send.   Routinely double-check all the recipient fields—especially when you're replying to a message. The original writer may have copied the message widely: Do you want to send your reply to that entire group or just to the original writer?

Include an appropriate signature.   Professional e-mail of any kind should include a signature that identifies you and provides contact information readers need. Your e-mail address alone may not be clear enough to identify who you are, especially if you are writing to your instructor. Be sure to set up a signature for your laptop, desktop, or mobile device.

But be careful: You may not want to provide readers with a *home* phone number or address since you don't know precisely who may see your e-mail message. When you send e-mail, the recipient can reach you simply by replying.

Consider, too, that a list of incoming e-mails on a cell phone typically previews just the first few lines of a message. If you want a reader's attention, make your point quickly.

Use standard grammar.   Professional e-mails should be almost as polished as business letters: At least give readers the courtesy of a quick review to catch humiliating gaffes or misspellings. ○ Emoticons and smiley faces have also disappeared from most professional communications.

Have a sensible e-mail address.   You might enjoy communicating with friends as HorribleHagar or DaisyGirl, but such an e-mail signature will undermine your credibility with a professor or potential employer. Save the oddball name for a private e-mail account.

Don't be a pain.   You just add to the daily clutter if you send unnecessary replies to e-mails—a pointless *thanks* or *Yes!* or *WooHoo!* Just as bad is CCing everyone on a list when you've received a query that needs to go to one person only: For example, when someone trying to arrange a meeting asks members of a group for available times and those members carbon copy their replies to all other members.

> **Your Turn**   Take a quick look at the formatting of the e-mails that appear on your mobile device. Many phones now have no problem displaying images, complex pages, or other textual features within e-mail. But note the limitations too. Images clutter a message on a small screen, so place them after your text. And you might not want to put any links you include too close together because they can be hard to select if they are side-by-side or beneath each other.

revise and edit
p. 452

How to start ▶ ● **Want to get a response?**
Explain your purpose clearly and logically.
See page 317.

14 Business Letters

communicate formally

The formal business letter remains an important instrument for sending information in professional situations. Though business letters can be transmitted electronically these days, legal letters or decisions about admissions to schools or programs often still arrive on paper, complete with a real signature.

- Responding to a summer internship opportunity, you outline your credentials for the position in a cover letter and attach your résumé.

- You send a brief letter to the director of admissions of a law school, graciously declining your acceptance into the program.

- You send a letter of complaint to an auto company, documenting the list of problems you've had with your SUV and indicating your intention to seek redress under your state's "lemon law."

- You write to a management company to accept the terms of a lease, enclosing a check for the security deposit on your future apartment.

UNDERSTANDING BUSINESS LETTERS.   As you would expect, business letters are generally formal in structure and tone, and follow a number of specific conventions, designed to make the document a suitable record or to support additional communication. Yet the principles for composing a business or job letter are not much different from those for a business e-mail. ○

want to get a ◀ response?

Explain your purpose clearly and logically.   Don't assume a reader will understand why you are writing. Use the first paragraph to announce your concern and explain your purpose, anticipating familiar *who, what, where, when, how,* and *why* questions. Be specific about names, titles, dates, and places. If you're applying for a job, scholarship, or admission to a program, name the specific position or program and mention that your résumé is attached. Remember that your letter may have a long life in a file cabinet: Write your document so that it will make sense months or years later.

Tell your readers what you want them to do.   Don't leave them guessing about how they should respond to your message. Lay out a clear agenda for accomplishing one task: Apply for a job, request information, or make an inquiry or complaint. Don't hesitate to ask for a reply, even by a specific date when that is necessary.

understand e-mail
p. 310

Write for your audience.   Quite often, you won't know the people to whom you are sending a business letter. So you have to construct your letter considering how an executive, employer, admissions officer, or complaints manager might be most effectively persuaded. Courtesy and goodwill go a long way—though you may have to be firm and impersonal in some situations. Avoid phony emotions or tributes.

A job application or cover letter (with your résumé attached) poses special challenges. You need to present your work and credentials in the best possible light without seeming full of yourself. Be succinct and specific, letting achievements speak mostly for themselves—though you can explain details that a reader might not appreciate. Focus on recent events and credentials and explain what skills and strengths you bring to the job. Speak in your own voice, clipped slightly by a formal style. O

Keep the letter focused and brief.   Like e-mails, business letters become hard to read when they extend beyond a page or two. A busy administrator or employee prefers a concise message, handsomely laid out on good stationery. Even a job-application letter should be relatively short, highlighting just your strongest credentials: Leave it to the accompanying résumé or dossier to flesh out the details.

Use a conventional form.   All business letters should include your address (called the *return address*), the date of the message, the address of the person to whom you are writing (called the *inside address*), a formal salutation or greeting, a closing, a signature in ink (when possible), and information about copies or enclosures.

Both *block format* and *modified-block format* are acceptable in business communication. In block forms, all elements are aligned against the left-hand margin (with the exception of the letterhead address at the top). In modified-block form, the return address, date, closing, and signature are aligned with the center of the page. In both cases, paragraphs in the body of the letter are set as single-spaced blocks of type, their first lines not indented, and with an extra line space between paragraphs.

define your style
p. 432

In indented form (not shown), the elements of the letter are arranged as in modified-block form, but the first lines of body paragraphs are indented five spaces, with no line spaces between the single-spaced paragraphs.

Distribute copies of your letter sensibly.   Copy anyone involved in a message, as well as anyone who might have a legitimate interest in your action. For example, in filing a product complaint with a company, you may also want to send your letter to the state office of consumer affairs. Copies are noted and listed at the bottom of the letter, introduced by the abbreviation *Cc* (for *courtesy copy*).

The following are two business letters: the first is a cover letter written by a student sending a résumé in a quest for a summer internship; the second is a concise letter of complaint.

Cover letter

In modified-block form, return address, date, closing, and signature are centered.

Opening paragraph clearly states thesis of letter: Nancy Linn wants this job.

Letter highlights key accomplishments succinctly and specifically.

Candidate repeatedly explains how internship fits career goals.

Additional contact information provided.

Courtesy copy of letter sent to advisor mentioned in first paragraph; can be contacted as reference.

                           1001 Harold Circle #10
                           Austin, TX 78712
                           June 28, 20--

Mr. Josh Greenwood
ABC Corporate Advisors, Inc.
9034 Brae Rd., Suite 1111
Austin, TX 78731

Dear Mr. Greenwood:

Rita Weeks, a prelaw advisor at the University of Texas at Austin, e-mailed me about an internship opportunity at your firm. Working at ABC Corporate Advisors sounds like an excellent chance for me to further my interests in finance and corporate law. I would like to apply for the position.

As my attached résumé demonstrates, I have already interned at an estate-planning law firm, where I have learned to serve the needs of an office of professionals and clients. I also have a record of achievement on campus: I have used my skills as a writer and speaker to obtain funding for the Honors Business Association at UT-Austin, for which I serve as vice president and financial director. By e-mailing and speaking with corporate recruiters, I raised $5,500 from Microsoft, ExxonMobil, Deloitte, and other companies and secured $2,400 from the University Co-op through written proposals.

I am ready now for a job that more closely relates to my academic training and career goal: becoming a certified financial and/or valuation analyst and corporate lawyer.

Please contact me at 210-555-0000 or NLINN@abcd.com to schedule an interview. Thank you for considering me as a potential intern. I look forward to meeting you.

                           Sincerely,

                           N. Linn
                           Nancy Linn

Enclosure: Résumé
CC: Rita Weeks

Complaint letter

John Humbert
95 Primrose Lane
Columbus, OH 43209

September 23, 2011

Home Design Magazine
3652 Delmar Drive
Prince, NY 10012

Dear *Home Design* Magazine:

I am a subscriber to your magazine, but I never received my July 2011 or August 2011 issues. When my subscription expires at the end of this year, please extend it two more months at no charge to make up for this error. Originally, my last issue would have been the December 2011 magazine. Since I have missed two issues and since my subscription was paid in full almost a year ago, please send me the January and February 2012 issues of *Home Design* at no additional charge.

Thank you for your attention.

Sincerely,

J. Humbert
John Humbert

Letterhead is preprinted stationery carrying the return address of the writer or institution. It may also include a corporate logo.

Allow two or three spaces between the date and address.

Allow one line space above and below the salutation. A colon follows the greeting.

The letter is in block form, with all major elements aligned with the left margin.

Getting the details right

Perhaps the most important detail in a business letter is keeping the format you use consistent and correct. Be sure to print your letter on good-quality paper or letterhead and to send it in a proper business envelope, one large enough to accommodate a page $8\frac{1}{2}$ inches wide.

Use consistent margins and spacing.   Generally, 1-inch margins all around work well, but you can use larger margins (up to $1\frac{1}{2}$ inches) when your message is short. The top margin can also be adjusted if you want to balance the letter on the page, though the body need not be centered.

Finesse the greeting.   Write to a particular person at a firm or institution. Address him or her as *Mr.* or *Ms.*—unless you actually know that a woman prefers *Mrs.* You may also address people by their full names: *Dear Margaret Hitchens.* When you don't have a name, fall back on *Dear Sir or Madam* or *To Whom It May Concern*, though these forms of address (especially *madam*) are increasingly dated. When it doesn't sound absurd, you can address the institution or entity: *Dear Exxon* or *Dear IRS*—again, this is not a preferred form.

Spell everything right.   Be scrupulous about the grammar and mechanics too—especially in a job-application letter. Until you get an interview, that piece of paper represents you to a potential client or employer. Would you hire someone who misspelled your company's name or made noticeable errors? O

Photocopy the letter as a record.   An important business letter needs a paper copy, even when you have an electronic version archived: The photocopied signature may mean something.

Don't forget the promised enclosures.   A résumé should routinely accompany a job-application letter. O

help with common errors p. 600

understand résumés p. 324

Fold the letter correctly and send it in a suitable envelope.
Business letters always go on $8\frac{1}{2} \times 11$-inch paper and are sent in standard business envelopes, generally $4\frac{1}{8} \times 9\frac{1}{2}$ inches. Fold the letter in three sections, trying to put the creases through white space in the letter so that the body of the message remains readable.

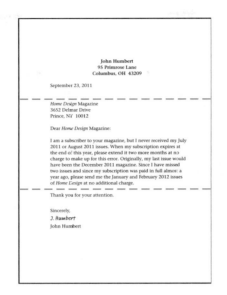

John Humbert
95 Primrose Lane
Columbus, OH 43209

September 23, 2011

Home Design Magazine
3652 Delmar Drive
Prince, NY 10012

Dear *Home Design* Magazine:

I am a subscriber to your magazine, but I never received my July 2011 or August 2011 issues. When my subscription expires at the end of this year, please extend it two more months at no charge to make up for this error. Originally, my last issue would have been the December 2011 magazine. Since I have missed two issues and since my subscription was paid in full almost a year ago, please send me the January and February 2012 issues of *Home Design* at no additional charge.

Thank you for your attention.

Sincerely,
J. Humbert
John Humbert

Your Turn   Have you received a business letter recently? If so, pull it out and take a minute to note the specific features described in this chapter. They are easy to overlook: letterhead, date, inside address, greeting, closing, attachments, spacing. Are their functions obvious and do they make sense? Now take a look at a recent e-mail you may have received from an institution or business (rather than a friend or colleague). What features does the business e-mail have in common with a business letter? In what ways are they different?

Résumés

**record
professional
achievements**

A one-page résumé usually accompanies any letter of application you send for a position or job. The résumé gathers and organizes details about your experiences at school, on the job, and in the community. In some careers, you may recap years of work and achievements in a longer, but similarly organized, document called a CV (curriculum vitae).

● Applying for a part-time position at a local day-care center, you assemble a résumé that chronicles your relevant experience.

● For an application to graduate school, you prepare a résumé that gives first priority to your accomplishments as a dean's list dual major in government and English.

● You modify your résumé slightly to highlight your internships with several law firms because you are applying for a paralegal clerk position at Baker Botts LLP.

● For a campus service scholarship, you tweak your résumé to emphasize activities more likely to interest college administrators than potential employers.

UNDERSTANDING RÉSUMÉS.   The point of a résumé is to provide a quick, easy-to-scan summary of your accomplishments to someone interested in hiring you. The document must be readable at a glance, meticulously accurate, and reasonably handsome. Think of it this way: A résumé is your one- or two-page chance to make a memorable first impression.

Contrary to what you may think, there's no standard form for résumés, but they do usually contain some mix of the following information:

- Basic contact data: your name, address, phone number, and e-mail address

- Educational attainments (usually college and above, once you have a BA, BS, or other postsecondary credential): degrees earned, where, and when

- Work experience: job titles, companies, dates of employment, with a brief list of the skills you used in specific jobs (such as customer service, sales, software programs, language proficiencies, and so on)

- Other accomplishments: extracurricular activities, community service, volunteer work, honors, awards, and so on. These may be broken into subcategories.

A strong résumé can be your ticket to the job or position you want.

Depending on the situation, you might also include the following elements:

● A brief statement of your career goals
● A list of people willing to serve as references (with their contact information)

You can add additional categories to your résumé too, whenever they might improve your chances at a job. The résumé you'll compile as your career evolves, for instance, may eventually include items such as administrative appointments, committee service, awards, patents, publications, lectures, participation in business organizations, community service, and so on. But keep the document brief. Ordinarily, a first résumé shouldn't exceed one page—though it may have to run longer if you are asked to provide references.

Résumés, which often resemble outlines without the numbers or letters, vary enormously in design. You have to decide on everything from fonts and headings to alignments and paper. You can choose to pay companies to fashion your résumé or buy special software to produce these documents. But your word processor has all the power you need to create a competent résumé on your own. Here's some advice.

Gather the necessary information.   You'll have to assemble this career data sooner or later. It's much simpler if you start in college and gradually build a full résumé over the years.

Don't guess or rely on memory for résumé information: Take the time necessary to get the data right. Verify your job titles and your months or years of employment; identify your major as it is named in your college catalog; make an accurate list of your achievements and activities without embellishing them. Don't turn an afternoon at a sandlot into "coaching high school baseball." Focus on attainments during your college years and beyond. Grade school and high school achievements don't mean much, unless you're LeBron James.

Decide on appropriate categories.   In most cases, right out of college or postsecondary school training, you'll use the résumé categories noted above. But you may vary their order and emphasis, depending on the job or career you pursue. In the past, one expensively printed résumé served all occasions; today you can—and should—tailor your electronically crafted résumé to individual job searches.

Arrange the information within categories in reverse chronological order. The most recent attainments come first in each of your categories. If such a list threatens to bury your most significant items, you have several options: Cut the lesser achievements from the list, break out special achievements in some consistent way, or highlight those special achievements in the cover letter that should always accompany a résumé. O

Design pages that are easy to read. Basic design principles aren't rocket science: Headings and key information should stand out and individual items should be clearly separated. The pages should look substantive but not cluttered. White space makes any document friendly, but too much in a résumé can suggest a lack of achievement. O

want to get ◄
a job?

In general, treat the résumé as a conservative document. This is not the time to experiment with fonts and flash or curlicues. Don't include a photograph either, even a good one.

Proofread every line in the résumé several times. Careful editing isn't a "detail" when it comes to résumés: It can be the whole ball game. When employers have more job candidates than they can handle, they may look for reasons to dismiss weak cases. Misspelled words, poor design of headings and text, and incomplete or confusing chronology are the kinds of mistakes that can terminate your job quest. O

Applying for a job need not be as dreary as it once was—or as sexist.

The following résumé, by Andrea Palladino, is arranged in reverse chronological order. Palladino uses a simple design that aligns the major headings and dates in a column down the left-hand margin and indents the detailed accomplishments to separate them, making them highly readable.

understand business letters p. 316

think visually p. 592

help with common errors p. 600

Contact information
centered at top of page
for quick reference. If
necessary, give both school
and permanent addresses.

Optional "career objective"
functions like thesis.

Alignments further empha-
size headings and dates.

Ample, but not excessive,
white space enhances
readability.

Andrea Palladino
600 Oak St.
Austin, TX 78705
(281) 555-1234

CAREER OBJECTIVE	Soon-to-be college graduate seeking full-time position that allows for regular interpersonal communication and continued professional growth.
EDUCATION 8/07–5/11	University of Texas at Austin – Psychology, BA
EXPERIENCE 3/10–Present	Writing Consultant University of Texas at Austin Undergraduate Writing Center – Austin, TX Tutor students at various stages of the writing process. Work with a variety of assignments. Attend professional development workshops.
5/10–Present	Child Care Provider CoCare Children's Services – Austin, TX Care for infants through children aged ten, including children with physical and mental disabilities. Change diapers, give food and comfort, engage children in stimulating play, and clean/disinfect toys after child care. Work on standby and substitute for coworkers when needed.
5/09–12/10	Salesperson/Stockperson Eloise's Collectibles – Katy, TX Unpacked new shipments, prepared outgoing shipments, and kept inventory. Interacted with customers and performed the duties of a cashier.
ACCOMPLISHMENTS 2009– Present	College Scholar for three years – acknowledgment of in-residence GPA of at least 3.50
10/11–Present	Big Brothers Big Sisters of Central Texas
Fall 2009	University of Texas at Austin Children's Research Lab – Research Assistant

Getting the details right

With its fussy dates, headings, columns, and margins, a résumé is all about the details. Fortunately, it is brief enough to make a thorough going-over easy. Here are some important considerations.

Don't leave unexplained gaps in your education or work career. Readers will wonder about blanks in your history (Are you a spy? Slacker? Felon?) and so may dismiss your application in favor of candidates whose career chronology raises no red flags. Simply account for any long periods (a year or so) you may have spent wandering the capitals of Europe or flipping burgers. Do so either in the résumé or in the job-application/cover letter—especially if the experiences contributed to your skills.

Be consistent. Keep the headings and alignments the same throughout the document. Express all dates in the same form: For example, if you abbreviate months and seasons, do so everywhere. Use hyphens between dates.

Protect your personal data. You don't have to volunteer information about your race, gender, age, or sexual orientation on a job application or résumé. Neither should you provide financial data, Social Security or credit card numbers, or other information you don't want in the public domain and that is not pertinent to your job search. However, you do need to be accurate and honest about the relevant job information: Any disparity about what you state on a résumé and your actual accomplishments may be a firing offense down the road.

Consider having your résumés designed and printed professionally. You may save time by letting someone else design and print your document, if you aren't computer savvy. If you do produce your own résumé, be sure to print it on high-quality paper. Ordinary printer paper won't cut it.

> **Your Turn** If you already have a résumé, open it up and check its features against the suggestions offered in this chapter. Consider how you might modify it for the different kinds of positions you may be applying for over the next several years. And if you don't yet have a résumé, now is an excellent time to draft one. You will more likely need it sooner than later.

16 Personal Statements

explain a person's experiences and goals

Preparing a short personal statement has become almost a ritual among people applying for admission to college, professional school, or graduate school, or for jobs, promotions, scholarships, internships, and even elective office.

- An application for an internship asks for an essay in which you explain how your career goals will contribute to a more tolerant and diverse society.

- All candidates for the student government offices you're interested in must file a personal statement explaining their positions. Your statement, limited to three hundred words, will be printed in the campus newspaper and posted online.

- You dust off the personal statement you wrote to apply to college to see what portions you can use in an essay required for admission to upper-division courses in the College of Communication.

UNDERSTANDING PERSONAL STATEMENTS.   Institutions that ask for personal statements are rarely interested in who you are. Rather, they want to see whether you can *represent* yourself as a person with whom they might want to be affiliated. That may seem harsh, but consider the personal statements you have already written. At best, they are a slice of your life—the verbal equivalent of you in full-dress mode.

TURNING A 20-FOOT
WALL INTO A CANVAS
TAKES VISION.

SO DOES
GETTING INTO
COLLEGE.

Get started at
KnowHow2GO.org
You've got what it takes.

Lumina   Ad Council   ACE

If you want a sense of what a school, business, or other institution expects in the essays they request from applicants, read whatever passes for that group's core values or mission statement, often available online. If their words sound a little stiff, inflated, and unrealistic, you've got it—except that you shouldn't actually sound as pretentious as an institution. A little blood has to flow through the veins of your personal statement, just not so much that someone in an office gets nervous about your emotional shape.

Hitting the right balance between displaying overwhelming competence and admitting human foibles in a personal state-ment is tough. Here's some advice for composing a successful essay.

Read the essay prompt carefully.   Essay topics are often deliberately open-ended to give you some freedom in pursuing a topic, but only answer the question actually posed, not one you'd prefer to deal with. Ideally, the question will focus on a specific aspect of your work or education; try to write about this even if the question is more general.

Be realistic about your audience.   Your personal statements are read by strangers. That's scary, but you can usually count on them to be reason-able people and well-disposed to give you a fair hearing. They measure you against other applicants—not unreachable standards of perfection.

Gather your material.   Don't repeat in your personal statement what's already on record in an application letter or résumé. Instead, look for inci-dents that will bring your résumé lines to life. Talk about the experiences that prepared you for the work you want to do or, perhaps, determined the direction of your life. If the prompt encourages personal reminiscences (e.g., *the person who influenced you the most*), think hard about how to convey those experiences to a stranger.

feeling lost?

Decide on a focus or theme.   Personal statements are short, so make the best use of a reader's time. Don't ramble about summer jobs or vague educational opportunities. Instead, find a theme that focuses on the strongest aspects of your application. If you're driven by a passion for research, arrange the elements of your life to illustrate this. If your best work is extracurricular, explain in a scholarship application how your commitment to people and activities makes you a more well-rounded student. In other words, turn your life into a thesis statement and make a clear point about yourself. O

Organize the piece conventionally.   Many personal statements take a narrative form, though they may also borrow some elements of reports and even proposals. Whatever structures you adopt for the essay, pay attention to the introduction, conclusion, and transitions: You cannot risk readers getting confused or lost. O

Try a high or middle style.   You don't want to be breezy or casual in an essay for law school or medical school, but a *personal* statement does invite a human voice. So a style that marries the correctness and formal vocabulary of a high style with the occasional untailored feel of the middle style might be perfect for many personal statements. O

The Academic Service Partnership Foundation asked candidates for an internship to prepare an essay addressing a series of questions. The prompt and one response to it follows.

ASPF NATIONAL INTERNSHIP PROGRAM

Please submit a 250- to 500-word typed essay answering the following three questions:

Specific questions limit reply, but also help to organize it.

1. Why do you want an internship with the ASPF?
2. What do you hope to accomplish in your academic and professional career goals?
3. What are your strengths and skills, and how would you use these in your internship?

p. 393

connect ideas
p. 416

define your style
p. 432

Michael Villaverde

April 14, 20--

The opportunity to work within a health-related government agency alongside top-notch professionals initially attracted me to the Academic Service Partnership Foundation (ASPF) National Internship Program. Participating in the ASPF's internship program would enable me to augment the health-services research skills I've gained working at the VERDICT Research Center in San Antonio and the M.D. Anderson Cancer Center in Houston. This internship could also help me gain experience in health policy and administration.

I support the ASPF's mission to foster closer relations between formal education and public service and believe that I could contribute to this mission. If selected as an ASPF intern, I will become an active alumnus of the program. I would love to do my part by advising younger students and recruiting future ASPF interns. Most important, I make it a point to improve the operations of programs from which I benefit. Any opportunities provided to me by the ASPF will be repaid in kind.

Other strengths I bring to the ASPF's National Internship Program are my broad educational background and dedication. My undergraduate studies will culminate in two honors degrees (finance and liberal arts) with additional premed course work. Afterward, I wish to enroll in a combined MD/PhD program in health-services research. Following my formal

Opening sentence states writer's thesis or intent; first two paragraphs address first question.

Essay uses first person (*I, me*) but is fairly formal in tone and vocabulary, between high and middle style.

Personal note slips through in enthusiasm author shows for internship opportunity.

This statement transitions smoothly into second issue raised in prompt.

Formidable and specific goals speak for themselves in straightforward language.

education, I will devote my career to seeing patients in a primary-care setting, researching health-care issues as a university faculty member, teaching bioethics, and developing public policy at a health-related government agency.

Another transition introduces third issue raised by prompt.

The course work at my undergraduate institution has provided me with basic laboratory and computer experience, but my strengths lie in oral and written communication. Comparing digital and film-screen mammography equipment for a project at M.D. Anderson honed my technical-writing skills and comprehension of statistical analysis. The qualitative analysis methods I learned at VERDICT while evaluating strategies used by the Veterans Health Administration in implementing clinical practice guidelines will be a significant resource to any prospective employer. By the end of this semester, I will also possess basic knowledge of Statistical Package for the Social Sciences (SPSS) software.

Qualifications offered are numerous and detailed.

During my internship I would like to research one of the following topics: health-care finance, health policy, or ethnic disparities in access to high-quality health care. I have read much about the Patient Protection and Affordable Care Act of 2010 and anticipate studying its implications. I would learn a great deal from working with officials responsible for the operation and strategic planning of a program like Medicare (or a nonprofit hospital system). The greater the prospects for multiple responsibilities, the more excited I will be to show up at work each day.

Special interest/concern is noted and is likely to impress reviewers of statement.

Final sentence affirms enthusiasm for technical internship.

Getting the details right

As with résumés, there's no room for errors or slips in personal statements. ○ They are a test of your writing skills, plain and simple, so you need to get the spelling, mechanics, and usage right. In addition, consider the following advice.

Don't get too artsy. A striking image or two may work well in the statement, as may the occasional metaphor or simile. But don't build your essay around a running theme, an extended analogy, or a pop-culture allusion that a reader might dismiss as hokey or simply not get. If a phrase or feature stands out too noticeably, change it, even though *you* may like it.

Use common sense. You probably already have the good grace not to offend gender, racial, religious, and ethnic groups in your personal statement. You should also take the time to read your essay from the point of view of people from less protected groups who may take umbrage at your dismissal of *old folks, fundamentalists,* or even *Republicans.* You don't know who may be reading your essay.

Write the essay yourself. It's the ethical thing to do. If you don't and you're caught, you're toast. You might ask someone to review your statement or take a draft to a writing center for a consultation. ○ This review or consult by a parent or English-major roommate should not purge your *self* from the essay. Remember, too, that wherever you arrive, you'll need to write at the level you display in the statement that got you there.

Your Turn Amused by the thought of your life as a thesis statement? Give it a try. Compose *three* thesis sentences that might be plausibly used to organize three different personal statements, emphasizing varying aspects of your life and career. Which statement do you think describes you best? Would it always be the best thesis for a personal statement? Why or why not?

---

help with common errors p. 600

peer review p. 458

How to start ▶ ● **First time writing a lab report?**
Look at model reports. See page 338.

17 Lab Reports

record a
scientific
experiment

In most courses in the natural or social sciences, you are expected to learn how to describe experiments systematically and report information accurately. It goes with the territory. The vehicle for such work is the familiar lab report.

● For a physics course, you describe an experiment that uses a series of collisions to demonstrate the conservation of energy.

● In an organic chemistry lab, you try to produce chemical luminescence and report your results.

● For a psychology class, you describe the results of an experiment you created to determine whether students taking examinations benefit from a good night's sleep the night before the test.

UNDERSTANDING LAB REPORTS.   Formal scientific papers published in academic journals have conventional features designed to convey information to readers professionally interested in the results of studies and experiments. The key elements of such a scientific paper are the following:

- Title page with the title clearly describing the contents of the paper; includes names of authors and their institutional affiliations

- Abstract (not always required) summarizing the main points in the paper

- Introduction explaining the purpose of the study or experiment and reviewing previous work on the subject (called a literature review)

- Description of materials and methods, explaining the factual and procedural details of the experiment

- Results section, tabulating and reporting the data

- Discussion of the results, interpreting the data

- References list or bibliography, documenting articles and books cited in the paper

- Figures, tables, and other supporting materials (if any)

For details about composing full scientific papers, consult the handbooks used in your particular field (and recommended by your instructor), such as *The CSE Manual for Authors, Editors, and Publishers* (7th edition, 2006) or the *Publication Manual of the American Psychological Association* (6th edition, 2009).

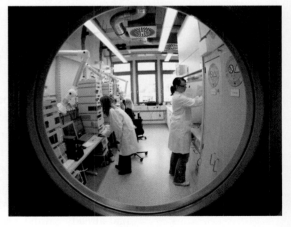

Lab reports borrow many of the features of the scientific papers published in academic journals, but are generally much shorter and tailored to specific situations. Typically, you prepare lab reports to describe the results of experiments you're assigned to perform in science courses. But you may also write lab reports to document original research done with colleagues or professors.

▶ first time writing
a lab report?

Follow instructions to the letter.   In a course with a lab, you typically receive precise instructions on how to compile a lab notebook or prepare and submit reports. Read these guidelines carefully and ask the instructor or teaching assistant questions about any specifications you do not understand. Each section of a lab report provides a specific kind of information that helps a reader understand and, possibly, repeat a procedure or an experiment.

Look at model reports.   Lab report requirements may vary not only from subject to subject but also from course to course. So ask the instructor whether sample reports might be available for a particular lab section. If so, study them closely. The best way to understand what your work should look like is to see a successful model.

Be efficient.   If an abstract is required, keep it brief. Use charts, tables, and graphs (as required) to report information and don't repeat that data elsewhere. Keep your reporting of results separate from the discussion and commentary.

Edit the final version.   In a lab report, editing means not only proofreading your language but also reviewing the structure of equations or formulas, assessing the clarity of methods or procedures sections, and checking any numbers, calculations, equations, or formulas. ○ Be sure to label all sections and items accurately, numbering any figures, tables, and charts. Use these numbers to refer to these items in the body of your report.

The following lab report was produced for a course in organic chemistry. It follows a structure defined in a full page of instructions. Some sections — such as "Main Reactions and Mechanisms" — are clearly tied to the specific subject matter of the chemistry class. Other sections — such as "Data and Results" — would be found in lab reports in many disciplines.

 Like any lab report, this one is mostly business. But there are informal moments ("Did it glow? Yes!"), probably reflecting the fact that the writer had already gained a sense of what was acceptable in this course: This was the seventh of more than a dozen required reports.

revise and edit
p. 452

Shane McNamee

Professor Lyman

Chemistry 300

March 22, 20--

Synthesis of Luminol

CH 300 Syllabus, Supplement I

INTRODUCTION

The purpose of this lab is to synthesize a chemiluminescent

product and observe chemiluminescence.

MAIN REACTIONS AND MECHANISMS

a.

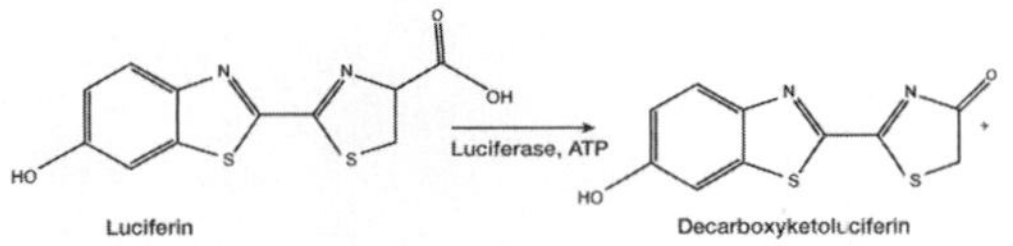

Luciferin   Decarboxyketoluciferin

b.

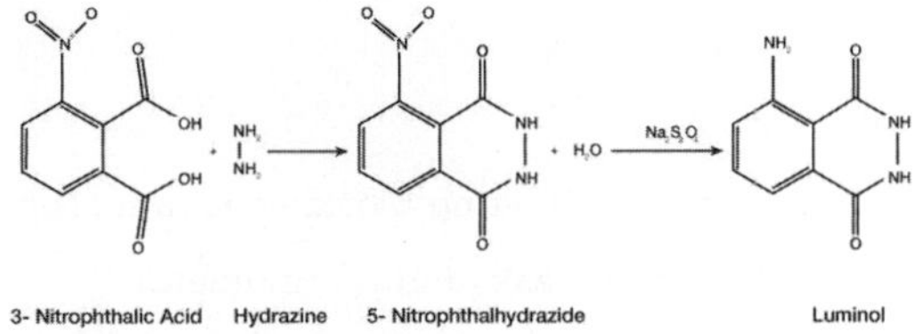

3- Nitrophthalic Acid   Hydrazine   5- Nitrophthalhydrazide   Luminol

Almost all lab reports use headings for their structure. "Introduction" functions as thesis.

"Materials and Methods" section starts here. (Assignment instructions specified different language for these headings.)

Synthesis of Luminol 2

c.

3- aminophthalate
Singlet state

3- aminophthalate
Triplet state

Proposed peroxide

3- aminophthalate
Ground state

TABLE OF REACTANTS AND PRODUCTS

Included 3-nitrophthalic acid, hydrazine solution, triethylene
glycol, NaOH, sodium hydrosulfite dihydrate, acetic acid,
luminol, potassium ferricyanide, hydrogen peroxide

SYNOPSIS OF PROCEDURE

APPARATUS:

5 ml conical vial, hot plate, heating block, spin vane, Hirsch
funnel, 250 ml Erlenmeyer flask, and thermometer

SYNTHESIS OF LUMINOL:

1. Heated 5 ml vial containing 200 mg 3-nitrophthalic acid
    and 0.4 ml aq 8% hydrazine solution until solid dissolved.

Abbreviations are not
followed by periods.

Synthesis of Luminol 3

2. Once dissolved, added 0.6 ml triethylene glycol and clamped vial in vertical position. Added spin vane and inserted thermometer into vial.

3. Brought solution to vigorous boil to boil away excess water. During this time, temperature should be around 110°C.

4. Once water boiled off, temperature rose to 215°C in a 3-4 minute period. Maintained the 215-220°C temperature for 2 minutes.

5. Removed the vial and cooled it to 100°C. While cooling, placed 10 ml water in Erlenmeyer flask and heated to boiling.

6. Once sample cooled to 100°C, added 3 ml boiling water.

7. Collected yellow crystals by vacuum filtration using a Hirsch funnel.

8. Transferred solid back to vial and added 1 ml of 3.0 M NaOH and stirred with a stirring rod until the solid was dissolved. Then added 0.6 g of fresh sodium hydrosulfite dihydrate to the deep brown-red solution.

9. Heated solution slightly under boiling for 5 minutes, taking care not to cause bumping. Then added 0.4 ml acetic acid.

10. Cooled tube in beaker of cool water, and collected solid luminol by vacuum filtration using Hirsch funnel.

△

Synthesis of Luminol 4

LIGHT-PRODUCING REACTION:

1. Combined two samples of luminol. Dissolved them in
    2 ml of 3 M NaOH and 18 ml water (solution A).

2. Next, prepared a solution of 4 ml 3% aqueous potassium
    ferricyanide, 4 ml 3% H_2O_2, and 32 ml H_2O (solution B).

3. Then, diluted 5 ml solution A with 35 ml water. In a
    dark place, poured diluted solution and solution B
    simultaneously into an Erlenmeyer flask. Swirled
    flask; looking for blue-green light.

DATA AND RESULTS

Did it glow? Yes!

DISCUSSION AND CONCLUSION

When a chemical reaction generates light, chemiluminescence
has occurred. The product of such a reaction is in an excited
electronic state and emits a photon. One example of
chemiluminescence is the luciferase-catalyzed reaction
of luciferin with molecular oxygen in the male firefly.
Chemiluminescence occurring through biochemical
processes is also called bioluminescence.

Luminol is synthesized through two steps. Hydrazine and
4-nitrophthalic acid react to produce 5-nitrophthalhydrazide,
which is reduced by sodium dithionite to form luminol. In
alkaline solution, luminol emits blue-green light when
mixed with H_2O_2 and potassium ferricyanide.

Standard notation is
used to describe chemical
reactions.

Data sections are rarely
this simple. Most would
require tables, charts, and
so on.

Synthesis of Luminol 5

Although the mechanism of this reaction isn't fully understood, chemists believe that a peroxide decays to form 3-diaminophthalate in an excited triplet state (two unpaired electrons with the same spin). Slowly, the 3-diaminophthalate converts to a singlet state (two unpaired electrons now have different spins), which then decays to the ground state, emitting light through fluorescence. In contrast, phosphorescence occurs in reactions where a triplet state emits photons while converting to a singlet state.

Blue-green light glowed for a fraction of a second when solutions A and B were mixed. This indicates that enough luminol was successfully synthesized to run the chemiluminescent reaction. Only a small amount of dissolved luminol was required, so a high yield was not necessary.

Getting the details right

Even the conventions of scientists vary, so it helps to know what sorts of issues may come up in preparing a lab report for a given course. Again, ask questions when you aren't sure what conventions to follow.

Keep the lab report impersonal. Keep yourself and any lab partners out of the work. In fact, most instructors will *require* that you use the third person and passive voice throughout: *The beaker was heated* rather than *We heated the beaker.* Though some instructors do allow the use of first-person pronouns in undergraduate work—preferring the clarity of active sentences—always check before using *I* or *we.* ○

Keep the style clear. Written for knowledgeable readers, lab reports needn't apologize for using technical terms, jargon, and scientific notation. However, sentences still need to be coherent and grammatical in structure and free of clutter. Avoid contractions, however, as well as any trendy or slang terms.

Follow the conventions. Learn the rules as they apply in particular fields. In general, however, you should italicize scientific names expressed in Latin, write out formulas and equations on separate lines, use only metric quantities and measures, use standard abbreviations, and narrate the materials and methods section in the past tense.

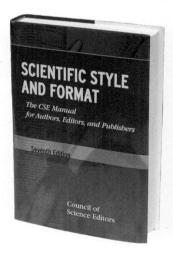

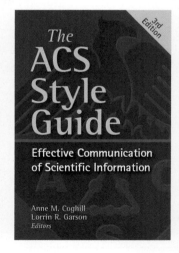

344

define your style
p. 432

Label charts, tables, and graphs carefully.   Any data you present graphically should make sense at a glance if your design is sensible and the labels are thorough and accurate. Don't leave readers wondering what the numbers in a column represent or what the scale of a drawing might be. **O**

Document the report correctly.   Most lab reports won't require documentation or a list of references. But a scientific paper will. Determine the documentation style manual used in the subject area and follow its guidelines closely. ○

> **Your Turn**   As a highly "formulaic" genre of writing, lab reports have well-defined elements that follow a predictable structure and precise guidelines. Can you identify other kinds of writing that are this conventional? Could the structure of the lab report, moving clearly from an introduction and methods to results and discussion, work in any writing situations outside of the laboratory?

display data
p. 584

understand citation
styles p. 501

How to start ▶ ● **Adapting material?**
Organize your presentation. See page 347.

18 Oral Reports

**present
information
to a live
audience**

In an oral report, you present material you have researched to an audience listening and watching rather than reading. So you must organize information clearly and find ways to convey your points powerfully, memorably, and sometimes graphically.

● For a psychology course, you use presentation software to review the results of an experiment you and several classmates designed to test which types of music were most conducive to studying for examinations.

● In a Shakespeare class, you use slides to give an oral report on Elizabethan theaters that draws upon research you are doing for your end-of-semester term paper.

● Prepping a crowd for a protest march, you use a bullhorn and a little humor to review the very serious ground rules for staging a peaceful demonstration on the grounds of the state capitol.

UNDERSTANDING ORAL REPORTS. Oral reports can be deceptive. When watching someone give an effective five-minute talk, you may assume the speaker spent less time preparing it than he or she would a ten-page paper. But be warned: Oral presentations require all the research, analysis, and drafting of any other type of assignment, and then some. After all the background work is done, the material needs to be distilled into its most important points and sold to an audience. Here is some advice for preparing effective oral reports.

Know your stuff. Having a firm grasp on your subject will make your presentation more effective—which is why you should base reports on serious research. Knowledge brings you confidence that will ease some anxieties about public speaking. You'll appear believable and persuasive to an audience. And you'll feel more comfortable when improvising or taking questions. If you are in command of your subject, you'll survive even if equipment fails or you misplace a note card.

Organize your presentation. If your report is based on material you've already written, reduce the text to an outline, memorize its key points (or put them on cards), and then practice speaking about each one. ○ If it helps, connect the main ideas to one or two strong examples listeners might later remember. Make the report *seem* spontaneous, but plan every detail.

adapting ◄ material?

The best equipment can't save a poorly prepared report.

The process is similar for an oral report built from scratch. First, study your subject. Then list the points you want to cover and arrange them in a way that will engage listeners—choosing a pattern of organization that fits your topic. Use note cards or the outlining tools in programs like Word or PowerPoint to explore options for structuring your talk.

Cover only a limited number of points. It's better to leave your listeners with two or three good ideas than to bore them with a string of underdeveloped concepts.

At the beginning of your report, tell your audience briefly what you intend to cover and in what order. Then at critical transitions in the report, remind listeners where you are by simply stating what comes next: *The second issue I wish to discuss . . . ; Now that we've examined the phenomenon, let's look at its consequences.* Don't be shy about making your main points this directly or worry about repetition. In an oral report, strategic repetition is your friend.

order ideas p. 408

△

Stay connected to your listeners.   For about thirty seconds, you'll probably have the spontaneous goodwill of an audience. After that, you've got to earn every minute of their continued attention. Begin by introducing yourself and your subject, if there is no one to perform that task. For longer reports, consider easing into your material with an anecdote that connects you, your subject, and your listeners. Self-deprecating humor usually works. (Short, in-class presentations won't need much, if any, warm-up material.)

Once the oral presentation begins, maintain eye contact with members of the audience. Watch their reactions. When it's clear you've made a point, move on. If you see puzzled looks, explain more. No speaker charms everyone, so don't let a random yawn or frown throw you. But if the whole crowd starts to snooze, you *are* the problem. Connect or lose 'em: pick up your pace; move on to the next point; skip to your best material. O

Be sure to speak *to* your listeners, not to your notes or text. Arrange your materials and print them large enough so that you can read them easily from a distance and not lose your place. If you look downward too often, you'll lose eye contact and your voice may be muffled, even with a microphone.

Use your voice and body.   Speak clearly and deliberately, and be sure people in the back of the room can hear you. Nervous speakers unconsciously speed up until they're racing to their conclusions. If you get skittish, calm yourself by taking a deep breath and smiling.

If the room is large and a fixed microphone doesn't confine you, move around on the stage to address more of the audience. Use gestures too. They are a natural part of public speaking, especially for arguments and personal narratives. If you get stuck behind a podium, be sure to scan the entire audience (not just speak to the middle of the room) and modulate your voice. Keep your body steady too: Don't rock as you speak.

Adapt your material to the time available.   If you know your subject well, don't worry about running out of things to say. Once they get rolling, most speakers have the opposite problem: They talk too much. So be realistic about how much you can cover within the assigned limit, especially if you have to take questions at the end. Tie your key ideas to fixed points on a

O

connect ideas
p. 416

clock or watch. Know where you need to be at a quarter, half, and three-quarters of the way through the available time.

When you finally get near the end, signal your conclusion and wrap up the report shortly thereafter, as promised. If you're taking questions after your presentation, follow up with *Any questions?*

Practice your presentation.   Any oral report needs several dry runs to increase your confidence and alert you to potential problems. Speak any material aloud *exactly* as you intend to deliver it and go through all the motions, especially if you will use media such as slides or video clips. Have one or more friends or classmates watch you practice and give you feedback.

Use the practice session to time the presentation too. If you practice only in your head, you will greatly underestimate the length of the report.

If your presentation is collaborative, choreograph the report with the full group, agreeing on the introductions, handoffs, and interactions with the audience. Who runs the computer? Who distributes the handouts and when? Who handles the question-and-answer session? Handoffs like these seem minor until they are fumbled on game day.

Prepare for the occasion.   Before the report, check out the locale and any equipment you will need. Be sure your laptop will connect to the multimedia projector in the room; know how to dim the lights; be sure a screen or electrical outlets are available.

Then dress up. A little spit and polish earns you the goodwill of most audiences. Your classmates may razz you about the tie or skirt, but it just proves they're paying attention. And that's a good thing.

The following PowerPoint presentation was created by Terri Sagastume, a resident of a small Florida town who opposes a proposed real-estate development, Edenlawn Estates, on property near his home. J&M Investments, the real-estate developer that recently purchased the property, hopes to create a new multistory condominium complex in place of the property's existing single-family homes. Sagastume's goal is to inform the public of the damage such a development would do to the surrounding area, and he is trying to convince his audience to sign a petition, which he will present to the local government in an effort to shut the project down.

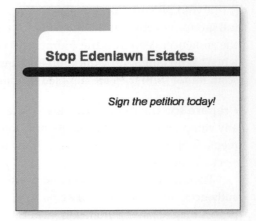

The slides themselves are extremely simple and brief: They are merely the bullet points that Sagastume uses to ground his presentation.

With the first slide as his backdrop, Sagastume provides a preview of his speech in three broad sections. First, he explains to his audience that the real-estate developer—a Miami-based conglomerate with no personal ties to the area—wants to change the existing building codes and zoning laws in order to maximize profits. Second, he reminds his audience of the reason those codes and laws are there, and that much could be lost if exceptions are made. And finally, he convinces his audience that, together, they can fight the big developer and win.

Getting the details right

There's nothing wrong with a report that relies on the spoken word alone. Still, audiences appreciate supporting material, including flip charts, handouts, slides, and visual or audio samplings. All such materials, clearly labeled and handsomely reproduced, should also be genuinely relevant to the report. Resist the temptation to show something just because it's cool.

Most oral reports use presentation software such as the dominant player in this field, PowerPoint. With presentation software, you create a sequence of slides to accompany an oral report, building the slides yourself or picking them from a gallery of ready-made designs and color schemes that fit different occasions. You can also choose individual layouts for slides to accommodate text only, text and photos, text and charts, images only, and so on.

Presentation software offers so many bells and whistles that novices tend to overdo it, allowing the software to dominate the report. Here's how to make PowerPoint or Keynote work for you.

Be certain you need presentation software. A short talk that makes only one or two points probably works better if viewers focus on you, not on a screen. Use presentation software to keep audiences on track through more complicated material, to highlight major issues or points, or to display images viewers really need to see. A little humor or eye candy is fine once in a while, but don't expect audiences to be impressed by glitz. What matters is the content of the report. O

For presentations, PowerPoint offers design templates such as this one.

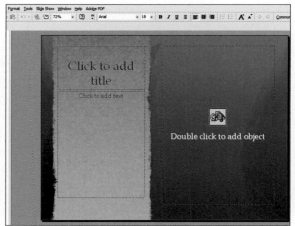

Use slides to introduce points, not cover them. If you find yourself reading your slides, you've put too much material on them. And you'll bore your audience to distraction. Put material on-screen that audiences need to see: main points, charts, and images directly relevant to the report (see the "Edenlawn Estates" slides on p. 350). It's fine, too, for a slide to outline your presentation at the beginning and to summarize your points at the end. In fact, it's helpful to have a slide that obviously signals a conclusion.

understand reports
p. 44

Use a simple and consistent design. Select one of the design templates provided or create a design of your own that fits your subject. A consistent design scheme will unify your report and minimize distractions. **O**

For academic presentations, choose simple designs and fonts. Make the text size large enough for viewers at the back of the room to read easily. For reasons of legibility, avoid elegant, playful, or eccentric fonts, including those that resemble handwriting or Old English styles. And don't use more than one or two fonts within the presentation. Use boldface very selectively for emphasis. If you have to boldface a font to make it visible at a distance, simply find a thicker font. Italics are fine for occasional use, but in some fonts they are hard to read at a distance.

Consider alternatives to slide-based presentations. Anything you build on a laptop can be projected onscreen. So you need not use conventional slide-based presentation software for your oral report if you can build materials on your own. For example, various interactive Web 2.0 applications, from social-network software to blogs and wikis, can be configured for oral presentations, as can mind-mapping software and PowerPoint alternatives such as Prezi. In Prezi, for example, sequential slides are replaced by words, images, and media presented on an unending canvas; images move, rotate, and zoom in and out to provide different perspectives on a subject.

> **Your Turn** Given the number of oral presentations and lectures you've sat through, most of them using PowerPoint, you could probably write your own chapter on this special assignment. Working with a small group, list five hallmarks of an effective oral report and five characteristics of a dismal one. Annotate the list with examples that you may recall from particular reports. Then compare the features your group has come up with to those generated by other groups.

think visually
p. 592

Map your own writing process.

Where are you in your process?	Look for more help here.	
Exploring Purpose and Topic	Find a topic	356
	Read closely	365
	Ask for help	379
	Choose a genre	390
	Develop a statement	393
	Develop ideas	412
	Interview and observe	478
Understanding Your Audience	Find a topic	356
	Collaborate	362
	Think critically	372
	Choose a genre	390
	Develop a statement	393
	Shape your work	406
	Develop ideas	412
	Connect ideas	416
	Refine your tone	432
	Plan a project	466
	Refine your search	472
	Interview and observe	478
	Find reliable sources	482
	Analyze claims and evidence	487
	Understand citation styles	501
Finding and Developing Materials	Choose a genre	390
	Develop a statement	393
	Develop a draft	398
	Connect ideas	416
	Define your style	432
	Respect your readers	440
	Sum up ideas	491

Where are you in your process?	Look for more help here.	

Creating a Structure ▶

Choose a genre	390
Develop a statement	393
Shape your work	406
Order ideas	408
Connect ideas	416
Shape a beginning	420
Shape an ending	425
Revise and edit	452
Think visually	592

Choosing a Style and Design ▶

Define your style	432
Improve your sentences	444
Sum up ideas	491
Restate ideas	494
Use quotations	497
Cite in MLA	503
Go multimodal	568
Display data	584
Think visually	592

Need more help?
Try these Visual Tutorials.

How to Browse for Ideas	360–61
How to Use the Writing Center	382–83
How to Revise Your Work	456–57
How to Insert a Comment in a Word Document	462–63
How to Cite from a Book (MLA)	516–17
How to Cite from a Magazine (MLA)	522–23
How to Cite from a Web Site (MLA)	526–27
How to Cite from a Database (MLA)	528–29
How to Cite from a Web Site (APA)	556–57
How to Cite from a Database (APA)	558–59
How to Insert an Image into a Word Document	578–79

reference

Ideas

part three

find a topic/
get an idea

19 **Brainstorming** 356

collaborate

20 **Brainstorming with Others** 362

read closely

21 **Smart Reading** 365

think critically/
avoid fallacies

22 **Critical Thinking** 372

ask for help

23 **Experts** 379

tackle hard stuff

24 **Writer's Block** 384

Need help organizing or drafting? See page 388.

19 Brainstorming

find a topic/
get an idea

A great deal of thinking occurs at the beginning of a project or assignment. How exactly will you fill ten or twenty pages with your thoughts on Incan architecture, the life cycle of dung beetles, or what you did last summer? What hasn't already been written about religion in America, cattle in Africa, or the cultural hegemony of Google? What do you do when you find yourself clueless or stuck or just overwhelmed by the possibilities—or lack thereof? Simple answer: Brainstorm.

Put a notion on the table and see where it goes—and what you might do with it or learn about it. Toy with an idea like a kitten with a catnip mouse. Push yourself to think through, around, over, and under a proposition. Dare to be politically incorrect or, alternatively, so conventional that your good behavior might scare even your elders.

But don't think of brainstorming as disordered and muddled. Consider the metaphor itself: Storms are awesomely organized events. They generate power by physical processes so complex that we're just beginning to understand them. Similarly, a first-rate brainstorming session spins ideas from the most complex chemistry in our bodies, the tumult of the human brain.

Naturally, you'll match brainstorming techniques to the type of writing you hope to produce. Beginning a personal tale about a trip to Wrigley Field, you might make a list of sensory details to jog your memory—the smell of hot dogs, the catcalls of fans, the green

356

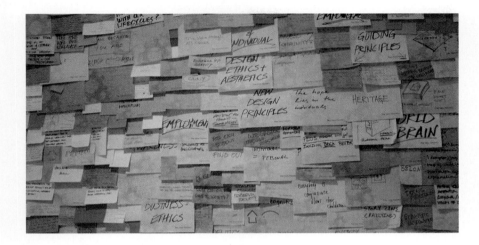

Chalkboards, flip charts, and even sticky notes can help you rapidly record your ideas.

grass of the outfield. ○ But for an assigned report on DNA fingerprinting, your brainstorming might itemize things you still must learn about the subject: what DNA fingerprinting is, how it is done, when it can be used, how reliable it is, and so on. ○

Find routines that support thinking.   Use whatever brainstorming techniques get you invested in a project. Jogging, swimming, knitting, or sipping brew at the coffeehouse may be your stimulus of choice. Such routine activities keep the body occupied, allowing insights to mature. Your thoughts do need to be captured and recorded, either in notes or, perhaps, voice memos.

One warning: Brainstorming activities of this kind can become simple procrastination. That comfortable chair in Starbucks might evolve into a spot too social for much thinking or writing. Recognize when your productivity has been compromised and change tactics.

Build lists.   Brainstorm to list potential topics or, if you already have a subject, to explore the major points you might cover. Add all items that come to mind: If you're too picky or detailed at the start, you defeat the power of brainstorming—in which one idea, written on paper or on a screen, suggests another, then another. Even grocery lists work this way.

understand
narratives p. 4

understand
reports p. 44

> Ideas won't keep; something must be done about them.

—Alfred North Whitehead

Lists work especially well when you already know something about a subject. For instance, preparing a letter to the editor in defense of collegiate sports, you can first inventory the arguments you've heard from friends or have made yourself. Then list the counterarguments you come up with as well. Write down everything that bubbles up, both reasonable and off-the-wall. Finally, winnow out the better items based on their quality or plausibility, and arrange them tentatively, perhaps pairing arguments and counterarguments. Even when you don't know much about a potential topic, assemble a list of basic questions that might lead to greater knowledge, to stimulate your ideas and thinking.

Map your ideas.   If you find a list too static as a prompt for writing, another way may be to explore the relationships between your ideas *visually*. Some writers use logic trees to represent their thinking, starting with a single general concept and breaking it into smaller and smaller parts. You can find examples of "tree diagrams" from many fields by using a search engine to investigate a keyword and then clicking the Image option.

Try freewriting.   Freewriting is a brainstorming technique of nonstop composing designed to loosen the bonds we sometimes use to clamp down on our own thinking. Typically, freewriting sessions begin slowly, with disconnected phrases and words. Suddenly, there's a spark and words stream onto the paper—but slow or fast, you must still keep writing. The moment you settle back in your chair, you break the circuit that makes freewriting work. By forcing yourself to write, you push yourself to think and, perhaps, to discover what really matters in a subject.

Like other brainstorming techniques, freewriting works best when you already have some knowledge of your subject. You might freewrite successfully about standardized testing or working at fast-food restaurants if you've experienced both; you'll stumble trying to freewrite on subjects you know next to nothing about, such as, perhaps, thermodynamics, ergonomics, or the career of Maria Callas. Freewriting tends to work best for personal narratives, personal statements, arguments, O and proposals, O and less well for reports and technical projects.

understand
argument p. 72

understand
proposals p. 176

Although freewriting comes in many forms, the basic formula is simple.

STAGE ONE

- Start with a blank screen or sheet of paper.
- Put your subject or title at the top of the page.
- Write on that subject nonstop for ten minutes.
- Don't stop typing or lift your pen from the paper during that time.
- Write nonsense if you must, but keep writing.

STAGE TWO

- Stop at ten minutes and review what you have written.
- Underscore or highlight the most intriguing idea, phrase, or sentence.
- Put the highlighted idea at the top of a new screen or sheet.
- Freewrite for another ten minutes on the new, more focused topic.

Use memory prompts.　When writing personal narratives, institutional histories, or even résumés, you might trigger ideas with photographs, yearbooks, diaries, or personal memorabilia. An image from a vacation may bring events worth writing about flooding back to you. Even checkbooks or credit card statements may help you reconstruct past events or see patterns in your life worth exploring in writing.

Search online for your ideas.　You can get lots of ideas by simply exploring most topics online through keywords. Indeed, determining those initial keywords and then following up with new terms you discover while browsing is in itself a potent form of brainstorming.

A photo album is a great place to look for writing ideas, because we tend to document meaningful moments.

Your Turn　If you have never used freewriting as a brainstorming activity, give it a try. Pick a general topic from among courses you are currently studying, news events that interest you, or activities you are deeply involved in: for example, the Japanese concept of Bushido, immigration reform, or unpaid internships. (You want a topic about which you have *some* knowledge or opinions.) Then follow the preceding directions. See what happens.

How to... Browse for ideas

Uncle Bob, who's a cop, complains about the "*CSI* effect." What is that?

I found a study by professors of law and psychology. What do they think?

Google | CSI effect

About 20,600,000 results (0.15 secon

▶ Scholarly articles for **CSI effect**
CSI Effect: Popular Fiction about Forensic S
... Concerning Scientific Evidence: Does the
The **CSI effect**: fact or fiction - Thomas - Cit

CSI effect - Wikipedia, the free encyclope
en.wikipedia.org/wiki/**CSI**_effect - Cached
The **CSI effect**, also known as the CSI syndrome a
in which the exaggerated portrayal of forensic scien
Background - Manifestations - Trials - References

The '**CSI Effect**': Does It Really Exist? | Na
www.nij.gov/journals/259/**csi-effect**.htm - Cached
by DE Shelton - Cited by 12 - Related articles
Mar 17, 2008 – Do law-related television shows like
influence juror expectations and demands for forens

/archive/csieffect.pdf

108% | Find

ARTICLE

THE *CSI* EFFECT: POPULAR FICTION ABOUT FORENSIC SCIENCE AFFECTS THE PUBLIC'S EXPECTATIONS ABOUT REAL FORENSIC SCIENCE

N.J. Schweitzer
Michael J. Saks*

ABSTRACT: Two of a number of hypotheses loosely referred to as the CSI Effect suggest that the television program and its spin-offs, which wildly exaggerate and glorify forensic science, affect the public, and in turn affect trials either by (a) burdening the prosecution by creating greater expectations about forensic science than can be delivered or (b) burdening the defense by creating exaggerated faith in the capabilities and reliability of the forensic sciences. The present study tested these hypotheses by presenting to mock jurors a simulated trial transcript that included the testimony of a forensic scientist. The case for conviction was relatively weak, unless the expert testimony could carry the case across the threshold of reasonable doubt. In addition to reacting to the trial evidence, respondents were asked about their television viewing habits. Compared to non-CSI viewers, CSI viewers were more critical of the forensic evidence presented at the trial, finding it less believable. Regarding their verdicts, 29% of non-CSI viewers said they would convict, compared to 18% of CSI viewers (not a statistically significant difference). Forensic science viewers expressed more confidence in their verdicts than did non-viewers. Viewers of general crime programs, however, did not differ significantly from their non-viewing counterparts on any of the other dependent measures, suggesting that skepticism toward the forensic science testimony was specific to those whose diet consisted of heavy doses of forensic science television programs.

1

Find reliable sources.

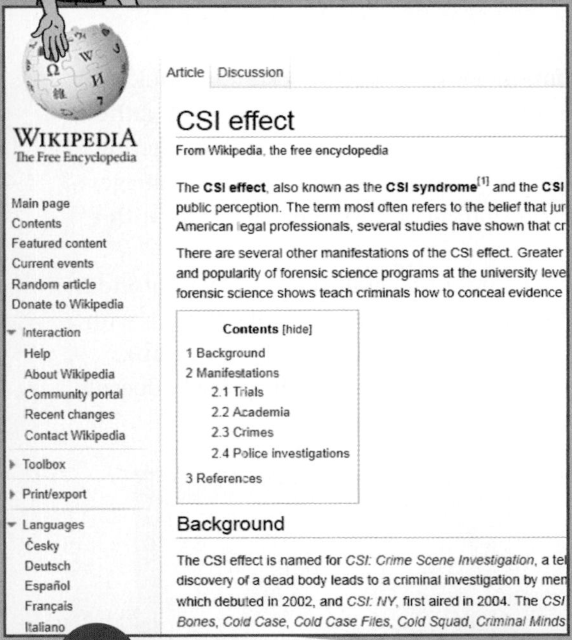
Article | Discussion

CSI effect

From Wikipedia, the free encyclopedia

The **CSI effect**, also known as the **CSI syndrome**[1] and the **CSI**
public perception. The term most often refers to the belief that jur
American legal professionals, several studies have shown that cr

There are several other manifestations of the CSI effect. Greater
and popularity of forensic science programs at the university leve
forensic science shows teach criminals how to conceal evidence

Contents [hide]

1 Background
2 Manifestations
2.1 Trials
2.2 Academia
2.3 Crimes
2.4 Police investigations
3 References

Background

The CSI effect is named for *CSI: Crime Scene Investigation*, a te
discovery of a dead body leads to a criminal investigation by men
which debuted in 2002, and *CSI: NY*, first aired in 2004. The *CSI*
Bones, Cold Case, Cold Case Files, Cold Squad, Criminal Minds

WIKIPEDIA
The Free Encyclopedia

Main page
Contents
Featured content
Current events
Random article
Donate to Wikipedia

Interaction
Help
About Wikipedia
Community portal
Recent changes
Contact Wikipedia

Toolbox

Print/export

Languages
Česky
Deutsch
Español
Français
Italiano

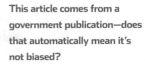

2

Stay alert to differing perspectives.

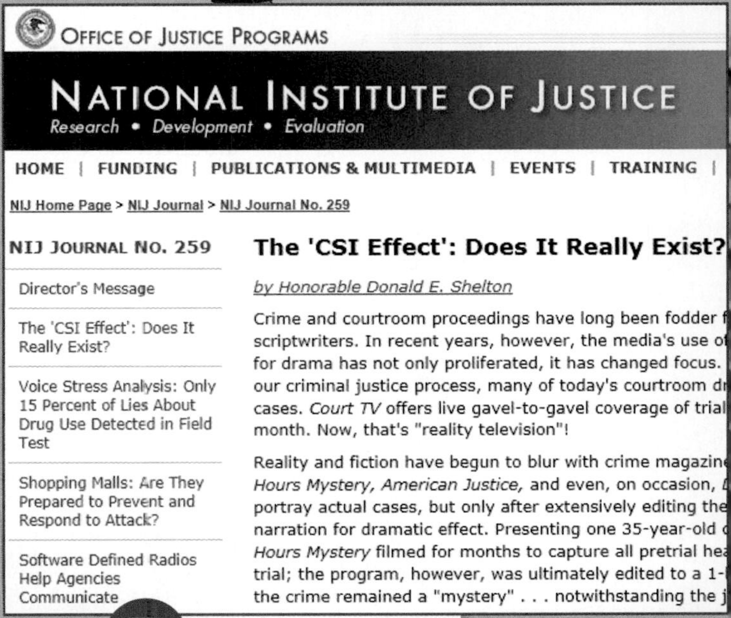
OFFICE OF JUSTICE PROGRAMS

NATIONAL INSTITUTE OF JUSTICE
Research • Development • Evaluation

HOME | FUNDING | PUBLICATIONS & MULTIMEDIA | EVENTS | TRAINING |

NIJ Home Page > NIJ Journal > NIJ Journal No. 259

NIJ JOURNAL NO. 259

Director's Message

The 'CSI Effect': Does It Really Exist?

Voice Stress Analysis: Only 15 Percent of Lies About Drug Use Detected in Field Test

Shopping Malls: Are They Prepared to Prevent and Respond to Attack?

Software Defined Radios Help Agencies Communicate

The 'CSI Effect': Does It Really Exist?

by Honorable Donald E. Shelton

Crime and courtroom proceedings have long been fodder f
scriptwriters. In recent years, however, the media's use o
for drama has not only proliferated, it has changed focus.
our criminal justice process, many of today's courtroom d
cases. *Court TV* offers live gavel-to-gavel coverage of trial
month. Now, that's "reality television"!

Reality and fiction have begun to blur with crime magazin
Hours Mystery, American Justice, and even, on occasion,
portray actual cases, but only after extensively editing the
narration for dramatic effect. Presenting one 35-year-old
Hours Mystery filmed for months to capture all pretrial he
trial; the program, however, was ultimately edited to a 1-
the crime remained a "mystery" . . . notwithstanding the j

3

Question claims.

20 Brainstorming with Others

collaborate

You've probably seen films or TV series that mock groupthink in corporations—wherein cowering yes-men and yes-women gather around a table to rubber-stamp the dumb ideas of a domineering CEO. Real group brainstorming is just the opposite. It encourages a freewheeling discovery and sharing of ideas among people with a stake in the outcome.

Group brainstorming comes in several varieties. The notorious college dorm-room bull session is a famous example, though with obvious defects. Such boozy late-night talk is likely to be frank, open-ended, wide-ranging, and passionate. But it typically doesn't lead anywhere or produce an agenda for action.

In academic or professional situations, formal brainstorming within a group requires specific strategies to produce solid results.

In academic and professional situations, formal brainstorming within a group requires specific strategies to produce solid results.

Choose a leader.   Leaders should be strong enough to keep discussions moving, cordial enough to encourage everyone to participate, and modest enough to draw out a range of opinions without pursuing agendas of their own. The leader probably shouldn't be the person with the most power in the group—not the CEO, chair of the department, or president of the student government. In fact, in serious brainstorming sessions, an outsider or trained facilitator might be the best choice.

Begin with a goal and set an agenda.   Most groups don't brainstorm for the pleasure of it. Some need or concern brings participants to the table—for instance, an assignment that requires a committee's response or a project that involves more work than one person can handle. The leader should get the group to agree on a goal and a simple agenda. Even if that goal is open-ended, it will help keep discussions on track. And both the goal and agenda can be written on a board or flip chart to keep the group on task. Without an agenda, brainstorming activity can dissolve into a bull session.

As the session evolves, a leader should help the group understand what it is accomplishing by stating and restating positions as they develop from discussion, posing important questions, and recording ideas as they emerge.

Set time limits.   Groups are most productive when working against reasonable time restraints. Given open-ended sessions (such as those dorm-room all-nighters), nothing productive may ever occur. But with only an hour or two for brainstorming, a group serious about its work will focus mightily. Time restraints also give a leader leverage to stifle the chatterers.

Encourage everyone to participate.   A leader or facilitator can call on the quiet types, but other participants can help, too, just by asking a colleague, "What do you think?" In a group setting, a reluctant participant's first contribution is usually the toughest to elicit, but it's worth any prodding: The silent observer in a group may come up with the sharpest insight.

Avoid premature criticism.   Leaders and participants alike need to encourage outside-the-box thinking and avoid a tendency to cut off contributions at the knees. No sneering, guffawing, or eye rolling—even when ideas *are* stupid. Early on, get every scheme, suggestion, and proposal on the blackboard or flip chart. Criticism and commentary can come later.

It might even help to open the session with everyone freewriting on a key idea for five or ten minutes as a warm-up, then reading their best ideas aloud. O

Test all ideas.   Sometimes, a group agrees too readily when a sudden good idea gains momentum. Such a notion should be challenged hard—even if it means someone has to play devil's advocate, that is, raise arguments or objections just to test the leading idea or claim. Even good ideas need to have their mettle proved.

Keep good records.   Many brainstorming sessions fail not because the ideas didn't emerge, but because no one bothered to catch them. Someone competent should take notes detailed enough to make sense a month later, when memories start to fade. Here again, a flip chart may be useful, since points written on it don't get erased. The facilitator should follow up on the session by seeing that the notes get organized, written up, and promptly distributed to the group.

Agree on an end product.   Effective brainstorming sessions should lead to action of some kind or, at least, a clear agenda for further discussion. Keeping an eye on the clock, the leader of the group should wind up general discussion early enough to push the group toward conclusions and plans for action. Not every brainstorming session reaches its goals, but participants will want closure on their work.

> **Your Turn**   Can you describe a time when a group brainstorming activity either generated great ideas or failed miserably? If so, briefly describe that incident and try to account for its success or failure. Be open-minded about the definition of "group activity." Your moment may have occurred among campers stranded by a flat tire or campus activists gathered to spread a political message.

get an idea
p. 356

Smart Reading **21**

There's probably no better strategy for generating ideas than reading. Reading can deepen your impressions of a subject you are studying, enrich your awareness, sharpen your critical acumen, and introduce you to alternative views. Reading also places you within a community of writers who have already thought about a subject.

Of course, not all reading serves the same purposes.

read closely

- You check out a dozen scholarly books to do research for a paper and then look for journal articles online.
- You consult stock market quotes and baseball box scores because you need info. *now*.
- You study an organization chart to figure out who actually controls the student government budget.
- You read an old diary to discover what life was like before photocopiers, air conditioning, and (*gulp!*) cell phones.
- You pack a *Twilight Saga* novel for pleasure reading on the Jersey shore.

Yet any of these reading experiences, as well as thousands of others, might lead to ideas for projects.

You've probably been thoroughly schooled in basic techniques of academic reading: Survey the table of contents, preread to get a sense of the whole, look up terms or concepts you don't know, summarize what you've read, and so on. Such suggestions are practical, especially for difficult scholarly or professional texts. Following is advice about reading to sharpen your college-level writing.

> If you don't have
> the time to read,
> you don't have
> the time or tools
> to write.

— Stephen King

Read to deepen what you already know.   Whatever your interests or experiences in life, you're not alone. Others have explored similar paths and probably written about them. Reading such work may give you confidence to bring your own thoughts to public attention. Whether your passion is tintype photography, skateboarding, or film fashions of the 1930s, you'll find excellent books on the subject by browsing library catalogs or even just checking Amazon.com. ○

For example, if you have worked at a fast-food franchise and know what goes on there, you might find a book like Eric Schlosser's *Fast Food Nation: The Dark Side of the All-American Meal* engrossing. You'll be drawn in because your experience makes you an informed critic. You can agree and disagree intelligently with Schlosser and, perhaps, see how his arguments might be extended or amended. At a minimum, you'll walk away from the book understanding even more about the fast-food industry and knowing the titles of dozens of additional sources, should you want to learn more.

Read above your level of knowledge.   It's comfortable to connect with people online who share your interests, but you'll often be chatting with people who don't know much more than you do. To find new ideas, push your reading to a higher and more demanding level. Spend some time with books and articles you can't blow right through. You'll know you are there when you find yourself looking up names, adding terms to your vocabulary, and feeling humbled at what you still need to learn about a subject. That's when thinking occurs and ideas germinate.

Read what makes you uncomfortable.   Most of us today have access to technologies that connect us to endless paths of information. But all those channels also mean that we can choose to read (or watch) only materials that confirm our existing beliefs and prejudices—and many people do. Yet such narrowness will be quickly exposed whenever you write on a controversial subject and find readers pushing back with facts and ideas you never considered before. Surprise! The world is more complicated than you thought. The solution is simple: Get out of the echo chamber and read more broadly, engaging with those who see the world differently.

refine your search
p. 472

Your Turn Working with a small group, make a list of the newspapers, Web sites, magazines, TV shows or networks, or other resources that members of the group use to gather their news and information about politics, society, and culture. Then try to locate these media resources along a ribbon that moves from the political far left to the political far right. Be prepared for considerable disagreement. When you are done, compare your placements with those of other groups working on the same project. What may account for your differences?

Far left _____ Left _____ Center _____ Right _____ Far right

Read against the grain. Skeptics and naysayers may be no fun at parties, but their habits may be worth emulating whenever you are reading. It makes sense to read with an open mind, giving reputable writers and their ideas a fair hearing. But you always want to raise questions about the assumptions writers make, the logic they use, the evidence they present, and the authorities and sources upon which they build their arguments.

Reading against the grain does not mean finding fault with everything, but rather letting nothing slip by without scrutiny. Treat the world around you as a text to be read and analyzed. ○ Ask questions. Why do so few men take liberal-arts courses? What topics does your campus paper avoid and why? Have your friendships changed now that you deal with people mostly online? Notice such phenomena, ponder their meaning, and write about them.

Read slowly. Browsing online has made many of us superficial readers. For serious texts, forget speed-reading and your own Web habits. Settle in for the duration. Find the thesis; look up unfamiliar words and names; don't jump to another article until you've finished the one in hand.

Annotate what you read. Find some way to record your reactions to whatever you read. If you own the text and don't mind marking it, highlighting pens and

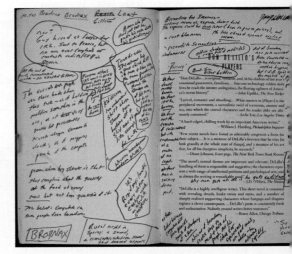

The late writer David Foster Wallace took copious notes when he read—in this case, the Don DeLillo novel *Players*.

think critically
p. 372

comments in the margin remain great tools for drawing your attention to weighty ideas. Electronic media and e-readers offer a range of built-in commenting tools. Even Post-it notes work in some circumstances. What's key is to interact with your reading.

Read visually.   Much information comes to us today not in words only but in visual formats that expand the way data can be presented. Whether in print or on screen, visual texts are inherently appealing, but don't assume they are simplistic or easy to interpret.

Consider how much information the humble campus map conveys, relying on nothing more than drawings, colors, symbols, and various legends or keys. When enhanced by sound and motion, as they routinely are in electronic environments, visual texts can become complex multimedia experiences.

When reading or using the following types of images and graphics, try the strategies suggested here.

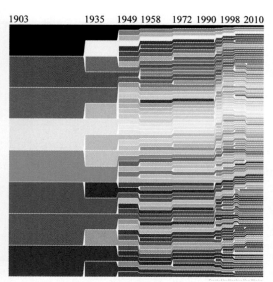

"Velo's Crayola Color Chart, 1903–2010"

- **Read an image showing a sequence.** Like a narrative, an image can break information into stages or steps. So study a graphic for its structural pattern: the way it gives order to its components. Elements may be arranged alphabetically, chronologically, or by degree or magnitude (for example, greater to lesser, cheaper to more expensive)—whatever works for the material. Begin your interpretation by paying attention to headings and navigation devices (especially for electronic images); then study any legends and keys, which will explain the meaning of symbols, colors, and other devices used in the graphic. An elegant chronological graphic like Stephen Von Worley's "Velo's Crayola Color Chart, 1903–2010" leaves some of the work of interpretation to you.

- **Read an image demonstrating a process.** Sequences grow more complicated when they begin to offer choices and alternative pathways. Flowcharts, for example, may display complicated options and feedback loops that you must navigate to reach a goal or conclusion. Look carefully at such diagrams to be sure you understand the meaning of intersections, lines and line graphics, and colors. For an excellent example of a complex flowchart, see "How Our Laws Are Made" on page 70.

- **Read an image displaying relationships and differences.** Many graphics use boundaries —lines, boxes, columns, contrasting colors, and so on—to highlight divisions. A seating guide to an auditorium might mimic its floor plan to guide you to your box and use colors to show the price difference between the loge and the mezzanine sections. More complicated are the charts, graphs, and tables you'll encounter in natural and social science courses. These items use visual elements to array information or to plot relationships between variables. So you have to carefully examine their labels, column titles, interpretive keys, and other devices to be certain that you understand them. You may also need to know the sources of the data they present, the scales used to express changes over time, and so on. For good reason, we talk about "studying" charts and graphs. In recent years, much attention has been paid to designing informative graphics to convey data memorably. "What Are We Eating?" prepared by Visualeconomics .com is an example of such an *infographic*.

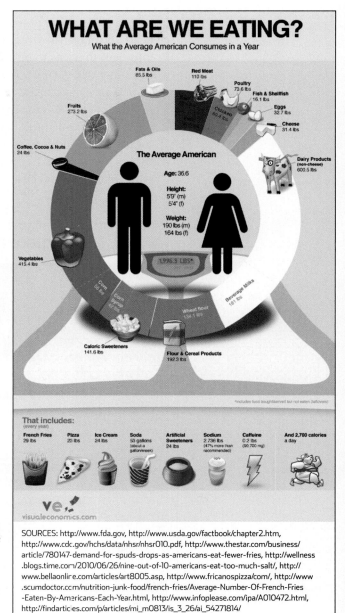

● **Read an image showing how items are connected.** Quite often, information needs to be presented in diagrams that show hierarchies and other ties. A family tree illustrates the genealogical connections among a person's ancestors. A site map displays the main pages and subpages of a Web site. An organizational chart (or "org. chart," as it is commonly called) lets you know who reports to whom within an organization. You may struggle with some diagrams of this sort, but that's usually a flaw in their design. These types of visuals should be self-explanatory and clear.

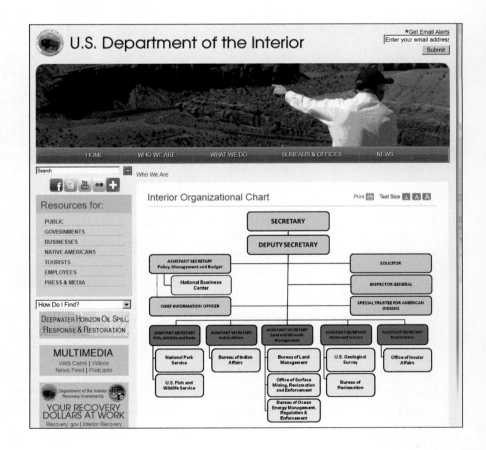

- **Read a map.** Surveys indicate that as many as one-third of drivers can't read a street map; weather maps may be just as puzzling. The problem is that while maps seem simple, they ask you to imagine the complications of real life reduced to symbols. On a map you must contend with direction, scale, geography, terrain, distance, boundaries, road symbols and names, place names, speed, and time. Hold the map wrong and you already have a problem. Weather maps introduce other variables. Yet the genius of a good map is the enormous amount of information it will offer once you master its symbols, keys, and scale. That's where to begin.

- **Read an image imitating three dimensions.** Many images, particularly in the fields of science and engineering, attempt to convey three-dimensional information in two dimensions, enabling viewers to understand how objects work, how parts mesh, or how the natural world functions (see "Geologic Hazards at Volcanoes"). Such cutaway or "exploded" drawings enable viewers to see relationships that would be very difficult to explain in words alone. And yet they require you to imagine how the various layers fit together when you see the parts either cut away or pulled apart. You may have to study such images to figure them out; not surprisingly, some 3-D information is better conveyed on video. **O**

≋USGS
science for a changing world

Geologic Hazards at Volcanoes

Prevailing Wind

Eruption Column

Eruption Cloud

Tephra (Ash) Fall

Acid Rain

Bombs

Lava Dome

Lava Dome Collapse

Debris Avalanche (Landslide)

Pyroclastic Flow

Vent

Fumaroles

Pyroclastic Flow

Lava Flow

Lahar (Mud or Debris Flow)

Conduit

Ground Water

Crack

Magma

Most volcano hazards are associated with eruptions. However, some hazards, such as lahars and debris avalanches, can occur even when a volcano is not erupting.

By Bobbie Myers and Carolyn Driedger 2008

Available from U.S. Geological Survey, Information Services, Box 25286, Federal Center, Denver, CO, 80225. 1-888-ASK-USGS
Digital files available at http://pubs.usgs.gov/gip/64

U.S. Department of the Interior
U.S. Geological Survey

Printed on recycled paper

General Information Product 64

22 Critical Thinking

think
critically/
avoid
fallacies

We all get antsy when our written work is criticized (or even edited) because the ideas we put on a page or screen emerge from our own thinking—writing is *us*. Granted, our words rarely express *exactly* who we are or what we've been imagining, but such distinctions get lost quickly when someone points to our work and says, "That's stupid" or "What nonsense!" The criticism cuts deep; it feels personal.

Fortunately, the surest way to avoid embarrassing criticism is also the best way to come up with ideas that look plausible when they find their way into print: *critical thinking*. Critical thinking is a term that describes mental habits that bolster logical reasoning and analysis. There are lots of ways to foster critical thinking, from following the general strategies of smart reading described in Chapter 21 to using the specific rhetorical tactics presented throughout the "Guide" section of this book. To report, argue, explain, or analyze well is, in effect, to practice critical thinking.

Here we focus on several aspects of critical thinking that you will find useful in college writing.

Think in terms of claims and reasons.　When you read reports, arguments, or analyses, chances are you begin by examining the claims writers make and the good reasons they have for offering them. Logically, then, when you write in these genres, you should expect the same scrutiny.

Claims are the passages in a text where you make an assertion, offer an argument, or present a hypothesis for which you intend to provide evidence.

> Using a cell phone while driving is dangerous.
>
> Playing video games can improve intelligence.
>
> Worrying about childhood obesity is futile.

Early in a work, you may state a *thesis* or goal for a project, but that's only one type of claim. ○ Sentences that make a specific point may occur just about anywhere in an article, report, or book. You'll need to offer clear claims as the topic sentences in many paragraphs, in transitional sentences, and in summary materials at various points in the work, especially at the conclusion. (The exception may be formal scientific writing, in which the hypothesis, results, and discussion will occur in specific sections of an article.) ○

Critical thinking really begins when you make sure that all such major claims in a text are accompanied by plausible supporting *reasons* either in the same sentence or in adjoining material. These reasons may be announced by expressions as straightforward as *because, if, to,* and *so.* Once you attach reasons to a claim, you have made a deeper commitment to it. You must then do the hard work of providing readers with convincing evidence, logic, or conditions for accepting your claim. Seeing your ideas fully stated on paper early in a project may even persuade you to abandon an implausible claim—one you cannot or do not want to defend.

> Using a cell phone while driving is dangerous *because* distractions are a proven cause of auto accidents.
>
> Playing video games can improve intelligence *if* they teach young gamers to make logical decisions quickly.
>
> ~~Worrying about childhood obesity is futile because there's nothing we can do about it.~~

Think in terms of premises and assumptions.   Underlying all important claims and reasons are the core principles and values upon which researchers and writers operate: These are called *premises* or *assumptions.*

develop a statement
p. 393

understand lab
reports p. 336

In oral arguments, when people say *I understand where you're coming from*, they signal that they get your assumptions. You want similar clarity and connection when writing reports and arguments, especially when your claims may be regarded as controversial or argumentative. Your assumptions can be specific or general, conventional or highly controversial, as in the following examples.

> We should discourage behaviors that contribute to traffic accidents. [specific]
>
> Improving intelligence is a desirable goal. [general]
>
> The physical world is organized by coherent and predictable principles. [conventional]
>
> Freedom is better than tyranny. [conventional]
>
> Exploiting the environment is better than preserving it. [controversial]

With some audiences, you may be able to assume that most readers agree with your underlying values. In such cases, your premises may simply be implied. But when your arguments are more controversial, you will need to take the time to explain and defend your assumptions. Naturally—and here's where the critical thinking comes in—you need to be aware of the premises upon which your arguments are built. Do they make sense? Can you defend your assumptions?

Your Turn   Working in a group, find an example of a short argument that impresses most of you. (Your instructor might suggest a particular article.) Carefully locate the claims within the piece that all of you regard as its most important, impressive, or controversial statements. Then see if you can formulate the premises or values upon which these claims rest. Try to state these premises as clearly as you can in a complete, declarative sentence. Are the assumptions you have uncovered statements that you agree with? If the assumptions are controversial, does the piece explain or defend them? Be prepared to present your group's analysis and conclusions in class.

Think in terms of evidence.   As you write, be sure that all your major claims as well as your assumptions (when they are controversial) are supported by *evidence*. A claim without evidence attached is just that—a barefaced assertion no better than a child's "Oh, yeah?" You should choose supporting material attentively, always weighing whether it is sufficient, complete, reliable, and unbiased. ○ Has an author you want to cite done original research and drawn on respectable sources or, instead, relied on evidence that seems flimsy or anecdotal? And can you offer enough evidence to make a convincing case? How much evidence might be too much? These are questions to ask routinely and persistently.

Anticipate objections.   Critical thinkers understand that serious issues have many dimensions—and rarely just two sides. That's because they have done their homework, which means trying to understand even those positions with which they strongly disagree. When you start writing with this kind of knowledgeable perspective, you'll hear voices of the loyal opposition in your head and can address objections even before potential readers make them. At a minimum, you will enhance your credibility. But more important, you'll have done the kind of thinking that makes you smarter.

Avoid logical fallacies.   Honest, fair-minded writers have nothing to hide. They name names, identify sources, and generate appropriate emotions. They acknowledge weakness in their arguments and concede readily when the opposition has a point. These are qualities you want to display in your serious academic and professional work.

One way to enhance your reputation as a writer and critical thinker is to avoid logical fallacies. *Fallacies* are rhetorical moves that corrupt solid reasoning—the verbal equivalent of sleight of hand. The following classic, but all too common, fallacies can undermine the integrity of your writing.

● **Appeals to false authority.** Be sure that any experts or authorities you cite on a topic have real credentials in the field and that their claims can be verified. Similarly, don't claim or imply knowledge, authority, or credentials yourself that you don't have. Be frank about your level of expertise. Framing yourself as an honest, if amateur, broker on a subject can even raise your credibility.

refine your search
p. 472

- *Ad hominem* attacks. In arguments of all kinds, you may be tempted to bolster your position by attacking the personal integrity of your opponents when character really isn't an issue. It's easy to resort to name-calling (*socialist, racist*) or character assassination, but it usually signals that your own case is weak.

- **Dogmatism**. Writers fall back on dogmatism whenever they want to give the impression, usually false, that they control the party line on an issue and have all the right answers. You are likely indulging in dogmatism when you begin a paragraph, *No serious person would disagree* or *How can anyone argue. . . .*

- **Either/or choices**. A shortcut to winning arguments, which even Socrates abused, is to reduce complex situations to simplistic choices: good/bad,

"*Either you left the TV on downstairs or we have whales again.*"

right/wrong, liberty/tyranny, smart/dumb, and so on. If you find yourself inclined to use some version of the *either/or* strategy, think again. Capable readers will see right through your tactic.

- **Scare tactics**. Avoid them. Arguments that make their appeals chiefly by raising fears—usually of the unknown—are automatically suspect. When fears are legitimate, provide evidence for the threat and don't overstate it.

- **Sentimental or emotional appeals**. Maybe it's okay for the Humane Society to decorate its pleas for cash with pictures of sad puppies, but you can see how the tactic might be abused. In your own work, be wary of using language that pushes buttons the same way, *oohing* and *aahing* readers out of their best judgment.

- **Hasty generalizations**. It is remarkably tempting to draw conclusions from just one or two poignant examples that fit your preconceived notions—or those of your intended audiences. But avoid the temptation to hang a claim on such scant evidence. Your integrity is at stake.

- **Faulty causality**. Just because two events or phenomena occur close together in time doesn't mean that one caused the other. (The Red Sox didn't start winning *because* you put on the lucky boxers.) People are fond of leaping to such easy conclusions, and many pundits and politicians do routinely exploit this weakness, particularly in situations involving economics, science, health, crime, and culture. Causal

relationships are almost always complicated, and you will get credit for dealing with them honestly. ○

- **Equivocations, evasions, and misstatements.** *Equivocations* are lies that look like truths; *evasions* simply avoid the truth entirely. Skilled readers know when a writer is using these devices, so avoid them.

- **Straw men.** *Straw men* are easy or habitual targets that writers aim at to win an argument. Often the issue in such an attack has long been defused or discredited: for example, welfare recipients driving Cadillacs, immigrants taking jobs from hard-working citizens, the rich not paying a fair share of taxes. When you resort to straw-man arguments, you signal to your readers that you may not have much else in your arsenal.

- **Slippery-slope arguments.** Take one wrong step off the righteous path and you'll slide all the way down the hill: That's the warning that slippery-slope arguments make. They aren't always inaccurate, but they are easy to overstate. Will using plastic bags really doom the planet? Maybe or maybe not. If you create a causal chain, be sure that you offer adequate support for every step and don't push beyond what's plausible.

- **Bandwagon appeals.** You haven't made an argument when you simply tell people it's time to cease debate and get with popular opinion. Too many bad decisions and policies get enacted that way. If you order readers to jump aboard a bandwagon, expect them to resist.

- **Faulty analogies.** Similes and analogies are worth applauding when they illuminate ideas or make them comprehensible or memorable. But seriously analyze the implications of any analogies you use. Calling a military action either "another Vietnam" or a "crusade" might raise serious issues, as does comparing one's opponents to "Commies" or the KKK. Readers have a right to be skeptical of writers who use such ploys.

understand causal
analysis p. 138

Experts 23

Forget about *expert* as an intimidating word. When you need help with your writing, seek advice from people who either know more about your subject than you do or have more experience developing such a project. Advice may come from different people, but that's not a problem: The more people you talk to, the better.

Knowledgeable people can get you on track quickly, confirming the merit of your topic ideas, cutting through issues irrelevant to your work, and directing you to the best resources.

ask for help

Talk with your instructor.   Don't be timid. Instructors hold office hours to answer your questions, especially about assignments. Save yourself time and, perhaps, much grief by getting early feedback on your ideas and topic. It's better to learn that your thesis is hopeless *before* you compose a first draft.

Just as important, your instructor might help you see aspects of a topic you hadn't noticed or direct you to indispensable sources. Don't write a paper only to please instructors, but you'd be foolish to ignore their counsel.

Take your ideas to the writing center.   Many student writers think the only time to use a campus writing center is when their teacher returns a draft on life support. Most writing center tutors prefer not to be seen as EMTs. So they are eager to assist at the start of a project, when you're still developing ideas. Tutors may not be experts on your subject, but they have seen enough bad papers to offer sensible advice for focusing a topic, shaping a thesis, or adapting a subject to an audience. ○ They also recognize when you're so clueless that you need to talk with your instructor pronto.

Find local experts.   Don't bother an expert for information you could find easily yourself in the library or online: Save human contacts for when you need serious help on a major writing project—a senior thesis, an important story for a campus periodical, a public presentation on a controversial subject. But, then, do take advantage of the human resources you have. Campuses are teeming with knowledgeable people and that doesn't just include faculty in their various disciplines. Staff and administrative personnel at your school can advise you on everything from trends in college admissions to local crime statistics.

Look to the local community for expertise and advice as well. Is there a paper to be written about declining audiences for foreign films? You couldn't call Pedro Almodóvar and get through, but you could chat with a few local theater owners or managers to learn what they think about the business. Their perceptions might change the direction of your project.

Check with librarians.   Campus librarians have lots of experience helping writers find information, steering them toward fertile topics and away from ideas that may not have much intellectual standing. Librarians can't be as specific or directive as, for example, your instructor, but they have just as firm a grasp on the resources available for a project and what sorts of topic ideas the library's resources will and will not support.

Chat with peers.   Peers aren't really experts, but an honest classroom conversation among fellow students can be an eye-opening experience. You'll likely see a wide spectrum of opinions (if the discussion is frank) and even be surprised by objections to your ideas that you hadn't anticipated. Peers often have a surprising range of knowledge and, if the group is diverse, your friends will bring a breadth of life experiences to the conversation. You might be eager to champion advances in medical technology, but someone

develop a statement
p. 393

from a community where hospitals can't afford high-tech gear might add a
wrinkle to your thinking.

Colleges and universities
often provide lists of faculty and staff with special
expertise in their fields.

Your Turn   If you were asked to identify yourself as an expert on a subject,
what would it be? Don't consider academic subjects only. Think about *any*
areas or activities about which you could confidently offer authoritative and
reliable advice. Make a list, and share it with your classmates. Do their lists
give you additional ideas?

1 Bring materials with you, including the assignment, previous drafts or outlines, comments from your instructor if you have any, a pen, and a notebook.

2 Be actively involved during the session, and arrive with specific goals in mind. Your tutor may ask questions about your writing process and your paper. Be prepared to think about and respond to your tutor's suggestions.

3 Keep revising. While the tutor may be able to help you with some aspects of your writing, you are ultimately responsible for the finished paper — and your grade.

24 Writer's Block

tackle hard
stuff

Waiting until the last minute to write a paper hasn't been defined as a medical problem yet. But give it time. Already a condition called *executive dysfunction* describes the inability of some children and adults to plan, organize, pace, and complete tasks. No doubt we've all experienced some of its symptoms, describing the state as *procrastination* when it comes to doing the laundry and *writer's block* when it applies to finishing papers on time.

Getting writing done isn't hard because the process is painful, but rather because it is so fragile and vulnerable to ridiculous excuses and distractions. Who hasn't vacuumed a floor or washed a car rather than compose a paragraph? Writing also comes with no guarantees, no necessary connection between labor put in and satisfactory pages churned out. Like baseball, writing is a game without time limits. When a paper isn't going well, you can stretch into fruitless twelfth and thirteenth innings with no end in sight. And if you do finish, readers may not like what you have done — even when you know the work is solid, based on honest reading, observation, and research. Such concerns are enough to give anyone writer's block.

So what do you do when you'd rather crack walnuts with your teeth than write a term paper?

Break the project into parts. Getting started is usually the hard part for writers simply because the project taken as a whole seems overwhelming. Even a simple one-page position paper can ruin a whole weekend, and a term paper—with its multiple drafts, abstract, notes, bibliography, tables, and graphs—stretches beyond the pale.

But what if, instead of thinking about how much time and energy the whole project will take, you divide it into manageable stages? Then you can do the work in chunks and celebrate the success that comes from completing each part. That position paper might be broken down into two, maybe three, less daunting steps: doing the assigned reading; brainstorming the paper; writing the page required. The same procedure makes a research paper less intimidating: You have more parts to manage, but you also have a strategy to finish them.

Set manageable goals.   Unless you are very disciplined, writing projects absorb all the time available for them. Worse, you'll likely expend more energy fretting than working. To gain control, set reasonable goals for completing the project and stick to them. In other words, don't dedicate a whole Saturday to preparing your résumé or working up a lab report; instead, commit yourself to the full and uninterrupted two hours the task will really take if you sit down and concentrate.

If you have trouble estimating how much time a project may require, consider that it is better to set a goal than to face an open-ended commitment. That's one good reason both teachers and publishers set deadlines.

Create a calendar.   For complicated assignments that extend over weeks or even months, create a calendar or timeline and stick with it. ○ First break the task into parts and estimate how much time each stage of the paper or other project will take. Knowing your own work habits, you can draw on past experience with similar assignments to construct a levelheaded plan. You'll feel better once you've got a road map leading to completion.

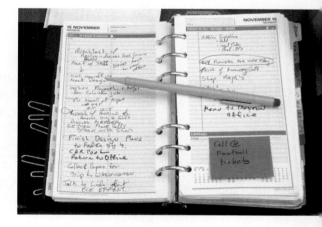

plan a project
p. 466

> Inspiration is wonderful when it happens, but the writer must develop an approach for the rest of the time. . . . The wait is simply too long.

— Leonard Bernstein

Don't draw up a schedule so elaborate that you build in failure by trying to manage too many events. Assume that some stages, especially research or drafting, may take more time than you originally expect. But do stick to your schedule, even if it means starting a draft with research still remaining or cutting off the drafting process to allow time for thorough revision.

Limit distractions.   Put yourself in a place that encourages writing and minimizes any temptations that might pull you away from your work. Schedule a specific time for writing and give it priority over all other activities, from paying your bills to feeding the dog. (On second thought, feed that dog to stop the barking.) Shut down your Facebook and e-mail accounts, turn off your cell phone, shuffle from the Killers to Bill Frisell on your iPod, start writing, and don't stop for an hour.

Do the parts you like first.   Movies aren't filmed in sequence and papers don't have to be written that way either. Compose those parts of a project that feel ready to go or interest you most. You can work on the transitions later to make the paper feel seamless, the way editors cut disparate scenes into coherent films. Once you have portions of a paper already composed you'll be more inclined to continue working on it: The project suddenly seems manageable.

Write a zero draft.   When you are *really* blocked, try a zero draft—that is, a version of the paper composed in one sitting, virtually nonstop. The process may resemble freewriting, but this time you aren't trawling for ideas. You're ready to write, having done the necessary brainstorming, reading, and research. You might even have a thesis and an outline. What you lack is the confidence to turn this preparation into coherent sentences. So repress your inhibitions by writing relentlessly, without pausing to reread and review your stuff. Keep at it for several hours if need be. Imagine you're writing an essay exam. ○

understand essay
exams p. 284

The draft you produce won't be elegant (though you might surprise yourself), and some spots might be rough indeed. But keep pushing until you've finished a full text, from introduction to conclusion. Put this version aside, delaying any revision for a few hours or even days. Then, instead of facing an empty tablet or screen, you have full pages of prose to work with.

Reward yourself.   People respond remarkably well to incentives, so promise yourself some prize correlated to the writing task you face. Finishing a position paper is probably worth a personal-size pizza. A term paper might earn you dinner and a movie. A dissertation is worth a used Honda Civic.

Your Turn   Do you have a good writer's block story to share? You might describe an odd thing you have done rather than start a paper — especially one that might seem far more arduous than putting words down on a page. Or maybe you have figured out an infallible method for overcoming writer's block. Or you have endured a roommate's endless excuses for failing to complete a writing assignment. Tell your story in a paragraph or two, which you will start writing *NOW*.

Shaping & Drafting

4

part four

choose a genre   **25** **Genre** 390

develop a statement   **26** **Thesis** 393

develop a draft   **27** **Strategies** 398

shape your work   **28** **Organization** 406

order ideas   **29** **Outlines** 408

develop ideas   **30** **Paragraphs** 412

connect ideas   **31** **Transitions** 416

shape a beginning   **32** **Introductions** 420

shape an ending   **33** **Conclusions** 425

name your work   **34** **Titles** 428

Need help developing your ideas? See page 412. / Need style help? See page 432.

25 Genre

choose a
genre

What's a *genre*? You already know. You use the concept of genre whenever you identify movies by type: *sci-fi films, westerns, action/ adventure films, romances* (a.k.a. "chick flicks"), *horror movies,* and so on. You surely recognize that movies have distinct *subgenres* too. Horror movies, for example, can be broken down into slasher pics, monster films, psychological thrillers, and more—all with well-established features and characteristics that audiences expect to encounter in a darkened theater.

Genre is also a term used to describe important categories of writing such as novels, short stories, poems, or nonfiction. Each of these genres can be clearly defined, described by their features, and taught by using formulas or templates.

But now consider a more dynamic view of *genre*, one that treats genres of writing not as fixed categories but as real-life responses to ever-changing situations. Simply put, writers have to figure out what they must do to achieve a goal and to reach particular readers. So they adapt a familiar form of writing to a specific moment, context, reader, and purpose. That's how genres are presented in this book.

For instance, in recent years, as more and more organizations and businesses have required potential job candidates to describe their lives and qualifications, the genre of the "personal statement" has evolved. Today, people recognize and expect such a task whenever they apply for internships, jobs, or scholarships. As a result, it's now possible to describe the strategies and conventional features of successful personal statements—and explain how writers can compose them successfully. You can find such information in Chapter 16.

But because genres respond to real-world situations, they change to fit the times. So when you learn a new genre, you don't necessarily acquire a hard-and-fast set of rules for writing; instead, you gain control over that genre's possibilities. That enables you to adapt its moves to your specific needs. So genres don't complicate your life; instead, they enable you to address widely varying writing situations.

> **Your Turn**   Generate a list of all the genres of writing or communication that you produce in a typical week in all aspects of your life, not just in school. How did you learn to produce those genres? Which did you learn on your own and which required formal instruction? Which have you yet to master? Compare your list of genres with those produced by classmates, noting in particular any types of writing they use that you don't.

Recognize the variety of genres.   Some genres of writing are broad and open-ended, such those presented in Part 1 of this book: personal narratives, reports, arguments, analyses, and so on. When you study genres like these, you encounter the basic strategies people use in school and the professional world. But when you actually write, you will usually produce a narrower version of these genres—one of those subgenres discussed earlier. So you won't compose a nonspecific report; you'll write a history term paper or sports column about college recruiting. You won't produce a generic evaluation; ◯ you'll write a movie or restaurant review or job assessment. In effect, you'll adapt a genre to your needs.

Part 2, "Special Assignments," covers a range of subgenres especially important to people studying in school or entering the job market—items such as the essay examination, résumé, personal statement, and oral report. In these chapters, you'll notice how down-to-earth and action oriented genres can be. They do bona fide work.

And that is how genres differ from the *strategies of writing* presented in Chapter 27, such as description, division, comparison, classification, and definition. ◯ These techniques are essential tools of writing, but they apply across a full range of genres. In writing a report or argument, you might need to illustrate a point, offer a description, or draw a comparison to make ideas stand out. But you would rarely just describe or compare or illustrate without making some larger point represented by a genre.

understand
evaluation p. 106

develop a draft
p. 398

Know how to use genres.   Many people think of genres chiefly in terms of their structures of organization. Naturally, when writing a book review or a psychology term paper, it makes sense to study examples of the genre, noting what elements go where. That's a useful first step.

But to understand a genre well, you must also recognize its typical aims, audiences, styles of language, special features, and characteristic media. Reports, for example, often rely on tables and graphs; a research paper always needs reliable sources and careful documentation; and arguments deploy lots of examples and evidence. Such matters are covered in the "Genres" and "Special Assignments" chapters in this book (see Chapters 1–18). Once you grasp the way genres work, you won't be intimidated by any of them.

Appreciate that genres change.   Genres in almost every medium always change: Consider how the vampire movie has evolved from Bela Lugosi's 1931 *Dracula* to today's *Twilight* series. Genres of writing typically alter in response to the needs of audiences and institutions. But we are probably more aware than ever of such evolution today because of the speed of technological developments.

Consider how personal communications have been transformed, moving from paper to e-mail to text message to Twitter feed, each new medium creating its own expectations and etiquette. In working with such rapidly changing technologies, you are actually learning how genres arise and evolve. So pay attention.

Name	Time	Artist	Album	Genre
☑ Believe Me Natalie	5:07	The Killers	Hot Fuss	Alternative
☑ 'A vucchella	3:16	Anton Guadagno, L...	Luciano Pavarotti –...	Classical
☑ Getting Better	2:48	The Beatles	Sgt. Pepper's Lonel...	Rock
☑ One More Night	2:25	Bob Dylan	Nashville Skyline	Folk
☑ I Will Find You	1:51	Clannad	The Last Of The M...	Soundtrack
☑ Losing Touch	4:15	The Killers	Day & Age	Alternative...

You may recognize the term *genre* from iTunes, where it heads the column labeling the types of music you download. What musical genres from your iTunes list probably wouldn't be found on this baby boomer's iPod?

Thesis 26

develop a
statement

A *thesis* is a statement in which a writer affirms or defends the specific idea that will focus or organize a paper. Typically, the thesis appears in an opening paragraph or section, but it may also emerge as the paper unfolds. In some cases, it may not be stated in classic form until the very conclusion. A thesis can be complex enough to require several sentences to explain, or a single sentence might suffice. But a thesis will be in the writing somewhere.

Offering a thesis is a move as necessary and, eventually, as instinctive to a writer as stepping on a clutch before shifting used to be to drivers. No thesis, no forward motion.

How do you write and frame a thesis? Consider the following advice.

Write a complete sentence. Phrases can identify topic areas, even intriguing ones, but they don't make the assertions or claims that provoke thinking and require support. Sentences do. ○ None of the following phrases comes close to providing direction for a paper.

Polygamy in the United States

Reasons for global warming

Economist Steven D. Levitt's controversial theory about declining crime rates

Make a significant claim or assertion.   *Significant* here means that the notion provokes discussion or inquiry. Give readers substance or controversy—in other words, a reason to spend time with your writing.

> Until communities recognize that polygamy persists in parts of the United States, girls and young women will continue to be exploited by the practice.

> Global warming won't stop until industrial nations either lower their standards of living or admit the need for more nuclear power.

Write a declarative sentence, not a question.   Questions may focus attention, but they are not assertions. So, while you might use a question to introduce a topic, don't rely on it to state your claim. A humdrum question acting as a thesis can provoke simplistic responses. There's always the danger, too, that in offering your thesis as a question, you invite strong reactions from readers—and not the ones you want. But introduce an idea as a statement and you gain more control. There is one exception to this guideline: Provocative questions can often help structure personal and exploratory writing.

Expect your thesis to mature.   Your initial thesis will likely grow more complicated as you learn more about your subject. That's natural. But avoid the misconception that a thesis is a statement that breaks a subject into three parts. Theses that follow this pattern too often read like shopping lists, with only re-mote connections between the ideas presented. Just putting the claims in such a tri-part statement into a relationship often makes for a more compelling thesis. The items in dark red type do that job in the second example below.

ORGINAL THESIS

Crime in the United States has declined because more people are in prison, the population is growing older, and DNA testing has made it harder to get away with murder.

REVISED THESIS

It is **much more likely** that crime in the United States has declined because more people are in prison **than because** the population is growing older **or** DNA testing has made it harder to get away with murder.

Introduce a thesis early in a project.   This sound guideline is especially applicable to academic projects and term papers. Instructors will usually want to know up front what the point of a paper will be, especially in reports and some arguments. Whether phrased as a single sentence or several, a thesis typically follows an introductory paragraph or two. Here's the thesis (highlighted in yellow) of Andrew Kleinfeld and Judith Kleinfeld's essay "Go Ahead, Call Us Cowboys," following an opening paragraph that offers a context for their claim.

> Everywhere, Americans are called *cowboys*. On foreign tongues, the reference to America's Western rural laborers is an insult. Cowboys, we are told, plundered the earth, arrogantly rode roughshod over neighbors, and were addicted to mindless violence. So some of us hang our heads in shame. We shouldn't. The cowboy is in fact our Homeric hero, an archetype that sticks because there's truth in it.

Or state a thesis late in a project.   In high school, you may have heard that the thesis statement is *always* the last sentence in the first paragraph. That may be so in conventional five-paragraph essays, but you'll rarely be asked to follow so predictable a pattern in college or elsewhere.

   In fact, it is not unusual, especially in some arguments, for a paper to build toward a thesis—and that statement may not appear until the final paragraph or sentence. ○ Such a strategy makes sense when a claim might not be convincing or rhetorically effective if stated baldly at the opening of the piece. Bret Stephens uses this strategy in an essay entitled "Just Like Stalingrad" to debunk frequent comparisons between former President George W. Bush and either Hitler or Stalin. Stephens's real concern turns out to be not these exaggerated comparisons themselves but rather what happens to language when it is abused by sloppy writers. The final two paragraphs of his essay summarize this case and, arguably, lead up to a thesis in the very last sentence of the essay—more rhetorically convincing there because it comes as something of a surprise.

> Care for language is more than a concern for purity. When one describes President Bush as a fascist, what words remain for real fascists? When one describes Fallujah as Stalingrad-like, how can we express, in the words that remain to the language, what Stalingrad was like?

○

understand
argument p. 72

George Orwell wrote that the English language "becomes ugly and inaccurate because our thoughts are foolish, but the slovenliness of our language makes it easier for us to have foolish thoughts." In taking care with language, we take care of ourselves.

– Wall Street Journal, June 23, 2004

Write a thesis to fit your audience and purpose.   Almost everything you write will have a purpose and a point (see the following table), but not

Type of Assignment	Thesis or Point
Narratives	Usually implied, not stated. (See thesis example on p. 9.)
Reports	Thesis usually previews material or explains its purpose. (See thesis example on p. 66.)
Arguments	Thesis makes an explicit and arguable claim. (See thesis example on p. 76.)
Evaluations	Thesis makes an explicit claim of value based on criteria of evaluation. (See thesis example on p. 127.)
Causal analyses	Thesis asserts or denies an explanatory or causal relationship, based on an analysis of evidence. (See thesis example on p. 141.)
Proposals	Thesis offers a proposal for action. (See thesis example on p. 181.)
Literary analyses	Thesis explains the point of the analysis. (See thesis example on p. 209.)
Rhetorical analyses	Thesis explains the point of the analysis. (See thesis example on p. 265.)
Essay examinations	Thesis previews the entire answer, like a mini-outline. (See thesis example on p. 288.)
Position papers	Thesis makes specific assertion about reading or issue raised in class. (See thesis example on p. 293.)
Annotated bibliographies	Each item may include a statement that describes or evaluates a source. (See example on p. 298.)
Synthesis papers	Thesis summarizes and paraphrases different sources on a specific topic. (See thesis example on p. 306.)
E-mails	Subject line may function as thesis or title. (See thesis example on p. 313.)
Business letters	Thesis states the intention for writing. (See thesis example on p. 320.)
Résumés	"Career objective" may function as a thesis. (See thesis example on p. 328.)
Personal statements	May state an explicit purpose or thesis or lead readers to inferences about qualifications. (See thesis example on p. 333.)
Lab reports	Thesis describes purpose of experiment. (See thesis example on p. 339.)
Oral reports	Introduction or preview slide describes purpose. (See thesis example on p. 350.)

every piece will have a formal thesis. In professional and scientific writing, readers want to know your claim immediately. For persuasive and exploratory writing, you might prefer to keep readers intrigued or have them track the path of your thinking, and delay the thesis until later.

Your Turn   Transform two or three of the following song titles into full-blown thesis statements that might be suitable in an academic paper or newspaper op-ed piece. If these titles don't inspire you, start with several song, album, or movie titles of your own choosing. Be sure that your theses are full, declarative sentences that make a significant assertion.

"Taxman"	"Lost in the Supermarket"
"Shark in the Water"	"Times Like These"
"Rain Is a Good Thing"	"Bleed American"
"Share the Ride"	"Especially in Michigan"
"I Don't Want Control of You"	"We Are Nowhere and It's Now"
"Waiting on the World to Change"	"I Turn My Camera On"
"All You Fascists"	"Someone Else's Problem"
"Concrete and Barbed Wire"	"Let the Idiot Speak"
"The Times They Are A-Changin'"	"Be True to Your School"

27 Strategies

develop a
draft

If *genres* represent forms of writing that serve specific aims and audiences, **O** then *strategies* describe patterns of writing that work across genres and are useful in many situations. This chapter looks at some of these essential tools, such as description, division, classification, definition, and comparison/contrast. It's true that you may sometimes write "descriptions" for their own sake, or "compare and contrast" just for the heck of it. But mostly you'll use these modes of writing while working within other genres.

Use description to set a scene.   Descriptions, which use language to recreate physical characteristics, can be impressive enough to stand on their own. But you'll often need descriptive passages to support other kinds of writing — perhaps a sentence to set the scene in a narrative or many paragraphs to bring a historical period alive in a term paper. Writers adapt descriptions to particular situations. In an explanation of an apparatus in a lab report, the language might be cold and technical, but in an opening chapter of a novel, the description would likely be richer and more connotative, as in the following paragraph.

> *Malpais*, translated literally from the Spanish, means "bad country." In New Mexico, it signifies specifically those great expanses of lava flow which make black patches on the map of the state. The malpais of the Checkerboard country lies just below Mount Taylor, having been produced by the same volcanic

398

choose a genre
p. 390

fault that, a millennium earlier, had thrust the mountain fifteen thousand feet into the sky. Now the mountain has worn down to a less spectacular eleven thousand feet and relatively modern eruptions from cracks at its base have sent successive floods of melted basalt flowing southward for forty miles to fill the long valley between Cebolleta Mesa and the Zuni Mountains.

—Tony Hillerman, *People of Darkness*

Descriptions always involve selection. Just as a photographer carefully frames a subject, you have to decide which elements (visual, aural, tactile, and so on) in a scene will convey the situation most accurately, efficiently, and memorably and then turn them into words. Think nouns first, then modifiers. Adjectives and adverbs are essential, but it's easy to ruin a description by overdressing the scene. Be specific, concrete, and honest. O

A smart procedure is to write down everything in a descriptive passage that you want to include, and then edit out any words or phrases that are not essential. Be careful, too, to build the scene in a way that a reader can follow, providing clear directions for the eyes and mind. The following paragraph is from an argument about music and identity that uses a variety of techniques to describe the fans of punk rock; note that the passage focuses as much on sound as sight, which is appropriate when dealing with music.

Few genres showcase the unifying power of music better than punk. Punk surfaced in the mid-1970s as a form of anticulture and quickly swelled to epic influence. Finding multitudes of fans worldwide in a matter of years, bands like the Ramones and the Clash offered a fast, brash, and unforgiving sound that sonically "scoffed" at usual genre conventions. And their fans began mimicking that desire to separate from the current culture. The type of person you would associate with punk music didn't exist, so fans re-created themselves to personify the ideas the music portrays. Much like the loud, careless, and in-your-face fury of the power chords that punk music hurls at listeners, "punks," as they were labeled, began doing everything "loudly." They used their bodies as canvasses for tattoos and piercings, while wearing their clothes down to the threads to refuse the "establishment's" idea of a member of society. And the effect back then was the same as it is today. Visually, this style connects listeners to the music and each other; when a punk sees one of his own (or hears him listening to punk music), the sense of kindred identity between the two is

improve your
sentences p. 444

△

unmistakable. And the way punks act, the jobs they take, and the items they consume all follow suit. Ironically, the music style that aimed to go against culture created an entirely new one.

–Jeremy Burchard

> **Your Turn**   Write a paragraph of about 200–250 words describing something or someone you love. This is a tough assignment because it calls for you to choose details that will convey a sentiment to readers that they won't initially share. If you can find a focus for the description, perhaps even a thesis, your job will be easier.

Use division to divide a subject.   This strategy of writing is so common you might not notice it in action. A division involves no more than breaking a subject into its major components or enumerating its parts. In a report for an art history class, you might use division to study a famous cathedral by listing and describing its major architectural features, one by one: facade, nave, towers, windows, and so on. Or in a sports column on the Big Ten's NCAA football championship prospects, you could just run through its roster of twelve teams. That's a reasonable structure for a review, given the topic.

Division also puts ideas into logical relationships that make them easier for readers to understand and use. The challenge comes when a subject doesn't break apart as neatly as a tangerine. Then you have to decide which parts are essential and which are subordinate. Divisions of this sort are more than mechanical exercises: They require your clear understanding of a subject. For example, in organizing a Web site for your school or college, you'd probably start by deciding which components of the school merit top-tier placement on the home page. **O** Such a decision will shape the entire project. (See the two examples on the next page.)

O

learn media
conventions p. 577

Your Turn As a strategy of writing (or organization), just how common is division? Look for examples of division in the texts you use or encounter during one day and keep a list. Then compare your list with those compiled by others. Which items on your list are straightforward examples of division and which shade into classification? (See the next strategy.) Does the difference matter?

Use classification to sort objects or ideas by consistent principles.
Classification breaks subjects into parts not by separating objects, but by clustering them according to meaningful or useful principles. Just think of all the ways that people can be classified:

By body type: endomorph, ectomorph, mesomorph

By hair color: black, brown, blond, red, gray, other

By weight: underweight, normal, overweight, obese

By sexual orientation: straight, bisexual, gay/lesbian, transgender

By race: black, Asian, white, other

By religion: Hindu, Buddhist, Muslim, Christian, Jew, other, no religion

Ideally, a principle of classification should apply to every member of the general class studied (in this case, people), and there would be no overlap among the resulting groups. But almost all useful efforts to classify complex phenomena—whether people, things, or ideas—have holes, gaps, or overlaps. Classifying people by religious beliefs, for instance, usually means mentioning the major groups and then lumping tens of millions of other people in a convenient category called "other."

Even scientists who organize everything from natural elements to species of birds run into problems with creatures that cross boundaries (plant or animal?) or discoveries that upset familiar categories. You'll wrestle with such problems routinely when, for instance, you argue about social policy: How do notions such as gay marriage or school vouchers fit into conventional classifications of "marriage" or "public education"? At some point, principles of classification evolve or change to maintain their explanatory power, because that's the rationale for any classification: to organize information accurately and perceptively.

> **Your Turn**   Not all classifications are equally important or useful. Begin with a large general category with which you are quite familiar: It might be sports franchises, politicians, horror movies, video games, cheeses, dogs, or some other topic. Next come up with three principles of division that you believe people less knowledgeable about your subject than you might find useful in understanding it better. Then, for fun, come up with three pointless or frivolous principles of division. For example, it might be important to classify politicians by education, political orientation, or region; it might be less useful to group them by hair color, weight, or their tastes in popular music. Or would it? Discuss your schemes of classification with your classmates.

Use definition to clarify meaning.   Definitions don't appear in dictionaries only. Like other strategies in this chapter, they occur in many genres. A definition might become the subject of a scientific report (what is a planet?), the bone of contention in a legal argument (how does the statute define *life*?), or the framework for a cultural analysis (can a comic book be a serious novel?). In all such cases, writers need to know how to construct valid definitions.

Though definitions come in various forms, the classic dictionary definition is based on principles of classification discussed in the previous section. Typically a term is defined first by placing it in a general class. Then its distinguishing features or characteristics are enumerated, separating it from other members of the larger class. You can see the principle operating in this comic paragraph, which first fits "dorks" into the general class of "somebody," that is to say, a *person*, and then claims two distinguishing characteristics.

> It's important to define what I truly mean by "dork," just so he or she doesn't get casually lumped in with "losers," "burnouts" and "lone psycho-path bullies." To me, **the dork is somebody who didn't fit in at school** and who **therefore sought consolation in a particular field** – computers, "Star Trek," theater, heavy metal, medieval war reenacts, fantasy, sports trivia, even isolation sports like cross-country and ice skating.
>
> – Ian R. Williams, "Twilight of the Dorks?" *Salon.com*, October 23, 2003

In much writing, definitions become crucial when a question is raised about whether a particular object does or does not meet the criteria to join a particular group. You engage in this kind of debate when you argue about what is or isn't a sport, a punk band, a progressive piece of legislation, a loyal Democrat, an act of terrorism, and so on. In outline form, the structure of such a discussion looks like this:

Defined group:

– General class

– Distinguishing characteristic 1

– Distinguishing characteristic 2 . . .

Controversial term

– Is/is not in the general class

– Does/does not share characteristic 1

– Does/does not share characteristic 2 . . .

Controversial term is/is not in the defined group

> **Your Turn**   Write a short argument in which you use a definition to determine whether someone or something does or does not deserve to be identified with a particular term. A classic example of such an argument, now settled by a federal court, is whether "cheerleading" is a "sport." (It's not.) Find a subject of your own, perhaps drawing from actual discussions or debates you have had with friends.

Use comparison and contrast to show similarity and difference.

We seem to think better when we place ideas or objects side-by-side. So it's not surprising that comparisons and contrasts play a role in all sorts of writing, especially reports, arguments, and analyses. Paragraphs are routinely organized to show how things are alike or different.

> The late 1960s and early 1970s were a time of cultural conflict, a battle between what I have called the beautiful people and the dutiful people. While Manhattan glitterati thronged Leonard Bernstein's apartment to celebrate the murderous Black Panthers, ordinary people in the outer boroughs and the far-flung suburbs of New Jersey like Hamilton Township were going to work, raising their families, and teaching their children to obey lawful authority and work their way up in the world.
>
> —Michael Barone, "The Beautiful People vs. the Dutiful People,"
> *U.S. News & World Report*, January 16, 2006

Much larger projects can be built on similar structures of comparison and/or contrast.

To keep extended comparisons on track, the simplest structure is to evaluate one subject at a time, running through its features completely before moving on to the next. Let's say you decided to contrast economic conditions in France and Germany. Here's how such a paper might look in a scratch outline if you focused on the countries one at a time. O

> France and Germany: An Economic Report Card
> I.   France
>   A. Rate of growth
>   B. Unemployment rate
>   C. Productivity

order ideas
p. 408

     D. Gross national product
     E. Debt
  II. Germany
     A. Rate of growth
     B. Unemployment rate
     C. Productivity
     D. Gross national product
     E. Debt

The disadvantage of evaluating subjects one at a time is that actual comparisons, for example, of rates of employment in the outline above, might appear pages apart. So in some cases, you might prefer a comparison-contrast structure that looks at features point by point. ⭕

France and Germany: An Economic Report Card
  I.   Rate of growth
     A. France
     B. Germany
  II. Unemployment rate
     A. France
     B. Germany
  III. Productivity
     A. France
     B. Germany
  IV. Gross national product
     A. France
     B. Germany
  V. Debt
     A. France
     B. Germany

Your Turn   Often, the most interesting and fiercely argued contrasts are to be found between things that appear to be quite similar, for example, senators from the same political party, or high-end cameras, or competing top shelf sports teams. Write a short comparison involving closely paired items that you know well. Use the piece to illuminate the differences for readers who might not care much about the differences. Show them why they might be wrong.

understand evaluation
p. 106

28 Organization

shape your
work

To describe the organization of their projects, writers often use metaphors or other figures of speech. They visualize the elements of their work linked by chains, frames, patterns, or even skeletons. Such structural concepts help writers keep their emerging ideas on track, giving them shape and consistency. Effective organization also makes life easier for readers who come fresh to any paper or project, wondering how its words and ideas will fit together.

In Parts 1 and 2, you'll find specific suggestions for structuring a wide variety of writing genres. The following general advice will help you organize your work.

Examine model documents.   Many types of writing are highly conventional—which simply means that they follow predictable patterns and formulas. So study the structure of several examples of any new genre you're expected to compose. Some structural elements are immediately obvious, such as headings or introductory and concluding sections. But look for more subtle moves too—for example, many editorials first describe a problem, then blame someone for it, and finally make a comment or offer a comparison. Working with models of a genre will point your project in the right direction.

Sketch out a plan or sequence.   Even if you are brainstorming, starting with a rough plan helps give a project direction and purpose. A scratch (or informal) outline or similar device puts your initial ideas on paper, suggests relationships between them (sequence, similarity, difference), and perhaps hints at flaws or omissions. Just as important, creating a structure makes a writing project suddenly seem more doable because you've broken a complex task into smaller, more manageable parts.

Visualize structure when appropriate.   Technology can make it easier to organize your project. Consider how deftly you can move the slides in a PowerPoint project until you find the most effective order. Pen and paper can work just as well for visualizing the relationships between elements in a project, whether you prepare an outline to separate divergent features in a comparison/contrast piece or notecards to map the administrative structure of a complex organization. Seeing these items can point to ways of organizing everything from a paper to a Web site. **O**

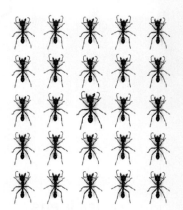

Your ideas won't march in rows like these ants, so you'll need a plan for your work.

Provide clear steps or signals for readers.   Just because you know how the parts of your paper or project fit together, don't assume readers will. You have to give them cues—which come in various forms, including titles, headings, captions, and, especially, transitional words and phrases. For example, in a narrative you might include transitional words to mark the passage of time (*next, then, before, afterward*). Or if you organize a project according to a principle of magnitude, you might give readers signals that clearly show a change from *best* to *worst*, *cheapest* to *most expensive*, *most common species* to *endangered*. And if you are writing to inform or report, you might also rely heavily on visuals to help make your point. **O**

Deliver on your commitments.   This is a basic principle of organization. If, for example, you promise in an introductory paragraph to offer two reasons in support of a claim, you need to offer two clearly identifiable reasons in that paper or readers will feel that they missed something. But commitments are broader than that: Narratives ordinarily lead somewhere, perhaps to a climax; editorials offer opinions; proposals offer and defend new ideas; evaluations make judgments. You can depart from these structural expectations, but you should do so knowing what readers expect and anticipating how they might react to your straying from the formula.

think visually
p. 592

order ideas
p. 408

29 Outlines

Despite what you may believe, outlines are designed to make writing easier, not harder, as they help you put ideas in manageable form. And you'll feel more confident when you begin with a plan. The trick is to start simple and let outlines evolve to fit your needs.

order ideas

Begin with scratch outlines. Many writers prefer working first with scratch, or informal, outlines—the verbal equivalent of the clever mechanical idea hurriedly sketched on a cocktail napkin.

In fact, the analogy is especially apt because good ideas often do evolve from simple, sometimes crude, notions that begin to make sense only when seen on paper. Both the Internet and the structure of the DNA molecule began with the visual equivalents of scratch outlines.

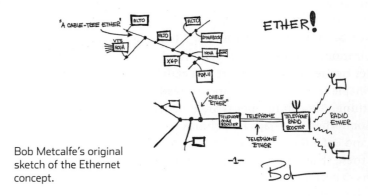

Bob Metcalfe's original sketch of the Ethernet concept.

List key ideas.   Write down your preliminary thoughts so you can see exactly what they are, eliminating any that obviously overlap. Keep these notes brief but specific, using words and phrases rather than complete sentences. Your initial scratch outline will likely resemble a mildly edited brainstorming list, like the one that follows.

> <u>Fuel-efficient vehicles</u>
> Hybrids
> Electric cars haven't worked well
> Europeans prefer diesels
> Strengths and weaknesses
> Costs might be high
> Mechanically reliable?

Once you have ideas, begin applying the three principles that make outlining such a powerful tool of organization: *relationship, subordination,* and *sequence.*

Look for relationships.   Examine the initial items on your list and try grouping *like* with *like*—or look for opposites and contrasts. Experiment with various arrangements or clusters. In the brief scratch outline above, for example, you might decide that the items fall into two distinct categories. The three types of fuel-efficient cars are obviously related, while the remaining items represent aspects of these vehicles.

Hybrids	Strengths
Electric cars	Weaknesses
Diesels	Costs
	Reliability

Subordinate ideas.   Outlines are built on this principle of subordination or hierarchy: You are systematically dividing a subject into topics and subtopics. So some ideas belong not only grouped with others but also under them—that is to say, they belong to a smaller subset within a larger set.

For instance, looking again at those simple groupings of fuel-efficient vehicles, you could argue that *cost* and *reliability* are items that fit better under either *strengths* or *weaknesses*. They are aspects of these larger categories. So you remove them from the outline for the moment.

You might notice, too, that your notes so far suggest a comparison/contrast structure for your project. (See "Use comparison and contrast to show similarity and difference" on p. 405 of Chapter 27, "Strategies.") Deciding to replace *strengths* and *weaknesses* with the slightly more aggressive terms *advantages* and *disadvantages*, you sketch out a rather more complex outline.

> Fuel-efficient vehicles
> Advantages
>   Hybrids
>   Electric cars
>   Diesels
> Disadvantages
>   Hybrids
>   Electric cars
>   Diesels

Decide on a sequence.   Now that you've moved from an initial list of ideas to a basic design, consider the order in which to present the material. You might arrange the items chronologically or by magnitude. Or your order might be determined rhetorically—by how you want readers to respond.

Let's say you drive a Prius and have done enough research to believe that hybrids represent the best option for saving on fuel costs. So you arrange the paper to end on that note, understanding that readers are most likely to remember what they read last. Reading the end of your paper, the audience will focus on the advantages of gas-electric hybrid vehicles.

> A. Disadvantages of fuel-efficient vehicles
>   1. Electrics
>   2. Diesels
>   3. Gas-electric hybrids
> B. Advantages of fuel-efficient vehicles
>   1. Electrics
>   2. Diesels
>   3. Gas-electric hybrids

Move up to a formal outline. You may be required to submit a formal outline with your final paper. By adhering to the following outline conventions, you can ferret out weaknesses in your thinking. ○

● Align the headings at every level (see example).

● Present at least two items at every heading level (I, A, and 1). If you can't find a second item to match the first in a new level of heads, perhaps the new level isn't needed.

● Present all items (except the thesis) as complete and parallel statements (not questions), properly punctuated.

● Place a topic sentence above the outline, underlined or italicized. That topic sentence sitting up top may keep you from wandering off-subject.

Thesis: <u>Though all fuel-efficient vehicles have technological strengths and weaknesses, hybrids currently represent the best option for drivers today.</u>

I. Currently available fuel-efficient vehicles have different technological problems.
   A. Electric vehicles lack versatility.
      1. Their batteries limit them to about one hundred miles before recharging.
      2. Their batteries are heavy, expensive, and slow to charge.
   B. Diesel vehicles can be truck-like.
      1. Their emissions are hard to clean up.
      2. Their fuel is smelly and toxic.
      3. Diesel fuel can be expensive.
   C. Gas-electric hybrids are technologically risky.
      1. They are heavy.
      2. Their dual propulsion systems (gas and electric) are complex.
II. Fuel-efficient vehicles have significant strengths.
   A. Electric vehicles are simple and civilized machines.
      1. They emit no measurable pollution where they are used.
      2. Their motors are almost silent and free of vibration.
   B. Diesels are robust vehicles suitable for all road conditions.
      1. Their engines are based on well-proven and strong technology.
      2. They burn fuel efficiently.
   C. Gas-electric hybrids combine advantages of other fuel-efficient vehicles.
      1. They work like electric vehicles in the city.
      2. They are as strong as diesels on the highway.
      3. They combine well-proven electric and internal-combustion technologies.

The fully electric Nissan Leaf has a range of one hundred miles per charge, but needs up to eight hours to charge.

develop a statement
p. 393

30 Paragraphs

develop ideas

Paragraphs are a practical invention, created to make long continuous blocks of writing easier to read by dividing them up. Because they give writers a physical way to shape ideas and transmit them to readers, paragraphs are a powerful tool. You've heard many rules and definitions over the years, but the fact is that paragraphs exist to help you develop and structure your ideas. Here are some helpful ways to think about them.

Make sure paragraphs lead somewhere.   Sometimes you'll use a straightforward topic sentence to state your point and introduce a claim that the rest of your paragraph will develop. ○ But, just as often, you may wait until the concluding sentences to make your point, or you may weave a key idea into the fabric of the entire paragraph (as in the first paragraph of the example that follows). Whatever your strategy, all paragraphs should do significant work: introduce a subject, move a narrative forward, offer a new argument or claim, provide support for a claim already made, contradict another point, amplify an idea, furnish more examples, even bring discussion to an end. It has to do *something* that readers see as purposeful and connected to what comes before and after.

For instance, reviewing the third album of the rock band Coldplay, music critic Jon Pareles leads his readers through an opening paragraph demanding enough to try any rocker's patience. What's he doing here? But then he delivers his death-blow in a second, much shorter, paragraph. Suddenly, you have no

develop a statement
p. 393

doubt where Pareles stands—and probably want to read the entire review, even if you like the band.

> There's nothing wrong with self-pity. As a spur to songwriting, it's right up there with lust, anger, and greed, and probably better than the remaining deadly sins. There's nothing wrong, either, with striving for musical grandeur, using every bit of skill and studio illusion to create a sound large enough to get lost in. Male sensitivity, a quality that's under siege in a pop culture full of unrepentant bullying and machismo, shouldn't be dismissed out of hand, no matter how risible it can be in practice. And building a sound on the lessons of past bands is virtually unavoidable.
>
> But put them all together and they add up to Coldplay, the most insufferable band of the decade.
>
> —"The Case Against Coldplay," *New York Times*, June 5, 2005

Develop ideas adequately.   Instructors who insist that paragraphs run a minimum number of sentences (say 6–10) are usually just tired of students who don't back up claims with details and evidence. ○ In fact, most writers don't count sentences when they build paragraphs. Instead, they develop a sense for paragraph length, matching the swell of their ideas to the habits of their intended readers.

Consider the following paragraph, which describes the last moments of the final Apollo moon mission in December 1972. The paragraph might be reduced to a single sentence: *All that remained of the 363-foot* Apollo 17 *launch vehicle was a 9-foot capsule recovered in the ocean.* But what would be lost? The pleasure of the full paragraph resides in the details the writer musters to support the final sentence, which contains his point.

> A powerful Sikorsky Sea King helicopter, already hovering nearby as they [the *Apollo 17* crew] hit the water, retrieved the astronauts and brought them to the carrier, where the spacecraft was recovered shortly later. The recovery crew saw not a gleaming instrument of exotic perfection, but a blasted, torn, and ragged survivor, its titanic strength utterly exhausted, a husk now a shell. The capsule they hauled out of the ocean was all that remained of the *Apollo 17* Saturn V. The journey had spent, incinerated, smashed, or blistered into atoms every other part of the colossal, 363-foot white rocket, leaving only this burnt and brutalized 9-foot capsule. A great shining army had set out over the horizon, and a

understand
argument p. 72

lone squadron had returned, savaged beyond recognition, collapsing into the arms of its rescuers, dead. Such was the price of reaching for another world.

— David West Reynolds, *Apollo: The Epic Journey to the Moon*

Organize paragraphs logically.   It would be surprising if paragraphs didn't borrow structural strategies used by full essays: thesis and support, division, classification, comparison/contrast. But it's ideas that drive the shape of paragraphs, not patterns of organization. Most writers don't pause to wonder whether their next paragraph should follow a narrative or cause-effect plan. They just write it, making sure it makes a point and offers sufficient evidence to keep readers engaged.

In fact, individual paragraphs in any longer piece can be organized many different ways. And because paragraphs are relatively short, you usually see their patterns unfold right before your eyes. The following two passages are from an essay by Jon Katz entitled "Do Dogs Think?" The paragraphs within them use structures Katz needs at that given moment.

Narrative paragraph describes changes in Blue's behavior.

Blue, Heather's normally affectionate and obedient Rottweiler, began tearing up the house shortly after Heather went back to work as an accountant after several years at home. The contents of the trash cans were strewn all over the house. A favorite comforter was destroyed. Then Blue began peeing all over Heather's expensive new living-room carpet and systematically ripped through cables and electrical wires.

Katz uses *causal* pattern to explore Blue's behavioral problem.

Lots of dogs get nervous when they don't know what's expected of them, and when they get anxious, they can also grow restless. Blue hadn't had to occupy time alone before. Dogs can get unnerved by this. They bark, chew, scratch, destroy. Getting yelled at and punished later doesn't help: The dog probably knows it's doing something wrong, but it has no idea what. Since there's nobody around to correct behaviors when the dog is alone, how could the dog know which behavior is the problem? Which action was wrong?

A simple *statement-proof* structure organizes this paragraph.

I don't believe that dogs act out of spite or that they can plot retribution, though countless dog owners swear otherwise. To punish or deceive requires the perpetrator to understand that his victim or object has a particular point of view and to consciously work to manipulate or thwart it. That requires mental processes dogs don't have.

Why will Clementine come instantly if she's looking at me, but not if she's sniffing deer droppings? Is it because she's being stubborn or, as many people tell me, going through "adolescence"? Or because, when following her keen predatory instincts, she simply doesn't hear me? Should my response be to tug at her leash or yell? Maybe I should be sure we've established eye contact before I give her a command, or better yet, offer a liver treat as an alternative to whatever's distracting her. But how do I establish eye contact when her nose is buried? Can I cluck or bark? Use a whistle or hoot like an owl?

I've found that coughing, of all things, fascinates her, catches her attention, and makes her head swivel, after which she responds. If you walk with us, you will hear me clearing my throat repeatedly. What can I say? It works. She looks at me, comes to me, gets rewarded.

– *Slate.com*, October 6, 2005

> The paragraphs in this passage together follow a *problem-solution* structure common in *proposal* arguments.

Design paragraphs for readability.   Paragraph breaks work best when they coincide with shifts or divisions within the writing itself. Readers understand that your thoughts have moved in some new direction. But paragraphs are often at the mercy of a text's physical environment as well. When you read a news items on the Web, the short paragraphs used in these single-column stories look fine. But hit the "print this article" link and the text suddenly sprawls across the screen, becoming difficult to read.

The point? You can manipulate the length and shape of paragraphs to suit the environment in which your words will appear.

Use paragraphs to manage transitions.   Paragraphs often furnish direction in a paper. An opening paragraph can be used to set the scene in a narrative or to preview the content in a report. ○ You might occasionally use very brief paragraphs—sometimes just a sentence or two long—to punctuate a piece by drawing attention to a turn in your thinking or offering a strong judgment. You've likely seen paragraphs that consist of nothing more than an indignant "Nonsense!" or a sarcastic "Nuts" or "Go figure." There's always a risk in penning a paragraph with so much attitude, but it's an option when the occasion calls for it. In longer papers, you might need full transitional paragraphs to summarize what has already been covered or to point the project in new directions.

shape a beginning
p. 420

31

Transitions

connect ideas

What exactly makes words, sentences, and ideas flow from paragraph to paragraph as fluidly as Michael Phelps slipping through the water at the Beijing Olympics? *Transitional words and phrases*, many writers would reply—thinking of words such as *and, but, however, neither . . . nor, first . . . second . . . third,* and so on. Placed where readers need them, these connecting words make a paper read smoothly. But they are only part of the story.

Almost any successful piece of writing is held together by more devices than most writers can consciously juggle. Fortunately, a few of the devices—such as connections between pronouns and their referents—almost take care of themselves. Here are some guidelines for making smooth transitions between ideas in paragraphs and sections of your writing.

Common Transitions

Connection or Consequence	Contrast	Correlation	Sequence or Time	Indication
and	but	if . . . then	first . . . second	this
or	yet	either . . . or	and then	that
so	however	from . . . to	initially	there
therefore	nevertheless		subsequently	for instance
moreover	on the contrary		before	for example
consequently	despite		after	in this case
hence	still		until	
	although		next	
			in conclusion	

Use appropriate transitional words and phrases.   There's nothing complicated or arcane about them: You'll recognize every word in any list of transitions. But be aware that they have different functions and uses, with subtle differences even between words as close in meaning as *but* and *yet*.

Transitional words are often found at the beginnings of sentences and paragraphs, simply because that's the place where readers expect a little guidance. There are no rules, per se, for positioning transitions—though they can be set off from the rest of the sentence with commas.

Use the right word or phrase to show time or sequence.   Readers often need specific words or phrases to help keep events in order. Such expressions can simply mark off stages: *first, second, third.* Or they might help readers keep track of more complicated passages of time.

Use sentence structure to connect ideas.   When you build sentences with similar structures, readers will infer that the ideas in them are related. Devices you can use to make this kind of linkage include *parallelism* O and *repetition*.

making a list?
p. 629

In the following example, the first three paragraphs of James P. Gannon's "America's Quiet Anger," you can see both strategies at work, setting up an emotional argument that continues in this pattern for another three paragraphs. Parallel items are highlighted.

> There is a quiet anger boiling in America.
>
> It is the anger of millions of hard-working citizens who pay their bills, send in their income taxes, maintain their homes and repay their mortgage loans – and see their government reward those who do not.
>
> It is the anger of small town and Middle American folks who have never been to Manhattan, who put their savings in a community bank and borrow from a local credit union, who watch Washington lawmakers and presidents of both parties hand billions in taxpayer bailouts to the reckless Wall Street titans who brought down the economy in 2008.
>
> – *American Spectator*, March 20, 2010

Pay attention to nouns and pronouns.   Understated transitions in a piece can occur between pronouns and their antecedents, but make sure the relationships between the nouns and pronouns are clear. ⃝ And, fortunately, readers usually don't mind encountering a pronoun over and over—except maybe *I*. Note how effortlessly Adam Nicolson moves between *George Abbot, he*, and *man* in the following paragraph from *God's Secretaries* (2003), in which he describes one of the men responsible for the King James translation of the Bible:

> George Abbot was perhaps the ugliest of them all, a morose, intemperate man, whose portraits exude a sullen rage. Even in death, he was portrayed on his tomb in Holy Trinity, Guilford, as a man of immense weight, with heavy, wrinkled brow and coldly open, staring eyes. He looks like a bruiser, a man of such conviction and seriousness that anyone would think twice about crossing him. What was it that made George Abbot so angry?

Use synonyms.   Simply by repeating a noun from sentence to sentence, you make an obvious and logical connection within a paper—whether you

help with common
errors p. 600

are naming an object, an idea, or a person. To avoid monotony, vary terms you have to use frequently. But don't strain with archaic or inappropriate synonyms that will distract the reader.

Note the sensible variants on the word *trailer* in the following paragraph.

> Hype and hysteria have always been a part of movie advertising, but the frenzy of film trailers today follows a visual style first introduced by music videos in the 1980s. The quick cut is everything, accompanied by a deafening soundtrack. Next time you go to a film, study the three or four previews that precede the main feature. How are these teasers constructed? What are their common features? What emotions or reactions do they raise in you? What might trailers say about the expectations of audiences today?

Use physical devices for transitions. You know all the ways movies manage transitions between scenes, from quick cuts to various kinds of dissolves. Writing has fewer visual techniques to mark transitions, but they are important. Titles and headings in lab reports, for instance, let your reader know precisely when you are moving from "Methods" to "Results" to "Discussion." ○ In books, you'll encounter chapter breaks as well as divisions within chapters, sometimes marked by asterisks or perhaps a blank space. Seeing these markers, readers expect that the narration is changing in some way. Even the numbers in a list or shaded boxes in a magazine can be effective transitional devices, moving readers from one place to another.

Read a draft aloud to locate weak transitions. The best way to test your transitions in a paper or project may be to listen to yourself. As you read, mark every point in the paper where you pause, stumble, or find yourself adding a transitional word or phrase not in the original text. Record even the smallest bobble because tiny slips have a way of cascading into bigger problems.

○ understand lab reports p. 336

32 Introductions

shape a
beginning

An introduction has to grab and hold a reader's attention, but that's not all. It also must introduce a topic, a writer, and a purpose. Like the music over a film's opening credits, an introduction tells readers what to expect. Any doubts about where the following opening lines are heading?

> Normal people don't like today's computers. Most loathe them because they can't fully understand their absurd complexity and arcane conventions. That's why the iPad will kill today's computers, just like the latter killed computers running with punchcards and command lines.
>
> —Jesus Diaz, "iPad Is the Future," *Gizmodo*, April 2010

> At a liquidation sale, every day is Black Friday. Customers hover outside the store before it opens like vultures waiting for a dying animal to become a fresh carcass.
>
> —Michael Nance, "Everything Must Go," May 2010

Of course, you will want to write introductions that fit your projects. In some cases a single line may be enough—as in an e-mail request for information. ○ A paragraph can provide all the push you need to get a short paper rolling. In a senior thesis or book, a preface or an entire chapter can set the stage for your project. Realize, too, that in longer projects, you'll write what amounts to an introduction for every new section or major division.

understand e-mail
p. 310

What should your introductory paragraphs accomplish? The following are some options.

Announce your project. In academic papers, introductions typically declare a subject directly and indicate how it will be developed. Quite often, an introductory paragraph or section leads directly to a thesis statement or a hypothesis. ○ This is a pattern you can use in many situations.

> In her novel *Wuthering Heights* (1847), Emily Brontë presents the story of the families of Wuthering Heights and Thrushcross Grange through the seemingly impartial perspective of Nelly Dean, a servant who grows up with the families. Upon closer inspection, however, it becomes apparent that Nelly acts as much more than a bystander in the tragic events taking place around her. In her status as an outsider with influence over the families, Nelly strikingly resembles the Byronic hero Heathcliff and competes with him for power. Although the author depicts Heathcliff as the more overt gothic hero, Brontë allows the reader to infer from Nelly's story her true character and role in the family. The author draws a parallel between Nelly Dean and Heathcliff in their relationships to the Earnshaw family, in their similar roles as tortured heroes, and in their competition for power within their adoptive families.
>
> — Manasi Deshpande, "Servant and Stranger: Nelly and Heathcliff in *Wuthering Heights*"

Paper opens by identifying its general topic or theme.

Detailed thesis states what paper will prove.

Preview your project. Sometimes you'll have to use an introductory section to set up the material to follow, helping readers to understand why an issue deserves their attention. You might, for example, present an anecdote, describe a trend, or point to some change or development readers may not have noticed. Then you can explore its significance or implications. In the following example, Gabriela Montell, a writer for *The Chronicle of Higher Education*, first describes a research study so she can then explain why she is interested in whether looks matter for college professors.

News article opens by getting readers interested in research study.

Researchers identified and study described in sufficient, but limited, detail.

Professors aren't known for fussing about their looks, but the results of a new study suggest they may have to if they want better teaching evaluations.

Daniel Hamermesh, a professor of economics at the University of Texas at Austin, and Amy Parker, one of his students, found that attractive professors consistently outscore their less comely colleagues by a significant margin on student evaluations of teaching. The findings, they say, raise serious questions about the use of student evaluations as a valid measure of teaching quality.

In their study, Mr. Hamermesh and Ms. Parker asked students to look at photographs of ninety-four professors and rate their beauty. Then they compared those ratings to the average student evaluation scores for the courses taught by those professors. The two found that the professors who had been rated among the most beautiful scored a point higher than those rated least beautiful (that's a substantial difference, since student evaluations don't generally vary by much).

Full story will examine implications of study for educators.

While it's not news that beauty trumps brains in many quarters, you would think that the ivory tower would be relatively exempt from such shallowness.

– "Do Good Looks Equal Good Evaluations?" October 15, 2003

Provide background information.   Decide what your readers need to know about a subject and then fill in the blanks. Provide too little background information on a subject and readers may find the remainder of the project confusing. Supply too much context and you lose fans quickly: Readers may assume that the paper has nothing new to offer them or may simply grow impatient.

And yet, even when readers know a subject well, you still need, especially in academic papers, to answer basic questions about the project or topic—*who, what, where, when, how,* and *why.* Name names in your introduction, offer accurate titles, furnish dates, and explain what your subject is. Imagine readers from just slightly outside your target audience who might not instantly recall, for instance, that Shakespeare wrote a play titled *Henry V* or that the *Deepwater Horizon* oil rig exploded in the Gulf of Mexico on April 20, 2010.

Catch the attention of readers.   Give them a reason to enter your text. You can invite them any number of ways—with a compelling incident or amusing story, with a recitation of surprising or intriguing facts, with a dramatic question, with a provocative description or quotation. For visual texts (like a brochure or poster), a cover, masthead, or headline can lead readers inside the project.

Naturally, any opening has to be in sync with the material that follows—not outrageously emotional if the argument is sober, not lighthearted and comic if the paper has a serious theme. It is hard to imagine a reader even modestly interested in history not being caught by the opening paragraph of Barbara Tuchman's *The First Salute* (1998):

> White puffs of gun smoke over a turquoise sea followed by the boom of cannon rose from an unassuming fort on the diminutive Dutch island of St. Eustatius in the West Indies on November 16, 1776. The guns of Fort Orange on St. Eustatius were returning the ritual salute on entering a foreign port of an American vessel, the *Andrew Doria*, as she came up the roadstead, flying at her mast the red-and-white-striped flag of the Continental Congress. In its responding salute the small voice of St. Eustatius was the first officially to greet the largest event of the century—the entry into the society of nations of a new Atlantic state destined to change the direction of history.

Set a tone.   Introductory material sends readers all sorts of signals, some of them almost subliminal. Make noticeable errors in grammar and usage in an opening section and you immediately lose credibility with your readers.

More typically, though, readers use your opening material to determine whether they belong to the audience you are addressing. A paper beginning with highly technical language signals that the territory is open to specialists only, while a more personal or colloquial style welcomes a broader audience. ○

Follow any required formulas.   Many genres of writing define how you may enter a subject. This is especially the case for technical material (lab reports, research articles, scholarly essays) and highly conventional genres

refine your tone
p. 432

such as business letters, job-application letters, and even e-mail. Quite often, these conventions are simple: A business letter opens with a formal salutation; a job letter announces that you are applying for a specific announced position. You cannot ignore these details without raising eyebrows and doubts. To get such introductions right, review models of the genre and follow them.

Write an introduction when you're ready.   The opening of a project— especially of longer efforts such as research papers and theses—can be notoriously difficult to compose. If you are blocked at the outset of a project, plunge directly into the body of the paper and see where things go. You can even write the opening section last. No one will know.

Similarly, if you write your introduction first, review it when you come to the end of the paper—and revise as necessary. ○ Sometimes, the promises you made at the beginning aren't the same ones you delivered on. When that's the case, recast the opening to reflect the paper's new content or revise the body of the paper to conform to important commitments made in the introduction.

> **Your Turn**   Examine the opening paragraphs in several chapters of this section of *How to Write Anything* (Chapters 25–34). What strategies do you notice? How do the chapter openers differ? Do you find any of the chapters more successful than others? Why?

revise and edit
p. 452

Conclusions  33

Composing introductions carries all the trepidations of asking for a first date. So conclusions should be much easier, right? By the time you write a conclusion, you've established a relationship with readers, provided necessary background, laid down arguments, and discussed important issues. All that remains is the verbal equivalent of a good-night kiss . . . Okay, maybe conclusions aren't that simple.

Like introductions, conclusions serve different purposes and audiences. A brief e-mail or memo may need no more sign-off than a simple closing: *regards, best, later.* A senior thesis, however, could require a whole chapter to wrap things up. Here are some of the options when writing conclusions.

Summarize your points, then connect them. In reports and arguments, use the concluding section to recap what you've covered and tie your major points together. The following is the systematic conclusion of a college report on a childhood developmental disorder, cri du chat syndrome (CDCS). Note that this summary paragraph also leads where many other scientific and scholarly articles do: to a call for additional research.

> Though research on CDCS remains far from abundant, existing studies prescribe early and ongoing intervention by a team of specialists, including speech-language pathologists,

**shape an
ending**

Major point

△

Major point

Conclusion ties together
main points made in paper,
using transitional words
and phrases.

physical and occupational therapists, various medical and educational
professionals, and parents. Such intervention has been shown to allow
individuals with CDCS to live happy, long, and full lives. The research,
however, indicates that the syndrome affects all aspects of a child's
development and should therefore be taken quite seriously. Most children
require numerous medical interventions, including surgery (especially to
correct heart defects), feeding tubes, body braces, and repeated treatment
of infections. Currently, the best attempts are being made to help young
children with CDCS reach developmental milestones earlier, communicate
effectively, and function as independently as possible. However, as the
authors of the aforementioned studies suggest, much more research is
needed to clarify the causes of varying degrees of disability, to identify
effective and innovative treatments/interventions (especially in the area of
education), and to individualize intervention plans.

–Marissa Dahlstrom, "Developmental Disorders: Cri du Chat Syndrome"

Reveal your point.   In some writing, including many arguments, you
may not want to disclose your key point until the very end, following a
convincing presentation of claims and evidence. ⬡ The paper unfolds a bit
like a mystery, keeping readers on edge, eager to discover your point. You
don't open with a thesis, nor do you tip your hand completely until the
conclusion.

Here, for example, are the concluding paragraphs of an article in which
Andrew Sullivan has been guiding readers through a city he argues has
grown more self-absorbed and alienated because of technologies like the
Internet and iPod. In his conclusion, Sullivan raises important questions
that lead toward his chief belief that we need to turn outward again to
enrich our lives.

We become masters of our own interests [thanks to technology],
more connected to people like us over the Internet, more instantly in touch
with anything we want, need, or think we want and think we need. Ever
tried a Stairmaster in silence? But what are we missing? That hilarious
shard of an overheard conversation that stays with you all day; the child
whose chatter on the pavement takes you back to your early memories;

understand argument
p. 72

birdsong; weather; accents; the laughter of others. And those thoughts that come not by filling your head with selected diversion, but by allowing your mind to wander aimlessly through the regular background noise of human and mechanical life.

> Details give argument power: Plugged in, we're missing a lot.

External stimulation can crowd out the interior mind. Even the boredom that we flee has its uses. We are forced to find our own means to overcome it.

And so we enrich our life from within, rather than from white wires. It's hard to give up, though, isn't it?

> Sullivan anticipates readers' objections and acknowledges his own weakness.

Not so long ago I was on a trip and realized I had left my iPod behind. Panic. But then something else. I noticed the rhythms of others again, the sound of the airplane, the opinions of the taxi driver, the small social cues that had been obscured before. I noticed how others related to each other. And I felt just a little bit connected again and a little more aware.

> Final anecdote drives home key point.

Try it. There's a world out there. And it has a soundtrack all its own.

> Three short concluding sentences punctuate the essay.

—"Society Is Dead: We Have Retreated into the iWorld," *New York Times*

Finish dramatically.   Arguments, personal narratives, and many other kinds of writing often call for conclusions that will influence readers and maybe change their opinions. Since final paragraphs are what many readers remember, it makes sense that they be powerfully written. Here's the conclusion of a lengthy personal essay by Shane McNamee on gay marriage that leads up to a poignant political appeal.

Forget for the moment the rainbow flags and pink triangles. Gay pride is not about being homosexual; it's about the integrity and courage it takes to be honest with yourself and your loved ones. It's about spending life with whomever you want and not worrying what the government or the neighbors think. Let's protect that truth, not some rigid view of sexual orientation or marriage. Keep gay marriage out of your church if you like, but if you value monogamy as I do, give me an alternative that doesn't involve dishonesty or a life of loneliness. Many upstanding gay citizens yearn for recognition of their loving, committed relationships. Unless you enjoy being lied to and are ready to send your gay friends and family on a Trail of Queers to Massachusetts or Canada—where gay marriage is legal—then consider letting them live as they wish.

> Deliberate repetition focuses readers on serious point.

> Conclusion makes direct appeal to readers, addressed as *you.*

> Final sentence appeals emotionally through both images and language.

—"Protecting What Really Matters"

34 Titles

Titles may not strike you as an important aspect of writing, but they can be. Sometimes the struggle to find a good title helps a writer shape a piece and define its main point. Of course, a proper title tells readers what a paper is about and makes finding the document later easier.

name your
work

Use titles to focus documents.   A too-broad title early on in a project is a sure sign that you have yet to find a workable subject. If all you have is "Sea Battles in World War II" or "Children in America," expect to do more reading and research. If no title comes to mind at all, you don't have a subject. ○ You're still exploring ideas.

Titles for academic papers need only be descriptive. Consider these items culled at random from one issue of the *Stanford Undergraduate Research Journal* (Spring 2008). As you might guess, scientific papers aimed at a knowledgeable audience of specialists have highly technical titles. Titles in the social sciences and liberal arts are slightly less intimidating, but just as focused on providing information about their subjects.

> "Molecular and Morphological Characterization of Two Species of Sea Cucumber, *Parastichopus parvimensis* and *Parastichopus californicus*, in Monterey, CA"
>
> — Christine O'Connell, Alison J. Haupt, Stephen R. Palumbi

develop a statement
p. 393

"Justifiers of the British Opium Trade: Arguments by Parliament, Traders, and the *Times* Leading Up to the Opium War"

–Christine Su

"The Incongruence of the Schopenhauerian Ending in Wagner's *Götterdämmerung*"

–James Locus

Create searchable titles.   For academic or professional papers, a title should make sense standing on its own and out of context. That way if the paper winds up in someone's bibliography or in an online database, readers know what your subject is. Your title should also include keywords by which it might be searched in a database or online.

"Rethinking the Threat of Domestic Terrorism"

If you must be clever or allusive, follow the cute title with a colon and an explanatory subtitle.

"'Out, Damn'd Spot!': Images of Conscience and Remorse in Shakespeare's *Macbeth*"

"Out, Damn'd Spot: Housebreaking Your Puppy"

Avoid whimsical or suggestive titles.   A bad title will haunt you like a silly screen name. At this point you may not worry about publication, but documents take on a life of their own when uploaded to the Web or listed on a résumé. Any document posted where the public can search for it online needs a levelheaded title, especially when you approach the job market.

Capitalize and punctuate titles carefully.   The guidelines for capitalizing titles vary between disciplines. See Chapters 49 and 50 for the MLA and APA guidelines, or consult the style manual for your discipline.

Your titles should avoid all caps, boldface, underscoring, and, with some exceptions, italics (titles within titles and foreign terms may be italicized; see examples above). For Web sites, newsletters, PowerPoint presentations, and so on, you can be bolder graphically. **O**

Titles tell readers what to expect.

think visually
p. 592

Style

part five

define your style/
refine your tone

35

High, Middle, and Low Style 432

respect your readers

36

Inclusive and Culturally Sensitive Style 440

improve your
sentences

37

Vigorous, Clear, Economical Style 444

Need help with revising and editing? See page 450. / Need help with common errors? See page 600.

35

High, Middle, and Low Style

define your style/refine your tone

We all have an ear for the way words work in sentences and paragraphs, for the distinctive melding of voice, tone, rhythm, and texture some call *style*. You might not be able to explain exactly why one paragraph sparkles and another is flat as day-old soda, but you know when writing feels energetic, precise, and clear or stodgy, lifeless, and plodding. Choices you make about sentence type, sentence length, vocabulary, pronouns, and punctuation *do* create distinctive verbal styles—which may or may not fit particular types of writing. ○

In fact, there are as many styles of writing as of dress. In most cases, language that is clear, active, and economical will do the job. But even such a bedrock style has variations. Since the time of the ancient Greeks, writers have imagined a "high" or formal style at one end of a scale and a "low" or colloquial style at the other, bracketing a just-right porridge in the middle. Style is more complex than that, but keeping the full range in mind reveals some of your options.

High, middle, and low styles of weddings: formal and traditional, less formal, and totally informal.

432

improve your sentences p. 444

Use high style for formal, scientific, and scholarly writing. You will find high style in professional journals, scholarly books, legal briefs, formal addresses, many editorials, some types of technical writing, and some wedding invitations. Use it yourself when a lot is at stake—in a scholarship application, for example, or a job letter, term paper, or thesis. High style is signaled by some combination of the following features—all of which can vary.

- Serious or professional subjects

- Knowledgeable or professional audiences

- Dominant third-person (*he, she, it, they*) or impersonal point of view

- Relatively complex and self-consciously patterned sentences (that display *parallelism, balance, repetition*), often in the passive voice

- Professional vocabulary, often abstract and technical

- No contractions, colloquial expressions, or nonstandard forms

- Conventional grammar and punctuation; standard document design

- Formal documentation, when required, often with notes and a bibliography

The following example is from a scholarly journal. The article uses a formal scientific style, appropriate when an expert in a field is writing for an audience of his or her peers.

Temperament is a construct closely related to personality. In human research, temperament has been defined by some researchers as the inherited, early appearing tendencies that continue throughout life and serve as the foundation for personality (A. H. Buss, 1995; Goldsmith et al., 1987). Although this definition is not adopted uniformly by human researchers (McCrae et al., 2000), animal researchers agree even less about how to define temperament (Budaev, 2000). In some cases, the word *temperament* appears to be used purely to avoid using the word *personality*, which some animal researchers associate with anthropomorphism. Thus, to ensure that my review captured all potentially relevant reports, I searched for studies that examined either personality or temperament.

—Sam D. Gosling, "From Mice to Men: What Can We Learn About Personality from Animal Research?" *Psychological Bulletin*

> Technical terms introduced and defined.

> Sources documented.

> Perspective generally impersonal—though *I* is used.

The following *New York Times* editorial also uses a formal style. This is common when dealing with serious political or social issues.

Tone of first paragraph is sober and direct.

Haiti, founded two centuries ago by ex-slaves who fought to regain their freedom, has again become a hub of human trafficking.

Key term is defined.

Today, tens of thousands of Haitian children live lives of modern-day bondage. Under the system known as *restavek*, a Creole word meaning "stay with," these children work for wealthier families in exchange for education and shelter. They frequently end up cruelly overworked, physically or sexually abused, and without access to education.

Vocabulary is fairly abstract.

The most effective way to root out this deeply oppressive but deeply ingrained system would be to attack the conditions that sustain it—chiefly, impoverished, environmentally unsustainable agriculture and a severe shortage of rural schools.

This is an area in which America can and should help. Washington has been quick to respond to political turmoil in Haiti, with its accompanying fears of uncontrollable refugee flows. But the frenzied flurries of international crisis management that follow typically leave no lasting results.

Borrows technical language of diplomacy and government.

A wiser, more promising alternative would be to help create long-term economic options by improving access to schools and creating sustainable agriculture. Meanwhile, the United States should work with nongovernmental organizations to battle the resigned acceptance by many Haitians of the restavek system. They could, for example, help local radio stations broadcast programs of open dialogue about how damaging the system is, and include restavek survivors or human-rights experts.

Voice throughout is that of a serious institution, not an individual.

The primary responsibility for eliminating the restavek system lies with the Haitian people and their government. After years of political crisis, there is a new democratically elected government. Eradicating the restavek system should be one of its top priorities, combining law enforcement efforts with attacks on the root social and economic causes.

Tone of final paragraph is more emotional than rest of editorial.

The former slaves who won Haiti's freedom two hundred years ago dreamed of something better for their children than restavek bondage. The time is overdue for helping those dreams become reality.

– "The Lost Children of Haiti," *New York Times*

Use middle style for personal, argumentative, and some academic writing.   This style, perhaps the most common, falls between the extremes. It is the language of journalism, popular books and magazines, professional memos and nonscientific reports, instructional guides and manuals, and most commercial Web sites. Use this style in position papers, letters to the editor, personal statements, and business e-mails and memos—even in some business and professional work, once you are comfortable with the people to whom you are writing. Middle style doesn't so much claim features of its own as walk a path between formal and everyday language. It may combine some of the following characteristics:

- Full range of topics, from serious to humorous
- General audiences
- Range of perspectives, including first (*I*) and second (*you*) person points of view
- More often a human rather than an institutional voice
- Sentences in active voice that are varied in complexity and length
- General vocabulary, more specific than abstract, with concrete nouns and action verbs and with unfamiliar terms or concepts defined
- Informal expressions, some dialogue, slang, and contractions
- Conventional grammar and reasonably correct formats
- Informal documentation, usually without notes

In the following article for the online magazine *Slate.com*, Joel Waldfogel, a professor of business and public policy, explains recent research in his field to a general audience—people who are not experts in either business or public policy.

It is well-documented that short people earn less money than tall people do. To be clear, pay does not vary lockstep by height. If your friend is taller than you are, then it's nearly a coin toss whether she earns more. But if you compare two large groups of people who are similar in every respect but height, the average pay for the taller group will be higher. Each additional inch of height adds roughly 2 percent to average annual earnings, for both men and women. So, if the average heights of our hypothetical groups

Expressions are casual.

Readers are addressed familiarly as *you*, and an example is offered to clarify the causal relationship.

were 6 feet and 5 feet 7 inches, the average pay difference between them would be 10 percent.

> But why? One possibility is height discrimination in favor of the tall. A second involves adolescence. A few years ago, Nicola Persico and Andrew Postlewaite of the University of Pennsylvania and Dan Silverman of the University of Michigan discovered that adult earnings are more sharply related to height at age sixteen than to adult height — suggesting, scarily, that the high-school social order determined the adult economic order. For boys at least, height at sixteen affects things like social and athletic success — scoring chicks and baskets or, as the authors put it, "participation in clubs and athletics." And maybe those things affect later earning power.

> That wasn't likely to make short people feel good, but the latest explanation is worse. In a new study, Anne Case and Christina Paxson, both of Princeton University, find that tall people earn more, on average, because they're smarter, on average. Yikes.

–Joel Waldfogel, "Short End," *Slate.com*

Transition between paragraphs reads like spoken English: easy and natural.

Sources cited, but not documented.

Highlights difference between his informality and high style of scholars.

A surprisingly informal expression ends the paragraph.

Next, in this excerpt from an article that appeared in the popular magazine *Psychology Today*, Ellen McGrath uses a conversational middle style to present scientific information to a general audience.

> Families often inherit a negative thinking style that carries the germ of depression. Typically it is a legacy passed from one generation to the next, a pattern of pessimism invoked to protect loved ones from disappointment or stress. But in fact, negative thinking patterns do just the opposite, eroding the mental health of all exposed.

> When Dad consistently expresses his disappointment in Josh for bringing home a B minus in chemistry although all the other grades are A's, he is exhibiting a kind of cognitive distortion that children learn to deploy on themselves — a mental filtering that screens out positive experience from consideration.

> Or perhaps the father envisions catastrophe, seeing such grades as foreclosing the possibility of a top college, thus dooming his son's future. It is their repetition over time that gives these events power to shape a person's belief system.

–Ellen McGrath, "Is Depression Contagious?" *Psychology Today*

Vocabulary is sophisticated but not technical.

Familiar example (fictional son is even named) illustrates technical term: cognitive distortion.

Phrase following dash offers further clarification helpful to educated, but nonexpert, readers.

Use a low style for personal, informal, and even playful writing.

Don't think of "low" here in a negative sense: A colloquial or informal style is
fine on occasions when you want or need to sound more at ease and open. Low
style can be right for your personal e-mails and instant messaging, of course,
as well as in many blogs, advertisements, magazines trying to be hip, personal
narratives, and humor writing. Low style has many of the following features:

● Everyday or off-the-wall subjects, often humorous or parodic

● In-group or specialized readers

● Highly personal and idiosyncratic points of view; lots of *I, me, you, us*,
  and dialogue

● Shorter sentences and irregular constructions, especially fragments

● Vocabulary from pop culture and the street—idiomatic, allusive, and
  obscure to outsiders

● Colloquial expressions resembling speech

● Unconventional grammar and mechanics and alternative formats

● No systematic acknowledgment of sources

Note the relaxed style this former college instructor uses in her blog.

TUESDAY, JANUARY 03, 2006

Dumpster diving

Stuff I've found in or near the dumpsters after the college kids move out of
our apartment complex between semesters:

- Brand new HP printer, all cords still attached
- Tall oak computer-printer stand on wheels
- Blank computer discs and CD-ROMs
- China tea set
- Funky 1950s plates and saucers, left in a box beside the garbage bin
- Unopened bottle of semi-expensive champagne (still in my fridge)
- Nearly full bottles of expensive shampoos and conditioners
- Leather camera bag
- Replacement car antenna, still in unopened package
- Framed movie posters

Stuff and *kids* immediately
signal casual tone—as
does the sentence
fragment.

Highly personal
parenthetical remark—and
slangy *fridge*.

"Really made out bigtime" is deliberately low, echoing student chatter.

Pause marked by ellipsis.

Article omitted at beginning of sentence makes advice seem casual.

One of my students told me about one of the rare perks of being a resident assistant in the dorm. She really made out bigtime with stuff left behind. One girl moved out and left all the dresser drawers loaded with clothes (and not by accident . . . she just didn't want to pack the stuff). Lots of students abandon bicycles, stereos, VCRs, TVs, sofas, and futons. Best days for scavenging are during final exams and right after.

> **Your Turn**   Over the next day, look for three pieces of writing that seem to you to represent examples of high, middle, and low style. Then study several paragraphs or a section of each in detail, paying attention to the features listed in the checklists for the three styles. How well do the pieces actually conform to the descriptions of high, middle, and low style? Where would you place your three examples on a continuum that moves from high to low? Do the pieces share some stylistic features? Do you find any variations of style within the individual passages you examined?

The very serious story told in the *9/11 Commission Report* was retold in *The 9/11 Report: A Graphic Adaptation* (p. 439). Creators Sid Jacobson and Ernie Colón use the colloquial visual style of a comic book to make the formidable data and conclusions of a government report accessible to a wider audience. O

choose a genre
p. 390

Panels combine verbal and visual elements to tell a story.

Political figures become characters in a real-life drama.

Sounds (*Shoom!*) are represented visually — as in superhero tales.

Real images (the photograph on the left) are sometimes juxtaposed with cartoon panels as part of the collage.

36 Inclusive and Culturally Sensitive Style

respect your
readers

Writers in school or business today need to remember how small and tightly connected the world has become and how readily people may be offended. When you compose any document electronically (including a Word file), it may sail quickly around the Web. You can't make every reader in this potential audience happy, but you can at least write respectfully, accurately, and, yes, honestly. Language that is both inclusive and culturally sensitive can and should have these qualities.

Avoid expressions that stereotype genders.   Largely purged from contemporary English usage are job titles that suggest that they are occupied exclusively by men or women. Gone are *poetess* and *stewardess, policeman* and *congressman, postman* and *woman scientist*. When referring to professions, even those still dominated by one gender or another, avoid using a gendered pronoun.

Don't strain sense to be politically correct. *Nun* and *NFL quarterback* are still gendered, as are *witch* and *warlock* — and *surrogate mother*. Here are some easy solutions.

STEREOTYPED   The postman came up the walk.

INCLUSIVE   The letter carrier came up the walk.

STEREOTYPED   Among all her other tasks, a nurse must also stay up-to-date on her medical education.

INCLUSIVE   Among all their other tasks, nurses must also stay up-to-date on their medical education.

Outdated Terms	Alternatives
postman	letter carrier, postal worker
mankind	humankind, people, humans
congressman	congressional representative
chairman	chair
policewoman	police officer
stewardess	flight attendant
actress, poetess	actor, poet
fireman	firefighter

Avoid expressions that stereotype races, ethnic groups, or religious groups.   Deliberate racial slurs these days tend to be rare in professional writing. But it is still not unusual to find clueless writers (and politicians) noting how "hardworking," "articulate," "athletic," "well-groomed," or "ambitious" members of minority and religious groups are. The praise rings hollow because it draws on old and brutal stereotypes. You have an obligation to learn the history and nature of such ethnic caricatures and grow beyond them. It's part of your education, no matter what group or groups you belong to.

Refer to people and groups by the expressions used in serious publications, understanding that almost all racial and ethnic terms are contested: *African American, black* (or *Black*), *Negro, people of color, Asian American, Hispanic, Mexican American, Cuban American, Native American, Indian, Inuit, Anglo, white* (or *White*). Even the ancient group of American Indians once called Anasazi now go by the more culturally and historically accurate Native Puebloans. While shifts of this sort may seem fussy or politically correct to some, it costs little to address people as they prefer, acknowledging both their humanity and our differences.

Be aware, too, that being part of an ethnic or racial group usually gives you license to say things about the group not open to outsiders. Chris Rock and Margaret Cho can joke about topics Jay Leno can't touch, using epithets that would cost the *Tonight Show* host his job. In academic and professional settings, show similar discretion in your language — though not in your treatment of serious subjects. Sensitivities of language should not become an excuse for avoiding open debate, nor a weapon to chill it. In the following table are suggestions for inclusive, culturally sensitive terms.

Outdated Terms	Alternatives
Eskimo	Inuit
Oriental	Asian American (better to specify country of origin)
Hispanic	Specify: Mexican, Cuban, Nicaraguan, and so on
Negro (acceptable to some)	African American, black
colored	people of color
a gay, the gays	gay, lesbian, gays and lesbians
cancer victim	cancer survivor
boys, girls (to refer to adults)	men, women
woman doctor	doctor
male nurse	nurse

Treat all people with respect.   This policy makes sense in all writing. Some slights may not be intended—against the elderly, for example. But writing that someone drives *like an old woman* manages to offend two groups. In other cases, you might mistakenly think that most readers share your prejudices or narrow vision when describing members of campus groups, religious groups, the military, gays and lesbians, athletes, and so on. You know the derogatory terms and references well enough, and you should avoid them if for no other reason than the golden rule. Everyone is a member of some group that has at one time or another been mocked or stereotyped. So writing that is respectful will itself be treated with respect.

Avoid sensational language.   It happens every semester. One or more students ask the instructor whether it's okay to use four-letter words in their papers. Some instructors tolerate expletives in personal narratives, but it is difficult to make a case for them in academic reports, research papers, or position papers unless they are part of quoted material—as they may be in writing about contemporary literature or song lyrics.

Certain kinds of writing do effectively push the limits of their audience or, rather, appreciate that their readers might occasionally enjoy seeing a subject justly skewered by a few well-chosen words. You'll see this gleeful meanness in book, movie, or music reviews, for example. ○ The following paragraph is from Richard Corliss's review of M. Night Shyamalan's fantasy epic, *The Last Airbender*, a film set in ancient China, which had been criticized for not casting enough ethnic Asians. Note that Corliss avoids offensive language, but he doesn't mince words either.

> You can relax, bloggers. The dearth of racially appropriate casting in the U.S. simply means that fewer Asians were humiliated by appearing in what is surely the worst botch of a fantasy epic since Ralph Bakshi's animated desecration of *The Lord of the Rings* back in 1978. The actors who didn't get to be in *The Last Airbender* are like the passengers who arrived too late to catch the final flight of the *Hindenburg*.
>
> —"*The Last Airbender:* Worst Movie Epic Ever?" *Time*, July 2, 2010

Your Turn   Write a paragraph or two about any pet peeve you may have with language use. Your problem may address a serious issue like insensitivities in naming your ethnicity, community, or beliefs. Or you may just be tired of a friend insisting that you describe Sweetie Pie as your "animal companion" rather than use that demeaning and hegemonic term "pet." You'll surely want to share your paragraph and also read what others have written.

understand
evaluation p. 106

37

Vigorous, Clear, Economical Style

improve your
sentences

Ordinarily, tips and tricks don't do much to enhance your skills as a writer. But a few guidelines, applied sensibly, can improve your sentences and paragraphs noticeably—and upgrade your credibility as a writer. You sound more professional and confident when every word and phrase pulls its weight.

Always consider the big picture in applying the following tips: Work with whole pages and paragraphs, not just individual sentences. Remember, too, that these are guidelines, not rules. Ignore them when your good sense suggests a better alternative.

Use strong, concrete subjects and objects.   Scholar Richard Lanham famously advised writers troubled by tangled sentences to ask, "Who is kicking who?" That's a memorable way of suggesting that readers shouldn't have to puzzle over what they read.

Lower the level of generality to add interest. Nouns should be as specific as possible so that sentences create images for readers.

ABSTRACT	SPECIFIC
bird	roadrunner
cactus	prickly pear
animal	coyote

Most readers can more readily imagine *students* than *constituencies*; they can picture a *school*, not an *academic institution*. A wordy sentence can seem almost hopeless until you start translating phrases like "current fiscal pressures" into everyday English.

WORDY   All of the separate constituencies at this academic institution must be invited to participate in the decision making process under the current fiscal pressures we face.

BETTER   Faculty, students, and staff at this school must all have a say during this current budget crunch.

Avoid clumsy noun phrases.   It's too easy to build massive noun phrases that sound impressive but give readers fits, especially as they accumulate in sentence after sentence. You can spot such phrases by various markers:

- Strings of prepositional phrases
- Verbs turned into nouns via endings such as *-ation* (*implement* becomes *implementation*)
- Lots of articles (*the*, *a*)
- Lots of heavily modified verbals

Such expressions are not always inaccurate or wrong, just tedious. They make your reader work hard for no reason. They are remarkably easy to pare down once you notice them.

WORDY   members of the student body at Arizona State

BETTER   students at Arizona State

WORDY   the manufacturing of products made up of steel

BETTER   making steel products

WORDY   the prioritization of decisions for policies of the student government

BETTER   the student government's priorities

Avoid sentences with long windups.   Get to the point quickly. The more stuff you pile up ahead of the main verb, the more readers have to remember. Most people today prefer sentences that put any lengthy modifying phrases and clauses *after* the verb. The following sentence from the Internal Revenue Service Web site keeps you waiting too long for a verb. It's easy to fix.

> Don't use words too big for the subject. Don't say "infinitely" when you mean "very"; otherwise you'll have no word left when you want to talk about something really infinite.

—C. S. Lewis

ORIGINAL	A new scam e-mail that appears to be a solicitation from the IRS and the U.S. government for charitable contributions to victims of the recent Southern California wildfires has been making the rounds.
REVISED	A new scam e-mail making the rounds asks for charitable contributions to victims of the recent Southern California wildfires. Though it appears to be from the IRS and the U.S. government, it is a fake.

Use action verbs when possible.   Verbs get as tangled up as nouns if you lose track of the action. Cut through the clutter.

WORDY VERB PHRASE	We must **make a decision** soon.
BETTER	We must **decide** soon.
WORDY VERB PHRASE	Students **are reliant** on credit cards.
BETTER	Students **rely** on credit cards.
WORDY VERB PHRASE	Engineers **proceeded to reinforce** the levee.
BETTER	Engineers **reinforced** the levee.

Avoid strings of prepositional phrases.   Prepositional phrases consist of a preposition and its object, which may take modifiers: *under* the spreading chestnut tree; *between* you and me; *in* the line *of* duty. You can't write without prepositional phrases. But use more than two or, rarely, three in a row and they drain the energy from your sentences. Try moving the prepositions or turning them into more compact modifiers. Sometimes you can alter the verb to eliminate a preposition, or it might be necessary to revise the sentence even more substantially.

TOO MANY PHRASES	We stood **in line** at the observatory **on the top of a hill in the mountains** to look **in a huge telescope** at the moons **of Saturn**.
BETTER	We **lined up** at the mountaintop observatory to view Saturn's moons **through a huge telescope**.

Don't repeat key words close together.   You can often improve the style of a passage just by making sure you haven't used a particular word or phrase too often—unless you repeat it deliberately for effect (*government of the people, by the people, for the people*). Your sentences will sound fresher after you have eliminated unintentional and pointless repetition.

This is a guideline to apply sensibly: Sometimes to be clear, especially in technical writing, you must repeat key nouns and verbs sentence after sentence.

> The *New Horizons* payload is incredibly power efficient, with the instruments collectively drawing only about 28 watts. The payload consists of three optical instruments, two plasma instruments, a dust sensor, and a radio science receiver/radiometer.
>
> —NASA, "*New Horizons* Spacecraft Ready for Flight"

Avoid doublings. In speech, we tend to repeat ourselves or say things two or three different ways to be sure listeners get the point. Such repetitions are natural, even appreciated. But in writing, the habit of doubling can be irritating. And it is very much a habit, backed by a long literary tradition comfortable with pairings such as *home and hearth, friend and colleague, tried and true, clean and sober, neat and tidy,* and so on.

Often, writers will add an extra noun or two to be sure they have covered the bases: *colleges and universities, books and articles, ideas and opinions*. There may be good reasons for a second (or third) item. But not infrequently, the doubling is just extra baggage that slows down the train. Leave it at the station.

Turn clauses into more direct modifiers. If you are fond of *that, which,* and *who* clauses, be sure you need them. You can sometimes save a word or two by pulling the modifiers out of the clause and moving them ahead of the words they embellish. Or you may be able to tighten a sentence just by cutting *that, which,* or *who*.

WORDY   Our football coach, who is nationally renowned, expected a raise.

BETTER   Our nationally renowned football coach expected a raise.

WORDY   Our football coach, who is nationally renowned and already rich, still expected a raise.

BETTER   Our football coach, nationally renowned and already rich, still expected a raise.

Cut introductory expressions such as *it is* and *there is/are* when you can.   Such expressions, called *expletives*, are just part of the way we say some things: *It is going to rain today. There is a tide in the affairs of men.* Some expletives are fine, but don't let them stand in for clearer and more specific subjects. Revise as necessary. But don't let an expletive substitute for a clearer expression.

WORDY   It is necessary that we reform the housing policies.

BETTER   We need to reform the housing policies.

WORDY   There were many incentives offered by the company to its sales force.

BETTER   The company offered its sales force many incentives.

Vary your sentence lengths and structures.   Sentences, like music, have rhythm. If all your sentences run about the same length or rarely vary from a predictable subject-verb-object pattern readers will grow bored without knowing why. Every so often, surprise them with a really short statement. Or begin with a longer-than-usual introductory phrase. Or try compound subjects or verbs, or attach a series of parallel modifiers to the verb or object. Or let a sentence roll toward a grand conclusion, as in the following example.

> [Carl] Newman is a singing encyclopedia of pop power. He has identified, cultured, and cloned the most buoyant elements of his favorite Squeeze, Raspberries, Supertramp, and Sparks records, and he's pretty pathological about making sure there's something unpredictable and catchy happening in a New Pornographers song every couple of seconds—a stereo flurry of *ooohs*, an extra beat or two bubbling up unexpectedly.
>
> —Douglas Wolk, "Something to Talk About," *Spin*

Listen to what you have written.   Read everything that matters aloud at least once. Then fix the words or phrases that cause you to pause or stumble. This is a great way to find problem spots. If you can't unravel your own writing, a reader won't be able to either. Better yet, persuade a friend or roommate to read your draft to you and take notes.

Cut a first draft by 25 percent—or more.   If you tend to be wordy, try to cut your first drafts by at least one-quarter. Put all your thoughts down

on the page when drafting a paper. But when editing, cut every unnecessary expression. Think of it as a competition. However, don't eliminate any
important ideas and facts. If possible, ask an honest friend to read your work
and point out where you might tighten your language.

I believe more in
the scissors than
I do in the pencil.

— Truman Capote

be wordy,
If you ~~are aware that you~~ tend to ~~say more than you need to in your writing,~~
                    ∧
                         your
~~then get in the habit of~~ trying to cut ~~the~~ first drafts ~~that you have written~~ by
                         ∧   P
at least one-quarter. ~~There may be good reasons for you to~~ put all your
                                                    ∧
thoughts ~~and ideas~~ down on the page when ~~you are in the process of~~

drafting a paper ~~or project~~. But when ~~you are in the process of~~ editing, ~~you~~
                                        expression.
~~should be sure to~~ cut every unnecessary ~~word that is not needed or~~
                                        ∧   T
~~necessary. You may find it advantageous to~~ think of it as a competition ~~or a~~   .
             However,   ∧   ∧
~~game. In making your cuts, it is important that you~~ don't eliminate any
        ∧   *and*   .
important ideas ~~that may be essential or~~ facts ~~that may be important.~~ If ~~you~~
                                        ∧   ∧
~~find it~~ possible, ~~you might consider~~ asking an honest friend ~~whom you trust~~
                work
to read your ~~writing~~ and ~~ask them to~~ point out ~~those places in your writing~~
            ∧   *tighten*   .
where you might ~~make~~ your language ~~tighter.~~
            ∧   ∧

Your Turn   Even if you think your prose is as stingy as Lean Cuisine, take a
first draft you have written and try the 25 percent challenge. Count the words
in the original version (or let your software do it for you) and then pare away
until you come in under quota. And, while you are at it, turn abstract nouns
and strung-out verbs into livelier expressions and eliminate long windups and
boring chains of prepositional phrases. When you are done, read the revised
version aloud — and then revise one more time.

Revising & Editing

part six

revise and edit

38 **Revising Your Own Work** 452

for the big picture 453

for flow 453

for details 454

comment/
peer review/
proofread

39 **Peer Editing** 458

peer editing guidelines 459

proofreading symbols 460

Need style help? See page 430. / Need help with common errors? See page 600.

38 Revising Your Own Work

How much time should you spend revising a draft? Decide this based on the importance of the document and the time available to complete it. A job-application letter, résumé, or term paper had better be perfect. But you shouldn't send even an e-mail without a quick review, if only to make certain you're sending it to the right people and that your tone is appropriate. Errors might not bother you, but don't assume that other readers are just as easygoing. Given a choice, a well-edited piece always trumps sloppy work.

How you revise your work is a different matter. Some people edit line by line, perfecting every sentence before moving on to the next. Others write whole drafts quickly and then revise, and others combine these methods.

In most cases, it makes sense to draft a project fairly quickly and then edit it. Why? Because revising is hierarchical: Some issues matter more to your work than others. You might spend hours on a draft, getting each comma right and deleting every word not pulling its weight. But then you read the whole thing and you get that sinking feeling: The paper doesn't meet the assignment or is aimed at the wrong audience. So you trash paragraph after carefully edited paragraph and reorganize many of your ideas. Maybe you even start from scratch.

Wouldn't it have been better to discover those big problems early on, before you put in so many hours polishing the punctuation? With major projects, consider revising and editing sequentially, starting with the big issues like content and organization. Think of *revising* as making sweeping changes, and *editing* as finessing the details.

Revise to see the big picture.   When you revise, be willing to overhaul your whole project. Of course, you'll need a draft first and it should be a real one with actual words on the page, not just good intentions. With media projects such as a Web site or blog, you might work with a site plan and page designs. ⭕ But nothing beats a prototype to test a project. Revisions at this top level may require wholesale rewrites of the paper, even starting over. Whatever it takes.

- **Does the project meet the assignment?** You really can get so wrapped up in a paper that you forget the original assignment. If you received an assignment sheet, go back and measure your draft by its requirements. If it asks for a report and you have argued, prepare for major revisions. Review, too, any requirements set for length or use of sources.

- **Does the project reach its intended audience?** Who will read your paper? Are your tone and the level of vocabulary right for these people? What kinds of sources have you used? You'll have to revise heavily if your project won't work for the assigned or intended audience.

- **Does the project do justice to its subject?** This is a tough question to address and you may want to get another reader's input. It might also help to review a successful model of the assignment before you revise your paper. Look for such work in magazines, newspapers, and textbooks. Or ask your instructor or a writing-center staff member to suggest examples. How well does yours compare? Be certain you treat your subject intelligently and thoroughly and have included all the parts required. (These requirements obviously vary from assignment to assignment.) If you find some sections of the paper wanting, admit it and fix the problems.

Edit to make the paper flow.   There are different opinions as to what *flow* means when applied to writing, but it's a good thing. Once you are confident that you've met the major requirements of an assignment, check how

A manuscript page from "Terrific Mother," a short story by Lorrie Moore.

think visually
p. 592

well you have coordinated all its various elements. Editing to improve flow takes time and can produce valuable changes in a paper. It's the stage that gets skipped in more hurried forms of communication.

- **Does the organization work for the reader?** You may understand how a project fits together, but is that structure clear to readers? If your paper needs a thesis, does it have one that readers can identify readily and will find challenging? Do your paragraphs develop coherent points? Pay particular attention to the opening sentences in those paragraphs: They must both connect to what you just wrote and preview the upcoming material.

- **Does the paper have smooth and frequent transitions?** Transitional words and phrases support the overall organization. They are road signs to help keep readers on track. Make sure transitions appear not only at the beginning of paragraphs but also throughout the project. To navigate media projects, readers need other devices, from the captions and boxes on brochures to headings and links on Web sites. ○

- **Is the paper readable?** Once you've got the basics in place, especially a sound organization, you can tinker to your heart's content with the language, varying sentence structures, choosing words to achieve the level of style you want, and paring away clumsy verbiage (which almost rhymes with *garbage*). Review the chapters on style and apply those suggestions to the paper at this stage.

Edit to get the details right.   Most people are perfectionists when it comes to things that matter to them, but have a hard time understanding the obsessions of others. In preparing your paper, you may wonder who cares whether a page number is in the right place, a figure is correctly captioned, or a title is italicized. You'd be surprised.

When editing a paper, nothing clears your mind as much as putting a draft aside for a few days and then looking at it with fresh eyes. You will be amazed at all the changes you will want to make. But you have to plan ahead to take advantage of this unsurpassed editing technique. Wait until the last minute to complete a project and you lose that opportunity.

- **Is the format correct right down to the details?** Many academic and professional projects follow templates from which you cannot vary. In

connect ideas
p. 416

fact, you may be expected to learn these requirements as a condition for entering a profession or major. So if you are asked to prepare a paper in Modern Language Association (MLA) or American Psychological Association (APA) style, for instance, invest the few minutes it takes to get details right for titles, margins, headings, and page number formats. ○ Give similar attention to the formats for lab reports, e-mails, Web sites, and so on. You'll look like a pro if you do.

● **Are the grammar and mechanics right?** Word-processing programs offer a surprising amount of help in these areas. But use this assistance only as a first line of defense, not as a replacement for carefully rereading every word yourself. Even then, you still have to pay close attention to errors you make habitually. You know what they are. ○

● **Is the spelling correct?** Spell-checkers pick up some obvious gaffes but may not be any help with proper nouns or other special items—such as your professor's last name. They also don't catch correctly spelled words that simply aren't the ones you meant to use: *the* instead of *then*, *rein* instead of *reign*, and so on.

Your Turn   Advice about revising can sound abstract, but the process is a real one you engage in regularly—or should. In a discussion with your colleagues (or in a paragraph or two), describe your habits of revision. Explore questions such as the following:

- Do you revise as you write, or do you prefer to wait until you have a full draft?
- How willing are you to make big changes in a draft?
- Have you ever been embarrassed or hurt by what seemed like minor errors?
- Do you know your specific areas of weakness, and how do you address them?
- Do you allow yourself enough time to give your projects a close second look? Should you?
- Have you ever had a surprising success with a paper you wrote at the last minute and turned in almost unrevised?

---

understand citation
styles p. 501

help with common
errors p. 600

1 Put the paper aside for a few days (or at least a few hours) before revising.

2 Print out the paper, clear space on your desk, and read with fresh eyes. Does the paper respond to the assignment? Will it make sense to readers?

3 Read your paper aloud to yourself, your roommate, your goldfish — anyone who will listen. Mark the parts that confuse you or your audience.

39 Peer Editing

Many people get nervous when asked to play editor, though such requests come all the time: "Read this for me?" Either they don't want to offend a colleague with their criticisms, or they have doubts about their own abilities. These are predictable reactions, but you need to get beyond them.

Your job in peer editing drafts is not to criticize other writers, but to help them. And you will accomplish that best by approaching any draft honestly, from the perspective of a typical reader. You may not grasp all the finer points of grammar, but you will know if a paper is boring, confusing, or unconvincing. Writers need this response: You really do have the expertise to give a classmate worthwhile feedback about issues that require attention.

And yet most peer editors in college or professional situations edit only minimally. They focus on tiny matters, such as misspellings or commas, and ignore arguments that completely lack evidence or paragraphs dull enough to kill small mammals. Frankly, spelling and punctuation errors are just easy to circle. It's much tougher to suggest that whole pages need to be redone or that a colleague should do better research. But there's nothing charitable about ignoring these deeper issues when a writer's grade or career may be on the line. So what should you do?

First, before you edit any project, agree on the ground rules for making comments. It is very easy to annotate electronic drafts since you won't have to touch or change the original file. But writers may be more protective of paper copies of their work. Always ask whether you may write comments on a paper and then make sure that your handwriting is legible and your remarks signed or initialed.

Peer edit the same way you revise your own work.   As suggested in Chapter 38, pay attention to global issues first. ○ Examine the purpose, audience, and subject matter of the project before dealing with its sentence structure, grammar, or mechanics. Deal with these major issues in a thoughtful and supportive written comment at the end of the paper. Use marginal comments and proofreading symbols (see p. 460) to highlight mechanical problems. But don't correct these items. Leave it to the writer to figure out what is wrong.

Be specific in identifying problems or opportunities.   For instance, it doesn't help a writer to read "organization is confusing." Instead, point to places in the draft that went off track. If one sentence or paragraph exemplifies a particular problem—or strength—highlight it in some fashion and mention it in the final comment. Nothing helps a writer less than vague complaints or cheerleading:

> *You did a real good job though I'm not sure you supported your thesis.*

It's far better to write something like the following:

> *Your thesis on the opening page is clear and challenging, but by the second page, you have forgotten what you are trying to prove. The paragraphs there don't seem tied to the original claim, nor do I find enough evidence to support the points you do make. Restructure these opening pages?*

Too tough? Not at all. The editor takes the paper seriously enough to explain why it's not working.

Offer suggestions for improvement.   You soften criticism when you follow it up with reasonable suggestions or strategies for revision. It's fine, too, to direct writers to resources they might use, from more authoritative

No passion in the world is equal to the passion to alter someone else's draft.

—H. G. Wells

revise and edit
p. 452

sources to better software. Avoid the tendency, however, to revise the paper for your colleague or to redesign it to suit your own interests and opinions.

Praise what is genuinely good in the paper.   An editor can easily overlook what's working well in a paper, and yet a writer needs that information as much as any pertinent criticism. Find something good to say, too, even about a paper that mostly doesn't work. You'll encourage the writer who may be facing some lengthy revisions. But don't make an issue of it. Writers will know immediately if you are scraping bottom to find something worthy of praise.

Use proofreading symbols.   Proofreading marks may seem fussy or impersonal, but they can be a useful way of quickly highlighting some basic errors or omissions. Here are some you might want to remember and use when editing a paper draft.

SP	Word misspelled (not a standard mark, but useful)
X	Check for error here (not a standard mark)
℣	Delete marked item
⌒	Close up space
∧	Insert word or phrase
⌄	Insert comma
⌄⌄	Insert quotation marks
≡	Capitalize
⊙	Insert period
∼	Transpose or reverse the items marked
¶	Begin new paragraph
#	Insert or open up space
(ital)	Italicize word or phrase

how *s*
It is amazing much of our day-to-day lives now depend on increasingly

SP (seemless) kinds of communication, our cell phones talking to our PDAs,

drawing e-mails from the air, sharing texts with each other, down loading

images, and taking pictures. Our communications now seem infinitely

layered a real-life *Alice in Wonderland* experience Messages don't begin

or end somewhere; they are part of a magical stream of information that

extends the reach of human intelligence, to make us all connected to

anything we want.

Keep comments tactful.   Treat another writer's work the way you'd like to have your own efforts treated. Slips in writing can be embarrassing enough without an editor tweeting about them.

Your Turn   Anderson Cooper of CNN reported on a teacher in North Carolina suspended without pay for two weeks for writing "Loser" on a sixth-grader's papers. Apparently the student wasn't offended because the teacher was known to be a "jokester," but administrators were. Did they overreact with the suspension (without pay), or should teachers and editors show discretion when commenting on something as personal as writing? Is there any room for sarcasm when peer editing? Make the case, one way or the other, in an exploratory paragraph.

How to... Insert a comment in a Word document

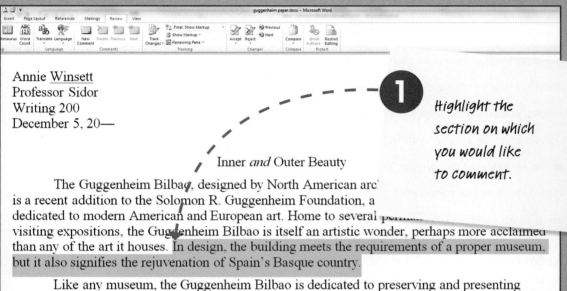

1 Highlight the section on which you would like to comment.

2 On the "Review" tab, click "New Comment."

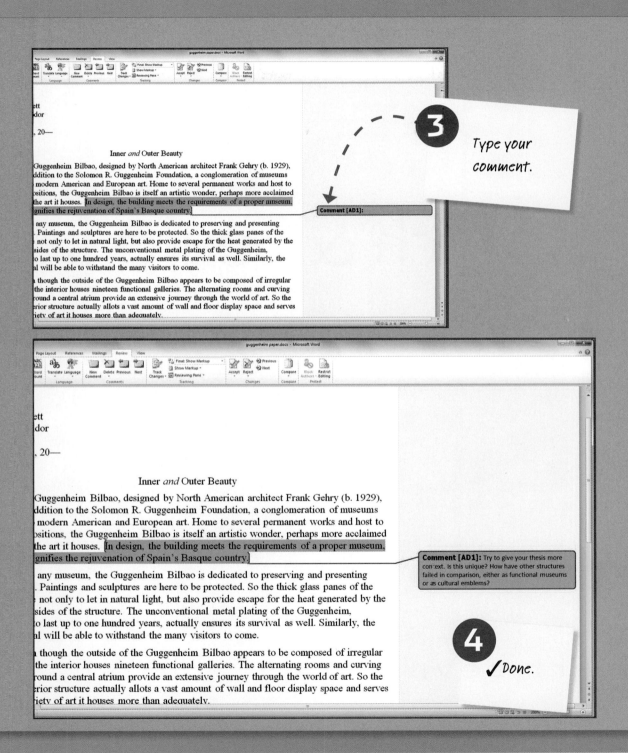

3 Type your comment.

4 ✓ Done.

Research & Sources

7

plan a project

40 **Beginning Your Research** 466

refine your search

41 **Finding Print and Online Sources** 472

interview and observe

42 **Doing Field Research** 478

find reliable sources

43 **Evaluating Sources** 482

analyze claims and
evidence/take notes

44 **Annotating Sources** 487

sum up ideas

45 **Summarizing Sources** 491

restate ideas

46 **Paraphrasing Sources** 494

avoid plagiarism/
use quotations

47 **Integrating Sources into Your Work** 497

understand citation
styles

48 **Documenting Sources** 501

cite in MLA

49 **MLA Documentation and Format** 503

in-text citations **505**
list of works cited **512**
paper format **537**

cite in APA

50 **APA Documentation and Format** 540

in-text citations **543**
list of references **549**
paper format **562**

40 Beginning Your Research

plan a project

Research can be part of any writing project. Creative writers spend long hours in a library gathering details about historical periods or contemporary events. Authors of reports conduct surveys and studies to confirm what they believe about a topic. And people engaged in arguments (ideally, at least) consult dozens of professional sources to be sure their claims are accurate and supported. ○

When doing research, you find out what is already known about a topic. For humanities courses, this involves examining a wide range of books, articles, and Web sources. In the social and natural sciences, you may also perform experiments or do field research to create and share new knowledge about a topic.

So where do you begin your research project and how do you keep from being swamped by the sheer quantity of information available? You need smart research strategies.

Know your assignment. Begin by reviewing the assignment sheet for a term paper or research project, when one is provided, and be sure you understand the kinds of research the paper requires. For a one-page position paper related to a class discussion, you might use only the reference section of the library and your textbook. An argument about current events will likely send you to newspapers, magazines, and Web sites, while a full-length term paper will draw on academic books and journals for support. (For details and advice on a wide variety of assignments, refer to Parts 1 and 2.)

choose a
genre p. 390

Come up with a plan.   Research takes time. You have to find sources, read them, record your findings, and then write about them. Most research projects also require full documentation and some type of formal presentation, either as a research paper or, perhaps, an oral report. This stuff cannot be scammed the night before. You can avoid mayhem by preparing a calendar that links specific tasks to specific dates. Simply creating the schedule (and you should keep it *simple*) might even jump-start your actual research. At a minimum, record important due dates in your day planner. Here's a basic schedule for a research paper with three deadlines.

Research is formalized curiosity. It is poking and prying with a purpose.

—Zora Neale Hurston

<u>Schedule: Research Paper</u>

February 20: Topic proposal due
___ Explore and select a topic
___ Do preliminary library/Web research
___ Define a thesis or hypothesis
___ Prepare an annotated bibliography

March 26: First draft due
___ Read, summarize, paraphrase, and synthesize sources
___ Organize the paper

April 16: Final draft due
___ Get peer feedback on draft
___ Revise the project
___ Check documentation
___ Edit the project

Find a manageable topic.   Keep in mind that any topic and thesis for a research project should present you with a reasonable problem to solve. (For advice on finding and developing topics, see Part 3.) Look for an idea or a question you can handle realistically within the scope of the assignment and the time available, and with the resources available to you.

When asked to submit a ten- or twenty-page term paper, some writers panic, thinking they need a topic broad or general enough to fill up all these blank pages. But the opposite is true. You will have more success finding helpful sources if you break off small but intriguing parts of much larger subjects.

> *not* Military Aircraft, *but* The Development of Jet Fighters in World War II
>
> *not* The History of Punk Rock, *but* The Influence of 1970s Punk Rock on Nirvana
>
> *not* Developmental Disorders in Children, *but* Cri du Chat Syndrome

Read widely at first to find a general subject; then narrow it down to a specific topic. Brainstorm this topic to come up with focused questions you might ask in your preliminary research. By the end of this early stage of the research process, your goal is to have turned a topic idea or phrase into a claim at least one full sentence long. ○

In the natural and social sciences, topics sometimes evolve from research problems already on the table in various fields. Presented with this research agenda in a course, you ordinarily begin with a "review of the literature" to determine what others have published on this issue in the major journals and what represents state-of-the-art thinking in the field. Then create an experiment in which your research question—offered as a claim called a *hypothesis*—either confirms the direction of ongoing work in the field or perhaps advances or changes it. In basic science courses, get plenty of advice from your instructor about formulating workable research questions and hypotheses.

Seek professional help.   During your preliminary research phase, you'll quickly discover that not all sources are equal. ○ They differ in purpose, method, media, audience, and authority. Until you get your legs as a researcher, never hesitate to ask questions about research tools and strategies: Get recommendations about the best available journals, books, and authors from teachers and reference librarians. Ask them which publishers, institutions, and experts carry the most intellectual weight in their fields. If your topic is highly specialized, plan to spend additional time tracking down sources outside of your own library.

develop a statement
p. 393

find reliable sources
p. 482

Distinguish between primary and secondary sources.   This basic distinction is worth keeping in mind as you approach a new subject and project: A *primary source* is a document that provides an eyewitness account of an event or phenomenon; a *secondary source* is a step or two removed, an article or book that interprets or reports on events and phenomena described in primary sources. The famous Zapruder film of the John F. Kennedy assassination in Dallas (November 22, 1963) is a memorable primary historical document; the many books or articles that draw on the film to comment on the assassination are secondary sources. Both types of sources are useful to you as a researcher.

Use primary sources when doing research that breaks new ground. Primary sources represent raw data—letters, journals, newspaper accounts, official documents, laws, court opinions, statistics, research reports, audio and video recordings, and so on. Working with primary materials, you generate your own ideas about a subject, free of anyone else's opinions or explanations. Or you can review the actual evidence others have used to make prior claims and arguments, perhaps reinterpreting their findings, correcting them, or bringing a new perspective to the subject.

Use secondary sources to learn what others have discovered or said about a subject. In many fields, you spend most of your time reviewing secondary materials, especially when researching areas of knowledge new to you. Secondary sources include scholarly books and articles, encyclopedias,

Web sites featuring government resources, such as Thomas or FedStats, and corporate annual reports provide primary material for analysis.

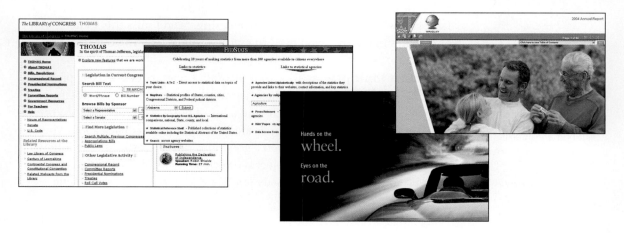

magazine pieces, and many Web sites. In academic assignments, you may find yourself moving easily between different kinds of materials, first reading a primary text like *Hamlet* and then reading various commentaries on it.

Record every source you examine.   Most writers and researchers download or photocopy sources rather than examine original copies in a library and take notes. However you plan on working, *you must* accurately record every source you encounter right from the start, gathering the following information:

- Authors, editors, translators, sponsors (of Web sites), or other major contributors
- Titles, subtitles, edition numbers, and volumes
- Publication information, including places of publication and publishers (for books); titles of magazines and journals, as well as volume and page numbers; dates of publication and access (the latter for online materials)
- Page numbers, URLs, electronic pathways, keywords, or other locators

You'll need these details later to document your sources.

It might seem obsessive to collect basic bibliographic data on books and articles you know you are unlikely to use. But when you expect to spend weeks or months on an assignment, log all material you examine so that later you won't have to backtrack, wondering, "Did I miss this source?" A log also comes in handy if you need to revisit a source later in your research.

Prepare a topic proposal.   Your instructor may request a topic proposal. Typically, this includes a topic idea, a draft thesis or hypothesis, potential sources, your intended approach, and a list of potential problems.

Remember that such proposals are written to get feedback about your project's feasibility, and that even a good idea raises questions. The following sample proposal for a short project is directed chiefly at classmates, who must respond via electronic discussion board as part of the assignment.

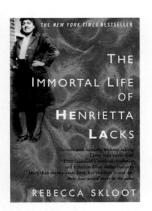

Books and magazines often provide secondary, not primary, information.

(*Nature* cover reprinted by permission from Macmillan Publishers Ltd.: NATURE, © January 2008.)

Eades 1

Micah Eades

Professor Kurtz

English 201

March 20, 20--

Causal Analysis Proposal: Awkward Atmospheres

People don't like going to the doctor's office. You wait in an office room decorated from the 1980s reading *Highlights* or last year's *Field & Stream* and listen to patients in the next room talking about the details of their proctology exam. Since I am planning a future as a primary care physician, I don't want people to dread coming to see me.

My paper will propose that patient dissatisfaction with visits to their physicians may not be due entirely to fear of upcoming medical examinations but rather to the unwelcoming atmosphere of most waiting and treatment rooms. More specifically, I will examine the negative effect that noise, poor interior design, and unsympathetic staff attitudes may have on patient comfort. I will propose that these factors have a much larger impact on patient well-being than previously expected. Additionally, I will propose possible remedies and ways to change these negative perceptions.

My biggest problem may be finding concrete evidence for my claims. For evidence, I do intend to cite the relatively few clinical studies that have been conducted on patient satisfaction and atmosphere. My audience will be a tough crowd: doctors who have neither an awareness of the problems I describe nor much desire to improve the ambience of their offices.

Title indicates that proposal responds to a specific assignment.

Opening paragraph offers a rationale for subject choice.

Describes planned content and structure of paper.

Has done enough research to know that literature on subject is not extensive.

Paper will be directed to a specific audience.

41 Finding Print and Online Sources

refine your
search

When beginning an academic research project, whether a brief report or a full term paper or thesis, you'll likely turn to three resources: local and school libraries, informational databases and indexes, and the Internet.

At the library are books, journals, and newspapers and other printed materials in a collection overseen by librarians to preserve information and support research. Often, the help of these librarians is necessary to locate and evaluate sources.

Also at a library or among its online resources are databases and indexes with electronic access to abstracts or full-text versions of up-to-date research materials in professional journals, magazines, and newspaper archives. Your library or school purchases licenses to allow you to use these password-protected resources—services such as *EBSCOhost*, *InfoTrac*, and *LexisNexis*.

And, of course, you can find endless streams of information online simply by exploring the Web, using search engines such as Google and Bing to locate data. Information on the Web varies hugely in quality, but covers just about every subject imaginable.

Whether working in a physical library, within a library catalog or an electronic database, or at home on your computer or mobile device, you need to know how to use the full capacity of research tools designed to search large bodies of information.

Learn to navigate the library catalog. All but the smallest or most specialized libraries now organize their collections electronically. Be sure you know how the electronic catalog works: It tells you if the library has an item you need, where it is on the shelves, and whether it has been checked out. You can search for most items by author, title, subject, keywords, and even call number.

Pay special attention to the terms or keywords used to index an item you've located in an electronic catalog. You can then use those terms to search for similar materials—an important way of generating leads on a topic.

Locate research guides. Another excellent option for starting an academic project is to use research sites prepared by libraries or universities to help researchers working in specific fields. Check to see whether your institution has developed such materials. Or simply search the phrase "library research guides" on the Web. Such sites identify resources both within and outside of academic institutions and may also give you suggestions for topic ideas or research areas. Use these guides carefully, since they may contain links to sites that libraries and schools cannot vouch for entirely. Some of the university-based materials may be restricted to students at the particular schools. But, even then, they may identify resources you can access through your own institution. The charts on pages 474 and 477 may help you identify databases for your subject.

You will probably begin your search with one or more multidisciplinary databases such as *LexisNexis Academic, Academic OneFile,* or *Academic Search Premier.* These resources cover a wide range of materials, including newspapers, respected magazines, and some professional journals. Most libraries

In addition to author, title, and publication information, the full entry for an item in a library catalog will also include subject headings. These terms may suggest additional avenues of research.

Research Guides and Databases	
Institution	**Subject Guides at**
Columbia University Library	www.columbia.edu/cu/lweb/eresources
New York Public Library	http://www.nypl.org/collections/ nypl-recommendations/research-guides
University of Chicago	http://guides.lib.uchicago.edu/home
University of Virginia	www.lib.virginia.edu/resguide.html
Electronic Books	www.lib.utexas.edu/books/etext.html
Infomine	http://infomine.ucr.edu
The Internet Public Library	www.ipl.org
Library of Congress Research and Reference Services	http://www.loc.gov/rr/

subscribe to one or more such information services, and these can be searched using keywords.

But for more in-depth work, focus on the databases within your specific discipline. There are, in fact, hundreds of such databases and tools, far too many to list here. Look for databases that present current materials at a level you can understand: Some online resources may be too specific or technical for your project. When working with a database for the first time, review the Help section or page to find the most efficient way to conduct your searches. Librarians, too, can offer professional advice on refining your search techniques.

Identify the best reference tools for your needs.   For encyclopedias, almanacs, historical records, maps, and so on, head to the reference section of your library and ask the librarian to direct you to the appropriate items.

Quite often, for instance, you'll need to trace the biographical facts of important people—dates of birth, countries of origin, schools attended, career paths, and so on. For current newsmakers, you might find enough fairly reliable data from a Web search or a Wikipedia entry. But to get the most accurate information on historical figures, consult more authoritative library tools such as the *Oxford Dictionary of National Biography* (focusing on the United Kingdom) or the *Dictionary of American Biography*. The British work is available in an up-to-date online version. Libraries also have more specialized biographical resources, both in print and online. Ask about them.

When you need information from old newspapers, you'll need more ingenuity. Libraries don't store newspapers, so local and selected national papers will be available only on microfilm. Just as limiting, few older papers are indexed. So, unless you know the approximate date of an event, you may have a tough time finding a story in the microfilmed copies of newspapers. Fortunately, both the *New York Times* and *Wall Street Journal* are indexed and available on microfilm in most major libraries. You'll also find older magazines on microfilm. These may be indexed (up to 1982) in print bibliographies such as the *Readers' Guide to Periodical Literature*. Ask a librarian for help.

When your library doesn't have the material you need, ask the librarian if it's possible to acquire the material from another facility through interlibrary loan. The loan process may take time, but if you plan ahead, you can get any reasonable item.

Use online sources intelligently.   Browsing the Web daily to check the sports scores and surf your favorite blogs and Web sites is a completely different matter than using the Web for research. Thanks to exhaustive search engines like Google and Bing, you can find facts on just about any subject — often too much information. And the quality of the results you turn up in a Web search will be uneven. Hits are generally returned by popularity, not reliability.

Improve your online research the same way you learn to navigate a library's academic databases: Study the Help screens that accompany the Web browser. Most offer advanced search options to help you turn up fewer and more pertinent materials.

Google's Help screen provides tips on how to search the Internet.

© 2011 Google

But you also need to exercise care with Web sources. Be certain you know who is responsible for the material (for instance, a government agency, a congressional office, a news service, a corporation), who is posting it, who is the author of the material or sponsor of the Web site, what the date of publication is, and so on. ○ A site's information is often skewed by those who pay its bills or run it; it can also be outdated, if no one regularly updates the site.

Keep current with Web developments too. Web companies such as Google are making more books and journal articles both searchable and available through their sites. Although these and other projects to broaden access to scholarly information do raise questions about copyright and the ownership of intellectual property, you should certainly take time to explore these tools as they become available.

For instance, a tool such as Google Scholar will direct you to academic sources and scholarly papers on a subject—exactly the kind of material you would want to use in a term paper or report. As an experiment, you might compare the hits you get on a topic with a regular Google search with those that turn up when you select the Scholar option. You'll quickly notice that the Scholar items are more serious and technical—and also more difficult to access. In some cases, you may see only an abstract of a journal article or the first page of the item. Yet the sources you locate may be worth a trip to the library to retrieve in their entirety.

find reliable sources
p. 482

Resources to Consult When Conducting Research

Source	What It Provides	Usefulness in Academic Research	Where to Find It
Scholarly Books	Fully documented and detailed primary research and analyses by scholars	Highly useful if not too high-level or technical	Library, Google Scholar
Scholarly Journals	Carefully documented primary research by scientists and scholars	Highly useful if not too high-level or technical	Library, databases
Newspapers	Accounts of current events	Useful as starting point	Library, microfilm, databases (*LexisNexis*), Internet
Magazines	Wide topic range, usually based on secondary research; written for popular audience	Useful if magazine has serious reputation	Libraries, newsstands, databases (*EBSCOhost*, *InfoTrac*), Internet
Encyclopedias (General or Discipline-Specific)	Brief articles	Useful as a starting point	Libraries, Internet
Wikipedia	Open-source encyclopedia: entries written/edited by online contributors	Not considered reliable for academic projects	Internet: www.wikipedia.org
Special Collections	Materials such as maps, paintings, artifacts, etc.	Highly useful for specialized projects	Libraries, museums; images available via Internet
Government, Academic, or Organization Web Sites	Vast data compilations of varying quality, some of it reviewed	Highly useful	Internet sites with URLs ending in *.gov, .edu,* or *.org*
Commercial Web Sites	Information on many subjects; quality varies	Useful if possible biases are known	Internet sites
Blogs	Controlled, often highly partisan discussions of specialized topics	Useful when affiliated with reputable sources such as newspapers	Internet
Personal Web Sites	Often idiosyncratic information	Rarely useful; content varies widely	Internet

42 Doing Field Research

interview and observe

While most research you do will be built on the work of others—that is, their books, articles, and fact-finding—you can strike out on your own in many situations. For instance, you might interview people with experiences or information related to the subject you're exploring. ○ Or you could support a claim by carefully observing and recording how people actually behave or think.

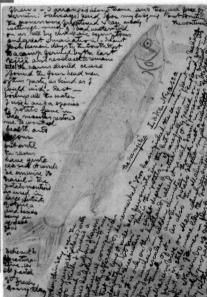

Field research is done in many ways and with different tools and media.

ask for help p. 379

Interview people with unique knowledge of your subject.   When considering whether an interview makes sense for your project, ask yourself the important question, "What do I expect to learn from the interviewee?" If the information you seek is readily available online or in print, don't waste everyone's time going through with an interview. If, on the other hand, this person provides a fresh perspective on your topic, a personal interview may make an excellent contribution to your research.

Interviews can be written or spoken. Written interviews, whether by e-mail or letter, allow you to keep questions and answers focused and provide a written record of your interviewee's exact words. But spoken interviews, both in person and on the phone, allow in-depth discussion of a topic and may lead to more memorable quotes or deeper insights. Be flexible in setting up the type of interview most convenient for your subject. For interviews, keep the following suggestions in mind:

- Request an interview formally by phone, confirming it with a follow-up e-mail.

- Give your subjects a compelling reason for meeting or corresponding with you; briefly explain your research project and why their knowledge or experience is important to your work.

- Let potential interviewees know how you chose them as subjects. If possible, provide a personal reference—a professor or administrator who can vouch for you.

- Prepare a set of thoughtful and relevant interview questions to encourage your subject to elaborate. Don't try to wing it in an interview.

- Think about how to phrase questions to open up the interview. Avoid questions that can be answered in one word, such as, *Did you enjoy your years in Asia?* Instead, ask, *What did you enjoy most about the decade you spent in Tokyo?*

- Start the interview by thanking the interviewee for his or her time and providing a brief reminder of your research project.

- Keep a written record of material you wish to quote. If necessary, confirm the exact wording with your interviewee.

- End the interview by again expressing your thanks.

- Follow up on the interview with a thank-you note or e-mail and, if the interviewee's contributions were substantial, send him or her a copy of the research paper.

- In your paper, give full credit to any people interviewed by properly documenting the information they provided. ○

If you conduct your interview in writing, request a response by a certain date—one or two weeks is reasonable for ten questions. Refer to Chapter 13 for e-mail etiquette and Chapter 14 for guidelines on writing business letters.

For telephone interviews, call from a place with good reception, where you will not be interrupted. Your cell phone should be fully charged or plugged in.

For an interview conducted in person, arrive at the predetermined meeting place on time and dressed professionally. If you wish to tape-record the interview, be sure to ask permission first.

Your Turn   Prepare a full set of questions you would use to interview a classmate about some *academic* issue—for example, his or her study habits, method for writing papers, or career objectives. Think about how you would sequence the questions, how you would follow up on the possible replies (if the interview were oral), and how you might avoid one-word replies that would give you little material for a report based on the interview. Write down your questions and then pair up with a classmate for a set of mutual interviews.

When you are done, write a one-page report based on what you learn and share the results with classmates.

Make careful and verifiable observations.   In writing either reports or arguments, especially those that focus on a specific local group or community, you might find yourself lacking enough data to move your claims beyond mere opinion. The point of systematic observation is to provide a clear, reliable, and verifiable way of studying a narrowly defined activity or phenomenon.

For example, an anecdote or a few random examples may not be enough to persuade administrators that the open meeting rooms in the student union are not being used efficiently. But you could probably construct a systematic observation of these facilities, showing exactly how many student groups use them, and on what basis, over a given period of time. This kind

understand citation
styles p. 501

of evidence carries far more weight than mere opinion because your readers can study exactly how you conducted your observations and accept or challenge your results.

Some situations can't be counted or measured as readily as the one described above. If, for example, you wanted to compare the various meeting rooms to determine whether those with windows facilitated more productive discussions than rooms without, your observations would need to be more qualitative. For example, to record whether meeting participants appeared alert or distracted, you might describe the tone of their voices and the general mood of the room. Numbers should figure in this observation as well; for instance, you could track how many people participated in the discussion or the number of tasks accomplished during the meeting.

To avoid bias in their observations, many researchers use double-column notebooks. In one column, they record the physical details of their observation as objectively as possible—descriptions, sounds, countable data, weather, time, circumstances, activity, and so on. In the second column, they record their interpretations and commentaries on the data.

In addition to careful and objective note-taking techniques, devices such as cameras, video recorders, and tape recorders provide reliable backup evidence about an event. Also, having more than one witness observe a situation can help verify your findings.

Learn more about fieldwork.   In those disciplines or college majors that use fieldwork, you will find guides or manuals to explain the details of such research procedures. You will also discover that fieldwork comes in many varieties, from naturalist observations and case studies to time studies and market research.

OBSERVABLE DATA	COMMENTARY
9/12/11 2 P.M. Meeting of Entertainment Committee Room MUB210 (no windows) 91 degrees outside Air conditioning broken People appear quiet, tired, hot	Heat and lack of a/c probably making everyone miserable.

A double-column notebook entry.

43 Evaluating Sources

find reliable
sources

In Chapter 41, you were steered in the direction of the best possible print and online sources for your research. But the fact is, all sources, no matter how prestigious, have strengths and weaknesses, biases and limitations. Even the most well-intentioned librarians have their prejudices. So evaluating sources is simply a routine and unavoidable part of any careful research process. Here are some strategies to use when making your own judgments about potential sources.

Preview source materials for their key features and strategies.   Give any source a quick once-over, looking for clues to its aim, content, and structure. Begin with the title and subtitle, taking seriously its key terms and qualifiers. A good title tells what a piece is—and is not—about. For many scholarly articles, the subtitle (which typically follows a colon) describes the substance of the argument.

Then scan the introduction (in a book) or abstract (in an article). From these items, you should be able to quickly grasp what the source covers, what its methods are, and what the author hopes to prove or accomplish.

Inspect the table of contents in a book or the headings in an article methodically, using them to grasp the overall structure of the work or to find specific information. Briefly review charts, tables, and illustrations, too, to discover what they offer. If a book has an index—and a serious book should—look for the key terms or subjects you are researching to see how well they are covered.

If the work appears promising, read its final section or chapter. Knowing how the source concludes gives considerable insight into its value for your research. Finally, look over the bibliography. The list of sources indicates how thorough the author has been and, not incidentally, points you to other materials you might want to examine.

Check who published or produced the source.   In general, books published by presses associated with colleges and universities (Harvard, Oxford, Stanford, etc.) are reputable sources for college papers. So are articles from professional journals described as *refereed* or *peer-reviewed*. These terms are used for journals in which the articles have been impartially evaluated by panels of experts prior to publication.

You can also usually rely on material from reputable commercial publishers and from established institutions and agencies. The *New York Times*, *Wall Street Journal*, CNN, Random House, Simon & Schuster, and the U.S. government make their ample share of mistakes, of course, but are generally considered to be more reliable than blogs or personal Web sites. But you always need to be cautious.

Check who wrote the work.   Ordinarily, you should cite authorities on your topic. Look for authors who are mentioned frequently and favorably within a field or whose works appear regularly in notes or bibliographies. Get familiar with these names.

The Web makes it possible to review the careers of many authors whom you might not recognize. Search for their names online to confirm that they are professional experts or reputable journalists. Avoid citing authors working too far beyond their areas of professional expertise. Celebrities especially like to cross boundaries, sometimes mistaking their passion for an issue for genuine mastery of the subject.

Consider the audience for a source.   What passes for adequate information in the general marketplace of ideas may not cut it when you're doing academic research. Many widely read books and articles that popularize a

You can learn a lot about a
source by previewing a few
basic elements.

ACADEMIC
PRESS

Available online at www.sciencedirect.com

SCIENCE @ DIRECT®

Journal of Research in Personality 36 (2002) 607–614

JOURNAL OF
RESEARCH IN
PERSONALITY

www.academicpress.com

Brief report

Are we barking up the right tree?
Evaluating a comparative approach to personality

Samuel D. Gosling * and Simine Vazire

Department of Psychology, University of Texas, Austin, TX, USA

Playful title nonetheless fits:
Article is about animals.

Abstract

Animal studies can enrich the field of human personality psychology by addressing questions that are difficult or impossible to address with human studies
alone. However, the benefits of a comparative approach to personality cannot be
reaped until the tenability of the personality construct has been established in animals. Using criteria established in the wake of the person–situation debate (Kenrick & Funder, 1988), the authors evaluate the status of personality traits in
animals. The animal literature provides strong evidence that personality does exist
in animals. That is, personality ratings of animals: (a) show strong levels of inte-
robserver agreement, (b) show evidence of validity in terms of predicting behaviors and real-world outcomes, and (c) do not merely reflect the implicit theories of
observers projected onto animals. Although much work remains to be done,
the preliminary groundwork has been laid for a comparative approach to personality.
© 2002 Elsevier Science (USA). All rights reserved.

Abstract previews entire
article.

Introduction

Personality characteristics have been examined in a broad range of non-
human species including chimpanzees, rhesus monkeys, ferrets, hyenas, rats,

Headings throughout
signal this is a research
article.

* Corresponding author. Fax: 1-512- 471-5935.
E-mail address: gosling@psy.utexas.edu (S.D. Gosling).

0092-6566/02/$ - see front matter © 2002 Elsevier Science (USA). All rights reserved.
PII: S0092-6566(02)00511-1

608   *Brief report / Journal of Research in Personality 36 (2002) 607 614*

sheep, rhinoceros, hedgehogs, zebra finches, garter snakes, guppies, and octopuses (for a full review, see Gosling, 2001). Such research is important because animal studies can be used to tackle questions that are difficult or impossible to address with human studies alone. By reaping the benefits of animal research, a comparative approach to personality can enrich the field of human personality psychology, providing unique opportunities to examine the biological, genetic, and environmental bases of personality, and to study personality development, personality-health links, and personality perception. However, all of these benefits hinge on the tenability of the personality construct in non-human animals. Thus, the purpose of the present paper is to address a key question in the animal domain: is personality real? That is, do personality traits reflect real properties of individuals or are they fictions in the minds of perceivers?

Thirty years ago, the question of the reality of personality occupied the attention of human-personality researchers, so our evaluation of the comparative approach to personality draws on the lessons learned in the human domain. Mischel's (1968) influential critique of research on human personality was the first of a series of direct challenges to the assumptions that personality exists and predicts meaningful real-world behaviors. Based on a review of the personality literature, Mischel (1968) pointed to the lack of evidence that individuals' behaviors are consistent across situations (Mischel & Peake, 1982). Over the next two decades, personality researchers garnered substantial empirical evidence to counter the critiques of personality. In an important article, Kenrick and Funder (1988) carefully analyzed the various arguments that had been leveled against personality and summarized the theoretical and empirical work refuting these arguments.

The recent appearance of studies of animal personality has elicited renewed debate about the status of personality traits. Gosling, Lilienfeld, and Marino (in press) proposed that the conditions put forward by Kenrick and Funder (1988) to evaluate the idea of human personality can be mobilized in the service of evaluating the idea of animal personality. Gosling et al. (in press) used these criteria to evaluate research on personality in non-human primates. In the present paper, we extend their analysis to the broader field of comparative psychology, considering research on nonhuman animals from several species and taxa. Kenrick and Funder's paper delineates three major criteria that must be met to establish the existence of personality traits: (1) assessments by independent observers must agree with one another; (2) these assessments must predict behaviors and real-world outcomes; and (3) observer ratings must be shown to reflect genuine attributes of the individuals rated, not merely the observers' implicit theories about how personality traits covary. Drawing on evidence from the animal-behavior literature, we evaluate whether these three criteria have been met with respect to animal personality.

Point of this brief study is defined at end of opening paragraph.

This page reviews literature on studies of animal personality.

Matt Damon shared his thoughts on President Obama at an interview about Damon's film *The Adjustment Bureau*. He may be one of your favorite actors, but don't cite him as a political expert in a research paper.

subject—such as climate change or problems with health-care costs—may, in fact, be based on more technical scholarly books and articles. For academic projects, rely primarily on those scholarly works themselves, even if you were inspired to choose a subject by reading respectable nonfiction. Glossy magazines shouldn't play a role in your research either, though the lines can get blurry. *People, O, Rolling Stone*, or *Spin* might be important in writing about popular culture or music, but not for much else. Similarly, Wikipedia is invaluable for a quick introduction to a subject, but don't cite it as an authority in an academic paper.

Establish how current a source is.   Scholarly work doesn't come with an expiration date, but you should base your research on the latest information. For fields in which research builds on previous work, the date of publication may even be highlighted by its system of documentation. Copyright pages, on the back of the title page, list the date of publication.

Check the source's documentation.   All serious scholarly and scientific research is documented. Claims are based on solid evidence backed up by formal notes, data are packed into charts and tables, and there will be a bibliography at the end. All of this is done so that readers can verify the claims an author makes.

In a news story, journalists may establish the credibility of their information by identifying their sources or, at a minimum, attributing their findings to reliable unnamed sources—and usually more than one. The authors of serious magazine pieces don't use footnotes and bibliographies either, but they, too, credit their major sources somewhere in the work. No serious claim should be left hanging. ⭕

For your own academic projects, avoid authors and sources with undocumented assertions. Sometimes you have to trust authors when they are writing about personal experiences or working as field reporters, but let readers know when your claims are based on uncorroborated personal accounts.

think critically
p. 372

Annotating Sources 44

Once you locate trustworthy sources, review them to identify the best ideas and most convincing evidence for your project. During this process of careful and critical reading, you annotate, summarize, ○ synthesize, ○ and paraphrase ○ your sources, in effect creating the notes you need to compose your paper.

Annotate sources to understand them.   Examine important sources closely enough to understand not only what they say but also how they reached their conclusions or compiled their data. In a sense, you have to become an expert on the sources you cite. To assist your analysis, you'll want to mark key texts with appropriate tools—notes in the margins, Post-it notes, electronic comments, and so forth. Simply making such comments will draw you deeper into a text and make you think about it more.

Read sources to identify claims.   Begin by noting and highlighting any specific claims, themes, or thesis statements a writer offers early in a text. Then pay attention to the way these ideas recur within the work, especially near the conclusion. At a minimum, decide whether a writer has made reasonable claims, developed them consistently, and delivered on promised evidence. In the example on pages 488–90 claims and reasons are highlighted in yellow.

Read sources to understand assumptions.   Finding and annotating the assumptions in a source can be *much* trickier than

analyze
claims and
evidence/
take notes

sum up ideas
p. 491

understand synthesis
papers p. 300

restate ideas
p. 494

locating claims. Highlight any assumptions stated outright in the source; they will be rare. More often, you have to infer the writer's assumptions, put them in your own words, and perhaps record them in marginal notes. Identifying controversial or debatable assumptions is particularly important. For instance, if a writer makes the claim that *America needs tighter border security to prevent terrorist attacks*, you draw the inference that the writer believes that terrorism is caused by people crossing inadequately patrolled borders. Is that assumption accurate? Should the writer explain or defend it? Raise such questions. The one key assumption in the example that follows is highlighted in orange.

Read sources to find evidence.   Look for evidence that authors use to support both their claims and their assumptions. Evidence can come in the form of data, examples, illustrations, or logical inferences. Since evidentiary sections make up the bulk of most academic materials you read, highlight only the key items—especially any facts or materials you intend to cite in your own project. Make sure no crucial point goes unsupported; if you find one, make a note of it. In the following example, key evidence is highlighted in blue.

Record your personal reactions to source material.   When reading multiple sources, you'll want a record of what you appreciated or objected to in them. To be certain you don't later mistake your personal comments for observations *from* the source, use first person or pose questions as you respond. Use personal annotations, too, to draw connections to other source materials you have read. In the following example, personal reactions appear on the left.

SANITY 101

Parents of adolescents usually strive for an aura of calm and reason. But just two words can trigger irrational behavior in parent and child alike: "college admissions."

CLAIM AND REASON: Fear of college admissions procedures is key point in editorial.

It's not an unreasonable response, actually, given the list of exasperating questions facing parents seeking to maximize their children's prospects: Do I tutor my child to boost college admissions test scores? Do I rely on the school admissions counselor or hire a private adviser? Do I hire a professional editor to shape my child's college essay?

CLAIM

The price tags behind those decisions drive up

EVIDENCE

the angst. A testing tutor "guaranteeing" a 200-point score boost on the SAT admissions test will charge roughly $2,400. Hiring a private college counselor can cost from $1,300 to $10,000. And hiring an essay editor can cost between $60 and $1,800. Wealthy suburbs are particularly lucrative for the college prep industry. Less affluent families are left with even greater reason to fret: Their children face an unfair disadvantage.

EVIDENCE:
Specific concerns support initial claim. They are the issues troubling parents most.

READER'S REACTION:
Why don't colleges realize how unfair their admissions policies might be to poorer applicants?

Now, private employers are stepping in to help out.

CLAIM

In a front-page article on Tuesday, *USA Today*'s education reporter Mary Beth Marklein revealed a range of counseling packages that companies are offering parents of college applicants, from brown-bag discussion lunches to Web-based programs that manage the entire admissions process.

EVIDENCE

It's thoughtful of the employers, but it shouldn't be necessary.

READER'S REACTION:
Might there be a parallel here to out-of-control sports programs? Why are schools so poorly administered?

Thanks to overanxious parents, aggressive college admissions officials and hustling college prep entrepreneurs, the admissions system has spun out of control. And the colleges have done little to restore sanity.

CLAIM:
This assertion, midway through editorial, may in fact be its thesis.

EVIDENCE

Take just one example, the "early decision" process in which seniors apply to a college by November 1 and promise to attend if admitted.

Early decision induces students to cram demanding courses into their junior year so they will appear on the application record. That makes an already stressful year for students and parents even more so. Plus, students must commit to a college long before they are ready. The real advantages of early decision go to colleges, which gain more control over their student mix and rise in national rankings by raising their acceptance rates.

Parents and students can combat the stress factor by keeping a few key facts in mind. While it's true that the very top colleges are ruthlessly selective—both Harvard and Yale accept slightly less than 10 percent of applicants—most colleges are barely selective. Of the 1,400 four-year colleges in the United States, only about 100 are very selective, and they aren't right for every student. Among the other 1,300, an acceptance rate of about 85 percent is more the norm.

And the best part of all: Many of those 1,300 colleges are more interested in educating your child than burnishing their rankings on lists of the "top" institutions. So the next time you hear the words "college admissions," don't instantly open your wallet. First, take a deep breath.

—Editorial/Opinion, *USA Today*, January 19, 2006

CLAIM AND REASON: Parents are worrying too much.

EVIDENCE: Statistics offer reasons not to fear college admissions procedures.

ASSUMPTION: Change "are" to "should be" and you have the assumption underlying this entire argument.

Your Turn With a classmate, exchange a draft of papers you are developing. Then read your colleague's paper as outlined in this chapter, imagining how you might use it as a source. First highlight major claims and reasons offered by the author; then identify any key assumptions in the paper. Bracket those sections of the project that primarily offer evidence. Finally, offer your personal reactions to various parts of the paper.

You might use highlighting pens of different colors to separate claims/reasons from assumptions and evidence, as in the sample essay.

Summarizing Sources

Once you determine that specific articles, books, and other texts deserve closer attention and you have read them critically—with an eye toward using their insights and data in your project—you're ready to summarize the material, putting ideas you've found into your own words. These brief summaries or fuller paraphrases can become the springboard for composing your paper. ○

sum up ideas

Use a summary to recap what a writer has said.   Look carefully for the main point and build your summary on it, making sure that this statement *does* reflect the actual content of the source, not your opinion of it. Be certain that the summary is *entirely* in your own words. Include the author and title of the work, too, so you can easily cite it later. The following is one summary of the *USA Today* editorial reprinted on pages 488–90, with all the required citation information:

> In "Sanity 101," the editors of *USA Today* (January 19, 2006) criticize current college admission practices, which, they argue, make students and parents alike fear that getting into an appropriate school is harder than it really is.
>
> Source: "Sanity 101." Editorial. *USA Today* 19 Jan. 2006: 10A. Print.

restate ideas
p. 494

∧

Be sure your summary is accurate and complete.   Even when a source makes several points, moves in contradictory directions, or offers a complex conclusion, your job is simply to describe what the material does. Don't embellish the material or blur the distinction between the source's words and yours. Include all bibliographical information (title, author, and date) from the source. The following summary of "Sanity 101" shows what can go wrong if you are not careful.

Omits title/source. Opening claim is not in editorial.

Editorial actually makes opposite point.

Summary improperly uses source's exact words. Might lead to inadvertent plagiarism later on.

> According to *USA Today*, most students get into the colleges they want. But admission into most colleges is so tough that many parents blow a fortune on tutors and counselors so that their kids can win early admission. But the paper's advice to parents is don't instantly open your wallet. First, take a deep breath.

Use a summary to record your take on a source.   In addition to reporting the contents of the material accurately, note also how the source might (or might not) contribute to your paper. But make certain that your comments won't be confused with claims made in the summarized article itself. The following are two acceptable sample summaries for "Sanity 101."

> In "Sanity 101," *USA Today* (January 19, 2006) describes the efforts of college applicants and parents to deal with the progressively more competitive admissions policies of elite institutions. The editorial claims that most schools, however, are far less selective. The article includes a reference to another *USA Today* piece by Mary Beth Marklein on the support some companies offer employees to assist them with college admissions issues.
>
> Source: "Sanity 101." Editorial. *USA Today* 19 Jan. 2006: 10A. Print.

> In an editorial (January 19, 2006) entitled "Sanity 101," *USA Today* counsels parents against worrying too much about hypercompetitive current college admission practices. In reality only a small percentage of schools are highly selective about admissions. The editorial doesn't provide the schools' side of the issue.
>
> Source: "Sanity 101." Editorial. *USA Today* 19 Jan. 2006: 10A. Print.

Prepare a summary to provide a useful record of a source. After reading a research source, you may decide that all you need is a brief description of it—the gist of it—recorded either on a card or in an electronic file (with complete bibliographic data). Such a summary reminds you that you have, in fact, seen and reviewed the source, which can be no small comfort when developing projects that stretch over several weeks or months. After you've examined dozens and dozens of sources, it's easy to forget what exactly you've already read.

Use summaries to prepare an annotated bibliography. In an annotated bibliography, brief summaries are provided for every item in an alphabetical list of sources. These summaries help readers understand the content and scope of materials. For more about annotated bibliographies, see Chapter 11. ⭕

Your Turn   Practice writing summaries by pairing up with a classmate and finding (probably online) a newspaper or blog page with a variety of opinion-oriented articles. For instance, check out the "Opinion" page in the *New York Times* or the home page of *Arts & Letters Daily* or the *Huffington Post*.

Agree on three or four pieces that both of you will summarize separately. Then write the paired summaries, being careful to identify the items, describe them accurately, and separate your recaps from any comments you make about the material you have read. When you are done, compare your summaries. Discuss their accuracy and make certain that neither of you has inadvertently borrowed language from the original articles.

---

understand annotated
bibliographies p. 296

46 Paraphrasing Sources

restate ideas

Paraphrases provide more complete records of the sources you examine than do summaries. ○ Like a summary, a paraphrase recaps a source's main point, but it also tracks the reasons and important evidence supporting that conclusion. Paraphrase any materials you expect to use extensively in a project. Then consider how the research materials you have gathered work in relationship to each other.

Identify the key claims and structure of the source.
Determine the main points made by the article, chapter, or text, and study how the work organizes information to support its claims. ○ Then be sure your paraphrase follows the same structure as the source. For example, your paraphrase will likely be arranged sequentially when a work has a story to tell, be arranged by topic when you're dealing with reported information, or be structured logically when you take notes from arguments or editorials.

Track the source faithfully.   A paraphrase should follow the reasoning of the source, moving through it succinctly but remaining faithful to its organization, tone, and, to some extent, style. In effect, you are preparing an abstract of the material, complete and readable in itself. So take compact and sensible notes, adapting the paraphrase to your needs—understanding that some materials will be more valuable for your project than others. ○

494

sum up ideas
p. 491

think critically
p. 372

take notes
p. 487

Record key pieces of evidence.   Thanks to photocopies and downloaded files, you don't usually have to copy data laboriously into your notes—and you probably shouldn't. (The chances of error greatly multiply whenever you copy information by hand.) But be certain that your paraphrase does record the reasons supporting all major claims in the source, as well as key evidence and facts. Key evidence proves a point or seals the deal. Also, keep track of page numbers for the important data so you can cite this material directly from your notes.

Be certain your notes are entirely in your own words.   If you borrow the language of sources as you paraphrase them, you'll likely slip into plagiarism when you compose your paper. Deliberately or not, you could find yourself copying phrases or sentences from the sources into your project.

When you are confident that you've paraphrased sources correctly, never borrowing their language, you may then safely transfer those notes directly into your project—giving the original writers due credit. In effect, you've begun to compose your own paper whenever you write competent paraphrases.

The following is a paraphrase of "Sanity 101," the complete, fully annotated text of which appears in Chapter 44 (pp. 488–90). Compare the paraphrase here to the summaries of the article that appear in Chapter 45 (pp. 491–92).

> In an editorial entitled "Sanity 101" (January 19, 2006), the editors of *USA Today* worry that many fearful parents are resorting to costly measures to help assure their child's college admission, some hiring private counselors and tutors that poorer families can't afford. Companies now even offer college admission assistance as part of employees' job packages. Colleges themselves are to blame for the hysteria, in part because of "early admission" practices that benefit them more than students. But parents and students should consider the facts. Only a handful of colleges are truly selective; most have acceptance rates near 85 percent. In addition, most schools care more about students than about their own rankings.

Avoid misleading or inaccurate paraphrasing.   Your notes won't be worth much if your paraphrases of sources distort the content of what you read. Don't rearrange the information, give it a spin you might prefer, or offer your own opinions on a subject. Make it clear, too, whenever your comments focus just on particular sections or chapters of a source, rather than on the entire piece. That way, you won't misread your notes months later and give readers a wrong impression about an article or book. The following is a paraphrase of "Sanity 101" that gets almost everything wrong.

Opening sentences follow language of editorial too closely, and also distort structure of editorial.

Paraphrase shifts tone, becoming much more colloquial than editorial.

Paraphrase borrows words and phrases too freely from original.

Paraphrase offers opinion on subject, its criticism of colleges going beyond original editorial.

Parents of teens usually try to be reasonable, the editors of *USA Today* complained on January 19, 2006. But the words "college admission" can make both child and parent irrational. The response is not unreasonable, given all the irritating questions facing parents seeking to improve their children's prospects. But the fact is that just a few colleges are highly selective. Most of the four-year schools in the country have acceptance rates of 85 percent. So high school students and parents should just chill and not blow their wallets on extra expenses. Rely on the school admissions counselor; don't hire a private adviser or professional editor to shape your child's college essay. A testing tutor might charge $2,400; a private college counselor can cost from $1,300 to $10,000. This is unfair to poorer families too, especially when companies start offering special admissions services to their employees. As always, the colleges are to blame, with their pushy "early admissions" programs, which make them look good in rankings but just screw their students.

Use your paraphrases to synthesize sources.   If you are asked to prepare a literature review or synthesis paper on a subject, begin that work by carefully summarizing and paraphrasing a range of reputable sources. For much more about synthesis and synthesis papers, see Chapter 12. O

Your Turn   Practice writing paraphrases by pairing up with a classmate and choosing a full essay to paraphrase from Part 1 of this book.
        Write your paraphrases of the agreed-upon essay separately, just as if you intended to cite the piece later in a report, research paper, or argument yourself. When both of you are done, compare your paraphrases. What did you identify as the main point(s) or thesis of the piece? What kind of structure did the article follow: for example, narrative, report, comparison/contrast, argument, and so on? What evidence or details from the article did you include in your paraphrases? How did your paraphrases compare in length?
        Discuss the differences. How might you account for them?

understand synthesis
papers p. 300

Integrating Sources into Your Work

47

When you integrate sources effectively into your work, you give readers information they need to identify paraphrased or quoted items and to understand how they may have been edited for clarity or accuracy.

Cue the reader in some way whenever you introduce borrowed material, whether it is summarized, paraphrased, or quoted directly.   Readers *always* need to be able to distinguish between your ideas and those you've obtained from other authors. So you must provide a signal whenever source material is introduced. Think of it as framing this material to set it off from your own words. Framing also enables you to offer an explanation or context for borrowed material, giving it the weight and power you believe it should have.

Often, all that's required for a frame is a brief signal phrase that identifies the author, title, or source you are drawing on.

> President Obama explained at a press conference that ". . .
>
> According to a report in *Scientific American*, . . .
>
> . . . ," said the former CEO of General Electric, arguing that ". . .
>
> In *Blink*, author Malcolm Gladwell makes some odd claims. For example, he . . .

avoid
plagiarism/
use quotations

MLA and APA Style

The examples in this section follow MLA (Modern Language Association) style, covered in Chapter 49. For information on APA (American Psychological Association) style, see Chapter 50.

At other times you'll need a clause or a complete sentence or more to incorporate borrowed material into a paper. Your frame can introduce, interrupt, follow, or even surround the words or ideas taken from sources, but be sure that your signal phrases are grammatical and lead naturally into the material.

Select an appropriate "verb of attribution" to frame borrowed material.   Note that source material is often introduced or framed by a "verb of attribution" or "signal verb." These verbs influence what readers think of borrowed ideas or quoted material.

Use more neutral signal verbs in reports, and descriptive or even biased terms in arguments. Note that, by MLA convention, verbs of attribution are usually in the present tense when talking about current work or ideas. (In APA, these verbs are generally in the past or present perfect tense.)

Verbs of Attribution		
Neutral	**Descriptive**	**Biased**
adds	acknowledges	admits
explains	argues	charges
finds	asserts	confesses
notes	believes	confuses
offers	claims	derides
observes	confirms	disputes
says	disagrees	evades
shows	responds	impugns
states	reveals	pretends
writes	suggests	smears

Use ellipsis marks [. . .] to shorten a lengthy quotation.   When quoting a source in your paper, it's not necessary to use every word or sentence, as long as the cuts you make don't distort the meaning of the original material. An ellipsis mark, formed from three spaced periods, shows where words, phrases, full sentences, or more have been removed from a quotation. The mark doesn't replace punctuation within a sentence. Thus, you might see a period or a comma immediately followed by an ellipsis mark.

ORIGINAL PASSAGE

Although gift giving has been a pillar of Hopi society, trade has also flourished in Hopi towns since prehistory, with a network that extended from the Great Plains to the Pacific Coast, and from the Great Basin, centered on present-day Nevada and Utah, to the Valley of Mexico. Manufactured goods, raw materials, and gems drove the trade, supplemented by exotic items such as parrots. The Hopis were producers as well, manufacturing large quantities of cotton cloth and ceramics for the trade. To this day, interhousehold trade and barter, especially for items of traditional manufacture for ceremonial use (such as basketry, bows, cloth, moccasins, pottery, and rattles), remain vigorous.

–Peter M. Whiteley, "Ties That Bind: Hopi Gift Culture and Its First Encounter with the United States," *Natural History*, November 2004, p. 26

> Highlighting shows words to be deleted when passage is quoted.

PASSAGE WITH ELLIPSES

Whiteley has characterized the practice this way:

> Although gift giving has been a pillar of Hopi society, trade has also flourished in Hopi towns since prehistory. . . . Manufactured goods, raw materials, and gems drove the trade, supplemented by exotic items such as parrots. The Hopis were producers as well, manufacturing large quantities of cotton cloth and ceramics for the trade. To this day, interhousehold trade and barter, especially for items of traditional manufacture for ceremonial use, . . . remain vigorous. (26)

> Ellipses show where words have been deleted.

Use brackets [ ] to insert explanatory material into a quotation.

By convention, readers understand that the bracketed words are not part of the original material.

> Writing in the *London Review of Books* (January 26, 2006), John Lancaster describes the fears of publishers: "At the moment Google says they have no intention of providing access to this content [scanned books still under copyright]; but why should anybody believe them?"

Use ellipsis marks, brackets, and other devices to make quoted materials suit the grammar of your sentences.   Sometimes, the structure of sentences you want to quote won't quite match the grammar, tense, or perspectives of your own surrounding prose. If necessary, cut up a quoted passage to slip appropriate sections into your own sentences, adding bracketed changes or explanations to smooth the transition.

ORIGINAL PASSAGE

Words to be quoted are highlighted.

Among Chandler's most charming sights are the business-casual dads joining their wives and kids for lunch in the mall food court. The food isn't the point, let alone whether it's from Subway or Dairy Queen. The restaurants merely provide the props and setting for the family time. When those kids grow up, they'll remember the food court as happily as an older generation recalls the diners and motels of Route 66 — not because of the businesses' innate appeal but because of the memories they evoke.

–Virginia Postrel, "In Defense of Chain Stores," *Atlantic Monthly*, December 2006

MATERIAL AS QUOTED

Words quoted from source are highlighted.

People who dislike chain stores should ponder the small-town America that cultural critic Virginia Postrel describes, one where "business-casual dads [join] their wives and kids for lunch in the mall food court," a place that future generations of kids will remember "as happily as an older generation recalls the diners and motels of Route 66."

Use [sic] to signal an obvious error in quoted material.   You don't want readers to blame a mistake on you, and yet you are obligated to reproduce a quotation exactly — including blunders in the original. You can highlight an error by putting *sic* (the Latin word for "thus") in brackets immediately following the mistake. The device says, in effect, that this is the way you found it.

The late Senator Edward Kennedy once took Supreme Court nominee Samuel Alito to task for his record: "In an era when America is still too divided by race and riches, Judge Alioto [sic] has not written one single opinion on the merits in favor of a person of color alleging race discrimination on the job."

Documenting Sources

48

Required to document your research paper? It seems simple in theory: List your sources and note where and how you use them. But the practice can be intimidating. For one thing, you have to follow rules for everything from capitalizing titles to captioning images. For another, documentation systems differ between fields. What worked for a Shakespeare paper won't transfer to your psychology research project. Bummer. What do you need to do?

Understand the point of documentation.   Documentation systems differ to serve the writers and researchers who use them. Modern Language Association (MLA) documentation, which you probably know from composition and literature classes, highlights author names, books, and article titles, and assumes that writers will be quoting a lot—as literature scholars do. American Psychological Association (APA) documentation, gospel in psychology and social sciences, focuses on publication dates because scholars in these fields value the latest research. Council of Science Editors (CSE) documentation, used in the hard sciences, provides predictably detailed advice for handling formulas and numbers.

So systems of documentation aren't arbitrary. Their rules simply anticipate problems researchers face when dealing with sources.

Understand what you accomplish through documentation.
First, you clearly identify the sources you have used. In a world awash with information, readers really do need to have reliable information about titles, authors, data, media of publication, and so on.

understand
citation
styles

By citing your sources, you certify the quality of your research and, in turn, receive credit for your labor. You also provide evidence for your claims. A shrewd reader or instructor can tell a lot from your bibliography alone.

Finally, when you document a paper, you encourage readers to follow up on your work. When you've done a good job, serious readers will want to know more about your subject. Both your citations and your bibliography enable them to take the next step in their research.

Style Guides Used in Various Disciplines

Field or Discipline	Documentation and Style Guides
Anthropology	*Chicago Manual of Style* (16th ed., 2010)
Biology	*Scientific Style and Format: The CSE Manual for Authors, Editors, and Publishers* (7th ed., 2006)
Business and management	*The Business Style Handbook: An A-to-Z Guide for Writing on the Job* (2002)
Chemistry	*The ACS Style Guide: Effective Communication of Scientific Information* (3rd ed., 2006)
Earth sciences	*Geowriting: A Guide to Writing, Editing, and Printing in Earth Science* (5th ed., 1995)
Engineering	Varies by area; *IEEE Standards Style Manual* (online)
Federal government	*United States Government Printing Office Manual* (30th ed., 2008)
History	*Chicago Manual of Style* (16th ed., 2010)
Humanities	*MLA Handbook for Writers of Research Papers* (7th ed., 2009)
Journalism	*The Associated Press Stylebook and Briefing on Media Law* (2011); *UPI Stylebook and Guide to Newswriting* (4th ed., 2004)
Law	*The Bluebook: A Uniform System of Citation* (19th ed., 2010)
Mathematics	*A Manual for Authors of Mathematical Papers* (8th ed., 1990)
Music	*Writing about Music: An Introductory Guide* (4th ed., 2008)
Nursing	*Writing for Publication in Nursing* (2nd ed., 2010)
Political science	*The Style Manual for Political Science* (2006)
Psychology	*Publication Manual of the American Psychological Association* (6th ed., 2010)
Sociology	*ASA Style Guide* (4th ed., 2010)

MLA Documentation and Format

The style of the Modern Language Association (MLA) is used in many humanities disciplines. For complete details about MLA style, consult the *MLA Handbook for Writers of Research Papers*, 7th ed. (2009). The basic details for documenting sources and formatting research papers in MLA style are presented below.

Document sources according to convention.   When you use sources in a research paper, you are required to cite the source, letting readers know that the information has been borrowed from somewhere else, and showing them how to find the original material if they would like to study it further. An MLA-style citation includes two parts: a brief in-text citation and a more detailed works cited entry to be included in a list at of the end of your paper.

In-text citations must include the author's name as well as the number of the page where the borrowed material can be found. The author's name (shaded in orange) is generally included in the signal phrase that introduces the passage, and the page number (shaded in yellow) is included in parentheses after the borrowed text.

> Frazier points out that the Wetherill-sponsored expedition to explore Chaco Canyon was roundly criticized (43).

Alternatively, the author's name can be included in parentheses along with the page number.

> The Wetherill-sponsored expedition to explore Chaco Canyon was roundly criticized (Frazier 43).

cite in MLA

503

At the end of the paper, in the works cited list, a more detailed citation includes the author's name as well as the title (shaded in green) and publication information about the source (shaded in blue).

Frazier, Kendrick. *People of Chaco: A Canyon and Its Culture.* Rev. ed. New York: Norton, 1999. Print.

Both in-text citations and works cited entries can vary greatly depending on the type of source cited (book, periodical, Web site, etc.). The following pages give specific examples of how to cite a wide range of sources in MLA style.

Directory of MLA In-Text Citations

1. Author named in signal phrase 505
2. Author named in parentheses 505
3. With block quotations 505
4. Two or three authors 506
5. Four or more authors 506
6. Group, corporate, or government author 506
7. Two or more works by the same author 506
8. Authors with same last name 507
9. Unidentified author 507
10. Multivolume work 507
11. Work in an anthology 507
12. Entry in a reference book 507
13. Literary work 508
14. Sacred work 508
15. Entire work 509
16. Secondary source 509
17. No page numbers 509
18. Multiple sources in the same citation 509

MLA in-text citation

1. Author Named in Signal Phrase

Include the author's name in the signal phrase that introduces the borrowed material. Follow the borrowed material with the page number of the source in parentheses. Note that the period comes after the parentheses. For a source without an author, see item 9; for a source without a page number, see item 17.

> According to Seabrook, "astronomy was a vital and practical form of knowledge" for the ancient Greeks (98).

2. Author Named in Parentheses

Follow the borrowed material with the author and page number of the source in parentheses, and end with a period. For a source without an author, see item 9; for a source without a page number, see item 17.

> For the ancient Greeks, "astronomy was a vital and practical form of knowledge" (Seabrook 98).

Note: Most of the examples below follow the style of item 1, but naming the author in parentheses (as shown in item 2) is also acceptable.

3. With Block Quotations

For quotations of four or more lines, MLA requires that you set off the borrowed material indented one inch from the left-hand margin. Include the author's name in the introductory text (or in the parentheses at the end). End the block quotation with the page number(s) in parentheses, *after* the end punctuation of the quoted material.

> Jake Page, writing in *American History*, underscores the significance of the well-organized Pueblo revolt:
>
>> Although their victory proved temporary, in the history of Indian-white relations in North America the Pueblo Indians were the only Native Americans to successfully oust European invaders from their territory. . . . Apart from the Pueblos, only the Seminoles were able to retain some of their homeland for any length of time, by waging war from the swamps of the Florida Everglades. (36)

4. Two or Three Authors

If your source has two or three authors, include all of their names in either the signal phrase or parentheses.

> Muhlheim and Heusser assert that the story "analyzes how crucially our actions are shaped by the society . . . in which we live" (29).

> According to some experts, "Children fear adult attempts to fix their social lives" (Thompson, Grace, and Cohen 8).

5. Four or More Authors

If your source has four or more authors, list the first author's name followed by "et al." (meaning "and others") in the signal phrase or parentheses.

> Hansen et al. estimate that the amount of fish caught and sold illegally worldwide is between 10 and 30 percent (974).

6. Group, Corporate, or Government Author

Treat the name of the group, corporation, or government agency just as you would any other author, including the name in either the signal phrase or the parentheses.

> The United States Environmental Protection Agency states that if a public water supply contains dangerous amounts of lead, the municipality is required to educate the public about the problems associated with lead in drinking water (3).

7. Two or More Works by the Same Author

If your paper includes two or more works by the same author, add a brief version of the works' titles (shaded in green) in parentheses to help readers locate the right source.

> Mills suggests that new assessments of older archaeological work, not new discoveries in the field, are revising the history of Chaco Canyon ("Recent Research" 66). She argues, for example, that new analysis of public spaces can teach us about the ritual of feasting in the Puebloan Southwest (Mills, "Performing the Feast" 211).

8. Authors with Same Last Name

If your paper includes two or more sources whose authors have the same last name, include a first initial with the last name in either the signal phrase or the parentheses.

> According to T. Smith, "as much as 60 percent of the computers sold in India are unbranded and made by local assemblers at about a third of the price of overseas brands" (12).

9. Unidentified Author

If the author of your work is unknown, include a brief title of the work in parentheses.

> The amount of protein that tilapia provides when eaten exceeds the amount that it consumes when alive, making it a sustainable fish ("Dream Fish" 26).

10. Multivolume Work

If you cite material from more than one volume of a multivolume work, include in the parentheses the volume number followed by a colon before the page number. (See also item 11, on p. 515, for including multivolume works in your works cited list.)

> Odekon defines *access-to-enterprise zones* as "geographic areas in which taxes and government regulations are lowered or eliminated as a way to stimulate business activity and create jobs" (1: 2).

11. Work in an Anthology

Include the author of the work in the signal phrase or parentheses. There is no need to refer to the editor of the anthology in the in-text citation; this and other details will be included in the works cited list at the end of your paper.

> Vonnegut suggests that *Hamlet* is considered such a masterpiece because "Shakespeare told us the truth, and [writers] so rarely tell us the truth" (354).

12. Entry in a Reference Book

In the signal phrase, include the author of the entry you are referring to, if there is an author. In the parentheses following the in-text citation, include the title of the entry and the page number(s) on which the entry appears.

> Willis points out that the Empire State Building, 1,250 feet tall and built in just over one year, was a record-breaking feat of engineering ("Empire State Building" 375-76).

For reference entries with no author (such as dictionaries), simply include the name of the article or entry in quotation marks along with the page reference in parentheses.

> *Black* is defined as a color "producing or reflecting comparatively little light and having no predominant hue" ("Black" 143).

13. Literary Work

Include as much information as possible to help readers locate your borrowed material. For classic novels, which are available in many editions, include the page number, followed by a semicolon, and additional information such as book ("bk."), volume ("vol."), or chapter ("ch.") numbers.

> At the climax of Brontë's *Jane Eyre,* Jane fears that her wedding is doomed, and her description of the chestnut tree that has been struck by lightning is ominous: "it stood up, black and riven: the trunk, split down the center, gaped ghastly" (274; vol. 2, ch. 25).

For classic poems and plays, include division numbers such as act, scene, and line numbers; do not include page numbers. Separate all numbers with periods. Use arabic (1, 2, 3, etc.) numerals instead of roman (I, II, III, etc.) unless your instructor prefers otherwise.

> In Homer's epic poem *The Iliad,* Agamemnon admits that he has been wrong to fight with Achilles, but he blames Zeus, whom he says "has given me bitterness, who drives me into unprofitable abuse and quarrels" (2.375-76).

14. Sacred Work

Instead of page numbers, include book, chapter, and verse numbers when citing material from sacred texts.

> Jesus' association with the sun is undeniable in this familiar passage from the Bible: "I am the light of the world. Whoever follows me will not walk in darkness, but will have the light of life" (John 8.12).

15. Entire Work

When referring to an entire work, there is no need to include page numbers in parentheses; simply include the author's name(s) in the signal phrase.

> Boyer and Nissenbaum argue that the witchcraft trials persisted because of the unique social and political environment that existed in Salem in 1692.

16. Secondary Source

To cite a source you found within another source, include the name of the original author in the signal phrase. In the parentheses, include the term "qtd. in" and give the author of the source where you found the quote, along with the page number. Note that your works cited entry for this material will be listed under the secondary source name (Pollan) rather than the original writer (Howard).

> Writing in 1943, Howard asserted that "artificial manures lead inevitably to artificial nutrition, artificial food, artificial animals, and finally to artificial men and women" (qtd. in Pollan 148).

17. No Page Numbers

If the work you are citing has no page numbers, include only the author's name (or the brief title, if there is no author) for your in-text citation.

> Gorman reported that in early 2007, hunger-striking enemy combatants at Guantanamo Bay were force-fed.

18. Multiple Sources in the Same Citation

If one statement in your paper can be attributed to multiple sources, alphabetically list all the authors with page numbers, separated by semicolons.

> Most historians agree that the Puritan religion played a significant role in the hysteria surrounding the Salem witchcraft trials (Karlsen 14; Norton 22; Reis 145).

Directory of MLA Works Cited Entries

AUTHOR INFORMATION

1. Single author 512
2. Two or three authors 512
3. Four or more authors 512
4. Corporate author 513
5. Unidentified author 513
6. Multiple works by the same author 513

BOOKS

7. Book: basic format 514
8. Author and editor 514
9. Edited collection 514
10. Work in an anthology or a collection 515
11. Multivolume work 515
12. Part of a series 515
13. Republished book 518
14. Later edition 518
15. Sacred work 518
16. Translation 519
17. Article in a reference book 519
18. Introduction, preface, foreword, or afterword 519
19. Title within a title 519

PERIODICALS

20. Article in a scholarly journal 520
21. Article in a scholarly journal with no volume number 520

22. Magazine article 520
23. Newspaper article 520
24. Editorial 521
25. Letter to the editor 521
26. Unsigned article 521
27. Review 524

ELECTRONIC SOURCES

28. Short work from a Web site 524
29. Entire Web site 524
30. Entire blog (Weblog) 524
31. Entry in a blog (Weblog) 525
32. Online book 525
33. Work from a library subscription service (such as *InfoTrac* or *FirstSearch*) 525
34. Work from an online periodical 530
35. Online posting 530
36. E-mail 530
37. CD-ROM 531
38. Podcast 531
39. Entry in a wiki 531

OTHER

40. Dissertation 531
41. Published conference proceedings 532
42. Government document 532
43. Pamphlet 532

44. Letter (personal and published) 533

45. Legal source 533

46. Lecture or public address 533

47. Interview 534

48. Television or radio program 534

49. Film or video recording 534

50. Sound recording 535

51. Musical composition 535

52. Live performance 535

53. Work of art 536

54. Map or chart 536

55. Cartoon or comic strip 536

56. Advertisement 536

General Guidelines for MLA Works Cited Entries

AUTHOR NAMES

- Authors listed at the start of an entry should be listed last name first and should end with a period.

- Subsequent author names, or the names of authors or editors listed in the middle of the entry, should be listed first name first.

DATES

- Dates should be formatted day month year: 27 May 2007.

- Use abbreviations for all months except for May, June, and July, which are short enough to spell out: Jan., Feb., Mar., Apr., Aug., Sept., Oct., Nov., Dec. (Months should always be spelled out in the text of your paper.)

TITLES

- Titles of long works—such as books, plays, periodicals, entire Web sites, and films—should be italicized. (Underlining is an acceptable alternative to italics, but note that whichever format you choose, you should be consistent throughout your paper.)

- Titles of short works—such as essays, articles, poems, and songs—should be placed in quotation marks.

PUBLICATION INFORMATION

- Include only the city name.

- Abbreviate familiar words such as "University" ("U") and "Press" ("P") in the publisher's name. Leave out terms such as "Inc." and "Corp."

- Include the medium of publication for each entry ("Print," "Web," "DVD," "Radio," etc.).

MLA works cited entries

AUTHOR INFORMATION

1. Single Author

Author's Last Name, First Name. *Book Title.* Publication City: Publisher, Year of Publication. Medium.

Will, George. *Men at Work: The Craft of Baseball.* New York: Macmillan, 1990. Print.

2. Two or Three Authors

List the authors in the order shown on the title page.

First Author's Last Name, First Name, and Second Author's First Name Last Name. *Book Title.* Publication City: Publisher, Year of Publication. Medium.

Mortenson, Greg, and David Oliver Relin. *Three Cups of Tea: One Man's Mission to Promote Peace . . . One School at a Time.* New York: Penguin, 2007. Print.

Clark, Ricky, George W. Knepper, and Ellice Ronsheim. *Quilts in Community: Ohio's Traditions.* Nashville: Rutledge, 1991. Print.

3. Four or More Authors

When a source has four or more authors, list only the name of the first author (last name first), followed by a comma and the Latin term "et al." (meaning "and others").

First Author's Last Name, First Name, et al. *Book Title.* Publication City: Publisher, Year of Publication. Medium.

Roark, James L., et al. *The American Promise: A History of the United States.* 4th ed. Boston: Bedford, 2009. Print.

4. Corporate Author

If a group or corporation rather than a person appears to be the author, include that name as the work's author in your list of works cited.

Name of Corporation. *Book Title.* Publication City: Publisher, Year of
  Publication. Medium.

Congressional Quarterly. *Presidential Elections: 1789-2004.* Washington:
  CQ, 2005. Print.

5. Unidentified Author

If the author of a work is unknown, begin the works cited entry with the title of the work.

Note that in the example given, "The New York Times" is not italicized because it is a title within a title (see item 19).

Book Title. Publication City: Publisher, Year of Publication. Medium.

The New York Times *Guide to Essential Knowledge: A Desk
  Reference for the Curious Mind.* New York: St. Martin's, 2004.
  Print.

6. Multiple Works by the Same Author

To cite two or more works by the same author in your list of works cited, organize the works alphabetically by title (ignoring introductory articles such as *The* and *A*). Include the author's name only for the first entry; for subsequent entries, type three hyphens followed by a period in place of the author's name.

Author's Last Name, First Name. *Title of Work.* Publication City:
  Publisher, Year of Publication. Medium.

---. *Title of Work.* Publication City: Publisher, Year of Publication.
  Medium.

Friedman, Thomas L. *The Lexus and the Olive Tree: Understanding
  Globalization.* New York: Farrar, 1999. Print.

---. *The World Is Flat: A Brief History of the Twenty-First Century.*
  New York: Farrar, 2005. Print.

BOOKS

7. Book: Basic Format

The example here is the basic format for a book with one author. For author variations, see items 1–6. For more information on the treatment of authors, dates, titles, and publication information, see the box on page 511. After listing the author's name, include the title (and subtitle, if any) of the book, italicized. Next give the publication city, publisher's name, and year. End with the medium of publication.

> Author's Last Name, First Name. *Book Title: Book Subtitle.* Publication
>   City: Publisher, Publication Year. Medium.

> Mah, Adeline Yen. *Falling Leaves: The True Story of an Unwanted
>   Chinese Daughter.* New York: Wiley, 1997. Print.

8. Author and Editor

Include the author's name first if you are referring to the text itself. If, however, you are citing material written by the editor, include the editor's name first, followed by a comma and "ed."

> Author's Last Name, First Name. *Book Title.* Year of Original Publication.
>   Ed. Editor's First Name Last Name. Publication City: Publisher, Year
>   of Publication. Medium.

> Editor's Last Name, First Name, ed. *Book Title.* Year of Original
>   Publication. By Author's First Name Last Name. Publication City:
>   Publisher, Year of Publication. Medium.

> Dickens, Charles. *Great Expectations.* 1861. Ed. Janice Carlisle. Boston:
>   Bedford, 1996. Print.

> Carlisle, Janice, ed. *Great Expectations.* 1861. By Charles Dickens.
>   Boston: Bedford, 1996. Print.

9. Edited Collection

> Editor's Last Name, First Name, ed. *Book Title.* Publication City: Publisher,
>   Year of Publication. Medium.

> Abbott, Megan, ed. *A Hell of a Woman: An Anthology of Female Noir.*
>   Houston: Busted Flush, 2007. Print.

10. Work in an Anthology or a Collection

Author's Last Name, First Name. "Title of Work." *Book Title.* Ed. Editor's
First Name Last Name. Publication City: Publisher, Year of Publication.
Page Numbers of Work. Medium.

Okpewho, Isidore. "The Cousins of Uncle Remus." *The Black Columbiad:
Defining Moments in African American Literature and Culture.* Ed.
Werner Sollors and Maria Diedrich. Cambridge: Harvard UP, 1994.
15-27. Print.

11. Multivolume Work

To cite one volume of a multivolume work, include the volume number after
the title. Including the volume number in your list of works cited means that
you do not need to list it in your in-text citation. To cite two or more
volumes, include the number of volumes after the title. In this case, you
would need to include the specific volume number in each of your in-text
citations for this source.

Author or Editor's Last Name, First Name. *Title of Work.* Vol. Number.
Publication City: Publisher, Year of Publication. Medium.

Odekon, Mehmet, ed. *Encyclopedia of World Poverty.* Vol. 2. Thousand
Oaks: Sage, 2006. Print.

Author or Editor's Last Name, First Name. *Title of Work.* Number of vols.
Publication City: Publisher, Year of Publication. Medium.

Odekon, Mehmet, ed. *Encyclopedia of World Poverty.* 3 vols. Thousand
Oaks: Sage, 2006. Print.

12. Part of a Series

After the title of the book, include the series title and number (if any) from
the title page.

Author or Editor's Last Name, First Name. *Title of Work.* Title and Number
of Series. Publication City: Publisher, Year of Publication. Medium.

Dixon, Kelly J. *Boomtown Saloons: Archaeology and History in Virginia
City.* Wilbur S. Shepperson Ser. in Nevada Hist. Reno: U of Nevada
P, 2005. Print.

How to...
Cite from a book (MLA)

BOOK COVER

TITLE PAGE

Andrews McMeel Publishing, LLC
Kansas City · Sydney · London

1 author

2 book title and subtitle

3 city of publication and publisher

When a publisher lists more than one city, use the first one.

COPYRIGHT PAGE

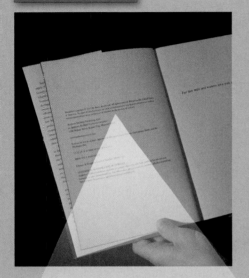

Tomatoland copyright © 2011 by Barry Estabrook.

QUOTED PAGE

145

4 year of publication   **5** page number   **6** medium

MLA
in-text
citation

Describing his vision for the new tomato breed, the seed company owner explained, "We were going to start with roadside growers and chefs. People who were interested in good flavor and good quality" (Estabrook 145).

1 **5**

MLA
works cited
entry

1 **2**

Estabrook, Barry. *Tomatoland: How Modern Industrial Agriculture Destroyed*

3 **4** **6**

Our Most Alluring Fruit. Kansas City: Andrews McMeel, 2011. Print.

13. Republished Book

If the book you are citing was previously published, include the original publication date after the title. If the new publication includes additional text, such as an introduction, include that, along with the name of its author, before the current publication information.

> Author's Last Name, First Name. *Title of Work.* Original Year of
>   Publication. New Material Author's First Name Last Name.
>   Publication City: Publisher, Year of Publication. Medium.

> Twain, Mark. *Life on the Mississippi.* 1883. Introd. Justin Kaplan.
>   New York: Penguin, 2001. Print.

14. Later Edition

Include the edition number as a numeral with letters ("2nd," "3rd," "4th," etc.) followed by "ed." after the book's title. If the edition is listed on the title page as "Revised," without a number, include "Rev. ed." after the title of the book.

> Author(s). *Title of Work.* Number ed. Publication City: Publisher, Year of
>   Publication. Medium.

> Hartt, Frederick, and David G. Wilkins. *History of Italian Renaissance
>   Art: Painting, Sculpture, Architecture.* 4th ed. New York: Abrams,
>   2006. Print.

15. Sacred Work

Include the title of the work as it is shown on the title page. If there is an editor or a translator listed, include the name after the title with either "Ed." or "Trans."

> *Title of Work.* Editor or Translator. Publication City: Publisher, Year of
>   Publication. Medium.

> *The New American Bible.* New York: Catholic Book, 1987. Print.

> *The Qur'an: A New Translation.* Trans. M. A. S. Abdel Haleem.
>   New York: Oxford UP, 2004. Print.

16. Translation

Original Author's Last Name, First Name. *Title of Work.* Trans. Translator's First Name Last Name. Publication City: Publisher, Year of Publication. Medium.

Fasce, Ferdinando. *An American Family: The Great War and Corporate Culture in America.* Trans. Ian Harvey. Columbus: Ohio State UP, 2002. Print.

17. Article in a Reference Book

If there is no article author, begin with the title of the article.

Article Author's Last Name, First Name. "Title of Article." *Book Title.* Publication City: Publisher, Year of Publication. Medium.

Lutzger, Michael A. "Peace Movements." *The Encyclopedia of New York City.* New Haven: Yale UP, 1995. Print.

"The History of the National Anthem." *The World Almanac and Book of Facts 2004.* New York: World Almanac, 2004. Print.

18. Introduction, Preface, Foreword, or Afterword

Book Part Author's Last Name, First Name. Name of Book Part. *Book Title.* Ed. Book Author or Editor's First Name Last Name. Publication City: Publisher, Year of Publication. Page Numbers. Medium.

Groening, Matt. Introduction. *Best American Nonrequired Reading 2006.* Ed. Dave Eggers. Boston: Houghton, 2006. xi-xvii. Print.

19. Title within a Title

If a book's title includes the title of another long work (play, book, or periodical) within it, do not italicize the internal title.

Author's Last Name, First Name. *Book Title* Title within Title. Publication City: Publisher, Year of Publication. Medium.

Norris, Margot. *A Companion to James Joyce's* Ulysses. Boston: Bedford, 1998. Print.

PERIODICALS

20. Article in a Scholarly Journal

List the author(s) first, then include the article title, the journal title (in italics), the volume number, the issue number, the publication year, the page numbers, and the publication medium.

> Author's Last Name, First Name. "Title of Article." *Title of Journal* Volume Number.Issue Number (Year of Publication): Page Numbers. Medium.

> Burt, Stephen, et al. "Does Poetry Have a Social Function?" *Poetry* 189.4 (2007): 297-309. Print.

21. Article in a Scholarly Journal with No Volume Number

Follow the format for scholarly journals (as shown in item 20), but list only the issue number before the year of publication.

> Author's Last Name, First Name. "Title of Article." *Title of Journal* Issue Number (Year of Publication): Page Numbers. Medium.

> Lee, Christopher. "Enacting the Asian Canadian." *Canadian Literature* 199 (2008): 6-27. Print.

22. Magazine Article

Include the date of publication rather than volume and issue numbers. (See abbreviation rules in the box on p. 511.) If page numbers are not consecutive, add "+" after the initial page.

> Author's Last Name, First Name. "Title of Article." *Title of Magazine* Date of Publication: Page Numbers. Medium.

> Fredenburg, Peter. "Mekong Harvests: Balancing Shrimp and Rice Farming in Vietnam." *World and I* Mar. 2002: 204+. Print.

23. Newspaper Article

If a specific edition is listed on the newspaper's masthead, such as "Late Edition" or "National Edition," include an abbreviation of this after the date. If page numbers are not consecutive, add "+" after the initial page.

Author's Last Name, First Name. "Title of Article." *Title of Newspaper* Date
    of Publication: Page Numbers. Medium.

Smith, Stephen. "Taunting May Affect Health of Obese Youths."
    Boston Globe 11 July 2007: A1+. Print.

Author's Last Name, First Name. "Title of Article." *Title of Newspaper* Date
    of Publication, Spec. ed.: Page Numbers. Medium.

Rohde, David. "Taliban Push Poppy Production to a Record Again."
    New York Times 26 Aug. 2007, natl. ed.: 3. Print.

If a newspaper numbers each section individually, without attaching
letters to the page numbers, include the section number in your citation.

Author's Last Name, First Name. "Title of Article." *Title of Newspaper* Date
    of Publication, sec. Section Number: Page Numbers. Medium.

Bowley, Graham. "Keeping Up with the Windsors." *New York Times*
    15 July 2007, sec. 3: 1+. Print.

24. Editorial

For a newspaper editorial, do not include an author, but do include the word
"Editorial," followed by a period, after the title of the article.

"Title of Article." Editorial. *Title of Newspaper* Date of Publication: Page
    Number(s). Medium.

"Living on Iraq Time." Editorial. *New York Times* 28 May 2007: A15.
    Print.

25. Letter to the Editor

Letter Writer's Last Name, First Name. Letter. *Title of Newspaper* Date of
    Publication: Page Number. Medium.

Zita, Ken. Letter. *Financial Times* 16 Aug. 2006: 8. Print.

26. Unsigned Article

"Title of Article." *Title of Newspaper* Date of Publication: Page Number. Medium.

"Justice Probes Lenders." *Washington Post* 26 July 2007: DO2. Print.

MAGAZINE COVER

ARTICLE

March 2010

By Marcus E. Raichle

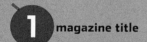

1 magazine title

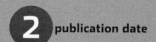

2 publication date

3 author

4 article title

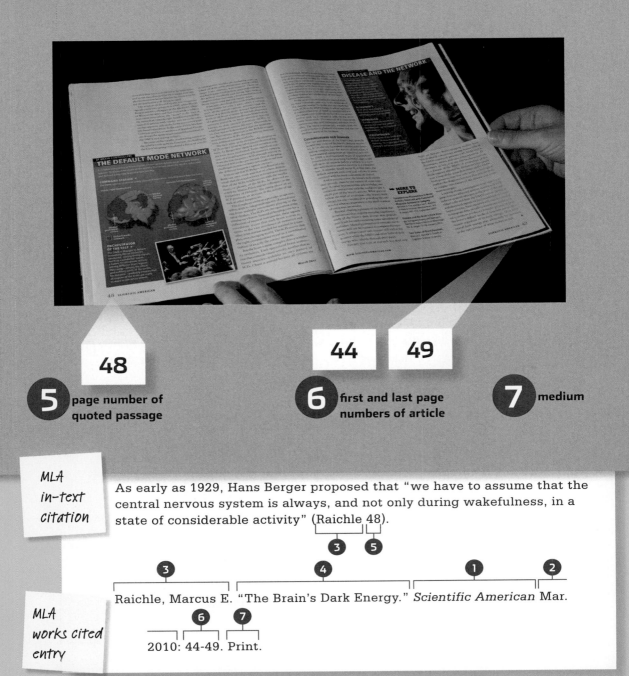

48

5 page number of quoted passage

44 **49**

6 first and last page numbers of article

7 medium

MLA in-text citation

As early as 1929, Hans Berger proposed that "we have to assume that the central nervous system is always, and not only during wakefulness, in a state of considerable activity" (Raichle 48).

3 **5**

3 **4** **1** **2**

Raichle, Marcus E. "The Brain's Dark Energy." *Scientific American* Mar.

6 **7**

2010: 44-49. Print.

MLA works cited entry

27. Review

Add "Rev. of" before the title of the work being reviewed.

> Review Author's Last Name, First Name. "Title of Review." Rev. of *Title of Work Being Reviewed*, by Author of Work Being Reviewed First Name Last Name. *Title of Publication in Which Review Appears* Volume.Issue (Year of Publication): Page Numbers. Medium.

> Levin, Yuval. "Diagnosis and Cure." Rev. of *Sick: The Untold Story of America's Health-Care Crisis and the People Who Pay the Price*, by Jonathan Cohn. *Commentary* 124.1 (2007): 80-82. Print.

ELECTRONIC SOURCES

28. Short Work from a Web Site

> Short Work Author's Last Name, First Name. "Title of Short Work." *Title of Web Site.* Name of Sponsoring Organization, Date of Publication or Most Recent Update. Medium. Date of Access.

> McFee, Gord. "Why 'Revisionism' Isn't." *The Holocaust History Project.* Holocaust Hist. Project, 15 May 1999. Web. 10 Sept. 2011.

29. Entire Web Site

> Short Work Author's Last Name, First Name. *Title of Web Site.* Name of Sponsoring Organization, Date of Publication or Most Recent Update. Medium. Date of Access.

> Myers, Robert, et al. *Exploring the Environment.* Wheeling Jesuit U, 28 Apr. 2005. Web. 12 Sept. 2007.

30. Entire blog (Weblog)

Include any of the following elements that are available. If there is no publisher or sponsoring organization, use the abbreviation "N.p."

> Blog Author's Last Name, First Name. *Title of Blog.* Name of Sponsoring Organization (if any), Date of Most Recent Post. Medium. Date of Access.

> Sellers, Heather. *Word after Word.* N.p., 26 Aug. 2011. Web. 14 Sep. 2011.

31. Entry in a blog (Weblog)

Entry Author's Last Name, First Name. "Title of Blog Entry." *Title of Blog.* Name of Sponsoring Organization (if any), Date of Entry. Medium. Date of Access.

Sellers, Heather. "East Coast." *Word after Word.* N.p., 7 Nov. 2007. Web. 30 Jan. 2008.

32. Online Book

Book Author's Last Name, First Name. *Title of Book.* Book Publication City: Book Publisher, Book Publication Year. *Title of Web Site.* Medium. Date of Access.

Riis, Jacob. *How the Other Half Lives.* New York: Scribner's, 1890. *Bartleby.com: Great Books Online.* Web. 6 Nov. 2010.

33. Work from a Library Subscription Service (such as *InfoTrac* or *FirstSearch*)

Follow the format for periodical articles as shown in items 20–27, above. If page numbers are not available, use the abbreviation "n. pag." End the citation with the database name (in italics), the publication medium ("Web"), and the date of access.

Article Author(s). "Title of Article." *Title of Periodical* Volume Number.Issue Number (Year of Publication): Page Numbers. *Name of Database.* Medium. Date of Access.

Cotugna, Nancy, and Connie Vickery. "Educating Early Childhood Teachers about Nutrition: A Collaborative Venture." *Childhood Education* 83.4 (2007): 194-98. *Academic OneFile.* Web. 10 July 2011.

How to...
Cite from a Web site (MLA)

TOP OF WEB PAGE

1 Web site title

2 article title

3 JAD ABUMRAD and ROBERT KRULWICH
author

4 August 17, 2010
update date

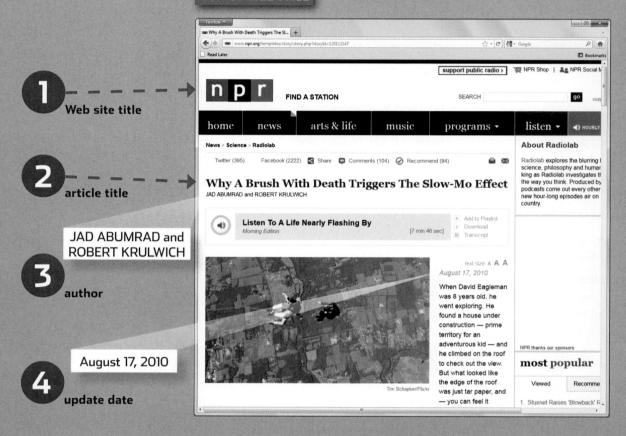

Firefox
Why A Brush With Death Triggers The Sl...

www.npr.org/templates/story/story.php?storyId=129112147

Google

Read Later

Bookmarks

support public radio >   NPR Shop | NPR Social

npr   FIND A STATION

SEARCH   go   sup

home   news   arts & life   music   programs ▾   listen ▾   HOURLY

News > Science > Radiolab

Twitter (395)   Facebook (2222)   Share   Comments (104)   Recommend (94)

Why A Brush With Death Triggers The Slow-Mo Effect
JAD ABUMRAD and ROBERT KRULWICH

Listen To A Life Nearly Flashing By
Morning Edition   [7 min 46 sec]

+ Add to Playlist
↓ Download
Transcript

text size A A A
August 17, 2010

When David Eagleman was 8 years old, he went exploring. He found a house under construction — prime territory for an adventurous kid — and he climbed on the roof to check out the view. But what looked like the edge of the roof was just tar paper, and — you can feel it

Tim Schapker/Flickr

About Radiolab
Radiolab explores the blurring science, philosophy and human king as Radiolab investigates t the way you think. Produced by podcasts come out every other new hour-long episodes air on country.

NPR thanks our sponsors

most popular
Viewed   Recomme

1. Stuxnet Raises 'Blowback' R

BOTTOM OF WEB PAGE

7 medium

Copyright 2011 NPR

5 Web site sponsor

August 25, 2011

6 date of access

MLA in-text citation

Dr. Eagleman suggests that moments of near-death panic prompt the brain to form memories of otherwise-ignored stimuli, and "when you read that back out, the experience feels like it must have taken a very long time" (Abumrad and Krulwich).

3

3   **2**

MLA works cited entry

Abumrad, Jad, and Robert Krulwich. "Why a Brush with Death Triggers the

1 5   4   7   6

Slow-Mo Effect." *NPR*. NPR, 17 Aug. 2010. Web. 25 Aug. 2011.

How to...
Cite from a database (MLA)

5 volume and issue number

6 publication date

7 name of database

DATABASE SCREEN

1 journal title

2 article title

3 author

4 page numbers

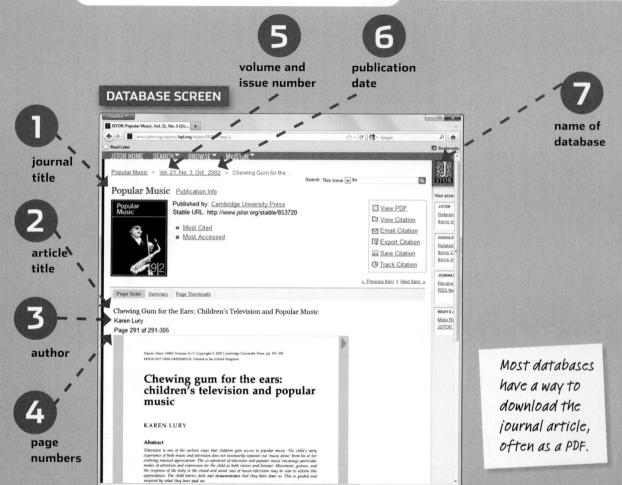

Most databases have a way to download the journal article, often as a PDF.

PDF VIEW

Use the PDF to double-check your citation elements. If you print the PDF, the medium is still Web, not print.

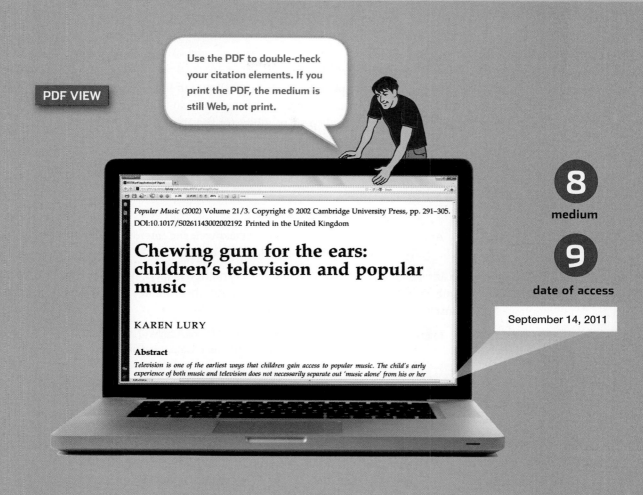

8 medium

9 date of access

September 14, 2011

Popular Music (2002) Volume 21/3. Copyright © 2002 Cambridge University Press, pp. 291–305.
DOI:10.1017/S0261143002002192 Printed in the United Kingdom

Chewing gum for the ears: children's television and popular music

KAREN LURY

Abstract

Television is one of the earliest ways that children gain access to popular music. The child's early experience of both music and television does not necessarily separate out 'music alone' from his or her

---

MLA in-text citation

Children accept even nonsensical lyrics as legitimate musical expression, and one researcher calls their tolerance "a mode of engagement carried productively into the adult's experience of popular songs" (Lury 300).

MLA works cited entry

Lury, Karen. "Chewing Gum for the Ears: Children's Television and

Popular Music." *Popular Music* 21.3 (2002): 291-305. *JSTOR*.

Web. 14 Sept. 2011.

34. Work from an Online Periodical

Follow the format for periodical articles as shown in items 20–27, above, listing the Web site name, in italics, as the periodical title. For articles in scholarly journals, include page numbers (or the abbreviation "n. pag." if page numbers are unavailable). End the citation with the publication medium ("Web") and the date of access.

> Journal Article Author(s). "Title of Article." *Title of Online Journal* Volume Number.Issue Number (Year of Publication): Page Numbers (or "n. pag."). Medium. Date of Access.

> Arora, Vibha, and Justin Scott-Coe. "Fieldwork and Interdisciplinary Research." *Reconstruction* 9.1 (2009): n. pag. Web. 13 Apr. 2009.

For articles appearing in online magazines and newspapers, list the publisher's name after the online periodical title. Page numbers are not required for nonscholarly articles published online.

> Magazine or Newspaper Article Author(s). "Title of Article." *Title of Online Periodical.* Periodical Publisher, Publication Date. Medium. Date of Access.

> Gogoi, Pallavi. "The Trouble with Business Ethics." *BusinessWeek.* McGraw, 25 June 2007. Web. 3 Oct. 2011.

35. Online Posting

> Post Author's Last Name, First Name. "Title (or Subject) of Post." *Title of Message Board.* Date of Post. Medium. Date of Access.

> Winkleman, Tallulah. "Reducing Your Food Miles." *Farm Folk City Folk Bulletin.* 13 July 2007. Web. 10 Sept. 2010.

36. E-mail

> E-mail Author's Last Name, First Name. "Subject of E-mail." Message to the author (or Name of Recipient). Date Sent. Medium.

> Gingrich, Newt. "Drill here. Drill now." Message to the author. 20 May 2008. E-mail.

37. CD-ROM

CD-ROM Author's (if any) Last Name, First Name. *Title of CD-ROM.*
Publication City: Publisher, Publication Year. Medium.

History through Art: The Twentieth Century. San Jose: Fogware,
2001. CD-ROM.

38. Podcast

For downloaded podcasts, include the file type, such as "MP3 file," as the
medium. If the file type is unknown, use the term "MP3 file."

"Title of Podcast." Names and Function of Pertinent Individual(s). *Title
of Web Site.* Name of Sponsoring Organization, Date of Publication.
Medium.

"Capping Pollution at the Source." Prod. Lester Graham. *The Environment
Report.* Nature Conservancy, 31 July 2006. MP3 file.

For podcasts that were listened to directly from the host Web site, list "Web"
as the medium and include an access date at the end.

39. Entry in a Wiki

Wiki content is continually edited by its users, so there is no author to cite.

"Title of Entry." *Title of Wiki.* Name of Sponsoring Organization, Date of
Publication or Most Recent Update. Medium. Date of Access.

"Emo." *Wikipedia.* Wikimedia Foundation, 24 June 2008. Web.
2 Feb. 2009.

OTHER

40. Dissertation

For unpublished dissertations, put the title in quotation marks.

Author's Last Name, First Name. "Dissertation Title." Diss. Name of
University, Year. Medium.

Mooney, John Alfonso. "Shadows of Dominion: White Men and Power
in Slavery, War, and the New South." Diss. U of Virginia, 2007.
Print.

If the dissertation is published as a book, italicize the title and include the publication information.

Author's Last Name, First Name. *Dissertation Title.* Diss. Name of University, Year. Publication City: Publisher, Publication Year. Medium.

Beetham, Christopher A. *Echoes of Scripture in the Letter of Paul to the Colossians.* Diss. Wheaton Coll. Graduate School, 2005. Boston: Brill, 2008. Print.

41. Published Conference Proceedings

List the editor(s) name(s), followed by "ed." or "eds." and italicize the title of the proceedings. Before the conference information, add "Proc. of" and follow with the conference title, dates, and location.

Editor(s), ed(s). *Title of Proceedings.* Proc. of Conference Title, Conference Date, Conference Location. Publication City: Publisher, Year. Medium.

Westfahl, G., and George Slusser, eds. *Nursery Realms: Children in the World of Science Fiction, Fantasy, and Horror.* Proc. of J. Lloyd Eaton Conf. on Science Fiction and Fantasy Lit., Jan. 1999, U of California, Riverside. Athens: U of Georgia P, 1999. Print.

42. Government Document

Begin by listing the government (usually a country or state) that issued the document, and then list the specific department or agency. Most U.S. government documents are published by the Washington-based Government Printing Office (GPO).

Government. Department or Agency. *Title of Document.* Publication City: Publisher, Date of Publication. Medium.

United States. Dept. of Labor. *Summary Data from the Consumer Price Index News Release.* Washington: GPO, Oct. 2006. Print.

43. Pamphlet

Pamphlet Title. Publication City: Publisher, Year of Publication. Medium.

50 Ways to Be Water Smart. West Palm Beach: South Florida Water Management Dist., 2006. Print.

44. Letter (Personal and Published)

For personal letters that you received, give the name of the letter writer followed by the description "Letter to the author." For publication medium, list "TS" ("typescript") for typed letters or "MS" ("manuscript") for handwritten letters. For e-mail, see item 36.

Letter Writer's Last Name, First Name. Letter to the author. Date of Letter. Medium.

Nader, Ralph. Letter to the author. 15 Oct. 2010. TS.

For published letters, list the letter writer as well as the recipient.

Letter Writer's Last Name, First Name. Letter to First Name Last Name.
    Date of Letter. *Title of Book.* Ed. Editor's First Name Last Name.
    Publication City: Publisher, Year. Medium.

Lincoln, Abraham. Letter to T. J. Pickett. 16 Apr. 1859. *Wit & Wisdom
    of Abraham Lincoln: As Reflected in His Letters and Speeches.*
    Ed. H. Jack Lang. Mechanicsburg: Stackpole, 2006. Print.

45. Legal Source

List the names of laws or acts (with no underlining or quotation marks), followed by the Public Law number and the date. Also give the Statutes at Large cataloging number and the medium. For other legal sources, refer to *The Bluebook: A Uniform System of Citation*, 19th ed. (Cambridge: Harvard Law Review Assn., 2010).

Title of Law. Pub. L. number. Stat. number. Date of Enactment. Medium.

No Child Left Behind Act of 2001. Pub. L. 107-110. Stat. 1425. 8 Jan.
    2002. Print.

46. Lecture or Public Address

For the medium, describe the type of speech ("Reading," "Address," "Lecture," etc.).

Speaker's Last Name, First Name. "Title of Speech." Name of Sponsoring
    Institution. Location of Speech. Date of Speech. Medium.

Wallace, David Foster. "Kenyon Commencement Speech." Kenyon
    College. Gambier. 21 May 2005. Address.

47. Interview

For published or broadcast interviews, give the title (if any), followed by the publication or broadcast information for the source that aired or published the interview. If there is no title, use "Interview" followed by a period.

> Interviewee's Last Name, First Name. "Title of Interview." *Book, Periodical, Web Site, or Program Title.* Publication or Broadcast Information (see specific entry for guidance). Medium.

> Rushdie, Salman. "Humanism and the Territory of Novelists." *Humanist* 67.4 (2007): 19-21. Print.

> Roth, Philip. Interview. *Fresh Air*. Natl. Public Radio. WQCS, Fort Pierce. 18 May 2006. Radio.

For interviews that you conduct yourself, include the name of the interviewee, interview type ("Personal interview," "E-mail interview," "Telephone interview," etc.), and date.

> Dean, Howard. E-mail interview. 3 May 2011.

48. Television or Radio Program

If you access an archived show online, include the access date after the medium.

> "Episode Title." *Program Title. or Series Title.* Network. Local Channel's Call Letters, City (if any). Air Date. Medium. Date of Access.

> "Poirot: Murder on the Orient Express." *Masterpiece*. PBS. WGBH, Boston. 22 May 2011. Television.

> "Past Deals Come Back to Haunt UAW." *Marketplace Morning Report*. Amer. Public Media. 29 June 2007. Web. 2 Nov. 2007.

49. Film or Video Recording

If you accessed the film via videocassette or DVD, include the distributor name and release date.

> *Film Title.* Dir. Director's First Name Last Name. Original Release Date. Distributor, Release Date of Recording. Medium.

> *Rear Window*. Dir. Alfred Hitchcock. 1954. Universal, 2001. DVD.

To highlight a particular individual's performance or contribution, begin
with that person's name, followed by a descriptive label (for example, "perf."
or "chor.").

> Stewart, James, perf. *Rear Window*. Dir. Alfred Hitchcock. 1954.
> Universal, 2001. DVD.

50. Sound Recording

> Performer's Last Name, First Name or Band's Name. "Title of Song." *Title
> of Album.* Record Label, Year. Medium.

> Thomas, Irma. "Time Is on My Side." *Live: Simply the Best*. Rounder,
> 1991. CD.

51. Musical Composition

Long works such as operas, ballets, and named symphonies should be
italicized. Additional information, such as key or movement, may be added
at the end.

> Composer's Last Name, First Name. *Title of Long Work.* Artists' names.
> Orchestra. Conductor. Manufacturer, Date. Medium.

> Mozart, Wolfgang Amadeus. *Le nozze di Figaro*. Perf. Alfred Poel,
> Cesare Siepi, Fernando Corena, and Hilde Gueden. Vienna
> Philharmonic Orchestra. Cond. Erich Kleiber. Decca, 1955. LP.

> Beethoven, Ludwig van. Sonata no. 16 in G major, op. 31. Perf. John
> O'Connor. Telarc, 1990. CD.

52. Live Performance

> *Performance Title.* By Author Name. Dir. Director Name. Perf. Performer
> Name(s). Theater or Venue Name, City. Date of Performance. Medium.

> *How to Succeed in Business without Really Trying*. By Frank Loesser.
> Dir. Rob Ashford. Perf. Daniel Radcliffe and John Larroquette. Al
> Hirschfeld Theatre, New York. 26 Mar. 2011. Performance.

53. Work of Art

Artist's Last Name, First Name. *Title of Artwork.* Date. Institution, City.

Sargent, John Singer. *The Daughters of Edward Darley Boit.* 1882. Museum of Fine Arts, Boston.

A publication medium is required only for reproduced works, such as in books or online. For works accessed on the Web, include an access date.

Kapoor, Anish. *Ishi's Light.* 2003. Tate Mod., London. *Tate Online.* Web. 4 Oct. 2007.

54. Map or Chart

Title of Map. Map. Publication City: Publisher Name, Year. Medium.

Northwest Territories and Yukon Territory. Map. Vancouver: Intl. Travel Maps, 1998. Print.

If you accessed the map online, include an access date.

Cambodia. Map. *Google Maps.* 2009. Web. 15 April 2009.

55. Cartoon or Comic Strip

Artist's Last Name, First Name. "Cartoon Title" (if given). Cartoon. *Title of Periodical* Date: Page Number. Medium.

Chast, Roz. "National Everything Awareness Day." Cartoon. *New Yorker* 3 Sept. 2007: 107. Print.

56. Advertisement

Product Name. Advertisement. *Title of Periodical* Date: Section Number: Page Number(s). Medium.

Louis Vuitton. Advertisement. *New York Times* 22 July 2007, sec. 9: 8-9. Print.

If you accessed the advertisement online, include an access date.

Dodge Journey. Advertisement. Dodge YouTube Channel 10 Sept. 2011. Web.

Format an MLA paper correctly.   You can now find software to format your academic papers in MLA style, but the key alignments for such documents are usually simple enough for you to manage on your own.

- Set up a header on the right-hand side of each page, one-half inch from the top. The header should include your last name and the page number.

- In the upper left on the first—or title—page, include your name, the instructor's name, the course title and/or number, and the date.

- Center the title above the first line of text.

- Use one-inch margins on all sides of the paper.

- Double-space the entire paper (including your name and course information, the title, and any block quotations).

- Indent paragraphs one-half inch.

- Use block quotations for quoted material of four or more lines. Indent block quotations one inch from the left margin.

- Do not include a separate title page unless your instructor requires one.

- When you document using MLA style, you'll need to create an alphabetically arranged works cited page at the end of the paper so that readers have a convenient list of all the books, articles, and other data you have used.

Miller 1

Melissa Miller

Professor Spahr

English 112

November 23, 20--

Distinguishing the *Other* in Two Works by Tolstoy

The Cossacks and the Chechens are two very different peoples; they share neither language nor religion. The Cossacks are Russian-speaking Christians, while the Chechens speak a Caucasian language and follow Islam. Certainly, Leo Tolstoy (1828-1910) knew these facts, since he spent a significant length of time in the Caucasus. However, it is difficult to distinguish them as different peoples in Tolstoy's work. The Cossacks in Tolstoy's novel of the same name (1863) and the Chechens in his story "A Prisoner in the Caucasus" (1872) share so many cultural and ethnic features—appearance, reverence for warriors and horses, their behavior—that they appear to be the same people. As a result, their deep cultural differences all but disappear to Tolstoy and his European readers.

From Tolstoy's descriptions of the Cossacks and the Chechens, they appear identical: Both groups are dark in complexion, wear *beshmets*, and are wild. The Cossack men have black beards and Maryanka has black eyes (*Cossacks* 30, 55), while Dina has black hair and a face like her father's, "the dark man" ("Prisoner" 316). In addition to the black, both groups are red in countenance: Uncle Yeroshka is "cinnamon-colored" (*Cossacks* 60), Maryanka is sunburned (93), and Kazi

Student's name, instructor's name, course title, and date appear in upper-left corner.

One-inch margin on all sides of page.

Half-inch indent for new paragraph.

Center the title.

Double-space all elements on title page.

Source and page number appear in parentheses.

Miller 6

Works Cited

Said, Edward W. *Orientalism*. New York: Vintage, 1976. Print.

Tolstoy, Leo. *The Cossacks*. New York: Scribner's, 1899. Print.

---. "A Prisoner in the Caucasus." *Walk in the Light and*
Twenty-three Tales. Maryknoll: Orbis, 2003. 78. Print.

"Works Cited" centered at top of page.

Entire page is double-spaced: no extra spaces between entries.

Begins on separate page.

Entries arranged alphabetically.

Second and subsequent lines of entries indent five spaces or one-half inch.

50 APA Documentation and Format

cite in APA

APA (American Psychological Association) style is used in many social science disciplines. For full details about APA style and documentation, consult the *Publication Manual of the American Psychological Association*, 6th ed. (2010). The basic details for documenting sources and formatting research papers in APA style are presented below.

Document sources according to convention.   When you use sources in a research paper, you are required to cite the source, letting readers know that the information has been borrowed from somewhere else and showing them how to find the original material if they would like to study it further. Like MLA style, APA includes two parts: a brief in-text citation and a more detailed reference entry.

In-text citations should include the author's name, the year the material was published, and the page number(s) that the borrowed material can be found on. The author's name and year of publication are generally included in a signal phrase that introduces the passage, and the page number is included in parentheses after the borrowed text. Note that for APA style, the verb in the signal phrase should be in the past tense (*reported*, as in the example on p. 541) or present perfect tense (*has reported*).

> Millman (2007) reported that college students around the country are participating in Harry Potter discussion groups, sports activities, and even courses for college credit (p. A4).

Alternatively, the author's name and year can be included in parentheses with the page number.

> College students around the country are participating in Harry Potter discussion groups, sports activities, and even courses for college credit (Millman, 2007, p. A4).

The list of references at the end of the paper contains a more detailed citation that repeats the author's name and publication year and includes the title and additional publication information about the source. Inclusive page numbers are included for periodical articles and parts of books.

> Millman, S. (2007). Generation hex. *The Chronicle of Higher Education,* 53(46), A4.

Both in-text citations and reference entries can vary greatly depending on the type of source cited (book, periodical, Web site, etc.). The following pages give specific examples of how to cite a wide range of sources in APA style.

Directory of APA In-Text Citations

1. Author named in signal phrase 543
2. Author named in parentheses 543
3. With block quotations 543
4. Two authors 543
5. Three to five authors 544
6. Six or more authors 544
7. Group, corporate, or government author 544
8. Two or more works by the same author 545
9. Authors with the same last name 545
10. Unknown author 545
11. Personal communication 545
12. Electronic source 546
13. Musical recording 546
14. Secondary source 546
15. Multiple sources in same citation 546

General Guidelines for In-Text Citations in APA Style

AUTHOR NAMES

- Give last names only, unless two authors have the same last name (see item 9 on p. 545) or if the source is a personal communication (see item 11 on p. 545). In these cases, include the first initial before the last name ("J. Smith").

DATES

- Give only the year in the in-text citation. The one exception to this rule is personal communications, which should include a full date (see item 11 on p. 545).

- Months and days for periodical publications should not be given with the year in in-text citations; this information will be provided as needed in the reference entry at the end of your paper.

- If you have two or more works by the same author in the same year, see item 8 on page 545.

- If you can't locate a date for your source, include the abbreviation "n.d." (for "no date") in place of the date in parentheses.

TITLES

- Titles of works generally do not need to be given in in-text citations. Exceptions include works with no author and two or more works by the same author. See items 8 and 10 on page 545 for details.

PAGE NUMBERS

- Include page numbers whenever possible in parentheses after borrowed material. Put "p." (or "pp.") before the page number(s).

- When you have a range of pages, list the full first and last page numbers (for example, "311-324"). If the borrowed material isn't printed on consecutive pages, list all the pages it appears on (for example, "A1, A4-A6").

- If page numbers are not available, use section names and/or paragraph (written as "para.") numbers when available to help a reader locate a specific quotation. See items 7 and 12 on pages 544 and 546 for examples.

APA in-text citation

1. Author Named in Signal Phrase

Doyle (2005) asserted that "although some immigrants are a burden on the welfare system, as a group they pay far more in taxes than they receive in government benefits, such as public education and social services" (p. 25).

2. Author Named in Parentheses

"Although some immigrants are a burden on the welfare system, as a group they pay far more in taxes than they receive in government benefits, such as public education and social services" (Doyle, 2005, p. 25).

3. With Block Quotations

For excerpts of forty or more words, indent the quoted material one-half inch and include the page number at the end of the quotation after the end punctuation.

Pollan (2006) suggested that the prized marbled meat that results from feeding corn to cattle (ruminants) may not be good for us:

> Yet this corn-fed meat is demonstrably less healthy for us, since it contains more saturated fat and less omega-3 fatty acids than the meat of animals fed grass. A growing body of research suggests that many of the health problems associated with eating beef are really problems with corn-fed beef. . . . In the same way ruminants are ill adapted to eating corn, humans in turn may be poorly adapted to eating ruminants that eat corn. (p. 75)

4. Two Authors

Note that if you name the authors in the parentheses, connect them with an ampersand (&).

Sharpe and Young (2005) reported that new understandings about tooth development, along with advances in stem cell technology, have brought researchers closer to the possibility of producing replacement teeth from human tissue (p. 36).

New understandings about tooth development, along with advances in stem cell technology, have brought researchers closer to the possibility of producing replacement teeth from human tissue (Sharpe & Young, 2005, p. 36).

5. Three to Five Authors

The first time you cite a source with three to five authors, list all their names in either the signal phrase or parentheses. If you cite the same source again in your paper, use just the first author's name followed by "et al."

> Swain, Scahill, Lombroso, King, and Leckman (2007) pointed out that "[a]lthough no ideal treatment for tics has been established, randomized clinical trials have clarified the short-term benefits of a number of agents" (p. 947).

> Swain et al. (2007) claimed that "[m]any tics are often under partial voluntary control, evidenced by patients' capacity to suppress them for brief periods of time" (p. 948).

6. Six or More Authors

List the first author's name only, followed by "et al."

> Grossoehme et al. (2007) examined the disparity between the number of pediatricians who claim that religion and spirituality are important factors in treating patients and those who actually use religion and spirituality in their practice (p. 968).

7. Group, Corporate, or Government Author

> The resolution called on the United States to ban all forms of torture in interrogation procedures (American Psychological Association [APA], 2007, para. 1). It also reasserted "the organization's absolute opposition to all forms of torture and abuse, regardless of circumstance" (APA, 2007, para. 5).

8. Two or More Works by the Same Author

To see reference list entries for these sources, see item 6 on page 550.

> Shermer (2005a) has reported that false acupuncture (in placebo
> experiments) is as effective as true acupuncture (p. 30).

> Shermer (2005b) has observed that psychics rely on vague and
> flattering statements, such as "You are wise in the ways of the world,
> a wisdom gained through hard experience rather than book learning,"
> to earn the trust of their clients (p. 6).

9. Authors with the Same Last Name

Distinguish the authors by including initials of their first names.

> M. Dunn (2003) argued that, in fact, the opposite may be true (p. 5).

10. Unknown Author

Identify the item by its title. However, if the author is actually listed as
"Anonymous," treat this term as the author in your citation.

> Tilapia provides more protein when eaten than it consumes when alive,
> making it a sustainable fish ("Dream Fish," 2007, 26).

> The book *Go Ask Alice* (Anonymous, 1971) portrayed the fictional life of
> a teenager who is destroyed by her addiction to drugs.

11. Personal Communication

If you cite personal letters or e-mails or your own interviews for your
research paper, cite these as personal communication in your in-text citation, including the author of the material (with first initial), the term
"personal communication," and the date. Personal communications should
not be included in your reference list.

> One instructor has argued that it is important to "make peer review a
> lot more than a proofreading/grammar/mechanics exercise" (J. Bone,
> personal communication, July 27, 2007).

To include the author of a personal communication in the signal phrase, use the following format:

> J. Bone (personal communication, July 27, 2007) has argued that it is important to "make peer review a lot more than a proofreading/ grammar/mechanics exercise."

12. Electronic Source

If page numbers are not given, use section names or paragraph numbers to help your readers track down the source.

> A recent report showed that, in 2006, "59 percent of KIPP fifth graders outperformed their local districts in reading, and 74 percent did so in mathematics" ("Charter Schools/Choice," 2007, para. 4).

13. Musical Recording

> In an ironic twist, Mick Jagger sings backup on the song "You're So Vain" (Simon, 1972, track 3).

14. Secondary Source

Include the name of the original author in the signal phrase. In the parentheses, add "as cited in," and give the author of the quoted material along with the date and page number. Note that your end-of-paper reference entry for this material will be listed under the secondary source name (Pollan) rather than the original writer (Howard).

> Writing in 1943, Howard asserted that "artificial manures lead inevitably to artificial nutrition, artificial food, artificial animals, and finally to artificial men and women" (as cited in Pollan, 2006, p. 148).

15. Multiple Sources in Same Citation

If one statement in your paper can be attributed to multiple sources, alphabetically list all the authors with dates, separated by semicolons.

> Most historians agree that the Puritan religion played a significant role in the hysteria surrounding the Salem witchcraft trials (Karlsen, 1998; Norton, 2002; Reis, 1997).

Directory of APA Reference Entries

AUTHOR INFORMATION

1. One author 549
2. Two authors 549
3. Three or more authors 549
4. Group, corporate, or government author 549
5. Unidentified author 549
6. Multiple works by the same author 550

BOOKS

7. Book: basic format 550
8. Author and editor 550
9. Work in an anthology or a collection 550
10. Edited collection 551
11. Multivolume work 551
12. Later edition 551
13. Translation 552
14. Article in a reference book 552

PERIODICALS

15. Article in a journal paginated by volume 552
16. Article in a journal paginated by issue 552
17. Magazine article 553

18. Newspaper article 553
19. Letter to the editor 553
20. Review 553

ELECTRONIC SOURCES

21. Article with a DOI 554
22. Article without a DOI 554
23. Article in Internet-only periodical 554
24. Multipage Web site 554
25. Part of a Web site 555
26. Online posting 555
27. Computer software 555
28. Entry in a blog (Weblog) 555
29. Podcast 555
30. Entry in a wiki 555

OTHER

31. Group, corporate, or government document 560
32. Published conference proceedings 560
33. Dissertation abstract 560
34. Film 561
35. Television program 561
36. Musical recording 561

General Guidelines for Reference Entries in APA Style

AUTHOR NAMES

- When an author's name appears *before* the title of the work, list it by last name followed by a comma and first initial followed by a period. (Middle initials may also be included.)
- If an author, editor, or other name is listed *after* the title, then the initial(s) precede the last name (see examples on pp. 000).
- When multiple authors are listed, their names should be separated by commas, and an ampersand (&) should precede the final author.

DATES

- For scholarly journals, include only the year (2007).
- For monthly magazines, include the year followed by a comma and the month (2007, May).
- For newspapers and weekly magazines, include the year, followed by a comma and the month and the day (2007, May 27).
- Access dates for electronic documents use the month-day-year format: "Retrieved May 27, 2007."
- Months should not be abbreviated.
- If a date is not available, use "n.d." (for "no date") in parentheses.

TITLES

- Titles of periodicals should be italicized, and all major words capitalized (*Psychology Today*; *Journal of Archaeological Research*).
- Titles of books, Web sites, and other nonperiodical long works should be italicized. Capitalize the first word of the title (and subtitle, if any) and proper nouns only (*Legacy of ashes: The history of the CIA*).
- For short works such as essays, articles, and chapters, capitalize the first word of the title (and subtitle, if any) and proper nouns only (The black sites: A rare look inside the CIA's secret interrogation program).

PAGE NUMBERS

- Reference entries for periodical articles and sections of books should include the range of pages: "245-257." For material in parentheses, include the abbreviation "p." or "pp." before the page numbers ("pp. A4-A5").
- If the pages are not continuous, list all the pages separated by commas: "245, 249, 301-306."

APA reference entries

AUTHOR INFORMATION

1. One Author

> Chopra, A. (2007). *King of Bollywood: Shah Rukh Khan and the seductive world of Indian cinema.* New York, NY: Warner Books.

2. Two Authors

> Johnson, M. E., & Vickers, C. (2005). *Threading the generations: A Mississippi family's quilt legacy.* Jackson, MS: University Press of Mississippi.

3. Three or More Authors

List every author up to and including seven; for a work with eight or more authors, give the first six names followed by three ellipsis dots and the last author's name.

> Thompson, M., Grace, C. O., & Cohen, L. J. (2001). *Best friends, worst enemies: Understanding the social lives of children.* New York, NY: Ballantine Books.

> Vitiello, B., Brent, D. A., Greenhill, L. L., Emslie, G., Wells, K., Walkup, J. T., . . . Zelazny, J. (2009). Depressive symptoms and clinical status during the treatment of adolescent suicide attempters (TASA) study. *Journal of the American Academy of Child & Adolescent Psychiatry, 48,* 997-1004.

4. Group, Corporate, or Government Author

In many cases, the group name is the same as the publisher. Instead of repeating the group name, use the term "Author" for the publisher's name.

> Society for the Protection of the Rights of the Child. (2003). *The state of Pakistan's children 2002.* Islamabad, Pakistan: Author.

5. Unidentified Author

If the author is listed on the work as "Anonymous," list that in your reference entry, alphabetizing accordingly. Otherwise, start with and alphabetize by title.

> Anonymous. (1971). *Go ask Alice.* New York, NY: Simon & Schuster.

> Dream fish. (2007, July/August). *Eating Well, 6,* 26-30.

6. Multiple Works by the Same Author

Shermer, M. (2003). I knew you would say that [Review of the book *Intuition: Its powers and perils*]. *Skeptic, 10*(1), 92-94.

Shermer, M. (2005a, August). Full of holes: The curious case of acupuncture. *Scientific American, 293*(2), 30.

Shermer, M. (2005b). *Science friction*. New York, NY: Henry Holt, 6.

BOOKS

7. Book: Basic Format

Author. (Publication Year). *Book title: Book subtitle.* Publication City, State (abbreviated) or Country of Publication: Publisher.

Mah, A. Y. (1997). *Falling leaves: The true story of an unwanted Chinese daughter.* New York, NY: John Wiley & Sons.

8. Author and Editor

Author. (Publication Year). *Book title: Book subtitle* (Editor's Initial(s). Editor's Last Name, Ed.). Publication City, State (abbreviated) or Country of Publication: Publisher.

Faulkner, W. (2004). *Essays, speeches, and public letters* (J. B. Meriwether, Ed.). New York, NY: Modern Library.

9. Work in an Anthology or a Collection

Begin with the author and date of the short work and include the title as you would a periodical title (no quotations and minimal capitalization). Then list "In" and the editor's first initial and last name followed by "Ed." in parentheses. Next give the anthology title and page numbers in parentheses. End with the publication information. If an anthology has two editors, connect them with an ampersand (&) and use "Eds."

Author. (Publication Year). Title of short work. In Editor's First Initial. Editor's Last Name (Ed.), *Title of anthology* (pp. Page Numbers). Publication City, State (abbreviated) or Country of Publication: Publisher.

Plimpton, G. (2002). Final twist of the drama. In N. Dawidoff (Ed.),
    Baseball: A literary anthology (pp. 457-475). New York, NY: Library
    of America.

For more than two editors, connect them with commas and an ampersand.
For large editorial boards, give the name of the lead editor followed by "et al."

J. Smith, L. Hoey, & R. Burns (Eds.)

N. Mallen et al. (Eds.)

10. Edited Collection

Editor. (Ed.). (Publication Year). *Book title: Book subtitle.* Publication
    City, State (abbreviated) or Country of Publication: Publisher.

Danquah, M. N. (Ed.). (2000). *Becoming American: Personal essays by
    first generation immigrant women.* New York, NY: Hyperion.

11. Multivolume Work

Author(s) or Editor(s) (Eds.). (Year of Publication). *Book title: Book
    subtitle* (Vols. volume numbers). Publication City, State (abbreviated)
    or Country of Publication: Publisher.

Lindahl, C., MacNamara, J., & Lindow, J. (Eds.). (2000). *Medieval folklore:
    An encyclopedia of myths, legends, tales, beliefs, and customs*
    (Vols. 1-2). Santa Barbara, CA: ABC-CLIO.

12. Later Edition

In parentheses include the edition type (such as "Rev." for "Revised" or
"Abr." for "Abridged") or number ("2nd," "3rd," "4th," etc.) as shown on the
title page, along with the abbreviation "ed." after the book title.

Author. (Publication Year). *Book title* (Edition Type or Number ed.). Publication
    City, State (abbreviated) or Country of Publication: Publisher.

Handlin, D. P. (2004). *American architecture* (2nd ed.). London, England:
    Thames and Hudson.

13. Translation

List the translator's initial, last name, and "Trans." in parentheses after the title. After the publication information, list "Original work published" and year in parentheses. Note that the period is omitted after the final parenthesis.

> Author. (Publication Year of Translation). *Book title* (Translator Initial(s). Last Name, Trans.). Publication City, State (abbreviated) or Country of Publication: Publisher. (Original work published Year)

> Camus, A. (1988). *The stranger* (M. Ward, Trans.). New York, NY: Knopf. (Original work published 1942)

14. Article in a Reference Book

> Article Author. (Publication Year). Article title. In Initial(s). Last Name of Editor (Ed.), *Reference book title* (pp. Page Numbers). Publication City, State (abbreviated) or Country of Publication: Publisher.

> Schwartz, J. (1995). Brownstones. In K. T. Jackson (Ed.), *Encyclopedia of New York City* (pp. 162-163). New Haven, CT: Yale University Press.

If a reference book entry has no author, begin with the title of the article.

> Article title. (Publication Year). In *Book title.* Publication City, State (abbreviated) or Country of Publication: Publisher.

> The history of the national anthem. (2004). In *The world almanac and book of facts 2004.* New York, NY: World Almanac Books.

PERIODICALS

15. Article in a Journal Paginated by Volume

> Article Author. (Publication Year). Title of article. *Title of Journal, Volume Number,* Page Numbers.

> Harwood, J. (2004). Relational, role, and social identity as expressed in grandparents' personal Web sites. *Communication Studies, 55,* 300-318.

16. Article in a Journal Paginated by Issue

> Article Author. (Publication Year). Title of article. *Title of Journal, Volume Number*(Issue Number), Page Numbers.

Clancy, S., & Simpson, L. (2002). Literacy learning for indigenous
students: Setting a research agenda. *Australian Journal of
Language and Literacy, 25*(2), 47-64.

17. Magazine Article

Article Author. (Publication Year, Month). Title of article. *Title of Magazine,
Volume Number*(Issue Number), Page Number(s).

Murrel, J. (2007, July). In the year of the storm: The topography of
resurrection in New Orleans. *Harper's Magazine, 315*(7), 35-52.

18. Newspaper Article

Article Author. (Publication Year, Month Day). Title of article. *Title of
Newspaper,* p. Page Number.

Dempsey, J. (2007, August 26). Germans ease curbs on skilled labor
from Eastern Europe. *The New York Times,* p. 8.

19. Letter to the Editor

Include "Letter to the editor" in brackets after the letter title (if any) and
before the period.

Author. (Publication Year, Month Day). Title of letter [Letter to the editor].
Title of Newspaper, p. Page Number.

Miller, E. D. (2007, August 29). It is the sworn duty of law officers to
uphold the law [Letter to the editor]. *The Stuart News,* p. A6.

20. Review

After the review title (if any), include in brackets "Review of the" and the
medium of the work being reviewed ("book," "film," "CD," etc.), followed by
the title of the work in italics. If the reviewed work is a book, include the
author's name after a comma; if it's a film or other media, include the year of
release.

Author Name. (Publication Year, Month Day). Title of review [Review of the
book *Book title,* by Author Name]. *Title of Periodical, Volume Number,*
Page Number.

Adams, L. (2007, July 15). The way west [Review of the book *Shadow
of the Silk Road,* by C. Thubron]. *The New York Times Book
Review, 1,* 10.

ELECTRONIC SOURCES

21. Article with a DOI

A DOI (digital object identifier) is a unique number assigned to specific content, such as a journal article. Include the DOI but not the database name or URL. Note that there is no period after the DOI.

> Thibedeau, H. (2009). Safer toys coming, but not with Santa Claus. *Canadian Medical Association Journal, 181*, E111-E112. doi:10.1503/cmaj.109-3003

22. Article without a DOI

Give the exact URL or the URL for the journal's home page if access requires a subscription. Do not give the database name. Note that there is no period after the URL.

> Moyo, J. (2009). Academic freedom and human rights in Zimbabwe. *Social Research, 76*, 611-614. Retrieved from http://www.socres.org/

23. Article in Internet-Only Periodical

An article published exclusively online is unlikely to have page numbers.

> Clark-Flory, T. (2007, August 31). Do we teach children to fear men? *Salon .com.* Retrieved from http://www.salon.com/mwt/broadsheet /2007/08/31/men/index.html

24. Multipage Web Site

Include a retrieval date before the URL if the material is likely to be changed or updated or if it lacks a set publication date. Do not add a period at the end of the entry.

> Web Site Author or Sponsor. (Date of Most Recent Update). *Title of Web site.* Retrieved date, from URL

> Annie E. Casey Foundation. (2007). *Kids count.* Retrieved September 9, 2007, from http://www.aecf.org/MajorInitiatives/KIDSCOUNT.aspx

> Hartmann, D., Gerteis, J., & Edgell, P. (2007). *American Mosaic Project.* Retrieved from http://www.soc.umn.edu/research/amp/

25. Part of a Web Site

Short Work Author. (Date of Most Recent Update). Title of short work. *Title of Web site.* Retrieved date, from URL

Taylor, W., Jr. (2005, November 16). A time to be thankful. *The Hopi Tribe Web site.* Retrieved from http://www.hopi.nsn.us/view_article .asp?id=116&cat=3

26. Online Posting

Post Author. (Year, Month Day of post). Title of post [Description of post]. Retrieved from URL

Winkleman, T. (2007, July 13). Reducing your food miles [Online forum comment]. Retrieved from http://tech.groups.yahoo.com/group /FFCFBulletin/message/220

27. Computer Software

If the software has an author or editor, the reference begins with that.

Title of software [Computer software]. (Publication Year). Publication City, State (abbreviated) or Country of Publication: Publisher.

History through art: The twentieth century [Computer software]. (2001). San Jose, CA: Fogware.

28. Entry in a blog (Weblog)

Sellers, H. (2008, June 21). Re: East Coast [Web log post]. Retrieved from http://heathersellers.com/blog/index.php

29. Podcast

Graham, L. (Producer). (2006, July 31). Capping pollution at the source. [Audio podcast]. *The environment report.* Retrieved from http://www.environmentreport.org/story.php3?story_id=3102

30. Entry in a Wiki

Article title. Posting date (if any). Retrieved date, from URL

Emo. (n.d.). Retrieved June 24, 2008, from http://en.wikipedia.org/wiki /Emo

How to...
Cite from a Web site (APA)

2 publisher of report (if not named as author)

3 report number

4 title of online report

5 author

1 publication date

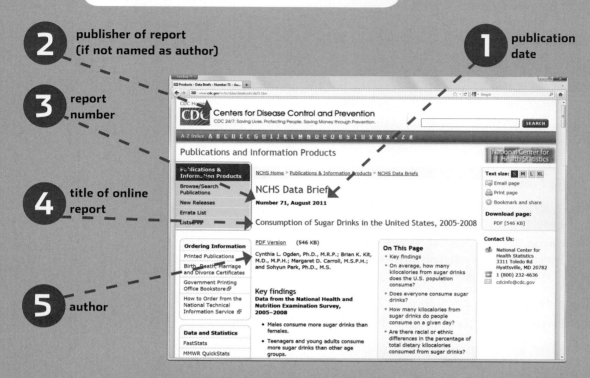

If you cite a source with three or more authors more than once in text, only list all of the authors the first time. Subsequent times only need the first author's last name, like this: (Ogden et al.).

SECTION BEING CITED

6 URL of section

7 section title

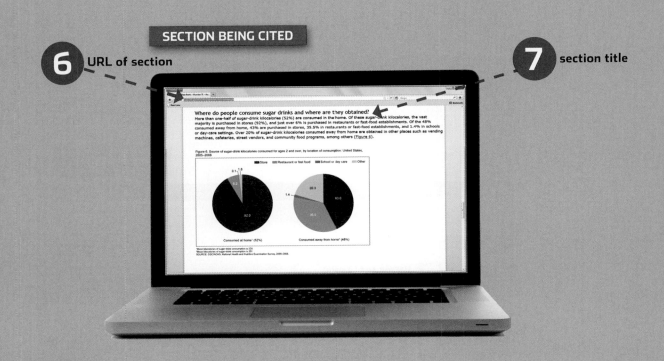

APA in-text citation

A nutrition survey of U.S. behavior between 2005 and 2008 found that an overwhelming 92% of sugar-drink kilocalories consumed outside the home were from drinks purchased in stores, not restaurants (Ogden, Kit, Carroll, & Park, 2011).

APA references list entry

Ogden, C. L., Kit, B. K., Carroll, M. D., & Park S. (2011, August). Where do people consume sugar drinks and where are they obtained? In *Consumption of sugar drinks in the United States, 2005–2008* (NCHS Data Brief No. 71). Retrieved from Centers for Disease Control and Prevention website: http://www.cdc.gov/nchs/data/databriefs/db71.htm#people

How to...
Cite from a database (APA)

DATABASE SCREEN

1 volume and issue number

2 periodical title

3 publication date

6 article title

5 author

4 DOI (digital object identifier)

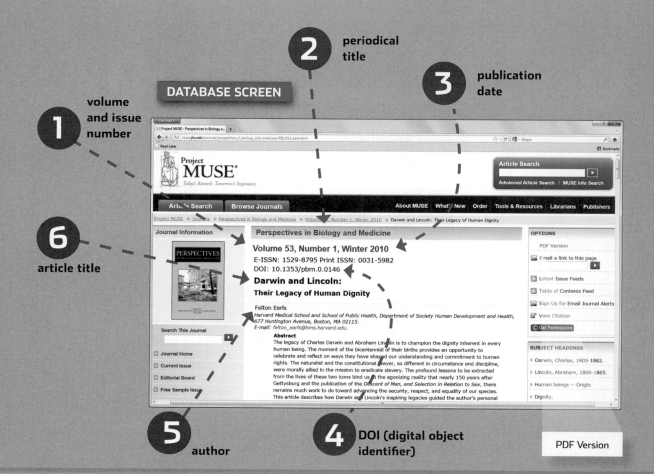

Project MUSE - Perspectives in Biology a...

muse.jhu.edu/journals/perspectives_in_biology_and_medicine/v053/53.1.earls.html

Read Later

Bookmarks

Project MUSE®
Today's Research. Tomorrow's Inspiration.

Article Search

Advanced Article Search | MUSE Info Search

Article Search | Browse Journals

About MUSE | What's New | Order | Tools & Resources | Librarians | Publishers

Project MUSE » Journals » Perspectives in Biology and Medicine » Volume 53, Number 1, Winter 2010 » Darwin and Lincoln: Their Legacy of Human Dignity

Journal Information

PERSPECTIVES

Perspectives in Biology and Medicine

Volume 53, Number 1, Winter 2010
E-ISSN: 1529-8795 Print ISSN: 0031-5982
DOI: 10.1353/pbm.0.0146

Darwin and Lincoln:
Their Legacy of Human Dignity

Felton Earls
Harvard Medical School and School of Public Health, Department of Society Human Development and Health, 677 Huntington Avenue, Boston, MA 02115.
E-mail: felton_earls@hms.harvard.edu.

Abstract
The legacy of Charles Darwin and Abraham Lincoln is to champion the dignity inherent in every human being. The moment of the bicentennial of their births provides an opportunity to celebrate and reflect on ways they have shaped our understanding and commitment to human rights. The naturalist and the constitutional lawyer, so different in circumstance and discipline, were morally allied in the mission to eradicate slavery. The profound lessons to be extracted from the lives of these two icons bind us to the agonizing reality that nearly 150 years after Gettysburg and the publication of the *Descent of Man, and Selection in Relation to Sex*, there remains much work to do toward advancing the security, respect, and equality of our species. This article describes how Darwin and Lincoln's inspiring legacies guided the author's personal

Search This Journal

☐ Journal Home
☐ Current Issue
☐ Editorial Board
☐ Free Sample Issue

OPTIONS

PDF Version

📧 Email a link to this page

📶 Latest Issue Feeds
📶 Table of Contents Feed
📧 Sign Up for Email Journal Alerts
View Citation
© Get Permissions

SUBJECT HEADINGS

▷ Darwin, Charles, 1809-1882.
▷ Lincoln, Abraham, 1809-1865.
▷ Human beings -- Origin.
▷ Dignity.

PDF Version

If you're reading an article in an Internet browser and aren't sure where to find the information you need, try viewing the article as a PDF, which usually shows what originally appeared in the print journal.

PDF VIEW (FIRST PAGE)

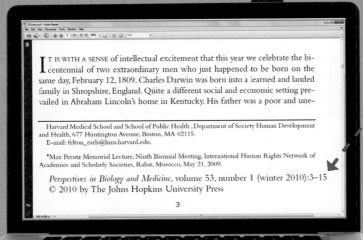

I T IS WITH A SENSE of intellectual excitement that this year we celebrate the bicentennial of two extraordinary men who just happened to be born on the same day, February 12, 1809. Charles Darwin was born into a learned and landed family in Shropshire, England. Quite a different social and economic setting prevailed in Abraham Lincoln's home in Kentucky. His father was a poor and une-

Harvard Medical School and School of Public Health , Department of Society Human Development and Health, 677 Huntington Avenue, Boston, MA 02115.
E-mail: felton_earls@hms.harvard.edu.

*Max Perutz Memorial Lecture, Ninth Biennial Meeting, International Human Rights Network of Academies and Scholarly Societies, Rabat, Morocco, May 21, 2009.

Perspectives in Biology and Medicine, volume 53, number 1 (winter 2010):3–15
© 2010 by The Johns Hopkins University Press

3

7 page range

APA in-text citation

It's important to note the contributions of Darwin and Lincoln to modern conceptions of human rights, "particularly the beliefs that scientists are free to pursue knowledge, no matter how different from or risky to the prevailing wisdom, and that one of the responsibilities of modern governments is to protect this right to rationality and critical inquiry" (Earls, 2011, 4).

5   **3**   **7**

APA references list entry

5   **3**   **6**
Earls, F. (2011, Winter). Darwin and Lincoln: Their legacy of human dignity.

2   **1**   **7**   **4**
Perspectives in Biology and Medicine, 53(1), 3-15. doi:10.1353/pbm.0.0146

OTHER

31. Group, Corporate, or Government Document

List the group or agency as the author, and include any identifying numbers. Many federal agencies' works are published by the U.S. Government Printing Office. If the group is also the publisher, use the word "Author" rather than repeating the group name at the end of the entry.

> Name of Group, Corporation, or Government Agency. (Publication Year). *Title of document* (Identifying number, if any). Publication City, State (abbreviated) or Country of Publication: Publisher.

> U.S. Department of Health and Human Services. (1995). *Disability among older persons: United States and Canada* (HE 20.6209:5/8). Washington, DC: U.S. Government Printing Office.

> Florida Department of Elder Affairs. (2006). *Making choices: A guide to end-of-life planning*. Tallahassee, FL: Author.

32. Published Conference Proceedings

> Editor(s). (Eds.). (Publication Year). *Proceedings of the Conference Name: Book title.* Publication City, State (abbreviated) or Country of Publication: Publisher.

> Bourguignon, F., Pleskovic, B., & Van Der Gaag, J. (Eds.). (2006). *Proceedings of the Annual World Bank Conference on Development Economics 2006: Securing development in an unstable world.* Washington, DC: World Bank.

33. Dissertation Abstract

For dissertations abstracted in *Dissertation Abstracts International*, include the author's name, date, and dissertation title. Then include the volume, issue, and page number. If you access the dissertation from an electronic database, identify the type of work ("Doctoral dissertation") before giving the database name and any identifying number. If you retrieve the abstract from the Web, include the name of the institution in the parentheses, and then give the URL.

Author. (Year of Publication). *Title of dissertation. Dissertation Abstracts International, Volume Number*(Issue Number), Page Number.

Berger, M. A. (2000). *The impact of organized sports participation on self-esteem in middle school children. Dissertation Abstracts International, 60*(11), 5762B.

Berger, M. A. (2000). *The impact of organized sports participation on self-esteem in middle school children* (Doctoral dissertation). Available from ProQuest Dissertations and Theses database. (730241441)

Berger, M. A. (2000). *The impact of organized sports participation on self-esteem in middle school children* (Doctoral dissertation. Pace University). Retrieved from http://digitalcommons.pace.edu /dissertations/AAI9950745/

34. Film

Writer(s), Producer(s), Director(s). (Release year). *Film title* [Motion picture]. Country of Origin: Movie Studio.

Haggis, P. (Writer/Director/Producer), & Moresco, B. (Writer/Producer). (2004). *Crash* [Motion picture]. United States: Lions Gate Films.

35. Television Program

Writer(s). Producer(s), Director(s). (Year of Release). Title of episode [Television series episode]. In Producer Initials. Last Name (Producer), *Title of series.* City, State (abbreviated) or Country of Publication: Broadcast Company.

Hochman, G. & Collins, M. (Writers), & Wolfinger, K. (Director). (2004). Ancient refuge in the Holy Land [Television series episode]. In P. S. Apsell (Producer), *NOVA.* Boston, MA: WGBH.

36. Musical Recording

Writer. (Copyright Year). Title of song [Recorded by Artist Name]. On *Album title* [Recording medium]. City of Recording, State (abbreviated) or Country of Publication: Record Label. (Recording Year).

Cornell, C. (1991). Rusty cage [Recorded by J. Cash]. On *Unchained* [CD]. Burbank, CA: American Recordings. (1994).

Format an APA paper correctly.   The following guidelines will help you prepare a manuscript using APA style.

- Set up a header on each page (including the title page, if your instructor requests one), one-half inch from the top. The header should include a brief title (shortened to no more than fifty characters) in cap/lowercase letters and the page number. Page numbers should appear in the upper right corner.

- Margins should be set at one inch on all sides of the paper.

- Check with your instructor to see if a title page is preferred. The title page should include the title of your paper, your name, the course title, your instructor's name, and the date. If included, the title page should be considered page number 1.

- If you include an abstract for your paper, put it on a separate page, immediately following the title page.

- All lines of text (including the title page, abstract, block quotations, and the list of references) should be double-spaced.

- Indent the first lines of paragraphs one-half inch or five spaces.

- Use block quotations for quoted material of four or more lines. Indent block quotations one inch from the left margin.

- When you document a paper using APA style, you'll need to create an alphabetically arranged references page at the end of the project so that readers have a convenient list of all the books, articles, and other data you have used in the paper or project.

Cri du Chat Syndrome 1

Short title in cap/lowercase is aligned at right, with arabic numerals used for page numbers.

Developmental Disorders:

Cri du Chat Syndrome

Full title centered in middle of page.

Marissa Dahlstrom

Course Title

Instructor's Name

Date

Writer's name, course name, instructor's name, and date are all centered.

Cri du Chat Syndrome 2

Developmental Disorders: Cri du Chat Syndrome

Developmental disorders pose a serious threat to young children. However, early detection, treatment, and intervention often allow a child to lead a fulfilling life. To detect a problem at the beginning of life, medical professionals and caregivers must recognize normal development as well as potential warning signs. Research provides this knowledge. In most cases, research also allows for accurate diagnosis and effective intervention. Such is the case with cri du chat syndrome (CDCS), also commonly known as cat cry syndrome, 5p-syndrome, and 5p-minus syndrome.

Cri du chat syndrome, a fairly rare genetic disorder first identified in 1963 by Dr. Jerome Lejeune, affects between 1 in 15,000 to 1 in 50,000 live births (Campbell, Carlin, Justen, & Baird, 2004). The syndrome is caused by partial deletion of chromosome number 5, specifically the portion labeled as 5p; hence the alternative name for the disorder (Five P-Minus Society). While the exact cause of the deletion is unknown, it is likely that "the majority of cases are due to spontaneous loss . . . during development of an egg or sperm. A minority of cases result from one parent carrying a rearrangement of chromosome 5 called a translocation" (Sondheimer, 2005). The deletion leads to many different symptoms and outcomes. Perhaps the most noted characteristic of children affected by this syndrome—a high-pitched cry resembling the mewing of a cat—explains Lejeune's choice of the name *cri du chat* syndrome. Pediatric nurse Mary Kugler writes that the cry is caused by "problems with the larynx and nervous system" (2006). Other symptoms, characteristics,

Center the title

This paper does not include an abstract; check with your instructor to find out whether an abstract is required.

The authors' names and publication date appear in parentheses.

A signal phrase including author's name introduces quotation, so only the date appears in parentheses.

Cri du Chat Syndrome 6

References

Campbell, D., Carlin M., Justen, J., III, & Baird, S. (2004).
Cri-du-chat syndrome: A topical overview. Retrieved from
http://www.fivepminus.org/online.htm

Denny, M., Marchand-Martella, N., Martella, R., Reilly, J. R., &
Reilly, J. F. (2000). Using parent-delivered graduated
guidance to teach functional living skills to a child with cri
du chat syndrome. *Education & Treatment of Children,*
23(4), 441.

Five P-Minus Society. (n.d.). *About 5P-syndrome.* Retrieved
from http://www.fivepminus.org/about.htm

Kugler, M. (2006). Cri-du-chat syndrome: Distinctive kitten-
like cry in infancy. Retrieved from http://rarediseases.
about.com/cs/criduchatsynd/a/010704.htm

McClean, P. (1997). Genomic analysis: *In situ* hybridization.
Retrieved from http://www.ndsu.nodak.edu/instruct
/mcclean/plsc431/genomic/genomic2.htm

Sarimski, K. (2003). Early play behavior in children with
5p-syndrome. *Journal of Intellectual Disability Research,*
47(2), 113-120.

Sondheimer, N. (2005). Cri du chat syndrome. In *MedlinePlus*
medical encyclopedia. Retrieved from http://www.nlm
.nih.gov/medlineplus/ency/article/001593.htm

Media & Design

part eight

go multimodal

51 **Understanding Digital Media** 568

learn media
conventions

52 **Digital Elements** 577

display data

53 **Tables, Graphs, and Infographics** 584

think visually

54 **Designing Print and Online
Documents** 592

51 Understanding Digital Media

go
multimodal

Schools, businesses, and professional organizations are finding innovative uses for new media tools and services such as blogs, wikis, digital video, web-mapping software, social networks, and more. The resulting texts—often spun from Web 2.0 interactive media technologies—represent genres much in flux. And yet they already play a role in many classrooms. You are employing new media if you contribute to a college service project hosted on a blog, schedule study sessions with classmates via Facebook, or use slide software to spiff up a report to the student government.

Plotting Flickr and Tweet locations in Europe produces this luminous map of the continent, suggesting the sweep of new media activity.

Choose a media format based on what you hope to accomplish.
A decision to compose with digital tools or to work in an environment
such as Facebook or Flickr should be based on what these new media offer
you. An electronic tool may support your project in ways that conventional
printed texts simply cannot—and that's the reason to select it. Various
media writing options are described in the following table.

Format	Elements	Purpose	Software Technology/Tools
Blogs	Topic-driven online discussion postings; interactive; text; images; video; links	Create communities (fan, political, academic); distribute news and information	Blogger; Moveable Type; Tumblr; WordPress
Web sites	Web-based information site; text; images; video; links; interactive posts	Compile and distribute information; establish presence on Web; sell merchandise, etc.	Dreamweaver; Drupal; WordPress
Wikis	Collaboratively authored linked texts and posts; Web-based; information; text; images; data	Create and edit collaborative documents based on community expertise; distribute and share information	DokuWiki; MediaWiki; Tiki Wiki
Podcasts	Digital file-based audio or (sometimes) video recording; downloadable; voice; music; episodic	Distribute mainly audio texts; document or archive audio texts and performances	Audacity; GarageBand
Maps	Interactive image maps; text; data; images	Give spatial or geographical dimension to data or texts; help users locate or visualize information	iMapBuilder; Google Earth; Google Maps
Video	Recorded images; live-action images; enhanced slides; animation; sound; music	Record events; provide visual documentation; create presentations; furnish instructions, etc.	Animoto; Camtasia; iMovie; Microsoft Movie Maker; Soundslides; Xtranormal
Remixes and mashups	Combined media; sampling; music; sound; images; video	Juxtapose or combine existing texts to create new perspectives; examine media conventions; explore new genres and texts	Audacity; Mixcraft

Use blogs to create communities. Blogs are moderated online discussions hosted by groups or individuals that typically focus on topics such as politics, news, sports, technology, and entertainment. They integrate individual postings, comments, images, videos, and lots of links; the busiest blogs are constantly updated, archived, and searchable.

Some college courses now use blogs to spur discussion of class materials, to distribute information, and to document research activities. An instructor may set up a site for a class or make the creation of a blog a course project. If blogging is part of a course assignment, understand the ground rules. Instructors often require a defined number of postings/comments of a specific length. Participate regularly by reading and commenting on other students' blogs or blog posts; by making substantive comments of your own on the assigned topic; and by contributing relevant images, videos, and links.

Keep your postings focused and title them descriptively; respond to others by commenting substantively on their ideas, asking pertinent questions, and suggesting links. Postings should be academic in style. Avoid the vitriol you may encounter on national sites: Remember that anyone—from your mother to a future employer—might read your remarks.

Create Web sites to share information. Not long ago, building Web sites was at the leading edge of technological savvy in the classroom. Today, blogs, wikis, and social networks are more efficient vehicles for many types of online communication. Still, Web sites remain essential because of their

This masthead appears on a Web site created by college students for a community development project in the small town of Mart, Texas (population 2,273).

The Mart Community Project   *Bringing Art to Mart*

Home   About   Events

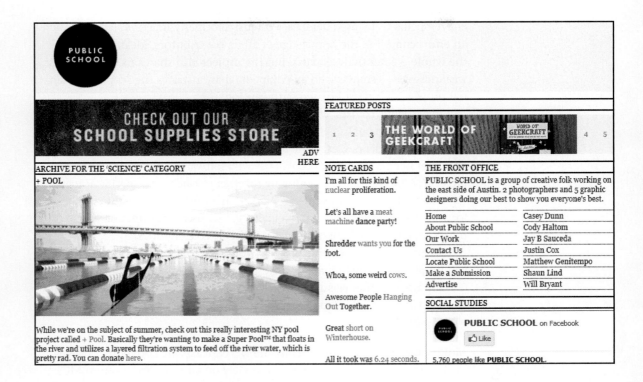

capacity to organize large amounts of text and information online. A Web site you create for a course might report research findings or provide a portal to information on a complex topic.

When creating a site with multiple pages, plan early on how to organize that information; the structure will depend on your purpose and audience. A simple site with sequential information (e.g., a photo essay) might lead readers through items one by one. More complicated sites may require a complex, hierarchical structure, with materials organized around careful topic divisions. The more comprehensive the site, the more deliberately you will need to map out its structure, allowing for easy navigation and growth.

Use wikis to collaborate with others.   If you have ever opened Wikipedia, you know what a wiki does: It enables a group to collaborate on the development of an ongoing online project—from a comprehensive

Public School is a Web site hosted by a small regional group of artists who are eager to showcase good design and talk about their own work. Note its use of school-themed design elements.

encyclopedia to focused databases on just about any imaginable topic. Such an effort combines the knowledge of all its contributors, ideally making the whole greater than its parts. But the project also shares its contributors' weaknesses. A resource such as Wikipedia demonstrates the scope of potential projects, but must be used with caution.

In academic courses, wikis have many applications. Instructors may ask class members to publish articles on an existing wiki—in which case you should read the site guidelines, examine its existing entries and templates, and then post your item. More likely you will use wiki software to develop a collaborative project for the course itself—bringing together research on a specific academic topic such as a historical event or a work of literature. A wiki might even be used for a service project in which participants gather useful information about nutrition, jobs, or arts opportunities for specific communities.

As always with electronic projects, you need to learn the software—which will involve not only uploading material to the wiki but also editing and developing texts that classmates have already placed there. If the assignment allows, parcel out wiki responsibilities to capitalize on the strengths of individual participants.

Make podcasts to share audio files. Podcasts are convenient downloadable audio or video files you can review on various devices from MP3 players to iPads. Often published in series, podcasts are an inexpensive way to share music, information, or media broadcasts.

Audio podcasts might be a way of sharing interviews you've made as part of a sociology project, an efficient method for explaining a complex procedure in an engineering course, or a tool for teaching or learning language skills. Depending on the intended audience, academic podcasts usually need to be scripted and edited.

Producing a podcast is a two-step process. First you must record the podcast; then you need to upload it to a Web site for distribution. Software such as GarageBand can do both.

Use maps to position ideas. You use mapping services such as Google Maps whenever you search online for a restaurant, store, or hotel. The service quickly provides maps and directions to available facilities, often embellished with links, information, and images. Not surprisingly, Google

Maps, the related Google Earth, and other mapping software are also finding classroom applications, as shown on these pages.

Multimedia maps also make it possible to display information such as economic trends, movements of people, climate data, and other variables

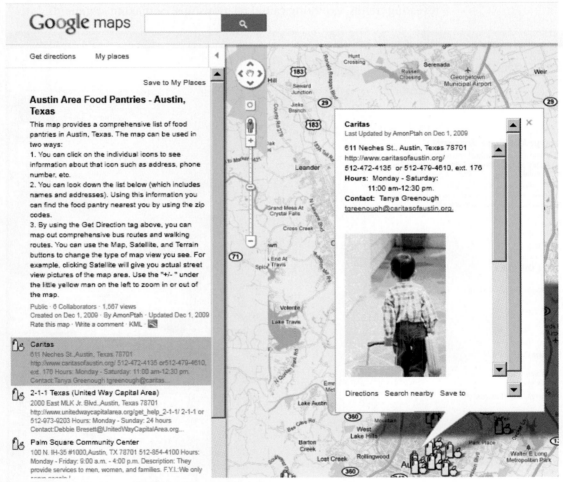

Students in a course called Writing in Digital Environments produced this Google Maps project to show where food pantries serve the community of Austin.

graphically and dynamically, using color, text, images, and video/audio clips to emphasize movement and change across space and time. Even literary texts can be mapped so that scholars or readers may track events or characters as they move in real or imaginary landscapes. Mapping thus becomes a vehicle for reporting and sharing information, telling personal stories, revealing trends, exploring causal relationships, or making arguments.

(Copyright © 2011 Google. Map data copyright © 2010 Europa Technologies, PPWK, Tele Atlas. Hala Herbly.)

English instructor Hala Herbly asked students to map the movements across Europe of the monster from Mary Shelley's novel *Frankenstein*.

Make "movies" to show and tell. Digital video is a medium that is easy and cheap to use. A video or cell phone camera can film any subject—from smart kitties to stupid boyfriends. Many simple items go viral on YouTube: Has anyone *not* seen "Charlie Bit Me"? But there are sophisticated ways to shape video narratives into worthwhile "small screen" presentations.

In a course assignment, you might be asked to develop a video that tells a story or makes an argument. Consider what you'd like to accomplish and then match your goals to available software resources. If you want to film an event, do interviews, or tell a story with actors, you need conventional software such as Microsoft Movie Maker or iMovie. With this software you can edit and mix digital scenes, refine the sound, add special effects, titles, and captioning, and so on. Such options enable you to achieve specific visual and rhetorical effects. If your subject is better served by animation, software such as Xtranormal gives you different choices.

You can construct nonnarrative kinds of video writing by combining text, film clips, still photos, and music. Software such as Animoto, Soundslides, or Camtasia provides the frameworks for such projects. If you have a concept, you can turn it into a clip and then upload it to a blog, presentation software, or Web sites with enormous audiences such as YouTube, Flickr, or Metacafe. To upload materials to Web sites, you'll establish an account and then follow the instructions for sending files.

Adriana Cervantes used Xtranormal to create a video for her college course on argument.

Try remixes and mashups to create something new. Combining media in unexpected ways may expose surprising relationships between vastly different kinds of texts. Already common in commercial music, design, and advertising, projects of this kind are now appearing in academic fields across various disciplines.

Mashups build texts by sampling and combining materials that may be poles apart, sometimes from within the same genre (in the movie *300*, does Leonidas channel the cartoon superhero Batman?) and sometimes across genres and media (do Walt Whitman's poems really work in Levi's Jeans "Go Forth" campaign?).

In 2007, Phil de Vellis reworked Apple's famous "1984" ad into a campaign spot for then-presidential candidate Barack Obama. The mashup entitled "Vote Different" became an icon of citizen media.

Such creative juxtapositions redefine what writing and composition mean: Just as DJs have been remixing music for decades, surprising audiences with unanticipated convergences, your own ideas and stories can be repurposed and reenergized through a "remix."

For instance, you could take a traditional argumentative essay and add photos, video, and art. Or you could transform it into a video or give it its own Facebook page, profile, and posts. You see this kind of remix in the music industry whenever artists take songs and develop them into videos or films.

Alternatively, a remix might allow you to illustrate your own ideas by references to other texts; for instance, you could fuse scenes from your favorite movies to explore a political position—just as a producer such as Kanye West samples from other songs to create the beat or the background for new songs. Mashups often take this form of sampling to the extreme, putting together disparate genres—as Danger Mouse did with the *Grey Album,* remixing the Beatles' *White Album* and Jay-Z's *Black Album.* Texts can also be remixed collaboratively: You can take your ideas, stories, or arguments and put them into conversation with those of your peers.

Part of the pleasure of this type of composing is in discovering new angles and ideas as you move texts around and recombine them. It is important, however, to develop creative strategies for citation when you are remixing: Keep track of everything you borrow and give creative credit wherever it is due.

Your Turn   Most of the software programs mentioned in this chapter have Web sites that describe their features, and some, such as Xtranormal, even include sample projects. Explore one or two of these programs online to learn about their capabilities. Then describe a new media project you would like to create using the software.

Digital Elements 52

Every day, you navigate an amazing variety of media, from video games and phone apps to e-readers and social networking sites, to name but a few. Yet creating academic or professional texts that use media effectively can be a challenge if you aren't familiar with some of the conventions, tools, or opportunities for introducing images, audio, and video. This chapter covers some of the basics.

learn media conventions

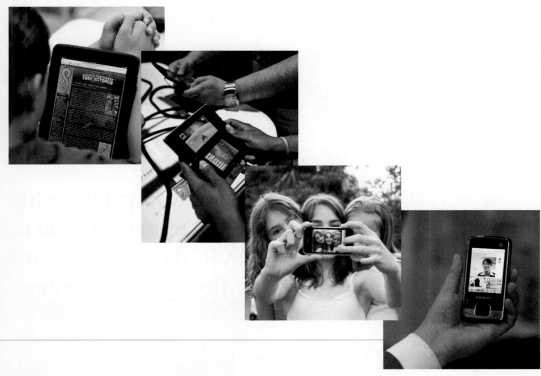

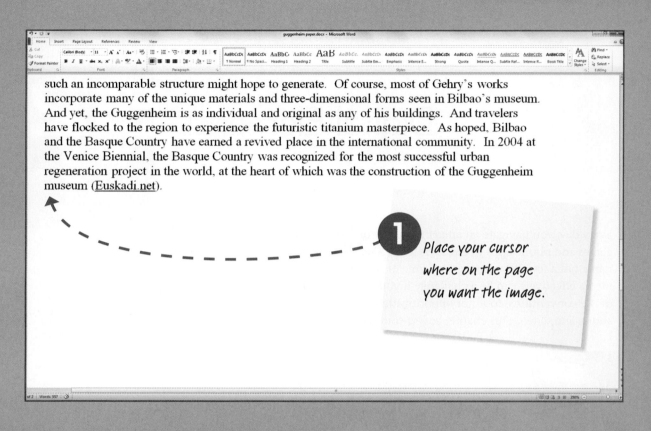

1 Place your cursor
where on the page
you want the image.

2 On the "Insert" tab,
click "Picture."

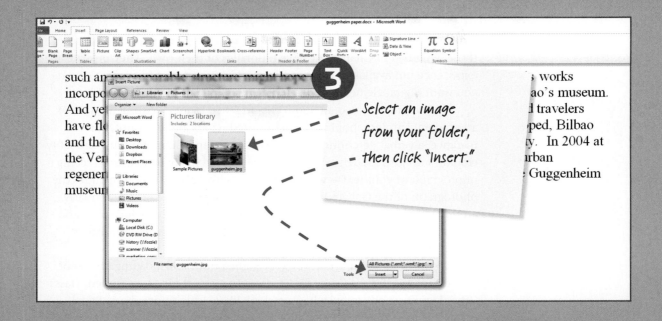

such an incomparable structure might hope ... works
incorpo... ...ao's museum.
And ye... ...d travelers
have fl... Select an image ...ped, Bilbao
and the... from your folder, ...ty. In 2004 at
the Ven... then click "Insert." ...urban
regener... ...e Guggenheim
museum...

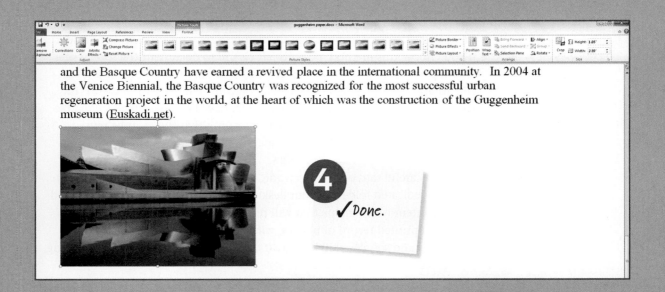

and the Basque Country have earned a revived place in the international community. In 2004 at
the Venice Biennial, the Basque Country was recognized for the most successful urban
regeneration project in the world, at the heart of which was the construction of the Guggenheim
museum (Euskadi.net).

✓ Done.

Have good reasons for using new media.   New media projects such as those described in Chapter 51 have rationales of their own: They provide an experience not available in conventional documents. But in academic work, you want digital elements to be purposeful, not mere eye candy or bling.

A photograph, video, or audio clip attached to an electronic version of an academic project should do what printed words alone cannot. For instance, a verbal description of the style of a Frank Gehry building probably wouldn't do justice to the subject. Readers would likely benefit from seeing a photograph in your text—which is exactly why Annie Winsett includes the photograph of the Guggenheim Bilbao in her report on page 67. Similarly, an oral report on Winston Churchill would appropriately include an audio file enabling the audience to hear clips from the British prime minister's famous wartime radio broadcasts of 1940.

On the other hand, what would be gained from downloading images of the current secretaries of state or defense into a report for a government class? Who doesn't already know what they look like? Using unnecessary digital embellishments contributes to clutter, the media equivalent of wordiness. ○

Download and save digital elements.   Most digital files on the Web can be saved on your computer simply by control clicking (or right clicking) on them and then transferring them to an appropriate location on your finder. If you choose this method, be *extremely careful* to document the source site; obtain permission if necessary. ○ You can also purchase whole libraries of clip art and stock photography, which you can then use without worrying about copyright infringement. Other media have been designated "creative commons" by their authors or owners, meaning that they can be reused and/or modified freely. Search for materials of this kind at sites such as <www.search.creativecommons.org>.

Keep careful tabs on the electronic content you collect for your project. Create a dedicated folder on your desktop, hard drive, or online archive and save each item with a name that will remind you where it came from. Keeping a printed record of images, with more detailed information about copyrights and sources, will be a great time-saver later, when you are putting your project or paper together.

improve your
sentences p. 444

understand citation
styles p. 501

Use tools to edit digital media.   Nonprint media texts often require as much revising and editing as traditional written ones. In fact, the tools for manipulating video, audio, and still-image files are among the most remarkable accomplishments of the digital revolution. If you are developing a podcast, an audio file can be tweaked a dozen ways using an audio editor like GarageBand or Audacity; such programs can also be used to create or refine musical clips. Comparable software is available for editing video clips.

You are apt to be familiar with tools for editing digital photographs. Even the simplest image-editing software enables users to adjust the tint, contrast, saturation, and sharpness of digital photographs. You might need to heighten the contrast of a PowerPoint image so that it projects better or adjust the tint in a portrait to purge the green from skin tones. Or you might use the cropping tool to select just the portion of an image you need for your project.

Image-editing software offers numerous options for enhancing picture files. Look for these options on palettes, toolbars, or dropdown menus.

Be aware, though, that when you enlarge a section of a larger digital image, it loses sharpness. And never crop an image in a way that distorts its meaning.

Sophisticated programs such as Photoshop allow you to do even more. Don't, however, tinker with the settings on professional photographs, even if you have permission to use them. Unless you have purchased the images from a stock photography library, or they are designated as "creative commons" material, they belong to someone else.

Use appropriate digital formats.   Working online, you quickly discover the various forms digital documents can take. Most of your academic work will be created in familiar word-processing, presentation, or spreadsheet software. Compatibility is rarely an issue today as you move your materials across computer platforms (PC to Mac) or download a presentation in a classroom for an oral report. Still, it never hurts to check ahead of time if, for example, you use Keynote or Prezi for a report rather than the more common PowerPoint.

Occasionally you need to save word-processing files in special formats. Sharing a file with someone using an older version of Word or Office may require saving a document in compatibility mode (.doc) rather than the now-standard .docx mode. Or moving across different applications may be easier if you use a plain text (.txt) or rich text format (.rtf)—in which case your document will lose some features, though the text will be preserved. When you want to share a document exactly as you wrote it and send it successfully across platforms, choose the .pdf mode. Files in .pdf form arrive exactly as you sent them, without any shifts in headings, alignments, or image locations; just as important, they cannot be easily altered.

Even if you have limited knowledge of differing image file formats (such as JPG, GIF, or TIFF), you probably understand that digital files come in varying sizes. The size of a digital-image file is directly related to the quality, or resolution, of the image. Attach a few high-resolution 14-megapixel photos to an e-mail and you'll clog the recipient's mailbox (or the e-mail will bounce back).

For most Web pages and online documents, compressed or lower-resolution images will be acceptable. On the other hand, if you intend to print an image—in a paper or brochure, for example—use the

At this size, the image downloaded from the Web is clear enough. But it would become distorted if you tried to enlarge it, because its resolution is too low.

highest-resolution image (the greatest number of pixels) available to assure maximum sharpness and quality.

Caption images correctly.   When using images or digital items in an academic paper, label, number, and caption them. Captions provide context for readers, so they know what an image, video, or audio file is and why they're considering it. If you also number your items (e.g., *Fig. 1.*), you can then direct readers to them unambiguously.

MLA and APA styles have different guidelines for captioning images and referring to them in the text, so consult the relevant guidebook before composing your captions. In general, however, captions should include the source of the image and any copyright and publication information. The photo on this page has not been previously published, but note that we still had to ask the photographer for permission to reprint.

Respect copyrights.   The images you find, whether online or in print, belong to someone. You cannot use someone else's property for commercial purposes — photographs, Web sites, brochures, posters, magazine articles, and so on — without permission. You may use a reasonable number of images in academic papers, but you must be careful not to go beyond "fair use," especially for any work you put online. Search the term "academic fair use" online for detailed guidelines.

Fig. 1. A boat ferries tourists from Zanzibar, Tanzania, to Prison Island, which was used as a quarantine station for yellow fever in the nineteenth century. (Courtesy Allie Goldstein.)

53

Tables, Graphs, and Infographics

Just as images and photographs are often the media of choice for conveying visual information, tables, graphs, and other "infographics" are essential tools for displaying numerical and statistical data. They take raw data and transform it into a story or picture readers can interpret.

Most such items are created in spreadsheet programs such as Excel that format charts and graphs and offer numerous design templates—though you will find basic graphics tools in Word and PowerPoint as well. More elaborate charts and graphs can be drawn with software such as Adobe Illustrator.

Creating effective tables and graphs is an art in itself, driven as always by purpose and audience. A table in a printed report that a reader will study can be rich in detail; a bar graph on screen for only a few moments must make its point quickly and memorably. Function always trumps appearance. Yet there's no question that handsome visual texts appeal to audiences. So spend the time necessary to design effective items. Use color to emphasize and clarify graphs, not just to decorate them. Label items clearly (avoiding symbols or keys that are hard to interpret), and don't add more detail than necessary.

In academic projects, be sure to label ("Fig.," "Table"), number, and caption your important graphic items, especially any that you mention in your text. Both MLA and APA style offer guidelines for handling labels; the APA rules are particularly detailed and specific.

display data

Often the most effective way to describe, explore, and summarize a set of numbers—even a very large set—is to look at pictures of those numbers.

—Edward R. Tufte

Use tables to present statistical data.   Tables can do all kinds of work. They
are essential for organizing and recording information as it comes in, for example, daily weather events: temperature, precipitation, wind velocities, and so on.
A table may also show trends or emphasize contrasts. In such cases, tables may
make an argument (in a print ad, for example) or readers may be left to interpret
complex data on their own—one of the pleasures of studying such material.

Tables typically consist of horizontal rows and vertical columns into
which you drop data. The axes of the chart provide different and significant
ways of presenting data, relating x to y: for example, in Table 1, lifetime
earnings is connected to education level.

In designing a table, determine how many horizontal rows and vertical
columns are needed, how to label them, and whether to use color or shading
to enhance the readability of the data. Software will provide templates to
suggest your options. Good tables can be very plain. In fact, many of the
tables on federal government Web sites, though packed with information,
are dirt simple and yet quite clear.

Table 1
Expected Lifetime Earnings Relative to High School Graduates, by Education Level

	Total Lifetime Earnings	Total Earnings Relative to High School Graduates	Present Value of Total Lifetime Earnings (3% Discount Rate)	Present Value Earnings Relative to HS Graduates (3% Discount Rate)
Not a High School Graduate	$941,370	0.74	$551,462	0.75
High School Graduate	1,266,730	1.00	738,609	1.00
Some College, No Degree	1,518,300	1.20	878,259	1.19
Associate Degree	1,620,730	1.28	943,181	1.28
Bachelor's Degree	2,054,380	1.62	1,189,836	1.61
Master's Degree	2,401,565	1.90	1,427,392	1.93
Doctoral Degree	3,073,240	2.43	1,748,716	2.37
Professional Degree	3,706,910	2.93	2,123,309	2.87
Bachelor's Degree or Higher	2,284,110	1.80	1,312,316	1.78

Sources: U.S. Census Bureau, 2006, PINC-03; calculations by the authors.

From College Board, *Education Pays: The Benefits of Higher Education for Individuals and Society,* 2007.

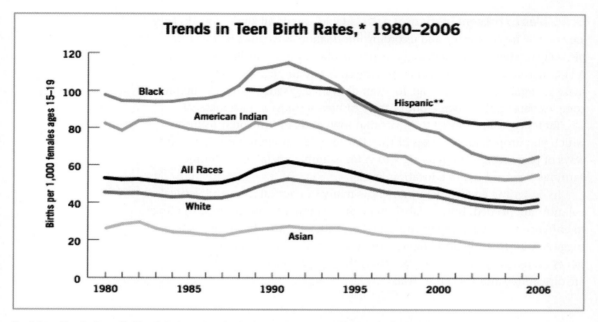

Trends in Teen Birth Rates,* 1980–2006

Fig. 1. Line Graph. From Children's Defense Fund, *The State of America's Children 2010* report.

Use line graphs to display changes or trends.   Line graphs are dynamic images, visually plotting and connecting variables on horizontal *x*- and vertical *y*-axes so that readers can see how relationships change or trends emerge, usually over time. As such, line graphs often contribute to political or social arguments by tracking fluctuations in income, unemployment, educational attainment, stock prices, and so on.

Properly designed, line graphs are easy to read and informative, especially when just a single variable is presented. But it is possible to plot several items on an axis, complicating the line graph but increasing the amount of information it offers (see fig. 1).

Use bar and column graphs to plot relationships within sets of data.   Column and bar graphs use rectangles to represent information either horizontally (bar graph) or vertically (column graph). In either form,

these graphs emphasize differences and can show changes over time; they
enable readers to grasp relationships that would otherwise take many words
to explain. Bar and column graphs present data precisely, if their *x*- and
y-axes are carefully drawn to scale. In Figure 2 , for example, a reader can
determine the number of major tornadoes in any of more than fifty years
and also note a slight trend toward fewer severe storms.

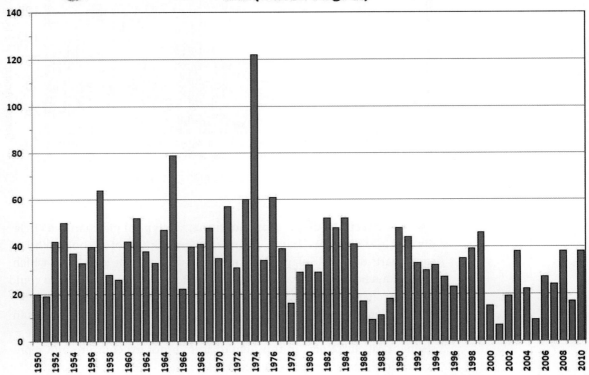

Number of Strong to Violent (EF3-EF5*)Tornadoes U.S. (March-August)

*Beginning in 2007, NOAA switched from the Fujita scale
to the Enhance Fujita scale for rating tornado strength.

Fig. 2. Number of Strong to Violent (EF3–EF5) Tornadoes. From NOAA Satellite and Information Service.

But it is easy to ask a single graphic image to do too much. For example, many readers probably find Figure 3 hard to interpret. Is the chart about the number of storms, their growing frequency, or their actual and adjusted costs? Storm effects in the background of the graphic just add to the clutter.

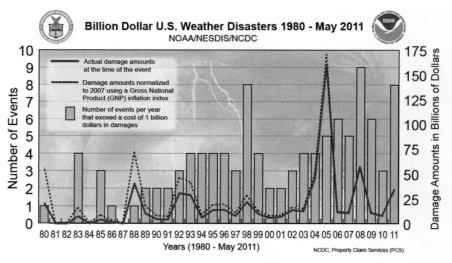

Fig. 3. Billion Dollar U.S. Weather Disasters 1980–2011. From NOAA Satellite and Information Service.

Use pie charts to display proportions.   A typical pie chart is a circle divided into segments that represent some proportion of a whole. While such charts do not display precise numbers well, they at least show which parts of a whole have greater or lesser significance. For instance, you could use a pie chart to depict the major categories of spending within the U.S. budget (defense, Social Security, Medicare, etc.). But since the segments in a typical pie chart need to total 100 percent, you would have to include a segment called "Other" in this item to account for expenditures not represented in the major categories (see fig. 4).

Pie-chart sections can be cut only so thin before they begin to lose clarity. If you wanted to use a pie chart to depict all significant federal outlays, you'd find yourself with thousands of slivers readers couldn't possibly distinguish. Better to transfer the data to a table, which could present each outlay in a separate row, page after page if necessary. A bar graph, too, might be able to handle more categories and translate data more effectively.

Use maps to display varying types of information.   Printed atlases or road maps deliver immense amounts of information, from the location and size of cities to the distances between them. But other kinds of data are now routinely laid atop geographic boundaries or displayed through technologies offered by services such as Google Maps. Everything from weather information to population movements (people, animals, plants) can be productively mapped.

Indeed, interactive technologies allow users to customize online maps to display just the information they want. The U.S. Bureau of Labor Statistics provides such a map to track employment statistics (see fig. 5). It is unlikely that you could produce a graphic this powerful, but it suggests options for presenting data.

Explore the possibilities of infographics.   People clearly enjoy using digital technologies to display information in groundbreaking ways. Under the rubric of "infographics," designers create data-driven visual texts about subjects from global warming to Halloween trends. One writer calls these focused presentations — freely combining charts, tables, timelines, maps, and other design elements — "visual essays." In some cases, infographics simply look like highly polished tables and charts (see fig. 6). But many presentations part ways with the academic conventions to tell livelier stories.

Various tools are available online to support the creation of infographics, including Many Eyes, Google Public Data Explorer, Wordle, and StatPlanet. For more about infographics and many examples, search the term online.

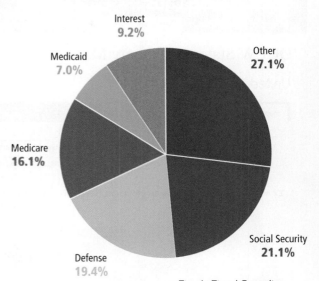

Federal Spending 2007
Actual fiscal year ended Oct. 31

Interest 9.2%
Other 27.1%
Medicaid 7.0%
Medicare 16.1%
Social Security 21.1%
Defense 19.4%

Fig. 4. Fiscal Spending 2007. From Congressional Budget Office.

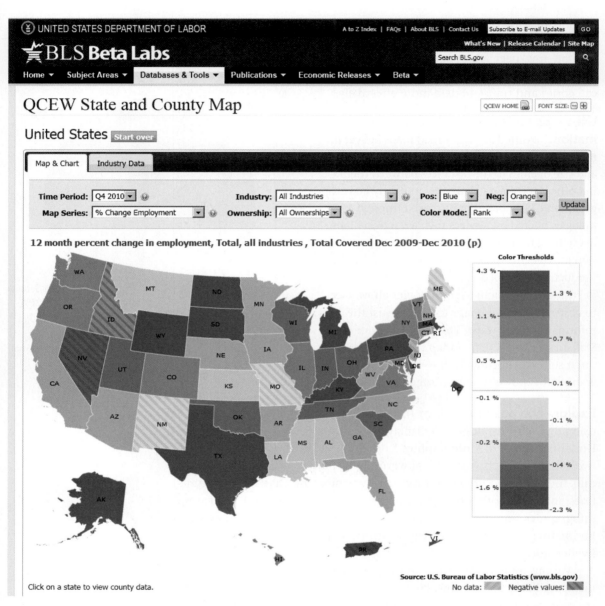

Fig. 5. Quarterly Census of Employment and Wages (QCEW) State and County Map. From U.S. Bureau of Labor Statistics, 2010.

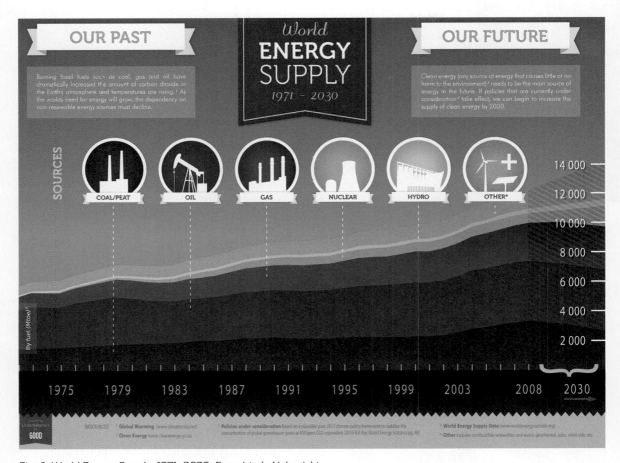

Fig. 6. World Energy Supply, 1971–2030. From Linda Nakanishi.

Your Turn   Examine Figure 6, "World Energy Supply," and then look online for additional examples of infographics. (They are readily available on sites such as VizWorld or Cool Infographics.) When you have sampled enough such items to have a sense of what the genre does, try to define the term "infographics" on your own. What do these charts have in common? What are their distinctive features?

54

Designing Print and Online Documents

think visually

Much advice about good visual design is common sense: You could guess that most academic and professional documents should look uncluttered, consistent, and balanced. But it is not always simple to translate abstract principles into practice. Nor are any visual qualities absolute. A balanced and consistent design is exactly what you want for research reports and government documents, but to create brochures or infographics, you may need more snap.

Understand the power of images. Most of us realize how powerful images can be, particularly when they perfectly capture a moment or make an argument that words alone struggle to express. The famous "Blue Marble" shot of the Earth taken by *Apollo 17* in 1972 is one such image—conveying both the wonder and fragility of our planet hanging in space. A very curious image of Osama bin Laden (see p. 593) had a similarly transformative (if much less memorable) impact in the summer of 2011, depicting, for our time, the banality of evil.

How do you diminish the ethos of an enemy like Osama bin Laden? Release a photo of him watching himself on TV. That's what the U.S. government did shortly after a team of Navy Seals killed the al-Qaeda leader in Pakistan in May 2011.

Visual texts can become potent tools in your own work. Use photographs to tell arresting stories or underscore important points. Videos can bring energy or provide visual evidence for an argument. And you can shape the visual elements of any page or screen—its colors, shapes, headings, type fonts, and so on—to make a text more appealing, focused, and accessible.

Keep page designs simple and uncluttered.   Simple doesn't mean a design should be simplistic, only that you shouldn't try to do more on a page than it (or your design skills) can handle. You want readers to find information they need, navigate your document without missteps, and grasp the structure of your project. Key information should stand out. If you keep the basic design uncomplicated, you can present lots of information without a page feeling cluttered.

Consider, for example, how cleverly Anthro Technology Furniture uses design cues as simple as *Step 1*, *Step 2*, and *Step 3* to guide consumers on a Web page through the complex process of configuring a workstation. Readers simply move left to right across a page, making specific choices. They don't feel overwhelmed by the options, even though the material is detailed.

Horizontal header guides reader across page.

Configuring the piece of furniture is broken into four easy steps.

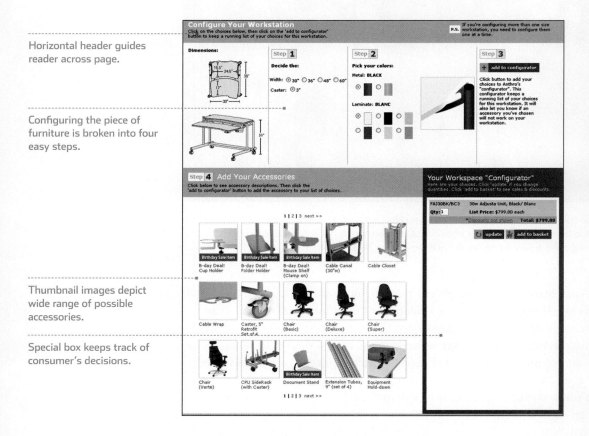

Thumbnail images depict wide range of possible accessories.

Special box keeps track of consumer's decisions.

Keep the design logical and consistent.   Readers need to be able to perceive the logic of a design quickly and then see those principles operating in elements throughout a document—especially on Web sites, in PowerPoint presentations, and in long papers.

Look to successful Web sites for models of logical and consistent design. Many sites build their pages around distinct horizontal and vertical columns that help readers locate information. A main menu generally appears near the top of the page, more detailed navigational links are usually found in a narrow side column, and featured stories often appear in wide columns in the center. To separate columns as well as individual items, the site designers use headlines, horizontal rules, images, or some combination of these devices. Handled well, pages are easy to navigate and thick with information, yet somehow seem uncluttered.

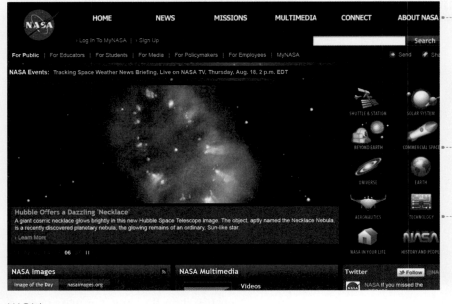

NASA home page

NASA's information-rich page has consistent horizontal orientation. The eye moves left to right to explore major options. Yet distinct horizontal sections also break the page into visually coherent segments.

Images are carefully aligned to convey information appealingly.

Full screen (not reproduced here) offers more than sixty links or options. Color scheme throughout the site is consistent: black, blue, and gray. Perhaps suggesting the vastness of space?

Keep the design balanced.   Think of balance as a dynamic term—what you hope to achieve *overall* in a design. You probably don't want many pages that, if split down the middle, would show mirror images. Strive for active designs, in which, for example, a large photograph on one side of a document is countered on the other by blocks of print and maybe several smaller images. The overall effect achieved is symmetry, even though the individual page elements may all differ in size and shape.

△

You can see conventional design principles at work on the front pages of most newspapers (print or online), where editors try to come up with a look that gives impact to the news. They have many elements to work with, including their paper's masthead, headlines of varying size, photographs and images, columns of copy, screened boxes, and much more. The pages of a newspaper can teach you a lot about design.

But you can learn, too, from the boundaries being pushed by designers of Web infographics (see Chapter 53), which use elaborate media effects to present information efficiently yet imaginatively. Unlike newspapers, magazines, or full Web sites, which must follow consistent specifications for page after page, a typical infographic focuses on a single theme or subject and chooses media tools best suited to the topic, whether graphs, flowcharts, maps, images, diagrams, or cutaways.

Use templates sensibly.   If you have the time and talent to design all of your own documents, that's terrific. But for many projects, you could do worse than to begin with the templates offered by many software products. The Project Gallery in Microsoft Office, for example, helps you create business letters, brochures, PowerPoint presentations, and more. It sets up a generic document, placing the document's margins, aligning key elements and graphics, and offering an array of customizations. No two projects based on the same template need look alike.

Colin Harman uses a simple Venn diagram to organize this infographic on design.

If you resist borrowing such materials from software, not wanting yet another part of your life packaged by corporate types, know that it is tough to design documents from scratch. Even if you intend to design an item yourself, consider examining a template to figure out how to assemble a complex document. Take what you learn from the model and then strike out on your own.

Front page of *The Plain Dealer*, March 29, 2011

To attract readers, a teaser for a sports story tops the simple masthead.

A full column with graphics in color summarizes the day's coverage and adds visual interest.

On the fold, a large image of President Obama dominates the page.

A story in a widened column is previewed by three parallel subheadings, adding variety to the design.

Local stories frame the page, their importance signaled by placement and headline size.

△

Coordinate your colors.   Your mother was right: Pay attention to colors and patterns when you dress and when you design color documents. To learn elementary principles of color coordination, try searching "color wheel" on the Web, but recognize that the subject is both complicated and more art than science. As an amateur, keep your design palettes relatively conventional and model your work on documents that you find particularly attractive.

For academic papers, the text is always black and the background is white. Color is fine in graphs and illustrations if the paper will be reviewed onscreen or printed in color. But be sure that no important elements are lost if the document is printed in black and white: A bar graph that relies on color to display differences might become unreadable. For Web sites and other projects, keep background colors light, if you use them at all, and maintain adequate contrast between text and background. Avoid either bright or pale fonts for passages of text.

Use headings if needed.   Readers appreciate headings as pathways through a text. In academic work, they should be descriptive rather than clever. If you have prepared a good scratch or topic outline, the major points may provide you with almost ready-made headings. O Like items in an outline, headings at the same level in a project should be roughly parallel in style. O

A short paper (three to five pages) doesn't require much more than a title. For longer papers (ten to twenty pages), it's possible to use top-level items from your outline as headings. For some projects, especially in the sciences, you must use the headings you're given. This is especially true for lab reports and scientific articles, and you shouldn't vary from the template.

Choose appropriate fonts.   There are likely dozens or even hundreds of fonts to work with on your computer, but, as with most other design elements, simple is generally best. Here is some basic information to help you choose the best font for your needs.

Serif fonts, such as Century, show thin flares and embellishments (called serifs; circled in the illustration on p. 599) at the tops and bottoms of their

O   O

order ideas p. 408

help with common
errors p. 600

letters and characters. These fonts have a traditional look: Note the newspaper masthead on page 597. In contrast, *sans serif* fonts, such as Helvetica, lack the decorations of serif fonts. They are smoother and more contemporary. For an example, see "Why we went in:" page 597.

Serif fonts are more readable than sans serif for extended passages of writing, such as papers. Headings in a sans serif font often contrast well in a document using serif-font text. Some designers prefer sans serif fonts for Web sites and PowerPoint presentations, especially for headings and smaller items.

Display and decorative fonts are designed to attract attention. Avoid them for academic and professional writing, but you may want to explore their use when creating posters, brochures, or special PowerPoint presentations. Beyond the few words of a heading, display fonts are hard to read: Never use them for extended passages of writing.

For typical academic projects, all text, headings, and other elements—including the title—are set in one font size, either 10 or 12 point. The standard font is Times New Roman. In professional or business projects, such as résumés, newsletters, or PowerPoint slides, you'll need to vary type sizes to distinguish headings, captions, and headlines from other elements. Examine your pages carefully in the draft stage to see that there is a balance between the larger and smaller fonts. The impact of a résumé in particular can be diluted by headings that overwhelm the career data. Be careful, too, with smaller sizes. Some fonts look crowded (and strain eyesight) if they dip below 10 points.

Boldfaced items stand out clearly on a page but only if they are rare. Too many boldfaced headings close together and your page looks heavy and cluttered. Of course, you should not use boldface as the regular text throughout your project. If you want an emphatic font, find one that looks that way in its regular form.

Century

Century, a serif font.

Helvetica

Helvetica, a sans serif font.

Common Errors

part nine

Spring or *spring*?

55 **Capitalization** 602

it's or *its*?

56 **Apostrophes** 605

need to connect ideas?

57 **Commas** 607

need a complete sentence?

58 **Comma Splices, Run-ons, and Fragments** 610

none are or *none is*?

59 **Subject/Verb Agreement** 614

lie or *lay*?

60 **Irregular Verbs** 618

their or *his* or *hers*?

61 **Pronoun/Antecedent Agreement** 620

sure what *it* means?

62 **Pronoun Reference** 622

I or *me*? *who* or *whom*?

63 **Pronoun Case** 624

are your descriptions clear?

64 **Misplaced and Dangling Modifiers** 627

making a list?

65 **Parallelism** 629

55 Capitalization

Spring or
spring?

In principle, the guidelines for capitalizing seem straightforward. You surely know to capitalize most proper nouns (and the proper adjectives formed from them), book and movie titles, the first words of sentences, and so on. But the fact is that you make many judgment calls when capitalizing, some of which will require a dictionary. (Ask your instructor if he or she can advise you on a good one.) Here are just a few of the special cases that can complicate your editing.

Capitalize the names of ethnic, religious, and political groups.   The names of these groups are considered proper nouns. Nonspecific groups, however, are lowercase.

South Korean	Native Americans	native peoples
Buddhists	Muslims	true believers
Tea Party	Democrats	political parties
the Bay City Council		the city council

Capitalize modifiers formed from proper nouns.   In some cases, such as *french fry*, the expressions have become so common that the adjective does not need to be capitalized. When in doubt, consult a dictionary.

PROPER NOUN	PROPER NOUN USED AS MODIFIER
French	French thought
Navajo	Navajo rug
Jew	Jewish lore
American	American history

Capitalize all words in titles except prepositions, articles, or conjunctions.   This is the basic rule for the titles of books, movies, long poems, and so on.

Dickens and the Dream of Cinema

In the Company of Cheerful Ladies

The variations and exceptions to this general rule, however, are numerous. MLA style specifies that the first and last words in titles always be capitalized, including any articles or prepositions.

The Guide to National Parks of the Southwest

To the Lighthouse

Such Stuff as Dreams Are Made Of

APA style doesn't make that qualification, but does specify that all words longer than four letters be capitalized in titles—even prepositions.

A Walk Among the Tombstones

Sleeping Through the Night and Other Lies

In all major styles, any word following a colon (or, much rarer, a dash) in a title is capitalized, even an article or preposition:

True Blood: All Together Now

The Exile: An Outlander Graphic Novel

Finally, note that in APA style *documentation*—that is, within the notes and on the references page, titles are capitalized differently. Only the first word in most titles, any proper nouns or adjectives, and any word following a colon are capitalized. All other words are in lowercase:

Bat predation and the evolution of frog vocalizations in the neotropics

Human aging: Usual and successful

Take care with compass points, directions, and specific geographical areas.   Points of the compass and simple directions are not capitalized when referring to general locations.

north	southwest
northern Ohio	eastern Canada
southern exposure	western horizons

But these same terms *are* capitalized when they refer to specific regions that are geographically, culturally, or politically significant (keep that dictionary handy!). Such terms are often preceded by the definite article, *the*.

the West	the Old South
the Third Coast	Southern California
Middle Eastern politics	the Western allies

Understand academic conventions.   Academic degrees are not capitalized, except when abbreviated.

bachelor of arts	doctor of medicine
MA	PhD

Specific course titles are capitalized, but they are lowercase when used as general subjects. Exception: Languages are always capitalized when referring to academic subjects.

Art History 101	Contemporary British Poetry
an art history course	an English literature paper

Capitalize months, days, holidays, and historical periods.   But don't capitalize the seasons.

January	winter
Monday	spring
Halloween	summer
the Enlightenment	fall

Apostrophes

56

Like gnats, apostrophes are small and irritating. They have two major functions: to signal that a noun is possessive and to indicate where letters have been left out in contractions. Apostrophes always need careful review.

Use apostrophes to form the possessive.   The basic rules for forming the possessive aren't complicated: For singular nouns, add 's to the end of the word:

> the wolf's lair
>
> the woman's portfolio
>
> IBM's profits
>
> Bush's foreign policy

Some possessives, while correct, look or sound awkward. In these cases, try an alternative:

ORIGINAL	REVISED
the class's photo	the class photo; the photo of the class
Bright Eyes's latest single	the latest single by Bright Eyes
in Kansas's budget	in the Kansas budget: in the budget of Kansas

it's or *its?*

For plural nouns that do not end in *s*, also add *'s* to the end of the word:

> men**'s** shoes   the mice**'s** cages   the geese**'s** nemesis

For plural nouns that do end in *s*, add an apostrophe after that terminal *s*:

> the wolves' pups
>
> the Bushes' foreign policies
>
> three senators' votes

Use apostrophes in contractions.   An apostrophe in a contraction takes the place of missing letters. Edit carefully, keeping in mind that a spell-checker doesn't help you with such blunders. It catches only words that make no sense without apostrophes, such as *dont* or *Ive*.

DRAFT	Its a shame that its come to this.
CORRECTED	It's (It is) a shame that it's (it has) come to this.
DRAFT	Whose got the list of whose going on the trip?
CORRECTED	Who's (Who has) got the list of who's (who is) going on the trip?

Don't use apostrophes with possessive pronouns.   The following possessives do not take apostrophes: *its, whose, his, hers, ours, yours,* and *theirs.*

DRAFT	We photographed the tower at it's best angle.
CORRECTED	We photographed the tower at its best angle.
DRAFT	The book is her's, not his.
CORRECTED	The book is hers, not his.
DRAFT	Their's may be an Oscar-winning film, but our's is still better.
CORRECTED	Theirs may be an Oscar-winning film, but ours is still better.

There is, inevitably, an exception. Indefinite pronouns such as *everybody, anybody, nobody,* and so on do show possession via *'s.*

> The film was everybody's favorite.
>
> Why it was so successful is anybody's guess.

Commas 57

The comma has more uses than any other punctuation mark—uses that can often seem complex. The following guidelines will help you handle commas in academic writing.

Use a comma and a coordinating conjunction to join two independent clauses.   An independent clause can stand on its own as a sentence. To join two of them, you need both a coordinating conjunction *and* a comma. A comma alone is not enough.

> Fiona's car broke down. She had to walk two miles to the train station.
>
> Fiona's car broke down, so she had to walk two miles to the train station.

There are several key points to remember here. Be sure you truly have two independent clauses, and not just a compound subject or verb. Also, make certain to include both a comma and a coordinating conjunction (*and, but, for, nor, or, so, yet*). Leaving out the coordinating conjunction creates an error known as a comma splice (see p. 610).

Use a comma after an introductory word group.   Introductory word groups are descriptive phrases or clauses that open a

need to connect ideas?

sentence. Separate these introductions from the main part of the sentence with a comma.

> Within two years of getting a degree in journalism, Ishan was writing for the *Wall Street Journal*.

For very brief introductory phrases, the comma may be omitted, but it is not wrong to leave it in.

> After college I plan to join the Marines.
> After college, I plan to join the Marines.

Use commas with transitional words and phrases. Transitional expressions such as *however* and *for example* should be set off within a sentence by a pair of commas.

> These fans can be among the first, however, to clamor for a new stadium to boost their favorite franchise.

If a transitional word or phrase opens a sentence, it should be followed by a comma.

> Moreover, studies have shown that trans fats can lower the amount of good cholesterol found in the body.

Put commas around nonrestrictive (that is, nonessential) elements. You'll know that a word or phrase is functioning as a nonrestrictive modifier if you can remove it from the sentence without destroying the overall meaning of the sentence.

> Cicero, ancient Rome's greatest orator and lawyer, was a self-made man.
> Cicero was a self-made man.

The second sentence is less informative, but still makes sense. See also the guideline on page 609, "Do not use commas to set off restrictive elements."

Use commas to separate items in a series. Commas are necessary when you have three or more items in a series.

> American highways were once ruled by powerful muscle cars such as Mustangs, GTOs, and Camaros.

Do not use commas to separate compound verbs.   Don't confuse a true compound sentence (with two independent clauses) with a sentence that simply has two verbs.

> DRAFT   They rumbled through city streets, and smoked down drag strips.
>
> CORRECTED   They rumbled through city streets and smoked down drag strips.

They rumbled through city streets is an independent clause, but *and smoked down drag strips* is not, because it doesn't have a subject. To join the two verbs, use *and* with no comma. If you have three or more verbs, however, treat them as items in a series and do separate them with commas.

> Muscle cars guzzled gasoline, burned rubber, and drove parents crazy.

Do not use a comma between subject and verb.   Perhaps it's obvious why such commas don't work when you try one in a short sentence.

> Keeping focused, can be difficult.

When a subject gets long and complicated, you might be more tempted to insert the comma, but it would still be both unnecessary and wrong. The comma in the following sentence should be omitted.

> Keeping focused on driving while simultaneously trying to operate a cell phone, can be difficult.

Do not use commas to set off restrictive elements.   Phrases you cannot remove from a sentence without significantly altering meaning are called *restrictive* or *essential*. They are modifiers that provide information needed to understand the subject.

> Only nation that recognize a right to free speech and free press should be eligible for seats on international human rights commissions.
>
> Students who have a perfect attendance record will earn three points for class participation.

Delete the highlighted phrases in the above examples and you are left with sentences that are vague or confusing. Put commas around the phrases and you create the false impression that they could be removed.

58 Comma Splices, Run-ons, and Fragments

need a complete sentence?

The sentence errors marked most often in college writing are comma splices, run-ons, and fragments.

Identify comma splices and run-ons.   A *comma splice* occurs when only a comma is used to join two independent clauses (an independent clause contains a complete subject and verb).

Identify a comma splice simply by reading the clauses on either side of a doubtful comma. If *both* clauses stand on their own as sentences (with their own subjects and verbs), it's a comma splice.

COMMA SPLICES   Officials at many elementary schools are trying to reduce childhood obesity on their campuses, research suggests that few of their strategies will work.

Some schools emphasize a need for more exercise, others have even gone so far as to reinstate recess.

A *run-on* sentence is similar to a comma splice, but it doesn't even include the comma to let readers take a break between independent clauses. The clauses bump together, confusing readers.

RUN-ON SENTENCES   Officials at many elementary schools are trying to reduce childhood obesity on their campuses research suggests that few of their strategies will work.

Some schools emphasize a need for more exercise others have even gone so far as to reinstate recess.

Fix comma splices and run-ons. To fix comma splices and run-ons, you can include a comma and a coordinating conjunction after the first independent clause to join it with the second clause.

Common Coordinating Conjunctions

and	or
but	so
for	yet
nor	

> Officials at many elementary schools are trying to reduce childhood obesity on their campuses, **but** research suggests that few of their strategies will work.

> Some schools emphasize a need for more exercise, **and** others have even gone so far as to reinstate recess.

Or you can use a semicolon to join the two clauses.

> Officials at many elementary schools are trying to reduce childhood obesity on their campuses; research suggests that few of their strategies will work.

> Some schools emphasize a need for more exercise; others have even gone so far as to reinstate recess.

Less frequently, colons or dashes may be used if the second clause summarizes or illustrates the main point of the first clause.

> Some schools have taken extreme measures: They have banned cookies, snacks, and other high-calorie foods from their vending machines.

Along with the semicolon (or colon or dash), you may wish to add a transitional word or phrase (such as *however* or *in fact*). If you do so, set off the transitional word or phrase with commas. O

> Officials at many elementary schools are trying to reduce childhood obesity on their campuses; research, **however,** suggests that few of their strategies will work.

> Some schools emphasize a need for more exercise—**in fact,** some have even gone so far as to reinstate recess.

You can also rewrite the sentence to make one of the clauses subordinate. Using a subordinating conjunction, revise so that one of the clauses in the sentence can no longer stand as a sentence on its own.

Common Subordinating Conjunctions

after	once
although	since
as	that
because	though
before	unless
except	until
if	when

> **Although** officials at many elementary schools are trying to reduce childhood obesity on their campuses, research suggests that few of their strategies will work.

connect ideas
p. 416

Or use end punctuation to create two independent sentences.

> Officials at many elementary schools are trying to reduce childhood obesity on their campuses. Research suggests that few of their strategies will work.

Identify sentence fragments.   A sentence fragment is a word group that lacks a subject, verb, or possibly both. As such, it is not a complete sentence and is not appropriate for most academic and professional writing.

FRAGMENT   Climatologists see much physical evidence of climate change. Especially in the receding of glaciers around the world.

Fix sentence fragments in your work.   You have two options for fixing sentence fragments. Attach the fragment to a nearby sentence:

COMPLETE SENTENCE   Climatologists see much physical evidence of climate change, especially in the receding of glaciers around the world.

Turn the fragment into its own sentence:

COMPLETE SENTENCE   Climatologists see much physical evidence of climate change. They are especially concerned by the receding of glaciers around the world.

Watch for fragments in the following situations.   Often a fragment will follow a complete sentence and start with a subordinating conjunction.

FRAGMENT   Climate change seems to be the product of human activity. Though some scientists believe sun cycles may explain the changing climate.

COMPLETE SENTENCE   Climate change seems to be the product of human activity, though some scientists believe sun cycles may explain the changing climate.

Participles (such as *breaking, seeking, finding*) and infinitives (such as *to break, to seek, to find*) can also lead you into fragments.

FRAGMENT   Of course, many people welcome the warmer weather. Upsetting scientists who fear governments will not act until global warming becomes irreversible.

COMPLETE SENTENCE Of course, many people welcome the warmer weather. Their attitude upsets scientists who fear governments will not act until global warming becomes irreversible.

Use deliberate fragments only in appropriate situations.   You'll find that fragments are common in advertising, fiction, and informal writing. In personal e-mail or on social networking sites, for example, expressions or clichés such as the following would likely be acceptable to your audience.

In your dreams.   Excellent!

Not on your life.   When pigs fly.

59 Subject/Verb Agreement

none are or
none is?

Verbs take many forms to express changing tenses, moods, and voices. To avoid common errors in choosing the correct verb form, follow these guidelines.

Be sure the verb agrees with its real subject. It's tempting to link a verb to the nouns closest to it (in dark red below) instead of the subject, but that's a mistake.

DRAFT   Cameras and professional lenses that cost as much as a small **car** makes photography an expensive hobby.

CORRECTED   Cameras and professional lenses that cost as much as a small car make photography an expensive hobby.

DRAFT   Bottled water from convenience **stores** or **groceries** usually cost far more per ounce than gasoline.

CORRECTED   Bottled water from convenience stores or groceries usually costs far more per ounce than gasoline.

Some indefinite pronouns are exceptions to this rule. See the chart on page 615.

Indefinite Pronouns		
Singular	**Plural**	**Variable**
anybody	both	all
anyone	few	any
anything	many	more
each	others	most
everybody	several	none
everyone		some
everything		
nobody		
no one		
nothing		
one		
somebody		
someone		
something		

In most cases, treat multiple subjects joined by *and* as plural. But when a subject with *and* clearly expresses a single notion, that subject is singular.

> Hip-hop, rock, and country are dominant forms of popular music today. [subject is plural]
>
> Blues and folk have their fans too. [subject is plural]
>
> Peanut butter and jelly is the sandwich of choice in our house. [subject is singular]
>
> Rock and roll often strikes a political chord. [subject is singular]

When singular subjects are followed by expressions such as *along with, together with,* or *as well as,* the subjects may feel plural, but technically they remain singular.

DRAFT   Esperanza Spalding, as well as Drake, Justin Bieber, Florence & the Machine, and Mumford & Sons, were competing for Best New Artist at the 2011 Grammys.

CORRECTED   Esperanza Spalding, as well as Drake, Justin Bieber, Florence & the Machine, and Mumford & Sons, was competing for Best New Artist at the 2011 Grammys.

If the corrected version sounds awkward, try revising the sentence.

CORRECTED   Esperanza Spalding, Drake, Justin Bieber, Florence & the Machine, and Mumford & Sons were all competing for Best New Artist at the 2011 Grammys.

When compound subjects are linked by *either . . . or* or *neither . . . nor,* make the verb agree with the nearer part of the subject.   Knowing this rule will make you one person among a thousand.

Neither my sisters nor my mother is a fan of Kanye West.

When possible, put the plural part of the subject closer to the verb to make it sound less awkward.

Neither my mother nor my sisters are fans of Kanye West.

Confirm whether an indefinite pronoun is singular, plural, or variable.   Most indefinite pronouns are singular, but consult the chart on page 615 to double-check.

Everybody complains about politics, but nobody does much about it.

Each of the women expects a promotion.

Something needs to be done about the budget crisis.

A few indefinite pronouns are obviously plural: *both, few, many, others, several.*

Many complain about politics, but few do much about it.

And some indefinite pronouns shift in number, depending on the prepositional phrases that modify them.

> All of the votes **are** in the ballot box.
> All of the fruit **is** spoiled.

> Most of the rules **are** less complicated.
> Most of the globe **is** covered by oceans.

> None of the rules **makes** sense.
> On the Security Council, **none** but the Russians **favor** the resolution.

Be consistent with collective nouns.   Many of these words describing a group can be treated as either singular or plural: *band, class, jury, choir, group, committee.*

> The **jury seems** to resent the lawyer's playing to its emotions.
> The **jury seem** to resent the lawyer's playing to their emotions.

> The **band was** unhappy with its latest release.
> The **band were** unhappy with their latest release.

A basic principle is to be consistent throughout a passage. If *the band* is singular the first time you mention it, keep it that way for the remainder of the project. Be sensible too. If a sentence sounds odd to your ear, modify it:

AWKWARD   The **band were** unhappy with their latest release.

BETTER   The **members** of the band **were** unhappy with their latest release.

60 Irregular Verbs

lie or *lay*?

Verbs are considered regular if they form the past and past participle—which you use to form various tenses—simply by adding *-d* or *-ed* to the base of the verb. Below are several regular verbs.

Base Form	Past Tense	Past Participle
smile	smiled	smiled
accept	accepted	accepted
manage	managed	managed

Unfortunately, the most common verbs in English are irregular. The chart on page 619 lists some of them. When in doubt about the proper form of a verb, check a dictionary.

Base Form	Past Tense	Past Participle
be	was, were	been
become	became	become
break	broke	broken
buy	bought	bought
choose	chose	chosen
come	came	come
dive	dived, dove	dived
do	did	done
drink	drank	drunk
drive	drove	driven
eat	ate	eaten
get	got	gotten
give	gave	given
go	went	gone
have	had	had
lay (to put or place)	laid	laid
lie (to recline)	lay	lain
ride	rode	ridden
ring	rang, rung	rung
rise	rose	risen
see	saw	seen
set	set	set
shine	shone, shined	shone, shined
sing	sang, sung	sung
sink	sank, sunk	sunk
speak	spoke	spoken
swear	swore	sworn
throw	threw	thrown
wake	woke, waked	woken, waked
write	wrote	written

61 Pronoun/Antecedent Agreement

their or *his*
or *hers*?

You already know that pronouns take the place of nouns. Antecedents are the words pronouns refer to. Since pronouns in their many forms stand in for nouns, they also share some of the same markers, such as gender and number.

SINGULAR/FEMININE	The **nun** merely smiled because **she** had taken a vow of silence.
SINGULAR/MASCULINE	The **NASCAR champion** complained that **he** got little media attention.
SINGULAR/NEUTER	The **chess team** took **itself** too seriously.
PLURAL	**Members of the chess team** took **themselves** too seriously.
PLURAL	**They** seemed awfully subdued for **pro athletes.**
PLURAL	The **bridge and groom** wrote **their** own ditzy vows.
PLURAL	**Many** in the terminal resented searches of **their** luggage.

The basic rule for managing pronouns and antecedents couldn't be simpler: Make sure pronouns you select have the same number and gender as the words they stand for.

DRAFT	When a **student** spends too much time on sorority activities, **they** may suffer academically.
CORRECTED	When a **student** spends too much time on sorority activities, **she** may suffer academically.

As always, though, there are confusing cases and numerous exceptions. The following guidelines can help you avoid common problems.

Check the number of indefinite pronouns.   Some of the most common singular indefinite pronouns—especially *anybody, everybody, everyone*—may seem plural, but they should be treated as singular. (For the complete list of indefinite pronouns, see the chart on p. 615 in Chapter 59.)

DRAFT   Has **everybody** completed **their** assignment by now?

CORRECTED   Has **everybody** completed **his or her** assignment by now?

If using *his or her* sounds awkward, revise the sentence.

Have **all students** completed **their** assignments by now?

Correct sexist pronoun usage.   Using *his* alone (instead of *his or her*) to refer to an indefinite pronoun is considered sexist unless it clearly refers only to males. ○

Treat collective nouns consistently.   Collective nouns—such as *team, herd, congregation, mob*, and so on—can be treated as either singular or plural.

The Roman **legion** marched until **it** reached **its** camp in Gaul.

The Roman **legion** marched until **they** reached **their** camp in Gaul.

Just be consistent and sensible in your usage. Treat a collective noun the same way, as either singular or plural, throughout a paper or project. And don't hesitate to modify a sentence when even a correct usage sounds awkward.

AWKWARD   The **team** smiled as **it** received **its** championship jerseys.

BETTER   **Members of the team** smiled as **they** received **their** championship jerseys.

respect your readers
p. 440

62 Pronoun Reference

sure what *it* means?

A pronoun should refer back clearly to a noun or pronoun (its *antecedent*), usually the one nearest to it that matches it in number and, when necessary, gender.

> **Consumers** will buy a **Rolex** because **they** covet **its** snob appeal.
>
> **Nancy Pelosi** spoke instead of **Harry Reid** because **she** had more interest in the legislation than **he** did.

If connections between pronouns and antecedents wobble within a single sentence or longer passage, readers will struggle. The following guidelines can help you avoid three common problems.

Clarify confusing pronoun antecedents. Revise sentences in which readers will find themselves wondering who is doing what to whom. Multiple revisions are usually possible, depending on how the confusing sentence could be interpreted.

CONFUSING	The **batter** collided with the **first baseman**, but **he** wasn't injured.
BETTER	The batter collided with the **first baseman**, **who** wasn't injured.
BETTER	The **batter** wasn't injured by **his** collision with the first baseman.

Make sure a pronoun has a plausible antecedent.   Sometimes the problem is that the antecedent doesn't actually exist—it is only implied. In these cases, either reconsider the antecedent/pronoun relationship or replace the pronoun with a noun.

CONFUSING   Grandmother had hip-replacement surgery two months ago, and it is already fully healed.

In the above sentence, the implied antecedent for *it* is *hip*, but the noun *hip* isn't in the sentence (*hip-replacement* is an adjective describing *surgery*).

BETTER   Grandmother had **her hip** replaced two months ago, and **she** is already fully healed.

BETTER   Grandmother had hip-replacement surgery two months ago, and **her hip** is already fully healed.

Be certain that the antecedent of *this, that,* or *which* isn't vague.
In the following example, a humble *this* is asked to shoulder the burden of a writer who hasn't quite figured out how to pull together all the ideas raised in the preceding sentence. What exactly might the antecedent for *this* be? It doesn't exist. To fix the problem, the writer needs to replace *this* with a more thoughtful analysis.

FINAL SENTENCE VAGUE

The university staff is underpaid, the labs are short on equipment, and campus maintenance is neglected. Moreover, we need two or three new parking garages to make up for the lots lost because of recent construction projects. Yet students cannot be expected to shoulder additional costs because tuition and fees are high already. **This** is a problem that must be solved.

FINAL SENTENCE CLARIFIED

How to fund both academic departments and infrastructure needs without increasing students' financial outlay is a problem that must be solved.

63 Pronoun Case

I or *me? who* or *whom?*

In spoken English, you hear it when you run into a problem with pronoun case.

> "Let's just keep this matter between **you** and . . . *ummmm* . . . **me**."
>
> "To **who** . . . I mean, uh . . . **whom** does this letter go?"
>
> "Hector is more of a people person than **her** . . . than **she is**."

Like nouns, pronouns can be subjects, objects, or possessives, and their forms vary to show which case they express in a sentence.

Subjective Pronouns	Objective Pronouns	Possessive Pronouns
I	me	my, mine
you	you	your, yours
he, she, it	him, her, it	his, her, hers, its
we	us	our, ours
they	them	their, theirs
who	whom	whose

Unfortunately, determining case is the problem. Here are some strategies for dealing with these common situations.

Use the subjective case for pronouns that are subjects. When pronouns are the only subject in a clause, they rarely cause a problem. But double the subject, and there's trouble.

> Sara and . . . **me** . . . , or is it Sara and **I** wrote the report?

To make the right choice, try answering the question for one subject at a time. You quickly recognize that *Sara* wrote the report, and *I* did the same thing. So one possible revision is:

> Sara and I wrote the report.

Or you can recast the sentence to avoid the difficulty in the first place.

> We wrote the report.

Use the objective case for pronouns that are objects. Again, choosing one objective pronoun is generally obvious, but with two objects, the choice is less clear. How do you decide what to do in the following sentence?

> The corporate attorney will represent both Geoff and I . . . Geoff and me?

Again, deal with one object at a time. Since the attorney will represent *me* and will also represent *Geoff*, a possible revision is:

> The corporate attorney will represent Geoff and me.

Or, to be more concise:

> The corporate attorney will represent us.

Use *whom* when appropriate. One simple pronoun choice brings many writers to their knees: *who* or *whom*. The rule, however, is the same as for other pronouns: Use the subjective case (*who*) for subjects and the objective case (*whom*) for objects. In some cases, the choice is obvious.

DRAFT	Whom wrote the report?
CORRECTED	Who wrote the report?

DRAFT	By who was the report written?
CORRECTED	By whom was the report written?

But this choice becomes tricky when you're dealing with subordinate clauses.

DRAFT	The shelter needs help from whomever can volunteer three hours per week.

The previous example may sound right because *whomever* immediately follows the preposition *from*. But, because the pronoun is the subject of a subordinate clause, it needs to be in the subjective case.

CORRECTED   The shelter needs help from **whoever** can volunteer three hours per week.

Finish comparisons to determine the right case.   Many times when writers make comparisons, they leave out some understood information.

> I've always thought John was more talented than Paul.

> (I've always thought John was more talented than Paul *was*.)

But leaving this information out can lead to confusion when it comes to choosing the correct pronoun case. Try the sentence, adding *him*.

DRAFT   I've always thought John was more talented than **him**.

I've always thought John was more talented than **him** *was*.

CORRECTED   I've always thought John was more talented than **he**.

If it sounds strange to use the correct pronoun, complete the sentence.

CORRECTED   I've always thought John was more talented than **he** was.

Don't be misled by an appositive.   An *appositive* is a word or phrase that amplifies or renames a noun or pronoun. In the example below, *Americans* is the appositive. First, try reading the sentence without it.

DRAFT   **Us** Americans must defend our civil rights.

APPOSITIVE CUT   **Us** must defend our civil rights. [*Us* can't be a subject.]

CORRECTED   **We** Americans must defend our civil rights.

Note that when the pronoun is contained within the appositive, as in the examples below, the pronoun follows the case of the word or words it renames.

SUBJECTIVE   The bloggers who were still in the running, Lucy, Cali, and **I**, wrote all night trying to outdo each other.

OBJECTIVE   The site was dominated by the bloggers who were still in the running, Lucy, Cali, and **me**.

Misplaced and Dangling Modifiers

64

In general, modifiers need to be close and obviously connected to the words they modify. When they aren't, readers may become confused—or amused.

Position modifiers close to the words they modify.

MISPLACED   Layered like a wedding cake, Mrs. DeLeon unveiled her model for the parade float.

Mrs. DeLeon is not layered like a wedding cake; the model for the parade float is.

REVISED   Mrs. DeLeon unveiled her model for the parade float, which was layered like a wedding cake.

Place adverbs such as *only, almost, especially*, and *even* carefully. If these modifiers are placed improperly, their purpose can be vague or ambiguous.

VAGUE   The speaker almost angered everyone in the room.

CLEARER   The speaker angered almost everyone in the room.

AMBIGUOUS   Joan only drove a stick shift.

CLEARER   Only Joan drove a stick shift.

CLEARER   Joan drove only a stick shift.

are your descriptions clear?

627

Don't allow a modifier to dangle.   A modifying word or phrase at the beginning of a sentence should be followed immediately by the subject it modifies. When it doesn't, the modifier is said to dangle.

DANGLING   **After picking me up at the airport,** San Francisco was introduced to me by my future business partner.

San Francisco didn't pick me up at the airport; my future business partner did. So *my future business partner* needs to be the subject of the sentence.

REVISED   **After picking me up at the airport,** my future business partner introduced me to San Francisco.

Parallelism  65

When items in sentences follow similar patterns of language, they are described as parallel. Parallel structure makes your writing easier to read and understand.

When possible, make compound items parallel. Don't confuse your readers by requiring them to untangle subjects, verbs, modifiers, or other items that could easily be parallel.

making a list?

NOT PARALLEL	Becoming a lawyer and to write a novel are Leslie's goals.
PARALLEL	Becoming a lawyer and writing a novel are Leslie's goals.
NOT PARALLEL	The university will demolish its old stadium and bricks from it are being sold.
PARALLEL	The university will demolish its old stadium and sell the bricks.
NOT PARALLEL	The TV anchor reported the story thoroughly and with compassion.
PARALLEL	The TV anchor reported the story thoroughly and compassionately.

Keep items in a series parallel.　A series should consist of all nouns, all adjectives, all verbs, and so on.

NOT PARALLEL　She was a fine new teacher—eager, very patient, and gets her work done.

PARALLEL　She was a fine new teacher—eager, very patient, and conscientious.

NOT PARALLEL　We expected to rehabilitate the historic property, break even on the investment, and to earn the goodwill of the community.

PARALLEL　We expected to rehabilitate the historic property, to break even on the investment, and to earn the goodwill of the community.

PARALLEL　We expected to rehabilitate the historic property, break even on the investment, and earn the goodwill of the community.

Keep headings and lists parallel.　If you use headings to break up the text of a document, use a similar language pattern and design for all of them. It may help to type the headings out separately from the text to make sure you are keeping them parallel. Items in a printed list should be parallel as well.

reader

Readings

part ten

66 Narratives 634

67 Reports 686

68 Arguments 735

69 Evaluations 764

70 Causal Analyses 799

71 Proposals 858

72 Literary Analyses 898

73 Rhetorical Analyses 969

Need help with critical reading? See page 365. / Need help analyzing claims and evidence? See page 487.

66 Narratives: Readings

LITERACY NARRATIVE
David Sedaris, *Me Talk Pretty One Day*   635

MEMOIR
Rob Sheffield, *Rumblefish*   642

GRAPHIC NARRATIVE (EXCERPT)
Lynda Barry, *Lost and Found*   654

REFLECTION
Naomi Shihab Nye, *Mint Snowball*   661

MEMOIR
Ira Sukrungruang, *Chop Suey*   664

LITERACY NARRATIVE
Jonathan Franzen, *The Comfort Zone*   668

See also Chapter 1:

REFLECTION
Mark Edmundson,
*The Pink Floyd Night
School,* 7

LITERACY NARRATIVE
Richard Rodriguez,
Strange Tools, 23

STUDENT MEMOIR
Miles Pequeno, *Check.
Mate?* 29

GRAPHIC NARRATIVE (EXCERPT)
Marjane Satrapi, from
Persepolis, 35

LITERACY NARRATIVE   David Sedaris has published six best-selling books of humorous personal essays and short fiction, and he frequently appears on the National Public Radio program *This American Life*. This essay, from his collection *Me Talk Pretty One Day* (2000), examines Sedaris's difficulties learning French and profiles his bumpy relationship with a tough teacher. This essay can be considered a literacy narrative — a personal essay that explores how we acquire language and communication skills, and how these experiences shape us as people.

DAVID SEDARIS

Me Talk Pretty One Day

At the age of forty-one, I am returning to school and have to think of myself as what my French textbook calls "a true debutant." After paying my tuition, I was issued a student ID, which allows me a discounted entry fee at movie theaters, puppet shows, and Festyland, a far-flung amusement park that advertises with billboards picturing a cartoon stegosaurus sitting in a canoe and eating what appears to be a ham sandwich.

I've moved to Paris with hopes of learning the language. My school is an easy ten-minute walk from my apartment, and on the first day of class I arrived early, watching as the returning students greeted one another in the school lobby. Vacations were recounted, and questions were raised concerning mutual friends with names like Kang and Vlatnya. Regardless of their nationalities, everyone spoke in what sounded to me like excellent French. Some accents were better than others, but the students exhibited an ease and confidence I found intimidating. As an added discomfort, they were all young, attractive, and well dressed, causing me to feel not unlike Pa Kettle trapped backstage after a fashion show.

The first day of class was nerve-racking because I knew I'd be expected to perform. That's the way they do it here — it's everybody into the language pool, sink or swim. The teacher marched in, deeply tanned from a recent vacation, and proceeded to rattle off a series of administrative announcements. I've spent quite a few summers in Normandy, and I took a monthlong French class before leaving New York. I'm not completely in the dark, yet I understood only half of what this woman was saying.

"If you have not *meimslsxp* or *lgpdmurct* by this time, then you should not be in this room. Has everyone *apzkiubjxow?* Everyone? Good, we shall begin." She spread out her lesson plan and sighed, saying, "All right, then, who knows the alphabet?"

It was startling because (a) I hadn't been asked that question in a while and (b) I realized, while laughing, that I myself did *not* know the alphabet. They're the same letters, but in France they're pronounced differently. I know the shape of the alphabet but had no idea what it actually sounded like.

"Ahh." The teacher went to the board and sketched the letter *a*. "Do we have anyone in the room whose first name commences with an *ahh?*"

Two Polish Annas raised their hands, and the teacher instructed them to present themselves by stating their names, nationalities, occupations, and a brief list of things they liked and disliked in this world. The first Anna hailed from an industrial town outside of Warsaw and had front teeth the size of tombstones. She worked as a seamstress, enjoyed quiet times with friends, and hated the mosquito.

"Oh, really," the teacher said. "How very interesting. I thought that everyone loved the mosquito, but here, in front of all the world, you claim to detest him. How is it that we've been blessed with someone as unique and original as you? Tell us, please."

The seamstress did not understand what was being said but knew that this was an occasion for shame. Her rabbity mouth huffed for breath, and she stared down at her lap as though the appropriate comeback were stitched somewhere alongside the zipper of her slacks.

The second Anna learned from the first and claimed to love sunshine and detest lies. It sounded like a translation of one of those Playmate of the Month data sheets, the answers always written in the same loopy handwriting. "Turn-ons: Mom's famous five-alarm chili! Turnoffs: insecurity and guys who come on too strong!!!!"

The two Polish Annas surely had clear notions of what they loved and hated, but like the rest of us, they were limited in terms of vocabulary, and this made them appear less than sophisticated. The teacher forged on, and we learned that Carlos, the Argentine bandoneon player, loved wine, music, and, in his words, "making sex with the womens of the world." Next came a beautiful young Yugoslav who identi- fied herself as an optimist, saying that she loved everything that life had to offer.

The teacher licked her lips, revealing a hint of the saucebox we would later come to know. She crouched low for her attack, placed her hands on the young woman's desk, and leaned close, saying, "Oh yeah? And do you love your little war?"

While the optimist struggled to defend herself, I scrambled to think of an answer to what had obviously become a trick question. How often is one asked what he loves in this world? More to the point, how often is one asked and then publicly ridiculed for his answer? I recalled my mother, flushed with wine, pounding the tabletop late one night, saying, "Love? I love a good steak cooked rare. I love my cat, and I love . . ." My sisters and I leaned forward, waiting to hear our names. "Tums," our mother said. "I love Tums."

The teacher killed some time accusing the Yugoslavian girl of masterminding a program of genocide, and I jotted frantic notes in the margins of my pad. While I can honestly say that I love leafing through medical textbooks devoted to severe dermatological conditions, the hobby is beyond the reach of my French vocabulary, and acting it out would only have invited controversy.

When called upon, I delivered an effortless list of things that I detest: blood sausage, intestinal pâtés, brain pudding. I'd learned these words the hard way. Hav- ing given it some thought, I then declared my love for IBM typewriters, the French word for *bruise,* and my electric floor waxer. It was a short list, but still I managed to mispronounce *IBM* and assign the wrong gender to both the floor waxer and the typewriter. The teacher's reaction led me to believe that these mistakes were capital crimes in the country of France.

"Were you always this *palicmkrexis*?" she asked. "Even a *fiuscrzsa ticiwelmun* knows that a typewriter is feminine."

I absorbed as much of her abuse as I could understand, thinking—but not saying—that I find it ridiculous to assign a gender to an inanimate object incapable of disrobing and making an occasional fool of itself. Why refer to Lady Crack Pipe or Good Sir Dishrag when these things could never live up to all that their sex implied?

The teacher proceeded to belittle everyone from German Eva, who hated laziness, to Japanese Yukari, who loved paintbrushes and soap. Italian, Thai, Dutch, Korean, and Chinese—we all left class foolishly believing that the worst was over. She'd shaken us up a little, but surely that was just an act designed to weed out the deadweight. We didn't know it then, but the coming months would teach us what it was like to spend time in the presence of a wild animal, something completely unpredictable. Her temperament was not based on a series of good and bad days but, rather, good and bad moments. We soon learned to dodge chalk and protect our heads and stomachs whenever she approached us with a question. She hadn't yet punched anyone, but it seemed wise to protect ourselves against the inevitable.

Though we were forbidden to speak anything but French, the teacher would occasionally use us to practice any of her five fluent languages.

"I hate you," she said to me one afternoon. Her English was flawless. "I really, really hate you." Call me sensitive, but I couldn't help but take it personally.

After being singled out as a lazy *kfdtinvfm*, I took to spending four hours a night on my homework, putting in even more time whenever we were assigned an essay. I suppose I could have gotten by with less, but I was determined to create some sort of identity for myself: David the hard worker, David the cut-up. We'd have one of those "complete this sentence" exercises, and I'd fool with the thing for hours, invariably settling on something like "A quick run around the lake? I'd love to! Just give me a moment while I strap on my wooden leg." The teacher, through word and action, conveyed the message that if this was my idea of an identity, she wanted nothing to do with it.

My fear and discomfort crept beyond the borders of the classroom and accompanied me out onto the wide boulevards. Stopping for a coffee, asking directions, depositing money in my bank account: these things were out of the question, as they involved having to speak. Before beginning school, there'd been no shutting me up, but now I was convinced that everything I said was wrong. When the phone rang, I ignored it. If someone asked me a question, I pretended to be deaf. I knew my fear was getting the best of me when I started wondering why they don't sell cuts of meat in vending machines.

My only comfort was the knowledge that I was not alone. Huddled in the hallways and making the most of our pathetic French, my fellow students and I engaged in the sort of conversation commonly overheard in refugee camps.

"Sometime me cry alone at night."

"That be common for I, also, but be more strong, you. Much work and someday you talk pretty. People start love you soon. Maybe tomorrow, okay."

Unlike the French class I had taken in New York, here there was no sense of competition. When the teacher poked a shy Korean in the eyelid with a freshly sharpened pencil, we took no comfort in the fact that, unlike Hyeyoon Cho, we all knew the irregular past tense of the verb *to defeat*. In all fairness, the teacher hadn't meant to stab the girl, but neither did she spend much time apologizing, saying only, "Well, you should have been *vkkdyo* more *kdeynfulh.*"

Over time it became impossible to believe that any of us would ever improve. Fall arrived and it rained every day, meaning we would now be scolded for the water dripping from our coats and umbrellas. It was mid-October when the teacher singled me out, saying, "Every day spent with you is like having a cesarean section."

And it struck me that, for the first time since arriving in France, I could understand every word that someone was saying.

Understanding doesn't mean that you can suddenly speak the language. Far from it. It's a small step, nothing more, yet its rewards are intoxicating and deceptive. The teacher continued her diatribe and I settled back, bathing in the subtle beauty of each new curse and insult.

"You exhaust me with your foolishness and reward my efforts with nothing but pain, do you understand me?"

The world opened up, and it was with great joy that I responded, "I know the thing that you speak exact now. Talk me more, you, plus, please, plus."

Reading the Genre

1. This is a literacy narrative about the acquisition of a second language. Who is the villain in this story? Who are the villains and heroes in your own literacy histories, and why? (For a description and another example of a literacy narrative, see Richard Rodriguez's essay "Strange Tools," on pp. 23–28. See also Lynda Barry's "Lost and Found," pp. 654–59, and Jonathan Franzen's "The Comfort Zone," pp. 668–84.)

2. How does David Sedaris use both English and a garbled form of French in this story for comedic effect? How are the two languages used to reveal his confusion, his failures, and his triumphs? (See "Use comparison and contrast to show similarity and difference," p. 404.)

3. Does this story end happily? Do literacy narratives have to have a happy ending? Do they have to have an epiphany? (For a definition of *epiphany*, see p. 16.)

4. Stories about schooling and education often reveal quite a bit about the group dynamic within a classroom. How does Sedaris represent the mood within this environment? How does he depict his fellow students and their collective feelings and shared experiences? (See "Develop major characters," p. 21.)

5. **WRITING:** Think about your own experiences learning a second language or dialect (a dialect can be thought of as the common vocabulary, grammar, and speech patterns of a group of people). What was it like being an outsider? Think about your struggles and successes in expressing yourself. What conclusions can you draw about the process of learning a new language or dialect?

6. **AUDIO ESSAY:** After you have drafted a narrative, listen to any episode of the NPR show *This American Life* (available for free on iTunes and at www .thisamericanlife.org). Now, rewrite a section of your story for an audience of radio listeners. (For more help, see Chapter 51, "Understanding Digital Media," p. 568, and Chapter 52, "Digital Elements," p. 577.) Record yourself reading the section aloud and then listen to your recording, thinking about what you would revise to make the story "sound" better. (If you are deaf or hard of hearing and use sign language, you might try making a video of yourself signing the narrative.)

MEMOIR   Rob Sheffield, a former radio D.J., is an editor and columnist for *Rolling Stone* magazine. His first wife, Renée Crist, who is his muse for this essay, passed away in 1997. You can read excerpts from his book *Love Is a Mix Tape* (2007) and listen to the music he refers to in this essay at www.randomhouse.com/crown/mixtape or at www.myspace.com/loveisamixtapethebook. Sheffield's newest book is a memoir about music entitled *Talking to Girls about Duran Duran*.

ROB SHEFFIELD

Rumblefish

A SIDE ONE DATE / TIME	**B** SIDE TWO DATE / TIME
Pavement: "Shoot the Singer"	R.E.M.: "Man on the Moon"
The Smiths: "Cemetry Gates"	10,000 Maniacs: "Candy Everybody Wants"
Belly: "Feed the Tree"	
Sloan: "Sugar Tune"	Royal Trux: "Sometimes"
L7: "Shove"	Bettie Serveert: "Palomine"
Lois: "Bonds in Seconds"	Morrissey: "We Hate It When Our Friends Become Successful"
Grenadine: "In a World Without Heroes"	
The Pooh Sticks: "Sugar Baby"	Mary Chapin Carpenter: "Passionate Kisses"
The Chills: "Part Past Part Fiction"	
Whitney Houston: "I'm Every Woman"	Pavement: "Texas Never Whispers"
L7: "Packin' A Rod"	Boy George: "The Crying Game"
	Belly: "Slow Dog"

The playback: late night, Brooklyn, a pot of coffee, and a chair by the window. I'm listening to a mix tape from 1993. Nobody can hear it but me. The neighbors are asleep. The skater kids who sit on my front steps, drink beer, and blast Polish hip-hop—they're gone for the night. The diner next door is closed, but the air is still full of borscht and kielbasa. This is where I live now. A different town, a different apartment, a different year.

This mix tape is just another piece of useless junk that Renée left behind. A category that I guess tonight includes me.

I should have gone to sleep hours ago. Instead, I was rummaging through old boxes, looking for some random paperwork, and I found this tape with her curly scribble on the label. She never played this one for me. She didn't write down the songs, so I have no idea what's in store. But I can already tell it's going to be a late night. It always is. I pop *Rumblefish* into my Panasonic RXC36 boombox on the kitchen counter, pour some more coffee, and let the music have its way with me. It's a date. Just me and Renée and some tunes she picked out.

All these tunes remind me of her now. It's like that old song, "88 Lines About 44 Women." Except it's 8,844 lines about one woman. We've done this before. We get together sometimes, in the dark, share a few songs. It's the closest we'll get to hearing each other's voices tonight.

The first song: *Pavement's "Shoot the Singer." Just a sad California boy, plucking his guitar and singing about a girl he likes. They were Renée's favorite band. She used to say, "There's a lot of room in my dress for these boys."*

Renée called this tape *Rumblefish*. I don't know why. She recorded it over a promo cassette by some band called Drunken Boat, who obviously didn't make a big impression, because she stuck her own label over their name, put Scotch tape over the punch holes, and made her own mix. She dated it "Ides o' March 1993." She also wrote this inspirational credo on the label:

> "You know what I'm doing — Just follow along!"
>   —Jennie Garth

Ah, the old Jennie Garth workout video, *Body in Progress*. Some nights you go to the mall with your squeeze, you're both a little wasted, and you come home with a Jennie Garth workout video. That's probably buried in one of these boxes, too. Neither of us ever threw anything away. We made a lot of mix tapes while we were together. Tapes for making out, tapes for dancing, tapes for falling asleep. Tapes for doing the dishes, for walking the dog. I kept them all. I have them piled up on my bookshelves, spilling out of my kitchen cabinets, scattered all over the bedroom floor. I don't even have pots or pans in my kitchen, just that old boombox on the counter, next to the sink. So many tapes.

I met Renée in Charlottesville, Virginia, when we were both twenty-three. When the bartender at the Eastern Standard put on a tape, Big Star's *Radio City,* she was the only other person in the room who perked up. So we drank bourbon and talked about music. We traded stories about the bands we liked, shows we'd seen. Renée loved the Replacements and Alex Chilton and the Meat Puppets. So did I.

I loved the Smiths. Renée hated the Smiths.

The second song on the tape is "Cemetry Gates" by the Smiths.

The first night we met, I told her the same thing I've told every single girl I've ever had a crush on: "I'll make you a tape!" Except this time, with this girl, it worked. When we were planning our wedding a year later, she said that instead of stepping on a glass at the end of the ceremony, she wanted to step on a cassette case, since that's what she'd been doing ever since she met me.

Falling in love with Renée was not the kind of thing you walk away from in one piece. I had no chance. She put a hitch in my git-along. She would wake up in the middle of the night and say things like "What if Bad Bad Leroy Brown was a girl?" or "Why don't they have commercials for salt like they do for milk?" Then she would fall back to sleep, while I would lie awake and give thanks for this alien creature beside whom I rested.

Renée was a real cool hell-raising Appalachian punk-rock girl. Her favorite song was the Rolling Stones' "Let's Spend the Night Together." Her favorite album was

Pavement's *Slanted and Enchanted*. She rooted for the Atlanta Braves and sewed her own silver vinyl pants. She knew which kind of screwdriver was which. She baked pies, but not very often. She could rap Roxanne Shante's "Go on Girl" all the way through. She called Eudora Welty "Miss Eudora." She had an MFA in fiction and never got any stories published, but she kept writing them anyway. She bought too many shoes and dyed her hair red. Her voice was full of the frazzle and crackle of music.

Renée was a country girl, three months older than me. She was born on November 21, 1965, the same day as Björk, in the Metropolitan Mobile Home Park in Northcross, Georgia. She grew up in southwest Virginia, with her parents, Buddy and Nadine, and her little sister. When she was three, Buddy was transferred to the defense plant in Pulaski County, and so her folks spent a summer building a house there. Renée used to sit in the backyard, feeding grass to the horses next door through the fence. She had glasses, curly brown hair, and a beagle named Snoopy. She went to Fairlawn Baptist Church and Pulaski High School and Hollins College. She got full-immersion baptized in Claytor Lake. The first record she ever owned was KC & the Sunshine Band's "Get Down Tonight." KC was her first love. I was her last.

I was a shy, skinny, Irish Catholic geek from Boston. I'd never met anybody like Renée before. I moved to Charlottesville for grad school, my plans all set: go down South, get my degree, then haul ass to the next town. The South was a scary new world. The first time I saw a possum in my driveway, I shook a bony fist at the sky and cursed this godforsaken rustic hellhole. I'm twenty-three! Life is passing me by! My ancestors spent centuries in the hills of County Kerry, waist-deep in sheep shit, getting shot at by English soldiers, and my grandparents crossed the ocean in coffin ships to come to America, just so I could get possum rabies?

Renée had never set foot north of Washington, D.C. For her, Charlottesville was the big bad city. She couldn't believe her eyes, just because there were *sidewalks* everywhere. Her ancestors were Appalachians from the hills of West Virginia; both of her grandfathers were coal miners. We had nothing in common, except we both loved music. It was the first connection we had, and we depended on it to keep us together. We did a lot of work to meet in the middle. Music brought us together. So now music was stuck with us.

I was lucky I got to be her guy for a while.

I remember this song. L7, punk-rock girls from L.A., the "Shove" single on Sub Pop. Renée did a Spin *cover story on them, right after she made this tape. She'd never seen California before. The girls in the band took her shopping and picked out some jeans for her.*

When we were married we lived in Charlottesville, in a moldy basement dump that flooded every time it rained. We often drove her creaky 1978 Chrysler LeBaron through the mountains, kicking around junk shops, looking for vinyl records and finding buried treasures on scratched-up 45s for a quarter a pop. She drove me up to the Meadow Muffin on Route 11, outside Stuart's Draft, for the finest banana milkshakes on the planet. Every afternoon, I picked Renée up from work. By night we'd head to Tokyo Rose, the local sushi bar, where bands played in the basement. We went to hear every band that came to town, whether we liked them or not. If we'd waited around for famous, successful, important bands to play Charlottesville, we would have been waiting a long time. Charlottesville was a small town; we had to make our own fun. Renée would primp for the shows, sew herself a new skirt. We knew we would see all of our friends there, including all the rock boys Renée had crushes on. The bassist—always the bassist. I'm six-five, so I would hang in the back with the other tall rock dudes and lean against the wall. Renée was five-two, and she definitely wasn't the type of gal to hang in the back, so she'd dart up front and run around and wag her tail. She made a scene. She would dive right into the crowd and let me just linger behind her, basking in her glow. Any band that was in town, Renée would invite them to crash at our place, even though there wasn't even enough room for us.

Belly? Aaaargh! Renée! Why are you doing this to me? This band blows homeless goats. I can't believe she liked this song enough to tape it.

I get sentimental over the music of the '90s. Deplorable, really. But I love it all. As far as I'm concerned, the '90s was the best era for music ever, even the stuff that I loathed at the time, even the stuff that gave me stomach cramps. Every note from those years is charged with life for me now. For instance, I hated Pearl Jam at the time. I thought they were pompous blowhards. Now, whenever a Pearl Jam song comes on the car radio, I find myself pounding my fist on the dashboard, screaming, "Pearl JAM! Pearl JAM! Now *this* is rock and roll! Jeremy's SPO-ken! But he's still al-LIIIIIIVE!"

I don't recall making the decision to love Pearl Jam. Hating them was a lot more fun.

1991. The year punk broke. The palindrome year. In the *Planet of the Apes* movies, it was the year of the ape revolution, but I'll settle for the 1991 we got. This was the year we got married. We knew it would be a big deal, and it was. The next few years were a rush. It was a glorious time for pop culture, the decade of Nirvana and Lollapalooza and *Clueless* and *My So-Called Life* and *Sassy* and *Pulp Fiction* and Greg Maddux and Garth Brooks and Green Day and Drew and Dre and Snoop and *Wayne's World*. It was the decade Johnny Depp got his *Winona Forever* tattoo, the decade Beavis and Butthead got butt-shaped tattoos on their butts. It was the decade of Kurt Cobain and Shania Twain and Taylor Dayne and Brandy Chastain. The boundaries of American culture were exploding, and music was leading the way.

There was a song Renée and I made up in the car, singing along with the radio.

Out on the road today, I saw a Sub Pop sticker on a Subaru.
A little voice inside my head said, yuppies smell teen spirit too.
I thought I knew what love was, but I was blind.
Those days are gone forever, whatever, never mind.

At the end of the working day, we rubbed each other's feet and sang Pavement songs to each other, and we knew every word was true. . . . I rubbed Lubriderm into her pantyhose burns. The Reagan-Bush nightmare was coming to an end, so close we could taste it. Nirvana was all over the radio. Corporate rock was dead. On *90210*, Dylan and Kelly were making out on the beach to "Damn, I Wish I Was Your Lover." We were young and in love and the world was changing.

When we weren't being students or working lame jobs, we were rock critics, freelancing for the *Village Voice* and *Spin* and *Option*. Our friends in other towns had fanzines, so we wrote for them, too. We were DJs on our local independent radio station, WTJU. Bands that would have been too weird, too feminist, too rough for the mainstream a year earlier suddenly *were* the mainstream, making their noise in public. Our subcultural secrets were out there, in the world, where they belonged. After work, Renée and I would cruise by Plan 9 Records and flip through the vinyl 45s. There was always something new we *had* to hear. We wrote as fast as we could, but still there was more great music out there than we had time to write about. Sometimes we got checks in the mail for writing, so we bought more records. Renée would hunker down over her typewriter and play the same Bratmobile single for hours, flipping it over every two and a half minutes, singing along. . . . Everything was changing, that was obvious. The world was so full of music, it seemed we could never run out. 'Twas bliss in that dawn to be alive, but to be young and overworked and underexposed and stuck in a nowhere town was very heaven. It was our time, the first one we had to ourselves.

It was a smashing time, and then it ended, because that's what times do.

Whitney Houston, "I'm Every Woman." Mmmmm. Whitney was so rad back then. What the hell happened?

Renée left a big mess behind: tapes, records, shoes, sewing patterns, piles of fabric she was planning to turn into skirts and handbags. Fashion mags and rock fanzines she was in the middle of reading. Novels jammed with bookmarks. Drafts of stories all over her desk. Pictures she'd ripped from magazines and taped up on the walls — Nirvana, PJ Harvey, John Travolta, Drew Barrymore, Shalom Harlow,

Mo Vaughn. A framed photo of the 1975 Red Sox. A big clay Mexican sun god she brought back from doing the L7 story in L.A. A stuffed pumpkin head from—well, no idea. Nutty things she sewed for herself, mod minidresses from fabric she found with little snow peas or Marilyn Monroe faces all over. She was in the middle of everything, living her big, messy, epic life, and none of us who loved her will ever catch up with her.

Renée loved to *do* things. That was mysterious to me, since I was more comfortable talking about things and never doing them. She liked passion. She liked adventure. I cowered from passion and talked myself out of adventure. Before I met her, I was just another hermit wolfboy, scared of life, hiding in my room with my records and my fanzines. One of Renée's friends asked her, "Does your boyfriend wear glasses?" She said, "No, he wears a Walkman." I was a wallflower who planned to stay that way, who never imagined anybody else to be. Suddenly, I got all tangled up in this girl's noisy, juicy, sparkly life. Without her, I didn't want to do anything, except keep being good at Renée. You know the story about Colonel Tom Parker, after Elvis died? The Colonel said, "Hell, I'll keep right on managing him." That's how I felt. Every tree in the woods, every car that passed me on the road, every song on the radio, all seemed to be Gloria Grahame at the end of *The Big Heat,* asking the same question: "What was your wife like?" It was the only conversation I was interested in.

Our friend Suzle told me her sister didn't understand—she always thought Suzle had one friend named "Robin Renée." How did Robin Renée turn into Rob and Renée, two different people?

The whole world got cheated out of Renée. I got cheated less than anybody, since I got more of her than anybody. But still, I wanted more of her. I wanted to be her guy forever and ever. I always pictured us growing old together, like William Holden and Ernest Borgnine in *The Wild Bunch,* side by side in our sleeping bags, drinking coffee and planning the next payroll heist. We only got five years. On our fifth anniversary, we drove out to Afton Mountain and checked into a motel. We got righteously wasted and blasted David Bowie's "Five Years" over and over. It's a song about how the world is going to end in five years, which forces everybody to seize the freedom to do whatever they want, to act out their craziest desires and devour the moment and not even think about the future.

"Five years!" we screamed in unison. "That's *aaaooowwwlll* we got!"

It *was* all we got. That was a good night. There were a lot of good nights. We got more of those than we had any right to expect, five years' worth, but I wanted more, anyway.

Another L7 song, "Packin' a Rod." It's a cover of an old L.A. hardcore punk anthem—Renée could have told you who did the original version, but I can't. And already we're at the end of side one. Eject. Flip it.

It's too late to sleep anyway. The coffee's gone cold, so I just heat up another pot. Tonight, I feel like my whole body is made out of memories. I'm a mix tape, a cassette that's been rewound so many times you can hear the fingerprints smudged on the tape.

Press play.

First song, side two: R.E.M.'s "Man on the Moon." Did Renée ever make a mix tape without R.E.M.? A whole generation of southern girls, raised on the promise of Michael Stipe.

I now get scared of forgetting anything about Renée, even the tiniest detail, even the bands on this tape I can't stand—if she touched them, I want to hear her fingerprints. Sometimes, I wake up in the middle of the night, my heart pounding, trying to remember: What was Renée's shoe size? What color were her eyes? What was her birthday, her grandparents' first names, that Willie Nelson song we heard on the radio in Atlanta? The memory comes back, hours or days later. It always comes back. But in the moment, I panic. I'm positive it's gone for good. I'm shaking from that sensation now, trying to remember some of this music. Nothing connects to the moment like music. I count on the music to bring me back—or, more precisely, to bring her forward.

There are some songs on this tape that nobody else on the planet remembers. I guarantee it. Like the Grenadine song "In a World Without Heroes." Grenadine wasn't even a real band—just a goofball side project. As far as we were concerned, though, this was easily the finest pseudo-Bowie limp-wristed fuzz-guitar indie-boy girl-worship ballad of 1992. We never convinced anyone else to agree. Not even our so-called friends would lie to us about this one.

Nobody ever liked it except me and Renée, and now she's gone, which means nobody remembers it. Not even the guy who wrote it. I know that for a fact, because Mark Robinson played a solo show at Tokyo Rose a few years later. When he asked for requests, we screamed for "In a World Without Heroes." He just stared and shook his head. A few songs later, with a little more liquid courage in us, we screamed for it again. He stopped asking for requests. So it's official: *nobody* likes this song.

A song nobody likes is a sad thing. But a love song nobody likes is hardly a thing at all.

Mary Chapin Carpenter. A big country-radio hit at the time. Wasn't she the one who wore leg-warmers?

The country singers understand. It's always that one song that gets you. You can hide, but the song comes to find you. Country singers are always twanging about that number on the jukebox they can't stand to hear you play, the one with the memories. If you're George Jones, it's 4–0–3–3. If you're Olivia Newton-John, it's B-17. If you're Johnny Paycheck, you can't stop yourself from going back to the bar where they play that song over and over, where they have a whole jukebox full of those songs. Johnny Paycheck called it "The Meanest Jukebox in Town."

Gangsters understand, too. In the old gangster movies, you're always running away to a new town, somewhere they won't know your mug shot. You can bury the dirty deeds of your past. Except the song follows you. In *Detour*, it's "I Can't Believe You're in Love with Me." The killer hears it on the truck-stop jukebox, and he realizes there's no escape from the girl. In *Gilda*, it's "Put the Blame on Mame." In *Dark Passage,* it's "Too Marvelous for Words." Barbara Stanwyck in *Clash by Night,* she's so cool and tough and unflappable, until she goes to a bar and gets jumped by a song on the jukebox, "I Hear a Rhapsody." She starts to ramble about a husband who died, and a small town where she used to sell sheet music. She's not so tough now. You can't get away from the meanest jukebox in town.

Pavement again. "Texas Never Whispers." One of our favorites. The tape creaks a little. I know it must be getting near the end.

I've been playing *Rumblefish* all night. By now, I know all the tunes. I'm writing down their titles, so I won't forget. I'm still staring out the window, but the sun won't rise for another couple of hours. The city lights are blinking through the trees of McCarren Park. The house across the street has a stuffed wooden owl whose head spins around every fifteen minutes, which is extremely annoying. The city is full of adventure, just a couple of subway stops away. But I'm not going anywhere.

We met on September 17, 1989. We got married on July 13, 1991. We were married for five years and ten months. Renée died on May 11, 1997, very suddenly and unexpectedly, at home with me, of a pulmonary embolism. She was thirty-one. She's buried in Pulaski County, Virginia, on the side of a hill, next to the Wal-Mart.

As soon as Side Two cuts off, right in the middle of a terrible Belly song, I sit there and wait for the final *ca-chunka.* Then I flip the tape and press play again. The first song is Pavement's "Shoot the Singer," which I just heard an hour ago. I have some unfinished business with these tunes. I'm going to be up for a while. Renée's not done with me yet.

Reading the Genre

1. This narrative has an "elegiac" tone—it is written in loving remembrance. What mood does this create for the reader? Can you find an example passage that is particularly successful in conveying this mood?

2. This is a personal, reflective narrative. But most important it is a memoir about a relationship. What does Sheffield reveal about himself, what does he reveal about Renée, and what does he reveal about the two of them together? What difficulties does an author face in writing about an intimate relationship?

3. Sheffield creates his own genre of narrative in this essay, by structuring the piece around the songs on his mix tape. Each song title then becomes a heading, a physical device that makes a transition between sections. (See Chapter 31, "Transitions," p. 416.) In this way, the essay relies on our understanding of the genre of the mix tape itself. What are the qualities and characteristics of a good mix tape (or mix CD, or playlist)? Can a good essay have the same qualities or characteristics as a good mix?

4. **WRITING:** In the last paragraph on page 644, Sheffield begins a list of things he remembers about Renée, beginning with "Renée was a real cool hell-raising Appalachian punk-rock girl." Each subsequent sentence in this paragraph begins with "she" or "her." Choose someone that you are close to, and list as many things about her or him as you can, in one long paragraph, beginning each sentence with *she* or *he*, *her* or *his*.

5. **MIX TAPE:** Create a list of songs that, together and in a particular order, say something about an important time in your life. Title the mix, and provide a brief description of the importance of each song. Try to quote from the lyrics of each song to provide examples of the song's meaning to you. (For more help, see Chapter 51, "Understanding Digital Media," p. 568, and Chapter 52, "Digital Elements," p. 577.) You can burn this mix to a CD and accompany it with liner notes or create a document with links to each song within it. Try to find a way to combine audio of the songs with your writing about them.

GRAPHIC NARRATIVE (EXCERPT)   Lynda Barry writes the weekly comic strip *Ernie Pook's Comeek*, found in many alternative weekly newspapers or at www.marlysmagazine.com. Barry's work is often funny but serious, sad but optimistic. When she writes about herself, as she does in this excerpt from the book *One! Hundred! Demons!* (2002), she is very honest about her own past. She currently teaches a popular writing workshop called Writing the Unthinkable. Barry has written seventeen books; her most recent is *Picture This: The Near-Sighted Monkey Book* (2010).

Lost and Found

Lynda Barry

AFTER I LEARNED TO READ, I LOVED GETTING HOME FROM SCHOOL AND WAITING FOR THE AFTERNOON PAPER. WE DIDN'T HAVE BOOKS IN THE HOUSE, BUT THE PAPER GAVE ME PLENTY TO WORK WITH.

THE FIRST SECTION I TURNED TO WAS THE CLASSIFIEDS. I ALWAYS READ THE "LOST AND FOUND" ADS, TRYING TO MEMORIZE DESCRIPTIONS OF DOGS AND CATS WHO WERE OUT THERE ALONE AND SCARED.

2 YR OLD M BRN+WHT CHIHUAHUA MIX. RD COLLAR. ANS TO "HENRY." REWARD.

"JINGLES" LOST 10/2. F GRAY TABBY. BLIND RT EYE NEEDS MEDICATION.

POOR JINGLES.

EACH QUARTER-INCH AD WAS LIKE A CHAPTER IN A BOOK. I'D IMAGINE THE WHOLE STORY: THE FREAKED-OUT PEOPLE, THE FREAKED-OUT ANIMALS, AND ME, ALWAYS COMING TO THE RESCUE AND NEVER ACCEPTING THE REWARD.

NO, KEEP THE FIVE HUNDRED DOLLARS, SIR. ALL I CARE ABOUT IS THAT HENRY IS HOME.

PLEASE, MA'AM, WHAT MY NAME IS DOESN'T MATTER. AND NEITHER DOES THE TEN THOUSAND DOLLARS. ALL THAT MATTERS IS JINGLES.

LIKE MOST WRITERS, I LOVED TO READ WHEN I WAS LITTLE, BUT UNTIL RECENTLY, I NEVER REALLY THOUGHT ABOUT SOME OF THE THINGS I ENJOYED READING MOST. THE CLASSIFIED ADS FASCINATED ME.

CRYPT IN MAUSOLEUM. PRIME LOC. EYE-LEVEL. BEST OFFER. EVENINGS.

SZ. 12 WEDDING DRESS. NEVER WORN. MUST SACRIFICE.

FILL DIRT, VERY CLEAN.

PARTY PIANIST. MY PIANO OR YOURS.

THEY GAVE ME SO MANY WEIRD BLANKS TO FILL IN. LIKE WHO WAS SELLING THEIR CRYPT? I ONLY KNEW THE WORD FROM HORROR MOVIES. ZOMBIES AND VAMPIRES CAME OUT OF THEM. THE AD SAID "EVENINGS." IT SEEMED LIKE SUCH AN OBVIOUS TRICK.

DING DONG

WHO IS IT?

UH, I'M HERE ABOUT THE CRYPT?

AAHHHH!!

SAME WITH THE WEDDING DRESS AD. WHO ELSE WAS GOING TO CALL ABOUT IT EXCEPT A MAIDEN? IT SAID "MUST SACRIFICE." WHO ELSE GOT SACRIFICED BUT MAIDENS? THE POLICE WOULD BE BAFFLED BY HOW MAIDENS KEPT DISAPPEARING.

HELLO?

YES?

YOU'VE GOT TO BE KIDDING.

OK.

NOT ANOTHER MAIDEN!

I'M AFRAID SO.

DANG!

WHEN I CAME FORWARD WITH THE SOLUTION TO THESE CRIMES, AT FIRST NO ONE WOULD BELIEVE ME. I EXPECTED THAT. I WATCHED A LOT OF MOVIES. NO ONE EVER BELIEVES KIDS AT FIRST. YOU HAVE TO WAIT UNTIL ALMOST THE END. YOU HAVE TO WAIT 'TIL YOUR LIFE IS IN DANGER.

CALLING ALL CARS! THAT KID WAS RIGHT ABOUT THE WANT ADS!

BUT NOW THE CRYPT-VAMPIRE AND THE WEDDING DRESS-ZOMBIE HAVE HER IN THEIR CLUTCHES! WE WERE SO STUPID! REPEAT! VERY STUPID!

MOSTLY I DIED IN MY CLAS-SIFIED STORIES. EVEN THEN I LOVED TRAGIC ENDINGS. PEO-PLE WOULD BE CRYING SO HARD. THEY'D COVER MY COFFIN WITH FILL DIRT, VERY CLEAN. THE PARTY PIANIST WOULD PLAY.

CHERISH IS THE WORD I USE TO DIS-CRI-IBE..

WHEN I READ ABOUT WRITER'S LIVES, THERE ARE USUALLY STORIES ABOUT WRITING FROM THE TIME THEY WERE LITTLE. I NEVER WROTE ANYTHING UN-TIL I WAS A TEENAGER, AND THEN IT WAS ONLY A DIARY THAT SAID THE SAME THING OVER AND OVER.

I thought Bill liked me but turns out he doesn't. I'm so depressed about Bill. He didn't call me. I can't stop thinking about Bill.

WRITERS TALK ABOUT ALL THE BOOKS THEY LOVED WHEN THEY WERE CHILDREN. CLASSIC STORIES I NEVER READ, BUT I LIED ABOUT BECAUSE I WAS SCARED IT WAS PROOF I WASN'T REALLY A WRITER.

AND WIND IN THE WILLOWS?

AH, YES.

AMAZING.

"THE LION, THE WITCH AND THE WARDROBE?"

INCREDIBLE. SAME WITH "WATERHEAD DOWN".

YOU MEAN "WATERSHIP".

UH, YEAH.

SUPER DRAMATICALLY EDUCATED. KNOWS ABOUT "STORY STRUC-TURE" AND "ARC" AND "PLOT POINTS"

JIVE-ASS FAKER WHO CAN'T SPELL AND HAS NO IDEA WHAT "STORY STRUCTURE" EVEN MEANS

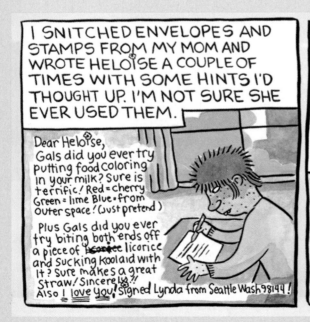

BUT ONLY CERTAIN PEOPLE WERE "ADVANCED" ENOUGH FOR WRITING AND LITERATURE. IN COLLEGE IT GOT EVEN WORSE. I LOVED THE WRONG KIND OF WRITING AND I NEVER COULD BREAK A STORY DOWN TO FIND THE SYMBOLIC MEANING, ALTHOUGH I SURE TRIED TO FAKE IT.

(3:30 AM)

In "The Bell Jar," Plath profounds her enumerated existential parthenogenesis using subvertible intra-mural insight on the dissimulation of her classic bummer of the 20th century.

MY TROUBLE ENDED WHEN I STARTED MAKING COMIC-STRIPS. IT'S NOT SOMETHING A PERSON HAS TO BE VERY "ADVANCED" TO DO. AT LEAST NOT IN THE MINDS OF LITERARY TYPES.

SO YOU'RE A CARTOONIST! HOW ADORABLE!

POLITICAL? NO. HUMOROUS? KINDA. WE'RE BOTH WRITERS.

SAY, MAYBE WE COULD COLLABORATE! WE WRITE IT AND YOU DRAW IT! HOW FUN!

NOBODY FEELS THE NEED TO PROVIDE DEEP CRITICAL IN-SIGHT TO SOMETHING WRITTEN BY HAND. MOSTLY THEY KEEP IT AS SHORT AS A WANT AD. THE WORST I GET IS, "TOO MANY WORDS. NOT FUNNY. DON'T GET THE JOKE." I CAN LIVE WITH THAT.

GALS, EVER FELT SO intimidated by the IDEA OF writing THAT you've never even given it a try? Think writing IS only FOR "writers"? Sure IS common!

ESPECIALLY BECAUSE I'M SURE THAT THE NINE-YEAR-OLD VERSION OF ME WHO MADE UP ALL THOSE "CLASSI-FIED STORIES" WOULD THINK THAT THIS ONE HAD A VERY HAPPY ENDING.

(and YES, Gals- the first thing I read in the paper is still the "lost and found")

LOST. SOMEWHERE AROUND PUBERTY. ABILITY TO MAKE UP STORIES. HAPPINESS DEPENDS ON IT. PLEASE WRITE.

Reading the Genre

1. Even though this essay is in comic form, it also addresses literacy directly, discussing the author's early reading experiences. As a literacy narrative, what does "Lost and Found" teach us about the author's approach to reading and writing? (For other examples of literacy narratives, see Richard Rodriguez's "Strange Tools" on pp. 23–28, David Sedaris's essay "Me Talk Pretty One Day" on pp. 635–40, and Jonathan Franzen's "The Comfort Zone" on pp. 668–84.)

2. Unlike many other comic authors, Lynda Barry provides descriptions for some of her pictures. Why do you think she does this, and how do these descriptions contribute to the essay?

3. How is Barry's artistic and storytelling style different from that of Marjane Satrapi in the excerpt from *Persepolis* (see pp. 36–42)?

4. If Barry had presented her story without images, do you think your response to it would be different? How do comics present information, and why might a writer or artist choose this medium? (See Chapter 35, "High, Middle, and Low Style," p. 432.)

5. **WRITING:** Craigslist might be the online equivalent of the newspaper classified section. Go to www.craigslist.org and find an advertised item that suggests a story to you. (Hint: Try looking at the lost and found section or the ads for free items.) Draw a picture of this item and write a short imaginative narrative about it. (See "Finding and developing materials," p. 14.)

6. **COMPOSING VISUALLY:** This essay comes from the book *One! Hundred! Demons!* The concept for the book comes from an ancient Japanese painting exercise in which artists painted about things that worried or challenged them. As she began painting and writing about her demons, Barry explains that "at first the demons freaked me, but then I started to love watching them come out of my paintbrush." Try drawing or writing about memories from your own past as a student. What have you struggled with? In writing about these memories, have you also come to better understand them?

REFLECTION   Poet and novelist Naomi Shihab Nye has written or edited more than twenty books and has won dozens of awards for her writing. Nye's mother is American and her father is Palestinian, and much of her writing is focused on helping people understand the similarities and differences between Middle Eastern and American cultures, and specifically on dispelling stereotypes about the Middle East.

NAOMI SHIHAB NYE

Mint Snowball

My great-grandfather on my mother's side ran a drugstore in a small town in central Illinois. He sold pills and rubbing alcohol from behind the big cash register and creamy ice cream from the soda fountain. My mother remembers the counter's long polished sweep, its shining face. She twirled on the stools. Dreamy fans. Wide summer afternoons. Clink of nickels in anybody's hand. He sold milkshakes, cherry Cokes, old-fashioned sandwiches. What did an old-fashioned sandwich look like? Dark wooden shelves. Silver spigots on chocolate dispensers.

My great-grandfather had one specialty: a Mint Snowball which he invented. Some people drove all the way in from Decatur just to taste it. First he stirred fresh mint leaves with sugar and secret ingredients in a small pot on the stove for a very long time. He concocted a flamboyant elixir of mint. Its scent clung to his fingers even after he washed his hands. Then he shaved ice into tiny particles and served it mounded in a glass dish. Permeated with mint syrup. Scoops of rich vanilla ice cream to each side. My mother took a bite of minty ice and ice cream mixed together. The Mint Snowball tasted like winter. She closed her eyes to see the Swiss village my great-grandfather's parents came from. Snow frosting the roofs. Glistening, dangling spokes of ice.

Before my great-grandfather died, he sold the recipe for the mint syrup to someone in town for one hundred dollars. This hurt my grandfather's feelings.

My grandfather thought he should have inherited it to carry on the tradition. As far as the family knew, the person who bought the recipe never used it. At least not in public. My mother had watched my grandfather make the syrup so often she thought she could replicate it. But what did he have in those little unmarked bottles? She experimented. Once she came close. She wrote down what she did. Now she has lost the paper.

Perhaps the clue to my entire personality connects to the lost Mint Snowball. I have always felt out-of-step with my environment, disjointed in the modern world. The crisp flush of cities makes me weep. Strip centers, poodle grooming and take-out Thai. I am angry over lost department stores, wistful for something I have never tasted or seen.

Although I know how to do everything one needs to know—change airplanes, find my exit off the interstate, charge gas, send a fax—there is something missing. Perhaps the stoop of my great-grandfather over the pan, the slow patient swish of his spoon. The spin of my mother on the high stool with her whole life in front of her, something fine and fragrant still to happen. When I breathe a handful of mint, even pathetic sprigs from my sunbaked Texas earth, I close my eyes. Little chips of ice on the tongue, their cool slide down. Can we follow the long river of the word "refreshment" back to its spring? Is there another land for me? Can I find any lasting solace in the color green?

Reading the Genre

1. Nye uses sentence fragments in this essay. Examine these incomplete sentences, particularly in the first two paragraphs of the essay. How is the content of each of these shorter sentences similar, and how does this work within the essay? (See Chapter 35, "High, Middle, and Low Style," p. 432; Chapter 57, "Commas," p. 607; and Chapter 58, "Comma Splices, Run-ons, and Fragments," p. 610.)

2. This narrative is divided into two parts. The perspective in the second part of the story radically shifts. How would you describe the perspective, or point of view, in the first half and in the second? What can the author do in the second half that she can't in the first? Why? (See Chapter 31, "Transitions," p. 416, and Chapter 34, "Titles," p. 428.)

3. **WRITING:** Consider the work history of your own family: What kind of work do your parents do, and what kind of work did their parents do? What kind of work does your extended family do? Are there specific skills or lessons, or even ways of looking at the world, that have been passed down in your family because of the sort of work your family has done? Write a short personal reflection on this topic.

4. **WRITING:** Visit a local business and interview the owner about the history of this business. Then, write a short narrative that tells the story of the business — how it began, what it specializes in, what makes it unique, how it has changed over the years, and so on. (See "Develop the setting to set the context and mood," p. 21.)

MEMOIR   Ira Sukrungruang writes and teaches creative nonfiction. He is the author of *Talk Thai: The Adventures of Buddhist Boy* (2010), a memoir of growing up Thai American, and the coeditor of *What Are You Looking At? The First Fat Fiction Anthology* (2003) and *Scoot Over, Skinny: The Fat Nonfiction Anthology* (2005). This story comes from the online journal *Brevity* (www.creativenonfiction.org/brevity), which collects very short creative nonfiction.

Brevity

Posted: Fall 2005
From: Ira Sukrungruang

Chop Suey

My mother was a champion bowler in Thailand. This was not what I knew of her. I knew only her expectations of me to be the perfect Thai boy. I knew her distaste for blonde American women she feared would seduce her son. I knew her distrust of the world she found herself in, a world of white faces and mackerel in a can. There were many things I didn't know about my mother when I was ten. She was what she was supposed to be. My mother.

At El-Mar Bowling Alley, I wanted to show her what I could do with the pins. I had bowled once before, at Dan Braun's birthday party. There, I had rolled the ball off the bumpers, knocking the pins over in a thunderous crash. I liked the sound of a bowling alley. I felt in control of the weather, the rumble of the ball on the wood floor like the coming of a storm, and the hollow explosion of the pins, distant lightning. At the bowling alley, men swore and smoked and drank.

My mother wore a light pink polo, jeans, and a golf visor. She put on a lot of powder to cover up the acne she got at 50. She poured Vapex, a strong smelling vapor rub, into her handkerchief, and covered her nose, complaining of the haze of smoke that floated over the lanes. My mother was the only woman in the place. We were the only non-white patrons.

I told her to watch me. I told her I was good. I set up, took sloppy and uneven steps, and lobbed my orange ball onto the lane with a loud thud. This time there were no bumpers. My ball veered straight for the gutter.

My mother said to try again. I did, and for the next nine frames, not one ball hit one pin. Embarrassed, I sat next to her. I put my head on her shoulder. She patted it for a while and said bowling wasn't an easy game.

My mother rose from her chair and said she wanted to try. She changed her shoes. She picked a ball from the rack, one splattered with colors. When she was ready, she lined herself up to the pins, the ball at eye level. In five concise steps, she brought the ball back, dipped her knees, and released it smoothly, as if her hand was an extension of the floor. The ball started on the right side of the lane and curled into the center. Strike.

She bowled again and knocked down more pins. She told me about her nearly perfect game, how in Thailand she was unbeatable.

I listened, amazed that my mother could bowl a 200, that she was good at something beyond what mothers were supposed to be good at, like cooking and punishing and sewing. I clapped. I said she should stop being a mother and become a bowler.

As she changed her shoes, a man with dark hair and a mustache approached our lane. In one hand he had a cigarette and a beer. He kept looking back at his buddies a few lanes over, all huddling and whispering. I stood beside my mother, wary of any stranger. My mother's smile disappeared. She rose off the chair.

"Hi," said the man.

My mother nodded.

"My friends over there," he pointed behind him, "well, we would like to thank you." His mustache twitched.

My mother pulled me closer to her leg, hugging her purse to her chest.

He began to talk slower, over-enunciating his words, repeating again. "We . . . would . . . like . . . to . . . thank . . ."

I tugged on my mother's arm, but she stood frozen.

". . . you . . . for . . . making . . . a . . . good . . . chop . . . suey. You people make good food."

The man looked back again, toasted his beer at his friends, laughing smoke from his lips.

My mother grabbed my hand and took one step toward the man. In that instant, I saw in her face the same resolve she had when she spanked, the same resolve when she scolded. In that instant, I thought my mother was going to hit the man. And for a moment, I thought the man saw the same thing in her eyes, and his smile disappeared from his face. Quickly, she smiled — too bright, too large — and said, "You're welcome."

Reading the Genre

1. This story begins as a pleasant memory of the author's youth but ends with a difficult and awkward encounter. This development comes as a surprise to readers, just as it did to Sukrungruang and his mother. When the story ends, what emotions are you left with as a reader? What would you have wanted to do if you had been in the bowling alley that day? (See Chapter 33, "Conclusions," p. 425.)

2. At the end of this story, in the dialogue between Sukrungruang's mother and the man with "dark hair and a mustache," Sukrungruang uses ellipses to insert pauses in the discussion. What effect do these pauses have on the story and on you as a reader? (See "Use dialogue," p. 20, and "Pace the story effectively," p. 12.)

3. It's not easy to realistically depict action in a personal narrative, but using just a few details, Sukrungruang does a good job of capturing the act of throwing a bowling ball. Reread his descriptions of his own bad bowling and his mother's excellent bowling. Try and identify the adjectives and adverbs that he uses, as well as the metaphors. (See "Use figures of speech," p. 19.)

4. **WRITING:** The events Ira Sukrungruang recounts in this story reveal a turning point in his life, a moment when he learns something important. Can you identify the turning points in your life when you discovered important things that you hadn't known before? Choose one of these moments and write a narrative about this event.

5. **WRITING:** Sukrungruang's narrative comes from a journal that publishes only nonfiction stories shorter than 750 words, and Naomi Shihab Nye's narrative (see pp. 661–62) was published in an anthology of very short essays. *Smith* magazine has recently taken the concept of brevity many steps further by asking writers to create six-word memoirs. Read some examples of these memoirs at www.smithmag.net/sixwords/, and then write a personal narrative in six words. You might also try writing your story as a 140-character "tweet."

LITERACY NARRATIVE   An award-winning essayist, journalist, and fiction writer, Jonathan Franzen is best-known for his novels *Freedom* (2010) and *The Corrections* (2001). This essay was published in the November 29, 2004, issue of the *New Yorker*. It can be considered a literacy narrative because it is organized around reading (comics, especially *Peanuts*), writing (a grade-school play), and other related activities (the "Homonym Spelldown"). Every scene seems to be about developing literacy in some way.

The Comfort Zone
Growing Up with Charlie Brown

JONATHAN FRANZEN

In May, 1970, a few nights after the Kent State shootings, my father and my brother Tom, who was nineteen, started fighting. They weren't fighting about the Vietnam War, which both of them opposed. The fight was probably about a lot of different things at once. But the immediate issue was Tom's summer job. He was a good artist, with a meticulous nature, and my father had encouraged him (you could even say forced him) to choose a college from a short list of schools with strong programs in architecture. Tom had deliberately chosen the most distant of these schools, Rice University, and he had just returned from his second year in Houston, where his adventures in late-sixties youth culture were pushing him toward majoring in film studies, not architecture. My father, however, had found him a plum summer job with Sverdrup & Parcel, the big engineering firm in St. Louis, whose senior partner, General Leif Sverdrup, had been a United States Army Corps of Engineers hero in the Philippines. It couldn't have been easy for my father, who was shy and morbidly principled, to pull the requisite strings at Sverdrup. But the office gestalt was hawkish and buzz-cut and generally inimical to bell-bottomed, lefty film-studies majors; and Tom didn't want to be there.

Up in the bedroom that he and I shared, the windows were open and the air had the stuffy wooden-house smell that came out every spring. I preferred the make-believe no-smell of air-conditioning, but my mother, whose subjective experience of temperature was notably consistent with low gas and electric bills, claimed to be a devotee of "fresh air," and the windows often stayed open until Memorial Day.

On my night table was the *Peanuts Treasury*, a large, thick hardcover compilation of daily and Sunday funnies by Charles M. Schulz. My mother had given it to me the previous Christmas, and I'd been rereading it at bedtime ever since. Like most of the nation's ten-year-olds, I had an intense, private relationship with Snoopy, the cartoon beagle. He was a solitary not-animal animal who lived among larger creatures of a different species, which was more or less my feeling in my own house. My brothers, who are nine and twelve years older than I, were less like siblings than like an extra, fun pair of quasi-parents. Although I had friends and was a Cub Scout in good standing, I spent a lot of time alone with talking animals. I was an obsessive rereader of A. A. Milne and the Narnia and Doctor Dolittle novels, and my involvement with my collection of stuffed animals was on the verge of becoming age-inappropriate. It was another point of kinship with Snoopy that he, too, liked animal games. He impersonated tigers and vultures and mountain lions, sharks, sea monsters, pythons, cows, piranhas, penguins, and vampire bats. He was the perfect sunny egoist, starring in his ridiculous fantasies and basking in everyone's attention. In a cartoon strip full of children, the dog was the character I recognized as a child.

Tom and my father had been talking in the living room when I went up to bed. Now, at some late and even stuffier hour, after I'd put aside the *Peanuts Treasury* and fallen asleep, Tom burst into our bedroom. He was shouting with harsh sarcasm. "You'll get over it! You'll forget about me! It'll be so much easier! You'll get over it!"

My father was offstage somewhere, making large abstract sounds. My mother was right behind Tom, sobbing at his shoulder, begging him to stop, to stop. He was pulling open dresser drawers, repacking bags he'd only recently unpacked. "You think you want me here," he said, "but you'll get over it."

What about me? my mother pleaded. *What about Jon?*

"You'll get over it!"

I was a small and fundamentally ridiculous person. Even if I'd dared sit up in bed, what could I have said? "Excuse me, I'm trying to sleep"? I lay still and followed the action through my eyelashes. There were further dramatic comings and goings, through some of which I may in fact have slept. Finally I heard Tom's feet pounding down the stairs and my mother's terrible cries, now nearly shrieks, receding after him: "Tom! Tom! Tom! Please! Tom!" And then the front door slammed.

Things like this had never happened in our house. The worst fight I'd ever witnessed was between Tom and our older brother, Bob, on the subject of Frank Zappa, whose music Tom admired and Bob one day dismissed with such patronizing disdain that Tom began to sneer at Bob's own favorite group, the Supremes, which led to bitter hostilities. But a scene of real wailing and doors slamming in the night was completely off the map. When I woke up the next morning, the memory of it already felt decades-old and semi-dreamlike and unmentionable.

My father had left for work, and my mother served me breakfast without comment. The food on the table, the jingles on the radio, and the walk to school all were unremarkable; and yet everything about the day was soaked in dread. At school that week, in Miss Niblack's class, we were rehearsing our fifth-grade play. The script, which I'd written, had a large number of bit parts and one very generous role that I'd created with my own memorization abilities in mind. The action took place on a boat, involved a taciturn villain named Mr. Scuba, and lacked the most rudimentary comedy, point, or moral. Not even I, who got to do most of the talking, enjoyed being in it. Its badness—my responsibility for its badness—became part of the day's general dread.

There was something dreadful about springtime itself, the way plants and animals lost control, the *Lord of the Flies* buzzing, the heat indoors. After school, instead of staying outside to play, I followed my dread home and cornered my mother in our dining room. I asked her about my upcoming class performance. Would Dad be in town for it? What about Bob? Would he be home from college yet? And what about Tom? Would Tom be there, too? This was quite plausibly an innocent line of questioning—I was a small glutton for attention, forever turning conversations to the subject of myself—and, for a while, my mother gave me plausibly innocent answers. Then she slumped into a chair, put her face in her hands, and began to weep.

"Didn't you hear anything last night?" she said.

"No."

"You didn't hear Tom and Dad shouting? You didn't hear doors slamming?"

"No!"

She gathered me in her arms, which was probably the main thing I'd been dreading. I stood there stiffly while she hugged me. "Tom and Dad had a terrible fight," she said. "After you went to bed. They had a terrible fight, and Tom got his things and left the house, and we don't know where he went."

"Oh."

"I thought we'd hear from him today, but he hasn't called, and I'm frantic, not knowing where he is. I'm just frantic!"

I squirmed a little in her grip.

"But this has nothing to do with you," she said. "It's between him and Dad and has nothing to do with you. I'm sure Tom's sorry he won't be here to see your play. Or maybe, who knows, he'll be back by Friday and he will see it."

"O.K."

"But I don't want you telling anyone he's gone until we know where he is. Will you agree not to tell anyone?"

"O.K.," I said, breaking free of her. "Can we turn the air-conditioning on?"

I was unaware of it, but an epidemic had broken out across the country. Late adolescents in suburbs like ours had suddenly gone berserk, running away to other cities to have sex and not attend college, ingesting every substance they could get their hands on, not just clashing with their parents but rejecting and annihilating everything about them. For a while, the parents were so frightened and so mystified and so ashamed that each family, especially mine, quarantined itself and suffered in isolation.

When I went upstairs, my bedroom felt like an overwarm sickroom. The clearest remaining vestige of Tom was the *Don't Look Back* poster that he'd taped to a flank of his dresser where Bob Dylan's psychedelic hair style wouldn't always be catching my mother's censorious eye. Tom's bed, neatly made, was the bed of a kid carried off by an epidemic.

In that unsettled season, as the so-called generation gap was rending the cultural landscape, Charles Schulz's work was almost uniquely beloved. Fifty-five million Americans had seen *A Charlie Brown Christmas* the previous December, for a Nielsen share of better than fifty per cent. The musical *You're a Good Man, Charlie Brown* was in its second sold-out year on Broadway. The astronauts of Apollo X, in their dress rehearsal for the first lunar landing, had christened their orbiter and landing vehicle Charlie Brown and Snoopy. Newspapers carrying *Peanuts* reached more than a hundred and fifty million readers, *Peanuts* collections were all over the best-seller lists, and if my own friends were any indication there was hardly a kid's bedroom in America without a *Peanuts* wastebasket or *Peanuts* bedsheets or a *Peanuts* gift book. Schulz, by a luxurious margin, was the most famous living artist on the planet.

To the countercultural mind, a begoggled beagle piloting a doghouse and getting shot down by the Red Baron was akin to Yossarian paddling a dinghy to Sweden. The strip's square panels were the only square thing about it. Wouldn't the country be better off listening to Linus Van Pelt than Robert McNamara? This was the era of flower children, not flower adults. But the strip appealed to older Americans as well. It was unfailingly inoffensive (Snoopy never lifted a leg) and was set in a safe, attractive suburb where the kids, except for Pigpen, whose image Ron McKernan of the Grateful Dead pointedly embraced, were clean and well spoken and conservatively dressed. Hippies and astronauts, the Pentagon and the antiwar movement, the rejecting kids and the rejected grown-ups were all of one mind here.

An exception was my own household. As far as I know, my father never in his life read a comic strip, and my mother's interest in the funnies was limited to a single-panel feature called *The Girls*, whose generic middle-aged matrons, with their weight problems and stinginess and poor driving skills and weakness for department-store bargains, she found just endlessly amusing.

I didn't buy comic books, or even *Mad* magazine, but I worshipped at the altars of Warner Bros. cartoons and the funnies section of the St. Louis *Post-Dispatch*. I read the section's black-and-white page first, skipping the dramatic features like *Steve Roper* and *Juliet Jones* and glancing at *Li'l Abner* only to satisfy myself that it was still trashy and repellent. On the full-color back page I read the strips strictly in reverse order of preference, doing my best to be amused by Dagwood Bumstead's midnight snacks and struggling to ignore the fact that Tiger and Punkinhead were the kind of messy, unreflective kids I disliked in real life, before treating myself to my favorite strip, *B.C.* The strip, by Johnny Hart, was caveman humor. Hart wrung hundreds of gags from the friendship between a flightless bird and a long-suffering tortoise who was constantly attempting unturtlish feats of agility and flexibility. Debts were always paid in clams; dinner was always roast leg of something. When I was done with *B.C.*, I was done with the paper.

The comics in St. Louis's other paper, the *Globe-Democrat*, which my parents didn't take, seemed bleak and foreign to me. *Broom Hilda* and *Animal Crackers* and *The Family Circus* were off-putting in the manner of the kid whose partially visible underpants, which had the name Cuttair hand-markered on the waistband, I'd stared at throughout my family's tour of the Canadian parliament. Although *The Family Circus* was resolutely unfunny, its panels clearly were based on some actual family's life and were aimed at an audience that recognized this life, which compelled me to posit an entire subspecies of humanity that found *The Family Circus* hilarious.

I knew very well, of course, why the *Globe-Democrat*'s funnies were so lame: the paper that carried *Peanuts* didn't *need* any other good strips. Indeed, I would have swapped the entire *Post-Dispatch* for a daily dose of Schulz. Only *Peanuts*, the strip we didn't get, dealt with stuff that really mattered. I didn't for a minute believe that the children in *Peanuts* were really children — they were so much more emphatic and cartoonishly *real* than anybody in my own neighborhood — but I nevertheless took their stories to be dispatches from a universe of childhood that was somehow more substantial and convincing than my own. Instead of playing kickball and foursquare, the way my friends and I did, the kids in *Peanuts* had real baseball teams, real football equipment, real fistfights. Their interactions with Snoopy were far richer than the chasings and bitings that constituted my own relationships with neighborhood dogs. Minor but incredible disasters, often involving new vocabulary words, befell them daily. Lucy was "blackballed from the Bluebirds." She knocked Charlie Brown's croquet ball so far that he had to call the other players from a phone booth. She gave Charlie Brown a signed document in which she swore not to pull the football away when he tried to kick it, but the "peculiar thing about this document," as she observed in the final frame, was that "it was never notarized." When Lucy smashed the bust of Beethoven on Schroeder's toy piano, it struck me as odd and funny that Schroeder had a closet full of identical replacement busts, but I accepted it as humanly possible, because Schulz had drawn it.

To the *Peanuts Treasury* I soon added two other equally strong hardcover collections, *Peanuts Revisited* and *Peanuts Classics*. A well-meaning relative once also gave me a copy of Robert Short's national best-seller, *The Gospel According to Peanuts*, but it couldn't have interested me less. *Peanuts* wasn't a portal to the Gospel. It was my gospel.

Chapter 1, verses 1–4, of what I knew about disillusionment: Charlie Brown passes the house of the Little Red-Haired Girl, the object of his eternal fruitless longing. He sits down with Snoopy and says, "I wish I had two ponies." He imagines offering one of the ponies to the Little Red-Haired Girl, riding out into the countryside with her, and sitting down with her beneath a tree. Suddenly, he's scowling at Snoopy and asking, "Why aren't you two ponies?" Snoopy, rolling his eyes, thinks, "I knew we'd get around to that."

Or Chapter 1, verses 26–32, of what I knew about the mysteries of etiquette: Linus is showing off his new wristwatch to everyone in the neighborhood.

"New watch!" he says proudly to Snoopy, who, after a hesitation, licks it. Linus's hair stands on end. "You licked my watch!" he cries. "It'll rust! It'll turn green! He's ruined it!" Snoopy is left looking mildly puzzled and thinking, "I thought it would have been impolite not to taste it."

Or Chapter 2, verses 6–12, of what I knew about fiction: Linus is annoying Lucy, wheedling and pleading with her to read him a story. To shut him up, she grabs a book, randomly opens it, and says, "A man was born, he lived and he died. The End!" She tosses the book aside, and Linus picks it up reverently. "What a fascinating account," he says. "It almost makes you wish you had known the fellow."

The perfect silliness of stuff like this, the koanlike inscrutability, entranced me even when I was ten. But many of the more elaborate sequences, especially the ones about Charlie Brown's humiliation and loneliness, made only a generic impression on me. In a classroom spelling bee that Charlie Brown has been looking forward to, the first word he's asked to spell is "maze." With a complacent smile, he produces "M-A-Y-S." The class screams with laughter. He returns to his seat and presses his face into his desktop, and when his teacher asks him what's wrong he yells at her and ends up in the principal's office. *Peanuts* was steeped in Schulz's awareness that for every winner in a competition there has to be a loser, if not twenty losers, or two thousand, but I personally enjoyed winning and couldn't see why so much fuss was made about the losers.

In the spring of 1970, Miss Niblack's class was studying homonyms to prepare for what she called the Homonym Spelldown. I did some desultory homonym drilling with my mother, rattling off "sleigh" for "slay" and "slough" for "slew" the way other kids roped softballs into center field. To me, the only halfway interesting question about the Spelldown was who was going to come in second. A new kid had joined our class that year, a shrimpy black-haired striver, Chris Toczko, who had it in his head that he and I were academic rivals. I was a nice enough little boy as long as you didn't compete on my turf. Toczko was annoyingly unaware that I, not he, by natural right, was the best student in the class. On the day of the Spelldown, he actually taunted me. He said he'd done a lot of studying and he was going to beat me! I looked down at the little pest and did not know what to say. I evidently mattered a lot more to him than he did to me.

For the Spelldown, we all stood by the blackboard, Miss Niblack calling out one half of a pair of homonyms and my classmates sitting down as soon as they had failed. Toczko was pale and trembling, but he knew his homonyms. He was the last kid standing, besides me, when Miss Niblack called out the word "liar." Toczko trembled and essayed, "L . . . I . . ." And I could see that I had beaten him. I waited impatiently while, with considerable anguish, he extracted two more letters from his marrow: "E . . . R?"

"I'm sorry, Chris, that's not a word," Miss Niblack said.

With a sharp laugh of triumph, not even waiting for Toczko to sit down, I stepped forward and sang out, "L-Y-R-E! *Lyre.* It's a stringed instrument."

I hadn't really doubted that I would win, but Toczko had got to me with his taunting, and my blood was up. I was the last person in class to realize that Toczko was having a meltdown. His face turned red and he began to cry, insisting angrily that "lier" *was* a word, it *was* a word.

I didn't care if it was a word or not. I knew my rights. Toczko's tears disturbed and disappointed me, as I made quite clear by fetching the classroom dictionary and showing him that "lier" wasn't in it. This was how both Toczko and I ended up in the principal's office.

I'd never been sent down before. I was interested to learn that the principal, Mr. Barnett, had a Webster's International Unabridged in his office. Toczko, who barely outweighed the dictionary, used two hands to open it and to roll back the pages to the "L" words. I stood at his shoulder and saw where his tiny, trembling index finger was pointing: *lier, n., one that lies (as in ambush).* Mr. Barnett immediately declared us co-winners of the Spelldown—a compromise that didn't seem quite fair to me, since I would surely have murdered Toczko if we'd gone another round. But his outburst had spooked me, and I decided it might be O.K., for once, to let somebody else win.

A few months after the Homonym Spelldown, just after summer vacation started, Toczko ran out into Grant Road and was killed by a car. What little I knew then about the world's badness I knew mainly from a camping trip, some years earlier, when I'd dropped a frog into a campfire and watched it shrivel and roll down the flat side of a log. My memory of that shrivelling and rolling was sui generis, distinct from my other memories. It was like a nagging, sick-making atom of rebuke in me. I felt similarly rebuked now when my mother, who knew nothing of Toczko's rivalry with me, told me that he was dead. She was weeping as she'd wept over Tom's disappearance some weeks earlier. She sat me down and made me write a letter of condolence to Toczko's mother. I was very much unaccustomed to considering the interior states of people other than myself, but it was impossible not to consider Mrs. Toczko's. Though I never met her, in the ensuing weeks I pictured her suffering so incessantly and vividly that I could almost see her: a tiny, trim, dark-haired woman who cried the way her son did.

"Everything I do makes me feel guilty," says Charlie Brown. He's at the beach, and he has just thrown a pebble into the water, and Linus has commented, "Nice going. . . . It took that stone four thousand years to get to shore, and now you've thrown it back."

I felt guilty about Toczko. I felt guilty about the little frog. I felt guilty about shunning my mother's hugs when she seemed to need them most. I felt guilty about the washcloths at the bottom of the stack in the linen closet, the older, thinner washcloths that we seldom used. I felt guilty for preferring my best shooter marbles, a solid-red agate and a solid-yellow agate, my king and my queen, to marbles farther down my rigid marble hierarchy. I felt guilty about the board games that I didn't like to play—Uncle Wiggily, U.S. Presidential Elections, Game of the States—and sometimes, when my friends weren't around, I opened the boxes and examined the pieces in the hope of making the games feel less forgotten. I felt guilty about neglecting the stiff-limbed, scratchy-pelted Mr. Bear, who had no voice and didn't mix well with my other stuffed animals. To avoid feeling guilty about them, too, I slept with one of them per night, according to a strict weekly schedule.

We laugh at dachshunds for humping our legs, but our own species is even more self-centered in its imaginings. There's no object so Other that it can't be anthropomorphized and shanghaied into conversation with us. Some objects are more amenable than others, however. The trouble with Mr. Bear was that he was more realistically bearlike than the other animals. He had a distinct, stern, feral persona; unlike our faceless washcloths, he was assertively Other. It was no wonder I couldn't speak through him. An old shoe is easier to invest with comic personality than is, say, a photograph of Cary Grant. The blanker the slate, the more easily we can fill it with our own image.

Our visual cortexes are wired to quickly recognize faces and then quickly subtract massive amounts of detail from them, zeroing in on their essential message: Is this person happy? Angry? Fearful? Individual faces may vary greatly, but a smirk on one is a lot like a smirk on another. Smirks are conceptual, not pictorial. Our brains are like cartoonists—and cartoonists are like our brains, simplifying and exaggerating, subordinating facial detail to abstract comic concepts.

Scott McCloud, in his cartoon treatise *Understanding Comics,* argues that the image you have of yourself when you're conversing is very different from your image of the person you're conversing with. Your interlocutor may produce universal smiles and universal frowns, and they may help you to identify with him emotionally, but he also has a particular nose and particular skin and particular hair that continually remind you that he's an Other. The image you have of your own face, by contrast, is highly cartoonish. When you feel yourself smile, you imagine a cartoon of smiling, not the complete skin-and-nose-and-hair package. It's precisely the simplicity and universality of cartoon faces, the absence of Otherly particulars, that invite us to love them as we love ourselves. The most widely loved (and profitable) faces in the modern world tend to be exceptionally basic and abstract cartoons: Mickey Mouse, the Simpsons, Tintin, and, simplest of all—barely more than a circle, two dots, and a horizontal line—Charlie Brown.

Schulz only ever wanted to be a cartoonist. He was born in St. Paul in 1922, the only child of a German father and a mother of Norwegian extraction. As an infant, he was nicknamed Sparky, after a horse in the then popular comic strip *Barney Google*. His father, who, like Charlie Brown's father, was a barber, bought six different newspapers on the weekend and read all the era's comics with his son. Schulz skipped a grade in elementary school and was the least mature kid in every class after that. Much of the existing Schulzian literature dwells on the Charlie Brownish traumas in his early life: his skinniness and pimples, his unpopularity with girls at school, the inexplicable rejection of a batch of his drawings by his high-school yearbook, and, some years later, the rejection of his marriage proposal by the real-life Little Red-Haired Girl, Donna Mae Johnson. Schulz himself spoke of his youth in a tone close to anger. "It took me a long time to become a human being," he told *Nemo* magazine in 1987.

> I was regarded by many as kind of sissyfied, which I resented because I really was not a sissy. I was not a tough guy, but . . . I was good at any sport where you threw things, or hit them, or caught them, or something like that. I hated things like swimming and tumbling and those kinds of things, so I was really not a sissy. [But] the coaches were so intolerant and there was no program for all of us. So I never regarded myself as being much and I never regarded myself as being good looking and I never had a date in high school, because I thought, who'd want to date me? So I didn't bother.

Schulz "didn't bother" going to art school, either—it would only have discouraged him, he said, to be around people who could draw better than he could. You could see a lack of confidence here. You could also see a kid who knew how to protect himself.

On the eve of Schulz's induction into the Army, his mother died of cancer. She was forty-eight and had suffered greatly, and Schulz later described the loss as an emotional catastrophe from which he almost did not recover. During basic training, he was depressed, withdrawn, and grieving. In the long run, though, the Army was good for him. He went into the service, he recalled later, as "a nothing person" and came out as a staff sergeant in charge of a machine-gun squadron. "I thought, By golly, if that isn't a man, I don't know what is," he said. "And I felt good about myself and that lasted about eight minutes, and then I went back to where I am now." After the war, Schulz returned to his childhood neighborhood, lived with his father, became intensely involved in a Christian youth group, and learned to draw kids. For the rest of his life, he virtually never drew adults. He avoided adult vices—didn't drink, didn't smoke, didn't swear—and, in his work, he spent more and more time in the imagined yards and sandlots of his childhood. But the world of *Peanuts* remained a deeply motherless place. Charlie Brown's dog may (or may not) cheer him up after a day of failures; his mother never does.

Although Schulz had been a social victim as a child, he'd also had the undivided attention of two loving parents. All his life, he was a prickly Minnesotan mixture of disabling inhibition and rugged self-confidence. In high school, after another student illustrated an essay with a watercolor drawing, Schulz was surprised when a teacher asked him why he hadn't done some illustrations himself. He didn't think it was fair to get academic credit for a talent that most kids didn't have. He never thought it was fair to draw caricatures. ("If somebody has a big nose," he said, "I'm sure that they regret the fact they have a big nose and who am I to point it out in gross caricature?") In later decades, when he had enormous bargaining power, he was reluctant to demand a larger or more flexible layout for *Peanuts,* because he didn't think it was fair to the papers that had been his loyal customers. His resentment of the name *Peanuts,* which his editors had given the strip in 1950, was still fresh in the eighties, when he was one of the ten highest-paid entertainers in America (behind Bill Cosby, ahead of Michael Jackson). "They didn't know when I walked in there that here was a fanatic," he told *Nemo.* "Here was a kid totally dedicated to what he was going to do. And to label then something that was going to be a life's work with a name like *Peanuts* was really insulting." To the suggestion that thirty-seven years might have softened the insult, Schulz said, "No, no. I hold a grudge, boy."

I never heard my father tell a joke. Sometimes he reminisced about a business colleague who ordered a "Scotch and Coke" and a "flander" fillet in a Dallas diner in July, and he could smile at his own embarrassments, his impolitic remarks at the office and his foolish mistakes on home-improvement projects, but there wasn't a silly bone in his body. He responded to other people's jokes with a wince or a grimace. As a boy, I told him a story I'd made up about a trash-hauling company cited for "fragrant violations." He shook his head, stone-faced, and said, "Not plausible."

In another archetypal *Peanuts* strip, Violet and Patty are abusing Charlie Brown in vicious stereo: "Go on home! We don't want you around here!" As he trudges away with his eyes on the ground, Violet remarks, "It's a strange thing about Charlie Brown. You almost never see him laugh."

My father only ever wanted not to be a child anymore. His parents were a pair of nineteenth-century Scandinavians caught up in a Hobbesian struggle to prevail in the swamps of north-central Minnesota. His popular, charismatic older brother drowned in a hunting accident when he was still a young man. His nutty and pretty and spoiled younger sister had an only daughter who died in a one-car accident when she was twenty-two. My father's parents also died in a one-car accident, but only after regaling him with prohibitions, demands, and criticisms for fifty years. He never said a harsh word about them. He never said a nice word, either.

The few childhood stories he told were about his dog, Spider, and his gang of friends in the invitingly named little town, Palisade, that his father and uncles had constructed among the swamps. The local high school was eight miles from Palisade. To attend, my father lived in a boarding house for a year and later commuted in his father's Model A. He was a social cipher, invisible after school. The most popular girl in his class, Romelle Erickson, was expected to be the valedictorian, and the school's "social crowd" was "shocked," my father told me many times, when it turned out that "the country boy," "Earl Who," had claimed the title.

When he registered at the University of Minnesota, in 1933, his father went with him and announced, at the head of the registration line, "He's going to be a civil engineer." For the rest of his life, my father was restless. He was studying philosophy at night school when he met my mother, and it took her four years to persuade him to have children. In his thirties, he agonized about whether to study medicine; in his forties, he was offered a partnership in a contracting firm which he almost dared to accept; in his fifties and sixties, he admonished me not to waste my life working for a corporation. In the end, though, he spent fifty years doing exactly what his father had told him to do.

My mother called him "oversensitive." She meant that it was easy to hurt his feelings, but the sensitivity was physical as well. When he was young, a doctor gave him a pinprick test that showed him to be allergic to "almost everything," including wheat, milk, and tomatoes. A different doctor, whose office was at the top of five long flights of stairs, greeted him with a blood-pressure test and immediately declared him unfit to fight the Nazis. Or so my father told me, with a shrugging gesture and an odd smile (as if to say, "What could I do?"), when I asked him why he hadn't been in the war. Even as a teen-ager, I sensed that his social awkwardness and sensitivities had been aggravated by not serving. He came from a family of pacifist Swedes, however, and was very happy not to be a soldier. He was happy that my brothers had college deferments and good luck with the lottery. Among his patriotic colleagues and the war-vet husbands of my mother's friends, he was such an outlier on the subject of Vietnam that he didn't dare talk about it. At home, in private, he aggressively declared that, if Tom had drawn a bad number, he personally would have driven him to Canada.

Tom was a second son in the mold of my father. He got poison ivy so bad it was like measles. He had a mid-October birthday and was perennially the youngest kid in his classes. On his only date in high school, he was so nervous that he forgot his baseball tickets and left the car idling in the street while he ran back inside; the car rolled down the hill, punched through an asphalt curb, and cleared two levels of a terraced garden before coming to rest on a neighbor's front lawn.

To me, it simply added to Tom's mystique that the car was not only still drivable but entirely undamaged. Neither he nor Bob could do any wrong in my eyes. They were expert whistlers and chess players, phenomenal wielders of tools and pencils, sole suppliers of whatever anecdotes and cultural data I was able to impress my friends with. In the margins of Tom's school copy of *A Portrait of the Artist,* he drew a two-hundred-page riffle-animation of a stick-figure pole-vaulter clearing a hurdle, landing on his head, and being carted away on a stretcher by stick-figure E.M.S. personnel; this seemed to me a masterwork of filmic art and science. But my father had told Tom: "You'd make a good architect, here are three schools to choose from." He said: "You're going to work for Sverdrup."

Tom was gone for five days before we heard from him. His call came on a Sunday after church. We were sitting on the screen porch, and my mother ran the length of the house to answer the phone. She sounded so ecstatic with relief I felt embarrassed for her. Tom had hitchhiked back to Houston and was doing deep-fry at a Church's Fried Chicken, hoping to save enough money to join his best friend in

Colorado. My mother kept asking him when he might come home, assuring him that he was welcome and that he wouldn't have to work at Sverdrup; but there was something toxic about us now which Tom obviously wanted nothing to do with.

Charles Schulz was the best comic-strip artist who ever lived. When *Peanuts* débuted, in October, 1950 (the same month Tom was born), the funny pages were full of musty holdovers from the thirties and forties. Even with the strip's strongest precursors, George Herriman's *Krazy Kat* and Elzie Segar's *Popeye,* you were aware of the severe constraints under which newspaper comics operated. The faces of Herriman's characters were too small to display more than rudimentary emotion, and so the burden of humor and sympathy came to rest on Herriman's language; his work read more like comic fable than like funny drawing. Popeye's face was proportionately larger than Krazy Kat's, but he was such a florid caricature that much of Segar's expressive budget was spent on nondiscretionary items, like Popeye's distended jaw and oversized nose; these were good jokes, but the same jokes every time. The very first *Peanuts* strip, by contrast, was all white space and big funny faces. It invited you right in. The minor character Shermy was speaking in neat letters and clear diction: "Here comes ol' Charlie Brown! Good ol' Charlie Brown . . . Yes, sir! Good ol' Charlie Brown . . . How I hate him!"

This first strip and the seven hundred and fifty-nine that immediately followed it have recently been published, complete and fully indexed, in a handsome volume from Fantagraphics Books. (This is the first in a series of twenty-five uniform volumes that will reproduce Schulz's entire daily oeuvre.) Even in Schulz's relatively primitive early work, you can appreciate what a breakthrough he made in drawing characters with large, visually uncluttered heads. Long limbs and big landscapes and fully articulated facial features—adult life, in short—were unaffordable luxuries. By dispensing with them, and by jumping from a funnies world of five or ten facial expressions into a world of fifty or a hundred, Schulz introduced a new informational dimension to the newspaper strip.

Although he later became famous for putting words like "depressed" and "inner tensions" and "emotional outlets" in the mouths of little kids, only a tiny percentage of his strips were actually drawn in the mock-psychological vein. His most important innovations were visual—he was all about *drawing funny*—and for most of my life as a fan I was curiously unconscious of this fact. In my imagination, *Peanuts* was a narrative, a collection of locales and scenes and sequences.

And, certainly, some comic strips do fit this description. Mike Doonesbury, for example, can be translated into words with minimal loss of information. Garry Trudeau is essentially a social novelist, his topical satire and intricate family dynamics and elaborate camera angles all serving to divert attention from the monotony of his comic expression. But Linus Van Pelt consists, first and foremost, of pen strokes. You'll never really understand him without seeing his hair stand on end. Translation into words inevitably diminishes Linus. As a cartoon, he's already a perfectly efficient vector of comic intention.

The purpose of a comic strip, Schulz liked to say, was to sell newspapers and to make people laugh. Although the formulation may look self-deprecating at first glance, in fact it is an oath of loyalty. When I. B. Singer, in his Nobel address, declared that the novelist's first responsibility is to be a storyteller, he didn't say "mere storyteller," and Schulz didn't say "merely make people laugh." He was loyal to the reader who wanted something funny from the funny pages. Just about anything—protesting against world hunger; getting a laugh out of words like "nooky"; dispensing wisdom; dying—is easier than real comedy.

Schulz never stopped trying to be funny. Around 1970, though, he began to drift away from aggressive humor and into melancholy reverie. There came tedious meanderings in Snoopyland with the unhilarious bird Woodstock and the unamusing beagle Spike. Certain leaden devices, such as Marcie's insistence on calling Peppermint Patty "sir," were heavily recycled. By the late eighties, the strip had grown so quiet that younger friends of mine seemed baffled by my fandom. It didn't help that later *Peanuts* anthologies loyally reprinted so many Spike and Marcie strips. The volumes that properly showcased Schulz's genius, the three hardcover collections from the sixties, had gone out of print. There were a few critical appreciations, most notably by Umberto Eco, who argued for Schulz's literary greatness in an essay written in the sixties and reprinted in the eighties (when Eco got famous). But the praise of a "low" genre by an old semiotic soldier in the culture wars couldn't help carrying an odor of provocation.

Still more harmful to Schulz's reputation were his own kitschy spinoffs. Even in the sixties, you had to fight through cloying Warm Puppy paraphernalia to reach the comedy; the cuteness levels in latter-day *Peanuts* TV specials tied my toes in knots. What first made *Peanuts Peanuts* was cruelty and failure, and yet every *Peanuts* greeting card and tchotchke and blimp had to feature somebody's sweet, crumpled smile. (You should go out and buy the new Fantagraphics book just to reward the publisher for putting a scowling Charlie Brown on the cover.) Everything about the billion-dollar *Peanuts* industry, which Schulz himself helped create, argued against him as an artist to be taken seriously. Far more than Disney, whose studios were churning out kitsch from the start, Schulz came to seem an icon of art's corruption by commerce, which sooner or later paints a smiling sales face on everything it touches. The fan who wants to see an artist sees a merchant instead. Why isn't he two ponies?

It's hard to repudiate a comic strip, however, when your memories of it are more vivid than your memories of your own life. When Charlie Brown went off to summer camp, I went along in my imagination. I heard him trying to make conversation with the fellow-camper who sat on his bunk and refused to say anything but "Shut up and leave me alone." I watched when he finally came home again and shouted to Lucy "I'm back!" and Lucy gave him a bored look and said, "Have you been away?"

I went to camp myself, in the summer of 1970. But, aside from an alarming personal-hygiene situation that seemed to have resulted from my peeing in some poison ivy, and which, for several days, I was convinced was either a fatal tumor or puberty, my camp experience paled beside Charlie Brown's. The best part of it was coming home and seeing Bob's new yellow Karmann Ghia waiting for me at the Y.M.C.A.

Tom was also home by then. He'd managed to make his way to his friend's house in Colorado, but the friend's parents weren't happy about harboring somebody else's runaway son, and so they'd sent Tom back to St. Louis. Officially, I was very excited that he was back. In truth, I was embarrassed to be around him. I was afraid that if I referred to his sickness and our quarantine I might trigger a relapse. I wanted to live in a *Peanuts* world where rage was funny and insecurity was lovable. The littlest kid in my *Peanuts* books, Sally Brown, grew older for a while and then hit a glass ceiling. I wanted everyone in my family to get along and nothing to change; but suddenly, after Tom ran away, it was as if the five of us looked around, asked why we should be spending time together, and failed to come up with many good answers.

For the first time, in the months that followed, my parents' conflicts became audible. My father came home on cool nights to complain about the house's "chill." My mother countered that the house wasn't cold if you were *doing housework all day*. My father marched into the dining room to adjust the thermostat and dramatically point to its "Comfort Zone," a pale-blue arc between 72 and 78 degrees. My mother said that she was *so hot*. And I decided, as always, not to voice my suspicion that the Comfort Zone referred to air-conditioning in the summer rather than heat in the winter. My father set the temperature at seventy-two and retreated to the den, which was situated directly above the furnace. There was a lull, and then big explosions. No matter what corner of the house I hid myself in, I could hear my father bellowing, "Leave the god-damned thermostat alone!"

"Earl, I didn't touch it!"

"You did! Again!"

"I didn't think I even moved it, I just *looked* at it, I didn't mean to change it."

"Again! You monkeyed with it again! I had it set where I wanted it. And you moved it down to seventy!"

"Well, if I did somehow change it, I'm sure I didn't mean to. You'd be hot, too, if you worked all day in the kitchen."

"All I ask at the end of a long day at work is that the temperature be set in the Comfort Zone."

"Earl, it is so hot in the kitchen. You don't know, because you're never *in* here, but it is *so* hot."

"The *low end* of the Comfort Zone! Not even the middle! The low end! It is not too much to ask!"

I wonder why "cartoonish" remains such a pejorative. It took me half my life to achieve seeing my parents as cartoons. And to become more perfectly a cartoon myself: what a victory that would be.

My father eventually applied technology to the problem of temperature. He bought a space heater to put behind his chair in the dining room, where he was bothered in winter by drafts from the bay window. Like so many of his appliance purchases, the heater was a pathetically cheap little thing, a wattage hog with a stertorous fan and a grinning orange mouth which dimmed the lights and drowned out conversation and produced a burning smell every time it cycled on. When I was in high school, he bought a quieter, more expensive model. One evening, my mother and I started reminiscing about the old model, caricaturing my father's temperature sensitivities, doing cartoons of the little heater's faults, the smoke and the buzzing, and my father got mad and left the table. He thought we were ganging up on him. He thought I was being cruel, and I was, but I was also forgiving him.

Reading the Genre

1. What kind of research did Franzen do to write this narrative? Make a list of the nonpersonal details he includes in the story—such as biographical information, historical facts, and other writers' literary analyses—and then comment on what this research adds to Franzen's own memories. (See Chapter 7, "Literary Analyses," p. 206.)

2. Franzen seems to jump from one scene to another, but this narrative does have a plot. Map the story along a timeline. What is the major action that moves the narrative along? How does Franzen tie the different scenes together? (See "Use physical devices for transitions," p. 419.)

3. This essay blends three genres: memoir, literary analysis, and literacy narrative. Focusing first on Franzen's literary analysis, what arguments does he make about Schulz's work? What evidence does he include to support his arguments? (For a literary analysis related to this essay, see Geraldine DeLuca's, "'I felt a Funeral, in my Brain': The Fragile Comedy of Charles Schulz," pp. 913–23.)

4. Compare "The Comfort Zone" with "Me Talk Pretty One Day" (pp. 635–40) and "Lost and Found" (pp. 654–59). What do all three narratives have in common, and how are they different?

5. **WRITING:** Franzen draws on close readings of his favorite comic strip to explain how he saw the world when he was young. Looking back at a favorite book, television show, or movie from your childhood, explore how you might have developed an understanding of the world through its characters. What truths about life did you learn from fiction? Write a narrative based on your reflections.

67 Reports: Readings

See also Chapter 2:

NEWS REPORT
Laura Layton, *Uranus's Second Ring-Moon System,* 47

INVESTIGATIVE REPORT
Tyghe Trimble, *The Running Shoe Debate: How Barefoot Runners Are Shaping the Shoe Industry,* 61

ACADEMIC REPORT
Annie Winsett, *Inner and Outer Beauty,* 66

FLOWCHART
Mike Wirth and Suzanne Cooper-Guasco, *How Our Laws Are Made,* 70

INFORMATIVE REPORT
Sharon Begley, *Learning to Love Climate "Adaptation"* 687

INFORMATIVE REPORT
David Wolman, *The Truth about Autism: Scientists Reconsider What They Think They Know* 691

INFORMATIVE REPORT
Kathryn Miles, *Dog Is Our Copilot* 703

LEGAL REPORT
Philip Deloria, *The* Cherokee Nation *Decision* 717

DESCRIPTIVE REPORT
Molly Young, *Sweatpants in Paradise* 726

INFORMATIVE REPORT   Sharon Begley is a senior science writer for *Newsweek* and the author of *Train Your Mind, Change Your Brain: How a New Science Reveals Our Extraordinary Potential to Transform Ourselves* (2007). In this article, first published in *Newsweek*, (January 2008), Begley takes a unique stance. Instead of reporting on global warming and measures to halt it, she focuses on the ways our society has prepared itself to adapt to and live with climate change.

Learning to Love Climate "Adaptation"

It's too late to stop global warming. Now we have to figure out how to survive it.

SHARON BEGLEY

Two words: airport runways. As scientists and policy types figure out what changes will be necessary to cope with global warming, it's obvious that massive sea walls will be required to hold back rising oceans, that enormous new reservoirs will be needed to cope with the alternating droughts and deluges that many regions will suffer, and that a crash program to develop heat- and drought-resistant crops would be a good idea if people are to keep eating. But it's the less-obvious yet no-less-necessary adaptations to climate change that are likely to wreak havoc. So, runways: hotter air, which we'll have more of in a greenhouse world, is less-dense air (hence, hot air rises). In less-dense air, says Bernoulli's principle, for planes to gain lift and stay aloft they need to take off faster. Ergo, airport runways will need to be longer to give planes the requisite ground speed before they're wheels up. Will someone please tell O'Hare?

It's such a polite, unthreatening word: *adapt*. The kind of thing you do as you roll with the punches or keep a stiff upper lip, modifying your behavior to a new situation. But as it will be used in 2008, *adaptation* is a euphemism for widespread, expensive changes that will be needed to cope with climate change. Although some adaptations will be modest and low tech, such as cities' establishing cooling centers to shelter residents during heat waves, others will require such herculean efforts and be so costly that we'll look back on the era beginning in 1988, when credible warnings of climate change reached critical mass, and wonder why we were so stupid as to blow the chance to keep global warming to nothing more extreme than a few more mild days in March.

According to the Intergovernmental Panel on Climate Change (which just picked up its Nobel Peace Prize), we are in for a minimum of 90 more years of warming no matter how many Hummers are junked in favor of Priuses. The reason is both atmospheric (greenhouse gases such as carbon dioxide remain aloft for about a century) and political (the world can't seem to summon the will to reduce greenhouse emissions). We are now at 385 parts per million of carbon dioxide, and there is no way, short of an asteroid impact that sends the world economy back to the Stone Age, to avoid reaching 450 ppm by mid-century, says Jay Gulledge of the Pew Center on Global Climate Change. Unfortunately, the effects of even 385 ppm are worse than forecast. More Arctic sea ice is melting, for instance, and global sea levels are rising faster. "Climate change is with us now, and the rates and impacts are greater than predicted," says Pew's Vicki Arroyo. "We have no choice but to talk about adaptation."

The required adaptations will be much more profound than turning up the air conditioning a notch come summertime. Melting glaciers will trigger "glacier lake outburst floods," warns the IPCC; if you have a child wondering which field to enter, dam engineering and building look like excellent bets. Permafrost is melting, so villages and roads in the (once) frozen north that are built on it will have to be relocated. Sea-level rise is inundating the wetlands and mangrove swamps that once absorbed storm surges; sea-wall design and construction will also be a growth industry, at least in areas that can afford it. For the tens of millions of Bangladeshis and other impoverished people living in coastal regions that will be underwater, inland areas can "adapt" by making room for unprecedented waves of environmental refugees. In a warmer world, the atmosphere holds more moisture. When moist air collides with Arctic air, freezing rain will fall, as it did in the nation's midsection in December, leaving tens of thousands of people without power for more than a week. Let's hope some smart utility engineers are figuring out how to build power lines that don't snap when they've got hundreds of pounds of ice on them.

Already some cities (New York, Seattle) and states (California, Alaska, Maryland, Oregon, Washington) have adaptation plans. Alaska is figuring out how to protect or relocate villages at risk from wave surges or flooding. California is beefing up its firefighting capacity because, in a greenhouse world, more forest fires will rage; it has also proposed desalinization plants for when seawater must substitute for rain that never fell and snowpack that never accumulated. Other locales are requiring new bridges to be built above anticipated storm surges (as for existing bridges, good luck) and developing heat-wave early-warning systems so they can ramp up cooling centers and get the word out to at-risk populations such as the elderly. They are vulnerable for both biological reasons (old bodies have trouble keeping cool) and social ones (they resist leaving their homes).

A trickle of money is beginning to fund such efforts. In August the Rockefeller Foundation announced a $70 million program on "climate-change resilience" to help the developing world in particular cope with what's coming. A climate bill in Congress would take some of the money raised from auctioning off permits to emit carbon dioxide and use it to fund adaptation research and programs (though other proposals would give the permits to industry gratis). Of course, if we do as competent a job adapting to climate change as we've done preventing it, too-short runways will be the least of our problems.

Reading the Genre

1. Reread the first and last sentences of this article. How does Begley grab your attention in the beginning and then drive home her point at the end? How important are these lines to an essay of this length, or to any report? (See Chapter 32, "Introductions," p . 420, and Chapter 33, "Conclusions," p. 425.)

2. What is the tone of this essay? How does the tone make this essay persuasive?

3. Look up the definitions of the terms *irony* and *hyperbole*. Then find lines in Begley's article that are particularly ironic or hyperbolic. How does irony or hyperbole work in a report? (See "Use language strategically," p. 74, and Chapter 35, "High, Middle, and Low Style," p. 432.)

4. What is the key word in this essay, and how does the author analyze it? How is this word a euphemism—a word or phrase that masks its own real meaning?

5. **WRITING:** Choose a popular euphemism that functions as doublespeak—language constructed to disguise its actual meaning. Example terms might be *right-sized, collateral damage, smart bomb, pre-owned,* or *job flexibility.* Perform a Google News search and report on the most recent and common uses of this euphemism. Then analyze how this term is used and what the use of this term reveals or conceals.

6. **COMPOSING VISUALLY:** Take one of the articles that turned up in your research for question 5 and convert it into a word cloud using the Wordle Web site (www.wordle.net). Examine the resulting graphic closely. What does the word cloud reveal to you about the article and the euphemistic term?

INFORMATIVE REPORT   A contributing editor for *Wired*, David Wolman has published articles about technology and science in dozens of magazines. He is also the author of two books: *A Left-Hand Turn around the World: Chasing the Mystery and Meaning of All Things Southpaw* (2005) and *Righting the Mother Tongue: From Olde English to Email, the Tangled Story of English Spelling* (2008).

Wired

From: David Wolman

The Truth about Autism: Scientists Reconsider What They *Think* They Know

The YouTube clip opens with a woman facing away from the camera, rocking back and forth, flapping her hands awkwardly, and emitting an eerie hum. She then performs strange repetitive behaviors: slapping a piece of paper against a window, running a hand lengthwise over a computer keyboard, twisting the knob of a drawer. She bats a necklace with her hand and nuzzles her face against the pages of a book. And you find yourself thinking: Who's shooting this footage of the handicapped lady, and why do I always get sucked into watching the latest viral video?

But then the words "A Translation" appear on a black screen, and for the next five minutes, 27-year-old Amanda Baggs—who is autistic and doesn't speak—describes in vivid and articulate terms what's going on inside her head as she carries out these seemingly bizarre actions. In a synthesized voice generated by a software application, she explains that touching, tasting, and smelling allow her to have a "constant conversation" with her surroundings. These forms of nonverbal stimuli constitute her "native language," Baggs explains, and are no better or worse than spoken language. Yet her failure to speak is seen as a deficit, she says, while other people's failure to learn her language is seen as natural and acceptable.

And you find yourself thinking: She might have a point.

In My Language

Baggs lives in a public housing project for the elderly and handicapped near downtown Burlington, Vermont. She has short black hair, a pointy nose, and round glasses. She usually wears a T-shirt and baggy pants, and she spends a scary amount of time—day

Amanda Baggs is at the forefront of a movement that's forcing researchers to rethink autism.

and night—on the Internet: blogging, hanging out in Second Life, and corresponding with her autie and aspie friends. (For the uninitiated, that's *autistic* and *Asperger's*.)

On a blustery afternoon, Baggs reclines on a red futon in the apartment of her neighbor (and best friend). She has a gray travel pillow wrapped around her neck, a keyboard resting on her lap, and a DynaVox VMax computer propped against her legs.

Like many people with autism, Baggs doesn't like to look you in the eye and needs help with tasks like preparing a meal and taking a shower. In conversation she'll occasionally grunt or sigh, but she stopped speaking altogether in her early twenties. Instead, she types 120 words a minute, which the DynaVox then translates into a synthesized female voice that sounds like a deadpan British schoolteacher.

The YouTube post, she says, was a political statement, designed to call attention to people's tendency to underestimate autistics. It wasn't her first video post, but this one took off. "When the number of viewers began to climb, I got scared out of my mind," Baggs says. As the hit count neared 100,000, her blog was flooded. At 200,000, scientists were inviting her to visit their labs. By 300,000, the TV people came calling, hearts warmed by the story of a young woman's fiery spirit and the rare glimpse into what has long been regarded as the solitary imprisonment of the autistic mind. "I've said a million times that I'm not trapped in my own world," Baggs says. "Yet what do most of these news stories lead with? Saying exactly that."

I tell her that I asked one of the world's leading authorities on autism to check out the video. The expert's opinion: Baggs must have had outside help creating it, perhaps from one of her caregivers. Her inability to talk, coupled with repetitive behaviors, lack of eye contact, and the need for assistance with everyday tasks are telltale signs of severe autism. Among all autistics, 75 percent are expected to score in the mentally retarded range on standard intelligence tests—that's an IQ of 70 or less.

People like Baggs fall at one end of an array of developmental syndromes known as autism spectrum disorders. The spectrum ranges from someone with severe disability and cognitive impairment to the socially awkward eccentric with Asperger's syndrome.

After I explain the scientist's doubts, Baggs grunts, and her mouth forms just a hint of a smirk as she lets loose a salvo on the keyboard. No one helped her shoot the video, edit it, and upload it to YouTube. She used a Sony Cybershot DSC-T1, a digital camera that can record up to 90 seconds of video (she has since upgraded). She then patched the footage together using the editing programs RAD Video Tools, VirtualDub, and DivXLand Media Subtitler. "My care provider wouldn't even know how to work the software," she says.

Baggs is part of an increasingly visible and highly networked community of autistics. Over the past decade, this group has benefited enormously from the Internet as well as innovations like type-to-speech software. Baggs may never have considered herself trapped in her own world, but thanks to technology, she can communicate with the same speed and specificity as someone using spoken language.

Autistics like Baggs are now leading a nascent civil rights movement. "I remember in '99," she says, "seeing a number of gay pride Web sites. I envied how many there were and wished there was something like that for autism. Now there is." The message: We're here. We're weird. Get used to it.

This movement is being fueled by a small but growing cadre of neuropsychological researchers who are taking a fresh look at the nature of autism itself. The condition,

they say, shouldn't be thought of as a disease to be eradicated. It may be that the autistic brain is not defective but simply different—an example of the variety of human development. These researchers assert that the focus on finding a cure for autism—the disease model—has kept science from asking fundamental questions about how autistic brains function.

A cornerstone of this new approach—call it the difference model—is that past research about autistic intelligence is flawed, perhaps catastrophically so, because the instruments used to measure intelligence are bogus. "If Amanda Baggs had walked into my clinic five years ago," says Massachusetts General Hospital neuroscientist Thomas Zeffiro, one of the leading proponents of the difference model, "I would have said she was a low-functioning autistic with significant cognitive impairment. And I would have been totally wrong."

Seventy years ago, a Baltimore psychiatrist named Leo Kanner began recording observations about children in his clinic who exhibited "fascinating peculiarities." Just as Kanner's landmark paper was about to be published, a pediatrician in Vienna named Hans Asperger was putting the finishing touches on a report about a similar patient population. Both men, independently, used the same word to describe and define the condition: *autist*, or *autism*, from the Greek *autos*, meaning self.

The children had very real deficits, especially when it came to the "failure to be integrated in a social group" (Asperger) or the inborn inability to form "affective contact" with other people (Kanner). The two doctors' other observations about language impairment, repetitive behaviors, and the desire for sameness still form much of the basis of autism diagnoses in the twenty-first century.

On the matter of autistic intelligence, Kanner spoke of an array of mental skills, "islets of ability"—vocabulary, memory, and problem-solving that "bespeak good intelligence." Asperger, too, was struck by "a particular originality of thought and experience." Yet over the years, those islets attracted scientific interest only when they were amazing—savant-level capabilities in areas such as music, mathematics, and drawing. For the millions of people with autism who weren't savants, the general view was that their condition was tragic, their brainpower lacking.

The test typically used to substantiate this view relies heavily on language, social interaction, and cultural knowledge—areas that autistic people, by definition, find difficult. About six years ago, Meredyth Goldberg Edelson, a professor of psychology at Willamette University in Oregon, reviewed 215 articles published over the past 71 years, all making or referring to this link between autism and mental retardation. She found that most of the papers (74 percent) lacked their own research data to back up the assumption. Thirty-nine percent of the articles weren't based on any data, and even the more rigorous studies often used questionable measures of intelligence. "Are the majority of autistics mentally retarded?" Goldberg Edelson asks. "Personally, I don't think they are, but we don't have the data to answer that."

Mike Merzenich, a professor of neuroscience at UC San Francisco, says the notion that 75 percent of autistic people are mentally retarded is "incredibly wrong and destructive." He has worked with a number of autistic children, many of whom are nonverbal and would have been plunked into the low-functioning category. "We label them as retarded because they can't express what they know," and then, as they grow older, we accept that they "can't do much beyond sit in the back of a warehouse somewhere and stuff letters in envelopes."

The irony is that this dearth of data persists even as autism receives an avalanche of attention. Organizations such as Autism Speaks advocate for research and resources. Celebrity parents like Toni Braxton, Ed Asner, and Jenny McCarthy get high-profile coverage on talk shows and TV news magazines. Newsweeklies raise fears of an autism epidemic. But is there an epidemic? There's certainly the perception of one. According to the Centers for Disease Control, one out of every 150 8-year-old children (in the areas of the US most recently studied) has an autism spectrum disorder, a prevalence much higher than in decades past, when the rate was thought to be in the range of four or five cases per 10,000 children. But no one knows whether this apparent explosion of cases is due to an actual rise in autism, changing diagnostic criteria, inconsistent survey techniques, or some combination of the three.

In his original paper in 1943, Kanner wrote that while many of the children he examined "were at one time or another looked upon as feebleminded, they are all unquestionably endowed with *good cognitive potentialities*." Sixty-five years later, though, little is known about those potentialities. As one researcher told me, "There's no money in the field for looking at differences" in the autistic brain. "But if you talk about trying to fix a problem—then the funding comes."

On the outskirts of Montreal sits a brick monolith, the Hôpital Rivière-des-Prairies. Once one of Canada's most notorious asylums, it now has a small number of resident psychiatric patients, but most of the space has been converted into clinics and research facilities.

One of the leading researchers here is Laurent Mottron, 55, a psychiatrist specializing in autism. Mottron, who grew up in postwar France, had a tough childhood. His family had a history of schizophrenia and Tourette syndrome, and he probably has what today would be diagnosed as attention deficit and hyperactivity disorder. Naturally, he went into psychiatry. By the early '80s, Mottron was doing clinical work at a school in Tours that catered to children with sensory impairment, including autism. "The view then," Mottron says, "was that these children could be reeled back to normalcy with play therapy and work on the parents' relationships"—a gentle way of saying that the parents, especially the mother, were to blame. (The theory that emotionally distant "refrigerator mothers" caused autism had by then been rejected in the US, but in France and many other countries, the view lingered.)

After only a few weeks on the job, Mottron decided the theories were crap. "These children were just of another kind," he says. "You couldn't turn someone autistic or make someone not autistic. It was hardwired." In 1986, Mottron began working with an autistic man who would later become known in the scientific literature as "E.C." A draftsman who specialized in mechanical drawings, E.C. had incredible savant skills in 3-D drawing. He could rotate objects in his mind and make technical drawings without the need for a single revision. After two years of working with E.C., Mottron made his second breakthrough—not about autistics this time but about the rest of us: People with standard-issue brains—so-called neurotypicals—don't have the perceptual abilities to do what E.C. could do. "It's just inconsistent with how our brains work," Mottron says.

From that day forward, he decided to challenge the disease model underlying most autism research. "I wanted to go as far as I could to show that their perception—their brains—are totally different." Not damaged. Not dysfunctional. Just different.

By the mid-1990s, Mottron was a faculty member at the University of Montreal, where he began publishing papers on "atypicalities of perception" in autistic subjects. When performing certain mental tasks—especially when tapping visual, spatial, and auditory functions—autistics have shown superior performance compared with neurotypicals. Call it the upside of autism. Dozens of studies—Mottron's and others—have demonstrated that people with autism spectrum disorder have a number of strengths: a higher prevalence of perfect pitch, enhanced ability with 3-D drawing and pattern recognition, more accurate graphic recall, and various superior memory skills.

Yet most scientists who come across these skills classify them as "anomalous peaks of ability," set them aside, and return to the questions that drive most research: What's wrong with the autistic brain? Can we find the genes responsible so that we can someday cure it? Is there a unifying theory of autism? With severe autistics, cognitive strengths are even more apt to be overlooked because these individuals have such obvious deficits and are so hard to test. People like Baggs don't speak, others may run out of the room, and still others might not be able to hold a pencil. And besides, if 75 percent of them are mentally retarded, well, why bother?

Mottron draws a parallel with homosexuality. Until 1974, psychiatry's bible, the *Diagnostic and Statistical Manual of Mental Disorders*, described being gay as a mental illness. Someday, Mottron says, we'll look back on today's ideas about autism with the same sense of shame that we now feel when talking about psychology's pre-1974 views on sexuality. "We want to break the idea that autism should definitely be suppressed," he says.

Michelle Dawson doesn't drive or cook. Public transit overwhelms her, and face-to-face interaction is an ordeal. She was employed as a postal worker in 1998 when she "came out of the closet" with her diagnosis of autism, which she received in the early '90s. After that, she claims, Canada Post harassed her to such a degree that she was forced to take a permanent leave of absence, starting in 2002. (Canada Post says Dawson was treated fairly.) To fight back, she went on an information-devouring rampage. "There's such a variety of human behavior. Why is my kind wrong?" she asks. She eventually began scouring the libraries of McGill University in Montreal to delve into the autism literature. She searched out journal articles using the online catalog and sat on the floor reading studies among the stacks.

Dawson, like Baggs, has become a reluctant spokesperson for this new view of autism. Both are prolific bloggers and correspond constantly with scientists, parents' groups, medical institutions, the courts, journalists, and anyone else who'll listen to their stories of how autistics are mistreated. Baggs has been using YouTube to make her point; Dawson's weapon is science.

In 2001, Dawson contacted Mottron, figuring that his clinic might help improve the quality of her life. Mottron tried to give her some advice on navigating the neurotypical world, but his tips on how to handle banking, shopping, and buses didn't help. After meeting with her a few times, Mottron began to suspect that what Dawson really needed was a sense of purpose. In 2003, he handed her one of his in-progress journal articles and asked her to copy-edit the grammar. So Dawson started reading. "I criticized his science almost immediately," she says.

Encouraged by Dawson's interest, Mottron sent her other papers. She responded with written critiques of his work. Then one day in early 2003, she called with a question. "I asked: 'How did they control for attention in that fMRI face study?' That caught his attention." Dawson had flagged an error that Mottron says most postdocs would have missed. He was impressed, and over the next few months he sought Dawson's input on other technical questions. Eventually, he invited her to collaborate with his research group, despite the fact that her only academic credential was a high school diploma.

Dawson has an incredible memory, but she's not a savant. What makes her unique, Mottron says, is her gift for scientific analysis—the way she can sniff through methodologies and statistical manipulation, hunting down tiny errors and weak links in logic.

Last summer, the peer-reviewed journal *Psychological Science* published a study titled "The Level and Nature of Autistic Intelligence." The lead author was Michelle

Dawson. The paper argues that autistic smarts have been underestimated because the tools for assessing intelligence depend on techniques ill-suited to autistics. The researchers administered two different intelligence tests to 51 children and adults diagnosed with autism and to 43 non-autistic children and adults.

The first test, known as the Wechsler Intelligence Scale, has helped solidify the notion of peaks of ability amid otherwise pervasive mental retardation among autistics. The other test is Raven's Progressive Matrices, which requires neither a race against the clock nor a proctor breathing down your neck. The Raven is considered as reliable as the Wechsler, but the Wechsler is far more commonly used. Perhaps that's because it requires less effort for the average test taker. Raven measures abstract reasoning—"effortful" operations like spotting patterns or solving geometric puzzles. In contrast, much of the Wechsler assesses crystallized skills like acquired vocabulary, making correct change, or knowing that milk goes in the fridge and cereal in the cupboard—learned information that most people intuit or recall almost automatically.

What the researchers found was that while non-autistic subjects scored just about the same—a little above average—on both tests, the autistic group scored much better on the Raven. Two individuals' scores swung from the mentally retarded range to the 94th percentile. More significantly, the subset of autistic children in the study scored roughly 30 percentile points higher on the Raven than they did on the more language-dependent Wechsler, pulling all but a couple of them out of the range for mental retardation.

A number of scientists shrugged off the results—of course autistics would do better on nonverbal tests. But Dawson and her coauthors saw something more. The "peaks of ability" on the Wechsler correlated strongly with the average scores on the Raven. The finding suggests the Wechsler scores give only a glimpse of the autistics' intelligence, whereas the Raven—the gold standard of fluid intelligence testing—reveals the true, or at least truer, level of general intelligence.

Yet to a remarkable degree, scientists conducting cognitive evaluations continue to use tests which presume that people who can't communicate the answer don't know the answer. The question is: Why? Greg Allen, an assistant professor of psychiatry at University of Texas Southwestern Medical Center, says that although most researchers know the Wechsler doesn't provide a good assessment of people with autism, there's pressure to use the test anyway. "Say you're submitting a grant to study autistic people by comparing them to a control group," he says. "The first question that comes up is: Did you control for IQ? Matching people on IQ is meant to clean up the methodology, but I think it can also end up damaging the study."

And that hurts autistic people, Dawson says. She makes a comparison with blindness. Of course blind people have a disability and need special accommodation. But you wouldn't give a blind person a test heavily dependent on vision and interpret their poor score as an accurate measure of intelligence. Mottron is unequivocal: Because of recent research, especially the Raven paper, it's clearer than ever that so-called low-functioning people like Amanda Baggs are more intelligent than once presumed. The Dawson paper was hardly conclusive, but it generated buzz among scientists and the media. Mottron's team is now collaborating with Massachusetts General Hospital's Zeffiro, a neuroimaging expert, to dig deeper. Zeffiro and company are looking for variable types of mental processing *without* asking, what's wrong with this brain? Their first study compares fMRI results from autistic and control subjects whose brains were imaged while they performed the Raven test. The group is currently crunching numbers for publication, and the study looks both perplexing and promising.

Surprisingly, they didn't find any variability in which parts of the brain lit up when subjects performed the tasks. "We thought we'd see different patterns of activation," Zeffiro says, "but it looks like the similarities outweigh the dissimilarities." When they examined participants' Raven scores together with response times, however, they noticed something odd. The two groups had the same error rates, but as an aggregate, the autistics completed the tasks 40 percent faster than the non-autistics. "They spent less time coming up with the same number of right answers. The only explanation we can see right now," Zeffiro says, is that autistic brains working on this set of tasks "seem to be engaged at a higher level of efficiency." That may have to do with greater connectivity within an area or areas of the brain. He and other researchers are already exploring this hypothesis using diffusion tensor imaging, which measures the density of brain wiring.

But critics of the difference model reject the whole idea that autism is merely another example of neuro-diversity. After all, being able to plan your meals for the week or ask for directions bespeaks important forms of intelligence. "If you pretend the areas that are troubled aren't there, you miss important aspects of the person," says Fred Volkmar, director of Yale's Child Study Center.

In the vast majority of journal articles, autism is referred to as a disorder, and the majority of neuro-psychiatric experts will tell you that the description fits—something is wrong with the autistic brain. UCSF's Merzenich, who agrees that conventional intelligence-testing tools are misleading, still doesn't think the difference model makes sense. Many autistics are probably smarter than we think, he says. But there's little question that more severe autism is characterized by what Merzenich terms "grossly abnormal" brain development that can lead to a "catastrophic end state." Denying this reality, he says, is misguided. Yale's Volkmar likens it to telling a physically disabled person: "You don't need a wheelchair. Walk!"

Meanwhile parents, educators, and autism advocates worry that focusing on the latent abilities and intelligence of autistic people may eventually lead to cuts in funding both for research into a cure and services provided by government. As one mother of an autistic boy told me, "There's no question that my son needs treatment and a cure."

Back in Burlington, Baggs is cueing up another YouTube clip. She angles her computer screen so I can see it. Set to the soundtrack of Queen's "Under Pressure," it's a montage of close-up videos showing behaviors like pen clicking, thumb twiddling, and finger tapping. The message: Why are some stress-related behaviors socially permissible, while others—like the rocking bodies and flapping arms commonly associated with autism—are not? Hit count for the video at last check: 80,000 and climbing.

Should autism be treated? Yes, says Baggs, it should be treated with respect. "People aren't interested in us functioning with the brains we have," she says, because autism is considered to be outside the range of normal variability. "I don't fit the stereotype of autism. But who does?" she asks, hammering especially hard on the keyboard. "The definition of autism is so fluid and changing every few years." What's exciting, she says, is that Mottron and other scientists have "found universal strengths where others usually look for universal deficits." Neuro-cognitive science, she says, is finally catching up to what she and many other adults with autism have been saying all along.

Baggs is working on some new videos. One project is tentatively titled "Am I a Person Yet?" She'll explore communication, empathy, self-reflection—core elements of the human experience that have at times been used to define personhood itself. And at various points during the clip, she'll ask: "Am I a person yet?" It's a provocative idea, and you might find yourself thinking: She has a point.

Reading the Genre

1. What are the key terms in this report? Reread the report and underline each key term and theory Wolman defines. How do the definitions help readers understand his subject?

2. Wolman reports on a contentious and controversial issue. How does he maintain objectivity? What strategies does he use to weigh the different sides of the issue, and what underlying assumptions does he explore? (See "Aim for objectivity," p. 46.)

3. Wolman interviews a parade of experts on his topic. When you write a report you won't likely have the same access to experts, but you can obtain the kinds of research and opinion that Wolman gets firsthand in other ways. Track down one of his sources using research databases and the Internet. Can you use this published research in the same ways that Wolman uses interviews? (See "Find reliable sources," p. 46; "Base reports on the best available sources," p. 52; and Chapter 43, "Evaluating Sources," p. 482.)

4. **WRITING:** Curious readers can find studies and opinion relevant to autistic ability anywhere from medical journals to the blogosphere. Conduct some additional research on the issue and write a short reflection on what you find.

5. **COMPOSING VISUALLY:** Watch Amanda Baggs's video "In My Language" on YouTube. What does it make you think or feel? Choose a visual medium, such as painting, collage, or photography, and attempt to express your response without words. (See Part 8, Media & Design, p. 566.)

INFORMATIVE REPORT   In her book *Adventures with Ari: A Puppy, a Leash, and Our Year Outdoors* (2009), Kathryn Miles makes an effort to see the world as her dog sees it, providing a unique perspective on the natural world and evolutionary theory. Miles, who teaches environmental writing at Unity College, published this article in the Winter 2008 issue of the journal *Ecotone*.

Dog Is Our Copilot

KATHRYN MILES

Could everything we know and love (or hate) about evolution depend upon a singularly pampered Victorian terrier? Perhaps not entirely. Then again, probably more than you might think.

Admittedly, Polly was no average dog. Sure, she looked ordinary enough—about fourteen inches tall, just shy of twenty pounds, and possessing a thin, athletic frame. She had a wiry white coat, built more for functionality than elegance. Even still, her face, what with its intelligent eyes, overturned ears, and slight beard, endeared her to Charles Darwin. She was rumored to be both clever and indulgent, consenting to any number of silly tricks for the amusement of visitors. She liked walks but loved curling up in her bed more. She was skilled at eliciting sympathy and engendering affection. She pined when her favorite human was away. In many ways, she was a typical family pet.

But she was also so much more. Polly was a direct descendant of a dog named Trump, who in turn was best known as being the first fox terrier owned by Parson John Russell. The parson was a man's man; he loved to hunt, and even after taking religious orders, he preferred to be called Jack by those who knew him. When he wasn't chasing foxes or administering the Eucharist, Jack Russell liked to experiment with dog genetics or, more specifically, coordinated breeding intended to bring out the most desirable traits in his terriers. He was surprisingly skilled at this pastime—so skilled, in fact, that he is credited with creating one of the first acknowledged dog breeds through speciation, or the process whereby one species is diverged into several. The dog world applauded his efforts by giving all members of this breed the moniker Jack Russell terrier.

Perhaps not surprisingly, Darwin was intrigued by Russell's tinkering in speciation. Darwin was also utterly enamored of the dogs that resulted—including our protagonist, Polly, whom Darwin adopted for his daughter Henrietta. Henrietta liked Polly just fine, but there was never a real connection between the two. So, when Henrietta set off for her new life as a married woman, she left Polly in the care of her doting father. As much as Darwin missed his daughter, he seemed more than pleased with his consolation prize.

Darwin adored dogs. In fact, he had managed to entwine just about every major relationship of his life with the existence of a dog. As a young boy, for instance, Darwin often felt oppressed by his regulated home life. According to his own account, on one day when he felt particularly confined, he became so frustrated he beat a puppy, thinking it would give him a sense of power. It didn't. Instead, it filled him with regret and a lifelong tenderness for the species. Meanwhile, he found other, less harmful modes of exerting sway in a relationship, like deliberately wooing his sister Caroline's dogs, vying for their affection as a way of making a sister jealous. It wasn't until college that Darwin found a dog of his own: a pointer he named Sappho, perhaps as a quiet emotional overture toward his cousin William Darwin Fox. For years Charles had adored William—and William's dog, Fan. He also loved the affection he could draw out from the latter and, in turn, the attention that he garnered from the former. During an extended stay with Charles, William repeatedly awoke at night to see that Charles had persuaded Fan to leave William's bed in favor of his own. William politely suggested that Charles find an unclaimed canine companion of his own.

And so he did in Sappho, who soon became Darwin's bosom confidant. Even after his friendship with Fox cooled, Darwin's affinity for Sappho—and dogs in general—remained strong. After Sappho, a parade of canines came in and out of Darwin's life: dogs by the name of Spark, Nina, Dash, Czar, Pincher, Snow, Bob, Bran, Ponto, and Shelah all shared his home. But the real love of his life—at least as far as puppy love is concerned—was Polly.

Part of Darwin's fascination with Polly was undoubtedly her deliberate breeding. But there were softer reasons for his interest, too. Polly proved to Darwin that dogs possess emotion and can feel. Thirteen years after the publication of *The Origin of Species*, he would point to the terrier's affection as further proof of both behavioral inheritance and the connection between humans and so-called lower animals.

Polly was no less taken with Charles Darwin. The dog accompanied him on his daily walks and was the only living creature permitted to lounge in his very private study. Darwin's son Francis described their relationship as one of mutual adoration. Polly would perform tricks only if asked by Charles; she would wait pensively at home while he toured for his books and his health; she would "go wild with excitement," according to Francis, when Darwin returned. Immediately upon his arrival, Darwin was said to bypass his family in order to greet Polly by pressing their faces together and whispering sweet nothings into her wiry ears. Darwin's wife, Emma, found this intimacy incomprehensible and wryly noted that an entire book could be written about it. "I think [Polly] has taken it into her head that [your father] is a very big puppy," Emma wrote to her daughter. "She is perfectly devoted to him; will only stay with him and leaves the room whenever he does. She lies upon him whenever she can, and licks his hands." Darwin, Emma also reported, returned the affection tenfold.

I love this fact about Darwin. I first discovered it when, like millions of other museumgoers, I visited the Darwin exhibit created by the American Museum of Natural History, which also toured the country. There I read the well-crafted placards and stood respectfully before the framed plant samples taken during the voyage of the *Beagle*. They were everything a display ought to be: lovely, informative, reverent. But they did not captivate me—at least not like Darwin's re-created study at Down House, which appeared near the end of the exhibit and waited quietly behind thick velvet ropes. Most of the other museumgoers walked right past this muted tableau. I almost skipped it too, until something caught my eye. There, next to a plain wooden writing desk and Regency mahogany chair, sat a small basket: a bed for a terrier-sized dog. With raised sides and a fleecy interior, it was precisely the kind of thing one might buy today at a big-box store specializing in impulse purchases for the doting pet owner. Darwin's study, like Polly's coat, was far more remarkable for its functionality than its elegance. He preferred furniture of the metaphoric sort: chairs that could be used to fetch books on upper shelves; divans that could hold coats as well as lounging readers. The inclusion of a small wicker bed, then, seemed uncharacteristically indulgent. This gave me pause. Could Darwin have belonged to that growing modern klatch of munificent pet owners? The sort who monogram sweaters for their dachshunds and buy frozen yogurt for their huskies? Really?

As it turns out, Darwin not only belonged to this set; he all but invented it.

Even knowing Darwin's biography, one finds it easy to forget that he had an emotional affinity for dogs and other domestic animals. His intellectual inheritance tends to overshadow the parts of life that were both sensitive and loving. Opponents of evolutionary theory like to posit a man tortured by his godlessness and the empty life it created; proponents often depict him as the archetypal eminent Victorian—staid and distantly contemplative. Neither offers an obvious venue for face-licking and fawning pet names. Besides, when we do talk about Darwin's interest in animals, we tend to emphasize his fascination with more mysterious creatures, like finches and tortoises, coral and barnacles. Or his continued interest in beetles, ants, and other creepy-crawlies. That's fair of course: all of these animals contributed to Darwin's sense of animal development and classification. Nevertheless, much of the theory underlying *The Origin of Species* is based not on the wild catalogue of animals he observed during his time on the *Beagle*, but rather on what he saw in animals closer to hearth and home. Of these, dogs proved particularly useful in his study.

But why?

Darwin never said specifically. However, we can wager a guess or two. First, dogs provide a bridge between what we know about the wild and the domestic. Their existence is one of tension: we deliberately invite them into our households, and yet we ask them to retain some semblance of their un-tamed selves. We want them to guard against intruders, to use their instinctual hunting capabilities, to adhere to pack mentalities. Then, at the end of the day, we want them to rest by the fireplace, play with the children, or hop in the car and enjoy a good ride around town. We are looking for a kind of metaphysical toggle switch between natural and cultivated. Dogs provide it. That was par-ticularly true in 1859, when *Canis lupus familiaris* was still very much a species in transition.

Two thousand years prior to *The Origin of Species*, Aristotle outlined several dog breeds in his *History of Animals*, including the Molossian, the Laconian, the Maltese, and the working sheepdog. This paltry number of dog breeds did not in-crease all that significantly over the next two millennia. In fact, Britain's first dog show (held, quite conveniently, in 1859) recognized just fourteen classes, all of which were some variation on pointers or setters. Nevertheless, the very definition of dog—with all of its possible permutations—was changing radically during the mid-nineteenth century, thanks to the growing interest in dog fancy. Suddenly dogs were far more than working animals: they were amusing hobbies, good friends, beloved members of many middle-class homes. As a result, the Victorian era witnessed an explosion in dog breeding and the creation of specific dog types, particularly of those dogs willing to exist as lap pets or entertaining indoor diversions.

This couldn't have happened at a better time for Darwin. His theory of evolution had found theoretical verification in his observations of other domestic animals, including pigeons, sheep, and even camels. None, however, showed the variety of traits witnessed in the dog. Darwin knew this, and he directed his inquiry accordingly. He began keeping a grisly assortment of greyhound fetuses, bulldog bones, and other unmentionables in his study. From this amalgamation of house pets and vivisected fetuses, Darwin found what he could not locate during his time on the *Beagle:* a systematic understanding of trait inheritance. Take, for instance, Polly, who was once accidentally burned on her back. When hair returned to the site of the wound, it was red instead of white. This change, Darwin proclaimed to his family, was proof of pangenesis: Polly's father, a red terrier, must have shed cell particles dictating attributes like fur color. These particles then must have remained latent during Polly's fetal development and arisen only now, as secondary growth characteristics.

Through this and other observations, Darwin was certain he had found the intergenerational verification he could not locate in *Beagle* ports of call. But I think dogs provided a more subjective benefit to Darwin's theory, too. The Victorians suffered from a self-professed collecting mania. From butterflies and beetles to spools and soup spoons, no assortment of curios was too inconsequential. By the time Darwin began his inquiry into the origin of species, designer dogs had become the newest, hottest thing to collect—and they were a lot more fun than insects wiggling on a pin. Victorians loved their increasing dog permutations at least in part because, like the young Darwin, they saw in dog attributes something they could control. Want a more effective otter hunter? Breed only those dogs showing chase prowess. Need a smaller dog for your London flat? Pair up the runts of two litters. Want utter adoration? Take the most gregarious, emotive animals and encourage a carnal love fest. Voilà! You've created your ideal dog.

This freedom appealed greatly to the Victorian culture as a whole. No one cried foul or screamed hubris—at least no one did loudly enough to make the annals of history. Darwin must have been aware of his epoch's penchant for dogs; he also understood that this love affair softened public approval for his ideas about the descent of genetic attributes. And why not? Breeding dogs was an increasingly popular pastime, an effective way to get the animal you wanted. So if a naturalist could quietly explain how you came into possession of your King Charles spaniel, or merely suggest that the creation of said spaniel was not so unlike your own arrival on this earth, maybe that might make the evolutionary pill a little easier to swallow.

In dogs Darwin found acceptable proof of human hubris: we can change a species. And if we can, then why couldn't nature, or why couldn't even that species, change itself? As far as Darwin was concerned, it could—and it did. All the time. But how?

Darwin couldn't say for sure. And the issue continued to plague him with more questions than answers. How did Polly relate to the family's larger, mixed breed, named Bob? Or to the greyhounds and bulldogs he had studied so fastidiously for *The Origin of Species*? And furthermore, what did the appearance of such breeds mean for the future of biology and ontology? Wouldn't it be so very interesting, he opined in *Origin*, if we could clear up this canine conundrum, "if, for instance, it could be shown that the grey-hound, bloodhound, terrier, spaniel, and bulldog . . . were the offspring of any single species. Such facts would have great weight in making us doubt about the immutability of the many very closely allied and natural species." Surely showing as much would solve these mysteries.

But proof of this connection remained elusive for Darwin. Instead, he conceded that different breeds must have evolved from different canids. In the years after the publication of *Origin*, Darwin maintained that Polly might best be considered a descendant of a fox, while Bob seemed more likely the relative of a dingo or jackal. The greyhounds and bulldogs in his study might have descended from wolves or coyotes or even some previously unknown species. He maintained this theory of descent—and the affection for *Canis familiaris*—right up until his death, in 1882.

What's become of this theory—and Darwin's beloved species—since then? For starters, we've disproven the theory of pangenesis and replaced it with a developing understanding of DNA. As for Darwin's multiple-progenitor theory of dog evolution, our contemporary iterations keep changing. In 1993, the American Society of Mammalogists, in conjunction with the Smithsonian Institution, concluded that wolves and domestic dogs maintained enough similarities to be considered part of the same species. They then applied the more nuanced distinction of "subspecies" to the domestic dog, changing its name from *Canis familiaris* to *Canis lupus familiaris*.

This was no act of mere semantics. Instead, it acknowledges the belief that dogs, through a combination of natural and artificial selection, descended from wolves. Most ethnologists now contend that ancient wolves accomplished this feat by self-selecting into two distinct groups. According to a study by Raymond and Lorna Coppinger, two of the leading experts on dog evolution, those wolves with less fear of humans and more interest in an easy meal started hanging around early settlements. The ones who didn't care for this kind of life stayed away. Eventually, these groups formed two different breeding pools. That's when there began to be serious differences in appearance and behavior. The self-domesticating wolves looked to settlement dumps for their meals, and the less concerned they were about humans, the bigger the meals they enjoyed. The more food they consumed there, the more energy they had for reproduction. Eventually, those wolves showing the friendliest and most engaging responses to humans were invited to continue their meals in our homes and common areas. By the time the Victorians arrived on the scene, these meals had become bacchanalian feasts.

And if you thought Victorians were indulgent about this invitation, consider our own behaviors. While Polly may have been perfectly content with a wicker bed and daily biscuit ration, these luxuries undoubtedly seem spartan to many contemporary dogs. Visit one of any number of online pet-supply sites and you'll see what I mean. Petco, for example, offers more than ninety dog beds to choose from. They range from the austere fleece donut bed (available in coral, eggshell, rose, and teal) to more elaborate settees like the Cleopatra Chaise in zebra and leopard print, the bamboo spindle bed, and the heated Therabed with eggshell memory foam. It's a wonder poor Polly could sleep at all. As for recreation, she had to content herself with daily saunters and silly pet tricks. Her descendants, on the other hand, have binkies and floppy disks, laser pointer games and motion-activated cosmic rainbow balls (dental rope not included). If they tire of these toys, one of the thousands of pet daycare centers across the country will happily pick up your bored basenjis or basset hounds and take them to dog camp, where they will enjoy social hour, recess, and snacks while you watch it all on a live video stream.

These trends in pet ownership represent a behavioral change in humans that even the dog-loving Darwin couldn't have fully predicted. True, we love our dogs just like the Victorians did. But somewhere along the line, we changed the way we demonstrate this love into nothing short of an entire consumer culture evolution. Consider this: on average, Americans now spend almost $41 billion annually on their pets. Dogs enjoy the lion's share of this output. According to the National Pet Owners Survey—a leading indicator of domestic animal spending—the average dog owner shells out $1,425 each year for his or her dog, including more than $100 for treats and toys. Each of us spends about another $250 on dog food. Do we question this expense? Not really. My dog, Ari, has a custom-made cedar doghouse, complete with shingles and trim. She hasn't spent a single moment inside it, since she much prefers our upholstered sofa. I regularly bake her biscuits made from the sort of organic ingredients generally reserved for use by celebrity chefs. Am I excessive? Maybe. But I am also not alone. I'm probably not even all that unusual or extreme in my doting.

People like me are good news for domestic canines.

Without a doubt, the latest trends in dog owner behavior have proven an evolutionary jackpot, at least in terms of dog population numbers. In spite of the fact that they are a relatively new species, four hundred million domestic dogs now occupy the planet—far outpacing the four hundred thousand wolves and even the four million coyotes thought to exist in the wild. And why not? Approximately seventy-five million pet dogs reside in the United States alone, and we're spending more than $22 billion making sure they're fat and sassy.

These figures make a lot of sense to people who study the success of canine populations. For every calorie a dog doesn't have to spend searching for food, that dog can devote one more bit of energy to enhancing sexual prowess and providing for a new litter of pups. And each time one domesticated dog reproduces, he or she passes on a genetic docility and willingness to ply human civilization. Pups frightened of humans tend to peel off from the existing population, taking their wary genes along with them. And, because of human responses to neoteny, we tend to reward those dogs who seem the most adorable in their infantile appearance and behavior. We encourage them to breed; we give them treats and opulent beds; we allow them to be adopted by people like Paris Hilton. As a result, there are more Chihuahuas on the planet than there are wolves. In the past ten years alone, Americans have registered more than 365,000 Chihuahuas with the American Kennel Club. That, of course, doesn't include nonregistered members of the breed or the hundreds of thousands of little dogs living in other countries. Just as staggering is the fact that Chihuahuas are ranked eleventh in terms of numbers of dogs registered with the AKC each year—well behind Shih Tzus, dachshunds, and retrievers.

But in spite of the obvious differences between a starlet's pocket companion and a timber wolf, scientists still believe that the basic blueprint for both animals has remained surprisingly similar over the past several hundred years. When it comes to wolves and domestic dogs, any genetic difference is best considered in terms of degree—and it is a very small degree. Ed Bangs, the wolf recovery coordinator for the U.S. Fish and Wildlife Service, explains the similarity this way: "Basically if you drop your beagle in a blender and look at the DNA it's pretty indistinguishable from a wild wolf." Such an assertion begs two questions for me. First, how closely related are wolves and beagles? Second, and perhaps more important, what kind of ghoulish cocktails are served at USFWS parties? I haven't yet found an answer to that second question. But I do know that DNA analysis of the aforementioned species reveals that wolves and domestic dogs share a whopping 99.8 percent of their DNA. According to the ethological scholar Robert K. Wayne, the next closest relative to the wolf is the coyote, which shares only 96 percent of its DNA with the wolf.

For well over a decade, this chromosomal link was enough to persuade scientists that Darwin was wrong: domestic dogs must have come from wolves, and only wolves. However, more recent mitochondrial analysis suggests that Darwin might have been on to something. Stanley Coren's recent book *Why Does My Dog Act That Way?* shows that although canine genome projects continue to support the hypothesis that the first domestic dog was a direct descendant of a wolf, additional evidence indicates that, over time, these early dogs probably also mated with dingoes, coyotes, jackals, and certain breeds of fox. Not exactly the direct descent Darwin was looking for, but closer than we once thought.

We might, then, be best served in viewing dogs and multiple wild canids as something between siblings and kissing cousins: close enough to be a part of the same genus and even interbreed, but worlds apart when it comes to a few key attributes—particularly those attributes that come to light in the natural world. This is the real power of genetic selection and species origination. That tiny fractional difference between dogs and their wild kin is all it takes to mold an eighty-pound timber wolf into any number of AKC toy breeds—including a wirehaired terrier like Polly.

Getting a wolf into the shape of a toy breed is where we demonstrate the real force of our Darwinian inheritance. Thanks to those human-induced

behavioral changes that include high-protein diets and state-of-the-art veteri-
nary care, dogs are surpassing their wild progenitors in more than just population numbers. The average life expectancy of a wolf is about seven years.
Compare this to Darwin's beloved pointers (fourteen years) or the Jack Russell terrier (sixteen years). In just about every category, domestic dogs trump
wolves when it comes to survival and life span. They also beat wolves and
even chimpanzees when it comes to interpreting human behavior and interacting with our species. Again, through selection, dogs and people have created an interspecies bond second to none.

We've also shown the extent, both legitimate and ludicrous, of genetic
selection. More than any other single species, dogs show tremendous range in
physical attributes. An average Newfoundland weighs in at approximately 150
pounds; a Yorkshire terrier rarely exceeds 5. The bloodhound possesses twice
as much skin as it needs, and its snout is almost as long as the rest of its head.
The Pekingese's face contains far more cat than dog, what with its petite ears
and very flat countenance, and you have to look awfully hard to see its taut skin
under all that fur. Its geographic cousin, the Chinese crested dog, is bald except
for enormous patches of hair on its equally enormous ears. Yet all of these dog
breeds (and the hundreds of others) are able to mate successfully.

We humans are almost completely responsible for this variance within *Canis
familiaris*. But that's not to say we've really helped all that much with dog evolution.
To the contrary, as much as we would like to believe we are in a mutually rewarding relationship or even one that benefits the canine species, many scholars speculate that we actually do a fair amount of harm. The Coppingers write that whether
through neglect and abuse or through the controlled reproduction of breeds, we not
only compromise the evolutionary development of canines, we also create situations
in which they can be hurt or even killed. For the most part, we humans don't mean
to do so—we just tend not to see things from a dog's point of view.

Our continued interest in designer dogs, for instance, is creating more
and more aesthetically appealing but physiologically problematic breeds.
Darwin referred to these breeds as "monsters," in the sense that they were gross,
Frankensteinian distortions of the evolutionary process. What struck Darwin as
most remarkable was their ability to reveal that their selection had been made
not on behalf of evolutionary development but, as Darwin puts it, for "man's use
or fancy." I doubt he'd be pleased with how right we've proven him over the past

century and a half. The contemporary bulldog, for instance, has a difficult time merely surviving as a breed. Females often have to give birth by cesarean section, and they all tend to have respiratory and joint problems. Even so, we continue to make bulldogs bigger and more physiologically problematic each year. Meanwhile, other dogs, like pugs and Boston terriers, have been so bred for their infantile appearance that their skulls can barely contain the eyeballs. Those dogs who manage to keep their eyes in their sockets run the risk of lacerations and abrasions to the eye, since they protrude to nearly the same degree as their noses.

None of this bodes well for dogs inside or outside the domestic realm. And the species has come to rely directly on humanity for its very survival. We embrace this dependency, and go out of our way to foster it. Meanwhile, natural selection necessitates that wild canids stay well out of view, keeping their numbers sparse and their genetics under lock and key, as it were.

There are exceptions within both species, of course. But these, too, are of our making.

In Chicago this past year, three different coyotes have been found wandering the downtown streets. And recently one entered a Quiznos sub shop in the city's busy shopping district. Remarkably, no one remembers him entering the store, but they certainly noticed when he hopped into the refrigerated drink case—presumably to cool an injury on his back leg. Millions of TV viewers watched as the coyote was captured, then taken to a wildlife rehabilitation center, where he was named Adrian. They sent text messages of support and offers to adopt the juvenile coyote. The next day, those same viewers fawned when the sub shop's manager brought Adrian a meat lover's sandwich.

Meanwhile, even the most bred of all show dogs are proving that you can't select out all that is wild in a dog. The show whippet Bohem C'est la Vie, or Vivi, famously escaped her crate at New York's JFK Airport in February 2006. In the days that followed, several airport employees spied her moving across the airport's five thousand acres, largely grass and swamp, but they were unable to catch her—even after tailing her in airport vehicles at speeds of thirty miles an hour. And in spite of her breed's "monstrous" weaknesses (like sensitivity to cold and sun, or a famously temperamental digestion), Vivi has remained on the loose ever since. In the year after her escape, animal rescue organizations received hundreds of calls from people who had spotted her in alleys or parks. The last such sighting was—fittingly—in a Queens cemetery, near the grave of Harry Houdini.

Animal behaviorists are divided on what has become of Vivi. Some think she has died or been captured, others maintain she has become feral and is living off the fat of the land. If that's true, it's probably because she has managed to find a career scavenging human-generated trash—further proof that contemporary dog survival depends on human tinkering. Somewhere in their genetic coding, all dogs seem to know this. They also seem to intuit, on a biological level, the truth in Darwin's observations about speciation and our ability to create animals that don't always resemble their genetic progenitors.

As for humans, we're more conflicted than ever.

Take our increased obsession with dog classification. Currently the AKC recognizes more than 150 official breeds, and it's preparing another six for eventual inclusion. The club is also becoming far more fastidious about what constitutes a breed standard. Once upon a time, Darwin's Polly would have been classified as a Jack Russell terrier without any debate. That was before purists worried that the colloquial use of the category to describe any scrappy little terrier was diluting the breed standard. So recently the AKC created the more rigid designation of the Parson Russell terrier, to distinguish the highbrow Pollys of the world from any shaggy interloper trying to pose as pure. In so doing, the club took away John Russell's jaunty nickname and replaced it with his formal title, emphasizing Russell's occupation: parson priest. This is perhaps ironic given the perceived discord between Russell's theology and the theory behind his biggest hobby.

Meanwhile, those individuals fed up with the eugenics of the AKC have broken away and formed their own organization, the American Canine Hybrid Club, or ACHC. Make no mistake, however: this is not an organization for lovers of mixed breeds and mutts. Members of the ACHC are very specific in their aims: to explore the creation of deliberate hybrids and the scope of evolutionary selection. The ACHC now recognizes more than four hundred new hybrid breeds, with names like the giant schnoodle, pogle, chiweenie, pom-a-poo, taco terrier, cock-a-chon, schneagle, and, my personal favorite, the rat-a-dorkie.

Not content with this amalgamation, a woman in California named Dawn Houston is now marketing the "puppykat." Houston told a reporter for the *Californian* that, after spying two stray cats with dog-like tendencies, she engaged them in a *Hustler*esque breeding orgy until she derived standard litters of creatures with down-turned ears, short tails, and a willingness to come when called. Houston has had tremendous success in marketing the so-called exotic breed—new owners are thrilled at how much like dogs their strange little cats behave, and they're thrilled by the amiability and loyalty of their misshapen new friends—perhaps proving once and for all that evolution and the human desire for companionship don't always square, at least as far as the advancement of a species is concerned.

But would Darwin agree?

When writing *The Origin of Species*, he chose to include an oft-overlooked subtitle: *The Preservation of Favoured Races in the Struggle for Life*. From Polly the Parson terrier to the idea behind pampered puppykats, no race has proven itself more favored than the contemporary dog, in all its cultural permutations. What began as Victorian dog fancy has evolved into something far more zealous on the part of *Homo sapiens sapiens*. We don't just fancy dogs; we exalt them. And because they acknowledge our affections so fetchingly, we increase our overtures tenfold. Our species may sometimes be misguided in how we demonstrate this favoritism, but that preference is commanding all the same. In our journey through science and genetic manipulation, what we know—and how we live—has become utterly intertwined with *Canis lupus familiaris*. Along the way, we've proven just how far selection can change the behavior of humans and animals alike. These days (and with all apologies to the writers at *Bark* magazine who coined the original phrase), dogs aren't just our copilots. When it comes to consumer spending and human lifestyle, sometimes dogs actually appear to be flying the plane. There's an important evolutionary lesson to be learned, particularly when it comes to understanding not only how we can effect change in a species, but also how that change can alter us.

Furthermore, we can learn far more than adaptive theory from our continued association with dogs. More than just companions and assistants, dogs are uniquely suited to translate the world for us. As ecological generalists, canines succeed in just about every biome: from the trash heaps of Tijuana to the streets of Tokyo, dogs know not only how to exist, but also how to thrive. They can take both the refuse of human civilization and its most consumer-based goods and find a way to make it benefit them: carrot tops and half-eaten sandwiches, deep-tissue massage and oatmeal-based conditioner, all work to advance the canine species. Meanwhile, these same dogs maintain a particular—and highly liminal—place in the environment, straddling the wild and the domestic as they continue to help humans sort out what it means for a species to descend.

Reading the Genre

1. What central cultural trend does Miles examine? What is her central scientific idea? How, according to Miles, do culture and science influence each other?

2. Create a skeleton outline that traces how Miles moves back and forth between time periods and shifts her focus between humans and dogs. How does she overcome the organizational difficulties involved in comparing two different cultures, as well as two different species? (See "Creating a structure," p. 54.)

3. What specific lessons, if any, does Miles want readers to learn? Do you feel free to draw your own conclusions? In what ways, is this report a persuasive text or an argument? (See "Aim for objectivity," p. 46.)

4. **WRITING:** Pick another species—from mice to cows to dolphins to horses— and write a report on current human attitudes toward, and interactions with, that particular class of animals. What does our treatment of these animals reveal about us?

5. **WRITING:** Design an experiment that would allow you to imagine the world through the senses of an animal, and then write a report on the experience from the animal's perspective. Some suggestions: Take a pet to a new park and report on the space through the pet's eyes; imagine you are a dog at a sidewalk café and describe what you see, hear, feel, smell, and taste; try to walk a cat on a leash and narrate the ordeal from the cat's point of view.

LEGAL REPORT   Philip Deloria, a descendant of the famous Sioux (Dakota) leader Tipi Sapa, is a well-known and highly regarded scholar. He teaches history, American culture, and Native American studies at the University of Michigan. Both of his books, *Playing Indian* (1998) and *Indians in Unexpected Places* (2004), were awarded prizes for academic excellence. The following essay appears in the book *A New Literary History of America* by Greil Marcus and Werner Sollors (2009).

PHILIP DELORIA

The *Cherokee Nation* Decision

This is a story about the law. For me, however, it begins elsewhere, with a cryptic little book, measuring three by five inches and covered with a crumbling leather binding. Open it to the title page—*A History of the Black Hawk War* by "An Old Resident of the Military Tract" (1832)—and you will think it a historical memoir, published locally at Fort Armstrong, Iowa. The Black Hawk War, which "opened up" the Mississippi Midwest to white settlement, did indeed take place in 1832. Continue reading, however, and you will find not history, but sixty-three pages of ciphered and mnemonic figures:

Indian

1. (I) g t t e a g o * w c t chief o # # t o o a t p
2. (I) # I I —-
3. (I) a a p Indians–- (II) I w a a r * –-# VI–-%
4. (II) y w s y t a p a Indians

And so it continues, through four tantalizing sections (Indian, Squaw, Warrior, and Braves). The book feels a bit like Poe, dark, desperate, and strange. Each section represents a role in the rituals of a white fraternal group that pretended, in its secret ceremonies, to be the Indian people so recently dispossessed in the war. Holding it I *feel* the 1830s, furtive and confused, a time of dark lanterns and sinister killings, treasure hunting and magic, secret ciphers, and houses (full of dead people and greasy playing cards) floating intact on the cresting Mississippi, with plenty of sorry to go around.

A fulcrum moment, these 1830s, of precarious cultural shifts, when the generative American contradiction between *killing Indians* and *becoming them* still lay close to the surface. That contradiction, long embodied in captivity narratives, frontier folk mythologies, and performances of Indian "American" identities, erupted in the 1830s into the realm of law. The eruption came in response to the crisis of an American nation that fully believed in its imperial destiny, yet spoke of its dominations only haltingly. It structures the lives, literatures, and politics of American Indian people—and thus *all* Americans—to the present day.

One phrase—"domestic dependent nations"—reordered the world of the 1830s. Authored by John Marshall, the chief justice of the U.S. Supreme Court, the three words translated the older cultural contradictions into new law and politics. If killing the Indian had allowed settlers to claim land and proclaim independence, "becoming" the Indian had let those same settlers incorporate themselves *into* the land, and lodge the ancient memory of Indian aboriginality in American souls. The new words applied (in reverse) the same contradictory structure of logic to Indian people themselves: somehow, they could be distinct nations—and yet be simultaneously incorporated within the American body politic. As nations, they might claim to be independent—and yet they were in fact dependent on the federal government.

John Marshall named Indian people as "domestic dependent nations" in the second of three closely linked legal cases involving the Cherokees. In the first case, *Johnson v. M'Intosh* (1823), Marshall wrote an unnecessarily elaborate opinion in which he codified the "discovery doctrine." He argued that, in the wake of contact between New World and Old, title to Indian lands no longer resided with Indian people but accrued instead to the European nation claiming first discovery. Indian people could sell the "claim" to their land, but only to the discovering sovereign—or a rightful successor, in most cases (conveniently) the United States. Marshall used this "discovery" argument carelessly, to prop up the land claims of Virginia militiamen, former comrades during the War for Independence. This set the legal terms for the second case, *Cherokee Nation v. Georgia*.

In 1828, the discovery of gold on Cherokee lands led the state of Georgia to try to eliminate the Cherokees. Earlier, Georgians had forsworn territorial claims in return for a federal promise to remove the Cherokees as soon as was practical. The passage in 1830 of the Indian Removal Act—which encouraged tribes to exchange their eastern land for territory west of the Mississippi—suggested that the time for Cherokee removal was at hand. President Andrew Jackson was more than sympathetic.

Before the violent dispossessions of Removal, however, Cherokees, Georgians, and the federal government fought over their respective sovereignties. The federal government claimed power over the individual states—which meant the continued validity of federally negotiated Indian treaties (with the Cherokees, for example). South Carolina and other states in the South claimed primacy for themselves, insisting that they could "nullify" federal laws they deemed unconstitutional. And within their state borders, Georgians confronted the Cherokee Nation, an independent society replete with a constitution, representative government, educational institutions, written language, and other appurtenances of "civilization," including chattel slavery.

Asserting its own state sovereignty, Georgia could hardly embrace the rising sovereign nation of the Cherokees. In 1828 the Georgia legislature passed an act to make Cherokee territory part of and subject to the laws of Georgia. The following year, a second act added a provision "to annul all laws and ordinances made by the Cherokee nation of Indians." In 1830 Georgia seized and sentenced to death George Tassells, a Cherokee man who had killed another Cherokee within the bounds of the Cherokee Nation—a case in which the Cherokee justice system had clear jurisdiction. After a failed appeal at the state level (Georgians used the "doctrine of discovery" to insist on their own jurisdiction), the Cherokees sought help from the U.S. Supreme Court, and John Marshall ordered a stay of execution. Georgia defied the Court (and suddenly, a dry legal narrative turns sinister: emergency sessions of the legislature, a rushed message on horseback from the governor—probably a dark lantern involved somewhere—and a hasty Christmas Eve hanging from a tree in a lonely field).

The Supreme Court said little about the legalized murder of Tassells, however, preferring to concentrate on *Cherokee Nation v. Georgia*, filed only days before by Cherokee chief John Ross in an effort to overturn Georgia's assertions of sovereignty. In the debate over the Indian Removal Act, many advocates insisted that Indian people *did* hold title to their lands—and thus national and territorial sovereignty, recognized through treaties and land purchases. The basis for this understanding, however, had been effectively undermined by the discovery doctrine. Brandishing a Supreme Court decision, Removal advocates argued that Indians had no title to their land and could be evicted at the pleasure of the United States, inheritor of the European rights of discovery.

Marshall ignored both the discovery doctrine and the defiance of Georgia (which refused to appear before the court), focusing instead on the question of jurisdiction. He framed the case around a grand historical narrative, and situated the Cherokees at a decisive turning point, one that required political recalibration. "If courts were permitted to indulge their sympathies," he wrote,

> a case better calculated to excite them can scarcely be imagined. A people once numerous, powerful, and truly independent, found by our ancestors in the quiet and uncontrolled possession of an ample domain, gradually sinking beneath our superior policy, our arts and our arms, have yielded their lands by successive treaties, each of which contains a solemn guarantee of the residue, until they retain no more of their formerly extensive territory than is deemed necessary to their comfortable subsistence. To preserve this remnant, the present application is made.

The key words—"independent," "powerful," "uncontrolled possession"—make the beginnings of his narrative clear. Indians were distinct, autonomous peoples ("nations" in a European sense). They formed alliances and negotiated treaties. The proper executive-branch office for Indian affairs was the War Department and the proper political relation was diplomacy or formal conflict. In the 1830s, however, Americans began saying out loud that after decades of conflicts, land cessions, removals, and dislocations, those relations had changed. Witness the key terms that seemed to shift the ground: "sinking beneath," "yielded their lands," "preserve this remnant."

The first rhetoric reflects a distinct form of colonial practice, characterized by warfare, treaties, a nation-to-nation relationship, and a cultural imagination that played with Indian otherness. The second calls into being a new and different kind of colonialism. Indian people were consolidated and segregated in regional spaces—the so-called Indian territory—the better to manage, reeducate, and incorporate them. This segregation enabled the development of American imperial governance based on the demographic shift from Indian to white, and the political transitions from mixed territory to white state and from Indian "nation" to Indian "tribe." The militiamen hunting down Black Hawk in 1832 engaged in exactly this process of containment. The results were clear: the states of Iowa, Illinois, and Wisconsin, the removal of many Indians from the Midwest, and a secret fraternal order with a book of coded rituals.

In this new form of colonialism, Indian nations could be viewed as something like states, though vastly inferior. The proper executive branch office for their oversight was now the Department of the Interior (the shift from the War Department was made in 1849) and the proper relationship would be that of a paternalistic guardian to its immature ward. Marshall's historical narrative—and American cultural production in general—repositioned 1830s Indians; once a foreign affairs problem, they were now a domestic issue.

And that is how it played out. The third article of the Constitution gives the Supreme Court jurisdiction over "controversies between a state or the citizens thereof, and foreign states, citizens, or subjects." Were the Cherokees a foreign state? If they were, then the Court would have jurisdiction and Marshall might indulge his sympathies and perhaps undo the damage he had caused. And yet, as foreign states, Indian nations would also be able to sign treaties with other nations, establish trade alliances with American enemies, and subject U.S. citizens to Indian laws, all acts the United States would construe as hostile. Despite any sympathies, the Court proved unwilling to see the Cherokees as a foreign nation.

So what were they? Indian tribes were distinct nations—but they existed in relation to the United States and within the borders it claimed. And so Marshall wrote: "It may well be doubted whether those tribes which reside within the acknowledged boundaries of the United States can, with strict accuracy, be denominated foreign nations. They may, more correctly, perhaps, be denominated domestic dependent nations . . . Their relation to the United States resembles that of a ward to his guardian." Lacking jurisdiction, John Marshall could not use the case to recall the unanticipated consequences of the discovery doctrine. But when the last of the three Cherokee cases came to the Court the following year, he reversed himself, ruling in *Worcester v. Georgia* that American Indian tribes were in fact sovereign nations and that they retained all sovereign rights not given up by treaty or lost in a just war. Cherokee claims to Cherokee homelands were guaranteed by those solemn federal treaties, and Georgia's claims to jurisdiction over those homelands were invalid.

It was too late. Southern courts responded to Marshall's decisions with their own cases—*Georgia v. Tassells* (1830), *Caldwell v. Alabama* (1831), and *Tennessee v. Forman* (1835)—each of which denied not only Marshall's belated assertion of tribal sovereignty but also the power of the Supreme Court itself. These Southern cases gave the doctrine of discovery new form, primarily around stark assertions of Indian racial inferiority. And, since Andrew Jackson's executive branch refused to enforce the Supreme Court's decision in *Worcester*, calling it "stillborn," it was the Southern decisions that structured Indian removal and the new colonialism of consolidation and reservation rule. They became the de facto legal precedents, even if *Worcester* theoretically dictated the rule of law.

The decision paved the way for the Trail of Tears, a forced migration to Indian territory in 1838 during which more than 4,000 Cherokees died. Similar removals and consolidations of Indians would become central to American policy over the next six decades. The federal government stopped making treaties in 1871, began reeducating Indian children in boarding schools, chopped up reservation land, and restricted tribes' religious practices. In law and politics, the paternalist language of guardians and wards was everywhere; indeed, it seemed to take precedence over "domestic dependent nations"—not to mention the idea that a tribe might have sovereignty.

These displacements existed in complex relation to the omnipresent cultural trope of the "vanishing" Indian. James Fenimore Cooper's *Last of the Mohicans* (1826) ends with noble Chingachgook alone, with no legacy or future. John Augustus Stone's *Metamora* (1829)—one of the most popular plays of the nineteenth century—finishes with tragic Indian death and a promising white future. John Mix Stanley's evocative painting *Last of the Race* (1857) shows a sad remnant of different tribes at sunset on the shores of the Pacific. And white fraternal orders in Iowa and elsewhere gathered at night, pretending to be now-departed Indians in order to perpetuate their memory.

And yet, Indian people did not vanish but began slowly reworking John Marshall's words. Some emphasized "domestic" and "dependent," focusing on American treaty obligations and using the language of "guardian" and "ward" to press the federal government for support for education, health, economic development, and other forms of assistance enshrined in treaty agreements. Others went in a different direction, skipping over "domestic" and "dependent" to argue for Indian nationhood and autonomy. In 1972, for example, following the Trail of Broken Treaties march on Washington, D.C., Indian activists demanded that all Indian people be governed by treaty relations, that the government restore a nation-to-nation relationship, ratify unapproved treaties, and establish a commission to review violations of treaty rights. Contemporary movements have pushed for Indian sovereignty, and they emphasize the word with a range of adjectives: political, legal, economic, intellectual, cultural.

When you hear about Indian casino gaming or tribal taxing authority or license plates, you are hearing—through the word "sovereignty"—the echoes of the *Cherokee Nation* decision. That decision has come full circle with the efforts of some Cherokees to dis-enroll Cherokee freedmen, the descendants of Cherokee-owned slaves guaranteed tribal citizenship under a treaty signed in 1866. The issue plays out on the grounds of Cherokee sovereignty (in the tribe's Supreme Court cases and electoral processes), nation-to-nation relations (in the Treaty of 1866), and guardianship oversight (in federal membership lists, a federal Indian blood quantum card, and a congressional effort to strip the Cherokees of federal recognition and funding). The complications of the 1830s—and sometimes their mood and tone—have continuously erupted into a series of presents.

Bibliography

Tim Alan Garrison, *The Legal Ideology of Removal: The Southern Judiciary and the Sovereignty of Native American Nations* (Athens, GA, 2002).

Lindsay G. Robertson, *Conquest by Law: How the Discovery of America Dispossessed Indigenous Peoples of Their Lands* (New York, 2005).

David E. Wilkins, *American Indian Sovereignty and the U.S. Supreme Court: The Masking of Justice* (Austin, TX, 1997).

Robert A. Williams, *The American Indian in Western Legal Thought: The Discourses of Conquest* (New York, 1990).

Reading the Genre

1. Deloria identifies several key terms in this report. What are they? How does Deloria explain them and their importance?

2. What strategy does Deloria use to organize information? (Hint: Take another look at the key terms from question 1.) How does the structure of the report make it accessible and easy to read? How does Deloria's organization help readers follow his argument?

3. In his conclusion, Deloria asks readers to consider how this legal history reaches into "a series of presents." What are some of the ways this happens? Where can we see the impact of the *Cherokee Nation* decision today?

4. Deloria quotes several historical figures and summarizes the work of four legal researchers in this report. How does he manage to include so much information efficiently, and how does he use it to support his thesis, or main idea? (See "Finding and developing materials," p. 52; "Find reliable sources," p. 46; "Base reports on the best available sources," p. 52; and Chapter 43, "Evaluating Sources," p. 482.)

5. **WRITING:** Deloria begins his report by stating that "this is a story about the law." The same is true, in a way, of any legal report. Choose a brief legal report from the Pew Research Web site (pewforum.org/Publications/Legal-reports/) and rewrite it as a short story. Try to follow the simplest narrative structure you can: Once upon a time there was a legal problem; it affected this group of characters; they decided to do some things about it; there was a struggle and a series of compromises and resolutions; this was the conclusion.

DESCRIPTIVE REPORT   Molly Young is a reporter and producer for the *Daily*, a news publication designed to be read exclusively on iPads. She writes regularly about the arts and cultural trends and has published articles in *Vice*, the *New York Observer*, *Details*, *n+1*, the *Economist*, and the magazine the *Believer*, where this piece appeared in 2010. She keeps a blog at http://mollyyoung.tumblr.com/.

Sweatpants in Paradise
The Exciting World of Immersive Retail

MOLLY YOUNG

1.

It is sometimes possible to define the depth of an experience by means of how radically it slows or hastens your sense of time. Swimming, fighting, nightmaring, enduring a migraine, having sex: these are all activities that move at exceptional rates. Shopping, too, and if you don't believe me, just enter a mall before sundown and see how you feel a few hours later when you reemerge into darkness. Depending on your mien and mood, this reemergence will feel sharply good or bad. The shopping wormhole affects everyone differently.

My father and I drove the other day to a mall in downtown San Francisco in order to exchange a pair of velour pants. San Francisco Centre contains more than 170 boutiques and is built like a gastropod shell with spiraling escalators and a white interior. There is a concierge and a family lounge. In some ways it's a fancy mall, but mostly it is like any other mall, with a food court and a lot of bathrooms and the smell of Bath & Body Works fragrances colliding in midair. "I feel like a robot," my dad said as an interactive map guided us to the correct store. All around us were young men and women moving slowly, and I was reminded of the fact that malls function secondarily as retail centers and primarily as promenades for people under thirty-five. Coupled or single, male or female: it doesn't matter. A day at the mall reveals display behavior as colorful as anything you'd see on safari.

We passed two chocolate boutiques and a place called The Art of Shaving on our way to the pants store, which was packed with shoppers and decorative jugs of candy. Painted in curly letters high on the wall was the phrase FOR NICE GIRLS WHO LIKE STUFF. While I waited for a new size of pants to be retrieved, I thought about this statement of purpose, and how blurry it was, and how accurate in its blurriness. FOR NICE GIRLS WHO LIKE STUFF exactly summed up the feelings of anticipation and anxious self-regard that a mall coaxes from shoppers. I thought of horoscopes and fog and mingling crowds while waiting for the pants to come out. Vague things. I felt united with every other customer in the mall, committed as we were to the promenade. It was soothing and stimulating at once.

This feeling, the communal purpose and the sense of display, points to what a mall has going for it that a website, for example, does not. A mall has the sound of music, the smell of Cinnabon, the knowledge of a shared experience, the social excitement of seeing and being seen. It is a place of latent sexual promise; the teenager's alternative to a bar. It is FOR NICE GIRLS WHO LIKE STUFF. People dress for the mall like they dress for a date.

2.

When I zipped into my velour outfit for the plane ride back to New York, it felt good, like wearing a caterpillar. Throughout the flight home I thought about the malls I was leaving behind and the mall-like stores that lay ahead of me in Manhattan. Bona fide malls do not exist at the center of New York City, but mall-size stores do, and of these there is one in particular—a new one—that interests me. I learned about it through a friend who had gotten stoned, wandered inside, and entered the shopping wormhole. She called me in San Francisco and said I should go straight to the Hollister Co. flagship store as soon as I got back to New York, and to go alone, which I did.

The Hollister store sits at the corner of Broadway and Houston in SoHo, a forty-thousand-square-foot block full of California-themed apparel. Topless men and girls without pants stand at the entrance, some wearing zinc oxide smeared across noses. The employees are selected for their insane good looks and friendliness, which creates the disorienting customer experience of receiving attention from people way out of your league over and over again. You can't avoid having a sexual experience at Hollister, even if it's just to stare at a greeter's bullet-hard nipples. Hollister's strategy may not be subtle, but it is clever. By literalizing the mall's sexual promise in actual naked flesh, the brand makes it unnecessary for shoppers to wander elsewhere. Rather than provide the neutral spaces of food courts and lobbies for promenading, the store offers a prefab (and make-believe) environment of sexual opportunity. It's the whole mall in one store!

There is a name for this tactic. Abercrombie & Fitch, which owns Hollister as well as the Abercrombie and now-defunct Ruehl brands, is among a growing corps of stores intent on targeting a customer's in-store experience as the main vehicle for its brand promotion. Abercrombie's 2009 annual report describes a shopping experience designed to stimulate "senses of sight, sound, smell, touch, and energy by utilizing visual presentation of merchandise, in-store marketing, music, fragrances, rich fabrics, and its sales associates to reinforce the aspirational lifestyles represented by the brands."

In practice this means a few things. It means that the Hollister store on Broadway is cramped and dimly lit, with narrow wallpapered rooms converging at a mezzanine lit up with live projections of Huntington Beach (waves waist-high and closing out). It means that a low-output fog machine pumps mist from the rafters while potted palms obstruct the floor at random places, both ingenious ways to slow down foot traffic. The store's official theme is "EPIC," and this is also the name of the brand's newest men's cologne, which hangs thick in the air. Things to buy at the store include distressed cargo pants, sweatpants embroidered with VARSITY CLUB SURFERS, sweatshirts designed to look like Spicoli's drug rug, and flip-flops on sale for $11.90. The tags on the women's clothing say BETTYS and the men's tags say DUDES. Music is a big deal at the store, almost a physical presence. A customer-service rep named Danielle told me that company policy dictates that the in-store music should hover between eighty and eighty-five decibels. (The level at which sustained exposure may result in hearing loss is ninety to ninety-five decibels.) The actual store sound track is unrecognizable yet generic; it is the music heard from the cars of popular kids in high-school movies.

3.

The real Hollister is a small California city in San Benito County about forty miles inland, just west of Interstate 5. In 1868 it was named for Colonel W. W. Hollister, who drove a flock of sheep across the country as early as 1851. The land was considered sacred by the Chumash Indians and is currently known for its business-friendly environment and mild winters. Though Hollister Co. displays the year 1922 on its logo, the brand was in fact launched in 2000 in

Columbus, Ohio. It is not clear why 1922 was selected as Hollister's origin point. Many things happened that year, none related to logo sweatpants: the Eskimo Pie was patented, Ernest Shackleton died, Hungary joined the League of Nations. If I had to guess at the significance of 1922 regarding Hollister, I'd point to three events that also occurred that year: The California grizzly bear was declared extinct, Helen Gurley Brown was born in Green Forest, Arkansas, and a meteorite landed near Blackstone, Virginia. In these three events we have the death of something authentically Californian, the birth of a woman who would encourage sartorial expressions of sexuality, and a random occurrence that no one could explain.

If Southern California surf culture is Hollister's guiding mythos, it is odd, too, that the company should name itself for a town twenty miles inland with declining home sales and greater-than-average earthquake activity. Did a lot of thought go into the choice? Or possibly none at all? It could be that "Hollister" just sounded more marketable than the nearby towns of Chualar and Molus. A fake testimony delivered by an imaginary dude on the Hollister website confirms the authenticity of the brand and its flagship:

> I headed out to SoHo to see what the EPIC Hollister store was all about. Born and bred in Southern California, I was curious to see what's up. As soon as I came in I was like—oh, this is gonna be big. . . .
> Everyone who works there is hot as hell—it looks like how you wish everyone looked on the beach. No grumpy old ladies screamin' at kids. The place is hooked-up, it's got everything. Dude, it's pretty spot-on to SoCal. . . . I got all mesmerized. . . .

But as its name suggests, "spot-on to SoCal" is exactly what Hollister isn't. What overwhelms a visitor more than the completeness of the flagship's fantasy is its specificity, first, and then its confusing lack of origin. To what movie, location, or lifestyle is Hollister referring with its potted plants and surf gear? How come we recognize it? Why is it cool?

4.

The night after I went to the Hollister flagship store for the first time, I woke up in the middle of the night, not sure whether I'd been sleeping or just lying prone long enough to feel like it. I got out of bed, turned on my computer, and opened a quarterly report for Abercrombie that I'd downloaded earlier in the week—one of those million-page PDF files that you avoid on the desktop for days until moments like the one at hand, when factors of concentration and boredom align into a PDF-reading mood.

When I opened the document, I saw that it was not a quarterly report at all but some sort of marketing memo from 2007, seemingly originating with Abercrombie but posted on Wikipedia without a source. Inside were bulletins about the company's financial performance and initiatives, including one designating $10 million for louvers and new signage. The document was illustrated with ad-campaign photographs and a picture of a bus. It contained bullet-pointed statements with nouns capitalized strangely, as though translated from German. For the quarter's accomplishments it listed:

- Introduce Fifth Concept in January 2008
- Currently implementing Core Retail Merchandising System
- Assembled strong and talented development team

and:

- Very excited about the business; great potential

I read the memo from start to finish and retained nothing, possibly because it meant nothing. But it meant nothing in relation to a retail giant with net sales in the billions and flagship stores in New York and London. What did it all mean? I went back to sleep.

5.

In 2008 IBM released an executive brief called "How Immersive Technology Can Revitalize the Shopping Experience." It outlined in lists and sidebars the future of shopping, and it accompanied a pair of stereoscopic goggles at that year's National Retail Federation Convention & Expo in New York City. The goggles were introduced as an in-store amenity that would allow customers to enter a 3-D virtual world when they visited their favorite store; for example, by viewing "a fashion show from Europe complete with music and smells," where, as a model walks down the runway, "her perfume will be noticeably in the air." IBM's brief poses the following questions:

Do individuals feel like your brand is relevant to their lifestyle? Do they understand the value of your brand experience over the commoditized products that you are selling? Or, as they wander from store to store, do your potential customers forget your brand as it blurs in their minds with those of competitors?

The solution IBM proposes to these problems is immersive retail, a strategy that aims to destabilize a current trend in consumer behavior that management advisers call *commoditization.* Commoditization describes the circumstance in which consumers care only about an item's price, perceiving no other difference between competitors. For retailers like Hollister—brands that produce basic items of OK quality for not-cheap prices—commoditization is an unfriendly concept.

Immersive retail is also a way to counter the allure of online shopping, which boils down to its convenience (what you need: an Internet connection and a finger) and privacy. Stereoscopic goggles are a prediction that convenience and privacy will soon fail to be sufficient inducements to spend. IBM describes the goals of immersive retail the way a party planner might envision a successful bar mitzvah, aiming for a "memorable, interactive, and emotional" experience full of "personalized dialogues." The paper explains that immersive retail "is more about involving the customer than it is about the merchandise." It is about shirtless male employees miming one-armed pushups on a rack of distressed jeans, yelling, *That's what I'm talkin' about!* and *Party at my house!* on a script every ten minutes. It's about filling a store with club chairs and issues of the *Surfer's Journal,* and about belly-button piercings that glint in the lamplight. "For stores in many retail segments to stay ahead of competitors," the brief explains, "they will need to generate the excitement of a theme park ride—and become a destination." Immersion retail presents clothes in the environment in which they are putatively designed to be worn, telling customers exactly what a product is supposed to mean.

6.

I do not think I am alone in recounting my teenage years in terms of things bought and the hopes invested in them. As a teenager in California, I wore sweatshirts and tight jeans like the ones Hollister sells, feeling always slightly paler and less experienced than the Kelseys and Jennifers of the world, as though the number of boys I'd hooked up with (zero) was embroidered across my trucker cap for all to see. These feelings rise anew when I enter the Hollister store, and I know why: despite its missteps, the brand nails certain aesthetic truths about my home state.

I attended community college with girls who resembled beta versions of the store's employees. To Mass Communications 110 they wore garments that insisted on comfort and conveyed the sexiness of total relaxation: sweatshirts, sheepskin boots, and thongs bisecting the slice of tanned upper butt that rose from low-cut jeans. It was a look of lazy, hygienic sexuality. The hottest girls always had brand-new socks, for example, and this was a key detail.

I'm lucky that I coincided with the trend. For one thing, it was an equalizing force. At a school made of both moneyed slackers and teenage mothers, the wealthy girls shopped at the same places as the non-wealthy girls. The former might have collected Tiffany bean pendants at home, but in the classroom it was possible for everyone to look basically the same.

Weed was another great equalizer. It is hard to overstate the importance of weed as a determining factor in the lives of West Coast teenagers. Weed was the reason girls selected clothes based on fuzziness, the reason boys sounded dumb, the reason we inflected every sentence as a question and used *like* and *you know* as phatic communications. In an era of T9 input, text messages begun with *I* would automatically fill in *mstoned*. Anyone familiar with the dim and spray-scented bedrooms of a weedy adolescence will recognize in Hollister's decor an environmental proxy of the average Friday night. Weed may not be for sale at Hollister, but its exigencies are everywhere.

One place we liked to visit while stoned was an interactive science museum in San Francisco called the Exploratorium. The Exploratorium is geared toward children but designed to be fun for adults, too, like a Pixar movie. It is vast, educational, and filled with exhibits that let you electrocute a pickle or dissect a cow eyeball. Inside the museum lies a geodesic structure called the Tactile Dome, which was introduced in 1971 as an experiment in sensory disorientation. The Dome is small, "about the size of a large weather balloon," and contains a three-dimensional labyrinth of pitch-black passages. A user takes off her shoes at the entrance, crawls through tunnels, climbs up a rope wall, and shoots down a slide into a pit of beans, all without the use of her eyesight. The passageway has thirteen chambers and no right angles, and various objects (keys, rubber toys) are hidden along the passageway for visitors to identify by touch. An early press release explained that visitors to the Dome "have compared the experience to being born again, turning yourself inside out head first, being swallowed by a whale, and inevitably, being enfolded in a giant womb." The maze takes about ten minutes from start to finish and stimulates both fear and lust, each arising from the heightened sensuality of short-term sightlessness. The final descent into beans is Dionysian.

Dr. August F. Coppola, a scientist,* and Carl Day, an architect, are the men responsible for the Tactile Dome. They spoke of the project at its inception as part of "an art revolution which uses people as participants" rather than "as targets at which to hurl artistic messages." The press release explained that both men "believe the revolution, if successful, will greatly affect not only art, advertising and industrial design but even life styles and basic beliefs."

With nothing to see and only one direction to go, the Tactile Dome offers the purest antidote I can find for immersive retail. It stokes the senses where Hollister dulls them; it offers ecstasy followed by self-reflection rather than headache. I don't doubt that Hollister's dulling effect is strategic. Engineers of immersive retail must understand that we buy things when we are bored and not when we're excited, alive, and metaphysically horny—that these feelings are just promises to get us in the door. Hollister is dark, sexy, and stimulating, but it won't turn your head inside out. The store has no slides and no rope nets, only stairs and emergency exits. And there is no bean pit at the end.

---

*Coppola is the brother of Francis Ford Coppola and the father of Nicolas Cage. The November 4, 2009, obituary in the *San Francisco Chronicle* notes that "Professor Coppola was often referred to as someone's relative. But his own charisma and immense intellect left lasting marks on California and on San Francisco." It continues, "Fascinated by touch and its taboos—he told the Exploratorium that 'the first commandment in life is given: "Don't touch"'—Professor Coppola's exhibit [the Tactile Dome] made touch mandatory. He later wrote *The Intimacy—a Novel,* about a man who interacts through touch."

Reading the Genre

1. How did Young supplement her field research for this report? Reread the article and in the margins, note what information Young gathered from sources. What kinds of sources did she use, and how did she access them? (See "Finding and developing materials," p. 52.)

2. What is Young's thesis, and how does she develop it? Underline each of her supporting claims. What evidence does she provide to back up her assertions?

3. Young divides her report into six sections. What is the function of each of these sections? Does Young's organization make sense to you? (See "Creating a structure," p. 54.)

4. **WRITING:** Visit a store as a researcher and write a short report on the shopping experience. Who shops there? How does this marketplace create a unique customer experience? What image or identity does the store create for itself, and how? What roles do employees play? Finally, what does this store offer to shoppers beyond the products themselves?

5. **COMPOSING VISUALLY:** Map the layout of the store you chose for question 4. Be creative: Label not just the physical features of the space, but also the different groups of people (shoppers, employees, managers, and so on) and the sensations they experience. (See "Read Visually," p. 368.)

Arguments: Readings

68

EDITORIAL
Maureen Dowd, *Don't Send in the Clones*   736

PROFILE
Nancy Gibbs, *Cool Running*   739

ARGUMENT FOR CHANGE
Emily Bazelon, *Hitting Bottom: Why America Should Outlaw Spanking*   743

ANALYSIS OF CULTURAL VALUES
Poranee Natadecha-Sponsel, *The Young, the Rich, and the Famous: Individualism as an American Cultural Value*   748

POLICY ARGUMENT
Daniel Engber, *Glutton Intolerance*   758

See also Chapter 3:

ARGUMENT TO
ADVANCE A THESIS
Scott Keyes,
*Stop Asking Me
My Major,* 75

EXPLORATORY ARGUMENT
Lynn Ehlers,
"Play 'Free Bird'!" 95

REFUTATION ARGUMENT
Cathy Young, *Duke's
Sexist Sexual Misconduct
Policy,* 101

VISUAL ARGUMENT
*Visualizing the BP Oil
Spill Disaster,* 104

EDITORIAL   Maureen Dowd is a prominent — if sometimes controversial — voice in American politics and culture. A Pulitzer Prize–winning journalist, she has been writing opinion columns and feature articles for the *New York Times* since 1995. Some of her favorites are collected in *Bushworld: Enter at Your Own Risk* (2004) and *Are Men Necessary? When Sexes Collide* (2005). This op-ed piece originally appeared in the *New York Times*.

Don't Send in the Clones

Maureen Dowd

For a time in college, I shared a dorm suite with three other girls.

We food shopped and ate dinner together but always squabbled over what groceries to buy. It got to the point where the only food we could agree on was corn, so that was what we got.

This upset my mother, who used to call me regularly to ominously demand: "Do you know why the Incas are extinct?"

This was B.G. (Before Google.) So I simply assumed that it either had to do with too much maize in the Inca diet or that Mom was just trying to scare me into healthier behavior — as when she attempted to ward off any tequila-tippling by calling to ask portentously: Do you know why so many tequila drinkers have nervous breakdowns?

Anyway, on one shopping expedition, I had a big fight with a roommate, no doubt over whether to get canned or frozen corn, creamed or whole kernel.

We were at a supermarket in a blighted part of D.C. My roommate got furious, stormed off in her car, and left me stranded. I called my brother Kevin to come get me. On the way back to school, he offered this advice: "Never pick a fight with the guy who's driving."

I took that to heart, literally and metaphorically. It has spared me plenty of problems since.

The serendipity of ending up with roommates that you like, despite your differences, or can't stand, despite your similarities, or grow to like, despite your reservations, is an experience that toughens you up and broadens you out for the rest of life.

So I was dubious when I read in the *Wall Street Journal* last week that students are relying more on online roommate matching services to avoid getting paired with strangers or peers with different political views, study habits, and messiness quotients.

A University of Florida official told the *Journal* that a quarter of incoming freshmen signed up to a Facebook application called RoomBug to seek out a roommate they thought would be more compatible than a random selection.

Other students are using URoomSurf. It makes matches with questions like these: How often do you shower? How neat are you? How outgoing are you? What's your study/party balance? Is it O.K. for your roommate to use your belongings?

I guess if I had used URoomSurf, I might have avoided those donnybrooks with one pill of a roommate, who yelled at me for such infractions as allegedly stretching out her sweater and eating a whole can of Campbell's Chunky Soup when I could have made do with half.

But co-habiting with snarly and moody roomies prepared me for the working world, where people can be outlandishly cantankerous over small stuff.

Just as rooming with Donna taught me humility. She was the sexiest girl on campus, an actress who would later brush off John Travolta in the Bee Gees–scored opening credits of *Saturday Night Fever*. And Susan, who wouldn't leave the room when it rained and who lost 20 pounds on an all-brownies diet, taught me to tolerate quirks.

I knew the lovely Susan would be my friend for life when I arrived in our freshman-year room shadowed by my mom, who was carrying a butcher knife, a can of Mace, and a letter opener.

Mom wanted us to be well armed against rapists—she wrote down instructions about how to insert the letter opener into an attacker's jugular—and Susan appreciated the gesture.

As in Darwinian evolution, cross-pollination with diverse strains promotes species development.

One young woman I know was appalled at first that the giggly cheerleader and former prom queen sharing her freshman room at the University of Pennsylvania put up 'N Sync posters "unironically." But in the end, she realized that just because her roommate loved 'N Sync and wore cute outfits did not necessarily mean she was shallow. And the prom queen realized that just because you hum when you write papers doesn't mean you're mentally ill. The prom queen lightened up the brooding, cynical, emo chick, and even got her to an 'N Sync concert—unironically.

Choosing roommates who are mirror images may fit with our narcissistic and microtargeted society, but it retards creativity and social growth. This reluctance to mix it up also has been reflected in the lack of full-throated political and cultural debates on campuses (as opposed to ersatz debates on cable TV), replaced by a quiet P.C. acceptance of differing views or an obnoxious stereotyping of anyone different.

As the *Times*'s Michiko Kakutani noted, the diminished debate syndrome at schools "suggests a closing off of the possibilities of growth and transformation."

Besides intensifying partisanship and conspiracy theories—think the birthers—the Internet divides the world more firmly into niches, birds of a feather avidly flocking together.

As you leave behind high school to redefine and even reinvent yourself as adult, you need exposure to an array of different ideas, backgrounds, and perspectives—not a cordon of clones.

College is not only where you hit the books. It also should be where you learn not to judge a book by its cover.

1. This essay about roommate selection also addressees the political climate on college campuses and in American media. What is Dowd's point? How does she encourage readers to think beyond college relationships?

2. What life lessons has Dowd learned from her roommates? What life lessons have *you* learned from the people you've lived with?

3. Dowd uses puns, or plays on words, in her title and in the last line of her essay. What are they? What does clever word play add to, or take away from, the effectiveness of Dowd's argument? (See Chapter 34, "Titles," p. 428; "Use language strategically," p. 74; and Part 5, "Style," p. 430.)

4. This essay originally appeared on the opinion page of the *New York Times.* Opinion sections of newspapers contain several short arguments about current issues like this one every day. How do you think that this length restriction shapes the style, tone, and form of argumentation in this essay?

5. **WRITING:** Think of another aspect of college existence that you have found unexpectedly challenging, such as grades, tuition, intramural sports, Greek life, finals, cafeterias, laundry, campus parking, or part-time work. Write a short opinion column for your campus newspaper about this aspect of college life: What have you learned from the challenges, and how, if at all, have such difficulties prepared you for life after graduation? What can other students learn from your experience?

PROFILE   Nancy Gibbs is executive editor for *Time* magazine where this essay appeared in 2008. It profiles the athlete and amputee Oscar Pistorius, his quest to compete in the 2008 Beijing Olympics, and the ethical issues raised by his success as a sprinter. You can find videos of Pistorius's races on YouTube. Pistorius is currently seeking to qualify for the 2012 Olympic Games.

Cool Running

NANCY GIBBS

It was only a matter of time before the challenge of Oscar Pistorius would run headlong into our cherished notions of what's equal, what's fair, and what's the difference between the two.

Democracy presumes that we're all created equal; competition proves we are not, or else every race would end in a tie. We talk about a level playing field because it's the least we can do in the face of nature's injustice. Some people are born strong or stretchy, or with a tungsten will. But Pistorius's advantage comes from what nature left out and technology replaced: his body ends at the knees, and from there to the ground it's a moral puzzle.

Born in South Africa without major bones in his legs and feet, he had his lower legs amputated before he was a year old. As he grew up, so did the science of prosthetics. Now twenty-one, Pistorius runs on carbon-fiber blades known as Cheetahs. He won gold in the 200 meter at the Athens Paralympics in 2004, breaking 22 seconds; but now his eye is on the Olympics in Beijing. It was up to the world body that governs track and field, the International Association of Athletics Federations (IAAF), to determine whether using Cheetahs is cheating.

A runner's stride is not perfectly efficient. Ankles waste energy — much more, it turns out, than Pistorius's J-shaped blades. He can run just as fast using less oxygen than his competitors (one describes the sound Pistorius makes as like being chased by a giant pair of scissors). On January 14, following the findings of the researcher who evaluated him, the IAAF disqualified Pistorius from Olympic competition. He is expected to appeal, arguing that the science of advantage is not that simple. Tom Hanks is interested in his life story. No matter what happens next, Pistorius is changing the nature of the games we play.

Our intuition tells us there's a difference between innate advantages and acquired ones. A swimmer born with webbed hands might have an edge, but a swimmer who had skin grafts to turn feet into flippers would pose a problem. Elite sport is unkind to the human body; high school linemen bulk up to an extent that may help the team but wreck their knees. What about the tall girl who wants her doctor to prescribe human growth hormone because her coach said three more inches of height would guarantee her that volleyball scholarship: Unfair, or just unwise? Where exactly is the boundary between dedication and deformity?

Imagine if Pistorius's blades made him exactly as biomechanically efficient as a normal runner. What should be the baseline: Normal for the average man? Or for the average Olympian? Cyclist Lance Armstrong was born with a heart

Oscar Pistorius, the South African sprinter.

and lungs that can make a mountain feel flat; he also trained harder than anyone on the planet. Where's the unfair advantage? George Eyser's wooden leg didn't stop him from winning six Olympic gymnastics medals, including in the parallel bars. But that was 1904; legs have improved since then.

The questions are worth asking because in them lies not just the future of our sports but of ourselves. Why should nature be allowed to play favorites but not parents? Science will soon deliver unto us all sorts of novel ways of redesigning our offspring or re-engineering ourselves that test what we mean by human. The fight over doping in baseball will seem quaint one day when players can dope not with drugs but with genes. Already there is black-market interest in therapies developed to treat muscular dystrophy but which could potentially be used to build super strong athletes.

But there is no honor in shortcuts. Today's dopers are like Rosie Ruiz's winning the marathon in 1980—because she took the subway. Are Pistorius's blades the equivalent of his attaching wheels to his running shoes? "We end up with these subtle, fascinating debates about what the meaning of competition is, and endless debate over where to draw the line," says Tom Murray, president of the Hastings Center, a bioethics think tank. "Don't underestimate how difficult it will be to evaluate all the technologies that are likely to filter into sport."

We honor heroes—in sports as in life—for grace and guts as well as natural gifts. When something comes easily, it's easy not to work at it, like the bright kid who coasts through class: talent taps persistence on the shoulder, says, You're not needed here. But put the two together, Tiger Woods's easy power and ferocious discipline—and he makes history. There's some sweet irony in the fact that before Pistorius came along, there was no need for the rules that now ban him. Only when the disabled runner challenged the able-bodied ones did officials institute a rule against springs and wheels and any artificial aids to running. That's a testimony to technology, but it is also a tribute to the sheer nerve and fierce will that got him to the starting line in the first place.

Reading the Genre

1. Gibbs frequently refers to values in this essay — shared "intuition," our "honor," "democracy," and "equality." What impact do these references have? Do you agree with her that most of society shares these values, or does Gibbs just *hope* that we all share these values? (See "Examine your core assumptions," p. 80.)

2. How does Gibbs address her audience? Why do you think she avoids speaking in the first person? (See Chapter 35, "High, Middle, and Low Style," p. 432.)

3. Gibbs poses several hypothetical situations in her essay. Look at each of these situations. How does exploring "what if" scenarios help us better evaluate the real questions raised by Oscar Pistorius's desire to compete in the 2008 Olympics?

4. How does Gibbs represent Oscar Pistorius himself? Do you get a feeling for who he is as a person? How does Gibbs describe his appearance, and how does she tell his story? How might Gibbs reveal more about Pistorius's personality?

5. **WRITING:** In a short essay, evaluate the ways that, as in athletics, successful students might have dedication and a work ethic, as well as natural gifts, but perhaps also technological or pharmacological advantages. Where should the line be drawn in our quest for success in school?

6. **WRITING:** Does technology give disabled athletes an unfair advantage? Write an imagined dialogue between Pistorius and a competing able-bodied runner, considering their different perspectives and the arguments each might make in favor of his or her own position.

ARGUMENT FOR CHANGE   Emily Bazelon is a senior editor at the online magazine *Slate.com*, where she writes about legal affairs. She takes part in a weekly *Slate* podcast called "The Gabfest," talking about current political issues with colleagues David Plotz and John Dickerson. Bazelon has also written for the *Atlantic, Mother Jones*, and the *Yale Law Journal*. In this essay, Bazelon examines an age-old domestic issue: spanking.

Slate.com

Posted: Thursday, Jan. 25, 2007, at 6:16 PM ET
From: Emily Bazelon

Hitting Bottom:
Why America Should Outlaw Spanking

Sally Lieber, the California assemblywoman who proposed a ban on spanking last week, must be sorry she ever opened her mouth. Before Lieber could introduce her bill, a poll showed that only 23 percent of respondents supported it. Some pediatricians disparaged the idea of outlawing spanking, and her fellow politicians called her crazy. Anyone with the slightest libertarian streak seems to believe that outlawing corporal punishment is silly. More government intrusion, and for what — to spare kids a few swats? Or, if you're pro-spanking, a spanking ban represents a sinister effort to take a crucial disciplinary tool out of the hands of good mothers and fathers — and to encourage the sort of permissive parenting that turns kids ratty and rotten.

Why, though, are we so eager to retain the right to hit our kids? Lieber's ban would apply only to children under the age of 4. Little kids may be the most infuriating; they are also the most vulnerable. And if you think that most spanking takes place in a fit of temper — and that banning it would gradually lead more parents to restrain themselves — then the idea of a hard-and-fast rule against it starts to seem not so ridiculous.

The purpose of Lieber's proposal isn't to send parents to jail, or children to foster care, because of a firm smack. Rather, it would make it easier for prosecutors to bring charges for instances of corporal punishment that they think are tantamount to child abuse. Currently, California law (and the law of other states) allows for spanking that is reasonable, age-appropriate, and does not carry a risk of serious injury. That forces judges to referee what's reasonable and what's not. How do they tell? Often, they may resort to looking for signs of injury. If a smack leaves a bruise or causes a fracture, it's illegal. If not, bombs away. In other words, allowing for "reasonable" spanking gives parents a lot of leeway to cause pain.

Who should we worry about more: The well-intentioned parent who smacks a child's bottom and gets hauled off to court, or the kid who keeps getting pounded because the cops can't find a bruise? A U.N. report on violence against children argues that "The de minimis principle — that the law does not concern itself with trivial matters" will keep minor assaults on children out of court, just as it does almost all minor assaults between adults. The U.N. Committee on the Rights of the Child has been urging countries to ban corporal punishment since 1996. The idea is that by making it illegal to hit your kids, countries will make hurting them socially unacceptable.

The United Nations has a lot of converting to do in this part of the world. Its report cites a survey showing that 84 percent of Americans believe that it's "sometimes necessary to discipline a child with a good hard spanking." On this front, we are in the company of the Koreans, 90 percent of whom reported thinking that corporal punishment is "necessary." On the other side of the spanking map are 19 countries that have banned spanking and three others that have partially banned it.

The grandmother of the bunch is Sweden, which passed a law against corporal punishment in 1979. The effects of that ban are cited by advocates on both sides of the spanking debate. Parents almost universally used corporal punishment on Swedish children born in the 1950s; the numbers dropped to 14 percent for kids born in the late 1980s, and only 8 percent of parents reported physically punishing their kids in 2000. Plus, only one child in Sweden died as the result of physical abuse by a parent between 1980 and 1996. Those statistics suggest that making spanking illegal contributes to making it less prevalent and also to making kids safer. On the other hand, reports to police of child abuse soared in the decades after the spanking ban, as did the incidence of juvenile violence. Did reports rise because frustrated, spanking-barred parents lashed out against their kids in other ways, or because the law made people more aware of child abuse? The latter is what occurred in the United States when reports of abuse spiked following the enactment of child-protective laws in the 1970s. Is the rise in kids beating on each other evidence of undisciplined, unruly child mobs, or the result of other unrelated forces? The data don't tell us, so take your pick.

A similar split exists in the American social-science literature. In a 2000 article in the *Clinical Child and Family Psychology Review,* Dr. Robert Larzelere (who approves of spanking if it's "conditional" and not abusive) reviewed 38 studies and found that spanking posed no harm to kids under the age of 7, and reduced misbehavior when deployed alongside milder punishments like scolding and timeouts. By contrast, a 2002 article in *Psychology Bulletin* by Dr. Elizabeth Gershoff (not a spanking fan) reviewed 88 studies and found an association between corporal punishment and a higher level of childhood aggression and a greater risk of physical abuse.

This is the sort of research impasse that leaves advocates free to argue what they will — and parents without much guidance. But one study stands out: An effort by University of California at Berkeley psychologist Diana Baumrind to tease out the effects of occasional spanking compared to frequent spanking and no spanking at all. Baumrind tracked about 100 white, middle-class families in the East Bay area of northern California from 1968 to 1980. The children who were hit frequently were more likely to be maladjusted. The ones who were occasionally spanked had slightly higher misbehavior scores than those who were not spanked at all. But this difference largely disappeared when Baumrind accounted for the children's poor behavior at a younger age. In other words, the kids who acted out as toddlers and preschoolers were more likely to act out later, whether they were spanked occasionally or never. Lots of spanking was bad for kids. A little didn't seem to matter.

Baumrind concluded that it is "*reliance* on physical punishment, not whether it is used at all, that is associated with harm to the child." The italics are mine. While Baumrind's evidence undercuts the abolitionist position, it doesn't justify spanking as a regular punishment. In addition, Baumrind draws a telling distinction between "impulsive and reactive" spanking and punishments that require "some restraint and forethought." In my experience as a very occasional (once or twice) spanker, impulsivity was what hitting my kid was all about. I know that I'm supposed to spank my sons more in sorrow than in anger. But does that really describe most parents, especially occasional spankers, when they raise their hand to their children? More often, I think, we strike kids when we're mad — enraged, in fact. Baumrind's findings suggest that occasional spankers don't need to worry about this much. I hope she's right. But her numbers are small: Only three children in her study weren't spanked at all. That's a tiny control group.

Baumrind argues that if the social-science research doesn't support an outright ban on spanking, then we shouldn't fight over the occasional spank, because it diverts attention from the larger problems of serious abuse and neglect. "Professional advice that categorically rejects any and all use of a disciplinary practice favored and considered functional by parents is more likely to alienate than educate them," she argues. The extremely negative reaction to Lieber's proposed ban is her best proof.

It's always difficult and awkward — and arguably misguided — to use the law as a tool for changing attitudes. In the case of corporal punishment, though, I'm not sure we'd be crazy to try. A hard-and-fast rule like Sweden's would infuriate and frustrate some perfectly loving parents. It would also make it easier for police and prosecutors to go after the really bad ones. The state would have more power over parents. But then parents have near infinite amounts of power over their kids.

1. How does Bazelon look at the many arguments against a ban on spanking? How does she address these arguments with her own refutations and arguments for a ban? Do you think that she fairly considers counterarguments? (See "Understand opposing claims and points of view," p. 74; "Anticipate objections," p. 375; and Chapter 22, "Critical Thinking," p. 372.)

2. Who are the key stakeholders in this debate — that is, whom does spanking directly affect, and who should care most about it? Make a list of people involved in this debate, and rank them in order of the impact that spanking has on their lives. How does Bazelon address these different stakeholders in the essay? Does she pay attention to the right people? How could identifying the stakeholders in an issue influence your own argumentative writing?

3. Bazelon uses hard evidence and other forms of research to support her arguments. Make an outline of her use of research: What kinds of research does she cite, what authority does it have, and how exactly does she use it to support her own claims? (See "Assemble your hard evidence," p. 86; "Creating a structure," p. 88; Chapter 43, "Evaluating Sources," p. 482; and Chapter 47, "Integrating Sources into Your Work," p. 497.)

4. **WRITING:** Many people find it easy to criticize or second-guess parents. Write a short argument paper that makes a few suggestions to parents about how to best raise children. Keep in mind that your audience of parents might not want your advice, so write accordingly, considering possible counterarguments.

ANALYSIS OF CULTURAL VALUES   Poranee Natadecha-Sponsel teaches philosophy, sociology, and religion at Chaminade University of Honolulu, Hawaii, where she focuses on the interconnectedness of religion and the environment, or "spiritual ecology." In this essay, Natadecha-Sponsel reflects on her experiences as a newcomer to American culture.

PORANEE NATADECHA-SPONSEL

The Young, the Rich, and the Famous: Individualism as an American Cultural Value

"Hi, how are you?" "Fine, thank you, and you?" These are greetings that everybody in America hears and says every day—salutations that come ready-made and packaged just like a hamburger and fries. There is no real expectation for any special information in response to these greetings. Do not, under any circumstances, take up anyone's time by responding in depth to the programmed query. What or how you may feel at the moment is of little, if any, importance. Thai people would immediately perceive that our concerned American friends are truly interested in our welfare, and this concern would require polite reciprocation by spelling out the details of our current condition. We become very disappointed when we have had enough experience in the United States to learn that we have bored, amused, or even frightened many of our American acquaintances by taking the greeting "How are you?" so literally. We were reacting like Thais, but in the American context where salutations have a different meaning, our detailed reactions were inappropriate. In Thai society, a greeting among acquaintances usually requests specific information about the other person's condition, such as "Where are you going?" or "Have you eaten?"

One of the American contexts in which this greeting is most confusing and ambiguous is at the hospital or clinic. In these sterile and ritualistic settings, I have always been uncertain exactly how to answer when the doctor or nurse asks "How are you?" If I deliver a packaged answer of "Fine," I wonder if I am telling a lie. After all, I am there in the first place precisely because I am not so fine. Finally, after debating for some time, I asked one nurse how she expected a patient to answer the query "How are you?" But after asking this question, I then wondered if it was rude to do so. However, she looked relieved after I explained to her that people from different cultures have different ways to greet other people and that for me to be asked how I am in the hospital results in awkwardness. Do I simply answer, "Fine, thank you," or do I reveal in accurate detail how I really feel at the moment? My suspicion was verified when the nurse declared that "How are you?" was really no more than a polite greeting and that she didn't expect any answer more elaborate than simply "Fine." However, she told me that some patients do answer her by describing every last ache and pain from which they are suffering.

A significant question that comes to mind is whether the verbal pattern of greetings reflects any social relationship in American culture. The apparently warm and sincere greeting may initially suggest interest in the person, yet the intention and expectations are, to me, quite superficial. For example, most often the person greets you quickly and then walks by to attend to other business without even waiting for your response! This type of greeting is just like a package of American fast food! The person eats the food quickly without enjoying the taste. The convenience is like many other American accoutrements of living such as cars, household appliances, efficient telephones, or simple, systematic, and predictable arrangements of groceries in the supermarket. However, usually when this greeting is delivered, it seems to lack a personal touch and genuine feeling. It is little more than ritualized behavior.

I have noticed that most Americans keep to themselves even at social gatherings. Conversation may revolve around many topics, but little, if anything, is revealed about oneself. Without talking much about oneself and not knowing much about others, social relations seem to remain at an abbreviated superficial level. How could one know a person without knowing something about him or her? How much does one need to know about a person to really know that person?

After living in this culture for more than a decade, I have learned that there are many topics that should not be mentioned in conversations with American acquaintances or even close friends. One's personal life and one's income are considered to be very private and even taboo topics. Unlike my Thai culture, Americans do not show interest or curiosity by asking such personal questions, especially when one just meets the individual for the first time. Many times I have been embarrassed by my Thai acquaintances who recently arrived at the University of Hawaii and the East-West Center. For instance, one day I was walking on campus with an American friend when we met another Thai woman to whom I had been introduced a few days earlier. The Thai woman came to write her doctoral dissertation at the East-West Center where the American woman worked, so I introduced them to each other. The American woman greeted my Thai companion in Thai language, which so impressed her that she felt immediately at ease. At once, she asked the American woman numerous personal questions such as, How long did you live in Thailand? Why were you there? How long were you married to the Thai man? Why did you divorce him? How long have you been divorced? Are you going to marry a Thai again or an American? How long have you been working here? How much do you earn? The American was stunned. However, she was very patient and more or less answered all those questions as succinctly as she could. I was so uncomfortable that I had to interrupt whenever I could to get her out of the awkward situation in which she had been forced into talking about things she considered personal. For people in Thai society, such questions would be appropriate and not considered too personal, let alone taboo.

The way Americans value their individual privacy continues to impress me. Americans seem to be open and yet there is a contradiction because they are also aloof and secretive. This is reflected in many of their behavior patterns. By Thai standards, the relationship between friends in American society seems to be somewhat superficial. Many Thai students, as well as other Asians, have felt that they could not find genuine friendship with Americans. For example, I met many American classmates who were very helpful and friendly while we were in the same class. We went out, exchanged phone calls, and did the same things as would good friends in Thailand. But those activities stopped suddenly when the semester ended.

Privacy as a component of the American cultural value of individualism is nurtured in the home as children grow up. From birth they are given their own individual, private space, a bedroom separate from that of their parents. American children are taught to become progressively independent, both emotionally and economically, from their family. They learn to help themselves at an early age. In comparison, in Thailand, when parents bring a new baby home from the hospital, it shares the parents' bedroom for two to three years and then shares another bedroom with older siblings of the same sex. Most Thai children do not have their own private room until they finish high school, and some do not have their own room until another sibling moves out, usually when the sibling gets married. In Thailand, there are strong bonds within the extended family. Older siblings regularly help their parents to care for younger ones. In this and other ways, the Thai family emphasizes the interdependence of its members.

I was accustomed to helping Thai babies who fell down to stand up again. Thus, in America when I saw babies fall, it was natural for me to try to help them back on their feet. Once at a summer camp for East-West Center participants, one of the supervisors brought his wife and their ten-month-old son with him. The baby was so cute that many students were playing with him. At one point he was trying to walk and fell, so all the Asian students, males and females, rushed to help him up.

Although the father and mother were nearby, they paid no attention to their fallen and crying baby. However, as the students were trying to help and comfort him, the parents told them to leave him alone; he would be all right on his own. The baby did get up and stopped crying without any assistance. Independence is yet another component of the American value of individualism.

Individualism is even reflected in the way Americans prepare, serve, and consume food. In a typical American meal, each person has a separate plate and is not supposed to share or taste food from other people's plates. My Thai friends and I are used to eating Thai style, in which you share food from a big serving dish in the middle of the table. Each person dishes a small amount from the serving dish onto his or her plate and finishes this portion before going on with the next portion of the same or a different serving dish. With the Thai pattern of eating, you regularly reach out to the serving dishes throughout the meal. But this way of eating is not considered appropriate in comparison to the common American practice where each person eats separately from his or her individual plate.

One time my American host, a divorcée who lived alone, invited a Thai girlfriend and myself to an American dinner at her home. When we were reaching out and eating a small portion of one thing at a time in Thai style, we were told to dish everything we wanted onto our plates at one time and that it was not considered polite to reach across the table. The proper American way was to have each kind of food piled up on your plate at once. If we were to eat in the same manner in Thailand, eyebrows would have been raised at the way we piled up food on our plates, and we would have been considered to be eating like pigs, greedy and inconsiderate of others who shared the meal at the table.

Individualism as a pivotal value in American culture is reflected in many other ways. Material wealth is not only a prime status marker in American society but also a guarantee and celebration of individualism—wealth allows the freedom to do almost anything, although usually within the limits of law. The pursuit of material wealth through individual achievement is instilled in Americans from the youngest age. For example, I was surprised to see an affluent American couple, who own a large ranch house and two BMW cars, send their nine-year-old son to deliver newspapers. He has to get up very early each morning to deliver the papers, even on Sunday! During summer vacation, the boy earns additional money by helping in his parents' gift shop from 10 A.M. to 5 P.M. His thirteen-year-old sister often earns money by babysitting, even at night.

In Thailand, only children from poorer families work to earn money to help the household. Middle- and high-income parents do not encourage their children to work until after they have finished their education. They provide economic support in order to free their children to concentrate on and excel in their studies. Beyond the regular schooling, families who can afford it pay for special tutoring as well as training in music, dance, or sports. However, children in low- and middle-income families help their parents with household chores and the care of younger children.

Many American children have been encouraged to get paid for their help around the house. They rarely get any gifts free of obligations. They even have to be good to get Santa's gifts at Christmas! As they grow up, they are conditioned to earn things they want; they learn that "there is no such thing as a free lunch." From an early age, children are taught to become progressively independent economically from their parents. Also, most young people are encouraged to leave home at college age to be on their own. From my viewpoint as a Thai, it seems that American family ties and closeness are not as strong as in Asian families whose children depend on family financial support until joining the work force after college age. Thereafter, it is the children's turn to help support their parents financially.

Modern American society and economy emphasize individualism in other ways. The nuclear family is more common than the extended family, and newlyweds usually establish their own independent household rather than initially living with either the husband's or the wife's parents. Parents and children appear to be close only when the children are very young. Most American parents seem to "lose" their children by the teenage years. They don't seem to belong to each other as closely as do Thai families. Even though I have seen more explicit affectionate expression among American family members than among Asian ones, the close interpersonal spirit seems to be lacking. Grandparents have relatively little to do with the grandchildren on any regular basis, in contrast to the extended family, which is more common in Thailand. The family and society seem to be graded by age to the point that grandparents, parents, and children are separated by generational subcultures that are evidently alienated from one another. Each group "does its own thing." Help and support are usually limited to whatever does not interfere with one's own life. In America, the locus of responsibility is more on the individual than on the family.

In one case I know of, a financially affluent grandmother with Alzheimer's disease is taken care of twenty-four hours a day by hired help in her own home. Her daughter visits and relieves the helper occasionally. The mature granddaughter, who has her own family, rarely visits. Yet they all live in the same neighborhood. However, each lives in a different house, and each is very independent. Although the mother worries about the grandmother, she cannot do much. Her husband also needs her, and she divides her time between him, her daughters and their children, and the grandmother. When the mother needs to go on a trip with her husband, a second hired attendant is required to care for the grandmother temporarily. When I asked why the granddaughter doesn't temporarily care for the grandmother, the reply was that she has her own life, and it would not be fair for the granddaughter to take care of the grandmother, even for a short period of time. Yet I wonder if it is fair for the grandmother to be left out. It seems to me that the value of individualism and its associated independence account for these apparent gaps in family ties and support.

In contrast to American society, in Thailand older parents with a long-term illness are asked to move in with their children and grandchildren if they are not already living with them. The children and grandchildren take turns attending to the grandparent, sometimes with help from live-in maids. Living together in the same house reinforces moral support among the generations within an extended family. The older generation is respected because of the previous economic, social, and moral support for their children and grandchildren. Family relations provide one of the most important contexts for being a "morally good person," which is traditionally the principal concern in the Buddhist society of Thailand.

In America, being young, rich, and/or famous allows one greater freedom and independence and thus promotes the American value of individualism. This is reflected in the mass appeal of major annual television events like the Super Bowl and the Academy Awards. The goal of superachievement is also seen in more mundane ways. For example, many parents encourage their children to take special courses and to work hard to excel in sports as a shortcut to becoming rich and famous. I know one mother who has taken her two sons to tennis classes and tournaments since the boys were six years old, hoping that at least one of them will be a future tennis star like Ivan Lendl. Other parents focus their children on acting, dancing, or musical talent. The children have to devote much time and hard work as well as sacrifice the ordinary activities of youth in order to develop and perform their natural talents and skills in prestigious programs. But those who excel in the sports and entertainment industries can become rich and famous, even at an early age, as for example Madonna, Tom Cruise, and Michael Jackson. Television and other media publicize these celebrities and thereby reinforce the American value of individualism, including personal achievement and financial success.

Although the American cultural values of individualism and the aspiration to become rich and famous have had some influence in Thailand, there is also cultural and religious resistance to these values. Strong social bonds, particularly within the extended family, and the hierarchical structure of the kingdom run counter to individualism. Also, youth gain social recognition through their academic achievement.

From the perspective of Theravada Buddhism, which strongly influences Thai culture, aspiring to be rich and famous would be an illustration of greed, and those who
have achieved wealth and fame do not celebrate it publicly as much as in American
society. Being a good, moral person is paramount, and ideally Buddhists emphasize
restraint and moderation.

Beyond talent and skill in the sports and entertainment industries, there are
many other ways that young Americans can pursue wealth. Investment is one route.
One American friend who is only a sophomore in college has already invested heavily in the stock market to start accumulating wealth. She is just one example of the
1980s trend for youth to be more concerned with their individual finances than with
social, political, and environmental issues. With less attention paid to public issues,
the expression of individualism seems to be magnified through emphasis on lucrative careers, financial investment, and material consumption—the "Yuppie" phenomenon. This includes new trends in dress, eating, housing (condominiums), and
cars (expensive European imports). Likewise, there appears to be less of a long-term
commitment to marriage. More young couples are living together without either
marriage or plans for future marriage. When such couples decide to get married,
prenuptial agreements are made to protect their assets. Traditional values of marriage, family, and sharing appear to be on the decline.

Individualism as one of the dominant values in American culture is expressed
in many ways. This value probably stems from the history of the society as a frontier
colony of immigrants in search of a better life with independence, freedom, and
the opportunity for advancement through personal achievement. However, in the
beliefs and customs of any culture there are some disadvantages as well as advantages.
Although Thais may admire the achievements and material wealth of American
society, there are costs, especially in the value of individualism and associated social
phenomena.

Reading the Genre

1. Natadecha-Sponsel, who is originally from Thailand, has lived in the United States for more than thirty years. What does she notice about America that people who have always lived in America might not notice? How does she get her readers to look more closely at American culture? (See "Understanding your audience," p. 82, and Chapter 36, "Inclusive and Culturally Sensitive Style," p. 440.)

2. How does the author set up her comparison of the United States and other cultures? Does she have an opinion about which culture is better? Is her purpose to help us choose which culture is best? (See "Compare and contrast," p. 123.)

3. Consider what this essay has to offer both an American reader and a non-American reader. How does Natadecha-Sponsel speak to both audiences?

4. How does Natadecha-Sponsel define the term *individualism*? Consider how she provides examples that illustrate what *individualism* means in America. How does each example help the reader understand what American individualism looks like to her? How does she connect these examples? (See Chapter 31, "Transitions," p. 416.)

5. **WRITING:** Create a "beginner's guide" to culture at your college or university. What would a new student (perhaps a foreign student) have to know to understand the cultural values at your school? Try to write about major cultural values — the big things that students believe in or assume to be inherently true — rather than cultural practices (like partying or studying). Which values would a new student find strange? Why?

6. **COMPOSE VISUALLY:** Look at your college's Web site and identify the key cultural values conveyed by the home page and other relevant sections. Do you feel comfortable with the site's portrayal of your school, its students, and their values? Create a sketch proposing a redesign of the Web site that reflects campus values as you understand them. (See "Read visually," p. 368.)

POLICY ARGUMENT   Daniel Engber writes a regular science column for *Slate.com* and has published articles in *Popular Mechanics, Popular Science, Salon,* and the *Chronicle of Higher Education.* A deliberately quirky writer, he has drawn on his graduate education in neuroscience to argue for distracting free-throw contestants at NBA games, for creating foolproof viral videos, and, in this article, for ending the backlash against obesity.

Slate.com

Posted: Monday, October 5, 2009, at 6:02 PM ET
From: Daniel Engber

Glutton Intolerance

What If a War on Obesity Only Makes the Problem Worse?

Just about every discussion of obesity and health care begins with the same purported fact: The diseases associated with excess weight are impoverishing the nation with $147 billion in unnecessary medical bills every year.

In my last column ("Give Us Your Tired, Your Poor, Your Big Fat Asses . . . "), I argued that obesity can also make us poor individually, since fat people face rampant discrimination on the job and marriage markets.

A recent paper from Yale's Rudd Center for Food Policy & Obesity hints at the scope of this anti-fat prejudice. We know, for example, that if you're fat, you make less money. Lots of studies have shown how body size plays out in the working world: According to one, women who are two standard deviations (or 64 pounds) overweight suffer a wage penalty of 9 percent; another found that severely obese white women lose out on one-quarter of their potential income. There's also evidence that obese women are less likely to attend college or maintain romantic relationships, even controlling for socioeconomic background. (One survey found that a few extra pounds could reduce a woman's chance of getting married by 20 percent.)

Heavy people may face discrimination in medical settings, too. The authors of the review, Rebecca Puhl and Chelsea Heuer, cite numerous surveys of anti-fat attitudes among health care workers, who tend to see obese patients as ugly, lazy, weak-willed, and lacking in motivation to improve their health. Doctors describe treating fatties as a waste of time, and the staff at teaching hospitals appear to single them out for derogatory jokes. Unsurprisingly, many obese people avoid seeing their primary care providers altogether, and those who do are less likely to be screened for breast, cervical, and colorectal cancers. (That's true even among those with health insurance and college degrees.)

These data points suggest a rather simple approach to America's obesity problem: Stop hating. If we weren't such unrepentant body bigots, fat people might earn more money, stay in school, and receive better medical care in hospitals and doctors' offices. All that would go a long way toward mitigating the health effects of excess weight — and its putative costs. But there's an even better reason to think that America's glutton intolerance is a threat to public health and the federal budget. Recent epidemiological research implies that the shame of being obese poses its own medical risk. Mental anguish harms the body; weight stigma can break your heart.

The victims of chronic stress or depression, whatever their size, tend to maintain higher levels of certain inflammatory chemicals in their bloodstream. Under normal circumstances — and over the short term — these cytokines help to control the body's response to dangerous situations like injury or illness. The chemicals create their own problems, though, when they stick around too long. A sustained or elevated stress response seems to increase your risk of heart disease, hypertension, and diabetes. That may explain some of the relationships between health and wealth: Blood tests show unusual cytokine activity among those of low socioeconomic status as well as patients with post-traumatic stress and panic disorders.

It turns out that obese people have unusual cytokine readings, too, and these are often taken as the cause of weight-related illness. According to one theory, the presence of visceral fat cells can set off a biochemical chain reaction that leads to the inflammatory response. (Fat cells may even secrete the cytokines themselves.) As a result, someone who's fat and someone who's chronically stressed will be at risk for many of the same diseases.

It may be that obesity and stress are independent risk factors that happen to affect the body in similar ways. Or maybe chronic stress leads to weight gain, which in turn causes inflammation.

According to epidemiologist Peter Muennig, there's another pathway from excess weight to disease. In his 2008 paper "The Body Politic: The Relationship Between

Stigma and Obesity-Associated Disease," Muennig argues that the stress and shame of being fat causes those cytokine abnormalities. In other words, obesity makes you sick by stressing you out.

According to Muennig's theory, the health effects of obesity should vary with the intensity of anti-fat bias — the more abuse you take, the worse the disease. Women are more likely than men to have eating disorders, and they face greater weight-based discrimination in the overweight range. (According to Puhl, men get harsher treatment when they're really obese.) And, sure enough, women are seven times more likely to experience significant illness or death as a result of being overweight. (Obese women are especially vulnerable to clinical depression, which is itself a risk factor for cardio-vascular disease.)

White people also appear to suffer disproportionately from weight-related illness, as compared with black people. According to Muennig, a black woman who's 5 feet 5 inches and less than 60 years old won't develop any weight-related risk of early death until she reaches 225 lbs. Meanwhile, a white woman of the same height and age group would hit the same threshold at 170 lbs. That fits with the idea that body-size norms differ among blacks and whites. (Black people also tend to be less susceptible to eating disorders and weight-based wage discrimination.)

There are some alternative explanations for these disparities. They might, for example, be an artifact of the crude way in which we measure obesity. Black people tend to have less abdominal fat (associated with cardiovascular disease) than white people given the same BMI reading, and women also tend to have more adipose tis-sue, and smaller waist-to-hip ratios, than men. But even the most accurate measures of fatness — like dual energy X-ray absorptiometry — don't really improve our ability to predict health outcomes across the population. It may be that the exact volume of adipose tissue in someone's body is less important than the way they look to others. (Muennig suggests that merely having "big bones" could be bad for your health.)

That's not to say obesity won't affect your body, independent of any social fac-tors. As Muennig points out, obese lab rodents aren't likely to suffer much emotional abuse from their fellow mice, but they seem to have higher levels of pro-inflammatory cytokines nonetheless. Still, there's plenty of evidence that body-shape discrimination plays a role in human disease outcomes. Shortness, for example, is associated with an increased risk of coronary heart disease, diabetes, and early death — as well as lower wages and fewer long-term relationships. For some reason, though, the health effects of being short are worse for men than they are for women. Could it be that the social consequences of height and weight go in opposite directions?

If anti-fat bias can affect our bodies, then it's worth considering how an all-out war on obesity plays out in terms of public health. When we reach out to poor communities and educate them about the risks of being overweight, we are, in effect, exporting the weight stigma that happens to be most prevalent among rich, white people. Indeed, Rebecca Puhl says the reported prevalence of weight discrimination has increased by two-thirds since the mid-1990s, while media coverage of the "obesity epidemic" has quintupled over roughly the same interval. (Meanwhile, the U.S. diet industry has just about doubled its annual revenues — to nearly $60 billion.)

We've worked hard to frame excess weight as a major health risk and a drain on the economy. The motivation is generous enough: Anti-obesity rhetoric encourages people to eat less and exercise more. But what if it also encourages discrimination? If that's the case, a war on obesity would come at a significant cost to the fattest Americans — in terms of lower wages, less education, and more stress-related illness.

Fat activists argue that the risks of such a policy far outweigh its potential benefits. (They say that doctors should encourage healthy lifestyles instead of trying to enforce an ideal body size.)

But few mainstream public-health advocates take such claims seriously. They point out that many interventions in poor communities focus on diet and exercise rather than weight per se. If BMI is used as a measure of success in these programs, that's because it's a quick way to see whether people really are pursuing a healthy lifestyle. For Kelly Brownell, director of the Rudd Center and a leading researcher on both health policy and weight bias, the dangers of discrimination are important but relatively modest. What about the idea that targeting obesity might be counterproductive for the fattest Americans? He doesn't buy it.

The fact is, very few researchers have tried to measure the combined health effects of anti-fat prejudice. Nor have legislators spent much effort on the social-consequences of weight stigma. Only a handful of cities — Washington, D.C.; San Francisco, and Santa Cruz, Calif. — have passed laws to protect the rights of obese people, and there's only one state — Michigan — that forbids employers from discriminating on the basis of body size. If you're victimized for being fat anywhere else in the United States, good luck. You can sue your employer under the Americans with Disabilities Act, but you'll have to prove that your weight condition is something like being wheelchair-bound or mentally retarded — not such a good way to reduce weight stigma overall.

Given the risks associated with weight stigma, we should at least reconsider our tendency to blame obesity for the country's health crisis. (I suggested last week that we could target poverty instead.) If obesity prevention measures do end up in the health bill, let's make sure they'll do more good than harm. The Rudd Center has called for a new federal ban on weight discrimination or an expansion of the Civil Rights Act. Both would go a long way toward protecting the two-thirds of all Americans who are classified as overweight or obese.

Reading the Genre

1. Engber opens his argument with an overview of recent scientific research on the costs of obesity, then startles readers with his thesis — "Stop hating" — in the fifth paragraph. Reread the article and locate other instances when Engber switches between academic and conversational style. What is the effect of these shifts? (See Chapter 35, "High, Middle, and Low Style," p. 432.)

2. Find Engber's restatement of his thesis in the last paragraph. How does the thesis change between Engber's introduction and his conclusion? (See Chapter 26, "Thesis," p. 393.)

3. Engber tests the logic of several theories, offers a range of possible causes for obesity, and considers the effects of being obese on individuals and on society. What do these causal analyses contribute to his argument? (See Chapter 5, "Causal Analyses," p. 138.)

4. Engber's article is thoroughly researched. Working from the sources he names in his text (you can find hyperlinks for each of them at www.slate.com/id/2231508/), create a list of works cited in MLA style or a references list in APA style. (See Chapter 49, "MLA Documentation and Format," p. 503, and Chapter 50, "APA Documentation and Format," p. 540.)

5. **WRITING:** Visit the Yale Rudd Center on Food Policy's "Hot Topics" Web page (www.yaleruddcenter.org/hot_topics.aspx) and select a food policy issue that interests you. Read five to ten of the articles and studies linked on the page, and then write an argumentative essay on your topic. Be sure to have a clearly expressed thesis and to document your sources as appropriate.

69 Evaluations: Readings

See also Chapter 4:

PRODUCT REVIEW
David Pogue, *Looking at the iPad from Two Angles,* **109**

ARTS REVIEW
Charles Isherwood, *Stomping onto Broadway with a Punk Temper Tantrum,* **127**

SOCIAL SATIRE
Jordyn Brown, *A Word from My Anti-Phone Soapbox,* **131**

VISUAL COMPARISON
Insurance Institute for Highway Safety, *Crash Test,* **136**

TELEVISION REVIEW
Carrie Brownstein, *So I Thought I Could Dance* **765**

SCIENTIFIC EVALUATION
Michio Kaku, *Force Fields* **769**

TECHNOLOGY REVIEW
Sasha Frere-Jones, *You, the D.J.* **783**

TELEVISION REVIEW
Nelle Engoron, *Why* Mad Men *Is Bad for Women* **788**

CONCERT REVIEW
Ann Powers, *Live Review: Lady Gaga at Staples Center* **795**

TELEVISION REVIEW   Carrie Brownstein, former guitarist and vocalist in the influential Portland band Sleater-Kinney, now performs with the band Wild Flag and appears on radio and television as a music critic and sketch comedian. The review here comes from the blog Monitor Mix (www.npr.org/blogs/monitormix), which she wrote for National Public Radio from 2007 to 2010. In Brownstein's words, the blog featured "writing and musings on music, but since music is often terrible," she often turned to "topics such as film, books, dogs, and television."

NPR.org

Posted: September 22, 2008, at 3:22 PM ET
From: Carrie Brownstein

So I Thought I Could Dance

I'm about to admit something embarrassing. Last night, I went with my family to see a live performance of the reality television show *So You Think You Can Dance.* They're fans of the program, and I love my family, so I went. No, I don't watch the show — I've never even seen it — but I'm not above reality television. For evidence of this, feel free to go back and read my post about *The Bachelor,* one of my more contentious entries, wherein people expressed major disappointment that I am not immune to, um, America.

So, while some of you were suffering through what sounds like a horrible Emmy broadcast, I was living inside of a television world and witnessing the mindset of the television viewer.

For those of you who don't know, *So You Think You Can Dance* (which from here on out will be known as *SYTYCD*) is a reality TV program wherein dancers from all genres come together and perform choreographed material in front of a live audience. Hip-hop dancers must learn to cha cha cha, ballroom dancers find their way into a breakdance routine, and modern dancers learn to do something other than float, flutter, and hug themselves. The dancers pair up and things get sexy. Or "sexy."

Portland was the second stop on the *SYTYCD* Season 4 tour. The performance took place at the Rose Garden, our giant sports stadium, which will also host an upcoming Celine Dion concert, as well as the Ice Capades. The first thing I noticed once we got to our seats was that, even though this was a live event, we were still essentially going to be watching TV. Like, the whole time. A Jumbotron provided the

A still from a first-season episode of the television show *So You Think You Can Dance.*

audience with season highlights, interviews with the cast members, and a Brady Bunch–esque segment with questions like "Which dancer likes to put ketchup and ranch dressing on everything?" In case you were wondering, the answer to that one was a dancer named Comfort.

No surprise here, but the entire show has been branded. Each dancer has his or her own look and personality. There's the wacky one, the intense one, the crybaby, the "this show saved me from my crappy life" guy, and so on. And when the dancers introduced the performances, they each came out in *SYTYCD* gear, of which there were copious amounts. And it was all for sale! There was even an intermission that seemed less about giving the dancers a rest and more about giving us a chance to go and purchase some of those souvenirs. I took the opportunity to buy a $4 bottle of water.

And, finally, there was the dancing itself. I really wanted it to be exciting. Some of these people don't just *think* they can dance; they really *can* dance. But, sadly, each piece was designed for our short, pitiful attention spans, which apparently give us about 45 seconds. All of the performances were culled from the TV show. The emcees would say, "Remember when Kate and Joshua did their piece that involved a bed?" The audience would scream. "Well, here it is!" More screams. And then Kate and Joshua would dance on a bed in a piece that was supposed to be about breaking up but made me feel about as emotional as I do about picking up dog poop. Most of the choreography told stories about love, as if all romance were merely an extension of a 14-year-old girl's imagination. The dances hinted at sex and flirtation, heartache and manipulation, but through a Disney-fied lens; magic, and magically sterile. The strangest moment — here is the music part, music-blogger purists! — came when one of the couples danced to the Mirah song "The Garden."

You'd think the live *SYTYCD* show would be an opportunity to prove that reality TV is sort of based in reality — that, in real life, the dancing is *better* than it is on TV. But when I looked at the stage from our swanky floor seats and then peeked at the Jumbotron, the dancing really did look more exciting on the Jumbotron. Somehow, even, more believable.

Most of my disappointment came from wanting to be part of something that seems surprisingly popular, to experience people enjoying an art form as unlikely as dance. In my naive hopes, I imagined more people buying season ballet tickets and checking out local dance troupes. Instead, however, I was reminded that what *SYTYCD* popularizes is not dance, but television, and bad television at that.

On the way out, I saw a guy whom I felt summed up the whole night. Wearing baggy gray sweatpants and carrying a program for the show in one arm, he had managed to stuff a 16-ounce paper cup of Coke into his right pants pocket. The straw hung out, dripping little bits of brown soda onto the floor. Other people's sense of satisfaction is a sadly beautiful thing.

Reading the Genre

1. In describing her blog, Brownstein admits that she is a bit of a "cynic and curmudgeon." She is obviously not a fan of the television show she examines in this review. What are the benefits of not liking the work you are evaluating? What are the drawbacks? (See "Make value judgments," p. 107.)

2. Brownstein writes about a reality television show. In what ways does she comment on this "reality"? What seems most real and most fake, and why does this matter?

3. Increasingly, television shows are, in Brownstein's words, a "television world" that has been fully "branded." The event that Brownstein attends is unique in that it centers on watching television, but it also renders the full "television world" and puts the "brand" right in the viewer's face. If a television screen is at the center of this experience, how would you describe or define all of the other things surrounding this screen, and what do they add to the show? What do these things demand of the audience? What does the audience get from this "world"?

4. **WRITING:** Watch an entire episode of a popular reality television show — preferably a show you aren't a fan of or don't already know well. Pay close attention to the show, as well as the commercials and the "world" around the show (product placement, tie-ins, promotions, and so on). Write an evaluation of the show with this entire "world" in mind.

5. **COMPOSING VISUALLY:** Reread question 3. Consider the idea that a television show also has a variety of other products, performances, and texts surrounding it, making it a "brand" and extending it into a "television world." Choose another heavily marketed show, such as *American Idol* or *Glee,* and create a chart with a television at the center. Draw lines out from the television to connect to the other entities that spin out of the show to promote it, brand it, and make it a "world." How do these things all structure the experience of the show? (For a cultural analysis of the show *Glee,* see pp. 238–45 in Chapter 7, "Literary Analyses.")

SCIENTIFIC EVALUATION   Michio Kaku is a theoretical physicist who specializes in string field theory—and in making scientific concepts understandable to a popular audience. This essay comes from his book *Physics of the Impossible* (2008), a collection of essays that examine the real science behind fictional ideas like death rays and invisibility cloaks.

MICHIO KAKU

Force Fields

I. When a distinguished but elderly scientist states that something is possible, he is almost certainly right. When he states that something is impossible, he is very probably wrong.

II. The only way of discovering the limits of the possible is to venture a little way past them into the impossible.

III. Any sufficiently advanced technology is indistinguishable from magic.

—Arthur C. Clarke's Three Laws

"**S**hields up!"

In countless *Star Trek* episodes this is the first order that Captain Kirk barks out to the crew, raising the force fields to protect the starship *Enterprise* against enemy fire.

So vital are force fields in *Star Trek* that the tide of the battle can be measured by how the force field is holding up. Whenever power is drained from the force fields, the *Enterprise* suffers more and more damaging blows to its hull, until finally surrender is inevitable.

So what is a force field? In science fiction it's deceptively simple: a thin, invisible yet impenetrable barrier able to deflect lasers and rockets alike. At first glance a force field looks so easy that its creation as a battlefield shield seems imminent. One expects that any day some enterprising inventor will announce the discovery of a defensive force field. But the truth is far more complicated.

In the same way that Edison's lightbulb revolutionized modern civilization, a force field could profoundly affect every aspect of our lives. The military could use force fields to become invulnerable, creating an impenetrable shield against enemy missiles and bullets. Bridges, superhighways, and roads could in theory be built by simply pressing a button. Entire cities could sprout instantly in the desert, with skyscrapers made entirely of force fields. Force fields erected over cities could enable their inhabitants to modify the effects of their weather—high winds, blizzards, tornados—at will. Cities could be built under the oceans within the safe canopy of a force field. Glass, steel, and mortar could be entirely replaced.

Yet oddly enough a force field is perhaps one of the most difficult devices to create in the laboratory. In fact, some physicists believe it might actually be impossible, without modifying its properties.

Michael Faraday

The concept of force fields originates from the work of the great nineteenth-century British scientist Michael Faraday.

Faraday was born to working-class parents (his father was a blacksmith) and eked out a meager existence as an apprentice bookbinder in the early 1800s. The young Faraday was fascinated by the enormous breakthroughs in uncovering the mysterious properties of two new forces: electricity and magnetism. Faraday devoured all he could concerning these topics and attended lectures by Professor Humphrey Davy of the Royal Institution in London.

One day Professor Davy severely damaged his eyes in a chemical accident and hired Faraday to be his secretary. Faraday slowly began to win the confidence of the scientists at the Royal Institution and was allowed to conduct important experiments of his own, although he was often slighted. Over the years Professor Davy grew increasingly jealous of the brilliance shown by his young assistant, who was a rising star in experimental circles, eventually eclipsing Davy's own fame. After Davy died in 1829 Faraday was free to make a series of stunning breakthroughs that led to the creation of generators that would energize entire cities and change the course of world civilization.

The key to Faraday's greatest discoveries was his "force fields." If one places iron filings over a magnet, one finds that the iron filings create a spiderweb-like pattern that fills up all of the space. These are Faraday's lines of force, which graphically describe how the force fields of electricity and magnetism permeate space. If one graphs the magnetic fields of the Earth, for example, one finds that the lines emanate from the north polar region and then fall back to the Earth in the south polar region. Similarly, if one were to graph the electric field lines of a lightning rod in a thunderstorm, one would find that the lines of force concentrate at the tip of the lightning rod. Empty space, to Faraday, was not empty at all, but was filled with lines of force that could make distant objects move. (Because of Faraday's poverty-stricken youth, he was illiterate in mathematics, and as a consequence his notebooks are full not of equations but of hand-drawn diagrams of these lines of force. Ironically, his lack of mathematical training led him to create the beautiful diagrams of lines of force that now can be found in any physics textbook. In science a physical picture is often more important than the mathematics used to describe it.)

Historians have speculated on how Faraday was led to his discovery of force fields, one of the most important concepts in all of science. In fact, the *sum total of all modern physics* is written in the language of Faraday's fields. In 1831, he made the key breakthrough regarding force fields that changed civilization forever. One day, he was moving a child's magnet over a coil of wire and he noticed that he was able to generate an electric current in the wire, without ever touching it. This meant that a magnet's invisible field could push electrons in a wire across empty space, creating a current.

Faraday's "force fields," which were previously thought to be useless, idle doodlings, were real, material forces that could move objects and generate power. Today the light that you are using to read this page is probably energized by Faraday's discovery about electromagnetism. A spinning magnet creates a force field that pushes the electrons in a wire, causing them to move in an electrical current. This electricity in the wire can then be used to light up a lightbulb. This same principle is used to generate electricity to power the cities of the world. Water flowing across a dam, for example, causes a huge magnet in a turbine to spin, which then pushes the electrons in a wire, forming an electric current that is sent across high-voltage wires into our homes.

In other words, the force fields of Michael Faraday are the forces that drive modern civilization, from electric bulldozers to today's computers, Internet, and iPods.

Faraday's force fields have been an inspiration for physicists for a century and a half. Einstein was so inspired by them that he wrote his theory of gravity in terms of force fields. I, too, was inspired by Faraday's work. Years ago I successfully wrote the theory of strings in terms of the force fields of Faraday, thereby founding string field theory. In physics when someone says, "He thinks like a line of force," it is meant as a great compliment.

The Four Forces

Over the last two thousand years one of the crowning achievements of physics has been the isolation and identification of the four forces that rule the universe. All of them can be described in the language of fields introduced by Faraday. Unfortunately, however, none of them has quite the properties of the force fields described in most science fiction. These forces are

1. *Gravity*, the silent force that keeps our feet on the ground, prevents the Earth and the stars from disintegrating, and holds the solar system and galaxy together. Without gravity, we would be flung off the Earth into space at the rate of 1,000 miles per hour by the spinning planet. The problem is that gravity has precisely the opposite properties of a force field found in science fiction. Gravity is

attractive, not repulsive; is extremely weak, relatively speaking; and works over enormous, astronomical distances. In other words, it is almost the opposite of the flat, thin, impenetrable barrier that one reads about in science fiction or one sees in science fiction movies. For example, it takes the entire planet Earth to attract a feather to the floor, but we can counteract Earth's gravity by lifting the feather with a finger. The action of our finger can counteract the gravity of an entire planet that weighs over six trillion trillion kilograms.

2. *Electromagnetism* (EM), the force that lights up our cities. Lasers, radio, TV, modern electronics, computers, the Internet, electricity, magnetism—all are consequences of the electromagnetic force. It is perhaps the most useful force ever harnessed by humans. Unlike gravity, it can be both attractive and repulsive. However, there are several reasons that it is unsuitable as a force field. First, it can be easily neutralized. Plastics and other insulators, for example, can easily penetrate a powerful electric or magnetic field. A piece of plastic thrown in a magnetic field would pass right through. Second, electromagnetism acts over large distances and cannot easily be focused onto a plane. The laws of the EM force are described by James Clerk Maxwell's equations, and these equations do not seem to admit force fields as solutions.

3 & 4. *The weak and strong nuclear forces.* The weak force is the force of radioactive decay. It is the force that heats up the center of the Earth, which is radioactive. It is the force behind volcanoes, earthquakes, and continental drift. The strong force holds the nucleus of the atom together. The energy of the sun and the stars originates from the nuclear force, which is responsible for lighting up the universe. The problem is that the nuclear force is a short-range force, acting mainly over the distance of a nucleus. Because it is so bound to the properties of nuclei, it is extremely hard to manipulate. At present the only ways we have of manipulating this force are to blow subatomic particles apart in atom smashers or to detonate atomic bombs.

Although the force fields used in science fiction may not conform to the known laws of physics, there are still loopholes that might make the creation of such a force field possible. First, there may be a fifth force, still unseen in the laboratory. Such a force might, for example, work over a distance of only a few inches to feet, rather than over astronomical distances. (Initial attempts to measure the presence of such a fifth force, however, have yielded negative results.)

Second, it may be possible to use a plasma to mimic some of the properties of a force field. A plasma is the "fourth state of matter." Solids, liquids, and gases make up the three familiar states of matter, but the most common form of matter in the universe is plasma, a gas of ionized atoms. Because the atoms of a plasma are ripped apart, with electrons torn off the atom, the atoms are electrically charged and can be easily manipulated by electric and magnetic fields.

Plasmas are the most plentiful form of visible matter in the universe, making up the sun, the stars, and interstellar gas. Plasmas are not familiar to us because they are only rarely found on the Earth, but we can see them in the form of lightning bolts, the sun, and the interior of your plasma TV.

Plasma Windows

As noted above, if a gas is heated to a high enough temperature, thereby creating a plasma, it can be molded and shaped by magnetic and electrical fields. It can, for example, be shaped in the form of a sheet or window. Moreover, this "plasma window" can be used to separate a vacuum from ordinary air. In principle, one might be able to prevent the air within a spaceship from leaking out into space, thereby creating a convenient, transparent interface between outer space and the spaceship.

In the *Star Trek* TV series, such a force field is used to separate the shuttle bay, containing small shuttle craft, from the vacuum of outer space. Not only is it a clever way to save money on props, but it is a device that is possible.

The plasma window was invented by physicist Ady Herschcovitch in 1995 at the Brookhaven National Laboratory in Long Island, New York. He developed it to solve the problem of how to weld metals using electron beams. A welder's acetylene torch uses a blast of hot gas to melt and then weld metal pieces together. But a beam of electrons can weld metals faster, cleaner, and more cheaply than ordinary methods. The problem with electron beam welding, however, is that it needs to be done in a vacuum. This requirement is quite inconvenient, because it means creating a vacuum box that may be as big as an entire room.

Dr. Herschcovitch invented the plasma window to solve this problem. Only 3 feet high and less than 1 foot in diameter, the plasma window heats gas to 12,000°F, creating a plasma that is trapped by electric and magnetic fields. These particles exert pressure, as in any gas, which prevents air from rushing into the vacuum chamber, thus separating air from the vacuum. (When one uses argon gas in the plasma window, it glows blue, like the force field in *Star Trek*.)

The plasma window has wide applications for space travel and industry. Many times, manufacturing processes need a vacuum to perform microfabrication and dry etching for industrial purposes, but working in a vacuum can be expensive. But with the plasma window one can cheaply contain a vacuum with the flick of a button.

But can the plasma window also be used as an impenetrable shield? Can it withstand a blast from a cannon? In the future, one can imagine a plasma window of much greater power and temperature, sufficient to damage or vaporize incoming projectiles. But to create a more realistic force field, like that found in science fiction, one would need a combination of several technologies stacked in layers. Each layer might not be strong enough alone to stop a cannon ball, but the combination might suffice.

The outer layer could be a supercharged plasma window, heated to temperatures high enough to vaporize metals. A second layer could be a curtain of high-energy laser beams. This curtain, containing thousands of crisscrossing laser beams, would create a lattice that would heat up objects that passed through it, effectively vaporizing them. . . .

And behind this laser curtain one might envision a lattice made of "carbon nanotubes," tiny tubes made of individual carbon atoms that are one atom thick and that are many times stronger than steel. Although the current world record for a carbon nanotube is only about 15 millimeters long, one can envision a day when we might be able to create carbon nanotubes of arbitrary length. Assuming that carbon nanotubes can be woven into a lattice, they could create a screen of enormous strength, capable of repelling most objects. The screen would be invisible, since each carbon nanotube is atomic in size, but the carbon nanotube lattice would be stronger than any ordinary material.

So, via a combination of plasma window, laser curtain, and carbon nanotube screen, one might imagine creating an invisible wall that would be nearly impenetrable by most means.

Yet even this multilayered shield would not completely fulfill all the properties of a science fiction force field—because it would be transparent and therefore incapable of stopping a laser beam. In a battle with laser cannons, the multilayered shield would be useless.

To stop a laser beam, the shield would also need to possess an advanced form of "photochromatics." This is the process used in sunglasses that darken by themselves upon exposure to UV radiation. Photochromatics are based on molecules that can exist in at least two states. In one state the molecule is transparent. But when it is exposed to UV radiation it instantly changes to the second form, which is opaque.

One day we might be able to use nanotechnology to produce a substance as tough as carbon nanotubes that can change its optical properties when exposed to laser light. In this way, a shield might be able to stop a laser blast as well as a particle beam or cannon fire. At present, however, photochromatics that can stop laser beams do not exist.

Magnetic Levitation

In science fiction, force fields have another purpose besides deflecting ray-gun blasts, and that is to serve as a platform to defy gravity. In the movie *Back to the Future*, Michael J. Fox rides a "hover board," which resembles a skateboard except that it floats over the street. Such an antigravity device is impossible given the laws of physics as we know them today. . . . But magnetically enhanced hover boards and hover cars could become a reality in the future, giving us the ability to levitate large objects at will. In the future, if "room- temperature superconductors" become a reality, one might be able to levitate objects using the power of magnetic force fields.

If we place two bar magnets next to each other with north poles opposite each other, the two magnets repel each other. (If we rotate the magnet, so that the north pole is close to the other south pole, then the two magnets attract each other.) This same principle, that north poles repel each other, can be used to lift enormous weights off the ground. Already several nations are building advanced magnetic levitation trains (maglev trains) that hover just above the railroad tracks using ordinary magnets. Because they have zero friction, they can attain record-breaking speeds, floating over a cushion of air.

In 1984 the world's first commercial automated maglev system began operation in the United Kingdom, running from Birmingham International Airport to the nearby Birmingham International railway station. Maglev trains have also been built in Germany, Japan, and Korea, although most of them have not been designed for high velocities. The first commercial maglev train operating at high velocities is the initial operating segment (IOS) demonstration line in Shanghai, which travels at a top speed of 268 miles per hour. The Japanese maglev train in Yamanashi prefecture attained a velocity of 361 miles per hour, even faster than the usual wheeled trains.

But these maglev devices are extremely expensive. One way to increase efficiency would be to use superconductors, which lose all electrical resistance when they are cooled down to near absolute zero. Superconductivity was discovered in 1911 by Heike Onnes. If certain substances are cooled to below 20 K above absolute zero, all electrical resistance is lost. Usually when we cool down the temperature of a metal, its resistance decreases gradually. (This is because random vibrations of the atom impede the flow of electrons in a wire. By reducing the temperature, these random motions are reduced, and hence electricity flows with less resistance.) But much to Onnes's surprise, he found that the resistance of certain materials fell abruptly to zero at a critical temperature.

Physicists immediately recognized the importance of this result. Power lines lose a significant amount of energy by transporting electricity across long distances. But if all resistance could be eliminated, electrical power could be transmitted almost for free. In fact, if electricity were made to circulate in a coil of wire, the electricity would circulate for millions of years, without any reduction in energy. Furthermore, magnets of incredible power could be made with little effort from these enormous electric currents. With these magnets, one could lift huge loads with ease.

Despite all these miraculous powers, the problem with superconductivity is that it is very expensive to immerse large magnets in vats of supercooled liquid. Huge refrigeration plants are required to keep liquids supercooled, making superconducting magnets prohibitively expensive.

But one day physicists may be able to create a "room-temperature superconductor," the holy grail of solid-state physicists. The invention of room-temperature superconductors in the laboratory would spark a second industrial revolution. Powerful magnetic fields capable of lifting cars and trains would become so cheap that hover cars might become economically feasible. With room-temperature superconductors, the fantastic flying cars seen in *Back to the Future, Minority Report,* and *Star Wars* might become a reality.

In principle, one might be able to wear a belt made of superconducting magnets that would enable one to effortlessly levitate off the ground. With such a belt, one could fly in the air like Superman. Room-temperature superconductors are so remarkable that they appear in numerous science fiction novels (such as the Ringworld series written by Larry Niven in 1970).

For decades physicists have searched for room-temperature superconductors without success. It has been a tedious, hit-or-miss process, testing one material after another. But in 1986 a new class of substances called "high-temperature superconductors" was found that became superconductors at about 90 degrees above absolute zero, or 90 K, creating a sensation in the world of physics. The floodgates seemed to open. Month after month, physicists raced one another to break the next world's record for a superconductor. For a brief moment it seemed as if the possibility of room-temperature superconductors would leap off the pages of science fiction novels and into our living rooms. But after a few years of moving at breakneck speed, research in high-temperature superconductors began to slow down.

At present the world's record for a high-temperature superconductor is held by a substance called mercury thallium barium calcium copper oxide, which becomes superconducting at 138 K (–135°C). This relatively high temperature is still a long way from room temperature. But this 138 K record is still important. Nitrogen liquefies at 77 K, and liquid nitrogen costs about as much as ordinary milk. Hence ordinary liquid nitrogen could be used to cool down these high-temperature superconductors rather cheaply. (Of course, room-temperature superconductors would need no cooling whatsoever.)

Embarrassingly enough, at present there is no theory explaining the properties of these high-temperature superconductors. In fact, a Nobel Prize is awaiting the enterprising physicist who can explain how high-temperature superconductors work. (These high-temperature superconductors are made of atoms arranged in distinctive layers. Many physicists theorize that this layering of the ceramic material makes it possible for electrons to flow freely within each layer, creating a superconductor. But precisely how this is done is still a mystery.)

Because of this lack of knowledge, physicists unfortunately resort to a hit-or-miss procedure to search for new high-temperature superconductors. This means that the fabled room-temperature superconductor may be discovered tomorrow, next year, or not at all. No one knows when, or if, such a substance will ever be found.

But if room-temperature superconductors are discovered, a tidal wave of commercial applications could be set off. Magnetic fields that are a million times more powerful than the Earth's magnetic field (which is .5 gauss) might become commonplace.

One common property of superconductivity is called the Meissner effect. If you place a magnet above a superconductor, the magnet will levitate, as if held upward by some invisible force. (The reason for the Meissner effect is that the magnet has the effect of creating a "mirror-image" magnet within the superconductor, so that the original magnet and the mirror-image magnet repel each other. Another way to see this is that magnetic fields cannot penetrate into a superconductor. Instead, magnetic fields are expelled. So if a magnet is held above a superconductor, its lines of force are expelled by the superconductor, and the lines of force then push the magnet upward, causing it to levitate.)

Using the Meissner effect, one can imagine a future in which the highways are made of these special ceramics. Then magnets placed in our belts or our tires could enable us to magically float to our destination, without any friction or energy loss.

The Meissner effect works only on magnetic materials, such as metals. But it is also possible to use superconducting magnets to levitate nonmagnetic materials, called paramagnets and diamagnets. These substances do not have magnetic properties of their own; they acquire their magnetic properties only in the presence of an external magnetic field. Paramagnets are attracted by an external magnet, while diamagnets are repelled by an external magnet.

Water, for example, is a diamagnet. Since all living things are made of water, they can levitate in the presence of a powerful magnetic field. In a magnetic field of about 15 teslas (30,000 times the Earth's field), scientists have levitated small animals, such as frogs. But if room-temperature superconductors become a reality, it should be possible to levitate large nonmagnetic objects as well, via their diamagnetic property.

In conclusion, force fields as commonly described in science fiction do not fit the description of the four forces of the universe. Yet it may be possible to simulate many of the properties of force fields by using a multilayered shield, consisting of plasma windows, laser curtains, carbon nanotubes, and photochromatics. But developing such a shield could be many decades, or even a century, away. And if room-temperature superconductors can be found, one might be able to use powerful magnetic fields to levitate cars and trains and soar in the air, as in science fiction movies.

Given these considerations, I would classify force fields as a Class I impossibility—that is, something that is impossible by today's technology, but possible, in modified form, within a century or so.

Reading the Genre

1. Kaku explains concepts on the cutting edge of theoretical physics. What strategies does he use to make these ideas understandable for readers who can't count themselves among the smartest scientists in the world? (See "Write for novices," p. 116.)

2. At several points in this essay, a scientist is evaluating science fiction. What is the effect of reading an evaluation of popular culture by a serious scientist? How does the writer establish *ethos*, or authority to analyze texts that are not in his field of expertise? How might you do the same in your own writing? (See "Consider and control your ethos," p. 82, and "Consider its use of rhetorical appeals," p. 260.)

3. What qualities does Kaku suggest are necessary for force fields to become possible? How does he state these criteria and then apply them? How does he try to convince readers that these are valid criteria? (See "Finding and developing materials," p. 117.)

4. Aside from the idea that having a force field would be fun, what uses (good or evil) does Kaku envision for this technology? What additional uses can you imagine?

5. **WRITING:** Choose a technology you use every day. Then write an imaginary evaluation based not on what this technology is capable of now, but on what it might be capable of in the future. What might cell phones or televisions do ten years from now, for instance?

6. **WRITING:** Create an advertisement for a force field. Your advertisement should explain the technology and markets and describe a way consumers might use the force field. You could make the advertisement in the form of a poster, a script for a television commercial, or an audio-recorded radio spot.

TECHNOLOGY REVIEW   Sasha Frere-Jones is a staff writer and pop-music critic for the *New Yorker* and the lifestyle and culture editor for the *Daily*, a newspaper that readers can access only through iPads. He is also an experimental photographer and a practicing musician. In this essay, first published in the June 14, 2010, issue of the *New Yorker*, he considers the changing shape of music broadcasting.

You, the D.J.

Online Music Moves to the Cloud

SASHA FRERE-JONES

No one knows what the future of the music business will look like, but the near future of *listening* to music looks a lot like 1960. People will listen, for free, to music that comes out of a stationary box that sits indoors. They'll listen to music that comes from an object that fits in the hand, and they'll listen to music in the car. That box was once a radio or a stereo; now it's a computer. The hand-held device that was once a plastic AM radio is now likely to be a smart phone. The car is still a car, though its stereo now plays satellite radio and MP3s. But behind the similarities is a series of subtle shifts in software and portability that may relocate the experience of listening—even if nobody has come close to replacing the concept of the radio d.j., whose job lingers as a template for much software.

"Of the twenty hours a week that an average American spends listening to music, only three of it is stuff you own. The rest is radio," Tim Westergren told me. Westergren is the founder of Pandora, one of several firms that have brought the radio model to the Internet. Pandora offers free, streaming music, not so different from the radio stations that many people grew up with, except that the d.j. is you, more or less. The company does not sell music—like normal radio, Internet radio is considered a promotional tool for recordings, even though the fees that it pays to labels are currently higher than those paid by terrestrial stations.

If you go to Pandora, on the Web or on a phone, you begin by picking a song or an artist, which then establishes a "station." Pandora's proprietary algorithm, in which a panel of musicians assesses about four hundred variables, like "bravado level in vocals" and "piano style," for each song, leads you from what you chose to a song that seems to fit with it, musically. You also have the option to teach the algorithm, by giving a song a thumbs up or a thumbs down. The company has captured a very large chunk of the Internet-radio audience—the service now has fifty million users, who listen an average of more than eleven hours a month.

The Pandora experience isn't much like being guided by a d.j. on a radio station—at least, not yet. (That delicious unpredictability is now approximated by the thousands of mixtapes and podcasts that are released by individuals on the Web, free of charge, every day.) I started my station with Public Image Ltd's "Poptones," a 1979 song that is loaded with bass, dissonant guitar, and the sinus bray of John Lydon, once known as Johnny Rotten. The band's sound is deeply indebted to reggae—the original bassist was named Jah Wobble—but I couldn't make a reggae song appear on my Poptones station. I did get lots of bands I like: the Minutemen, the Birthday Party, and Fugazi, who all make aggressive music that, like Public Image's, is heavy on articulate rhythm and acidic guitar.

After skipping six songs, I received this message on my iPhone app: "Sorry, our music licenses force us to limit the number of songs you may skip." Pandora is acting like a radio station, not like a replacement for a potential sale—you can't keep skipping until it plays what you want.

On a recent car trip I took through Florida, Pandora was perfect: I plugged in my phone, hit a couple of buttons, and was rewarded with ninety minutes of instrumental hip-hop.

The most popular alternative to the broadcast model is "on demand," which usually charges a subscription fee in return for the ability to choose exactly which song you'd like to hear. In Europe, the most prominent such service is Spotify, a Swedish company that has grown rapidly in the past year. In America, where Spotify has yet to début, one of the biggest on-demand players is MOG, a new service that offers a wide array of listening options, the least expensive of which costs five dollars a month. MOG offers the option of streaming 320-kilobyte-per-second files, the highest available digital quality, though customers have been reluctant to pay extra for greater audio fidelity.

With MOG, you can play entire albums, create playlists, or let the service perform the same kind of algorithmic radio function that Pandora provides. (While listening to a song, you pull a slider all the way to the right; the software suggests related artists and tracks.) You can also share playlists with other users. I looked up the German rock band Can, and saw, on the right side of my Web browser, a small box called "Popular Playlists Featuring Can." I clicked on one playlist called "Irritation Mix," created by a user named Scotfree, whose avatar picture looks like Iron Man. The Can track included was the spacey instrumental "Spray," from the 1973 album *Future Days*. The rest of the playlist leaned on seventies rock—the Faces, Mott the Hoople, Iggy & the Stooges—but used recent tracks to keep things pleasantly unpredictable: Lady Sovereign's bubbly dance track "Blah Blah" and a track called "Johnny Depp," by the sixties revivalists Chocolat, from Montreal.

I didn't care for a few of the songs, but the experience was much more like grappling with a d.j. than like watching a piece of software operate. I learned about two bands I didn't know, was reminded of beloved tracks I had forgotten, and didn't listen to anything I already had in mind. Scotfree's playlist didn't last as long as a good d.j.'s shift; the burden is on the user to find other appealing users and more lists, and to build the experience. In some ways, it's an improvement on the radio model: the number of potentially appealing d.j.s here dwarfs what you might have once found on radio.

The broadcast and on-demand models are governed by different rules, but they share one important feature: neither depends on downloading files or finding storage space on a personal computer. Lurking behind these models are two enormous companies that will likely change the landscape of online audio in a matter of months: Google and Apple. Google will soon offer a streaming music service for its Android phone that, like all of these services, uses the increasingly vital concept of the cloud—your music is all on a server, which you can access from any computer or smart phone, with little trouble and no wires. Apple, whose iTunes store is the biggest music retailer in America, bought the online streaming service Lala last year and then promptly shut it down. This suggests that there may soon be an iTunes.com, a Web-based streaming system that will leave behind the model of buying discrete tracks. In music's new model, fees are charged not necessarily so that you can physically possess a file but so that you can have that song whenever you want it.

An album "collection" is no longer relevant for many listeners. Limited only by the number of songs offered by any service—MOG offers nearly eight million—they can create as many playlists as they like, and access them from almost any device. Whoever comes up with the most powerful and elegant version of the streaming model will have a very big portal. If iTunes becomes a dominant radio force, it could control an overwhelming portion of the music business. Google owns YouTube, which already serves as a sort of ad-hoc radio station for many young people. If Google's streaming service works well with its Android applications and creates a music-bundling system, it, too, could take over a large share of the market.

While using these services, I kept thinking about an early-eighties drum machine called the Roland TR-808, which has seduced generations of musicians with its heavy kick-drum sound and the oddly human swing of its clock. Whoever programmed this box had more impact on dance music than the hundreds of better-known musicians who used the device. Similarly, the anonymous programmers who write the algorithms that control the series of songs in these streaming services may end up having a huge effect on the way that people think of musical narrative—what follows what, and who sounds best with whom. Sometimes we will be the d.j.s, and sometimes the machines will be, and we may be surprised by which we prefer.

Reading the Genre

1. Because the author is evaluating relatively new technologies, he needs to explain how those technologies work. How does he do so? Are his explanations accessible and understandable? Could the explanations be improved? (See "Understanding your audience," p. 115.)

2. How does Frere-Jones test the services he evaluates? How does he use his personal experience to support his assertions?

3. This evaluation examines the functions of music delivery systems but glosses over the motivations people might have for using them. How important is it to consider motivation for any electronic medium — such as e-mail, text messaging, social networking, and so on? Do different people have different uses for the same technologies and different reasons for using them? (See Chapter 51, "Understanding Digital Media," p. 568, and Chapter 52, "Digital Elements," p. 577.)

4. Frere-Jones makes at least one assumption in this essay: that his readers share his musical tastes. But do they? Choose one of Frere-Jones's criteria for evaluation and explain why you agree or disagree with it. (See "Establish and defend criteria," p. 108, and Chapter 22, "Critical Thinking," p. 372.)

5. **WRITING:** How do *you* listen to music? Write an evaluation of the technologies and devices that you use most often to listen to music.

6. **WRITING:** This essay evaluates several new technologies against one old one. Create a chart that lists the positive and negative qualities Frere-Jones cites for each method of listening to music. Does any one method emerge as the best option? (See "Compare and contrast," p. 123.)

TELEVISION REVIEW   Nelle Engoron is a freelance writer and editor. She blogs about television, movies, and related topics for Open Salon, a reader forum hosted by *Salon.com* (http://open.salon.com/blog/silkstone).

Salon.com

Posted: Friday, July 23, 2010, at 8:10 ET
From: Nelle Engoron

Why *Mad Men* Is Bad for Women

I've Championed the Show for Its Smart Depiction of Sexism — but as the Fourth Season Approaches, I'm Not so Sure

As a child of the 1950s and '60s who entered the workforce in the still-discriminatory '70s, I have deeply appreciated *Mad Men*'s frank and searing depiction of women's lives both at home and at work. Created by enormously talented and

meticulous artists, *Mad Men* often feels so real and compelling to those of us who lived through those times that watching it sometimes revives painful memories.

But as we approach the start of the fourth season, I fear that I've been wrong about its treatment of womanhood. The message that many women, especially those under 40, seem to have taken from the show is not relief or gratitude at what's changed, nor an understanding of the past, but something quite different: Those fashions are cool! God, Don's hot! Are you a Joan or a Peggy? Let's dress up like them, have a *Mad Men* party, and drink martinis!

I'm also increasingly disturbed by the striking difference in how men and women are portrayed — all the more curious and distressing since, although it was created by a man (Matthew Weiner), *Mad Men* is notable for the number of women on its creative staff. Even as it depicts rampant sexism, the show sides with the men. The men get off scot-free (if not scotch-free) while the women are subjected to repeated humiliation and misfortune, which is invariably attributed to their own flaws and poor choices.

In the skilled hands of *Mad Men*'s writers, directors, and the actor Jon Hamm, Don Draper is a complex and alluring character who continues to win our sympathy despite his frequent affairs, excessive drinking, rough handling of women, and outright desertions of his family. His callous treatment of his wife, whose suspicions he dismisses as paranoia, whose desires for connection he spurns, and whose grief at the loss of her mother he deems worthy of psychiatric treatment, is just short of despicable. Don doesn't merely deceive Betty; he also belittles her, playing mind games to get her to doubt herself rather than him.

And yet Don is the suave hero of the show, enjoying an uncanny creativity, a successful and lucrative career, a succession of beautiful women who fall into his arms, and a wife who initially forgives and embraces him when he spills all his secrets (although she does change her mind not long afterward). As the famous *Saturday Night Live* parody, "Don Draper's Guide to Women," astutely pointed out, his magnetism — despite the show's historical realism — is a James Bond fantasy. It is only in the penultimate episode of the third season that Don seems in any danger of being penalized for his transgressions.

The other men on the show are equally flawed and yet suffer very little. Roger Sterling is a raging alcoholic who abandons the loyal wife who stands up to him in order to marry a pretty young thing who lies down for him. Personifying the rich boy who is "born on third base and thinks he hit a triple," Roger's sole talent, for converting Stoli into lewd comments, is portrayed as catnip not just for clients but even put-upon secretaries. While Don's darkness is used to seduce the viewer, Roger provides comic relief, his open sexism and racism played strictly for laughs. So far Roger's only punishment has been a couple of heart attacks that not only didn't slow him down but actually rejuvenated him and drove him into the arms of a sultry young trophy wife.

Another rich boy, Pete Campbell, publicly demeans Peggy on her first day of work, a tactic that mysteriously causes her to sleep with him not long afterward, thus consigning her to a secret pregnancy and hidden torment. Pete thoughtlessly cheats on the wife who obviously loves him, apparently rapes a neighbor's au pair, breezes through his days in expense-account-fueled meetings with clients — while constantly whining about how life isn't fair to him. Upon finding out about his child with Peggy and having her reject his offer of love, he is temporarily dazed but then grows closer to the wife who adores him, forging what increasingly looks like a marriage of like-minded souls.

While some of the lesser male characters are more appealing — the gaffe-prone Harry in particular (although even he cheats on his wife) or even the terminally shallow but good-natured Ken Cosgrove (who we just know is headed for corporate success) — the only truly sympathetic male character is a gay man, Sal Romano, in large part because he is suffering oppression as well. Yet even Sal is guilty of marrying a woman under false pretenses and making her feel inadequate when he doesn't love her the way she does him.

Hardly an admirable portrait of manhood, and yet the costs to the men of their bad behavior seem minimal — other than of course for Sal, who loses his job due to sexual harassment (thus dramatically co-opting a fate usually endured by women). By contrast, the women not only suffer but also do so with the clear message that the fault lies not in society, but in themselves.

Betty has always represented the *Feminine Mystique*-era woman, privileged yet imprisoned by the restrictions of her life. Beautiful enough to have been a professional model, fluent in Italian, and possessing a degree from Bryn Mawr, she nonetheless knew she had to marry before her sell-by date arrived and to produce children even if she didn't really want them. After all, what were the alternatives? To stay single and be a waitress, teacher, or secretary? To have only furtive sexual relationships in order to avoid social disapproval and to constantly worry about an unwanted pregnancy? To give up on having children even if you wanted them but didn't want a husband? No, understandably enough, Betty made the same choice that most women did: selling her sexual appeal to gain financial security and ensure social approval.

But our sympathy for Betty is undermined by the extreme simplicity of her character, which is that of a child in a beautiful woman's body. How much more powerful would this show be if she were a smarter, more mature woman who found herself trapped in suburban hell, instead of a shallow princess who can't come up with more than "I have thoughts" when composing a love letter and who consistently behaves like a petulant 5-year-old, albeit one armed with a cigarette and a glass of wine?

Being stuck in a life of mind-numbing domesticity is tragic only when the person is capable of — and desirous of — much more. But Betty seems less limited by her situation than by her intellect and character. We have no sense of what she'd do with her life if she hadn't married, other than perhaps be a Holly Golightly party girl in Europe. Even when she finally leaves Don, it's not to become independent but only to go to another man who wants to marry her and take care of her every little need.

While the pressures of the traditional maternal role deserve serious examination, Betty's coldness to her children (other than her new baby) repels any sympathy we might have. She takes no joy in her children, snapping at them to behave and thoughtlessly passing on her own repressive conditioning, like when she shuts down her daughter's grief at her beloved grandfather's death. Superficial and self-focused, Betty seems to enjoy very little, other than sex and the occasional party or jaunt to Italy — even her horseback riding is a clenched affair full of frustration and anger. Such unrelieved negativity undercuts the very real sufferings of women in her era, making Betty an ungrateful, whiny princess rather than an example of how even privilege can be a prison when it is challenge and autonomy that you desire instead.

Unlike Betty, Peggy chose a career, progressing from the "new girl in the office" to the New Woman just beginning to appear in the business world. But Peggy's success has been shrouded not only by what she has been given to endure — a secret pregnancy that left her nearly catatonic and locked in a mental ward, the surrender of her baby, the gibes of sexist co-workers, the fumbling and hostile attentions of Pete, and most humiliatingly of all, having sex with a man named Duck — but also by how her character has been constructed.

While smart, creative, and brave, Peggy isn't allowed to be a full, rounded person and is instead portrayed as socially inept, humorless, and utterly unable to connect with either men or women, remaining friendless and loveless. Her stiffness, introversion, and social missteps are painful to watch, and her awkward attempts to be more "feminine" fall flat. In the third season, she was finally allowed a measure of sexual satisfaction, but only in a tawdry, loveless connection with a repugnant older man. Denied a satisfying romantic life, she lives to work and is molding herself into a female Don Draper, but minus the spouse and kids.

Yet instead of being a biting commentary on the social strictures of the time — when women truly did have to choose between the rare opportunity of a professional career and marriage and family — Peggy's isolation is portrayed as the logical result of her social clumsiness and ambition. She's not penalized for her choices (a valid historical point) but instead seems to be making the best use of a stunted personality by forging a career rather than ending up a lonely old maid. Watching her, I've increasingly wondered why we can't have an attractive, happy, fully sexual, intelligent female character with a great personality on this show?

Which brings me to Joan.

There's no way around it: Joan starts out the show as a bitch. In the first episode, she suggests that Peggy go home, cut eyeholes in a paper bag, put it over her head, and figure out what she needs to change about herself. Ouch.

But Joan is also portrayed as the one woman who has power. The classic queen bee of a female workplace, Joan rules the secretarial pool with a manicured hand, her prow of a bust gliding through the office like a warship going into battle. She rules the waves, both permanent and rollered, and takes no crap from anyone. What has made Joan delicious to many women is the way she handles the men on the show, her honey-eyed tones belying the razor-sharp put-downs she doles out not just to dazzled office boys but to the firm's partners. And yet Joan is also impeccably professional, handling clients as adroitly as any accounts man, and keeping the office running as smoothly as Mussolini's trains.

Perhaps most satisfyingly of all, Joan is initially portrayed as being as fully in control of her sexuality as she is the rest of her life. Carrying on a secret affair with Roger, she resists his attempts to confine her (symbolized by that bird in a cage he gives her), insisting on staying a free woman who chooses what — or who — she wants to do.

Unlike the other secretaries, she doesn't seem confined by her female-ghetto job, but triumphant in it. We believe her when she tells Peggy that she wouldn't want her copywriter position.

Joan's contentment is disturbed when she gets a chance to do media work and discovers that she's a natural at it. Yet as quickly as the opportunity to use her talents is given, it's taken away, and she faces the classic career bitch-slap of having to train a younger guy to do the same job, and for more money. So far, a great little history lesson about women's struggles at work to gain recognition.

But both Joan's discovery of her ambition and her disappointment are soon pushed to the side by the other development that's been scripted for her, which is to give up her satisfying single life and marry a handsome young doctor. In perhaps the most wrenching event of the entire series, not only is there no happy ending for Joan, but her supposedly "perfect" fiancé rapes her on the floor of Don's office in retaliation for what he senses about her sexual past. The free bird's wings have been clipped, if not broken.

At this point, Joan could have both retained her autonomy and restored her dignity by dumping the guy. But no, she married him. And continues to apparently love him as well as literally support him, after his promising career fizzles out. Many women have made the choice to stick with even more violent men, but this is "our Joanie" (as fans often call her), a strong woman who seemed the least likely person to take anything lying down, much less rape. We expected her to find the nearest letter opener and do a little surgery on Dr. Cut-Up, or failing that, at least leave the jerk. The one woman who had a career, autonomy, and a satisfying sex life is punished as surely as if we were reading *The Scarlet Letter*. Even worse, she embraces not only her punishment but also her punisher.

Of the minor female characters on the show — the vapid Jane who finds blackface hysterical, the hapless amateur chiropodist Lois, the succession of giggly secretaries so inept they can barely answer phones, the catty and racist housewives — the less said the better. Ironically, a show that has launched a slew of fashion trends has also made womanhood seem singularly unattractive. The men triumph despite who they are and what they do, while the women suffer as a result of both their character and their choices. The men are mad, all right, but the women on this show are increasingly crazy-making. I may need that martini, after all.

Reading the Genre

1. Engoron's evaluation begins with an appreciation of the positive qualities of the television series *Mad Men*. How does this strategy help to establish her *ethos*? How does praising some parts of the show allow Engoron to be more critical in later parts of the essay? (See "Consider its use of rhetorical appeals," p. 260, and Chapter 22, "Critical Thinking," p. 372.)

2. At what points in her essay does Engoron rely on literary analysis to evaluate the success of *Mad Men*? (See Chapter 7, "Literary Analyses," p. 206.) What other aspects of the show would lend themselves to this strategy? Pick one such aspect and write a paragraph analyzing it as though it were literature.

3. What is Engoron's underlying assumption about how television characters (especially women) should be depicted? What criteria does she use to determine if the depiction of characters is fair, and how does she support these criteria? (See "Establish and defend criteria," p. 108 and Chapter 22, "Critical Thinking," p. 372.)

4. Has your opinion of any television show changed over time? How has your opinion changed? Form a thesis statement that states how your opinion has changed about this television show. (See Chapter 26, "Thesis," p. 393 and "Expect your thesis to mature," p. 394.)

5. **WRITING:** Choose a television show that depicts your own generation and evaluate it based on what it says about gender roles. Concentrate on characters one at a time, as Engoron does. Does this show do a good or bad job of representing you and your peers? Why do you think so?

CONCERT REVIEW   Ann Powers, a music critic for National Public Radio, has also written for the *Los Angeles Times, New York Times,* and *Village Voice.* Her books include *Weird Like Us: My Bohemian America; Piece by Piece,* which she cowrote with musician Tori Amos; and *Rock She Wrote: Women Write about Rock, Pop, and Rap,* which she coedited. This article first appeared on the *Los Angeles Times* music blog.

Pop & Hiss

Posted: August 12, 2010, at 9:06 AM
From: Ann Powers

Live Review:
Lady Gaga at Staples Center

When Lady Gaga breathes, it's an event. That's not just hyperbole. The pop art star's gasps, coming fast and frequent as she stopped to pose during her Staples Center concert Wednesday, played an important role in her performance.

The sound of Gaga's exertion kept things real, on a gut level, despite the many fantastical outfits, elaborate sets, and dreamlike films featured in this arena-sized reworking of her Monster Ball show. It reminded the audience that this self-created freak deity is also a woman working hard, testing the limits of her 24-year-old body. Panting, sweating, even sometimes breaking into a little sob, Gaga continually shattered the fancy frames she puts around her music, stepping through the fantasy to force an encounter with the "very naked girl with a foul mouth" who still lives, she insists, within those intricate costumes.

Since the Monster Ball last came to Los Angeles last December in its Nokia Theatre-sized version, Gaga and her collaborators have grown the sets and expanded the show's arc. The arena setup allowed the star and her dancers to writhe and shimmy on a ramp in the midst of the crowd, providing up-close views of her Barbie Fairytopia-on-acid outfit, her sequined biker chick unitard, and her patent leather espionage ensemble, to name a few. As she moved through her many hits — "Poker Face," "Bad Romance," "Just Dance," and "Alejandro" among them — the main stage housed props like a steaming yellow taxi and a mini-subway train, as well as Gaga's lascivious dancers and her cartoonishly hard rocking band.

When it was first mounted in theaters, the Monster Ball was an impression-istic journey into Gaga's fluorescent subconscious, with a strong moral: Embrace individuality and practice compassion to gain happiness. Standing up for the com-munity of "freaks" — club kids, drag queens, metalheads, free thinkers in gen-eral — with whom she identifies, Gaga presented herself as the glorious spawn of the cultural underground's long, daring history, crediting her fans (her "Little Mon-sters") for building the bohemias that nurtured her.

The revamped show has a firmer storyline, not unlike the one employed by Rihanna this same summer. The Bajan singer's show invoked dreams; Gaga's is more like a fairy tale. Over two hours, she and her dancers journeyed through a neon-lit New York alleyway, onto a subway train, through a spooky forest, and into a kind of church, where Gaga sacrificed herself in baptismal fake blood while decrying religious bigotry. Finally, she faced a toothy giant octopus — the "Fame Monster" of her second album's title — and emerged triumphantly as Cinderella of her own grand fete.

Some elements remained from the older staging of the Monster Ball, notably the films that took over when Gaga disappeared to change her costumes. She's switched out her costumes, of course — to not do so would be to fail her fans, who crave her sartorial genius nearly as much as they love her gift for pop hooks. On one level, Gaga is a drag performer, with one silver boot in a half-hidden world of gay and lesbian gender-benders and the other in the more mainstream realms of glam rock and fash-ion diva-tude. Her explicit identification with the gay, lesbian, bisexual, and transgen-der community is a step into the light that shows how things have changed in the course of Gaga's lifetime; what Madonna said less directly in her videos and songs, her inheritor now can scream.

The Staples Center Monster Ball made clear how much that scream belongs to classic rock, and how in future projects she may begin to redefine that genre. There's a bit of Courtney Love in Gaga's rougher rock voice, and singing her power ballads "Speech-less" and "You and I" — in a sequence at a flaming piano that was a high point of the performance — she occasionally recalled Steven Tyler of Aerosmith. Gaga writes excel-lent danceable pop hits, but when her material takes on a rock edge, it seems to open her up. Her piano may spew flames, but that effect isn't necessary when she's simply pouring out her heart on one of her more direct power ballads.

Now that she has achieved her goal of staging a visually unforgettable spectacle, it might be wise of Gaga to focus on that less posed, though still flamboyant, aspect of her talent. The problems with the Monster Ball remain ones that afflict giant pop productions: The pacing suffered greatly from too many breaks for costume changes, and too often, the prerecorded music such productions nearly always require during dance-heavy sequences took over and Gaga's vocals were either obscured or seemingly absent. A talented vocalist, Gaga needs to figure out how to manage to really deliver in concert. If her new material allows, she might become more of a traditional rock-style performer — and rewrite rock's rules while she's at it. We'll see when she returns to Staples Center in March of 2011.

For this summer, though, the Monster Ball, which will also fill Staples tonight, stands as enough of an achievement. Turning the phrase, "You look fabulous!" into a rallying cry, Gaga spun a wild web around her basic message of love and tolerance, but the essence was surprisingly simple. "I don't want you to leave loving me more," she said. "I want you to leave loving yourself more." In other words, Little Monsters, just breathe.

Reading the Genre

1. As an evaluation of a live concert, this essay focuses on more than just the music. In fact, Powers hardly talks about Lady Gaga's music at all. What does she evaluate, then? (See "Decide on your criteria," p. 117 and Chapter 22, "Critical Thinking," p. 372.)

2. How does Powers compare and contrast in this essay? Who does Powers compare Lady Gaga to, and how do these references help Powers make an argument? (See "Compare and contrast," p. 123, and Chapter 27, "Strategies," p. 398.)

3. Lady Gaga's concerts draw huge audiences. But how does Powers identify exactly who might be in this audience? What does this identification do for her evaluation?

4. **WRITING:** Powers focuses on one motif in this review: breath. She starts the essay and ends it by discussing breathing. Lady Gaga's breathing, panting, sobbing, screaming, the "rallying cry" of the audience—these elements lend the essay a feeling, even a soundtrack. Go online and view a performance yourself: a concert or poetry reading or freestyle rap or dance routine. Then, as Powers does, choose one detail to focus on. Look just at a dancer's feet, or turn the sound off and zoom in on a performer's eyes as he or she reads a poem. Write about just this one detail, and try to argue why this one detail is important to the performance.

5. **VIDEO:** Building on the writing you do for question 4, use video-editing software to cut out everything but what you want to focus on—that breathing, those eyes or those feet, perhaps—and accompany your writing with this new video.

Causal Analyses: Readings

70

TECHNOLOGY ANALYSIS
Nicholas Carr, *Is Google Making Us Stupid?* 800

CULTURAL ANALYSIS
Natalie Angier, *Almost Before We Spoke, We Swore* 811

CULTURAL ANALYSIS
Alex Williams, *Here I Am Taking My Own Picture* 818

CAUSAL ANALYSIS
Virginia Postrel, *Pop Psychology* 823

EXPLORATORY ESSAY
Tricia Rose, *Hip Hop Causes Violence* 829

See also Chapter 5:
CAUSAL ANALYSIS
Jonah Goldberg, *Global Warming and the Sun,* 141
RESEARCH STUDY
Kyu-heong Kim, *Bending the Rules for ESL Writers,* 157
EXPLORATORY ESSAY
Liza Mundy, *What's Really behind the Plunge in Teen Pregnancy?* 165
CULTURAL ANALYSIS
Charles Paul Freund, *The Politics of Pants,* 170

TECHNOLOGY ANALYSIS   Information-technology writer Nicholas Carr is the author of *Does IT Matter?* (2004) and *The Big Switch* (2009). His most recent book, *The Shallows* (2010), investigates "what the Internet is doing to our brains." The following article on the same subject sparked a great deal of debate when it first appeared in the *Atlantic* in 2008.

Is Google Making Us Stupid?

What the Internet Is Doing to Our Brains

NICHOLAS CARR

"**D**ave, stop. Stop, will you? Stop, Dave. Will you stop, Dave?" So the supercomputer HAL pleads with the implacable astronaut Dave Bowman in a famous and weirdly poignant scene toward the end of Stanley Kubrick's *2001: A Space Odyssey*. Bowman, having nearly been sent to a deep-space death by the malfunctioning machine, is calmly, coldly disconnecting the memory circuits that control its artificial "brain." "Dave, my mind is going," HAL says, forlornly. "I can feel it. I can feel it."

I can feel it, too. Over the past few years I've had an uncomfortable sense that someone, or something, has been tinkering with my brain, remapping the neural circuitry, reprogramming the memory. My mind isn't going—so far as I can tell—but it's changing. I'm not thinking the way I used to think. I can feel it most strongly when I'm reading. Immersing myself in a book or a lengthy article used to be easy. My mind would get caught up in the narrative or the turns of the argument, and I'd spend hours strolling through long stretches of prose. That's rarely the case anymore. Now my concentration often starts to drift after two or three pages. I get fidgety, lose the thread, begin looking for something else to do. I feel as if I'm always dragging my wayward brain back to the text. The deep reading that used to come naturally has become a struggle.

I think I know what's going on. For more than a decade now, I've been spending a lot of time online, searching and surfing and sometimes adding to the great databases of the Internet. The Web has been a godsend to me as a writer. Research that once required days in the stacks or periodical rooms of libraries can now be done in minutes. A few Google searches, some quick clicks on hyperlinks, and I've got the telltale fact or pithy quote I was after. Even when I'm not working, I'm as likely as not to be foraging in the Web's info-thickets, reading and writing e-mails, scanning headlines and blog posts, watching videos and listening to podcasts, or just tripping from link to link to link. (Unlike footnotes, to which they're sometimes likened, hyperlinks don't merely point to related works; they propel you toward them.)

For me, as for others, the Net is becoming a universal medium, the conduit for most of the information that flows through my eyes and ears and into my mind. The advantages of having immediate access to such an incredibly rich store of information are many, and they've been widely described and duly applauded. "The perfect recall of silicon memory," *Wired's* Clive Thompson has written, "can be an enormous boon to thinking." But that boon comes at a price. As the media theorist Marshall McLuhan pointed out in the 1960s, media are not just passive channels of information. They supply the stuff of thought, but they also shape the process of thought. And what the Net seems to be doing is chipping away my capacity for concentration and contemplation. My mind now expects to take in information the way the Net distributes it: in a swiftly moving stream of particles. Once I was a scuba diver in the sea of words. Now I zip along the surface like a guy on a Jet Ski.

I'm not the only one. When I mention my troubles with reading to friends and acquaintances—literary types, most of them—many say they're having similar experiences. The more they use the Web, the more they have to fight to stay focused on long pieces of writing. Some of the bloggers I follow have also begun mentioning the phenomenon. Scott Karp, who writes a blog about online media, recently confessed that he has stopped reading books altogether. "I was a lit major in college, and used to be [a] voracious book reader," he wrote. "What happened?" He speculates on the answer: "What if I do all my reading on the web not so much because the way I read has changed, i.e. I'm just seeking convenience, but because the way I THINK has changed?"

Bruce Friedman, who blogs regularly about the use of computers in medicine, also has described how the Internet has altered his mental habits. "I now have almost totally lost the ability to read and absorb a longish article on the web or in print," he wrote earlier this year. A pathologist who has long been on the faculty of the University of Michigan Medical School, Friedman elaborated on his comment in a telephone conversation with me. His thinking, he said, has taken on a "staccato" quality, reflecting the way he quickly scans short passages of text from many sources online. "I can't read *War and Peace* anymore," he admitted. "I've lost the ability to do that. Even a blog post of more than three or four paragraphs is too much to absorb. I skim it."

Anecdotes alone don't prove much. And we still await the long-term neurological and psychological experiments that will provide a definitive picture of how Internet use affects cognition. But a recently published study of online research habits, conducted by scholars from University College London, suggests that we may well be in the midst of a sea change in the way we read and think. As part of the five-year research program, the scholars examined computer logs documenting the behavior of visitors to two popular research sites, one operated by the British Library and one by a U.K. educational consortium, that provide access to journal articles, e-books, and other sources of written information. They found that people using the sites exhibited "a form of skimming activity," hopping from one source to another and rarely returning to any source they'd already visited. They typically read no more than one or two pages of an article or book before they would "bounce" out to another site. Sometimes they'd save a long article, but there's no evidence that they ever went back and actually read it. The authors of the study report:

> It is clear that users are not reading online in the traditional sense; indeed there are signs that new forms of "reading" are emerging as users "power browse" horizontally through titles, contents pages, and abstracts going for quick wins. It almost seems that they go online to avoid reading in the traditional sense.

Thanks to the ubiquity of text on the Internet, not to mention the popularity of text-messaging on cell phones, we may well be reading more today than we did in the 1970s or 1980s, when television was our medium of choice. But it's a different kind of reading, and behind it lies a different kind of thinking—perhaps even a new sense of the self. "We are not only *what* we read," says Maryanne Wolf, a developmental psychologist at Tufts University and the author of *Proust and the Squid: The Story and Science of the Reading Brain*. "We are *how* we read." Wolf worries that the style of reading promoted by the Net, a style that puts "efficiency" and "immediacy" above all else, may be weakening our capacity for the kind of deep reading that emerged when an earlier technology, the printing press, made long and complex works of prose commonplace. When we read online, she says, we tend to become "mere decoders of information." Our ability to interpret text, to make the rich mental connections that form when we read deeply and without distraction, remains largely disengaged.

Reading, explains Wolf, is not an instinctive skill for human beings. It's not etched into our genes the way speech is. We have to teach our minds how to translate the symbolic characters we see into the language we understand. And the media or other technologies we use in learning and practicing the craft of reading play an important part in shaping the neural circuits inside our brains. Experiments demonstrate that readers of ideograms, such as the Chinese, develop a mental circuitry for reading that is very different from the circuitry found in those of us whose written language employs an alphabet. The variations extend across many regions of the brain, including those that govern such essential cognitive functions as memory and the interpretation of visual and auditory stimuli. We can expect as well that the circuits woven by our use of the Net will be different from those woven by our reading of books and other printed works.

Sometime in 1882, Friedrich Nietzsche bought a typewriter—a Malling-Hansen Writing Ball, to be precise. His vision was failing, and keeping his eyes focused on a page had become exhausting and painful, often bringing on crushing headaches. He had been forced to curtail his writing, and he feared that he would soon have to give it up. The typewriter rescued him, at least for a time. Once he had mastered touch-typing, he was able to write with his eyes closed, using only the tips of his fingers. Words could once again flow from his mind to the page.

But the machine had a subtler effect on his work. One of Nietzsche's friends, a composer, noticed a change in the style of his writing. His already terse prose had become even tighter, more telegraphic. "Perhaps you will through this instrument even take to a new idiom," the friend wrote in a letter, noting that, in his own work, his "'thoughts' in music and language often depend on the quality of pen and paper."

"You are right," Nietzsche replied, "our writing equipment takes part in the forming of our thoughts." Under the sway of the machine, writes the German media scholar Friedrich A. Kittler, Nietzsche's prose "changed from arguments to aphorisms, from thoughts to puns, from rhetoric to telegram style."

The human brain is almost infinitely malleable. People used to think that our mental meshwork, the dense connections formed among the 100 billion or so neurons inside our skulls, was largely fixed by the time we reached adulthood. But brain researchers have discovered that that's not the case. James Olds, a professor of neuroscience who directs the Krasnow Institute for Advanced Study at George Mason University, says that even the adult mind "is very plastic." Nerve cells routinely break old connections and form new ones. "The brain," according to Olds, "has the ability to reprogram itself on the fly, altering the way it functions."

As we use what the sociologist Daniel Bell has called our "intellectual technologies"—the tools that extend our mental rather than our physical capacities—we inevitably begin to take on the qualities of those technologies. The mechanical clock, which came into common use in the 14th century, provides a compelling example. In *Technics and Civilization*, the historian and cultural critic Lewis Mumford described how the clock "disassociated time from human events and helped create the belief in an independent world of mathematically measurable sequences." The "abstract framework of divided time" became "the point of reference for both action and thought."

The clock's methodical ticking helped bring into being the scientific mind and the scientific man. But it also took something away. As the late MIT computer scientist Joseph Weizenbaum observed in his 1976 book, *Computer Power and Human Reason: From Judgment to Calculation*, the conception of the world that emerged from the widespread use of timekeeping instruments "remains an impoverished version of the older one, for it rests on a rejection of those direct experiences that formed the basis for, and indeed constituted, the old reality." In deciding when to eat, to work, to sleep, to rise, we stopped listening to our senses and started obeying the clock.

The process of adapting to new intellectual technologies is reflected in the changing metaphors we use to explain ourselves to ourselves. When the mechanical clock arrived, people began thinking of their brains as operating "like clockwork." Today, in the age of software, we have come to think of them as operating "like computers." But the changes, neuroscience tells us, go much deeper than metaphor. Thanks to our brain's plasticity, the adaptation occurs also at a biological level.

The Internet promises to have particularly far-reaching effects on cognition. In a paper published in 1936, the British mathematician Alan Turing proved that a digital computer, which at the time existed only as a theoretical machine, could be programmed to perform the function of any other information-processing device. And that's what we're seeing today. The Internet, an immeasurably power-ful computing system, is subsuming most of our other intellectual technologies. It's becoming our map and our clock, our printing press and our typewriter, our calculator and our telephone, and our radio and TV.

When the Net absorbs a medium, that medium is re-created in the Net's image. It injects the medium's content with hyperlinks, blinking ads, and other digital gewgaws, and it surrounds the content with the content of all the other media it has absorbed. A new e-mail message, for instance, may announce its arrival as we're glancing over the latest headlines at a newspaper's site. The result is to scatter our attention and diffuse our concentration.

The Net's influence doesn't end at the edges of a computer screen, either. As people's minds become attuned to the crazy quilt of Internet media, tradi-tional media have to adapt to the audience's new expectations. Television pro-grams add text crawls and pop-up ads, and magazines and newspapers shorten their articles, introduce capsule summaries, and crowd their pages with easy-to-browse info-snippets. When, in March of this year, the *New York Times* decided to devote the second and third pages of every edition to article abstracts, its design director, Tom Bodkin, explained that the "shortcuts" would give har-ried readers a quick "taste" of the day's news, sparing them the "less efficient" method of actually turning the pages and reading the articles. Old media have little choice but to play by the new-media rules.

Never has a communications system played so many roles in our lives — or exerted such broad influence over our thoughts — as the Internet does today. Yet, for all that's been written about the Net, there's been little consideration of how, exactly, it's reprogramming us. The Net's intellectual ethic remains obscure.

About the same time that Nietzsche started using his typewriter, an ear-nest young man named Frederick Winslow Taylor carried a stopwatch into the Midvale Steel plant in Philadelphia and began a historic series of experiments aimed at improving the efficiency of the plant's machinists. With the approval of Midvale's owners, he recruited a group of factory hands, set them to work on various metalworking machines, and recorded and timed their every movement as well as the operations of the machines. By breaking down every job into a sequence of small, discrete steps and then testing different ways of performing each one, Taylor created a set of precise instructions — an "algorithm," we might say today — for how each worker should work. Midvale's employees grumbled about the strict new regime, claiming that it turned them into little more than automatons, but the factory's productivity soared.

More than a hundred years after the invention of the steam engine, the Industrial Revolution had at last found its philosophy and its philosopher. Taylor's tight industrial choreography—his "system," as he liked to call it—was embraced by manufacturers throughout the country and, in time, around the world. Seeking maximum speed, maximum efficiency, and maximum output, factory owners used time-and-motion studies to organize their work and configure the jobs of their workers. The goal, as Taylor defined it in his celebrated 1911 treatise, *The Principles of Scientific Management*, was to identify and adopt, for every job, the "one best method" of work and thereby to effect "the gradual substitution of science for rule of thumb throughout the mechanic arts." Once his system was applied to all acts of manual labor, Taylor assured his followers, it would bring about a restructuring not only of industry but of society, creating a utopia of perfect efficiency. "In the past the man has been first," he declared; "in the future the system must be first."

Taylor's system is still very much with us; it remains the ethic of industrial manufacturing. And now, thanks to the growing power that computer engineers and software coders wield over our intellectual lives, Taylor's ethic is beginning to govern the realm of the mind as well. The Internet is a machine designed for the efficient and automated collection, transmission, and manipulation of information, and its legions of programmers are intent on finding the "one best method"—the perfect algorithm—to carry out every mental movement of what we've come to describe as "knowledge work."

Google's headquarters, in Mountain View, California—the Googleplex—is the Internet's high church, and the religion practiced inside its walls is Taylorism. Google, says its chief executive, Eric Schmidt, is "a company that's founded around the science of measurement," and it is striving to "systematize everything" it does. Drawing on the terabytes of behavioral data it collects through its search engine and other sites, it carries out thousands of experiments a day, according to the *Harvard Business Review*, and it uses the results to refine the algorithms that increasingly control how people find information and extract meaning from it. What Taylor did for the work of the hand, Google is doing for the work of the mind.

The company has declared that its mission is "to organize the world's information and make it universally accessible and useful." It seeks to develop "the perfect search engine," which it defines as something that "understands exactly what you mean and gives you back exactly what you want." In Google's view, information is a kind of commodity, a utilitarian resource that can be mined and processed with industrial efficiency. The more pieces of information we can "access" and the faster we can extract their gist, the more productive we become as thinkers.

Where does it end? Sergey Brin and Larry Page, the gifted young men who founded Google while pursuing doctoral degrees in computer science at Stanford, speak frequently of their desire to turn their search engine into an artificial intelligence, a HAL-like machine that might be connected directly to our brains. "The ultimate search engine is something as smart as people—or smarter," Page said in a speech a few years back. "For us, working on search is a way to work on artificial intelligence." In a 2004 interview with *Newsweek*, Brin said, "Certainly if you had all the world's information directly attached to your brain, or an artificial brain that was smarter than your brain, you'd be better off." Last year, Page told a convention of scientists that Google is "really trying to build artificial intelligence and to do it on a large scale."

Such an ambition is a natural one, even an admirable one, for a pair of math whizzes with vast quantities of cash at their disposal and a small army of computer scientists in their employ. A fundamentally scientific enterprise, Google is motivated by a desire to use technology, in Eric Schmidt's words, "to solve problems that have never been solved before," and artificial intelligence is the hardest problem out there. Why wouldn't Brin and Page want to be the ones to crack it?

Still, their easy assumption that we'd all "be better off" if our brains were supplemented, or even replaced, by an artificial intelligence is unsettling. It suggests a belief that intelligence is the output of a mechanical process, a series of discrete steps that can be isolated, measured, and optimized. In Google's world, the world we enter when we go online, there's little place for the fuzziness of contemplation. Ambiguity is not an opening for insight but a bug to be fixed. The human brain is just an outdated computer that needs a faster processor and a bigger hard drive.

The idea that our minds should operate as high-speed data-processing machines is not only built into the workings of the Internet, it is the network's reigning business model as well. The faster we surf across the Web—the more links we click and pages we view—the more opportunities Google and other companies gain to collect information about us and to feed us advertisements. Most of the proprietors of the commercial Internet have a financial stake in collecting the crumbs of data we leave behind as we flit from link to link—the more crumbs, the better. The last thing these companies want is to encourage leisurely reading or slow, concentrated thought. It's in their economic interest to drive us to distraction.

Maybe I'm just a worrywart. Just as there's a tendency to glorify technological progress, there's a countertendency to expect the worst of every new tool or machine. In Plato's *Phaedrus*, Socrates bemoaned the development of writing. He feared that, as people came to rely on the written word as a substitute for the knowledge they used to carry inside their heads, they would, in the words of one of the dialogue's characters, "cease to exercise their memory and become forgetful." And because they would be able to "receive a quantity of information without proper instruction," they would "be thought very knowledgeable when they are for the most part quite ignorant." They would be "filled with the conceit of wisdom instead of real wisdom." Socrates wasn't wrong—the new technology did often have the effects he feared—but he was shortsighted. He couldn't foresee the many ways that writing and reading would serve to spread information, spur fresh ideas, and expand human knowledge (if not wisdom).

The arrival of Gutenberg's printing press, in the 15th century, set off another round of teeth gnashing. The Italian humanist Hieronimo Squarciafico worried that the easy availability of books would lead to intellectual laziness, making men "less studious" and weakening their minds. Others argued that cheaply printed books and broadsheets would undermine religious authority, demean the work of scholars and scribes, and spread sedition and debauchery. As New York University professor Clay Shirky notes, "Most of the arguments made against the printing press were correct, even prescient." But, again, the doomsayers were unable to imagine the myriad blessings that the printed word would deliver.

So, yes, you should be skeptical of my skepticism. Perhaps those who dismiss critics of the Internet as Luddites or nostalgists will be proved correct, and from our hyperactive, data-stoked minds will spring a golden age of intellectual discovery and universal wisdom. Then again, the Net isn't the alphabet, and although it may replace the printing press, it produces something altogether different. The kind of deep reading that a sequence of printed pages promotes is valuable not just for the knowledge we acquire from the author's words but for the intellectual vibrations those words set off within our own minds. In the quiet spaces opened up by the sustained, undistracted reading of a book, or by any other act of contemplation, for that matter, we make our own associations, draw our own inferences and analogies, foster our own ideas. Deep reading, as Maryanne Wolf argues, is indistinguishable from deep thinking.

If we lose those quiet spaces, or fill them up with "content," we will sacrifice something important not only in our selves but in our culture. In a recent essay, the playwright Richard Foreman eloquently described what's at stake:

> I come from a tradition of Western culture, in which the ideal (my ideal) was the complex, dense, and "cathedral-like" structure of the highly educated and articulate personality—a man or woman who carried inside themselves a personally constructed and unique version of the entire heritage of the West. [But now] I see within us all (myself included) the replacement of complex inner density with a new kind of self—evolving under the pressure of information overload and the technology of the "instantly available."

As we are drained of our "inner repertory of dense cultural inheritance," Foreman concluded, we risk turning into "'pancake people'—spread wide and thin as we connect with that vast network of information accessed by the mere touch of a button."

I'm haunted by that scene in *2001*. What makes it so poignant, and so weird, is the computer's emotional response to the disassembly of its mind: its despair as one circuit after another goes dark, its childlike pleading with the astronaut—"I can feel it. I can feel it. I'm afraid"—and its final reversion to what can only be called a state of innocence. HAL's outpouring of feeling contrasts with the emotionlessness that characterizes the human figures in the film, who go about their business with an almost robotic efficiency. Their thoughts and actions feel scripted, as if they're following the steps of an algorithm. In the world of *2001*, people have become so machinelike that the most human character turns out to be a machine. That's the essence of Kubrick's dark prophecy: as we come to rely on computers to mediate our understanding of the world, it is our own intelligence that flattens into artificial intelligence.

Reading the Genre

1. Using your Web browser's "history" function and your own memory, create a log of your computer activity for one evening. Map out where you go online and on your desktop, what for, and for how long. In light of Carr's article, explain how your habits might affect your thinking.

2. How does Carr adapt his writing for an audience that may not share his extensive understanding of information technology? (See "Understanding your audience," p. 147, and Chapter 35, "High, Middle, and Low Style," p. 432.)

3. Why is the title question important? What is at stake? Why is it important, rhetorically, to show all that is at stake?

4. Carr writes that changing "intellectual technologies" have changed the metaphors people use to describe themselves, which in turn have changed how the human mind works. (We used to think "like clockwork," for instance, but now we "process" information.) Choose your favorite technology and investigate the similarities between the way it functions and the way you think.

5. **WRITING:** Has technology affected your brain? Focusing on one example from personal experience, write a causal analysis essay that explores your answer to this question. (See "Finding and developing materials," p. 149.)

6. **TIMELINE:** Convert the examples in Carr's article into a timeline of technological innovation. Include a column that summarizes the worries skeptics have voiced about each new technology. Have these worries proven to be justified?

CULTURAL ANALYSIS Pulitzer Prize–winning *New York Times* science writer Natalie Angier is the author of four critically acclaimed books, including the best seller *Woman: An Intimate Geography* (1999). Her most recent, *The Canon: A Whirligig Tour of the Beautiful Basics of Science* (2008), provides a guide to the major theories of science. The following article, published in 2005 in the *New York Times*, uses linguistic and psychological research to try to explain a very common phenomenon: swearing.

Almost Before We Spoke, We Swore

Natalie Angier

Incensed by what it sees as a virtual pandemic of verbal vulgarity issuing from the diverse likes of Howard Stern, Bono of U2, and Robert Novak, the United States Senate is poised to consider a bill that would sharply increase the penalty for obscenity on the air.

By raising the fines that would be levied against offending broadcasters some fifteenfold, to a fee of about $500,000 per crudity broadcast, and by threatening to revoke the licenses of repeat polluters, the Senate seeks to return to the public square the gentler tenor of yesteryear, when seldom were heard any scurrilous words, and famous guys were not foul mouthed all day.

Yet researchers who study the evolution of language and the psychology of swearing say that they have no idea what mystic model of linguistic gentility the critics might have in mind. Cursing, they say, is a human universal. Every language, dialect, or patois ever studied, living or dead, spoken by millions or by a small tribe, turns out to have its share of forbidden speech, some variant on comedian George Carlin's famous list of the seven dirty words that are not supposed to be uttered on radio or television.

Young children will memorize the illicit inventory long before they can grasp its sense, said John McWhorter, a scholar of linguistics at the Manhattan Institute and the author of *The Power of Babel,* and literary giants have always constructed their art on its spine.

The Jacobean dramatist Ben Jonson peppered his plays with fackings and "peremptorie Asses," and Shakespeare could hardly quill a stanza without inserting profanities of the day like "zounds" or "sblood" — offensive contractions of "God's wounds" and "God's blood" — or some wondrous sexual pun.

The title *Much Ado About Nothing,* Dr. McWhorter said, is a word play on *Much Ado About an O Thing,* the *O thing* being a reference to female genitalia.

Even the quintessential Good Book abounds in naughty passages like the men in II Kings 18:27 who, as the comparatively tame King James translation puts it, "eat their own dung, and drink their own piss."

In fact, said Guy Deutscher, a linguist at the University of Leiden in the Netherlands and the author of *The Unfolding of Language: An Evolutionary Tour of Mankind's Greatest Invention,* the earliest writings, which date from 5,000 years ago, include their share of off-color descriptions of the human form and its ever-colorful functions. And the written record is merely a reflection of an oral tradition that Dr. Deutscher and many other psychologists and evolutionary linguists suspect dates from the rise of the human larynx, if not before.

Some researchers are so impressed by the depth and power of strong language that they are using it as a peephole into the architecture of the brain, as a means of probing the tangled, cryptic bonds between the newer, "higher" regions of the brain in charge of intellect, reason, and planning, and the older, more "bestial" neural neighborhoods that give birth to our emotions.

Researchers point out that cursing is often an amalgam of raw, spontaneous feeling and targeted, gimlet-eyed cunning. When one person curses at another, they say, the curser rarely spews obscenities and insults at random, but rather will assess the object of his wrath, and adjust the content of the "uncontrollable" outburst accordingly.

Because cursing calls on the thinking and feeling pathways of the brain in roughly equal measure and with handily assessable fervor, scientists say that by studying the neural circuitry behind it they are gaining new insights into how the different domains of the brain communicate — and all for the sake of a well-venomed retort.

Other investigators have examined the physiology of cursing, how our senses and reflexes react to the sound or sight of an obscene word. They have determined that hearing a curse elicits a literal rise out of people. When electrodermal wires are placed on people's arms and fingertips to study their skin conductance patterns and the subjects then hear a few obscenities spoken clearly and firmly, participants show signs of instant arousal.

Their skin conductance patterns spike, the hairs on their arms rise, their pulse quickens, and their breathing becomes shallow.

Interestingly, said Kate Burridge, a professor of linguistics at Monash University in Melbourne, Australia, a similar reaction occurs among university students and others who pride themselves on being educated when they listen to bad grammar or slang expressions that they regard as irritating, illiterate, or déclassé.

"People can feel very passionate about language," she said, "as though it were a cherished artifact that must be protected at all cost against the depravities of barbarians and lexical aliens."

Dr. Burridge and a colleague at Monash, Keith Allan, are the authors of *Forbidden Words: Taboo and the Censoring of Language,* which will be published early next year [2006] by the Cambridge University Press.

Researchers have also found that obscenities can get under one's goosebumped skin and then refuse to budge. In one study, scientists started with the familiar Stroop test, in which subjects are flashed a series of words written in different colors and are asked to react by calling out the colors of the words rather than the words themselves.

If the subjects see the word *chair* written in yellow letters, they are supposed to say "yellow."

The researchers then inserted a number of obscenities and vulgarities in the standard lineup. Charting participants' immediate and delayed responses, the researchers found that, first of all, people needed significantly more time to trill out the colors of the curse words than they did for neutral terms like *chair.*

The experience of seeing titillating text obviously distracted the participants from the color-coding task at hand. Yet those risqué interpolations left their mark. In subsequent memory quizzes, not only were participants much better at recalling the naughty words than they were the neutrals, but that superior recall also applied to the tints of the tainted words, as well as to their sense.

Yes, it is tough to toil in the shadow of trash. When researchers in another study asked participants to quickly scan lists of words that included obscenities and then to recall as many of the words as possible, the subjects were, once again, best at rehashing the curses — and worst at summoning up whatever unobjectionable entries happened to precede or follow the bad bits.

Yet as much as bad language can deliver a jolt, it can help wash away stress and anger. In some settings, the free flow of foul language may signal not hostility or social pathology, but harmony and tranquillity.

"Studies show that if you're with a group of close friends, the more relaxed you are, the more you swear," Dr. Burridge said. "It's a way of saying: 'I'm so comfortable here I can let off steam. I can say whatever I like.'"

Evidence also suggests that cursing can be an effective means of venting aggression and thereby forestalling physical violence.

With the help of a small army of students and volunteers, Timothy B. Jay, a professor of psychology at Massachusetts College of Liberal Arts in North Adams and the author of *Cursing in America* and *Why We Curse,* has explored the dynamics of cursing in great detail.

The investigators have found, among other things, that men generally curse more than women, unless said women are in a sorority, and that university provosts swear more than librarians or the staff members of the university day care center.

Regardless of who is cursing or what the provocation may be, Dr. Jay said, the rationale for the eruption is often the same.

"Time and again, people have told me that cursing is a coping mechanism for them, a way of reducing stress," he said in a telephone interview. "It's a form of anger management that is often underappreciated."

Indeed, chimpanzees engage in what appears to be a kind of cursing match as a means of venting aggression and avoiding a potentially dangerous physical clash.

Frans de Waal, a professor of primate behavior at Emory University in Atlanta, said that when chimpanzees were angry "they will grunt or spit or make an abrupt, upsweeping gesture that, if a human were to do it, you'd recognize it as aggressive."

Such behaviors are threat gestures, Professor de Waal said, and they are all a good sign.

"A chimpanzee who is really gearing up for a fight doesn't waste time with gestures, but just goes ahead and attacks," he added.

By the same token, he said, nothing is more deadly than a person who is too enraged for expletives — who cleanly and quietly picks up a gun and starts shooting.

Researchers have also examined how words attain the status of forbidden speech and how the evolution of coarse language affects the smoother sheets of civil discourse stacked above it. They have found that what counts as taboo language in a given culture is often a mirror into that culture's fears and fixations.

"In some cultures, swear words are drawn mainly from sex and bodily functions, whereas in others, they're drawn mainly from the domain of religion," Dr. Deutscher said.

In societies where the purity and honor of women is of paramount importance, he said, "it's not surprising that many swear words are variations on the 'son of a whore' theme or refer graphically to the genitalia of the person's mother or sisters."

The very concept of a swear word or an oath originates from the profound importance that ancient cultures placed on swearing by the name of a god or gods. In ancient Babylon, swearing by the name of a god was meant to give absolute certainty against lying, Dr. Deutscher said, "and people believed that swearing falsely by a god would bring the terrible wrath of that god upon them." A warning against any abuse of the sacred oath is reflected in the biblical commandment that one must not "take the Lord's name in vain," and even today courtroom witnesses swear on the Bible that they are telling the whole truth and nothing but.

Among Christians, the stricture against taking the Lord's name in vain extended to casual allusions to God's son or the son's corporeal sufferings — no mention of the blood or the wounds or the body, and that goes for clever contractions, too. Nowadays, the phrase "Oh, golly!" may be considered almost comically wholesome, but it was not always so. "Golly" is a compaction of "God's body" and, thus, was once a profanity.

Yet neither biblical commandment nor the most zealous Victorian censor can elide from the human mind its hand-wringing over the unruly human body, its chronic, embarrassing demands, and its sad decay. Discomfort over body functions never sleeps, Dr. Burridge said, and the need for an ever-fresh selection of euphemisms about dirty subjects has long served as an impressive engine of linguistic invention.

Once a word becomes too closely associated with a specific body function, she said, once it becomes too evocative of what should not be evoked, it starts to enter the realm of the taboo and must be replaced by a new, gauzier euphemism.

For example, the word *toilet* stems from the French word for "little towel" and was originally a pleasantly indirect way of referring to the place where the chamber pot or its equivalent resides. But *toilet* has since come to mean the porcelain fixture itself, and so sounds too blunt to use in polite company. Instead, you ask your tuxedoed waiter for directions to the ladies' room or the restroom or, if you must, the bathroom.

Similarly, the word *coffin* originally meant an ordinary box, but once it became associated with death, that was it for a "shoe coffin" or "thinking outside the coffin." The taboo sense of a word, Dr. Burridge said, "always drives out any other senses it might have had."

Scientists have lately sought to map the neural topography of forbidden speech by studying Tourette's patients who suffer from coprolalia, the pathological and uncontrollable urge to curse. Tourette's syndrome is a neurological disorder of unknown origin characterized predominantly by chronic motor and vocal tics, a constant grimacing or pushing of one's glasses up the bridge of one's nose or emitting a stream of small yips or grunts.

Just a small percentage of Tourette's patients have coprolalia—estimates range from 8 to 30 percent—and patient advocates are dismayed by popular portrayals of Tourette's as a humorous and invariably scatological condition. But for those who do have coprolalia, said Dr. Carlos Singer, director of the division of movement disorders at the University of Miami School of Medicine, the symptom is often the most devastating and humiliating aspect of their condition.

Not only can it be shocking to people to hear a loud volley of expletives erupt for no apparent reason, sometimes from the mouth of a child or young teenager, but the curses can also be provocative and personal, florid slurs against the race, sexual identity, or body size of a passer-by, for example, or deliberate and repeated lewd references to an old lover's name while in the arms of a current partner or spouse.

Reporting in *The Archives of General Psychiatry*, Dr. David A. Silbersweig, a director of neuropsychiatry and neuroimaging at the Weill Medical College of Cornell University, and his colleagues described their use of PET scans to measure cerebral blood flow and identify which regions of the brain are galvanized in Tourette's patients during episodes of tics and coprolalia.

They found strong activation of the basal ganglia, a quartet of neuron clusters deep in the forebrain at roughly the level of the mid-forehead, that are known to help coordinate body movement along with activation of crucial regions of the left rear forebrain that participate in comprehending and generating speech, most notably Broca's area.

The researchers also saw arousal of neural circuits that interact with the limbic system, the wishbone-shape throne of human emotions, and, significantly, of the "executive" realms of the brain, where decisions to act or desist from acting may be carried out: the neural source, scientists said, of whatever conscience, civility, or free will humans can claim.

That the brain's executive overseer is ablaze in an outburst of coprolalia, Dr. Silbersweig said, demonstrates how complex an act the urge to speak the unspeakable may be, and not only in the case of Tourette's. The person is gripped by a desire to curse, to voice something wildly inappropriate. Higher-order linguistic circuits are tapped, to contrive the content of the curse. The brain's impulse control center struggles to short-circuit the collusion between limbic system urge and neocortical craft, and it may succeed for a time.

Yet the urge mounts, until at last the speech pathways fire, the verboten is spoken, and archaic and refined brains alike must shoulder the blame.

Reading the Genre

1. How does the author manage to write an article about swearing with so little swearing in it? What effect does this have on you as a reader? Does it increase your "urge to speak the unspeakable"? If so, why?

2. At its simplest, a causal analysis asks *why something happens*. What claims does Angier make about why we swear? How does she support her claims?

3. Angier uses a range of sources to explore why people swear. List all her sources; then make notes about where each source gets his or her authority and how each source explains the predominance of swearing. Are some sources more persuasive? (See "Find reliable sources," p. 46; Chapter 22, "Critical Thinking," p. 372; Chapter 43, "Evaluating Sources," p. 482; and Chapter 44, "Annotating Sources," p. 487.)

4. In response to Angier's article, consider a causal analysis of an opposite inclination: Why do people refrain from swearing? What are some of the social, cultural, professional, familial, and personal forces that require people to speak politely? What are some good reasons for clean language? (See Chapter 22, "Critical Thinking," p. 372, and Chapter 35, "High, Middle, and Low Style," p. 432.)

5. **WRITING:** Do the media mold the way people speak? Watch a popular television show or listen to a song. Analyze the language of the television characters or that of the song lyrics. Can you make inferences about how these texts might influence audiences to speak similarly—using the same terms, dialects, and styles? Write a short causal analysis.

CULTURAL ANALYSIS   Alex Williams writes about technology, media, and culture for the *New York Times* and *New York* magazine. The following article first appeared in 2006 in the *New York Times*.

Here I Am Taking My Own Picture

Alex Williams

Morgan Adams, a recent college graduate, decided that her picture on her home page at MySpace.com had lingered a little too long, a full month. To snap a new one she called on the only photographer she thought she could trust: herself.

In her bedroom in Lubbock, Texas, Ms. Adams, 21, tried out a variety of poses—coy, friendly, sultry, goofy—in the kind of performance young people have engaged in privately for generations before a mirror. But Ms. Adams's mirror was a Web cam, and her journey of self-expression, documented in five digital self-portraits, was soon visible to the 56 million registered users of MySpace.

"Everyone's a little narcissistic," Ms. Adams said. "Being able to take pictures of yourself in privacy allows you to do it without inhibitions. Each person takes better pictures of themselves than anyone else can because they know their own bodies, they know their own minds."

The era of cheap, lightweight digital cameras—in cellphones, in computers, in hip pockets, even on key chains—has meant that people who did not consider themselves photography buffs as recently as five years ago are filling ever-larger hard drives with thousands of images from their lives.

And one particular kind of image has especially soared in popularity, particularly among the young: the self-portrait, which has become a kind of folk art for the digital age.

Framing themselves at arm's length, teenagers snap their own pictures and pass the cameras to friends at school or e-mail the images or upload them to the Internet. For a generation raised on a mantra of self-esteem, striking a heroic, sultry, or brooding pose and sharing it with the world comes naturally.

"It's a huge phenomenon," said Matt Polazzo, the coordinator of student affairs at Stuyvesant High School in Manhattan, referring to the compulsive habit of teenagers to snap everything in their lives, especially self-portraits. "Just yesterday I had a girl sitting on the couch in my office," he said. "She took out her cellphone and said, 'Here, I'm going to show you a picture of my best friend,' snapped a picture of herself, and showed it to me, all in one fluid motion."

Art historians say that the popularity of the self-portrait is unprecedented in the century-long history of the snapshot. "I think it is probably a new genre of photography," said Guy Stricherz, the author of *Americans in Kodachrome, 1945–65* (Twin Palms, 2002), which includes snapshots culled from 500 American families. Mr. Stricherz said he reviewed more than 100,000 pictures over 17 years in compiling the book but found fewer than 100 self-portraits. These days you can find as many by clicking through a few home pages on MySpace, Friendster, or similar social networking sites.

Jeff Gluck, a public relations executive, who lives in Woodcliff Lake, New Jersey, and his wife, Elizabeth, often find one of their two oldest daughters, ages 10 and 13, taking pictures of themselves with cellphone cameras. They do it in the back seat of the car or on the sofa watching television. When not mugging for their own cameras, the girls experiment with the family camera. "Many times with our regular digital camera I'll go to download photos at the computer, and I'll find six pictures of one of the kids that they obviously took themselves," Mr. Gluck said.

To a certain extent new technology is driving the new self-portraiture. Cellphone cameras and other digital cameras are sold with wide-angle lenses that allow a picture taken at arm's length to remain in focus. Computers are essentially $1,000 darkrooms that permit sophisticated manipulation of images.

But technology alone can't explain the trend. Even in previous generations when cameras were cheap, they were generally reserved for special occasions. "In 1960 a person just wouldn't take a Kodak Brownie picture of themselves," Mr. Stricherz said. "It would have been considered too self-aggrandizing."

Psychologists and others who study teenagers say the digital self-portraiture is an extension of behavior typical of the young, like trying on different identities, which earlier generations might have expressed through clothing and hairstyles. "Most of what I've been seeing is taking place in the bedroom," said Kathryn C. Montgomery, a professor of communication at American University, referring to teenage self-portraits. Dr. Montgomery studies the relation of teenagers to the digital media. "It's a locus of teen life where they are forming their identities, and now it's also a private studio where they can develop who they are. What better tool could they have than one that allows them to take pictures of themselves and manipulate them like never before?"

To Jeffrey Jensen Arnett, a developmental psychologist, digital self-portraiture is a high-tech way of expressing an impulse among teenagers and young adults that psychologists call "the imaginary audience."

"This is the idea that adolescents think people are more interested in them than they actually are, that people are always looking at them and taking note of what they are doing, even if it is just walking across the school cafeteria," said Dr. Arnett, who is a Fulbright scholar at the University of Copenhagen.

To Dr. Arnett, the role-playing evident in many self-portraits found online is "a form of pretend: the adolescent version of children dressing up." Others speculate that today's young people are different from earlier generations because they are more comfortable with public self-exposure.

"When I was a kid I didn't want my picture taken," said Jim Taylor, a trend consultant at the Harrison Group in Waterbury, Connecticut. "But these kids are fabulous self-marketers."

He added: "They see celebrities expressing their self-worth and want to join the party. This is a free forum to do so."

"Self-branding is a big deal for kids, and self-produced entertainment is a big deal," Mr. Taylor said. In their pictures, ordinary young women metamorphose into glamour queens or pinup girls, thanks to a few well-rehearsed come-hither poses and mood lighting reminiscent of an old Hollywood studio portrait. Average boys turn themselves into brooding antiheroes by gazing intently into their camera lens in a darkened room, face half buried in shadow.

"There's always a theatrical quality to their shots," Mr. Taylor said. "Kids love melancholy and sadness. There is lots of obvious symbolism about whether they see themselves as an actress, a model, a Christ figure, or a Hamlet."

Young people have become so candid in sharing their intimate images online that some parents and lawmakers are concerned. This month the attorney general of Connecticut, Richard Blumenthal, promised an investigation into MySpace, spurred by complaints of parents that minors could have access to sexual images on the site or could post suggestive pictures that could make them vulnerable to sexual predators. Members have included pictures of themselves in scanty attire or suggestive poses. For many, MySpace functions as a dating site.

But the operators of the Web site, which is owned by the News Corporation, the media conglomerate controlled by Rupert Murdoch, insist that a third of the work force is devoted to policing the site for inappropriate material. Offending members can be banned from the network, and MySpace says it will contact law enforcement officials in serious cases.

Not everyone who compulsively snaps self-portraits sees it as a journey of self-discovery. Tim Zebal, 23, an audio engineer in San Francisco, posted on MySpace an arresting shot of himself taken at a dramatic angle, wearing a billowing shirt and framed in a baroque gold mirror. "I had a new camera phone and snapped a picture in the mirror of a bar restroom," Mr. Zebal explained in an e-mail message. "I thought it looked cool. That's it."

Amber Davidson, 19, a freshman at Concordia College in Moorhead, Minnesota, refreshes her self-portrait on MySpace every couple of weeks and puts a lot of thought into it.

"There's been a big increase in creativity over the past couple of years," she said, referring to the self-portraits on the site. "A lot of people get inspired by what they see in other people's pictures."

Her MySpace home page contains five self-portraits created by pointing the camera toward herself, arm outstretched. She composed each shot so that the arm holding the camera is invisible. In one, Ms. Davidson wears a black-and-white spaghetti-strap dress and peers up winsomely at a camera over her head. It took about 15 tries to get it right, she said. "I don't want people to think I'm sitting there taking all these pictures of myself, even though I kind of am."

Since endless experimentation with digital photography costs little or nothing (you just delete the duds), many young camera owners like Ms. Davidson have practiced their art to the point where they have stumbled across sophisticated portraiture techniques of lighting, composition, and camera angle that were once the province of professionals.

Take that shot with the camera held high above the head, so common on MySpace that some members refer to it as "the helicopter shot." It is a fairly sophisticated technique.

"Shooting from higher up stretches the neck muscles, and there is no double chin," said Ken White, the chairman of the fine-art photography department at the Rochester Institute of Technology, adding that it also accentuates the jaw line. "It is a glamorizing view."

In the era of the blog, when many deem the most trivial and personal information fit for public consumption, the self-reference of the new portraiture feels natural. "In a funny way I don't see this as photography anymore," said Fred Ritchin, an associate professor in the photography and imaging department at the Tisch School of the Arts at New York University. "It's communication. It's all an extension of cellphones, texting, and e-mailing."

Many users consider digital self-portraits whimsical and ultimately disposable.

"People want pictures of a new hairstyle, outfit, or makeup, and they want to show it to their friends," Tom Anderson, the president of MySpace, said in an e-mail message. But, he added, "I suppose all folk art comes from necessity of some sort."

Reading the Genre

1. Williams suggests that self-portraiture is a new online genre. (See Chapter 25, "Genre," p. 390.) What kinds of portraits does he mention (for example, the "helicopter shot")? Building on the examples Williams offers, can you identify other types of online portraits?

2. In what ways have technological advances allowed for the huge increase in the popularity of these self-portraits? What technologies are involved, and what do these new tools and networking sites allow? (See Chapter 51, "Understanding Digital Media," p. 568, and Chapter 54, "Designing Print and Online Documents," p. 592.)

3. Williams implies not only that new technologies have led to the ubiquity of these kinds of photos but also that the photos say something important about how technology has influenced a generation. How do the photographs themselves show a shift in our culture?

4. Look at some of the newest features of Facebook. How do site participants use these features? How do these features shape the way people interact?

5. **WRITING:** Write a list of rules for Facebook users — what should this site be used for, what should users avoid, and so on. Think about all the possible audiences for a person's Facebook page. Choose one specific rule and write a short explanation of why Facebook users should follow it, and what might happen if they don't.

CAUSAL ANALYSIS   Virginia Postrel, a columnist at the *Wall Street Journal,* has written for the *Atlantic,* the *New York Times, Forbes, Reason,* and *Inc.* magazine. She has also published two books: *The Future and Its Enemies* (1998), a celebration of progress, and *The Substance of Style* (2003), an argument that aesthetic values have trumped practical values in American culture. The following article first appeared in the *Atlantic* magazine in 2008.

Pop Psychology

VIRGINIA POSTREL

In these uncertain economic times, we'd all like a guaranteed investment. Here's one: it pays a 24-cent dividend every four weeks for sixty weeks, fifteen dividends in all. Then it disappears. Unlike a bond, this security has no redemption value. It simply provides guaranteed dividends. It involves no tricky derivatives or unknown risks. And it carries absolutely no danger of default. What would you pay for it?

Before financially sophisticated readers drag out their calculators, look up interest rates, and compute the present value of those future payments, I have a confession to make. You can't buy this security, and it doesn't really pay dividends every four weeks. It pays every four *minutes,* in a computer lab, to volunteers in economic experiments.

For more than two decades, economists have been running versions of the same experiment. They take a bunch of volunteers, usually undergraduates but sometimes businesspeople or graduate students; divide them into experimental groups of roughly a dozen; give each person money and shares to trade with; and pay dividends of 24 cents at the end of each of fifteen rounds, each lasting a few minutes. (Sometimes the 24 cents is a flat amount; more often there's an equal chance of getting 0, 8, 28, or 60 cents, which averages out to 24 cents.) All participants are given the same information, but they can't talk to one another, and they interact only through their trading screens. Then the researchers watch what happens, repeating the same experiment with different small groups to get a larger picture.

The great thing about a laboratory experiment is that you can control the environment. Wall Street securities carry uncertainties—more, lately, than many people expected—but this experimental security is a sure thing. "The fundamental value is unambiguously defined," says the economist Charles Noussair, a professor at Tilburg University in the Netherlands, who has run many of these experiments. "It's the expected value of the future dividend stream at any given time": 15 times 24 cents, or $3.60 at the end of the first round; 14 times 24 cents, or $3.36 at the end of the second; $3.12 at the end of the third; and so on down to zero. Participants don't even have to do the math. They can see the total expected dividends on their computer screens.

Here, finally, is a security with security—no doubt about its true value, no hidden risks, no crazy ups and downs, no bubbles and panics. The trading price should stick close to the expected value.

At least that's what economists would have thought before Vernon Smith, who won a 2002 Nobel Prize for developing experimental economics, first ran the test in the mid-1980s. But that's not what happens. Again and again, in experiment after experiment, the trading price runs up way above fundamental value. Then, as the fifteenth round nears, it crashes. The problem doesn't seem to be that participants are bored and fooling around. The difference between a good trading performance and a bad one is about eighty dollars for a three-hour session, enough to motivate cash-strapped students to do their best. Besides, Noussair emphasizes, "you don't just get random noise. You get bubbles and crashes"—90 percent of the time.

So much for security.

These lab results should give pause not only to people who believe in efficient markets but also to those who think we can banish bubbles simply by curbing corruption and imposing more regulation. Asset markets, it seems, suffer from irrepressible effervescence. Bubbles happen, even in the most controlled conditions.

Experimental bubbles are particularly surprising because in laboratory markets that mimic the production of goods and services, prices rise and fall as economic theory predicts, reaching a neat equilibrium where supply meets demand. But, like real-world purchasers of haircuts or refrigerators, buyers in those markets need to know only how much they themselves value the good. If the price is less than the value to you, you buy. If not, you don't, and vice versa for sellers.

Financial assets, whether in the lab or the real world, are trickier to judge: can I flip this security to a buyer who will pay more than I think it's worth? In an experimental market, where the value of the security is clearly specified, "worth" shouldn't vary with taste, cash needs, or risk calculations. Based on future dividends, you know for sure that the security's current value is, say, $3.12. But—here's the wrinkle—you don't know that I'm as savvy as you are. Maybe I'm confused. Even if I'm not, you don't know whether I know that you know it's worth $3.12. Besides, as long as a clueless greater fool who might pay $3.50 is out there, we smart people may decide to pay $3.25 in the hope of making a profit. It doesn't matter that we know the security is worth $3.12. For the price to track the fundamental value, says Noussair, "everybody has to know that everybody knows that everybody is rational." That's rarely the case. Rather, "if you put people in asset markets, the first thing they do is not try to figure out the fundamental value. They try to buy low and sell high." That speculation creates a bubble.

In fact, the people who make the most money in these experiments aren't the ones who stick to fundamentals. They're the speculators who buy a lot at the beginning and sell midway through, taking advantage of "momentum traders," who jump in when the market is going up, don't sell until it's going down, and wind up with the least money at the end. ("I have a lot of relatives and friends who are momentum traders," comments Noussair.) Bubbles start to pop when the momentum traders run out of money and can no longer push prices up.

But people do learn. By the third time the same group goes through a fifteen-round market, the bubble usually disappears. Everybody knows what the security is worth and realizes that everybody else knows the same thing. Or at least that's what economists assumed was happening. But work that Noussair and his coauthors published in the December 2007 *American Economic Review* suggests that traders don't reason that way.

In this version of the experiment, participants took part in the fifteen-round market four times in a row. Before each session, the researchers asked the traders what they thought would happen to prices. The first time, participants didn't expect a bubble, but in later markets they did. With each successive session, however, they predicted the bubble would peak later and reach a higher price than it actually did. Expecting the future to look like the past, they traded accordingly, selling earlier and at lower prices than in the previous session, hoping to realize a profit before the bubble burst. Those trades, of course, changed the market pattern. Prices were lower, and they peaked closer to the beginning of the session. By the fourth round, the price stuck close to the security's fundamental value—not because traders were going for the rational price but because they were trying to avoid getting caught in a bubble.

"Prices converge toward fundamentals ahead of beliefs," the economists conclude. Traders literally learn from experience, basing their expectations and behavior not on logical inference but on what has happened in the past. After enough rounds, markets work their way toward a stable price.

If experience eliminates bubbles in the lab, you might expect that more-experienced traders in the real world (or what experimental economists prefer to call "field markets") would produce fewer financial crises. When asset markets run into trouble, maybe it's because there are too many newbies: all those dot-com day traders, twenty-something house flippers, and newly minted MBAs. As Alan Greenspan told Congress in October 2008, "It was the failure to properly price such risky assets that precipitated the crisis." People didn't know what they were doing. What markets need are more old hands.

Alas, once again the situation is not so simple. Even experienced traders can make big mistakes when conditions change. In research published in the June 2008 *American Economic Review*, Vernon Smith and his collaborators first ran the standard experiment, putting groups through the fifteen-round market twice. Then the researchers changed three conditions: they mixed up the groups, so participants weren't trading with familiar faces; they increased the range of possible dividends, replacing four possible outcomes (0, 8, 28, or 60), averaging 24, with five (0, 1, 8, 28, or 98), averaging 27; finally, they doubled the amount of cash and halved the number of shares in the market. The participants then completed a third round. These changes were based on previous research showing that more cash and bigger dividend spreads exacerbate bubbles.

Sure enough, under the new conditions, the experienced traders generated a bubble just as big as if they'd never been in the lab. It didn't last quite as long, however, or involve as much volume. "Participants seem to be tacitly aware that there will be a crash," the economists write, "and consequently exit from the market (sell) earlier, causing the crash to start earlier." Even so, the price peaks far above the fundamental value. "Bubbles," the economists conclude, "are the funny and unpredictable phenomena that happen on the way to the 'rational' predicted equilibrium *if the environment is held constant long enough.*"

For those of us who invest our money outside the lab, this research carries two implications.

First, beware of markets with too much cash chasing too few good deals. When the Federal Reserve cuts interest rates, it effectively frees up more cash to buy financial instruments. When lenders lower down-payment requirements, they do the same for the housing market. All that cash encourages investment mistakes.

Second, big changes can turn even experienced traders into ignorant novices. Those changes could be the rise of new industries like the dot-coms of the 1990s or new derivative securities created by slicing up and repackaging mortgages. I asked the Caltech economist Charles Plott, one of the pioneers of experimental economics, whether the recent financial crisis might have come from this kind of inexperience. "I think that's a good thesis," he said. With so many new instruments, "it could be that the inexperienced heads are not people but the organizations themselves. The organizations haven't learned how to deal with the risk or identify the risk or understand the risk."

Here the bubble experiments meet up with another large body of experimental research, first developed by Plott and his collaborators. This work explores how speculative markets can pool information from lots of people ("the wisdom of crowds") and arrive at accurate predictions—for example, who's going to win the presidency or the World Series. These markets work, Plott explains, because people with good information rush in early, leading prices to reflect what they know and setting a trajectory that others follow. "It's a kind of cascade, a good cascade, just what should happen," he says. But sometimes the process "can go bananas" and create a bubble, usually when good information is scarce and people follow leaders who don't in fact know much.

That may be what happened on Wall Street, Plott suggests. "Now we have new instruments. We have 'leaders,' who one would ordinarily think know something, getting in there very aggressively and everybody cuing on them—as they have done in the past, and as markets should. But in this case, there might be a bubble." And when you have a bubble, you will get a crash.

△

PART 10　READINGS

Reading the Genre

1. Postrel examines a laboratory experiment that economists have been conducting for almost thirty years. How does she assess the experiment's strengths and limitations? (See "Appreciate your limits," p. 140.)

2. What key economic terms does Postrel discuss? How does she define them for a popular audience?

3. Researchers began conducting the stock trading experiment in the 1980s. What recent economic problems does Postrel suggest their findings might have helped to predict or avoid?

4. **WRITING:** Search Google Scholar or a library database for works by Charles Noussair, one of the economists Postrel interviews. Read one of his articles — perhaps about consumer buying habits, international trade, or investment bubbles — and write a short summary that focuses on how Noussair describes causes. (See Chapter 45, "Summarizing Sources," p. 491.)

5. **FLOWCHART:** Search the Web for models of decision trees and flowcharts, and then present the basic process of the 24-cent dividend experiment in graphic form. (See Chapter 53, "Tables, Graphs, and Infographics," p. 584.)

EXPLORATORY ESSAY   Tricia Rose teaches Africana studies at Brown University. Her first book, *Black Noise: Rap Music and Black Culture in Contemporary America* (1994), revolutionized academic study of popular music. The essay reprinted here originally appeared as a chapter in Rose's *The Hip Hop Wars: What We Talk about When We Talk about Hip Hop — and Why It Matters* (2008), a book that examines both sides of ten controversial issues surrounding hip-hop music and culture.

TRICIA ROSE

Hip Hop Causes Violence

I'm giving you my opinion that says he is not an artist, he's a thug. . . . [Y]ou can't draw a line in the sand and say Ludacris, because he is a subversive guy that, number one advocates violence, number two, narcotics selling and all the other things, he's not as bad as Pol Pot [Cambodian communist] so we'll put a Pepsi can in his hand.

— Bill O'Reilly, on the subject of Ludacris as a Pepsi celebrity representative, *The O'Reilly Factor*, August 28, 2002

Ronald Ray Howard was executed Thursday [October 6, 2005] for fatally shooting a state trooper, a slaying his trial attorneys argued was prompted by Howard's listening to anti-police rap music. . . . Howard's trial attorney, Allen Tanner, told a reporter: "He grew up in the ghetto and disliked police, and these were his heroes . . . these rappers . . . telling him if you're pulled over, just blast away. It affected him." Howard didn't say for certain that rap music was responsible for his crime. [But he did say:] "All my experiences with police have never been good, whether I've been doing something bad or not."

— David Carson (www.txexecutions.org/reports/350.asp, October 7, 2005)

I would say to Radio 1, do you realize that some of the stuff you play on Saturday nights encourages people to carry guns and knives?

— David Cameron, British politician, www.BBC.com, June 7, 2006

Akey aspect of much of the criticism that has been leveled at hip hop is the claim that it glorifies, encourages, and thus causes violence. This argument goes as far back as the middle to late 1980s—the so-called golden age of hip hop—when politically radical hip hop artists, such as Public Enemy, who referred to direct and sometimes armed resistance against racism "by any means necessary," were considered advocates of violence. It is important to zero in on the specific issue of violence because this was the most highly visible criticism of hip hop for over a decade. The concern over hip hop and violence peaked in the early to mid-1990s when groups like N.W.A. from Los Angeles found significant commercial success through a gang-oriented repertoire of stories related especially to antipolice sentiment. N.W.A.'s 1989 song "*uck the Police"—with lyrics boasting that when they are done, "it's gonna be a bloodbath of cops dyin' in LA"—was at the epicenter of growing fears that rappers' tales of aggression and frustration (which many critics mistakenly perceived as simply pro-criminal statements of intent) were stirring up violent behavior among young listeners. The 1992 debut commercial single for Snoop Doggy Dogg, "Deep Cover" (from the film of the same name), garnered attention because of Snoop's laconic rap style, Dr. Dre's extra-funky beats, and the chorus phrase "187 on a undercover cop" ("187" is the police code for homicide). As what we now call gangsta rap began to move to the commercial center stage, the worry that increasing portrayals of violence in rap lyrics might encourage fans to imitate them evolved into a belief that the rappers were *themselves* criminals— representing their own violent acts in the form of rhyme. Snoop's own criminal problems authenticated his lyrics and added to the alarm about gangsta rap. As this shift in commercial hip hop has solidified, many vocal public critics have begun to characterize violence-portraying lyrics as autobiographical thuggery to a soundtrack. In turn, this link of violent lyrics in hip hop and behavior has been used in the legal arena by both defense and prosecuting attorneys. As the above epigraphs reveal, hip hop lyrics have indeed been considered strong influences. Increasingly, this connection has been extended into the realm of establishing character in murder trials. Prosecutors around the country have buttressed their cases with defendants' penned lyrics as evidence of their criminal-mindedness.

The criticism that hip hop advocates and thus causes violence relies on the unsubstantiated but widely held belief that listening to violent stories or consuming violent images *directly* encourages violent behavior. This concern was raised vis-à-vis violent video games during the 1980s, but also more recently, in relation to heavy metal music. Although the direct link between consumption and action may appear to be commonsensical, studies have been unable to provide evidence that confirms it. Recent challenges to the video game industry's sale of exceptionally gory and violent video games were stymied by the absence of such data and confirmation. Direct behavioral effect is, of course, a difficult thing to prove in scientific terms, since many recent and past factors—both individual and social—can contribute to a person's actions at any given time. The absence of direct proof doesn't mean that such imagery and lyrics are without negative impact. I am not arguing *for* the regular consumption of highly violent images and stories, nor am I saying that what we consume has no impact on us. Clearly, everything around us, past and present, has an impact on us, to one degree or another. Studies do show that violent music lyrics have been documented as increasing aggressive thoughts and feelings. High-saturation levels of violent imagery and action (in our simulated wars and fights in sports, film, music, and television but also, more significantly, in our real wars in the Middle East) clearly do not support patient, peaceful, cooperative actions and responses in our everyday lives.

However, the argument for one-to-one causal linking among storytelling, consumption, and individual action should be questioned, given the limited evidence to support this claim. And, even more important, the blatantly selective application of worries about violence in some aspects of popular culture and everyday life should be challenged for its targeting of individuals and groups who are already overly and problematically associated with violence. So, what may appear to be genuine concern over violence in entertainment winds up stigmatizing some expressions (rap music) and the groups with which they are associated (black youth). A vivid example of this highly selective application took place during the 1992 presidential campaign when George W. Bush said it was "sick" to produce a record that he said glorified the killing of police officers, but saw no contradiction between this statement and his acceptance of support and endorsement from Arnold Schwarzenegger. As one [*New York Times*] reporter put it: "I stand against those who use films or records or television or video games to glorify killing law enforcement officers," said Mr. Bush, who counts among his top supporters the actor Arnold Schwarzenegger, whose character in the movies *Terminator* and *Terminator II: Judgment Day* kills or maims dozens of policemen.

We live in a popular cultural world in which violent stories, images, lyrics, and performances occupy a wide cross-section of genres and mediums. Television shows such as *24* and *Law and Order*; Hollywood fare such as gangster, action, suspense, murder-driven, war, and horror films; video games; metal musics; and novels — together, these comprise a diverse and highly accessible palette of violent images attached to compelling characters and bolstered by high-budget realistic sets and backdrops. Although anti-violence groups mention many of these genres and mediums, the bulk of the popular criticism about violence in popular culture is leveled at hip hop, and the fear-driven nature of the commentary is distinct from responses to the many other sources of violent imagery. There are three important differences between the criticisms of hip hop and rappers and those leveled at other music, films, shows, and videos — most of which, unlike rap music, are produced (not just consumed) primarily by whites.

First, hip hop gets extra attention for its violent content, and the *perception* of violence is heightened when it appears in rap music form rather than in some other popular genre of music featuring violent imagery. Rappers such as Lil' Jon, Ludacris,

50 Cent, and T.I. who claim that there is violence throughout popular culture and that they get overly singled out are right: Some violent imagery and lyrics in popular culture are responded to or perceived differently from others. Social psychologist Carrie B. Fried studied this issue and concluded that the perception of violence in rap music lyrics is affected by larger societal perceptions and stereotypes of African-Americans. In her study, she asked participants to respond to lyrics from a folk song about killing a police officer. To some of the participants the song was presented as rap; and to others, as country. Her study supports the hypothesis that lyrics presented as rap music are judged more harshly than the same lyrics presented as country music. She concluded that these identical lyrics seem more violent when featured in rap, perhaps because of the association of rap with the stereotypes of African-Americans.

Nevertheless, saying that there is violence elsewhere and that one is being unfairly singled out in connection with it isn't the best argument to make. Rappers' claims that violence is everywhere isn't a compelling case for hip hop's heightened investment in violent storytelling, especially for those of us who are worried about the extra levels of destructive forces working against poor black people. It is important, however, to pay close attention to the issue of unfair targeting, blame, and the compounded effect this perception of blacks as more violent has on black youth.

Second, many critics of hip hop tend to interpret lyrics literally and as a direct reflection of the artist who performs them. They equate rappers with thugs, see rappers as a threat to the larger society, and then use this "causal analysis" (that hip hop causes violence) to justify a variety of agendas: more police in black communities, more prisons to accommodate larger numbers of black and brown young people, and more censorship of expression. For these critics, hip hop is criminal propaganda. This literal approach, which extends beyond the individual to characterize an entire racial and class group, is rarely applied to violence-oriented mediums produced by whites.

Despite the caricature-like quality of many of hip hop's cultivated images and the similarity of many of its stories, critics often characterize rappers as speaking entirely autobiographically, implying that their stories of car-jacking, killing witnesses to crimes, hitting women, selling drugs, and beating up and killing opponents are statements of fact, truthful self-portraits. Thus, for instance, the rhyme in Lil' Wayne's "Damage Is Done" that describes him as running away with a "hammer in my jeans, dead body behind me, cops'll never find me" would be interpreted by many critics as a description of actual events. This assumption—that rappers are creating rhymed autobiographies—is the result of both rappers' own investment in perpetuating the idea that everything they say is true to their life experience (given that the genre has grown out of the African-American tradition of boasting in the first person) and the genre's investment in the pretense of no pretense. That is, the genre's promoters capitalize on the illusion that the artists are not performing but "keeping it real"—telling the truth, wearing outfits on stage that they'd wear in the street (no costumes), remaining exactly as they'd be if they were not famous, except richer. Part of this "keeping it real" ethos is a laudable effort to continue to identify with many of their fans, who don't see their style or life experiences represented anywhere else, from their own points of view; part of it is the result of conformity to the genre's conventions. It makes rappers more accessible, more reflective of some of the lived experiences and conditions that shape the lives of some of their fans. And it gives fans a sense that they themselves have the potential to reach celebrity status, to gain social value and prestige while remaining "true" to street life and culture, turning what traps them into an imagined gateway to success.

But this hyper-investment in the fiction of full-time autobiography in hip hop, especially for those artists who have adopted gangsta personas, has been exaggerated and distorted by a powerful history of racial images of black men as "naturally" violent and criminal. These false and racially motivated stereotypes were promoted throughout the last two centuries to justify both slavery and the violence, containment, and revised disenfranchisement that followed emancipation; and they persisted throughout the twentieth century to justify the development of urban seg-regation. In the early part of the twentieth century, well-respected scientists pursu-ing the "genetic" basis of racial and ethnic hierarchy embraced the view that blacks were biologically inferior, labeling them not only less intelligent but also more prone to crime and violence. These racial associations have been reinforced, directly and indirectly, through a variety of social outlets and institutions and, even today, continue to be circulated in contemporary scientific circles. In 2007, for example, Nobel laureate biologist Jim Watson said that he was "inherently gloomy about the prospects of Africa" because "all our social policies are based on the fact that their intelligence is the same as ours, whereas all the testing says not really." He went on to say that while he hoped everyone was equal, "people who have to deal with black employees find this is not true." And in the now-infamous, widely challenged 1994 book *The Bell Curve*, Richard J. Herrnstein and Charles Murray argued that it is highly likely that genes partly explain racial differences in IQ testing and intel-ligence and also claimed that intelligence is an important predictor of income, job performance, unwed pregnancy, and crime. Thus the pseudoscientific circle was closed: Blacks are genetically less intelligent, and intelligence level predicts income, performance, criminality, and sexually unsanctioned behavior; therefore, blacks are genetically disposed toward poverty, crime, and unwed motherhood.

This history of association of blacks with ignorance, sexual deviance, violence, and criminality has not only contributed to the believability of hip hop artists' ficti-tious autobiographical tales among fans from various racial groups but has also helped explain the excessive anxiety about the popularity and allure of these artists. The American public has long feared black criminality and violence as particularly anxiety-producing threats to whites — and the convincing "performance" of black criminality taps into these fears. So, both the voyeuristic pleasure of believing that hip hop artists are criminal minded and the exaggerated fear of them are deeply connected. Hip hop has successfully traded on this history of scientific racism and its embedded impact on perceptions of poor black people, and has also been significantly criticized because of it.

A third central difference between the criticism of hip hop and rappers and the criticism leveled at other forms of popular culture has to do with the way the artists themselves are perceived in relation to their audiences and to society. Hip hop's violence is criticized at a heightened level and on different grounds from the vast array of violent images in American culture, and these disparities in perception are very important. While heavy metal and other nonblack musical forms that contain substantial levels of violent imagery are likewise challenged by anti-violence critics, the operative assumption is that this music and its violence-peddling creators will negatively influence otherwise innocent listeners. Therefore (according to these critics), metal, video games, and violent movies influence otherwise nonviolent teenagers, encouraging them to act violently. From this perspective, "our youth" must be protected from these outside negative, aggressive influences.

In the case of rap, the assumption is that the artists and their autobiographically styled lyrics represent an existing and already threatening violent black youth culture that must be prevented from affecting society at large. The quote from Bill O'Reilly at the outset of this chapter reflects this approach. For O'Reilly, Ludacris is advocating violence and selling narcotics. Allowing him to be a representative for Pepsi would, as O'Reilly's logic goes, be similar to giving power to Pol Pot, the Cambodian leader of the brutal Khmer Rouge government, allowing a "subversive" guy access to legitimate power. This difference in interpretation — such that black rappers are viewed as leaders of an invading and destructively violent force that undermines society — has a dramatic effect on both the nature of the criticism and the larger perceptions of black youth that propel the ways in which they are treated. It sets the terms of how we respond, whom we police, and whom we protect.

Tales of violence in hip hop share important similarities with the overall in-vestment in violence as entertainment (and political problem solving) in American culture, but they have more localized origins as well—namely, the damaging and terrible changes in black urban America over the past forty or so years. Although hip hop's penchant for stories with violent elements isn't purely a matter of documen-tary or autobiography, these stories are deeply connected to real social conditions and their impact on the lives of those who live them, close up. My point here may be confusing: On the one hand, I am saying that rappers are not the autobiographers they are often believed to be and that seeing them that way has contributed to the attacks they specifically face. But, on the other hand, I am also saying that much of what listeners hear in hip hop stories of violence is reflective of larger real-life social conditions. How can both be true?

This is a crucial yet often improperly made distinction: Hip hop is not pure fiction or fantasy (such as might emerge from the mind of horror writer Stephen King), but neither is it unmediated reality and social advocacy for violence. Nor is rap a product of individual imagination (disconnected from lived experiences and social conditions) or sociological documentation or autobiography (an exact depic-tion of reality and personal action). Yet conversations about violence in hip hop strategically deploy both of these arguments. Defenders call it fiction, just like other artists' work, whereas critics want to emphasize rappers' own claims to be keeping it real as proof that these stories "advocate violence" or, as British politician David Cameron suggested, "[encourage] people to carry guns and knives."

Neither of these positions moves us toward a more empowering understanding of violent storytelling and imagery in hip hop or toward the fashioning of a produc-tive, pro-youth position that recognizes the impact of these powerfully oppressive images without either accepting or excusing their negative effects. This is the line we must straddle: acknowledging the realities of discrimination and social policies that have created the conditions for the most dangerous and fractured black urban communities and, at the same time, not accepting or excusing the behaviors that are deeply connected to these local, social conditions.

The origins for the depth of investment in hip hop's myriad but context-specific stories involving guns, drugs, street culture, and crime are directly related to a combination of drastic changes in social life, community, and policies of neglect that destroyed neighborhood stability in much of black urban America. These local, social condition–based origins matter because the causal assumption that violent material when consumed increases violent actions underestimates the environmental forces at work. Although hip hop's violence has been marketed and exaggerated, its origins in violent urban communities and the reasons these communities became so violent must be understood. This context helps explain why hip hop's poorest inner-city fans and artists remain so invested in such stories. Rather than creating violence out of whole cloth, these stories are better understood as a distorted and profitable reflection of the everyday lives of too many poor black youth over the past forty or so years.

While context is crucial for explaining what we hear in a good deal of hip hop, context as justification for rap's constant repetition of violent storytelling is highly problematic. Rapper Tupac, for example, claimed that he was hoping to reveal the conditions in a powerful way to incite change: "I'm gonna show the most graphic details about what I see in my community and hopefully they'll stop it. Quick." Unfortunately, profits increased with increasingly violent, criminal-oriented rap while conditions remained and worsened. Despite the reality that these real conditions are not being changed because of rappers' stories and, instead, have become fodder for corporate profits, rappers continue to justify the use of black urban community distress and criminal icons along these lines, thus maintaining their value as a revenue stream. 50 Cent defended his lyrics, claiming that "[i]t's a reflection of the environment that I come from," and Jay-Z has confessed that "it's important for rappers to exaggerate 'life in the ghetto' because this is the only way the underclass can make its voice heard."

This context—the destruction of black community in urban America since the mid-1970s—has five central elements, each of which exacerbates the others, causing the serious dismantling of stable communities and resulting in several forms of social breakdown, one of which is increased violence.

High Levels of Chronic Joblessness

The issue of black and brown teen joblessness took on crisis proportions during the first two decades of hip hop's emergence. Unemployment and very low-paying, unstable employment have been concentrated in poor minority urban communities since the early part of the twentieth century, but this lengthy history of how race limits working-class opportunity took an especially pernicious turn in the 1980s and continued through the 1990s and beyond. What many scholars and economists call "permanent unemployment" or "chronic joblessness" began to plague poor black and brown communities, and the younger adults in these communities began to understand that traditional avenues for working-class job stability were becoming closed to them.

The effects of deindustrialization—the swift and extensive loss of unionized, well-paying manufacturing jobs out of urban areas to rural and nonunionized regions and out of the country entirely—hit all workers hard and dramatically undercut working-class economic mobility. This loss was accompanied by a growth in low-wage "service" jobs, which tended to be part-time and to offer limited or no benefits and few opportunities for upward mobility. Owing to both historical and contemporary forms of racial discrimination in the job market, these overall changes have been especially devastating for black communities. Indeed, blacks continued to be last hired and thus first fired when factories closed, and they were disproportionately kept in lower-level positions where upward advancement and skill-building (and thus job rehiring opportunities) are limited. During Ronald Reagan's second term, for example, more than one-third of black families earned incomes below the poverty line. By contrast, poverty rates hovered between 8 and 9 percent among white families. During the same period, black teenagers' already high levels of unemployment increased from 38.9 to 43.6 percent nationally, and in some regions, such as the Midwestern cities in the Great Lakes region, the figures were as high as 50 to 70 percent. By contrast, white teenage unemployment was around 13 percent.

Chronic and very high levels of unemployment and the poverty it creates, especially when magnified by long-standing injustice and discrimination, produce not only economic crisis but deep instabilities within families and across communities. These, in turn, result in higher levels of homelessness, street crime, and illegal income-generating activities (such as the drug trade), and alienation, rage, and violence.

Dramatic Loss of Affordable Housing/Urban Renewal

The legacies of thirty years of "urban renewal" began to bear rotten fruit in the middle to late 1970s. Dubbed "negro removal" by James Baldwin, the urban renewal programs designed to "clear slums" because they were considered "eyesores" proved to be terribly ill-conceived forms of neighborhood destruction that had a disproportionately negative impact on poor black urban communities. While the migration of millions of black people to cities in the twentieth century was met with forced urban housing segregation (producing what we now call black ghettos), those neighborhoods were also sources of community strength and general stability. Yes, poverty, discrimination, and other urban problems persisted, but areas like Watts in Los Angeles, Harlem in New York City, East St. Louis, and the Hill District in Pittsburgh became stable, multiclass communities where black people, as scholar Earl Lewis maintained, "turned segregation into congregation."

Urban renewal, especially during and after the 1960s, destroyed these low-income but highly network-rich and socially stable communities to make room for private development, sports arenas, hotels, trade centers, and high-income luxury buildings.

Far from being a plan to create affordable housing, it created the massive housing crisis we still face today. By the summer of 1967, 400,000 residential units in urban renewal areas had been demolished; only 10,760 low-rent public housing units were built on these sites. In 1968, the Kerner Commission report pointed out that

> [i]n Detroit a maximum of 758 low-income units have been assisted through (federal) programs since 1956. . . . Yet, since 1960, approximately 8,000 low-income units have been demolished for urban renewal. . . . Similarly in Newark, since 1959, a maximum of 3,760 low-income housing units have been assisted through the programs considered. . . . [D]uring the same period, more than 12,000 families, mostly low income, have been displaced by such public uses of urban renewal, public housing and highways.

This pattern of demolishing and not replacing thousands of units of existing affordable housing in poor black communities had a devastating impact in black communities all around the country, creating the constellation of symptoms in many major cities that we see today.

This was not just a housing problem, although the homeless crisis it produced was immense. The physical destruction of so many buildings was accompanied by the demolition of most of the adjacent venues and stores that served as community adhesive. Corner stores, music clubs, social clubs, beauty parlors, and barber shops were also displaced or destroyed, fraying community networks and patterns of connection. Social psychologist Mindy Fullilove refers to the destruction caused by urban renewal as "root shock," the "traumatic stress reaction to the destruction of all or part of one's emotional ecosystem." She astutely contextualizes this widespread destruction of housing and the social networks around it as one that destroyed communities, resulting in social disarray and increased levels of violence:

> Root shock, at the level of the individual, is a profound emotional upheaval. . . . [It] undermines trust, increases anxiety, . . . destabilizes relationships, destroys social, emotional, and financial resources, and increases the risk for every kind of

stress-related disease, from depression to heart attack. Root shock, at the level of the local community, . . . ruptures bonds, dispersing people to all the directions of the compass. . . . The great epidemics of drug addiction, the collapse of the black family, and the rise in incarceration of black men—all of these catastrophes followed the civil rights movement, they did not precede it. Though there are a number of causes of this dysfunction that cannot be disputed—the loss of manufacturing jobs, in particular—the current situation of Black America cannot be understood without a full and complete accounting of the social, economic, cultural, political, and emotional losses that followed the bulldozing of 1,600 neighborhoods.

Drug-Trade Expansion

The emergence of very cheap, addictive, and profitable drugs, such as PCP, but especially crack cocaine, in the mid-1980s made bad matters worse. The bleak economic reality of high levels of chronic joblessness and the loss of community networks produced by the destruction of black communities and massive housing demolition created not only a financial incentive for dealing hard drugs but an emotional one as well. The desire for drugs is directly linked to the longing to numb pain and suffering. Cheap, easily accessible, and highly addictive drugs like crack are especially alluring to the poor and others who face not only their own personal demons but also demons unleashed by society that are largely beyond their control. The affordability and profitability of crack created quick wealth for otherwise chronically unemployed people turned street dealers and fostered violent drug-gang turf wars and a whole generation of people in the clutches of a highly addictive drug.

This was at once a new phenomenon and part of a long history of black communities' serving as commercial shopping zones for all drug users from all class positions and racial backgrounds; crack's notoriously addictive qualities and low price—coupled with inattention to attacking drug distribution at higher levels—created a flourishing local and violent drug trade that spurred, expanded, and intensified gang activities in poor black and brown communities. The impact of drug addiction on the social public sphere was dramatic. The street sex trades became more linked to drugs; women especially, but also men who needed only a small amount of cash to get high, began selling themselves to support their crack habit. Drug addiction, which also fueled the spread of HIV/AIDS, was both a symptom and a cause of the extraordinary breakdown of poor black urban communities nationwide. Many rappers such as Jay-Z, 50 Cent, and T.I. are known for transforming themselves from drug dealers to rap moguls. Lyrics that reflect their history as drug dealers abound. Consider, for example, the chorus for 50 Cent's "Bloodhound": "I love to pump crack, I love to stay strapped."

But the crisis was so widespread that a whole generation of black comedians such as Chris Rock, David Chapelle, and others who grew up in and around this very dark period in black urban America came out with popular, biting, powerful routines and dark jokes about crack addiction and its impact on black communities. In a sense, the ground-level impact of crack, unemployment, and community destruction became a generational experience for many black youth. In a *Rolling Stone* interview, Chris Rock talked about the deep effects that crack had on the economic, social, and gender relations in black communities. The interviewer asked him: "How about crack? So many of your jokes and characters revolve around crack." Rock replies: "Basically, whatever was going on when you started getting laid will stick with you for the rest of your life. So crack was just a big part of my life, between my friends selling it or girls I use to like getting hooked on it. White people had the Internet; the ghetto had crack. . . . I have never been to war, but I survived that shit. I lost friends and family members. The whole neighborhood was kinda on crack. Especially living in Bed-Stuy [in Brooklyn], man." And in one of many David Chapelle skits featuring the memorable crack-head Tyrone Biggums, Biggums says: "Why do you think I car-jacked you, Rhonda?" Rhonda replies, "Cause the cops found you in it three hours later asleep, high on crack!" Biggums responds: "That's impossible, Rhonda. How can you sleep when you're high on crack? Chinese riddle for you."

AK-47: Automatic Weapons and the Drug Economy

If this highly profitable illegal drug trade had been protected just by fists and knives, it would have been violent but not nearly as deadly. Instead, this always violent young men's drug trade was fueled by easy access to guns, especially high-powered automatic weaponry. Given the financial incentives of crack, drug dealers used the most powerful weapons available to protect their businesses. And, increasingly, those not involved in selling drugs, especially young black men who were considered part of the same age and gender demographic, felt they had to carry guns to protect themselves.

Neighborhood turf wars have a long bloody history in immigrant and working-class communities; tales of street peril among white male immigrant youth over 100 years ago bear a striking resemblance to descriptions of today's invisible neighborhood boundaries and the dangerous street conflict they give rise to. But what really escalated this situation was the emergence of the highly lucrative crack trade and the flooding of poor urban communities with guns, especially semiautomatic ones. (Geoffrey Canada's book *Fist, Stick, Knife, Gun* chronicles the impact of the availability of this increasingly deadly weaponry and its impact on adolescent male violence.) Few young men fifty years ago lost their lives in street skirmishes, bloody and frequent though they were, as access to deadly weapons was extremely limited then and the reasons for such turf battles were personal rather than wedded to the extremely lucrative high-stakes drug trade. Greedy high-level drug dealers and gun dealers, enabled both by the gun lobby and by terribly misguided and neglectful public policy, turned a long-standing problem into a life-threatening crisis of extraordinary proportions.

Government/Police Response: Incarceration over Rehabilitation

The 1980s "war on drugs" was really a war on the communities that bore the brunt of the drug crisis. The police and federal resource emphasis on low-level street dealers and the criminalization (rather than rehabilitation) of drug users resulted in the treatment of ravaged communities as war zones. The LAPD, for example, is considered legendary for its use of military strategies, developed during the war in Vietnam, on U.S. citizens in South Central Los Angeles. This slash-and-burn approach, one that failed to address the roots of the problem and barely distinguished between the drug dealers and the communities as a whole, turned poor black communities into occupied territories. Helicopter surveillance and small tanks equipped with battering rams were hallmarks of the LAPD policing in South Central LA in the middle to late 1980s. Housing projects were equipped with police substations, and young black males were routinely picked up for "potential gang activity." Their names were placed in a database; many were intimidated and brutalized. And yet the government failed to enact effective community-building responses such as rehabilitation, meaningful and stable jobs, well-supervised recreational outlets, and social services to enhance the support networks around children.

The criminal justice system reinforced this warlike strategy by defining crack offenses as more criminal than other drug offenses, applying and effectively justifying longer sentences (especially those dubbed "maximum minimum" sentences) for crack users and dealers, who were poor and predominantly black, than for users of cocaine, a drug more often consumed by middle-class and white drug users. In fact, although crack and cocaine possess the same active ingredient, crack cocaine is the only drug whereby the first offense of simple possession can initiate a federal mandatory minimum sentence. Possession of five grams of crack will trigger a five-year mandatory minimum sentence. By contrast, according to the U.S. Sentencing Commission, "simple possession of any quantity of any other substance by a first-time offender — including powder cocaine — is a misdemeanor offense punishable by a maximum of one year in prison." Owing to the designation of drug users as criminals rather than as people in need of rehabilitation (and given the special targeting of crack users and dealers over all other drug users), the black prison population skyrocketed and so did the parolee population. In 1986, before mandatory minimums for crack offenses went into effect, the average federal drug offense sentence for blacks was 11 percent higher than for whites; four years later—after these harsher and targeted laws were implemented, the average federal drug offense sentence was 49 percent higher for blacks. In 1997, the U.S. Sentencing Commission report found that "nearly 90 percent of the offenders convicted in federal court for crack cocaine distribution are African-American while the majority of crack cocaine users are white. Thus, sentences appear to be harsher and more severe for racial minorities than others as a result of this law." The extensive denial of the ways that race and racism shaped and consolidated violence, instability, and poverty continued to fuel misguided and mean-spirited policies that focused far more on emphasizing personal behavioral responsibility and punishment than on community support and collective responsibility.

The "war on drugs" policy that favored punishment over other social responses was singularly responsible for the incredible expansion of the prison industrial complex and the heavy impact this had on poor black communities. Between 1970 and 1982 the U.S. prison population doubled in size; between 1982 and 1999, it increased again threefold. Within the United States today are only 5 percent of the world's inhabitants but 25 percent of the world's prisoners. Of the 2 million Americans currently behind bars, black men and women, who comprise around 12 percent of the national population, are profoundly overrepresented. Currently, black men make up 40 percent of prisoners in federal, state, and local prisons. Researchers anticipate that this trend will continue; based on current policies and conditions, they say that 30 percent of black men born today can expect to spend some time in prison. Among current black male prisoners, a disproportionately high number come from a small number of predominantly or entirely minority neighborhoods in big cities where aggressive street-level policing and profiling are heavily practiced. Over half of the adult male inmates from New York City come from fourteen districts in the Bronx, Manhattan, and Brooklyn, even though men in those areas make up just 17 percent of the city's total population. Numbers like these inspired the Justice Mapping Center to examine prison spending by neighborhood and by city block. Center founders Eric Cadora and Charles Swartz discovered what they dubbed "million-dollar blocks," neighborhoods where "so many residents were sent to state prison that the total cost of their incarceration will be more than one million dollars." In Brooklyn alone, there were thirty-five such blocks. Rates of incarceration among black women have also risen dramatically and disproportionately. Almost half of the female prison population are black, and many of these women are locked up for nonviolent offenses (theft, forgery, prostitution, and drugs) that are directly linked to the forces of community destruction addressed in this chapter. The community-wide impact of these disproportionate and racially specific levels of policing and incarceration is staggering.

These are the architectural signposts of today's ghettos. The violence that takes place within them has been created not only by racial discrimination long ago but also by assaults on poor black communities since the 1960s. The high levels of crime, police brutality, violence, drugs, and instability that define poor black urban communities are the direct result of chronic and high levels of concentrated jobless-ness, loss of affordable housing, community demolition, the crack explosion, the impact of easily accessible and highly deadly weapons used to defend the lucrative drug trade, and incarceration strategies that have criminalized large swaths of the African-American population. While not all of these factors were unique to poor black urban America, some were, and others were highly concentrated there. These recent conditions, along with compounding factors such as the long-term effects of economic, social, and political forms of racial discrimination, intensified the dra-matic demise of working-class and poor black urban communities.

Hip hop emerged in this context, and thus the tales of drug dealing, pimping, petty crime, dropping out of school, and joining a gang are more aptly seen as reflec-tions of the violence experienced in these areas than as origins of the violence. The drive to point out and criticize violence in rappers' stories as the cause of violence in poor black communities is often a disgraceful extension of the overemphasis on individual (decontextualized) personal behavior and the deep denial of larger social responsibility for creating and fostering these contexts.

The violent stories that characterize many hip hop lyrics are tales from this landscape, told from the ground-level perspective of circumstances as lived experience, not historical or sociological analysis. When we understand the depths of this reality, the actual destruction and violence that these societally manufactured conditions have fostered, then the violent lyrics take on a different character.

Why is it so difficult to understand that this highly vulnerable and dismantled community of chronically poor and racially-discriminated-against young people is in need of protection and advocacy? Why are we turning youth (through attacks on rap) into the agents of their own demise, seeing black kids as the source of violence in America while denying the extraordinary violence done to them?

My foregoing summary of the five causes of destruction of black communities—*chronic joblessness, loss of affordable housing, drug-trade expansion, automatic weapons and the drug economy,* and *incarceration instead of rehabilitation*—is not meant to encourage a blithe reaction to violent stories in hip hop, nor to cause readers to say, "Well, this is their reality." The prevalence of such stories in hip hop and the fact that they too often valorize violence (sometimes even serving as seductive tales of predatory action against other poor black people) are signs of a crisis for which the nation as a whole is responsible; the stories and rhymes themselves are not the primary source of the crisis. Attacking the rappers individually—calling them thugs and criminals while studiously avoiding the state of poor black urban America, or, worse, blaming these conditions entirely or even primarily on black people themselves—is a disturbing aspect of the hip hop wars. This stance reflects a long-term drive to deny the continued power and influence of institutional racism, sustains a racialized "us" versus "them" philosophy that enables the maintenance of racial and class inequality, and, in effect, extends the very logic that drove many of these mean-spirited and disempowering urban policies in the first place.

Culture is a means by which we learn how to engage with the world, and thus constant depictions of violence can have a normative effect. While this effect is not direct and absolute, there is ample evidence that people are deeply influenced by their surroundings and the social conditions impinging on them. Compared to children growing up in secure and stable environments, those who live in violence- or crime-ridden communities are at greater risk for exhibiting criminal and violent behavior. Our visually mediated culture is a large part of the surroundings and social conditions that shape us. If we are treated in violent ways, if we are forced by circumstance to survive in places where violent conflict is a matter of everyday life, and if we consume many violent images, we are more at risk—not only for exhibiting higher levels of violent behavior but, more important, for experiencing less trust and intimacy, increased fear, and a greater need for self-protection.

So, hip hop's extensive repertoire of stories about violence, guns, drugs, crime, and prison is compounded by everyday life for those who have little or no option but to reside in the poorest and most troubled neighborhoods and communities. Such stories become more powerful in this context, providing an image of everyday realities that can overemphasize the worst of what young people in these places face. On behalf of these kids, not the ones who listen vicariously from afar, we should be concerned about how and how often street crime and the drug trade are depicted—not because they represent the infusion of violence in American culture but because they sound an alarm about the levels of violence and social decay created by policies, public opinion, and neglect.

We must pay close attention to violence in hip hop, but we should not treat the tales of violence in hip hop in dangerous isolation from the many crucial contexts for its existence. Decontextualization—taking the violence expressed in hip hop lyrics and storytelling and examining them out of context—has a number of problematic effects both for the art form and for black people in general. Not only are the larger nonblack cultural reasons for these violent themes ignored but, worse, these reasons are attributed to black people themselves. So, the issue, once decontextualized, becomes violence as a black cultural problem, not violence as a larger social problem with tragic consequences for the most vulnerable. This approach does nothing to help us think through and reduce violence in black communities or in American society more broadly, nor to reduce our collective appetite for violent entertainment or our use of violence as a means to achieve success and secure opportunity. It does, however, contribute to the further targeting and criminalization of poor black youth; it helps us imagine that this is "their problem," which only "they" can fix by acting right.

Another negative effect of taking hip hop's lyrical tales of violence out of social context is that their distinctive style of expression overshadows all similarities between them and other styles of violent storytelling. Because the particular *brand* of poor urban black and Latino male street culture that many rappers detail in their rhymes is unfamiliar to many whites (who because of continued patterns of residential segregation do not live in these overwhelmingly black and brown neighborhoods), these unfamiliar listeners often equate black style of expression with content. Although tales of violent street culture have various ethnic and racial origins, the fascination with black versions of such street culture creates the illusion that violent street culture is itself a black cultural thing.

Poor white ethnic neighborhoods have long had their own forms of violent street culture, but the fact that their slang, style, and rhetoric are not generally perceived as racially distinctive contributes to the misreading of black street crime and street culture as a cultural matter rather than as an outgrowth of larger social patterns. This lack of local familiarity with black style among white fans adds to the allure of its expression in hip hop. It also encourages a false sense of black ownership of street culture and crime among blacks. Thus, black language, clothing, and other distinctions in style override the deep similarities between black and other ethnic (white and nonwhite) forms of violent street culture. The lack of regular day-to-day contact between races (facilitated by sustained housing and school segregation) enhances this miscue. Many white fans come to "know" these neighborhoods and their residents through mass media portraits (Hollywood film, television programming, news coverage, rap music lyrics, and videos), which only reinforce the fixation and reduce the recognition of cross-racial examples of violent male street cultures.

These factors, when taken together, create a web that looks something like this: We support policies that destroy black communities, and communities with great instability often experience more violence. Then, we rely on long-standing racist perceptions of black men as more violent, fear them more, and then treat them with more violence in response, which results in both more violence and more incarceration. Next, because we associate these men with violence, the stories they tell about violence are perceived as "authentic black expression," which activates a familiar kind of racial voyeurism and expands the market for their particular stories of crime and violence, which, in turn, confirms the perception that black men are more violent. This creates economic opportunity for performing and celebrating violent storytelling. Round and round we go.

But what is the actual role of violence in lyrics written by young people who live in communities that are struggling to stem the tide of real violence? Are these lyrics celebrations of the violence that shapes their lives—statements in support of the gangs, drugs, and crime about which they rap and rhyme? Or do they reflect a process of emotional and social management—a means by which these young people manage the lived reality of violence by telling their stories (a well-known process of healing in therapeutic and psychological circles)? Do these stories contribute to the violence these young people experience? Or are their stories about violence an outgrowth of the day-to-day threats they face, and do such stories relieve or reduce actual violence by responding to real violence with metaphor?

Or can *both* be true? Can violent lyrics and imagery reflect a real condition and at the same time contribute to creating it? The nub of the problem is this: At what point do stories that emanate from an overly violent day-to-day life begin to encourage and support that aspect of everyday life and undercut the communities' antiviolent efforts?

The question remains as to how we should examine and respond to the images and stories about violence that emanate from people who live in communities plagued by violence. We must continue to discuss whether we should attack the lyrics and the lyricists as causing violence or the conditions that foster violence. Clearly, we should challenge artists who have profited handsomely by constantly reinforcing the worst forms of predatory behavior against poor black communities. But to do so while denying the reality of their circumstances is mean-spirited and ineffectual.

In the song "Trouble" on the CD *Kingdom Come* (Roc-A-Fella Records, 2006), Jay-Z raps about his desire to stop hustling, but says he's only "pretending to be different," praying to god, in the chorus, because he'll never change. Both his longing to change and the bravado that accompanies his return to the game heighten the impact of the song. Jay-Z, a consummate braggadocio-style rapper, reestablishes his dominance over all around him. At one point he raps: "The meek shall perish." He goes on to say, "I'll roof you little nigga, I'm a project terrorist." His unrepentant character (self?) brags about being a person who rules with violent disregard and terrorizes people who live in the projects, an already terrorizing place to be. How should black poor people respond to this character? With pride? Affirmatively? Supportively? Since the song does not offer a critique of this "project terrorist," and given the charisma that Jay-Z imparts through his rhymes, one could perceive it as a glorification of a person terrorizing the most vulnerable members of black American society and demanding that we support his creative rights to profit from it. Why aren't street-level rappers like Jay-Z fashioning countless tales of youthful outrage at such a predator? This is a powerful example of how the art of bragging wedded to the icon of the violent street hustler—in communities where street hustling is a vibrant and destructive force—ends up having the power to celebrate predatory behavior.

In a 2007 *Rolling Stone* interview, Jay-Z acknowledged that the drug wars of which he was a part are hostile to black people and black communities: "When dealers are in the middle of it, they don't realize what they're doing, they don't humanize the people that's using the drugs, they don't humanize the neighborhood. It's not until you mature, and then you look back on it like, 'I was causing a lot of destruction around the neighborhood.'" But where are all the highly commercially successful lyrics that make this crucial point, that de-glamorize the drug trade, that reject gangsta worldviews, that humanize black people? This is the central problem with the expressions of violence and drug-dealer-turned-rapper stories in hip hop: They do not publicly reinforce the transition from "project terrorist" to "project humanist." Far too much pleasure, fame, style, and celebration go to the game, to the hustle, to the dehumanizing rhetoric of taking advantage of black people.

Without making overly blanket, ill-informed generalizations about the creativity in hip hop, we need to be alarmed about storytelling that offers little critique of violence against black people. There are brilliant stories in hip hop that capture the day-to-day reality of dealing with violence but do not seem to glorify it. Consider, for example, the lyrics for Nas's "Gangsta Tears," which tap into the pain, loss, and seemingly permanent cycle of retribution. But such sorrowful tales are a decreasing proportion of what sells records in hip hop, serving instead as "alternative" fare on corporate radio. Far too many of the most financially successful lyricists in hip hop—Jay-Z, 50 Cent, T.I., and Lil' Wayne, among others—overemphasize and glorify violent tales and gang personas because these are profitable. They no longer tell tales from the darkside, with the hopes of contributing to a devaluing of "the life" and producing radical, empowered youth. Instead, there is too much getting rich from the exploitation of black suffering.

Despite the wrong-headed, decontextualized, and unfairly targeted claims about hip hop causing violence, there is some truth to them. It is silly to claim that what we consume, witness, and participate in has no impact on us as individuals and as a society. When a society turns a blind eye to violent behavior and allows its culture and politics to be saturated in violence, it will normalize violence among its citizenry and perhaps also indirectly contribute to violent behavior among some of its citizens. And if we are going to rail about violence in hip hop, we should rail twice as hard about the depths of violence young black people experience, seeing them as the recipients and inheritors of violence rather than solely as its perpetrators. Where is all the media-supported outrage about this?

The combination of denial of the larger forces and the self-congratulatory story of hyper-individual responsibility most readily expressed by white middle-class leaders is more than dishonest; it is itself a form of social violence against the young people who are most vulnerable and who need all of us to make a real and serious commitment to restoring the kinds of institutions and opportunities that keep chaos, violence, and social root shock at bay. The refusal to acknowledge our national culpability for these conditions continues not only the legacy of denying the deep injuries done to African-Americans but also the long-standing use of the expression of black pain from these injuries as "evidence" of black people's own responsibility for these larger circumstances. The depths of the commercial success associated with violent, gang, and street culture as "authentic" hip hop has given violent black masculinity a seal of approval, thus encouraging these behaviors among the kids who are most at risk, and who "need" to embrace this model if manhood is to survive. What began as a form of releasing and healing has become yet another lucrative but destructive economy for young poor black men.

The day-to-day violence that plagues poor communities must be taken into account both as a crucial context for explaining some of what we hear in hip hop and as a reality that compounds the power of violent storytelling. The allure of celebrities whose cachet depends partly on their relationship to a criminal/drug underworld is surely a form of social idolization that might encourage already-vulnerable kids to participate in the lucrative drug trade in neighborhoods where good-paying jobs are nearly nonexistent. A good deal of 50 Cent's initial promotional campaign relied on the fact that he sold crack, that his mother was a crack user, that he was shot nine times and wore a bulletproof vest to protect him against enemies. We can't constantly make violence sexy for young people who find themselves mired in violent social spaces that are mostly not of their making and then expect them not to valorize violent action.

Some of this impact is going to be behavioral, and the behaviors in question should be vociferously challenged and rejected. Black people do not need "project terrorists"! The projects and "million-dollar blocks" are bad enough. Of course, the drive to pathologize black people (and to make pathologized blackness the only "true" and profitable blackness) makes such criticism of black behavior very tricky. But we must confront this dilemma with courage and honesty. Our efforts to support, sustain, and rebuild black communities must permanently join the five major causes of destruction I've listed above to their individual and collective consequences. Neither social responsibility nor individual responsibility should be talked about in isolation. Focusing on hip hop as a cause of violence is just as irresponsible as defending it by pointing to social conditions as a justification for perpetuating gang, gun, and drug slang, iconography, and lifestyles in the music. Despite the finger pointing, both positions in the hip hop wars propagate the myth that black people are themselves violent, and both downplay the violence done to them. Both seem to accept the larger social context as it is; neither challenges American society to change the playing field.

Unbiased, socially just forms of concern about violence will and do focus on directly helping communities reduce violence rather than pointing the finger at and railing about lyrics and images as the cause. Working as many local leaders and community groups do in the communities most directly affected by street crime and other acts of daily violence, activists don't advocate more force, violence, and policing but, on the contrary, strongly advocate for nonviolent conflict resolution in schools, at home, and in other places where children spend a great deal of their time. They also call for access to resources for families to help resolve conflict. Indeed, our response to youth crimes should result in extensive conflict resolution counseling and other highly supervised programs designed to reverse their direction, not placement in ever more violent adult incarceration facilities.

The most effective way to enact concern over violence is to (1) express this concern for black youth, and the real violence they face, in the form of activist social change; and (2) stop being hypocritical about violence. In other words, we must avoid the duplicity involved in expressing outrage at hip hop's violence while remaining virtually silent about the ways that our society condones violence and uses it both as social policy (internationally and at home) and as entertainment. This effort would have to address head-on the social worlds this nation has formed by creating, maintaining, and exacerbating the conditions in ghettos. It would have to confront violence against black youth — direct and indirect — that is part of everyday life but all too often goes unchallenged as a crisis for *our* society unless it spills *out* of the ghetto. Until this happens, those who rail about hip hop's violence but refuse to take into account the forces working against these communities do so not on behalf of the thousands of kids and young adults who have been left to fend for themselves but, rather, against them.

Reading the Genre

1. Why, according to Rose, do critics blame hip-hop music for violence? How does she show that such concerns oversimplify cause and effect?

2. Rose cites other scholars to both ground and extend her causal analysis. To what effect? Find examples of her use of secondary sources, and consider what the use of each of these sources allows Rose to do as a writer. (See Chapter 43, "Evaluating Sources," p. 482.)

3. Find passages where it is obvious that Rose is carefully handling material that may be sensitive. How does she maintain her impartiality? How is she able to address readers across a range of perspectives? (See Chapter 36, "Inclusive and Culturally Sensitive Style," p. 440.)

4. This essay examines multiple causes of "the destruction of black communities." What are these causes? How does Rose use five separate causal analyses to argue that contributing factors have had a greater negative impact on urban life than hip-hop has? (See "Creating a structure," p. 152, and "Finding and developing materials," p. 149.)

5. In addition to discussing the causes of urban violence, Rose addresses the effects of interpreting hip-hop music out of context. What does she say those effects are? Why is it so important to understand the context surrounding this genre of music?

6. **WRITING:** Rose offers Nas's "Gangsta Tears" as an example of a hip-hop song that critiques violence instead of glorifying it. Using this song, or another example from your listening experience, write a short essay arguing that hip-hop music can have a beneficial effect. In your analysis, investigate the lyrics closely and consider the ways they might promote positive change.

71

Proposals: Readings

See also Chapter 6:

TRIAL BALLOON
Barrett Seaman, *How Bingeing Became the New College Sport,* 179

FORMAL PROPOSAL
Donald Lazere, *A Core Curriculum for Civic Literacy,* 192

MANIFESTO
Katelyn Vincent, *Technology Time-out,* 198

VISUAL PROPOSAL
Pallettruth.com, *Asian Longhorned Beetles from Wood Pallets Invading NYC!* 204

PROPOSAL FOR CHANGE
Bill Gates and Melinda Gates, *Educating America's Young People for the Global Economy* 859

PROPOSAL FOR CHANGE
Eileen McDonagh and Laura Pappano, *Time to Change the Rules* 872

PROPOSAL FOR CHANGE
Thomas L. Friedman, *Start-Ups, Not Bailouts* 884

SATIRICAL PROPOSAL
Kembrew McLeod, *A Modest Free Market Proposal for Education Reform* 887

PROPOSAL FOR CHANGE
Peter Singer, *"One Person, One Share" of the Atmosphere* 892

PROPOSAL FOR CHANGE   Bill Gates is the billionaire cofounder and chairman of Microsoft. Together, Melinda and Bill run the Gates Foundation, the largest private philanthropic foundation in the world. Much of their recent charitable work has been focused on American education, and this essay surveys the current state of American schools, proposing solutions for the future.

BILL GATES AND MELINDA GATES

Educating America's Young People for the Global Economy

It's easy when talking about education reform to get lost in the statistics: the dropout rates, the test scores, and the spending figures. Certainly numbers make problems quantifiable; they help us to see where systems break down and how they might be fixed.

But while statistics help us define the need for reform, it's the people—the students, the teachers, and the principals—who make those numbers real. It's too easy to forget that education reform isn't about jobs, or policy, or statistics. It's about real people.

We have had the privilege of visiting many schools over the past decade and learning about the challenges they face. Melinda often reflects on her experience of meeting a young woman at a public high school in south Los Angeles. She was preparing to become a manicurist in a salon. That's a fine choice—if it's a real choice. But for her, it wasn't. She had no option to go on to college if she wanted to. She was locked in a course of study that—even if she aced it—would not prepare her for any postsecondary studies. In one of her math classes, she was learning to read the back of a can of soup.

We have met many young people on this same path. They graduate from high school without ever knowing how far behind they are. They get a job, but they cannot survive on the income, so they enroll at a community college part-time. They have to take remedial math and English. But college is expensive, they don't earn college credit for remedial classes, and the classes aren't offered at times that fit their work schedule. So they drop out. Many factors are to blame, but the biggest reason is that their education did not prepare them to earn a degree beyond high school. They were never given the opportunity to do what it takes to improve their lives.

This is why we've made improving America's education system a priority for our foundation.

We've taken on some tough issues: eradicating malaria, developing disease-resistant seed for farmers in the developing world, and combating family homelessness in the Pacific Northwest. But we often say to each other that, out of everything our foundation does, improving education in America may be the toughest challenge we've taken on.

We created our foundation with the belief that all people—regardless of background, circumstance, or geography—should have the chance to lead healthy and productive lives. In the United States, we chose to focus on education because it is the surest path to opportunity. Achieving that opportunity should be within reach for hundreds of thousands more young people in this country.

The students, parents, teachers, innovators, and community leaders whom we have met during the past ten years give us great optimism that we are all on the cusp of deep and lasting improvement in our public schools.

For much of America's history, its public schools were the subject of great civic pride. They were the cornerstone of our fundamental belief that through hard work and opportunity, young people could become anything they wanted to be. Our high schools were established generations ago when good-paying factory jobs were plentiful. We prepared only a fraction of students for college because for most Americans, college wasn't necessary to earn a wage that would let them support a family.[1]

But those days are gone. The global economy now is primarily based on knowledge and technology. Critical thinking and problem-solving skills are paramount, as are the abilities to innovate and to collaborate with others.

These are the traits today's employers value in their workers. We both know this firsthand from our experiences at Microsoft. Companies like Microsoft increasingly need highly skilled and well-educated workers in order to remain strong and grow. America must ensure that our young people are well positioned for these jobs.

But despite the best efforts of many committed educators, our high schools have not adapted. Classes are still separated into forty-minute chunks; the learning day ends at 3 p.m.; schools shut down for a long summer vacation—all vestiges of our agrarian and industrial past.

It goes deeper. Many schools do not have the data to tell us how a student is or is not progressing and why. We do not have clear, consistent standards across states that are based on the evidence of what colleges and employers need. And in most schools there is little room for taking a new approach to education.

As a result, many students end up bored and disengaged from their high school curriculum.[2] They're native to a digital age, but they're shoehorned into an archaic learning model. The results are devastating.

Today, nearly a third of our students fail to graduate from high school with their class.[3] For those who do graduate and make it to a community college, roughly 60 percent will need to take at least one remedial class.[4] For low-income students or those of color, the deck is stacked high against them. Only about 19 percent of Hispanics between the ages of twenty-five and thirty-four earn a degree from a two-year or four-year school. For African Americans, it's 29 percent.[5]

Those numbers simply aren't good enough for a strong America and a vibrant, competitive economy. A recent report from the Center on Education and the Workforce at Georgetown University shows why.

The report, *Help Wanted: Projections of Jobs and Education Requirements Through 2018*, forecasted that over the next eight years, 63 percent of all American jobs will require some sort of postsecondary education. What's more, American employers will need nearly 22 million new workers with postsecondary degrees. But the center's research shows that our higher education system will fall short of that mark by 3 million graduates.[6]

That's a pretty compelling argument for why we need an improved education system in the United States. It also affirms the importance of our foundation's recent work with higher education institutions, where we and our partners are working to dramatically increase college graduation rates.

Although we have one of the lowest high school graduation rates in the industrialized world,[7] America nevertheless excels at sending many of those students who do graduate high school to college — since 1980, enrollments at postsecondary institutions have increased by more than half.[8] Unfortunately, only about half of those college students will earn a degree. For minority and low-income students the graduation rates are much, much worse.[9]

And so as our foundation has gotten deeper into our postsecondary work over the past two years, it's become increasingly clear that even those students who make it through high school with decent grades still are not prepared for college-level work. Even when we set our sights on colleges and universities, we still end up at the original problem: high school.

Our foundation has been working for nearly a decade to improve high school graduation rates and college readiness. When we started, we were primarily focused on making schools smaller. We hoped that if we could make schools more personalized and engaging, we could drive down dropout rates and increase student achievement. The results of that early effort were mixed, and at the same time highly enlightening.

Some of the schools we worked with made strong gains, but many of the schools that were involved in our initial focus never showed much improvement.[10] When we examined why that was, we saw that successful schools made more than structural changes to the size or organization of the school. Their improvement seemed to be spurred by what was happening inside the classroom, where excellent teaching, high standards, and a strong curriculum took precedent.

In retrospect, it seems so simple: *Great teaching* explained the difference in student achievement among those schools. And it also explained why success was so spotty. Results that depend on great teaching can't be replicated on campuses that lack great teachers. Studies show that the impact on student learning of having an effective teacher is greater than the impact of any other factor inside a school.[11] For example, being taught for four years by a teacher in the top quarter of ability versus a teacher in the bottom quarter can help eliminate the achievement gap in test scores for African-American students.[12]

As we move forward in our education efforts, our strategy has at its heart the relationship and interactions that take place between students and teachers in the classroom. In short, we're now focused on effective teaching: identifying it, nurturing it, studying it, and replicating it. Of course, principals, parents, and others must be fully invested in the success of the education system as well.

But we realize that to be truly effective, teachers need support. They need clear and consistent college-ready standards to which they can teach. They need constructive, meaningful feedback and opportunities to grow and improve. They need information and data on their students' strengths and weaknesses. And they need to be part of the process to create those systems along the way.

How do you set up a system so that every teacher has access to each of these things?

We're supporting groundbreaking research in partnership with schools, teachers' unions, and communities across the country to answer this basic question. We're also on a quest to discover what makes an effective teacher. What can we do to put an effective teacher in every classroom, every year?

To achieve this, we must understand what makes an effective teacher. We know which teachers produce great student outcomes based on standardized tests, but we do not know the specific ingredients that make these teachers great.

To find out, we launched Intensive Partnerships for Effective Teaching in the fall of 2009 to support bold local plans to study and transform how teachers are recruited, rewarded, and retained. Our partnerships were launched in Hillsborough County, Florida; Memphis, Tennessee; Pittsburgh, Pennsylvania; and a group of charter schools in Los Angeles called The College-Ready Promise. Schools in these districts teach more than 350,000 students, and we believe they can be national models.

We are especially optimistic because in each place all the players are working together: administrators, teachers and their unions, elected officials, community leaders, and parents.

We know that a reform will never take root and flourish if teachers don't support it. We are partnering with the American Federation of Teachers to support innovative ideas for evaluating teachers, including a pay-for-performance plan based on multiple measures of student learning. And in our Intensive Partnerships for Effective Teaching sites, educators are helping overturn decades of entrenched policies in favor of new ways to recruit, develop, assign, evaluate, retain, compensate, and promote teachers. This is truly remarkable work because so much progress has come so quickly.

At the heart of our collaboration is an effort to create fair and reliable measures of teacher effectiveness that are tied to gains in student achievement. This is a sea change because, for the most part, public schools have seldom meaningfully coupled their teacher evaluations with student achievement.

Most teachers are evaluated by an administrator only two or three times a year. Typically, school principals or their assistants will briefly drop in to a teacher's classroom to observe a lesson. Based on what the administrator sees during that twenty minutes or so, he or she will fill out a standard evaluation form, along with checking off boxes for things like "arrives on time" and "maintains professional appearance."[13]

There is very little professional feedback on or analysis of what the administrators saw, or how the teacher could be better. There is rarely an attempt to correlate the administrator's observations to how much, or how little, the students in the class learned.[14]

From our conversations with teachers and union leaders, it's clear that many educators are frustrated that they do not get the help they need to coax more from their students. In 2008 and 2009, our foundation partnered with Scholastic Inc. to conduct a national survey, and we heard from some 40,000 teachers on crucial questions facing the profession. The survey reveals that teachers overwhelmingly believe that professional development is crucial to their success and that of their students, and that they want more feedback about their performance in the classroom.[15]

We also found that they want to be rewarded for their results. And this is where things get really exciting.

Through our Measures of Effective Teaching effort, we're using technology, data, and research to help educators develop new, fair evaluations that will give teachers the feedback they crave.

But to provide that kind of feedback, you have to get into classrooms. You have to stay for more than twenty minutes. And you have to do more than check off a bunch of boxes. This project is going to emphasize classes with big achievement gains, and we'll try to puzzle out what those teachers did that was so effective.

This research will give districts the information they need to make better use of investments in public education. America spends about $8 billion a year to reward teachers who have earned master's degrees, even though some evidence says that in most cases a teacher's master's degree does nothing to improve student achievement. Our nation is spending billions funding salary schedules based on a seniority system, even though the evidence says that after the first five years, seniority does not impact student achievement. We've spent billions to reduce class size, even though there is no strong evidence that reducing class size in high school improves student performance.[16]

We need to invest in approaches and methods where there is evidence of significant student gains and achievement. The research our partners are conducting will give districts the evidence they need to create fair evaluation systems that base compensation on student achievement and pay teachers what they're worth.

We're already seeing it happen. In Pittsburgh, the school district and the teachers' union recently ratified a new contract that both sides are calling a new way of doing business. The five-year agreement includes new incentives for teachers, including a pilot program that could grant teachers up to $8,000 in extra pay a year, provided students make substantial academic gains. Teachers, administrators, and board members have all called this new contract historic.[17]

We don't think it's possible to overstate the importance of the work school districts such as Pittsburgh are taking on. They've made creating and nurturing effective teachers the center of their work.

But even this probably isn't enough. Even the most effective and successful educators need guidance on what to teach and when to teach it. Our survey with Scholastic revealed that teachers favor establishing clear and common academic standards, so that must be a priority as well.[18]

The Common Core Standards initiative, a movement led by the nation's governors and state school superintendents, has brought together parents, teachers, principals, researchers, and other education experts to develop consistent, rigorous academic standards for math and English.

We believe that high standards for all students are indispensable to high achievement. In an era when technology makes it easy to forge friendships and business partnerships around the globe, there's no reason that the academic standards in Washington state shouldn't be as high as standards in Maine or anywhere else.

Even as these standards set the bar for the skills and knowledge all young people should have when they graduate high school, they still allow for a flexible approach. Different states, different regions, and different teachers in different cultures will teach to these standards in different ways. But all students will be taught to the same high standards, wherever they were born and no matter where they go to school.

These things—measuring, defining, and nurturing effective teaching along with adopting college-ready academic standards—are critically important to ensuring that every child in every classroom is prepared for success.

Finally, our school system desperately needs innovation, particularly when it comes to bringing technology into the classroom. Charter schools are important because they have enormous latitude for innovation. Public charter schools can identify effective ways to bring technology into the classroom, and those approaches can then be replicated in traditional public schools.

For example, we've been really impressed by Rocketship Education in San Jose, California. The leaders at Rocketship divided the curriculum into two parts. The first is a critical-thinking component, which is taught by master teachers in the traditional classroom. The second is a basic-skills component, which they discovered can be taught effectively in an online learning lab.

The results have been excellent. Students at both Rocketship campuses are scoring higher on state tests than those from wealthy districts like Palo Alto, even though almost 80 percent come from low-income families, and almost that many are English language learners.[19]

This is a challenging and exciting time in education. There is definitely a convergence of ideas and opportunity around education reform and a belief that all children need and deserve an education that prepares them for the demands of college and careers. Many national and local leaders, teachers, parents, and others share a desire to dramatically improve education for all children in America regardless of their background or circumstance. Many have been working on these issues for a long time.

We are optimistic that change is within reach. But we must all advocate for what works. We must all be willing to make tough choices. Once evidence and best practices are in hand, we need to work to replicate these approaches and policies.

Parents and students everywhere want the same thing—the opportunity to learn and achieve at the highest level—and they are willing to work hard to experience it. Our challenge is to provide them with that opportunity, no matter what kind of school they attend and no matter whether they are from a poor neighborhood or a more affluent community.

When we look ahead to the next ten years, we are reminded of KIPP, a charter school in Houston where we saw great teachers in action. The results are clear: KIPP graduates more than 95 percent of its students, compared to the district average of 70 percent. Almost 90 percent of the graduates go on to a four-year college.[20] If we commit to a country where this is a reality for all young people, we'll raise the next generation of Americans to be better educated, more creative, more productive, and ready to compete at the leading edge of the knowledge economy.

That's a change that will enhance the life of every American—and it's one we're ready to help make.

Notes

1. David Angus and Jeffrey Mirel, *The Failed Promise of the American High School 1890–1995* (New York: Teachers College Press, 1999).

2. John M. Bridgeland, John J. DiIulio Jr., and Karen Burke Morison, *The Silent Epidemic* (Washington, DC: Civic Enterprises, 2006).

3. Editorial Projects in Education, "Diplomas Count," *Education Week* 29, no. 34 (June 10, 2010).

4. Thomas Bailey, "Challenge and Opportunity: Rethinking the Role and Function of Developmental Education in Community College," CCRC Working Paper No. 14, Community College Research Center, 2008.

5. Calculations based on U.S. Census Bureau, "Educational Attainment in the United States: 2009," *Current Population Survey, 2009 Annual Social and Economic Supplement*, www.census.gov/population/www/socdemo/education/cps2009.html.

6. Anthony P. Carnevale, Nicole Smith, and Jeff Strohl, *Help Wanted: Projections of Jobs and Education Requirements Through 2018* (Washington, DC: Georgetown University Center on Education and the Workforce, 2010).

7. Organisation for Economic Co-operation and Development, "Indicator A2: How Many Students Finish Secondary Education and Access Tertiary Education?" in *Education at a Glance 2009: OECD Indicators* (Paris: OECD, 2009). The United States' 2007 graduation rate was eighteenth out of twenty-five OECD nations.

8. Thomas Snyder and Sally Dillow, *Digest of Education Statistics: 2009* (Washington, DC: National Center for Education Statistics, U.S. Department of Education, 2009).

9. Laura G. Knapp, Janice E. Kelly-Reid, and Scott A. Ginder, *Enrollment in Postsecondary Institutions, Fall 2008; Graduation Rates, 2002 & 2005 Cohorts; and Financial Statistics, Fiscal Year 2008* (Washington, DC: National Center for Education Statistics, U.S. Department of Education, April 2010). Note: Graduation rates are for first-time, full-time students graduating in 150 percent normal time.

10. Becky Smerdon, Barbara Means, et al., *Evaluation of the Bill & Melinda Gates Foundation's High School Grants Initiative: 2001–2005 Final Report* (Washington, DC: American Institutes for Research; Menlo Park, CA: SRI International, 2006).

11. Steven G. Rivkin, Eric A. Hanushek, and John F. Kain, "Teachers, Schools, and Academic Achievement," *Econometrica* 73, no. 2 (March 2005): 417–58.

12.   Robert Gordon, Thomas J. Kane, and Douglas O. Staiger, *Identifying Effective Teachers Using Performance on the Job* (Washington, DC: Hamilton Project, Brookings Institution, 2006).

13.   Stephen Newton, "Stull Evaluations and Student Performance," Los Angeles Unified School District, http://notebook.lausd.net/pls/ptl/docs/PAGE/CA_LAUSD/FLDR_ ORGANIZATIONS/FLDR_PLCY_RES_DEV/PAR_DIVISION_MAIN/RESEARCH_ UNIT/PUBLICATIONS/POLICY_ REPORTS/IMPACT_STULL_186.PDF.

14.   Kim Marshall, "It's Time to Rethink Teacher Supervision and Evaluation," *Phi Delta Kappan,* June 2005.

15.   Scholastic and Bill & Melinda Gates Foundation, *Primary Sources: America's Teachers on America's Schools* (New York: Scholastic Inc., 2010).

16.   Marguerite Roza, *Frozen Assets: Rethinking Teacher Contracts Could Free Billions for School Reform* (Washington, DC: Education Sector, 2007).

17.   Valerie Russ, "Teachers, School District Approve Contract," *Philadelphia Daily News,* January 23, 2010.

18.   Scholastic and Bill & Melinda Gates Foundation, *Primary Sources.*

19.   "Rocketship Education 2009 Academic Results Highest Performing in San Jose and Santa Clara County, Tops Palo Alto Unified," www.rsed.org/news/RSED%2009%20 Results%20Release%209.16%20FINAL.doc.

20.   Mike Feinberg, personal communications, 2010.

Reading the Genre

1. The authors spend the first section of this proposal recounting their own personal encounters with the American educational system, and throughout the essay they continue to mention themselves and their foundation. Why should the focus be on Bill and Melinda and the Gates Foundation? What does this establish for the authors and the essay?

2. What will the "new knowledge economy" look like? In what ways are the authors invested in this new economy themselves? If you are not familiar with the Gateses or with Microsoft, perform some Internet research.

3. In addition to proposing their own solutions to fix schools, the authors also identify the strategies that have not worked or have come up short. Then they examine school districts that are doing successful work. Create a chart of positive and negative educational experiences from your own life. Compare the strategies that the Gateses write about to what has worked (and failed) in your own experience. (See "Examine prior solutions," p. 187.)

4. **WRITING:** Now that you have read this essay from your own perspective, reread it from a new, imagined perspective. Imagine you are a young teacher, a veteran teacher, a software developer, a high school dropout, or a Microsoft shareholder. As you read through the essay, pay attention to the issues that would affect you. Write a response to the essay from this imagined perspective: What do you agree with and what do you disagree with?

5. **INFOGRAPHIC:** This proposal is full of statistics. The Gates Foundation Web site (www.gatesfoundation.org/college-ready-education) also contains lots of interesting data about education. Use data from both that site and this essay to create an "infographic" — an image that conveys the numbers from your chart or graph, but does so using symbols and images. (See Chapter 53, "Tables, Graphs, and Infographics," p. 584.)

PROPOSAL FOR CHANGE   Laura Pappano is an award-winning journalist, and Eileen McDonagh teaches political science at Northeastern University. Together, they write a blog hosted by the news and opinion site the Huffington Post (www.huffingtonpost.com/eileen-mcdonagh-and-laura-pappano). The following essay is from their book *Playing with the Boys: Why Separate Is Not Equal in Sports* (2008).

EILEEN MCDONAGH AND LAURA PAPPANO

Time to Change the Rules

Sports matter precisely because they are more than play. Organized athletics reveal our beliefs and biases and offer a proving ground for the lessons we care about. Sports culture may be steeped in tradition and resistant to reinterpretation. But we must try. We must be able to recast our athletic heroes as girls and women. We must reimagine games and rules and opportunities so that women and men can compete more often on the same field.

The idea of change in sport is as old as the notion of tradition in sport. Regardless of how organic it feels or for how long it has been woven into nationalistic rituals, sport is human-made. Athletic rules change constantly, seeking ways to draw larger audiences, speed up play, or improve player safety. On the eve of Wimbledon in 2003, for example, one newspaper polled tennis fans and concluded "millions are switching off 'boring' tennis" because it had become a contest of power serves. The newspaper survey of tennis aficionados, not mere average citizens, revealed half of respondents believed the solution was to adjust the game by reducing the pressure inside tennis balls to make them slower.[1]

There is, in other words, nothing "pure" or unalterable about sports. The practice of realigning conferences or jumping divisions is a constant in organized athletics. Players are traded and teams carry on. It should not be impossible to set goals at end marks other than winning a championship or selling more tickets. It should be possible to make gender equity a goal too.

Sport holds a distinguished place in our society. In his analysis of American fitness from 1890 to 1940 Donald J. Mrozek observes that "the genteel preacher, doctor, or teacher came to tolerate the public display and physical assertiveness of organized sport and athletics by seeing with them new means for ingraining the principles of ethical conduct."[2] At the very moment organized sport could have been rejected as a crude intrusion into American life, it had the fortune of being seized on by the upper-middle class and cast as a noble pursuit, an enterprise that developed physical health and moral character. As a result, Mrozek asserts, organized sport has become "a key building block of the mass culture."[3]

Sport today, despite its dark side, remains idealized as a vessel of positive social values. Players, fans, and parents may misbehave at sporting events, but we continue to emphasize the positive lessons. We prefer the romanticized image of athletics as a wholesome contest in which the rules are plain, the play fair, and the victors gracious. The clarity of games, whether Saturday morning youth soccer or the U.S. Open in tennis, is welcomed in a world in which things are not often as they seem and the final outcome is elusive.

Despite the starry-eyed glamour afforded American sport, despite the good to individual lives, it has been a barrier to gender equity. The time has come to acknowledge this and rethink the structure of American sport to support fair play and a just society. While many point to the progress women have made in terms of athletic achievement and public visibility, it does not erase the larger fact: females have been accommodated and tolerated, not treated as equals and promoted. There have been small adjustments and concessions to "let the girls play," but organized sport has resisted deep change. The solution is not to "let" females play, but to open our eyes to inequalities that have become routine business in organized sport that are barriers to women athletes.

We need reform at several levels. It is not work for one segment of society, but for all, from the personal to the governmental, from attitudes of coaches to institutional rules. Here are ten recommendations intended as a starting point.

1. *Accept a new, gender-neutral view of sports.*   We must challenge the stereotype that males are naturally superior athletes and consider the individual first. There are more athletic differences among individuals than between athletes which are based only on gender. This means challenging biases that label some sports as female and others as male. Girls can race cars; boys can figure-skate. Parents, teachers, neighbors, community leaders, and others whose impressions shape attitudes from youth must recognize and challenge ingrained stereotypes. Support children in playing whatever sport they choose; encourage girls to play sports that are not traditionally considered female and boys to play in sports that are not traditionally male.

2. *Increase opportunities for coed sports at every level.*   We need more events in which males and females play together. At the professional level, we must have more models of sex-integrated sporting events, even if they are initially special promotional events outside of regular circuit play. At recreational, youth, middle and high school levels, we must stop the reflexive sex segregation of sports. There must be more coed teams and more coed opportunities for competition. This means dividing teams by ability with the goal of increasing participation so that more individuals — even those males who are not stellar athletes — may find an appropriate level of competition.

3. *Gender-blind sports rules.*   The International Olympic Committee, as well as governing bodies of various men's and women's sports, should eliminate rule differences between male and female versions of a sport which reflect outmoded beliefs about male and female capabilities or that merely serve to differentiate male and female play. Wherever reasonable, the size of play areas, the length of games and races, the points needed to win, or other measures in a sport should be the same for males and females.

4. *Require parity in ticket prices, promotion, and salaries at educational institutions.* We must close the gap between pay for coaches of male teams and coaches of female teams. In addition, there should be no difference in ticket prices between men's and women's college and high school sporting events. College promotions offices should be required to put as much media effort into promoting women's sporting events as they do promoting men's.

5. *Equal television time for women's sports.* Much as the federal government requires broadcasters to devote regularly scheduled time to educational broadcasting for children for the privilege of using the airwaves, broadcasters should be required to devote equal time to programs on women's athletics or to covering women's events. As has happened with children's programming, these demands will likely yield new media stars and capture for broadcasters a new pool of viewers.

6. *Better print and online news coverage for women's sports.* Too many newspapers and mainstream online news and sports sites still cover women's sport events as charity work. The stories of female athletes and competition are just as compelling as stories about male athletes. The more people learn about an athlete, the more they will care and seek coverage. More television coverage of women's sports will drive increased interest in and reporting on female athletes. If sports editors value women's athletics as more than the occasional soft feature, people will look for those stories. They are looking for them now, and they're missing.

7. *Women must "speak" sports.* Athletics are important in our society and women opt out at their peril. Just as it is important to vote and be informed about local, national, and international political events, following sports can promote one's inclusion in business, professional, and everyday public life. Many women are already sports fans, consumers, and participants. They are already benefiting from sports as a key feminist tool.

8. *Feminist power play: bringing athletics into the network.* Men long ago created a power network that includes leaders in business, politics — and sports. Powerful women gather around business and political issues, but we must widen the circle so that there are more frequent and visible networking crossovers among high-profile female athletes, coaches, and team owners, and politicians and business leaders. We must help each other. Ruth Ann Marshall, president of the Americas for MasterCard, for example, decided to have MasterCard sponsor LPGA players like Dottie Pepper and sponsor Women's World Cup soccer. Such forward-thinking acts must be replicated by women in power. This is not charity. Raising the profile of female athletes and business and political leaders broadens public recognition for women and normalizes female competence and power.

9. *If you can, buy the team — or at least a ticket.* We need women to support women's athletics. Buy a season ticket to the WNBA franchise. Attend and support female athletic events. Take your children to see women play. If you can afford it, buy a team. More women must be at the owner's table, whether in women's leagues (precious few choices at the moment) or in men's. We must drive change from outside as well as from within. Even an act as simple as having your March Madness office pool include the Women's NCAA basketball tournament — not just the men's — raises awareness of compelling women's play. There is no apologetic stance needed: the women have game and more people need to know about it.

10. *Strengthen Title IX.* Title IX may have seemed appropriate when it was passed in 1972, but it never demanded equality. We now need financial equality, even if that means dramatically scaling back men's college football and basketball programs, some of which hardly resemble programs suitable for educational institutions. If the NFL or the NBA wants a development league, they should build it. Colleges should value men's and women's Olympic sports as part of

their educational mission. Title IX also must be more aggressively enforced. And finally, Title IX must *not* permit coercive sex segregation that prevents girls from "playing with the boys."

Sports: The Next Frontier

In the United States, the act of defining sex difference has defined inequality. The long-standing image of women as weak and physically inferior to males has ensured stark sex differentiation and in the past barred females from higher education, kept them from the right to vote, and created barriers in the workplace. In many cases, women embraced these limitations, agreeing it was not their "place" to occupy the same social and economic space as men.

Integrating higher education, permitting women to vote, and outlawing sex bias at work have been crucial steps not just for women, but also for American society. Organized athletics represents the next goal in the quest for equal participation. Familiar arguments of female physical and biological differences drive sex-separate athletic programs, differentiated male and female rules (not based on actual physical differences), and sex-differentiated expectations.

In fact, the barriers female athletes face today are not chiefly physical but social and cultural. One has only to look internationally to see the limiting power of social gender bias. When Lima Azima finished last in the 100-meter race at the World Track and Field Championships in Paris in August 2003, no one blamed her athletic ability. Her victory was in overcoming impressive obstacles to become the first Afghan woman ever to compete in a major worldwide sports event. She wore long baggy pants to other runners' sleek, form-fitting uniforms. She struggled with the starting blocks, had never worn proper running shoes (Adidas donated shoes for the race), and had not been permitted to train outdoors or in front of men. Merely participating was success.[4]

In Bangladesh, the women's soccer team has faced protests from conservative Muslim groups that consider their play immoral. In October 2004, the women's team played despite a demonstration by 500 activists in Dhaka carrying placards reading, among other slogans: "Stop un-Islamic activities, protect sanctity of womanhood." Moulana Abdur Rashid, deputy chief of the Islamic Constitution Movement, warned that "the national sport council will be put under siege . . . if the satanic women's football league is not abandoned immediately."[5]

The pervasive belief that athletics will keep women from being womanly persists. Research at the University of Nigeria found 51 percent of women were concerned that playing a sport would lead them to develop masculine features and therefore they chose not to participate. Many worried that athletics could affect menstruation and reproduction, and that they could be injured, which kept parents from encouraging daughters to play sports.[6]

Females in some minority groups avoid sports because of similar cultural messages. For example, only 43 percent of Hispanic high school sophomore girls play at least one interscholastic sport, compared with 52 percent of non-Hispanic sophomore girls. The issue is not money but cultural habits in which girls are not encouraged to stay after school for sports because they are expected at home to help with family obligations. Raul Hodgers, athletic director at Desert View High School in Tucson, Arizona (the school is 80 percent Hispanic), noted that "most of these girls are athletically inclined, but it is difficult to acclimate parents to the idea of kids staying after school."[7] And he was referring to girls, not boys.

In some parts of the developing world the demands of daily survival make sports appear trivial, while in other developing nations women are restricted to private spheres of home and child rearing, excluding them from public realms of work and sport.[8] And yet it is clear that athletics can be potent diplomatic and ideological tools.

The Chinese have earned international attention for athletics, winning 32 Gold Medals at the 2004 Athens Olympics, second only to the Americans. The Chinese government urged all Chinese citizens to learn from those athletic victories. "The excellent performance by China's athletes again shows the spirit of the Chinese nation's unremitting efforts to improve itself," the government said in broadcasts on state-run television. "The motherland is proud of you, and the people are proud of you."[9]

Nationalism

The rise of China's athletic profile on the international stage (NBA star Yao Ming has also helped) is seen as clear evidence of a nation on the road to economic dominance. Interestingly, success of Chinese women athletes, in part, has been attributed to a cultural norm in which an athlete's Chinese identity is viewed as more important than her gender identity. "Any polarization of males versus females is therefore overwhelmed by feelings of 'China versus the world,'" noted one researcher. "This is a phenomenon starkly at variance with the historical 'male versus female' dichotomy common in Western sporting nations, but is closer to the situation that existed in much of Eastern Europe and Cuban sport."[10]

It may be socially convenient to differentiate sports by sex. However, it thwarts power sharing and equality between the sexes. When Little League lawyers and physicians in 1974 argued to a New Jersey civil rights hearing officer that "boys like to be with boys and girls like to be with girls" in their failed quest to keep girls off the diamond, they echoed a cultural belief: regardless of whether boys and girls can or should play together, many don't want to.[11]

Although girls are now permitted to play Little League, and modest numbers actually do, most choose softball instead. Talk with parents and you hear similar sentiments: their daughters don't want to play with boys and boys don't want to play with girls. Whether the sport is baseball, basketball, ice hockey, wrestling, or soccer, the presumption is that athletes prefer to compete with players of their own sex. Adults, even in social tennis, gravitate to same-sex play. Organized sport truly is the most sex-segregated secular institution in our society. More than a reflection of actual physical differences between males and females, it reveals cultural norms and our present comfort zone. We have been conditioned—and our children are being conditioned—to believe this is *the right way* to play.

Sharing power depends on sharing turf in the Oval Office, Congress, state houses, local government, boardrooms, CEO suites—and on the playing field. Opening power structures to greater male-female cooperation means including more females in athletic opportunities with males, inviting more women to the business golf outing, seeing more females pick-and-roll in a pick-up, recreational league, or after-work basketball game.

This must start when children are young. Just as the drive for increasing racial and ethnic diversity is considered critical to preparing children for the future, we must teach children from the time they step onto the gymnasium floor on Saturday mornings to play Itty Bitty Basketball that girls and boys can pass to one another, and either can drive to the hoop.

The Family and Community

This requires a new way of thinking and an active effort by parents and youth sports leaders. It is critical we get out of the gender role habits that dominate in sports and the rest of life. It matters for players and for fans. It matters for athletes, coaches, organizers, media members, and sponsors. The challenge, in other words, demands a break from a sex-segregated past that stretches back well more than a century.

The Government

It is recognized now that women can and should have educational opportunities equal with men. This, in turn, serves as a foundation for equal employment opportunities. As a nation we want women to enter nontraditional educational and employment fields, through government- and foundation-sponsored programs aimed at encouraging women to enter such fields as math, science, and engineering.

Sports

We must do the same thing in sports. The family, the community, and government must press girls to explore nontraditional sports. We need role models. Girls must see women playing football and being referees in high-profile professional sports, including football, basketball (there's just one), and baseball. Just as the government encourages sex integration — rather than sex segregation — in math, science, and engineering, it must encourage sex integration in athletic programs. Sports is the next battleground in the fight for gender equality. The roots of sex discrimination must be challenged head-on. There are physical biological differences between the sexes. But they are not as great as we have supposed, and the female difference is not necessarily a lacking. Women are not inherently weak and in need of protection.

Not all women will support this drive. In every era, as women sought to gain equal access to education, to voting and workplace rights, other women were their fiercest adversaries. Women didn't want to take on male roles that meant learning, earning, and having a voice in our democracy. We know there is no justice without responsibility. More than ever we need women's voices in the halls of power, at the helms of corporations, and being celebrated for their athletic prowess. Women are starting to gain recognition for physical ability, mental acuity, and the ability to compete. And, yes, "*thank God* we ain't what we was."

However, we are not yet what we ought to be. Females playing sports with males must become standard practice, not the exception. And as surprising, if not difficult, as this idea may be for some, it is an idea that is gaining ground. When sports writer Dave Anderson, for example, speculated about how Tiger Woods's infant daughter, Sam Alexis, might handle her father's legacy, he noted that "maybe she'll want to try to win the most majors on the women's Tour, *if not the men's Tour.*"[12] *Exactly.* Playing with the boys should be an option, if not the norm, for her and for all girls and women, if we are to become *what we ought to be.*

Notes

1. Anthony King, "Wimbledon Fans Falling Out of Love with the Power Game," *Daily Telegraph,* June 23, 2003, 7.
2. Donald Mrozek, "Sport in American Life: From National Health to Personal Fulfillment, 1890–1940," in Kathryn Grover, ed., *Fitness in American Culture: Images of Health, Sport, and the Body, 1830–1940* (Rochester, NY: Margaret Woodbury Strong Museum, 1989), 19.
3. Mrozek, "Sport in American Life," 24.
4. "Runners Make History," *Syracuse Post-Standard,* August 21, 2004, 6; "Track and Field," *Syracuse Post-Standard,* August 24, 2003, D2.
5. "Bangladesh Group Protests against Women's Soccer," *Gleaner* (Kingston, Jamaica), October 18, 2004, 12.
6. S. U. Anyanwu, "Issues and Patterns of Women's Participation in Sport in Nigeria," *International Review for Sport Sociology* 15 (1980): 878–895. Cited in R. Chappell, "Sport in Developing Countries: Opportunities for Girls and Women," *Women in Sport and Physical Activity Journal* 8, no. 2 (1999): 1.
7. MaryJo Sylwester, "Hispanic Girls in Sports Held Back by Tradition," *USA Today,* March 29, 2005, 1.
8. Robert Chappell, *Sport in Developing Countries* (Roehampton University, 2007).
9. "Chinese Athletes Cash in on Medalist Status: China's Communist Rulers Cast Olympians as Model Workers," www.msnbc.msn.com/id/5867721.
10. James Riordan, "Chinese Women and Sport Success, Sexuality, Suspicion," *Women in Sport and Physical Activity Journal* 9, no. 1 (2000): 87.
11. Dr. Thomas Johnson, psychiatrist from San Diego, testifying in support of Little League. Summary of proceedings for hearing, State of New Jersey, Department of Law and Public Safety, Division on Civil Rights, November 8, 1973, 3, National Organization for Women papers, National Task Force on Sports file (31.10), Schlesinger Library, Radcliffe Institute for Advanced Study.
12. Dave Anderson, "Now Woods May Be Compared to Nicklaus as a Father," *New York Times,* Thursday, June 21, 2007, E16, emphasis added.

1. In a report, it is important both to identify an issue and to show the significance of the issue. (See "Define a problem," p. 178 and Chapter 27, "Strategies," p. 398.) How do McDonagh and Pappano define the issue at the heart
   of this essay? What do they argue about how far-reaching this problem is?

2. What audience do the authors target in this essay? Is their intended audience
   male or female? How wide or specific is the audience? How might their
   audience create change? How does the authors' choice of audience affect the
   essay? (See "Understanding your audience," p. 184, and "Target the proposal," p. 178.)

3. How does the section entitled "Sports: The Next Frontier" build on the recommendations in this proposal? Is it important for proposal writers to open up
   larger questions, consider wider implications, and test their ideas? How does
   doing so alter their arguments?

4. Review the authors' use of headings and subheadings in this excerpt. What is
   the rhetorical purpose of these headings? How do you think the authors made
   decisions about what words and phrases to use for these headings? (See
   Chapter 54, "Designing Print and Online Documents," p. 592.)

5. **WRITING:** Imagining that you have been recruited to help Pappano and
   McDonagh accomplish their goals, choose just one of the ten suggestions
   from this essay and develop a concrete plan—at least five strategies—that
   will help to implement this suggestion. Make sure that your recommendations
   are reasonable, specific, and realistic. Use clear language to describe how the
   plan can be followed.

PROPOSAL FOR CHANGE   A three-time Pulitzer Prize–winner, Thomas L. Friedman is a columnist for the *New York Times* and the author of five best-selling books, including *Longitudes and Attitudes: Exploring the World after September 11* (2002) and *The World Is Flat: A Brief History of the Twenty-first Century* (2005). This essay builds on ideas presented in his 2009 book, *Hot, Flat, and Crowded 2.0: Why We Need a Green Revolution—And How It Can Renew America* (2009).

Start-Ups, Not Bailouts

Thomas L. Friedman

Here's my fun fact for the day, provided courtesy of Robert Litan, who directs research at the Kauffman Foundation, which specializes in promoting innovation in America: "Between 1980 and 2005, virtually all net new jobs created in the U.S. were created by firms that were 5 years old or less," said Litan. "That is about 40 million jobs. That means the established firms created no new net jobs during that period."

Message: If we want to bring down unemployment in a sustainable way, neither rescuing General Motors nor funding more road construction will do it. We need to create a big bushel of new companies—fast. We've got to get more Americans working again for their own dignity—and to generate the rising incomes and wealth we need to pay for existing entitlements, as well as all the new investments we'll need to make. It was just reported that Social Security this year will pay out more in benefits than it receives in payroll taxes—a red line we were not expected to cross until at least 2016.

But you cannot say this often enough: Good-paying jobs don't come from bailouts. They come from start-ups. And where do start-ups come from? They come from smart, creative, inspired risk-takers. How do we get more of those? There are only two ways: grow more by improving our schools or import more by recruiting talented immigrants. Surely, we need to do both, and we need to start by breaking the deadlock in Congress over immigration, so we can develop a much more strategic approach to attracting more of the world's creative risk-takers. "Roughly 25 percent of successful high-tech start-ups over the last decade were founded or co-founded by immigrants," said Litan. Think Sergey Brin, the Russian-born co-founder of Google, or Vinod Khosla, the India-born co-founder of Sun Microsystems.

That is no surprise. After all, Craig Mundie, the chief research and strategy officer of Microsoft, asks: What made America this incredible engine of prosperity? It was immigration, plus free markets. Because we were so open to immigration—and immigrants are by definition high-aspiring risk-takers, ready to leave their native lands in search of greater opportunities—"we as a country accumulated a disproportionate share of the world's high-I.Q. risk-takers."

In addition, because of our vibrant and meritocratic university system, the best foreign students who wanted the best education also came here, and many of them also stayed. In its heyday, our unique system also attracted a disproportionate share of high-I.Q. risk-takers to high government service. So when you put all this together, with our free markets and democracy, it made it easy here for creative, high-I.Q. risk-takers to raise capital for their ideas and commercialize them. In short, America had a very powerful, self-reinforcing engine for growing innovative new companies.

"When you get this happy coincidence of high-I.Q. risk-takers in government and a society that is biased toward high-I.Q. risk-takers, you get these above-average returns as a country," argued Mundie. "What is common to Singapore, Israel, and America? They were all built by high-I.Q. risk-takers and all thrived—but only in the U.S. did it happen at a large scale and with global diversity, so you had this really rich cross-section."

What is worrisome about America today is the combination of cutbacks in higher education, restrictions on immigration, and a toxic public space that dissuades talented people from going into govern-

ment. Together, all of these trends are slowly eating away at our differentiated edge in attracting and enabling the world's biggest mass of smart, creative risk-takers.

It isn't drastic, but it is a decline—at a time when technology is allowing other countries to leverage and empower more of their own high-I.Q. risk-takers. If we don't reverse this trend, over time, "we could lose our most important competitive edge—the only edge from which sustainable advantage accrues"—having the world's biggest and most diverse pool of high-I.Q. risk-takers, said Mundie. "If we don't have that competitive edge, our standard of living will eventually revert to the global mean."

Right now we have thousands of foreign students in America and one million engineers, scientists, and other highly skilled workers here on H-1B temporary visas, which require them to return home when the visas expire. That's nuts. "We ought to have a 'job-creators visa' for people already here," said Litan. "And once you've hired, say, 5 or 10 American nonfamily members, you should get a green card."

We need health care, financial reform, and education reform. But we also need to be thinking just as seriously and urgently about what are the ingredients that foster entrepreneurship—how new businesses are catalyzed, inspired, and enabled and how we enlist more people to do that—so no one ever says about America what that officer says to Tom Cruise in *Top Gun*: "Son, your ego's writing checks your body can't cash."

Reading the Genre

1. Make a list of the problematic trends Friedman identifies. How does he propose to overcome them?

2. Does Friedman consider counterarguments in this essay? Suggest possible objections to his proposal. How might Friedman respond? (See Chapter 22, "Critical Thinking," p. 372; "Understand opposing claims," p. 74; and "Qualify your claim," p. 80.)

3. Who is the primary audience for this proposal? Whom would Friedman consider his ideal readers? (See "Understanding your audience," p. 11, and "Target the proposal," p. 178.)

4. **WRITING:** Friedman writes at length about the "high-I.Q. risk-taker." Create a profile of this hypothetical person. (For a sample profile, see Nancy Gibbs, "Cool Running," p. 739.)

5. **WRITING:** Friedman mentions that American schools need improvement, but he doesn't elaborate. What, in your opinion, are some of the problems with higher education today? Pick the problem that strikes you as most important and write your own proposal for change.

6. **PRESENTING DATA:** Friedman cites several statistics in this essay. Translate some of them into graphic form to reinforce (or dispute) Friedman's argument. (See Chapter 53, "Tables, Graphs, and Infographics," p. 584.)

SATIRICAL PROPOSAL   Kembrew McLeod is an activist, music critic, and documentary film producer. He focuses his work on issues of copyright and intellectual property and famously made an ironic point in 1997 by registering the phrase "Freedom of Expression" as a U.S. trademark. McLeod's books include *Owning Culture: Authorship, Ownership, and Intellectual Property* (2001) and *Freedom of Expression: Resistance and Repression in the Age of Intellectual Property* (2005). He teaches communication at the University of Iowa and enjoys playing pranks.

The Huffington Post

Posted: June 29, 2010, at 12:58 PM
From: Kembrew McLeod

A Modest Free Market Proposal for Education Reform

Times are tough for public universities. Over the past quarter century, state legislatures have slashed college budgets — cuts that have only accelerated during this economic meltdown. We have been told to do more with less, make sacrifices, and be self-sufficient — and I couldn't agree more. Unlike those socialists lining up to mainline milk from the nanny state, there are many of us who favor fiscally sound solutions. We should teach our children well by following dogmatically free market principles that reject government meddling.

My modest proposal is multi-pronged and forward thinking. It would hand over all aspects of academic life to private companies, creating a university system that is more efficient, profitable even. In re-imagining how higher education can be rebooted, we need to ask ourselves, "What would a liberal arts education look like if McDonald's funded it?" Killing many birds with one lethal stone, we can simultaneously solve the problems created by overstuffed state budgets, overpaid professors, and — as an added, unexpected bonus — plagiarism. Let me explain.

The first part of the plan involves the sponsorship of classes, in which companies would exchange cash and services for the prominent placement of their logos on syllabi and in teaching spaces. This is a no-brainer, especially because on-campus branding has expanded in recent years. Under this plan, rational economic decisions would play a greater role in determining course offerings; less popular, unprofitable classes would necessarily fall by the wayside.

My second proposal will be more controversial, for it involves radically rethinking the way undergraduate students approach their coursework. These days, professors fret over undergrads using the services of "research assistance" companies — businesses that sell finished papers on every imaginable subject. Rather than siding with these fuddy-duddies, we should instead embrace this shift in student work habits. After all, the free market is influencing the decisions our students make, and it would be disastrous to regulate an emerging marketplace during these uncertain times.

It also seems morally wrong to force undergrads to waste their time on reading, researching, writing, and revising when their labor could be better spent working service jobs and other entry-level positions. This will allow them to buy pre-packaged papers and still have spending money left over to inject into the economy — a win-win.

Only lazy students who are not gainfully employed would lose out. Additionally, those who carefully manage their money (or whose families have already done so) can purchase higher quality papers that will earn them better grades: a one-dollar, one-vote approach to learning. While it is true that this shift in pedagogy will hurt some businesses — such as companies that produce plagiarism-detecting software such as TurnItIn.com — the overall fiscal impact for society will be positive.

The third and final part of my plan takes the economic potential of education to the next level, offering great rewards with virtually no risk. Still, I anticipate that some old school professors will be alarmed by my suggestion that we should use this new education/business model to train future faculty. It's only fair that if we allow undergraduates to use research assistance companies, grad students should be allowed to do so as well. One such business, PhD-Dissertations.com, is leading the charge on this front. (When I first came across this website, I thought, Why hasn't anyone thought of this before? Talk about an untapped market!)

By no longer having to conduct original research themselves, graduate students will have more hours to spend in the classroom as adjunct instructors. Let's do the math. PhD-Dissertations.com charges $17.00 per page, which adds up to $3,400 for a 200-page dissertation (plus, their website states that, "A discount of 10% applies to orders of 75+ pages!"). Although this might seem like a lot of money, consider the fact that most colleges pay adjuncts roughly the same, between $3,000 and $4,000, for each course taught per semester. Therefore, by just adding one extra course to his or her roster, a graduate student can pay for an entire dissertation in less than one academic year — while at the same time serving the university's undergraduate teaching needs. Once this new generation of scholar/project managers enters the profession, there will be no more need for traditional professors.

Following this course of action, universities can be transformed into a well-oiled machine that will generate more credit hours and, therefore, more tuition dollars. For years, college deans have argued that we need to find cheaper ways to process more students through the system. Predictably, many tenured radicals derisively use the phrase "credit factory" to describe this approach, but I think the industrial process is an apt metaphor for how universities should conduct their business. Fast food is another good model to follow, a point that is underscored on PhD-Dissertations. com's Frequently Asked Questions page:

> Will the material be one-of-a-kind and unique? Yes, of course. As they say at Jack-in-the-Box, "We don't make it until you order it." We write all custom research materials from scratch, based on the specifications provided to us. Unlike other services with no sense of academic integrity, we do not copy-and-paste from writings that are freely available on the Internet.

Some will surely complain about this approach's "intellectually corrosive" effects, but these people — who have a practically medieval, pre-capitalist concept of what universities should do — are wrong. In fact, a legitimized research assistance industry will most definitely improve the quality of scholarly research and writing. Because these companies exist in the private sector, they naturally do a more efficient job than researchers in bloated college bureaucracies, which have extensive, wasteful workforce redundancies. In today's universities, some scholars examine similar topics, but using different perspectives. In other words, they hire multiple people to do a job fit for one!

Corporate research factories, on the other hand, can maximize the resources needed to produce top-notch scholarship better than any state-funded school. This is because research assistance companies have a streamlined division of labor: one specialized staff researcher writes, another proofreads, a different employee fact checks, and another administrator can manage the whole project. As is noted on the homepage for Student Network Resources, which owns PhD-Dissertations.com, "we created a highly advanced project management system for clients and writers to connect on a large scale"; only in the private sector can you achieve this level of efficiency.

Hard times call for tough choices and new ideas, which my plan will deliver. By creating synergistic links between universities and corporate sponsors — and by privatizing the work done by undergraduate student/workers and professors-in-training — we can create a lighter, leaner educational system that can better adapt to the realities of a changing world. More importantly, this approach will foster economic growth by turning the process of learning into a frictionless series of commodity exchanges. After all, what could go wrong?

Reading the Genre

1. This proposal is made up of three connected proposals. What are they, and how seriously does McLeod expect readers to take them?

2. Satire — the use of wit and irony to make a serious point — is a form of social commentary. What is McLeod criticizing with his use of satire?

3. Look up the meaning of *hyperbole* and consider how McLeod uses overstatement as a persuasive tool. Could this strategy work in a proposal that is not a satire? (See "Defend the proposal," p. 188.)

4. **WRITING:** Because this is a satirical proposal, McLeod doesn't expect readers to follow through on his suggestions. Try to imagine real solutions to the problems McLeod addresses, and write a serious proposal for change.

5. **WRITING:** Using McLeod's satirical approach for inspiration, propose an outlandish change to another aspect of university life, beyond academics.

PROPOSAL FOR CHANGE   Peter Singer is a Princeton philosopher whose views on bioethics — animal rights, euthanasia, and reproduction, specifically — have been highly controversial. Singer is a utilitarian: He judges the morality of an action by its outcome. The essay first appeared in People and Place, a blog about "ideas that connect us."

People and Place

Posted: March 25, 2009, at 9:40 PM
From: Peter Singer

"One Person, One Share" of the Atmosphere

For most of human existence, people living only short distances apart might as well have been living in separate worlds. A river, a mountain range, a stretch of forest or desert: these were enough to cut people off from each other.

As a result, our moral intuitions evolved to deal with problems within our community, rather than with the impact of our actions on those far away. Resources like the atmosphere and the oceans seemed unlimited, and we have had no inhibitions against making the fullest use of them.

Over the past few centuries the isolation has dwindled, and now people living on opposite sides of the world are linked in ways previously unimaginable. Problems like climate change have revealed that by driving your car, you could be releasing carbon dioxide that is part of a causal chain leading to lethal floods in Bangladesh.

How can our ethics take account of this new situation?

"Enough and as Good"

Imagine that we live in a village in which everyone puts their wastes down a giant sink. The capacity of the sink to dispose of our wastes seems limitless, and as long as that situation continues, it is reasonable to believe that we are leaving "enough and as good" for others. No matter how much we pour down the sink, others can do the same.

This phrase "enough and as good" comes from John Locke's *Second Treatise on Civil Government*, published in 1690. In that work Locke says that the earth and its contents "belong to mankind in common." How, then, can there be private property? Because our labor is our own, and hence when we mix our labor with the land and its products, we make them our own. It has this effect, Locke says, as long as our appropriation does not prevent there being "enough and as good left in common for others."

Locke's justification of the acquisition of private property is the classic historical account of how property can be legitimately acquired, and it has served as the starting point for more recent discussions.

Now imagine that conditions change, so that the sink's capacity to carry away our wastes is used to the full. At this point, when we continue to throw our wastes down the sink we are no longer leaving "enough and as good" for others, and hence our right to unchecked waste disposal becomes questionable.

Think of that giant sink as our atmosphere and our wastes as carbon dioxide and other greenhouse gases. Once we have used up the atmosphere's capacity to absorb our gases without harmful consequences, it has become a finite resource on which various parties have competing claims. The problem is to allocate those claims justly.

Defining Equitable Distribution

During the 2000 U.S. presidential election, when the candidates were asked in a televised debate what they would do about global warming, George W. Bush said:

> I'll tell you one thing I'm not going to do is I'm not going to let the United States carry the burden for cleaning up the world's air, like the Kyoto treaty would have done. China and India were exempted from that treaty. I think we need to be more even-handed.

As president, Bush frequently repeated this line of reasoning. Indeed, the issue of what constitutes even-handedness, or fairness or equity, is perhaps the greatest hurdle to international action on climate change. But was Bush right to say that it is not even-handed to expect the United States to restrict its emissions before China and India begin to restrict theirs?

There are various principles that people use to judge what is fair or even-handed. In political philosophy, it is common to follow Robert Nozick, who distinguished between *historical principles* and *time-slice principles*.

A historical principle is one that says: To understand whether a given distribution of goods is just or unjust, we must ask how the situation came about; we must know its history. Are the parties entitled, by an originally justifiable acquisition and a chain of legitimate transfers, to the holdings they now have? If so, the present distribution is just. If not, rectification or compensation will be needed to produce a just distribution.

Looking at data for 1900 to 1999, we find that the United States, for example, with about 5 percent of the world's population, was responsible for about 30 percent of carbon dioxide emissions from fossil fuels, the primary source of greenhouse gases. Most of this carbon dioxide is still up in the atmosphere, contributing to global warming.

In this case, the application of the historical principle might be called "the polluter pays" or "you broke it, you fix it." It would assign responsibility proportionate to the amount that each country has contributed, a view that puts a heavy burden on the developed nations.

In their defense, it might be argued that at the time when the developed nations contributed most of their greenhouse gases into the atmosphere, they could not know of its limits in absorbing those gases. It would therefore be fairer to make a fresh start now and set standards that look to the future, rather than to the past.

This is the idea behind the time-slice principle. It looks at the existing distribution at a particular moment in time and asks whether that distribution satisfies some idea of fairness — irrespective of any preceding sequence of events.

An Equal Share for Everyone

If we begin by asking, "Why should anyone have a greater claim to part of the global atmospheric sink than any other?" then the first, and simplest response is: "No reason at all." Everyone has the same claim to part of the atmospheric sink as everyone else. This kind of equality seems self-evidently fair, at least as a starting point for discussion.

The Kyoto Protocol aimed to achieve a level for developed nations that was 5 percent below 1990 levels. Suppose that we focus on emissions for the entire planet and aim just to stabilize them. If we choose a target of 1996 emissions levels, then the allocation per person works out conveniently to about 1 metric ton of carbon per year. This becomes the basic equitable entitlement for every human being on the planet. (Note that emissions are sometimes expressed in terms of tons of carbon dioxide, rather than tons of carbon. One ton of carbon is equivalent to 3.7 tons of carbon dioxide.)

Now compare actual emissions for some key nations. In 2004, the United States produced 5.61 tons of carbon per person per year, while Japan, Germany, and the U.K. each produced less than 3 tons. China was at 1.05 and India at 0.34. This means that to reach an equal per capita annual emission limit of 1 ton, India would be able to increase its emissions three times. China, on the other hand, would need to stabilize its current emissions, and the United States would have to reduce its emissions to one-fifth of present levels.

One objection to this approach is that it gives countries an insufficient incentive to do anything about population growth. We can meet this objection by setting national allocations that are tied to a specified population, rather than letting them rise with an increase in population.

But since different countries have different proportions of young people about to reach reproductive age, this provision might produce greater hardship in countries that have younger populations. To overcome this, the per capita allocation could be based on an estimate of a country's population at some future date. Countries would then receive a reward in terms of an increased emission quota per citizen if they achieved a lower population than had been expected.

A Proposal

Each of these principles of fairness, or others, could be defended as the best one to take. I propose, both because of its simplicity, and hence its suitability as a political compromise, and because it seems likely to increase global welfare, that we support the principle of equal per capita shares of the capacity of the atmospheric sink, tied to the current projections of population growth per country for 2050.

Some will say that this is excessively harsh on industrialized nations, which will have to cut back the most on their output of greenhouse gases. Yet the one person, one share principle is more indulgent to the industrialized nations than some others, including the historical principle.

Allocating on the basis of equal per capita shares will be tremendously dislocating for the industrialized nations, and the mechanism of emissions trading can make this transition much easier. Emissions trading works on a simple economic principle: If you can buy something more cheaply than you can produce it yourself, you are better off buying it than making it. In this case, what you can buy will be a transferable quota to produce greenhouse gases, allocated on the basis of an equal per capita share.

Appropriate Scale

The ancient Greek iconoclast Diogenes, when asked what country he came from, is said to have replied: "I am a citizen of the world." Until recently, such thoughts have been the dreams of idealists. But now we are beginning to live in a global community. The impact of human activity on our atmosphere exemplifies the need for human beings to act globally. On this issue, as well as others, the planet should become the basic unit for our ethical thinking.

Reading the Genre

1. This essay is organized into five distinct sections. What does Singer do in each of them? How do the headings help readers follow his logic? (See "Creating a structure," p. 189, and Chapter 28, "Organization," p. 406.)

2. Where and how does Singer handle opposing viewpoints? Does he treat objections fairly? (See "Address counterpoints when necessary," p. 89, and Chapter 22, "Critical Thinking," p. 372.)

3. Notice Singer's use of personal pronouns — *we* and *they* especially — in this essay. How does the author's word choice influence the tone of his proposal? (See Chapter 35, "High, Middle, and Low Style," p. 432.)

4. How does this proposal incorporate research? How does Singer use hard evidence to support his claims about ethics and fairness? (See "Assemble your hard evidence," p. 86, and "Read sources to find evidence," p. 488.)

5. **WRITING:** Before he gets to his proposal, Singer reviews a series of alternative philosophies and acknowledges that "each of these principles of fairness, or others, could be defended as the best one to take." Choose a principle other than the "equal per capita shares" approach that Singer advocates, and fashion a proposal around that idea of fairness. You might, for instance, support the "historical principle," defend George W. Bush's view, or argue for an approach that aggressively targets emission reduction rather than stabilization. (See "Examine prior solutions," p. 187.)

6. **PRESENTING DATA:** Choose one set of statistics discussed in this essay and present it in a visual format. (See Chapter 53, "Tables, Graphs, and Infographics," p. 584.)

72 Literary Analyses: Readings

See also Chapter 7:

LITERARY
INTERPRETATION
Kelsi Stayart,
*Authentic Beauty in
Morrison's
The Bluest Eye,* 209

CLOSE READING
Kanaka Sathasivan,
Insanity: Two Women, 232

CULTURAL ANALYSIS
Kelli Marshall, *Show
Musical Good, Paired
Segments Better:* Glee's
Unevenness Explained, 238

PHOTOGRAPHS AS
LITERARY TEXTS
Dorothea Lange, *Jobless
on Edge of Pea Field,
Imperial Valley,
California,* 246
Walker Evans, *Burroughs
Family Cabin, Hale County,
Alabama,* 247
Gordon Parks, *American
Gothic,* 248

FORMAL ANALYSIS
Adam Bradley, *Rap Poetry 101*   899

TEXTUAL ANALYSIS
Charles Schulz, *Peanuts* (cartoon)   913
Geraldine DeLuca, *"I felt a Funeral, in my Brain":
The Fragile Comedy of Charles Schulz*   914

TEXTUAL ANALYSIS
Joni Mitchell, *"Woodstock"* (song lyrics)   925
Camille Paglia, *"Woodstock"*   927

HISTORICAL ANALYSIS
Sara Buttsworth, *CinderBella:* Twilight, *Fairy Tales, and the
Twenty-First-Century American Dream*   935

CULTURAL ANALYSIS
Gish Jen, *Holden Raises Hell*   961

FORMAL ANALYSIS   Adam Bradley teaches literature at the University of Colorado, Boulder. An expert scholar on both hip-hop poetics and the writer Ralph Ellison, he is the coeditor of the *Yale Anthology of Rap* (2010) and of Ellison's posthumously published (and unfinished) novel *Three Days Before the Shooting . . .* (2010). This essay comes from *Book of Rhymes* (2009), an in-depth analysis of rap as poetry.

ADAM BRADLEY

Rap Poetry 101

Prologue

This is hip hop. You are in a small club, standing room only. Maybe it's the Roots or Common or some underground group about to perform. Bodies press tightly against you. Blue wreaths of smoke hang just above your head. From the four-foot speakers at the front of the stage, you hear the DJ spinning hip-hop classics—A Tribe Called Quest, De La Soul, Rakim—charging the crowd as it waits, five minutes, ten minutes, longer, for the show to begin.

As the music fades to silence, a disembodied voice over the PA system announces the headliner. Lights grow warm, blue turns to yellow, then to red. The first beat hits hard, and the crowd roars as the MC—the rapper, hip hop's lyrical master of ceremonies—glides to the front of the stage. Hands reach for the sky. Heads bob to the beat. The crowd is a living thing, animated by the rhythm. It can go on like this for hours.

Now imagine this. It happens just as the performance reaches its peak. First the melody drops out, then the bass, and finally the drums. The stage is now silent and empty save for a lone MC, kicking rhymes a cappella. His voice fades from a shout to a whisper, then finally to nothing at all. As he turns to leave, you notice something stranger still: lyrics projected in bold print against the back of the stage. It's like you're looking directly into an MC's book of rhymes. The words scroll along in clear, neat lines against the wall. People stand amazed. Some begin to boo. Some start to leave.

But you remain, transfixed by the words. You notice new things in the familiar lyrics: wordplay, metaphors and similes, rhymes upon rhymes, even within the lines. You notice structures and forms, sound and silence. You even start to hear a beat; it comes from the language itself, a rhythm the words produce in your mind. You're bobbing your head again. People around you, those who remain, are doing it too. There's a group of you, smaller than before but strong, rocking to an inaudible beat.

The change is subtle at first. Maybe it's a stage light flickering back to life. Maybe it's a snare hit punctuating that inaudible rhythm. But now the lights burn brighter, the beat hits harder than ever, the MC bounds back on stage, the crowd reaches a frenzy. It's the same song, just remixed.

Through the boom of the bass you can still somehow hear the low rhythm the words make. Lines of lyrics pass across your mind's eye while the sound from the speakers vibrates your eardrums. For the first time you see how the two fit together—the sight and the sound. Rap hasn't changed, but you have. This is the poetry of hip hop.

Rap Poetry 101

I start to think and then I sink
into the paper like I was ink.
When I'm writing I'm trapped in between the lines,
I escape when I finish the rhyme . . .
      —Eric B. & Rakim, "I Know You Got Soul"

A book of rhymes is where MCs write lyrics. It is the basic tool of the rapper's craft. Nas raps about "writin' in my book of rhymes, all the words pass the margin." Mos Def boasts about sketching "lyrics so visual / they rent my rhyme books at your nearest home video." They both know what Rakim knew before them, that the book of rhymes is where rap becomes poetry.

Every rap song is a poem waiting to be performed. Written or freestyled, rap has a poetic structure that can be reproduced, a deliberate form an MC creates for each rhyme that differentiates it, if only in small ways, from every other rhyme ever conceived. Like all poetry, rap is defined by the art of the line. Metrical poets choose the length of their lines to correspond to particular rhythms—they write in iambic pentameter or whatever other meter suits their desires. Free verse poets employ conscious line breaks to govern the reader's pace, to emphasize particular words, or to accomplish any one of a host of other poetic objectives. In a successful poem, line breaks are never casual or accidental. Rewrite a poem in prose and you'll see it deflate like a punctured lung, expelling life like so much air.

Line breaks are the skeletal system of lyric poetry. They give poems their shape and distinguish them from all other forms of literature. While prose writers usually break their lines wherever the page demands—when they reach the margin, when the computer drops their word to the next line—poets claim that power for themselves, ending lines in ways that underscore the specific design of their verse. Rap poets are no different.

Rap is poetry, but its popularity relies in part on people not recognizing it as such. After all, rap is for good times; we play it in our cars, hear it at parties and at clubs. By contrast, most people associate poetry with hard work; it is something to be studied in school or puzzled over for hidden insights. Poetry stands at an almost unfathomable distance from our daily lives, or at least so it seems given how infrequently we seek it out.

This hasn't always been the case; poetry once had a prized place in both public and private affairs. At births and deaths, weddings and funerals, festivals and family gatherings, people would recite poetry to give shape to their feelings. Its relative absence today says something about us—our culture's short attention span, perhaps, or the dominance of other forms of entertainment—but also about poetry itself. While the last century saw an explosion of poetic productivity, it also marked a decided shift toward abstraction. As the poet Adrian Mitchell observed, "Most people ignore poetry because most poetry ignores most people."

Rap never ignores its listeners. Quite the contrary, it aggressively asserts itself, often without invitation, upon our consciousness. Whether boomed out of a passing car, played at a sports stadium, or piped into a mall while we shop, rap is all around us. Most often, it expresses its meaning quite plainly. No expertise is required to listen. You don't need to take an introductory course or read a handbook; you don't need to watch an instructional video or follow an online tutorial. But, as with most things in life, the pleasure to be gained from rap increases exponentially with just a little studied attention.

Rap is public art, and rappers are perhaps our greatest public poets, extending a tradition of lyricism that spans continents and stretches back thousands of years. Thanks to the engines of global commerce, rap is now the most widely disseminated poetry in the history of the world. Of course, not all rap is great poetry, but collectively it has revolutionized the way our culture relates to the spoken word. Rappers at their best make the familiar unfamiliar through rhythm, rhyme, and wordplay. They refresh the language by fashioning patterned and heightened variations of everyday speech. They expand our understanding of human experience by telling stories we might not otherwise hear. The best MCs—like Rakim, Jay-Z, Tupac, and many others—deserve consideration alongside the giants of American poetry. We ignore them at our own expense.

Hip hop emerged out of urban poverty to become one of the most vital cultural forces of the past century. The South Bronx may seem an unlikely place to have birthed a new movement in poetry. But in defiance of inferior educational opportunities and poor housing standards, a generation of young people—mostly black and brown—conceived innovations in rhythm, rhyme, and wordplay that would change the English language itself. In *Can't Stop, Won't Stop: A History of the Hip-Hop Generation,* Jeff Chang vividly describes how rap's rise from the 1970s through the early 1980s was accompanied by a host of social and economic forces that would seem to stifle creative expression under the weight of despair. "An enormous amount of creative energy was now ready to be released from the bottom of American society," he writes, "and the staggering implications of this moment eventually would echo around the world." As one of the South Bronx's own, rap legend KRS-One, explains, "Rap was the final conclusion of a generation of creative people oppressed with the reality of lack."

Hip hop's first generation fashioned an art form that draws not only from the legacy of Western verse, but from the folk idioms of the African diaspora; the musical legacy of jazz, blues, and funk; and the creative capacities conditioned by the often harsh realities of people's everyday surroundings. These artists commandeered the English language, the forms of William Shakespeare and Emily Dickinson, as well as those of Sonia Sanchez and Amiri Baraka, to serve their own expressive and imaginative purposes. Rap gave voice to a group hardly heard before by America at large, certainly never heard in their own often profane, always assertive words. Over time, the poetry and music they made would command the ears of their block, their borough, the nation, and eventually the world.

While rap may be new-school music, it is old-school poetry. Rather than resembling the dominant contemporary form of free verse — or even the freeform structure of its hip-hop cousin, spoken word, or slam poetry, rap bears a stronger affinity to some of poetry's oldest forms, such as the strong-stress meter of *Beowulf* and the ballad stanzas of the bardic past. As in metrical verse, the lengths of rap's lines are governed by established rhythms — in rap's case, the rhythm of the beat itself.

The beat in rap is poetic meter rendered audible. Rap follows a dual rhythmic relationship whereby the MC is liberated to pursue innovations of syncopation and stress that would sound chaotic without the regularity of the musical rhythm. The beat and the MC's flow, or cadence, work together to satisfy the audience's musical and poetic expectations: most notably, that rap establish and maintain rhythmic patterns while creatively disrupting those patterns, through syncopation and other pleasing forms of rhythmic surprise.

Simply put, a rap verse is the product of one type of rhythm (that of language) being fitted to another (that of music). Great pop lyricists, Irving Berlin or John Lennon or Stevie Wonder, match their words not only to the rhythm of the music, but to melodies and harmonies as well. For the most part, MCs need concern themselves only with the beat. This fundamental difference means that MCs resemble literary poets in ways that most other songwriters do not. Like all poets, rappers write primarily with a beat in mind. Rap's reliance on spare, beat-driven accompaniment foregrounds the poetic identity of the language.

Divorced from most considerations of melody and harmony, rap lyrics are liberated to live their lives as pure expressions of poetic and musical rhythm. Even when rap employs rich melodies and harmonies — as is often the case, for instance, in the music of Kanye West — rhythm remains the central element of sound. This puts rap's dual rhythms in even closer proximity to one another than they might usually be in other musical genres. Skilled MCs underscore the rhythm of the track in the rhythm of their flows and the patterns of their rhymes. As a consequence, the lyrics rappers write are more readily separated from their specific musical contexts and presented in written form as poetry. The rhythm comes alive on the page because so much of it is embedded in the language itself.

Many of the reasonable arguments critics offer to distinguish musical lyrics from literary poetry do not apply to rap. One of the most common objections, voiced best by the critic Simon Frith, is that musical lyrics do not need to generate the highly sophisticated poetic effects that create the "music" of verse written for the page. Indeed, the argument goes, if a lyric is too poetically developed it will likely distract from the music itself. A good poem makes for a lousy lyric, and a great lyric for a second-rate poem. Rap defies such conventional wisdom. By unburdening itself from the requirements of musical form, rap is free to generate its own poetic textures independent of the music. Another objection is that popular lyric lacks much of the formal structure of literary verse. Rap challenges this objection as well by crafting intricate structures of sound and rhyme, creating some of the most scrupulously formal poetry composed today.

Rap's poetry can usefully be approached as literary verse while still recognizing its essential identity as music. There's no need to disparage one to respect the other. In fact, perhaps more than any other lyrical form, rap demands that we acknowledge its dual identity as word and song.

The fact that rap is music does not disqualify it as poetry; quite the contrary, it asserts rap's poetic identity all the more. The ancient Greeks called their lyrical poetry *ta mele*, which means "poems to be sung." For them and for later generations, poetry, in the words of Walter Pater, "aspires towards the condition of music." It has only been since the early twentieth century that music has taken a backseat to meaning in poetry. As the poet Edward Hirsch writes, "The lyric poem always walks the line between speaking and singing. . . . Poetry is not speech exactly — verbal art is deliberately different than the way that people actually talk — and yet it is always in relationship to speech, to the spoken word."

Like all poetry, rap is not speech exactly, nor is it precisely song, and yet it employs elements of both. Rap's earliest performers understood this. On "Adventures of Super Rhymes (Rap)" from 1980, just months after rap's emergence on mainstream radio, Jimmy Spicer attempted to define this new form:

> It's the new thing, makes you wanna swing
> While us MCs rap, doin' our thing
> It's not singin' like it used to be

No, it's rappin' to the rhythm of the sure-shot beat
It goes one for the money, two for the show
You got my beat, now here I go

Rap is an oral poetry, so it naturally relies more heavily than literary poetry on devices of sound. The MC's poetic toolbox shares many of the same basic instruments as the literary poet's, but it also includes others specifically suited to the demands of oral expression. These include copious use of rhyme, both as a mnemonic device and as a form of rhythmic pleasure; as well as poetic tropes that rely upon sonic identity, like homonyms and puns. Add to this those elements the MC draws from music—tonal quality, vocal inflection, and so forth—and rap reveals itself as a poetry uniquely fitted to oral performance.

Earlier pop lyricists like Cole Porter or Lorenz Hart labored over their lyrics; they were not simply popular entertainers, they were poets. Great MCs represent a continuation and an amplification of this vital tradition of lyrical craft. The lyrics to Porter's "I Got You Under My Skin" are engaging when read on the page without their melodic accompaniment; the best rap lyrics are equally engrossing, even without the specific context of their performances. Rap has no sheet music because it doesn't need it—rapping itself rarely has harmonies and melodies to transcribe—but it *does* have a written form worth reconstructing, one that testifies to its value, both as music and as poetry. That form begins with a faithful transcription of lyrics.

Rap lyrics are routinely mistranscribed, not simply on the numerous websites offering lyrics to go, but even on an artist's own liner notes and in hip-hop books and periodicals. The same rhyme might be written dozens of different ways—different line breaks, different punctuation, even different words. The goal should be to transcribe rap verses in such a way that they represent on the page as closely as possible what we hear with our ears.

The standardized transcription method proposed here may differ from those used by MCs in their own rhyme books. Tupac, for instance, counted his bars by couplets. Rappers compose their verses in any number of ways; what they write need only make sense to them. But an audience requires a standardized form organized around objective principles rather than subjective habits. Serious readers need a common way of transcribing rap lyrics so that they can discuss rap's formal attributes with one another without confusion.

Transcribing rap lyrics is a small but essential skill, easily acquired. The only prerequisite is being able to count to four in time to the beat. Transcribing lyrics to the beat is an intuitive way of translating the lyricism that we hear into poetry that we can read, without sacrificing the specific relationship of words to music laid down by the MC's performance. By preserving the integrity of each line in relation to the beat, we give rap the respect it deserves as poetry. Sloppy transcriptions make it all but impossible to glean anything but the most basic insights into the verse. Careful ones, on the other hand, let us see into the inner workings of the MC's craft through the lyrical artifact of its creation.

The MC's most basic challenge is this: When given a beat, what do you do? The beat is rap's beginning. Whether it's the hiccups and burps of a Timbaland track, the percussive assault of a Just Blaze beat, knuckles knocking on a lunchroom table, a human beatbox, or simply the metronomic rhythm in an MC's head as he spits a cappella rhymes, the beat defines the limits of lyrical possibility. In transcribing rap lyrics, we must have a way of representing the beat on the page.

The vast majority of rap beats are in 4/4 time, which means that each musical measure (or bar) comprises four quarter-note beats. For the rapper, one beat in a bar is akin to the literary poet's metrical foot. Just as the fifth metrical foot marks the end of a pentameter line, the fourth beat of a given bar marks the end of the

MC's line. One line, in other words, is what an MC can deliver in a single musical measure—one poetic line equals one musical bar. So when an MC spits sixteen bars, we should understand this as sixteen lines of rap verse.

To demonstrate this method of lyrical transcription, let's take a fairly straightforward example: Melle Mel's first verse on Grandmaster Flash and the Furious Five's classic "The Message."

> One   TWO   Three   FOUR
> Standing on the front stoop, hangin' out the window,
> watching all the cars go by, roaring as the breezes blow.

Notice how the naturally emphasized words ("standing," "front," "hangin'," "window," etc.) fall on the strong beats. These are two fairly regular lines, hence the near uniformity of the pair and the strong-beat accents on particular words. The words are in lockstep with the beat. Mark the beginning of each poetic line on the one and the end of the line on the four.

Not all lines, however, are so easily transcribed; many complications can occur in the process of transcription. Consider the famous opening lines from this very same song:

> One   TWO   Three FOUR
> Broken glass everywhere,
> people pissin' on the stairs, you know they just don't care.

Looking at the two lines on the page, one might think that they had been incorrectly transcribed. The only thing that suggests they belong together is the end rhyme ("everywhere" and "care"). How can each of these lines—the first half as long as the second, and with fewer than half the total syllables—take up the same four-beat measure? The answer has everything to do with performance. Melle Mel delivers the first line with a combination of dramatic pause and exaggerated emphasis. He begins rhyming a little behind the beat, includes a caesura (a strong phrasal pause within the line) between "glass" and "everywhere," and then dramatically extenuates the pronunciation of "everywhere." Were it not for an accurate transcription, these poetic effects would be lost.

Sometimes rap poets devise intricate structures that give logical shape to their creations. Using patterns of rhyme, rhythm, and line, these structures reinforce an individual verse's fusion of form and meaning. While literary poetry often follows highly regularized forms—a sonnet, a villanelle, a ballad stanza—rap is rarely so formally explicit, favoring instead those structures drawn naturally from oral expression. Upon occasion, however, rap takes on more formal structures, either by happenstance or by conscious design. For instance, Long Beach's Crooked I begins the second verse of "What That Mean" by inserting an alternating quatrain, switching up the song's established pattern of rhyming consecutive lines.

> Shorty saw him comin' in a glare
> I pass by like a giant blur
> What she really saw was Tim Duncan in the air
> Wasn't nothin' but a Flyin' Spur

By rhyming two pairs of perfect rhymes *abab* ("glare" with "air" and "blur" with "spur"), Crooked I fashions a duality of sound that underscores the two perspectives he describes: that of the woman onlooker and that of the MC in his speeding car. By temporarily denying the listener's expectation of rhyme, he creates a sense of heightened anticipation and increased attention. Using this new rhyme pattern shines a spotlight on the playful metaphor at the center of the verse: what the woman saw was the San Antonio Spurs' MVP Tim Duncan in the air, otherwise known as a flying Spur, otherwise known as his luxury automobile, a Bentley Continental Flying Spur. The mental process of deciphering the metaphor, nearly instantaneous for those familiar with the reference and likely indecipherable for anyone else, is facilitated by the rhyming structure of the verse. Rhyme and wordplay work together to create a sense of poetic satisfaction.

Rap's poetry is best exemplified in these small moments that reveal conscious artistry at work in places we might least expect. It is this sense of craft that connects the best poetry of the past with the best rap of today. Consider the following two verses side by side: on the left is Langston Hughes's "Sylvester's Dying Bed," written in 1931; on the right is a transcription of Ice-T's "6 'N the Mornin'," released in 1987. Though distanced by time, these lyrics are joined by form.

Hughes's form relies upon splitting the conventional four-beat line in half, a pattern I have followed with Ice-T's verse for the purposes of comparison; I might just as easily have rewritten Hughes's lines as two sets of rhyming couplets. This adjustment aside, the two lyrics are nearly identical in form. Each employs a two-beat line (or a four-beat line cut in two) with an *abcb* rhyme pattern. They even share the same syntactical units, with *end stops* (a grammatical pause for punctuation at the end of a line of verse) on lines two, four, six, and eight. Both draw upon the rhythms of the vernacular, the language as actually spoken. This formal echo, reaching across more than a half century of black poetic expression, suggests a natural affinity of forms.

I woke up this mornin'	Six in the mornin'
'Bout half past three.	Police at my door.
All the womens in town	Fresh Adidas squeak
Was gathered round me.	Across my bathroom floor.
Sweet gals was a-moanin',	Out my back window,
"Sylvester's gonna die!"	I made my escape.
And a hundred pretty mamas	Don't even get a chance
Bowed their heads to cry.	To grab my old school tape.

Rap lyrics properly transcribed reveal themselves in ways not possible when listening to rap alone. Seeing rap on the page, we understand it for what it is:

a small machine of words. We distinguish end rhymes from internal rhymes, end-stopped lines from enjambed ones, patterns from disruptions. Of course, nothing can replace the listening experience, whether in your headphones or at a show. Rather than replacing the music, reading rap as poetry heightens both enjoyment and understanding. Looking at rhymes on the page slows things down, allowing listeners — now readers — to discover familiar rhymes as if for the first time.

Walt Whitman once proclaimed that "great poets need great audiences." For over thirty years, rap has produced more than its share of great poets. Now it is our turn to become a great audience, repaying their efforts with the kind of close attention to language that rap's poetry deserves.

Reading the Genre

1. What is the thesis of this literary analysis? How does Bradley use both rap lyrics and other writers' analyses as evidence to support his claims? Are you persuaded by his argument? (See "Use texts for evidence," p. 208; "Find good sources," p. 223; and "Read sources to find evidence," p. 488.)

2. This essay opens with a scene in a club. How does Bradley's introduction set up and support his main idea? (See Chapter 32, "Introductions," p. 420.)

3. Bradley compares the genres of poetry and rap lyrics. What similarities does he find? How does the comparison support his argument that rap is a form of poetry? (See "Focus on its genre," p. 222.)

4. **WRITING:** Pick your favorite hip-hop song or select one from *Billboard*'s list of recent hits (www.billboard.com/charts/r-b-hip-hop-songs#/charts/r-b-hip -hop-songs). Using the terminology that Bradley introduces and the method of transcription he describes, write a literary analysis essay of the song's lyrics.

5. **PERFORMANCE:** Bradley's analysis asks readers to imagine hip-hop songs without music to appreciate the lyrics as poetry. Try doing the opposite: Choose a traditional poem and perform it as a rap. Consider what the music video might look like for this poem.

TEXTUAL ANALYSIS   Geraldine DeLuca teaches English at Brooklyn College and is the cofounder of *The Lion and the Unicorn*, a journal devoted to the "serious, ongoing discussion of literature for children." The following analysis honors Charles Schulz, the creator of the *Peanuts* comic strip, and seeks to connect his life and his work. This essay can be seen as a form of biographical criticism—literary analysis that focuses on the facts of an author's life and family background to gain insights into his or her writing. A sample *Peanuts* strip precedes the analysis. The title of this essay comes from the Emily Dickinson poem of the same name, which can be found on page 231. (For another essay about the *Peanuts* strip, see Jonathan Franzen's "The Comfort Zone," on pp. 668–84.)

"I felt a Funeral, in my Brain": The Fragile Comedy of Charles Schulz

GERALDINE DELUCA

I was never a devoted follower of the *Peanuts* comic strip, yet I'm moved by the news of Charles Schulz's death. Here was a man in love with his work and the characters he'd created. In a career that lasted nearly fifty years, he never missed a daily deadline. . . . Last night, on the eve of publication of his final strip, he died. His work and his life ended on the same day. . . .

Despite his success, Charles Schulz struggled all his life with depression and anxiety. "I suppose I have always felt apprehensive and anxious," he once said. "I have compared it to the feeling that you have when you get up on the morning of a funeral."

—"Sy Safransky's Notebook"

My own reaction to Schulz's death was similar to Safransky's. The *Peanuts* strip was not something I followed particularly, but I found myself upset for days when Schulz died. Partly it may have been that I was reeling from the recent, unexpected death of my sister and felt, as I've read in a poem some-where, that the door to my brain had been blown open. My defenses were down. And maybe I was sad because I recognized that his were too, always, that he was suffering just as we were, and keeping the faith. Perhaps that is one reason why we loved him, because, as Linus says, he was the "Charlie Browniest," the most vulnerable, because he lived in a psychic universe in which he woke each day to a funeral, and out of that depression and anxiety, he drew his wonderful strip.

By most measures, Schulz's life was a great success story. He had a reason-able childhood with loving if restrained parents. His father, like Charlie Brown's, was a barber. His strip was early on appreciated, and his work grew steadily. He married and had children. He got divorced, but then he married again and had a happy relationship with his second wife. He had a daily and a Sunday strip, and he collaborated with like-minded souls (Bill Melendez, Lee Mendelson, Vince Guaraldi) to make videos that were faithful to his low-key sensibility. *Peanuts* artifacts proliferated throughout the country; he made many millions of dollars, and every day, until a few months before his death, he did what he loved: he drew his strip. "You don't work all your life to get to do something," he told his biographer, Rheta Grimsley Johnson, "so that you can have time not to do it" (41).

The defining trauma of his life seems to have been the loss of his mother. She died of cancer in 1943, shortly after he was drafted into the army. Her illness was protracted and painful, and the last time he saw her was on a weekend pass during basic training. She told him that they should say goodbye because they would probably not see each other again, and she died the next day (Johnson 51). Although he spent most of his tour of duty in Kentucky, in 1945 he was shipped to Europe where, moving across France, Germany, and Austria, he participated in the liberation of Dachau, Munich, and Berchtesgaden. Another loss, less tragic, but still weighty to Schulz, was his rejection by the young woman who became in the strip Charlie Brown's unrequited love, "the little red haired girl."

Lucy would say, "Get over it." But what kind of therapist is she? And why is she the therapist to begin with? Perhaps because, despite the hip surface of the strip, therapy is not the route to salvation in *Peanuts*. Schulz's characters do not get over great losses. They do not change. In *The Gospel according to Peanuts,* Robert Short suggests a view of life that was probably more congenial to Schulz, which is that we are flawed souls who occasionally have a redemptive experience, a moment of release, of joy, but then we revert to our old patterns and we suffer again. It was in Schulz's nature to suffer. He was shy, even agoraphobic, Johnson says. He was known to get off planes before take-off. What seemed to help him was a small congregation, a carefully charted life, the routine of his work. When he returned from the war, he began attending church services and studying the Bible; he began drawing cartoons, and his artist's thin skin kept him close to those painful states of feeling that are so well depicted in his strip.

The world of *Peanuts* is a suburban pastoral where none of the characters has reached puberty, all the love is unrequited, and sexual experience remains unknown. The kids spend their time playing baseball; flying kites; attending ordinary, boring schools. From time to time, they stage Christmas pageants that affirm after all, despite shameless displays of acquisitiveness, that the true meaning of Christmas is not aluminum trees and excesses of presents but a scrawny evergreen and the birth of Christ. But moments of such serenity don't override the failure, exasperation, unfulfilled desire, greed, and existential dread that haunt Schulz's characters. There is much that they don't understand that pulls on them. Despite their sheltered lives, there are hints of mortality. Snoopy periodically comments on the falling leaves, here in pointedly heroic terms — as if to say, see what happens when you step into the world: "The first leaf to make the courageous leap! The first leaf to depart from home! The first leaf to plunge into the unknown! / The first leaf to die!!" (Short 110). In a tender scene, Charlie Brown and Linus crouch before a seedling together, and Charlie Brown says, "It's a shame that we won't be around to see it when it's fully grown." "Why," Linus asks, "where are we going?" (Short 56).

The characters are offshoots of Schulz's psyche, humor figures, defined mostly by a single trait, an unruly pantheon of narcissists whose legs rotate toward and away from wholeness. Because they are children, their outrageous behavior charms us. They seem to speak from just below the surface where the unconscious intrudes upon consciousness. Driven by their desires and fears, they blurt out their truths or hold onto their blanket or take pratfalls or fall asleep at their desks. They move in bands, and they alternately insult and embrace one another. Like many comic characters, they are rigid, self-absorbed, stuck. Sometimes they hug each other or get kissed by the dog or find a lost library book, and they declare a moment of happiness. But then they assume their worried look again.

The drawings are deceptively simple and enormously expressive. Round, oversized faces, distinguished by the curve of a cheek or a hairdo, are composed of two dots for eyes, dashes for eyebrows, a line for a mouth that turns into a kidney-shaped opening when they howl. The compact little bodies literally get blown away. They spin in the air like pinwheels. They get tangled in kite strings and hang upside down from trees. Sometimes they stand behind a wall, two heads projecting — Charlie Brown and Linus — contemplating life's dilemmas. Sometimes they insult each other — Lucy figures largely here — and then one walks away, leaving a blank space where the other now stands alone.

Short calls attention to the acuteness of Schulz's vision in defining a moral universe. His strips often read like parables, and this was evident from their inception. The first *Peanuts* strip appeared on October 2, 1950. It was a renaming by Schulz's editors of a strip called *Li'l Folks,* and the drawing is rudimentary compared to the more evolved, precise style that developed in the next few years. But the strip goes to the heart of the human condition. Charlie Brown is walking toward Shermy and another child. Shermy says, "Well! Here comes ol' Charlie Brown! / Good ol' Charlie Brown. Yes sir! / Good ol' Charlie Brown. / How I hate him!" Charlie Brown is wearing a little smile, apparently unaware that hatred is being directed his way. But on some level, given who he is, he must feel it. And Shermy, who watches him, looks caught and perplexed by his own feeling.

Johnson says that Schulz regretted this famous first strip because he thought hatred was an "inappropriate emotion" (x). But the strip's power lies in the truth of those feelings of unexamined hatred that children discover early and carry around. And if the polite, affable Schulz worried about what he was saying, the artist in him followed a deeper vision and keener sense of honesty. His strip is full of inappropriate emotions. That is part of its brilliance. To Short, it is as if Schulz "speaks in tongues," a conduit for little gems that his own more censorious part would find discomfiting but that he knows enough to publish.

At the heart of the strip are the characters who seem to mirror Schulz's personality most closely, the three males, Charlie Brown, Snoopy, and Linus. Charlie Brown, Schulz says, is "everyman." "When I was small," he writes, "I believed that my face was so bland that people would not recognize me if they saw me someplace other than where they normally would. . . . It was this weird kind of thinking that prompted Charlie Brown's round ordinary face" (*Peanuts: A Golden Celebration* 14). While he is often the butt of jokes, a melancholy soul who seems to stand outside the circle, he also carries moral weight. When his sister Sally (who is frequently depicted working on her homework) writes in script, "Christmas is getting all you can get while the getting is good," Charlie Brown says, "**Giving!** The only real joy is **giving!**" This understanding is part of his heavy burden of consciousness, and most of the time he doesn't know what to do with it.

Snoopy, by contrast, is happy. He is a dog, first of all, and perhaps for that reason, relieved of some of the dour knowledge that plagues Charlie Brown. And he is a dog who ponders his own contentment, who requires only that his dog dish be filled with food. When characters yell at him, he is as likely as not to kiss them. In his relatively carefree state, he can create discomfort in others, like his tiny friend Woodstock the bird, whom he often knocks around without knowing it. Unlike Charlie Brown, Snoopy is resistant to insult. When Lucy tells him that his manuscript "A Sad Story" is "a dumb story," he thinks to himself, "that's what makes it so sad" (*Peanuts: AGC* 138). Happiness, Schulz implies through Snoopy, involves a certain degree of obliviousness, a thick skin, so to speak. And it is in Snoopy that Schulz invests the artist part of himself. Sitting on top of his doghouse, suggesting the small-scale, domestic nature of Schulz's work, Snoopy taps out his corny stories. He is the dreamer, the world famous hockey star, the world famous astronaut, and most notably the World War One Flying Ace, battling his nemesis, the Red Baron. He is insulated from the perceptions that trouble his owner, Charlie Brown. And he has the outlet of his art.

The blanket-carrying Linus represents the philosopher in Schulz, the seeker, the man of faith. Early on in the strip, Linus confuses Halloween with Christmas and introduces the Great Pumpkin. In the video *It's the Great Pumpkin, Charlie Brown,* he tells Sally that the Great Pumpkin will come to his pumpkin patch because it is a "sincere" patch, free of hypocrisy. The Great Pumpkin respects sincerity, Linus says. And when he comes, he'll bring toys to all the children. Sally, who claims to love him and who, to Linus's distress, calls him her "sweet Babboo," is furious with him when it turns out that the Great Pumpkin isn't coming, that there will be no presents. So she finally departs in a huff, leaving him alone with his belief, a troubled-looking child who nonetheless often demonstrates the preacherly eloquence, inner calm, and spacy imagination of a visionary.

The girls, on the other hand, have a more aggressive energy. Lucy, of course, can be relentlessly terrible. Schulz writes that "Lucy comes from the part of me that's capable of saying mean and sarcastic things" (*Peanuts: AGC* 25). To say the least. She is the devouring mother, the one who wants to tell everyone exactly what she thinks of them. Whereas Charlie Brown swallows his anger and gets depressed, Lucy lashes out to defend against her own anxieties. Other people's happiness makes her uncomfortable because it contrasts with her own inherently irascible state, and she tries to argue characters out of their good moods. When she sees Snoopy gaily dancing, she yells, "**Stop it!** Stop it this instant! With all the trouble there is in this world, you have no right to be so happy!" (*Peanuts: AGC* 24). When Charlie Brown's little sister Sally is born, Lucy is furious that Charlie Brown is pleased. She tells him, "I suppose it's never occurred to you that overpopulation is a serious problem?!" (*Go Fly a Kite, Charlie Brown*). "It's the wrong time" for new babies, she tells Linus. He stands with his blanket pressed against his face, his dot eyes pondering her position. Then he turns to her and replies, "What are you gonna do with all those babies who are lined up waiting to be born? / You just can't tell them to go away and **wait** for another thousand years, can you? **Can you?**" (*Go Fly a Kite*). When she fails to discourage Charlie Brown on the grounds of overpopulation and world strife, she finds a more personal approach:

> You think having a baby sister is great, don't you? / From now on you're going to have to **share** the affection of your mother and dad! But you think you won't mind that, don't you! / You think It'll be fifty-fifty, don't you? Well, it won't! With a baby sister, it'll be fifty-one–forty-nine! Maybe even **sixty-forty!** (*Go Fly a Kite*)

Her weak spot is Schroeder, the Beethoven enthusiast. She leans on his toy piano, grotesquely vying for his attention, grinning her awful grin, at times even throwing his piano up a tree or down a sewer, so that he'll have to notice her. Lucy is the control freak, the merciless, insatiable one who doesn't trust, whose own strategies never get her the love she wants.

Occasionally she has a sweeter moment, most notably when talking to Rerun, whom she calls Rerun because he's just another baby brother, a re-run of Linus. Rerun doesn't seem to suffer Lucy's wrath. She treats him patiently, like a parent with her youngest child. And to her credit, when Linus falls asleep in the pumpkin patch — long after she has put on her witch mask and led the charge against him for being so stupid as to wait out there all night — Lucy is the one who gets out of bed and brings him home. So she is not completely without scruples. Perhaps the best one can say about her is that she offers intermittent positive reinforcement, creating in a character like Linus the look of a child whose hair is always standing on end.

The other girls, Sally, Marcie, and Peppermint Patty, seem a little further from Schulz's nerve endings. They express his exasperation and bewilderment with the daily insults and injustices of life, but they seem to be "other," constructs of a social world rather than manifestations of Schulz's psyche. Sally is frequently depicted in school settings, always trying unsuccessfully and with little sense of ethics to make her way there. When she has to do yet another science project, she steals Woodstock's newly constructed home and offers it as a prehistoric bird's nest. When she gets a C on her coat hanger sculpture, she protests,

> Was I judged on the piece of sculpture itself? If so, is it not true that time alone can judge a work of art? / Or was I judged on my talent? If so, is it right that I be judged on a part of life over which I have no control? . . . Was I judged on what I had learned about this project? If so, then were not you, my teacher, also being judged on your ability to transmit your knowledge to me? Are you willing to share my C? (*Peanuts: AGC* 89)

Schulz says he based this strip on a similar experience of his son's, and he used Sally to dramatize it, "for she is a character who expresses indignation well, and who is completely bewildered by all the things she has to go through in school" (*Peanuts: AGC* 89). Sometimes she stands outside the school and talks to the building because maybe that's what it feels like to talk to teachers: like talking to a wall.

Marcie and Peppermint Patty are often written into the same strips, and they too are likely to be found in school. Marcie is very smart, very well behaved, hopeless at sports, and Schulz muses that "she seems to have to put up with some kind of pressure from home to be a good student" (*Around* 30). Peppermint Patty, by contrast, is a great athlete and an unsuccessful student. She was introduced as a character from another school on the working-class side of town when Schulz decided that Charlie Brown needed an opposing baseball team. In the videos, she has a hip, tough way of talking, she wears Birkenstock-type sandals, and she calls Charlie Brown "Chuck."

> Her most notable trait is that she always falls asleep in school. About her history, Schulz speculates: We have received some vague hints that Peppermint Patty does not have a mother and that her father travels a little bit, which means that Patty sometimes stays up quite late at night because she doesn't like being home alone, which is why she is sleepy the next day. But, we really don't know what happened to her mother. Was there a breakup in the marriage, or did her mother die? We don't know. I wonder if we will ever find out. (*Around* 30)

Schulz writes that the "narcolepsy people" at Stanford University told him that Peppermint Patty should be sent to a sleep-disorder center. The suggestion reflects the tension in the strip between the artist's particular, freewheeling vision and the social function he is perceived to serve for his readers. If Peppermint Patty is falling asleep, is it enough to say that she goes to bed too late or that she's tuning out because she thinks her teacher hates her? To his readership, she may stand for children who are ignored or discriminated against in school—children with disabilities, children whose family situations or social worlds make learning more difficult. If her father leaves her alone at night, shouldn't the child welfare people be notified? Schulz seemed to understand that he bore a responsibility to take care of his characters because his readers included so many children. He must have recognized that he was perceived as a small, consistent moral voice in an often immoral universe. But he was writing stories, not case studies. If Peppermint Patty falls asleep in school, then that's what she does. Kids fall asleep in school all the time. She is a fictional character. So mostly he demurred gracefully because it was his nature not to want to offend, and then he did what he wanted.

And out of his deep sympathy for the condition of children, Schulz created interesting, psychologically astute strips around Peppermint Patty. When she gets an F on her test, she tells Franklin, the boy who sits in front of her, that the reason she fails all the time is that she has a big nose and the teacher doesn't like her looks. "Your paper is blank," Franklin points out. But that's irrelevant to her. If the teacher doesn't like your looks, why bother writing the test? In another series of strips, Schulz reinforces this notion of teacher prejudice and affirms Patty's way of seeing. The studious Marcie, who pays attention to things like contests, tells Peppermint Patty that she, Patty, has won the "All-City School Essay Contest." "You wrote about looking at clouds, remember? Anyway, you won. . . . Congratulations." In the next strip, Peppermint Patty says to Charlie Brown:

> Explain this, if you can, Chuck. Everyone in our class had to write an essay on what we did during Christmas vacation. / When I got mine back, the teacher had given me a "D minus." Well, I'm used to that, right, Chuck? Right! / Now, guess what. All those essays went into a city essay contest, and I won! Explain that, Chuck.

Snoopy, lying on his doghouse, thinks, "Never listen to reviewers" (*Peanuts: AGC* 137). So, like other characters, but more pointedly because she seems to be "at risk," a motherless child, one who, for whatever reason, is not doing well in school, Peppermint Patty represents the promise of the unpromising child. And Schulz stands up for her not by having her diagnosed and fixed but by reminding us of the value of her eccentricity. She may not perform in conventional ways, but, perhaps for that very reason, she notices the clouds.

This is not to say, of course, that there are not children who need intervention and special help, but that doesn't seem to be the way things work in Schulz's world. In a spiritual sense, he seemed to say, we are radically unfixable. And as far as his strip is concerned, comedy thrives on eccentricity, on the tension between the "normal" center toward which the characters are supposed to be integrating themselves and their aberrations. In the correspondence course in drawing that Schulz took when he was a young man, he a got a C– in "Drawing of Children." Despite our best knowledge and all the experts who would tell us how to be, life unfurls itself in surprising ways. And to be normal or to succeed all the time is, he points out, not funny. Failure is funny. A character in a ridiculous situation is funny. Repetition is funny. Never learning from one's mistakes is funny. The success of his strip rested on his being able to do endless turns on a rather restricted repertoire, finding in the situation of a group of children who essentially never learn continued ways to explore the dilemma of being human.

Schulz appealed to a huge and wide-ranging audience. He had the most successful comic strip in newspaper history. *Peanuts* was carried in 2,600 newspapers across 75 countries and was translated into 21 languages. He regarded himself as writing for adults. Yet many of the small books compiled from those strips became *Weekly Reader* books for children, and he respected that audience as well. His videos too were remarkably successful. Nat Gertler writes of *A Charlie Brown Christmas*:

> This unlikely piece, which the network brass feared too slow-moving, too religious, too innocent, and sounding too much of jazz and amateur kid voices, pulled in an unbelievable 45 share and won an Emmy and a Peabody. Suddenly . . . CBS decided that *Peanuts* was a good thing after all. (Gertler)

Schulz appealed to what was "cool" in our culture, and yet he quoted the Bible regularly. He had simply found himself a permanent place in the American sensibility, drawn from a homely and authentic vision that he never seemed to compromise.

It is a commonplace to say that comedy derives from pain, that the artist flees from life and then writes about it. That certainly seems to be the case with Schulz. And one senses in his strip the great pleasure he derived from letting his art unfold freely, year after year, to an appreciative audience. You're not crazy, he told us. If you think your life is bad, climb into my imagination for a moment. You're bound to feel better. His success didn't ease the depression, the agoraphobia, and his wife learned to travel without him. To friends who moved across the country, he could only say goodbye. As he got older, he even stopped listening to music because its beauty was too painful to bear. The strip keeps trying to define that elusive state, happiness, but as Lucy tells Snoopy, "Just because you're happy today, doesn't mean you'll be happy tomorrow! / Happiness isn't everything, you know! / It'll never bring you peace of mind" (*Peanuts: AGC* 25). And what will bring peace of mind? Maybe getting lost in one's work, transmuting all that angst into art. And still, even if one feels relaxed on going to bed, one may wake as if to face a funeral.

Works Cited

Gertler, Nat. "Bill Melendez: A Brief Biography." *Peanuts Book List*. Web.

Johnson, Rheta Grimsley. *Good Grief: The Story of Charles M. Schulz*. Kansas City: Andrews and McMeel/United Features Syndicate, 1995. Print.

Safransky, Sy. "Sy Safransky's Notebook." *The Sun* [Chapel Hill, NC] August 2000: 47. Print.

Schulz, Charles M. *Around the World in 45 Years*. Kansas City: Andrews and McMeel/United Features Syndicate, 1994. Print.

———. *Go Fly a Kite, Charlie Brown*. 1959. New York: Holt, Rinehart and Winston, 1960. Print.

———. *Peanuts: A Golden Celebration: The Art and the Story of the World's Best-Loved Comic Strip*. Ed. David Larkin. New York: HarperCollins, 1999. Print.

Short, Robert L. *The Gospel According to Peanuts*. Richmond, VA: John Knox P, 1964. Print.

Δ

Reading the Genre

1. This essay might be seen as a form of encomium—an essay that honors the memory of someone who has died. How does DeLuca honor Schulz? By memorializing him, does she also place his work in a particular light?

2. DeLuca sets up parallels between characters in the comic strip and aspects of Charles Schulz's life and personality: How are these comparisons structured, and how does she make them persuasive? (See Chapter 21, "Smart Reading," p. 365.)

3. What major themes does DeLuca identify in *Peanuts*? In what way does she focus on and explore these themes? How is her essay organized around these themes? (See "Focus on its meanings, themes, and interpretations," p. 221, and Chapter 28, "Organization," p. 406.)

4. DeLuca describes a *Peanuts* strip so that we understand it without seeing it. How does she manage this and then use these examples to ground her analysis? See the example *Peanuts* strip on page 913, and describe it for someone who can't see it. (See "Focus on its meanings, themes, and interpretations," p. 221.)

5. **WRITING:** Choose any comic strip from your local newspaper and follow it for a week. Or visit the comic's Web site and look at the seven most recent strips. What is the dominant theme of this comic? Choose three examples of action, dialogue, or imagery from the strips that illustrate this theme, and describe these things for readers who cannot see the strips themselves. Use these examples to support your thesis about the theme of the comic.

TEXTUAL ANALYSIS   Camille Paglia is a culture critic and professor of humanities and media studies at the University of the Arts in Philadelphia. A founding contributor for *Salon.com*, she publishes articles in dozens of magazines and newspapers worldwide. This essay on Joni Mitchell comes from her most recent book, *Break, Burn, Blow: Camille Paglia Reads Forty-Three of the World's Best Poems* (2005). Mitchell is the only songwriter among this group of the world's best poets; Paglia defends her choice of the singer, and through her analysis of the song "Woodstock," reveals the complexity of Mitchell's writing. The song lyrics are reprinted before the essay.

JONI MITCHELL

Woodstock

I came upon a child of God
He was walking along the road
And I asked him, where are you going
And this he told me

I'm going on down to Yasgur's farm   5
I'm going to join in a rock 'n' roll band
I'm going to camp out on the land
And try and get my soul free

We are stardust
We are golden   10
And we've got to get ourselves
Back to the garden

Then can I walk beside you
I have come here to lose the smog
And I feel to be a cog   15
In something turning

Well, maybe it is just the time of year
Or maybe it's the time of man
I don't know who I am
But life is for learning   20

We are stardust
We are golden
And we've got to get ourselves
Back to the garden

By the time we got to Woodstock   25
We were half a million strong
And everywhere there was song
And celebration

And I dreamed I saw the bombers
Riding shotgun in the sky   30
And they were turning into butterflies
Above our nation

We are stardust
    million-year-old carbon
We are golden   35
    caught in the devil's bargain
And we've got to get ourselves
Back to the garden

CAMILLE PAGLIA

"Woodstock"

In the 1960s, young people who might once have become poets took up the guitar and turned troubadour. The best rock lyrics of that decade and the next were based on the ballad tradition, where anonymous songs with universal themes of love and strife had been refined over centuries by the shapely symmetry of the four-line stanza. But few lyrics, stripped of melody, make a successful transition to the printed page. Joni Mitchell's "Woodstock" is a rare exception. This is an important modern poem — possibly the most popular and influential poem composed in English since Sylvia Plath's "Daddy."

"Woodstock" is known worldwide as a lively, hard-driving hit single by Crosby, Stills, Nash, and Young (from their 1970 *Déjà Vu* album). This virtuoso rock band, which had actually performed at the Woodstock Music Festival in August 1969, treats Mitchell's lyric uncritically as a rousing anthem for the hippie counterculture. Their "Woodstock" is a stomping hoedown. But Joni Mitchell's interpretation of the song on her album *Ladies of the Canyon* (also 1970), where she accompanies herself on electric piano, is completely different. With its slow, jazz-inflected pacing, her "Woodstock" is a moody and at times heartbreakingly melancholy art song. It shows the heady visions of the sixties counterculture already receding and evaporating.

In the sleeve notes and other published sources, the verses of "Woodstock" are run together with few or no stanza breaks. Hence the song's wonderfully economical structure is insufficiently appreciated. My tentative transcription follows the sleeve in omitting punctuation but restores the ballad form by dividing lines where rhymes occur. "Woodstock" is organized in nesting triads: its nine stanzas fall into three parts, each climaxing in a one-stanza refrain. In Mitchell's recording, the three refrains are signaled by the entrance of background scat singers — her own voice overdubbed. At the end, this eerie chorus contributes two off-rhymed lines that I insert in italics.

Mitchell the poet and artist has cast herself in the lyric as a wanderer on the road to Woodstock, beckoning as a promised land for those fleeing an oppressive society. She meets another traveler, whose story takes up the rest of part one (1–12). Hence "Woodstock" opens with precisely the same donnée as does Shelley's "Ozymandias" ("I met a traveller from an antique land / Who said . . ."). Responding with her own story, Mitchell's persona repeats her companion's hymnlike summation ("We are stardust / We are golden") to indicate her understanding and acceptance of its message (13–24). Now comrades, they arrive at Woodstock and merge with a community of astounding size. From that assembly rises a mystical dream of peace on earth and of mankind's reconnection to nature (25–38).

The song's treatment by a male supergroup automatically altered it. The four musicians, bellying up front and center, are buddies — the merry, nomadic "rock 'n' roll band" whom the lyric's young man yearns to join (6). But Mitchell's radical gender drama is missing. Presented in her voice, the lyric's protagonist is Everywoman. The wayfarers' chance encounter on the road to Woodstock is thus a reunion of Adam and Eve searching for Eden — the "garden" of the song's master metaphor (12). They long to recover their innocence, to restart human history. The song's utopian political project contains a call for reform of sexual relations. Following Walt Whitman or Jack Kerouac, the modern woman writer takes to the road, as cloistered Emily Dickinson could never do. She and her casual companion are peers on life's journey. Free love — "hooking up" in sixties slang — exalts spontaneity over the coercion of contract.

The rambler is "a child of God," like Jesus' disciples on the road to Emmaus, because he desires salvation — but not through organized religion (1). He has shed his old identity and abandoned family, friends, property, and career. Like her, he is a refugee. Indifferent to his social status, she honors him in the moment. And she asks no favors or deference as a woman. Her question — "where are you going" — implies. Where is this generation headed (3)? Is it progressing, or drifting? Does it aim to achieve, or merely to experience? And if the latter, how can raw sensation be bequeathed to posterity without the framing of intellect or art?

He's on his way to "Yasgur's farm" — the festival site on six hundred acres of rolling pastureland in upstate New York, a working dairy farm owned by the paternal Max Yasgur (5). It is nowhere near the real Woodstock, an art colony town seventy miles away. Most of those who flocked to the three-day Woodstock festival were the white, middle-class children of an affluent, industrialized nation cut off from its agrarian roots. In Mitchell's song, their goal, "Yasgur's farm," becomes a hippie reworking of Yahweh's garden. The young man planning "to camp out on the land" to free his soul is a survivalist searching for primal nature (7–8). Michael Wadleigh's epic documentary film *Woodstock* (1970) records the violent gale and torrents of rain on the second day that turned the field into a morass. The "rock 'n' roll band" coveted by the traveler is ultimately the festival audience itself, united in music — an adoptive family of brothers and sisters who were rocked by lightning and who rolled in the mud.

"We are stardust / We are golden": the refrain is a humanistic profession of faith in possibility (9–10). Mankind was created not by a stern overlord but by sacred nature itself. It's as if the earth were pollinated by meteor showers. To be golden means to be blessed by luck: divinity is within. "We've got to get ourselves / Back to the garden": Woodstock pilgrims need no Good Shepherd or mediating priesthood (11–12). When perception is adjusted, the earth is paradise now. The woman wanderer is touched by the stranger's sense of mission: "Then can I walk beside you" (13)? Woman as equal partner rejects the burden of suspicion and guilt for man's Fall. She too is a truth seeker: she has "come here to lose the smog" — the smoke that gets in our eyes from romantic love and from the cult of competition and celebrity in our polluted metropolises (14). She feels egotistic preoccupations lifting as she becomes "a cog / In something turning"—the great wheel of karma or of astrological cycle (15–16). (Woodstock was initially called an "Aquarian Exposition" to mark the dawning of the harmonious Age of Aquarius.)

The impulse for migration to Woodstock could be "just the time of year," when summer juices surge and vacationers flock to mountains or sea (17). But if it's "the time of man" (a gender-neutral term), Woodstock's mass movement is an epochal transformation (18). The lyric's apocalyptic theme can be understood as a healing amelioration of the modernist pessimism of Yeats's "The Second Coming"—a poem that Mitchell would daringly rewrite for a 1991 album. Yeats's sinister beast slouching toward Bethlehem has become a generation embarked on a spiritual quest.

"I don't know who I am": the road to Woodstock leads to self-knowledge or self-deception (19). As a name, "Woodstock" is fortuitously organic, with associations of forest and stalk or lineage: streaming toward their open-air sanctuary, the pilgrims are nature's stock, fleeing a synthetic culture of plastics and pesticides. (In her raffish hit song "Big Yellow Taxi," Mitchell says, "They paved paradise / And put up a parking lot / . . . Hey farmer farmer / Put away that DDT now.") The festival-goers believe, rightly or wrongly, that music is prophetic truth. "Life is for learning," for expansion of consciousness rather than accumulation of wealth or power, "the devil's bargain" (compare Wordsworth's "sordid boon"; 20, 36). The returning refrain hammers the point home: we own everything in nature's garden but are blinded by ambition and greed.

The lyric seems to take breath when the pair, with near ecstasy, realize their journey has been shared by so many others: "By the time we got to Woodstock / We were half a million strong" (25–26). The first "we" is two; the second, by heady alchemy, has become a vast multitude. It's as if Adam and Eve are seeing the future—the birth of Woodstock nation, forged of Romantic ideals of reverence for nature and the brotherhood of man. As the two melt into the half million, there is an exhilarating sense of personal grievances and traumas set aside for a common cause. The crowd is "strong" in its coalescence, however momentary. "Everywhere there was song / And celebration": duty and the work ethic yield to the pleasure principle, as music breaks down barriers and inhibitions (27–28). The group triumphs, for good or ill.

The artist's "I" reemerges from the surging "we" of the Woodstock moment: "I dreamed I saw the bombers / Riding shotgun in the sky / And they were turning into butterflies / Above our nation" (29–32). Is this a shamanistic or psychedelic hallucination? Or is it a magic metamorphosis produced by the roaring engine of rock, with its droning amps and bone-shuddering vibration, eddying up from the earth? The bombers are the war machine then deployed in Vietnam. During her childhood, Joni Mitchell's father was a flight lieutenant in the Royal Canadian Air Force. Thus "Woodstock" aligns the modern military with mythic father figures and sky gods, as in William Blake's engraving *The Ancient of Days,* where Yahweh, crouched in a dark cloud, launches spears of sunlight from his rigidly out-thrust down-stretched hand.

"Riding shotgun" means guarding a stagecoach in the Wild West. Why are the bombers on alert—to smite foreign enemies, or to monitor domestic subversives? Rebel children are the nation's new frontier. The bombers, Pharaoh's pursuing chariots, can destroy but not create; they helplessly follow social change from a distance. Their alteration to butterflies "above our nation" suggests an erasure of borders, restoring the continental expanse of pre-Columbian North America. It's as if mistrust and aggression could be wished away and nationalistic rivalries purged around the world. The impossibility of this lovely dream does not negate its value. Perhaps the armored warplanes are chrysalises hatching evolved new men, the pilots floating down on parachutes to join the festival of peace. But we cannot live as flitting butterflies. Civilization requires internal and external protections and is far more complex and productive than the sixties credo of Flower Power ever comprehended.

In spatial design, "Woodstock" tracks along the wanderers' narrow path, then suddenly expands horizontally at its destination, where the half million have gathered. Buoyed by "song," the lyric now swells vertically to the sky, where it bewitches and exorcizes its harassers. Finally, it sweeps backward in time to take in geology: we are "million-year-old carbon" (34). Our Darwinian origins are a primeval swamp of lizards and plants, crushed to a fertile matrix. We are kin to rocks and minerals, the lowest of the low in Judeo-Christianity's great chain of being. What injects life into the song's stardust and carbon is not the Lord's breath but music. By affirming our shared genetic past, furthermore, Mitchell's metaphor conflates the races: we are carbon copies of one another. If at the cellular level we're all carbon black, then racial differences are trivial and superficial. And carbon under pressure transmutes to the visionary clarity of diamond.

The grandeur of Mitchell's lyric, with its vast expanse of space and time, is somewhat obscured in its carefree performance by Crosby, Stills, Nash, and Young, who are true believers in the revolutionary promise of Woodstock nation. By literally re-creating the "song and celebration," their bouncy, infectious rock rendition permits no alternative view of the festival, even though by the time their record was released, the disastrous Altamont concert had already occurred, exposing the fragility of Woodstock's aspirations. (*Gimme Shelter,* the Maysles brothers' 1970 documentary on the all-day festival at Altamont Speedway near San Francisco, captures the discord and violence leading to a murder in front of the stage.) CSN&Y's evangelical version of "Woodstock" was meant to convert its listeners to pacifism and solidarity. But six months after release of their single, the group had bitterly broken up. They themselves couldn't hold it together. And Mitchell's love affairs with two band members (Crosby and Nash) also ended.

In the hesitations and ravaged vibrato of her recording of "Woodstock," Joni Mitchell confides her doubts about her own splendid vision. Partly because she did not perform at Woodstock, her version has more distance and detachment. Her delivery makes lavish use of dynamics, so that we feel affirmation, then a fading of confidence and will. This "Woodstock" is a harrowing lament for hopes dashed and energies tragically wasted. It's an elegy for an entire generation, flamingly altruistic yet hedonistic and self-absorbed, bold yet naive, abundantly gifted yet plagued by self-destruction. These contradictions were on massive display at Woodstock, where the music was pitifully dependent on capitalist technology and where the noble experiment in pure democracy was sometimes indistinguishable from squalid regression to the primal horde.

An extended coda begins, as if the song doesn't want to end. The lyrics dissolve into pure music—Woodstock's essence. The coda, with its broken syllables, is a crooning lullaby that turns into a warning wail. Mitchell is skeptical about groups; she longs to join but sees the traps. When her voice falls away, her reverberating piano goes on by stops and starts. The entire power of "Woodstock" is that what is imagined in it was *not* achieved. Woodstock the festival has become a haunting memory. Mitchell's final notes hang, quaver, and fade. Cold reality triumphs over art's beautiful dreams.

Reading the Genre

1. Paglia closely reads every line and word of the song "Woodstock." How does this reading allow her to suggest that the song is telling one particular story? Do you think there could be other meanings, or do you think Paglia got it right? (See "Examine the text closely," p. 221, and Chapter 21, "Smart Reading," p. 365.)

2. Is Paglia's reading shaped by the fact that a woman wrote this song? How important is it in literary analysis to consider a text's author, and why?

3. Paglia writes about the different recorded performances of the song. In what ways does the song's meaning change when the song is performed by different bands, with different instrumentation, or in different venues?

4. How does Paglia describe the social context in which the song was written? What would change if the song were written and performed today? (See "Focus on its social connections," p. 223.)

5. **WRITING:** Read lyrics written by one of your favorite artists (song lyrics are readily available online). Do a close, line-by-line and word-by-word analysis of the song. Using this close reading, what assertions can you make about the subject of the song? Support these claims by finding out more about who the author is, how and where the song has been performed, and what social context the song was written in. (See Chapter 41, "Finding Print and Online Sources," p. 472.)

6. **WRITING:** Watch some footage, on YouTube or DVD, of one of your favorite bands performing live and write an analysis that focuses not on the lyrics or the music, but on the performance itself. Consider, for example, the stage set, the lighting, the band members' movements, and their interaction with the crowd.

HISTORICAL ANALYSIS   A historian and cultural critic, Sara Buttsworth teaches at the University of Auckland in New Zealand. She has published books and academic essays on subjects ranging from World War II to *The Lord of the Rings* and *Buffy the Vampire Slayer*. In this essay, she applies her expertise in folklore to a fresh reading of Stephenie Meyer's popular *Twilight* series.

SARA BUTTSWORTH

CinderBella: *Twilight*, Fairy Tales, and the Twenty-First-Century American Dream

Forget Princess, I want to be a Vampire!
— T-shirt slogan, 2009

Preface

Once upon a time there was a dark forest of deep green where magical creatures simultaneously offered succor and peril, sanctuary and slaughter. At the edge of this forest lived a girl with skin as white as snow, a luscious blush to her cheeks, dark hair that rippled down her back, and a smell more tempting than ripe apples. The girl, whose name meant "beauty," lived in exile with her father, for whom she kept house, cleaning and cooking with good will. She liked to read and had feet that would not dance and a mind that was silent to the probing of others. Bella and her father were not poor exactly, but they had little to spare. Peerless as she was, she had no real friends among her own kind. Instead, she fell in love with an outsider—a prince who had the face of an angel, beastly appetites, and skin that reflected sunlight better than any glass slipper. Bella did not always heed warnings never to stray from paths in the forest and was therefore lucky to be befriended by the wolves living there—guardians of the forest and the "provincial town" of Forks. The wolves cared not that Bella wore no hood of red, only that her blood continued to pump through her veins, lending its color to her pale cheeks—and that she did not become the handsome prince's next meal.

The Dreams of Lambs and Lions

The novels (and film adaptations) of the *Twilight Saga* operate in the dreamlike realm of the fairy tale, where horror and romance coexist. Bella's quest for eternal youth and a literal happily-forever-after follows a tradition that has often governed the behavior of young women in different ways through the centuries. This tradition has its roots in the storytelling of peasants around their hearths. The stories began to be much more formally didactic for the emerging middle classes when Charles Perrault and his contemporaries transformed oral folktales into their literary *contes des fées* ("fairy tales") for the glittering salons of Paris society in the seventeenth and eighteenth centuries. Once fixed on paper, folktales were later recast and redefined by the morality of the Brothers Grimm in the nineteenth century and were later broadcast worldwide by Disney studios throughout the twentieth and into the twenty-first centuries.[1]

The personal details of young women like Bella Swan have changed over the centuries, along with the cultural contexts of the stories in which they appear, displaying various skills, virtues, and levels of intellect. Throughout the twentieth century, particularly with the standardized morality and global reach of Disney films, heroines—even the feisty ones of the latter part of the period—have continued to be rewarded for, but never rescued from, their patience, passivity, and pallid beauty.

Stephenie Meyer's stories are a gripping read from beginning to end partly because of their fairy-tale appeal, which, far from being "timeless," is very much of *this* time. References to heroines and romantic couples (both doomed and happy) outside the folkloric realm abound in the *Twilight* novels: the writings of Shake-speare, Emily Brontë, and Jane Austen are Bella's staple entertainment. But Bella's story, with its stance on premarital sex, fidelity, self-sacrifice for a prolife attitude, and the questions it begs about how young women in a "postfeminist" age are supposed to be able to "have it all," make Meyer's work very much a fairy tale of the twenty-first century.

The *Twilight* novels make use of a number of important factors that have remained constant in fairy-tale texts. Perhaps the most important fairy-tale factor Meyer has employed is the transformative power of "survival tale[s] with hope."[2] As characters within fairy tales survive the challenges they meet, they are transformed and attain their hearts' desires. Meyer's heroine is no exception to the personal transformation that is undergone by so many fairy-tale protagonists. And it is no great leap to see Bella's story as a "survival tale with hope." So, in considering the *Twilight Saga*, it is not the resemblance to fairy tales that poses a quandary. Rather,

the problem lies in deciding which fairy tale it resembles the most. Fragments of *Snow White*, *Cinderella*, *Beauty and the Beast*, and *Little Red Riding Hood* are *all* discernible throughout Meyer's work, so which story is it that binds this romance together?

The answer to this question is a story within a story. The fairy tale most apparent in these books is actually the American Dream—another story of "survival with hope" that has been handed down through the generations and adapted to changing cultural ideals and socioeconomic contexts. Bella comes from a lower-middle-class background. Her father, Charlie, is a small-town chief of police, and her mother, Renée, has a non-descript occupation (other than being Charlie's, and then Phil's, wife) and level of education that, foreshadowing her own child's early marriage and motherhood, seems to have been cut short by early marriage and pregnancy. Renée did not marry up in the same way that Bella does, and her neglected offspring certainly climbs up an entire socioeconomic beanstalk in marrying into the extremely wealthy Cullen family.

Bella may not have worn rags at the beginning of her story, but by its end she certainly has unfettered access to riches both materially and in terms of opportunities. And throughout the *Twilight* series, the American conviction that the United States is unique among nations, following different rules and pursuing a destiny different from that of other cultures (that is, the "exceptionalism" of the United States on the world stage), an idea that has been at the center of the American Dream since the Puritans, is evident in its heroine, its vampires, and its werewolves, glittering as brightly as diamonds in the sun. What Bella's story illustrates above all else, however, is that the American Dream tradition for young women in the early twenty-first century remains a variant of *Cinderella*. With or without glass slippers, it is the right marriage that elevates one out of the dark cabin in the woods to the sunlit castle on the hill.

As surely as Old World stories tell of Jack's winning a king's ransom by way of a handful of magic beans, and Dick Whittington becoming lord mayor of London in reluctantly parting with his cat, the American Dream posits that upward mobility can be, and is, a reality. Anyone, according to this fairy tale, can grow up to be president—if he is a boy that is (and history suggests that those who have had any real hope of gaining access to this Dream have also been overwhelmingly white, the current U.S. president notwithstanding). What it means for a man to reach his goals has changed over time; Puritans tended to focus on community and being closer to God, for example, whereas by the mid-twentieth century the emphasis had shifted toward each person's freedom to develop an individual identity. The individual successes that have been the dream since the late nineteenth century have continued to dominate and tend to preclude any analysis of how class, race, or gender can be barriers to success.[3] But the possibility of transformation in a single person's life, rather than collective revolution, is the key to the fairy-tale kingdom of the American Dream. Many staple fairy tales of European origin feed into this utopian vision of individual, community, and national success—if the fool can marry the princess and become king, why not become president? The mythical success of the "everyman" is all around us.

But what if you are a girl: Can you become president or will you always just be someone else's queen? The Cinderella myth is alive and kicking up its glass slippers in a plethora of literary and cinematic texts produced in the late twentieth and early twenty-first centuries, to the extent that an entire "princess culture" has emerged.[4] The American Dream continues to be regularly invoked and reinvented, from popular fiction to popular film to the speeches and treatises of successive U.S. presidents, including Barack Obama (one of his books even has the American Dream in its title: *The Audacity of Hope: Thoughts on Reclaiming the American Dream*). Just how accessible is this goal for young women? The *Twilight* stories are very much a part of this nexus of myths as tales of upward mobility, standing at the crossroads between the Old World and the New. Peppered with direct and indirect fairy-tale references and a reverence for baseball, the ending that allows Bella to "have it all" consists of early marriage, dying young, and staying pretty.[5] Throughout Meyer's saga, Bella is in many ways as blank as her 1950 Walt Disney predecessor, and other than her delicious smell, it is that and her unselfishness (like Beauty's and Cinderella's before her) that attract Edward, her prince.

This chapter explores the *Twilight* novels in the context of fairy-tale tradition, including the American Dream, and the ways in which this tradition can shed light on just how tight the glass slipper is. The analysis is divided into two parts, the first on the American Dream, and the second on Cinderella stories — although obviously teasing these apart completely is not entirely possible, and fairy-tale references abound in both. The characters of Carlisle and Edward best illustrate some of the changes in the tradition of American Dream stories. And just as the Cullen male leaders best exemplify this tradition, the Quileutes represent those who have been, and continue to be, consistently excluded from it. The Cullen coven and Bella illustrate the ongoing importance of American culture's vision of itself as "different" from other nations, not only in their "cross-species" relationships and "puritan" diet, but in relation to the European vampire aristocracy, the Volturi.

The second part of the analysis focuses more on the female characters, especially Bella, Esme, and Rosalie, who are all heiresses to the legacies left behind by their fairy-tale predecessors — for the most part the heroines of twentieth-century cinematic tales. Both sections demonstrate the ways in which the Cullen family (of which Bella is really a part right from the beginning, almost as if she was "born to be a vampire" of the Cullen ilk) represents the different ideals of individual morality for men and women, individual success, social mobility, and the unique aspects of American culture that are the dreams any American Cinderella's heart might harbor. (*Breaking Dawn,* 524.)

Creatures of the Night: Defenders of the Dream

The transformative power of the fairy tale, and of fairy-tale heroes, is often one of turning established hierarchies on their heads. This fantasy is as crucial for the

American Dream, where an individual can attain wealth and power regardless of his origins or structural or social obstacles, as it is for its fairy-tale siblings. The fool can be king for a day, for a lifetime, or for several, but the fool does not want to get rid of the social order that oppresses him. He merely wants to be on top of it. The hierarchies of society remain intact in the traditional folktale, but he who was at the bottom manages through hard work, perseverance, and sometimes dumb luck, to end up in a far loftier position than the one from which he started out.[6]

Th*e Twilight Saga* can also be seen as upending literary hierarchies in some ways, since vampires are not necessarily villains. Rather than the transgression, excess, and sexual deviance that have traditionally been keys to vampire stories, the Cullens and their friends represent chastity, morality, and restraint.[7] Interestingly, while the Cullens represent such a break with literary vampire traditions, they do not seek to overturn the vampire order. In the same way, to be opposed to their own great material wealth would jeopardize their ability to move through both vampire and human worlds (and other than perhaps Carlisle, none of the Cullens would ever really dream of questioning their right to fabulous riches). While they live outside many human systems of operation, they do use them to their advantage. Much as the Puritans represented a break from the "evils" of the Old World they fled as they sought Utopia in the New, the Cullen family, headed by Carlisle, represents a break from the excesses and cruelties of Old World vampirism. The New World is still the place to make your fortune, however, and, through hard work, to gain access to a little piece of paradise in this world and the hereafter.

Long before Thomas Jefferson wrote "life, liberty, and the pursuit of happiness" into the Declaration of Independence in 1776, before Abraham Lincoln ascended from a log cabin to the White House, and before Horatio Alger penned his popular fictions of rags-to-riches glory for those who worked hard and cared for others in the late 1860s, the Puritans arrived in the New World with their Spartan ways and their hopes of attaining a better life in the now and in heaven. Cultural historian

Jim Cullen (not to be confused with Meyer's Cullens), in his book *The American Dream: A Short History of an Idea That Shaped a Nation*, stresses free will and individual choice as the key to the freedoms Americans have always held dear; he also examines how the Declaration had its roots in the hopes and fears of the Puritans who arrived in North America more than a century before.[8] The story and character of Carlisle, father of the Cullen coven, can be viewed alongside these ancestors of the Founding Fathers.

In describing Carlisle as having been born the son of a seventeenth-century Protestant preacher, Meyer invokes memories of the Puritans, the religious reform movement that inspired small groups to break away from the Anglican Church in Britain and seek freedom from persecution in the new colonies on the East Coast of North America. The characterization of Carlisle's father as a leader of witch hunts, which leads to the literal demonizing of his own son, roots the entire Cullen family history in a search for freedom from persecution as they pursue a different way of life. The Puritan nature of the Cullens, while not evident in the trappings of wealth with which they surround themselves, is instead expressed through something even more basic to their identities: how they sustain their bodies through diet. It is their diet and desire to treat humans as people rather than as "pets" or "snacks" that sets them apart from the Old World vampires—the Volturi and most of their followers.

In refusing to drink human blood, Carlisle sets an example that baffles the "nighttime patrons of the arts," Aro, Caius, and Marcus, who attempted to "cure his aversion to 'his natural food source' as they called it." (*Twilight*, 297.) It is unclear what these attempts entailed. However, the impressions of the Volturi created in *New Moon*, *Eclipse*, and *Breaking Dawn* convey the idea that had they stopped feeling so indulgent in Carlisle's direction, the Volturi would not have hesitated to use a number of forms of coercion and persecution to achieve conformity. So, feeling that there was no hope of continuing his "religion" of caring for others and not sucking the life out of them, Carlisle fled seventeenth-century Italy and began a lonely extended life that eventually found him transforming Edward on his deathbed three centuries later. Freedom from persecution, a "puritan" diet, and an ethic of caring that leads Carlisle to transform only those who are close to death (and who become a part of his "family" rather than followers in a retinue) are among the ways in which Meyer reflects the notion that Americans (even if they are vampires!) have a unique culture among the nations, which is crucial to the American Dream.[9] Through dint of hard work and self-sacrifice, Carlisle overcame his appetites to the extent that, rather than living apart from people, he could live among them and be a pillar of the various communities through which he moved. As he says while dealing with Bella's injured arm in the opening chapters of *New Moon*, "Like everything in life, I just had to decide what to do with what I was given." (*New Moon*, 35.)

Hard work and a strong moral center led Carlisle to a life of which he is proud. His diet means he maintains the ethics of Puritanism, but his profession and long life mean he can still achieve the luxuries that only great wealth can afford. Political scientist Cal Jillson has claimed that like Puritans, for Quakers (a similar breakaway seventeenth-century sect), "[W]orking, saving, and investing led to prosperity and enhanced one's role in the community because thriving was taken to be a visible sign that one was living in the light of the Lord's grace." But it was the very material success that followed their Protestant work ethic that inevitably undermined the communitarian emphasis of the early Puritan and Quaker communities: as they became wealthier, they often ceased to live as simply as their founders had.[10] There appears to be no such conflict for the New World vampires of the Cullen coven. Excess, in the vampire world it seems, is largely related to food.

The subtle differences between the characterizations of Edward and Carlisle move *Twilight*'s American Dream into the twentieth century in terms of values and aspirations. While Carlisle does represent individual success, he is also the founder of a community and completely bound to it. Where Carlisle's commitment to his little coven has much to do with faith, Edward's is based on love and loyalty—and his affections can waver, depending on which sibling he interacts with and whether or not their behavior accords with his own code of conduct.[11] He is much more of a loner than Carlisle, and this very much makes Edward a twentieth-century man.

Edward becomes a vampire in 1918 as Spanish influenza wreaks its havoc worldwide and kills more people than died in combat during the whole four years of World War I. Edward's pre-vampire life is sketchy, but he appears to have been from a well-off upper-middle-class family. Prior to contracting influenza, Edward was about to join the army (although he would mostly likely have missed out on World War I action, as the war was nearly over by this stage). Following his "transformation," Edward discovers a talent for mind reading and, with a minor rebellious detour, does his best to live up to Carlisle's example. Here we see a dream become a legacy passed down from one generation to the next. In Edward's case, and the case of the other vampires who are friends and allies of the Cullens, while they ultimately come together as a community, it is their personal independence that is to be defended at all costs.

Edward's many gifts are stressed throughout the four novels, including his capacity to read minds, his musical abilities, his determination, and his intellect, which helps him to earn a number of degrees in medical science. What separates, and perhaps elevates, Edward above his brothers and sisters is how he uses all of his extra time. For example, in *Breaking Dawn*, when Charlie is first introduced to the newly transformed Bella, we see a family no longer as interested in maintaining the need for the human charade of winding down for the evening: where Emmett and Rosalie are involved in constructing a massive house of cards, transient and trivial, Edward moves to the piano—a demonstration not only of skill but of talent. Edward is the only one of the Cullen children who demonstrates more than a fleeting interest in education and research, and his qualifications are far more worthy than the display of high school graduation caps in the *Twilight* film indicates. He does not need to sleep and therefore works on honing his particular skills and interests. It is this work ethic and the desire to use, rather than squander, the gifts he has that make him the perfect heir to Carlisle's legacies. It is not just his good looks that make him the prince of this American fairy tale: it is his morality, his intellect, and his unswerving commitment to his family's way of life that crown him in Bella's eyes.

Both Carlisle and Edward demonstrate through their chosen lifestyles the emphasis on a unique, individual destiny that is so important to the American Dream. However, other than diet, morality, and hard work, there is another element crucial to the national mythologies of the United States. To this end, I would like to make a slight detour here to discuss a minor character from *Breaking Dawn* who not only invokes the Founding Fathers and the spirit of the Wars of Independence, but who also exemplifies one of the ongoing themes of the twenty-first-century American Dream: individual freedoms. We meet Garrett as the Cullens begin to gather their friends and allies in preparation for the impending doom of a visit from the Volturi. One of the first things we hear him utter is, "The redcoats are coming, the redcoats are coming." (*Breaking Dawn*, 680.) Garrett takes us back to Paul Revere's famous midnight ride, one of the most mythologized events of the American Revolutionary War. In what has become known as the original national conflict for autonomy and freedom from Old World dictatorship, the Revolutionary War is where and when Garrett became a vampire. And Garrett calls the Volturi out:

> "The Volturi care nothing for the death of the child. They seek the death of our free will. . . . So come, I say! Let's hear no more lying rationalizations. Be honest in your intents as we will be honest in ours. We will defend our freedom. You will or will not attack it. Choose now, and let these witnesses see the true issue debated here." [. . .]
> Aro smiled. "A very pretty speech, my revolutionary friend."
> Garrett remained poised for attack. "Revolutionary?" he growled. "Who am I revolting against, might I ask? Are you my king? Do you wish me to call you *master*, too, like your sycophantic guard?"
> "Peace Garrett," Aro said tolerantly. "I meant only to refer to your time of birth. Still a patriot, I see." (*Breaking Dawn*, 719.)

Garrett seeks to expose not only the Volturi's aristocratic pretensions, but also the Machiavellian power games with which they seek to direct all talent to their will and whims. Once again Meyer invokes an event that has become integral to American historical mythology. And because vampires are almost unkillable, Garrett's response places freedom from autocracy (and aristocracy) at the forefront of the stories of her individual vampires. Here, too, we see the idea of a unique American destiny at work. It is not only differences in diet that separate the Cullens and some of their friends from their Old World counterparts, but the value they place on individual talent and individual free will. No one is forced to join the Cullens' stand against the Volturi, and talents are not turned on friends except for training purposes. This forms a sharp contrast to the "guard" of the Volturi, who do indeed call Aro, Caius, and Marcus *master*, and whose minds and talents are bent to their masters' will through the talents of vampires like Chelsea, who is able to alter how people feel about one another and weaken the bonds between them, and Jane, who can inflict excruciating pain from a distance with her mind.

In spite of different story arcs for female characters (see below), Meyer also puts distance between the Old and the New Worlds in their treatment of women. While there are females with active talents in the Volturi retinue, these "wives" are never mentioned by name and hover like prized yet useless possessions in the confrontation with the Cullens. The women of the Cullen family and friends all have their own names and their own talents — put to use in the defense of what they hold dear. So once again we see the New World vampires standing against those of the Old and demonstrating the power and value of free will and individual choice.

A unique nature and destiny is also demonstrated by the Quileute wolves — they are not the same as the Children of the Moon, whom Marcus hunted almost to extinction. Their alliance with the vampires of Forks is completely unprecedented. But Jacob Black and his pack, even in this fairy tale, operate outside the magical realm of the American Dream, much as Native Americans have sought their own sovereignty and been excluded from opportunities for educational and material success in colonial and postcolonial North America. The Founding Fathers' City on the Hill came into existence only because they conquered the indigenous populations.[12] Younger Native Americans continue to struggle with the poverty and social problems endemic on many reservations, which keeps them from the material, community, and individual successes promised by the American Dream. The alternative Native American dreams of their own nation and self-determination cannot coexist with the dominant and dominating hegemony of the United States.

The Quileutes in Meyer's story are bound *to* their roles as guardians — which are crucial — and *by* the boundaries of the reservation, their territory. While Jacob, who ditches school on "the Rez" and excels as a mechanic, is worthy, moral, and magical, he is never on equal footing with the wealthy, white, upper-class Edward. While Bella may flirt with Jacob, and momentarily toy with the idea that she and he should have been together, Jacob was never going to be the prince in her story. He is not white, unnaturally beautiful, or wealthy. He cannot, by virtue of his race, species as shape-shifter/wolf, and socioeconomic position help her to rise, socially or economically, nor can he even help her to "evolve" into a being like himself, as Edward can. The American Dream may allow Beauty to befriend the wolf, but in order to live (or die?) the dream that says she *can* have it all, she must marry the Beast/Prince and herself become transformed.

CinderBella and Her Sisters

Much like Hansel scattering breadcrumbs through the dark forest, Meyer has peppered her books with fairy-tale references. The very cover of *Twilight* tempts the reader, Snow White–like, with its rosy red apple.[13] Isabella Swan's own name is itself a fairy-tale signifier, her first name meaning "beauty" in its abbreviated form, and the surname reminiscent of many tales, from the "Swan Maidens" to "Six Swans" to the "Ugly Duckling" (the latter's transformative aspect is one that Bella by inference applies to herself, since in her own mind she does not fulfill the beautiful potential of her name until her "undead" life). But what of the American Dream for our fairy-tale heroine?

J. Emmett Winn points to a number of Cinderella stories, such as *Working Girl* (1988) and *Pretty Woman* (1990), which incidentally is also a Disney film, as examples of ongoing mythologies of the American Dream.[14] Beautiful, hardworking, and moral (in spite of Vivian's occupation as a prostitute in *Pretty Woman*), the female characters Winn discusses rise above their circumstances and enrich the lives of those around them. However, Winn does little to discuss the fact that Cinderella stories are the specifically *feminine* form of the American Dream. From drudgery and strong expressions of morality to sartorial transformation, these stories bear striking similarities. Even when the woman in question attains a desired career as a part of her new life, it is always through her relationship to a man. While for men the ways to achieve their dreams, and even the dreams themselves, have changed over time, for women landing the prince remains a constant in the climax to their stories. Carlisle and Edward are shining examples of masculinity and progress, whereas Bella is depicted as old for her years and is by implication an old-fashioned heroine.

The *Twilight Saga*'s female characters follow narrative arcs that color them as either worthy, and therefore accepting of their fates, or as shallow and selfish and therefore open to criticism and punishment of some sort. Bella's story and those of Esme and Rosalie echo the fairy-tale legacies of both pre- and post-Perrault stories. The clearest influences in these stories, however, largely seem to come from the twentieth-century productions of Disney studios. Meyer's grim tales are inflected by twenty-first-century sexual politics. With their focus on "morality" at the expense of education, or honesty about teenage sexuality, they are in some ways more conservative than their seventeenth-century predecessors.[15] While Bella may flirt with her wolf to gain information, and get into bed with him to get warm, she remains fully clothed at all times. She bears little resemblance to the pre-Perrault Little Red Riding Hood, who does a striptease for the wolf before escaping out the back door: her attempts to help in the battle against Victoria's minions in *Eclipse* consist of self-sacrifice and self-harm, not cunning.[16] And while Edward climbs to her room every night, all activity between him and Bella remains charged yet chaste. Unlike the story of Rapunzel, there is no punishment for promiscuity and giving birth to illegitimate twins for our twenty-first-century heroine—she does not let down her hair until she is properly married.[17]

When Bella first meets Esme, she is reminded of an ingénue of the silent-film era. Moments later, Bella observes that "[I]t was like meeting a fairy tale—Snow White in the flesh." (*Twilight*, 282.) The reference to silent films and Snow White hearken back to the original American celluloid Cinderella, Clara Bow in *It* (1927). This reference, despite the "waves of caramel colored hair," intersects neatly with Walt Disney's first feature-length animated film, *Snow White and the Seven Dwarfs*, released in 1937. Both Clara Bow's character, Betty Lou, and Snow White know "someday my prince will come," both have pale complexions, and both have heart-shaped faces framed by bobbed hair. But there are some differences worthy of examination. Clara Bow's It-girl is the classic flapper of the 1920s, a time of frivolity, flagrant displays of wealth, and unease about changes in the postwar sexual behavior and roles of women. The "It" factor refers to sexuality. As hemlines rose, women gained the vote, and more and more women entered the workplace, Clara Bow's portrayal of Betty Lou encompassed both the hedonism and the anxiety of the era.[18] Despite the monumental changes that were occurring, the ideal presented by Hollywood's dream factory was still marriage, even in a text such as *It*. However, the flighty, manipulative, and sexualized behavior of Betty Lou, in spite of the Cinderella ending that implies that she was a "good girl," suggests that ultimately Esme more nearly resembles Disney's *Snow White*.

Carlisle is Esme's prince, and his "kiss" saves her life following her suicide attempt after losing a child. Esme has hobbies in architecture and the restoration of furniture and buildings, but this is described as something in which she dabbles rather than the "calling" pursued by Carlisle. This interest in houses is an extension of Esme as "homemaker," much like Disney's Snow White, who whistles while she works and worries terribly that the dwarfs have no mother. And the cottage Esme constructs for Bella and Edward is also straight out of *Snow White* or 1959's *Sleeping Beauty*. Esme's mothering instincts and her capacity for love and devotion are what make her the ideal companion for Carlisle. She is devoted to her "children" in spite of the threat that having a human girl in their midst poses; she wouldn't care if Bella had "a third eye and webbed feet" if it made Edward happy. (*Twilight*, 286.) While Esme may be the (unbeating) heart of the Cullen family, however, it is Carlisle who is its head and the leader of their way of life.

At the end of the Great Depression, *Snow White*, whose princess Esme resembles so strikingly, marked the beginning of Walt Disney's dominance as the chief peddler of fairy tales and dreams—and not only to an American audience. Walt Disney is himself representative of the American Dream in the early twentieth century: having pulled himself up by his bootstraps, he built his success in the 1930s, when destitution and despair were the lot of so many, and ended up the chief controller and dictator of the "happiest place on earth."[19] For many people growing up in the twentieth and twenty-first centuries, Disney *is* the chief source for fairy tales. This all-American studio and corporation have taken tales that originated in Europe and retold and repackaged them to the entire world in a kind of reverse colonization of the imagination. Often known as the "great sanitizer," "Disney's trademarked innocence operates on a systematic sanitization of violence, sexuality, and political struggle," purging these where they had been present in earlier versions of these fairy tales.[20] But as Naomi Wood pointed out, the "squeaky clean" feel of Disney texts was a part of the "American prurience that was so appealing and acceptable to his audiences."[21]

Certainly the "classic" Disney princesses in *Snow White*, *Cinderella*, and *Sleeping Beauty* represent beautiful heroines whose excellence in the domestic arts and beautiful bell-like singing voices are what commend them—much like the "feminine ideals" of the mid-twentieth century. *Cinderella* makes wishes on soap bubbles and passively receives the gifts of her fairy godmother. It is not she who seeks to find her own way to the ball, but her furry companions who go to work, making a dress fit for royalty. She is beautiful and blond—and blank. Her identity is defined first by her subordinate position in her family there among the cinders, and then as the "wife" of Prince Charming. Her dreams go no further than being on the arm of someone who can elevate her from being a servant in one household to presiding over another—neither of which belongs to her. The 1950 Disney *Cinderella* does not need to be named to be present in *Twilight*, but a direct reference does tie the two texts together. The spells of Cinderella's fairy godmother shimmer when Carlisle engages Jacob in a discussion of his DNA:

> "Your family's divergence from humanity is much more interesting. Magical almost."
> "Bibbidi-Bobbidi-Boo," I mumbled. He was just like Bella with all the magic garbage. (*Breaking Dawn*, 237.)

Jacob introduces another princess, *Sleeping Beauty*, overtly into Meyer's text in his less than cordial relationship with Rosalie: "The look on Rosalie's face made it clear that I wasn't welcome to one of them. It made me wonder what Sleepless Beauty needed a bed for anyway. Was she that possessive of her props?" (*Breaking Dawn*, 253.)

Rosalie's long blond hair and breathtaking beauty, even among the Botticellian vampires, reinforce the connection to the 1959 animated feature. Rosalie herself has told her story as a fairy tale gone awry.

Renowned for her physical beauty, Rosalie was the daughter of an aspiring middle-class family in the 1930s, a family that never felt the effects of the Great Depression. While the Hales had wealth, their position in banking suggests that their material well-being was at the expense of others who lost everything during the hardships of the early 1930s. So while they fulfilled the upwardly mobile part of American mythology, they did not possess the other requirement of moral strength and a willingness to help others.[22] Dreams of wealth without the desire or the capacity to improve the lives of those around you are empty dreams. And in *Twilight* the princess of such dreams, Rosalie, was similarly without substance. Rosalie, in *Eclipse*, attempts to explain to Bella why she should hold on to being human. For Rosalie, being turned into a vampire was more a punishment than a reward: a punishment for a shallow existence premised on little more than her good looks and her sense of entitlement. The fairy tale that had been promised in life — "This was everything they'd dreamed of. And Royce seemed to be everything I'd dreamed of. The fairy tale prince, come to make me a princess. Everything I wanted, yet it was still no more than I expected. We were engaged before I'd known him for two months." — ended in gang rape. (*Eclipse*, 157.) Beauty is a potential trap in many fairy tales, and without the moral center of self-sacrificing devotion of a true fairy-tale heroine, Rosalie's unhappiness continues in her afterlife.

It would be wrong to imply that Disney heroines have not changed over time, even though, ultimately, the end result of fulfillment through marriage has been maintained. Ariel (*The Little Mermaid*, 1989) and Belle (*Beauty and the Beast*, 1991), the two princesses who essentially rebooted the appeal of Disney animated magic for a new generation, represented significant change from their sweet, mop-wielding, predecessors. Both heroines have been somewhat influenced by feminism in their intellectual curiosity and their possession of much more bravery and capacity for action than Cinderella. Ultimately they too marry to rise socially, above the sea and out of "this provincial life," and their dreams of new ideas and experiences fade with the closing kisses of these stories. The women in the *Twilight* novels also exhibit feminist traits, both historical and contemporary, or they would simply have no appeal to a twenty-first-century audience. But they too have their eyes on the prize of marital bliss.

For example, Rosalie's whole existence seems to revolve around just being beautiful—but there are tongue-in-cheek references to her skills as a mechanic in both the books and the *Twilight* movie. This is more than a jibe at the incongruity of a beautiful blond emerging from underneath a car. It resonates with skills Rosalie may well have acquired during World War II, when in a time of national emergency women were being told (by a woman also called Rosie), "We can do it!" and encouraged to take on the jobs and skills of men, before being encouraged back to the kitchen and the bedroom at war's end.[23] But technical skill is not required of these radiant women and is indulged because they will never need to use it as a profession, unlike Jacob, whose class and ethnic background in these depictions seem to necessitate knowledge of a "trade" rather than aspiration to a profession.

Bella is introduced to the reader as sacrificing the life she loved in the sun so that her irresponsible mother can pursue her own happiness. Renée's happiness itself revolves around remarriage to a minor league ballplayer, her own entrée to the American Dream through "the American pastime." Bella then moves into the dark and gothic atmosphere of the town where her father is the chief of police, but like so many fairy-tale fathers, he is benign but largely absent. Bella may not sing while she does housework, but she takes on the role of housewife for her father much like her 1950 predecessor. Bella's blankness of mind for Edward poses a mystery, and it is one of the things that attract him. Along with devotion, beauty, and self-sacrifice, this feminine silence is often present in many fairy tales and has over many centuries acted both as a punishment of young women and a feature that attracts male fairy-tale heroes.[24] Her silence of mind and her silence with regard to keeping the secret of the Cullens' existence both become gifts in the end, since Bella's blankness becomes the means of saving her entire family from the games of the Volturi.

Bella toys with the idea of college but mainly as a device for the only ambition she ever clearly expresses—maintaining her hold on Edward. Before her relationship with Edward solidifies, we hear of Bella working to supplement her meager college fund, and we later learn she has applied to a university in Alaska (mainly because she could use this as a ruse to disguise her own transformation into a vampire). However, we never know what it is she might like to study or what she might like to pursue in terms of a career. Much like Belle in *Beauty and the Beast*, Bella does not really fit into "provincial" Forks. Like Belle, her longings for more are not clearly articulated, and this "more" seems to be fulfilled by both Beauties' choice of Beasts.

Beauty and the Beast was first published in French in the first half of the eighteenth century (translated into English in 1759), and includes clear evidence of class struggle and the aspirations of the merchant class for the trappings and privileges of the aristocracy.[25] It is a part of what folklorists call the "Cinderella cycle" of tales, and follows a familiar trajectory of feminine self-sacrifice and devotion being ultimately rewarded through marriage. The Disney text subtracts the element of class conflict, despite the obvious socioeconomic differences between Belle and the Beast. In this way, and in dressing Belle in a way reminiscent of the cinematic version of the original American fairy tale *The Wizard of Oz*, we have a truly American fairy tale that fits with the "classless" society of American Dream mythology.

Pre-vamp Bella makes a great deal of not accepting expensive gifts—a part of her "morality" is her rejection of the trappings that highlight the inequalities between herself and Edward. Along with Bella's father's profession, other indicators of Bella's class difference from the Cullens are constant throughout the *Twilight* novels. Like any Cinderella, her premarriage wardrobe is scanty and occasionally supplemented by the good fairy Alice. Bella's father's profession and income mean that the house they live in is small and shabby, and she has access only to antiquated communications technologies. Bella's car is an ancient Chevy truck that, while safe, has none of the style or speed of any of the vehicles in the Cullens' garage. CinderBella never complains about her circumstances, and that is a part of her charm. But where she protests extravagance extended in her direction before her nuptials, she has no such qualms in accepting the benefits of the Cullens' wealth after marriage, especially when this can assist her transition from human to vampire.

Conclusion: What Price the Glass Slipper?

The *Twilight Saga* is very much a twenty-first-century morality tale with a fairy-story ending. It is also a "survival story with hope" that invokes and enacts the premises, and promises, of the American Dream in all of its forms, both masculine and feminine. The Cullens represent morality, wealth, and the unique qualities of the New World vampires from the seventeenth century to the present. They work hard at staying secret, staying together, and maintaining their "vegetarian" diet. Bella makes sacrifices to keep her family happy and never complains about her limited lot in life. Her selflessness and character as a good girl mark her as exceptional in portrayals of young women in contemporary popular culture. She is also an exceptional "newborn" vampire—even for her New World family. But the things that make Bella's narrative an extraordinary vampire story make her a rather ordinary Cinderella. Beyond being a Cullen, she has no ambition, and unlike Carlisle and Edward, she seems unlikely to carve out her own separate path. And while the ultimate battle may take place after Edward and Bella's wedding, and while Bella plays an active role in her family's defense, the curtains still close on a kiss to last forever after.

Edward laughs off what in Meyer's saga are merely myths about vampires. However, the "truths" communicated by the American fairy tale remain. Moral good little girls can marry princes and become more talented through that marriage, stay beautiful, and never need to worry about juggling work and child care—but only if they adhere to whatever society dictates as moral and good, and only if they accept marriage as the ultimate happy ending. Bella fulfills the self-sacrifice quotient required of a fairy-tale heroine in the numerous conflict scenarios where she offers herself up to fate in order to try to save those around her. She is often selfish and self-indulgent but always self-sacrificing when it comes to those she loves.

Bella works hard, remains a virgin until marriage, and refuses an abortion even when her own life is at stake. And she is rewarded. In the ultimate wish fulfillment, Bella escapes the pains of aging in a society that purports to venerate knowledge but is really enamored of that most fleeting of shiny toys—youth. "Forget Princess, I want to be a Vampire" sums up an entire culture whose ideal of having it all conflicts with the realities of income differences and sexual inequality that still characterize American society. All happily-ever-afters come at a cost, and the price Bella pays is her life.

Notes

1. Fairy-tale theorists, such as Jack Zipes and Robert Darnton, argue that the roles for women in such tales were much more fluid in the oral storytelling cultures that predated Perrault. In fixing the tales in published literature (at a time when private and public spheres and a strict demarcation of gender roles were becoming more rigid for emerging middle classes) that had a strongly didactic function, the strictures on feminine behavior became much more apparent. Even in the literary traditions of the seventeenth, eighteenth, and nineteenth centuries, however, there is much variation according to changing behavioral norms and the socioeconomic, cultural, and religious backgrounds and genders of the authors. There have, of course, been many more producers of fairy-tale texts than the three cited in this section, but these are the three most well-known examples in the progression from oral to literary to cinematic texts. See, for example, Jack Zipes, "Breaking the Disney Spell," in Elizabeth Bell, Linda Haas, and Laura Sells, eds., *From Mouse to Mermaid: The Politics of Film, Gender, and Culture* (Bloomington and Indianapolis: Indiana Univ. Press, 1995), 21–42; Jack Zipes, *Why Fairy Tales Stick: The Evolution and Relevance of a Genre* (New York: Routledge, 2006); and Robert Darnton, *The Great Cat Massacre and Other Episodes in French Cultural Theory* (New York: Basic Books, 1984), 9–74. There remains, as Zipes points out in a number of his works, great potential for subversion in the fairy tale even in the face of such monolithic dream factories as Disney studio.

2. Zipes, *Why Fairy Tales Stick*, 27.

3. See Cal Jillson, *Pursuing the American Dream: Opportunity and Exclusion over Four Centuries* (Lawrence: Univ. Press of Kansas, 2004). See also J. Emmett Winn, *The American Dream and Contemporary Hollywood Cinema* (New York: Continuum, 2007).

4. Peggy Orenstein, "What's Wrong with Cinderella?" *New York Times*, December 24, 2006, www.nytimes.com/2006/12/24/magazine/24princess.t.html.

5. I wish I could claim to have ownership of the "dying young, staying pretty" idea. I first heard it articulated in the season 2 episode of *Buffy the Vampire Slayer*, "Lie to Me," where a former friend of Buffy's, Billy Fordham, who has terminal brain cancer, articulates it as the ideal of every American teen. Fordham's quip may have origins in a famous quote supposedly attributable to 1950s teen idol James Dean: "Live fast, die young, and leave a beautiful corpse." There is also a 1979 song by punk band Blondie titled "Die Young, Stay Pretty."

6. Darnton, *The Great Cat Massacre*, 59.

7. In fact, Bella herself makes reference to some of these tales: "It seemed that most vampire myths centered around beautiful women as demons and children as victims; they also seemed like constructs created to explain away the high mortality rates for young children and to give men an excuse for infidelity." (*Twilight*, 116.) What she doesn't mention is the voluptuousness and inferred homosexuality of many male and female vampires in literary and cinematic texts, including Bram Stoker's *Dracula*, which was first published in 1897, and Joseph Sheridan Le Fanu's *Carmilla*, published in 1892, to all of their cinematic incarnations throughout the twentieth century. It is highly unlikely that any homosexual vampires exist in the Cullen-verse, and while the consumption of blood can incite a fury, its orgiastic quality seems to relate more to gluttony than to sex. For commentary on aspects of sexual transgression in *Dracula* see, for example, Christopher Craft, "Kiss Me with Those Red Lips: Gender and Inversion in Bram Stoker's *Dracula*." *Representations* 8 (Autumn 1984): 107–133.

8. Jim Cullen, *The American Dream: A Short History of an Idea That Shaped a Nation* (New York: Oxford Univ. Press, 2003), 10, 38.

9. "American exceptionalism" is a term originally coined by Alexis de Tocqueville, the famous French writer who was so enamored of the nascent democracy in the United States in the nineteenth century. Originally this was intended to convey a sense

of difference through a nation made up of immigrants making a new life distinct from the old. A factor that encouraged this "difference" was life on the frontier. The term has come into much wider usage in the twentieth century, particularly after World War II, and has come to stand for the things that make America distinct and distinctly "virtuous" in contrast to the rest of the world. For an overview of the history of this idea, see Deborah Madsen, *American Exceptionalism* (Edinburgh: Edinburgh Univ. Press, 1998).

10. Jillson, *Pursuing the American Dream*, 29.

11. This is not to say that Carlisle's feelings are not those of love and loyalty, but he has a commitment to a bigger picture in his faith in God and God's will.

12. Jillson, *Pursuing the American Dream*, 58.

13. "What's with the Apple?" is an FAQ on Meyer's Web site, to which she responds with the following:

> The apple on the cover of *Twilight* represents "forbidden fruit." I used the scripture from Genesis (located just after the table of contents) because I loved the phrase "the fruit of the knowledge of good and evil." Isn't this exactly what Bella ends up with? A working knowledge of what good is, and what evil is. The nice thing about the apple is it has so many symbolic roots. You've got the apple in Snow White, one bite and you're frozen forever in a state of not-quite death. Then you have Paris and the golden apple in Greek mythology—look how much trouble *that* started. Apples are quite the versatile fruit. In the end, I love the beautiful simplicity of the picture. To me it says: *choice*.
>
> The Official Website of Stephenie Meyer, FAQ page, www.stepheniemeyer.com/twilight_faq.html.

14. J. Emmett Winn, *The American Dream in Contemporary Hollywood Cinema* (New York: Continuum Books, 2007).

15. Abstinence classes instead of sex education, in addition to abstinence pledges and leagues in high schools, have been a part of a growing politics of the religious right in the United States, which in spite of/because of these attempts to keep young people ignorant and/or chaste "leads the industrialized world in teen-pregnancy, abortion, and sexually transmitted disease rates." Susan Rose, "Going Too Far? Sex, Sin and Social Policy," *Social Forces* 84, no. 2 (December 2005): 1207.

16. For an involved and fascinating examination of all the incarnations of Little Red Riding Hood, see Jack Zipes, ed., *The Trials and Tribulations of Little Red Riding Hood* (New York: Routledge, 1993).

17. In the first edition of *Die Kinder und Hausmärchen der Brüder Grimm,* published in 1812, Rapunzel falls very obviously pregnant and reveals herself to the witch in asking: "Tell me Godmother, why my clothes are so tight and don't fit me any longer?" "Wicked Child," cried the Fairy. In the second edition, published in 1819, Rapunzel betrays herself thus: "Tell me, Godmother, why is it you are so much harder to pull up than the young prince?" Friedrich Panzer, ed., *Die Kinder und Hausmärchen der Brüder Grimm,* cited by Maria Tatar in *The Hard Facts of the Grimms' Fairy Tales* (Princeton, NJ: Princeton Univ. Press, 1987), 18.

18. See Cynthia Felando, "Clara Bow Is *It,*" in *Film Stars: Hollywood and Beyond,* ed. Andy Willis (Manchester, Eng.: Manchester Univ. Press, 2004), 8–24.

19. Elizabeth Bell, Lynda Haas, and Laura Sells, "Introduction: Walt's in the Movies," in Bell, Haas, and Sells, *From Mouse to Mermaid,* 2–3.

20. Ibid., 7.

21. Naomi Wood, "Domesticating Dreams in Walt Disney's *Cinderella,*" *The Lion and the Unicorn* 20, no. 1 (1996), muse.jhu.edu/journals/lion_and_the_unicorn/v020/20 .lwood.html.

22. See Jillson, *Pursuing the American Dream,* 71, where he uses *The Great Gatsby* (first published in 1925) as an example of the bankruptcy of the dream where only the pursuit of material wealth is present.

23. For an examination of the not-so-successful campaigns to mobilize American women during World War II, see D'Ann Campbell, *Women at War with America: Private Lives in a Patriotic Era* (Cambridge, MA: Harvard Univ. Press, 1984). "Rosie the Riveter" has become an icon for the mobilization of women and a recognition of women's skills. At the time, however, this was not enough to overcome much of the backlash against women who joined untraditional trades and professions in the war effort.

24. Successive chapters of Marina Warner's *From the Beast to the Blonde: Fairy Tales and Their Tellers* (London: Chatto and Windus, 1994) discuss the history and power of the myth of feminine silence.

25. Jerry Griswold, *The Meanings of Beauty and the Beast: A Handbook* (Toronto: Broadview Press, 2004), 27, 59.

Reading the Genre

1. Buttsworth's analysis focuses on similarities between the *Twilight* novels and traditional fairy tales. What, according to the author, are the major characteristics of fairy tales as a genre? How does she see those characteristics mirrored in Stephenie Meyer's vampire stories? (See Chapter 25, "Genre," p. 390.)

2. How does defining the *Twilight* series as fairy tale enable Buttsworth to critique cultural values? What set of values does she target, and what conclusions does she reach? (See "Focus on its social connections," p. 223.)

3. **WRITING:** Choose another cultural text that shares conventions with the fairy tale genre — possibilities include novels like *The Hunger Games* by Suzanne Collins or the *Harry Potter* series by J. K. Rowling, the movies *Slumdog Millionaire* (2008) or *The Princess Bride* (1987), and reality television shows like *American Idol* or *The Bachelor* — and write a literary analysis of that text focusing on the ways that it does or does not conform to the conventions of the fairy tale genre.

4. **WRITING:** Vampire stories have become tremendously popular in film, literature, and television. Choose three contemporary vampire texts and compare them in an essay. What themes seem consistent? What themes are unique to each text?

5. **COMPOSING VISUALLY:** Write and illustrate an original fairy tale. In your story, upend some of the conventions of the genre to create new possibilities for young female characters.

CULTURAL ANALYSIS   Gish Jen is a novelist, short story writer, and literary critic. Her books include, *Who's Irish?* (1999), *Typical American* (1991), *Mona in the Promised Land* (1997), *The Love Wife* (2004), and *World and Town* (2010). She also contributes to the *New Yorker*, the *Atlantic*, the *New York Times*, *Ploughshares*, and the *New Republic*. This essay first appeared in *A New Literary History of America* (2009), edited by Greil Marcus and Werner Sollors.

GISH JEN

Holden Raises Hell

The Catcher in the Rye

Some critics don't like it. *Catholic World* notes its "formidably excessive use of amateur swearing and coarse language," and there seems to be some question as to whether an alienated, hard-drinking, chain-smoking flunkie like its adolescent protagonist, Holden Caulfield, is going to prove a good influence on the young. Other critics, though, "chuckle and . . . even laugh aloud," and many compare Holden to Huck Finn. Sociologist David Riesman, who has just published *The Lonely Crowd* (1950), assigns *Catcher* to his Harvard undergrads as a case study. Still, the overall critical reception is within the normal bounds of book publishing; Harcourt Brace, which rejected the book, does not yet have much to live down. As for sales, well, the book has done fine in hardcover but, what with the recent invention of the perfect binding—a book binding using glue rather than stitching—there is now the paperback to consider. Doesn't *Catcher* seem like the sort of book that might do well in the new format?

And so it does, going on to sell over 60 million copies. Moreover, in 1956, some dam in critical interest seems to burst. Study after study is published; the 1950s are dubbed "the Decade of Salinger"; contemporaneous writers complain of neglect. Holden Caulfield is compared not only to Huck Finn but to Billy Budd,

David Copperfield, Natty Bumppo, Quentin Compson, Ishmael, Peter Pan, Hamlet, Jesus Christ, Adam, Stephen Dedalus, and Leopold Bloom put together. What critic George Steiner calls the "Salinger industry" swells fantastically, until it sits like a large, determined bird on a bunker-like egg.

Where did this start? In a 1940 letter to a friend, a twenty-one-year-old Salinger describes his novel in progress as "autobiographical"; decades later, too, in an interview with a high school reporter—the only interview he's ever given—Salinger says, "My boyhood was very much the same as that of the boy in the book." Of course, there are differences. Unlike Holden, Salinger is, among other things, a half-Jewish, half-Catholic brotherless World War II vet who attended a military academy. He did, though, like Holden, flunk out of prep school, and he was also, like Holden, manager of his high school fencing team, in which capacity he really did, according to his daughter, Margaret, once lose the team gear en route to a meet.

More important, Salinger seems to have shared Holden's disaffection. Numerous youthful acquaintances remember him as sardonic, rant-prone, a loner. Margaret Salinger likewise traces the alienation in the book to him, though it does not reflect for her either her father's innate temperament or difficult adolescence so much as his experiences of anti-Semitism and, as an adult, war. Where Salinger fought in some of the bloodiest and most senseless campaigns of World War II and apparently suffered a nervous breakdown toward its end, shortly after which—while still in Europe—he is known to have been working on *Catcher*—it is hardly surprising that Holden's reactions should evoke not only adolescent turmoil but also the awful seesaw of a vet's return to civilian life. Holden may be a rebel without a cause, but he is not a rebel without an explanation: it is easy to read the death of his brother as a stand-in for unspeakable trauma. And witness the notable vehemence with which Holden talks about the war—declaring, for instance, "I'm sort of glad they've got the atomic bomb invented. If there's ever another war, I'm going to sit right the hell on top of it. I'll volunteer for it, I swear to God I will."

But what of Margaret Salinger's theory regarding anti-Semitism? She characterizes Salinger as sensitive about his Jewishness, with good cause: a few years before her father's arrival at the military academy, the picture of a Jewish student who had graduated second in the class was printed on a perforated page in the yearbook, so it could be torn out. We note, too, in Ian Hamilton's unofficial biography, a letter from the father of a girl to whom Salinger once proposed, describing him as "an odd fellow. He didn't mingle much with the other guests [at their Daytona Beach hotel] . . . He was—well, is he Jewish? I thought that might explain the way he acted . . . I thought he had a chip on his shoulder."

Interestingly, Salinger's sister, in an interview, while supporting the anti-Semitism thesis, focuses on his in-betweenness as well. "It wasn't nice to be part-Jewish in those days," she says. "It was no asset to be Jewish either, but at least you belonged somewhere. This way you were neither fish nor fowl." Additionally complicating the picture is the fact that Salinger seems to have grown up revered by his Irish-Catholic mother but disparaged by his Jewish father, who wanted him to enter the family food-import business. Fish and fowl, adored and criticized, Salinger was remembered by some military academy classmates as a guy whose conversation "was laced with sarcasm," but by others as "a regular guy," and by teachers as "quiet, thoughtful, always anxious to please." Strikingly, this sometimes scathing student wrote a class song so convincingly straight ("Goodbyes are said, we march ahead / Success we go to find. / Our forms are gone from Valley Forge / Our hearts are left behind") it is still sung at graduation. He edited the yearbook, too, with what so completely passed as earnest conscientiousness that though it is tempting, given his active interest in acting, to view his activities as virtuoso performances of deep subterfuge, they might also be imagined to have been painfully disconcerting. Holden's description of himself as "the most terrific liar you ever saw" might well have applied to Salinger, and Salinger's own judgment of his divided nature, in this era before "situational selves," might well have involved the word that haunts his book, "phony."

A poignant part of Salinger's genius seems, in any case, to include the way that he transmutes—as he perhaps feels he must—his particular issues and injuries into a more enigmatic "autobiography" of alienation. And it can only be counted ironic that the result comes to exemplify American authenticity: like James Dean, Holden Caulfield is for many the very picture of the postwar rebel. Young, crude, misunderstood, he stands up to conformist pressures, is drawn to innocence, et cetera. Never mind that Holden is white, male, straight, sophisticated, rich, and a product of the 1940s; he personifies anguished resistance to '50s America—indeed, for many, America's truest self. Whether Salinger intended his creation to assume anything like this role—indeed, if he had any notion of the projection of a national identity as a desirable literary goal (as did his contemporary, John Updike, for example)—is unclear.

And is there not something if not phony, then at least a little wacky, about Holden's enshrinement in American culture? To some degree, academia took its cue from the culture; *Catcher*'s skyrocketing sales amid the mid-'50s "youthquake" fairly demanded explanation. Critics like George Steiner saw the book as all too fitting for the paperback market—short, easy to read, and flattering "the very ignorance and moral shallowness of his young readers." But others saw its success as a promising development, indicative of something enduringly young, defiant, and truth-loving in the American spirit. Drawing on the work of Donald Pease, critic Leerom Medovoi has described how a new cold war American canon arose around this time, in which American Renaissance works like *Moby-Dick* and *Adventures of Huckleberry Finn* were cast as a "coherent tradition that dramatized the emergence of American freedom as a literary ideal, somehow already waging its heroic struggle against a prefigured totalitarianism." He provocatively describes how *Catcher* came to join those works and how the lot of them, read as national allegories, located the very essence of Americanness in principled dissent, even as McCarthyism cast it as un-American.

No doubt other scholars, being scholars, disagree. Still, Medovoi's ideas may, in conjunction with the book's Mona Lisa–like ambiguity, help explain how *Catcher in the Rye* came to occupy what by other measures seems a strangely high place in American letters, for it strays notably from mainstream literary values. The novel is, to begin with, often precious and sentimental. What's more, while the critic Alfred Kazin is, I think, on the mark in ascribing the excitement of Salinger's stories to his "intense, his almost compulsive need to fill in each inch of his canvas, each moment of his scene," the writing in *Catcher* is nowhere near so alive with *moti mentali*. And the whole, too, is slight. Salinger, who has published only this one novel to date, once characterized himself as "a dash man and not a miler"; and indeed, though *Catcher*'s opening episodes explode with life, the whole reads like a novella that only just managed to shed its diminutive. It does not develop appreciatively through its middle, for example; Holden neither deepens nor comes to share the stage with other characters. Instead the book starts to feel narrow and maniacally one-note; reading, one wonders whether its real contribution lies in its anticipation of Christopher Lasch's *The Culture of Narcissism*. In contrast to, say, *The Great Gatsby*, this is manifestly not a book to be studied for insight into the novel form.

Unless, that is, one is interested in how a book can hit home with no evidence of its author's ever having read Henry James's "The Art of Fiction." *Catcher* demonstrates, among other things, how variously and mysteriously novels finally work, and how even sophisticated audiences tend to genuflect to art but yield to testimony. We are enthralled by voices that tell it like it is. Or, in the case of *Catcher*, that seem to. My sixteen-year-old son—who has, coincidentally, been reading *Catcher* for his tenth-grade English class even as I write—puts it this way: "You feel [with *Catcher*] like you're in on the real story," but in the end *Catcher* is a break from reality rather than a source of information about it. He likens Holden's appeal to that of Harry Potter: just as Harry speaks to children because Harry is like them, only "special" and able to do magic, Holden interests my son because Holden rebels and "gets away with it" in a way my son guesses—rightly—he would never. In short, one part of *Catcher*'s appeal lies in its purveyance of fantasy. This can have value—helping an audience reflect on the real limits of its freedom, for example—but can support solipsism, too. Alfred Kazin takes the harsh view, characterizing Salinger's audience as "the vast number who have been released by our society to think of themselves as endlessly sensitive, spiritually alone, [and] gifted, and whose suffering lies in the narrowing of their consciousness to themselves"—ranks that would no doubt include Mark David Chapman, who had a copy of *Catcher* in his pocket when he assassinated "phony" John Lennon, as well as John Hinckley who, also under Holden's influence, attempted to assassinate Ronald Reagan.

Other explanations of the book's popularity, though, must include its outrageous humor and must-read status, as well as its author's celebrity. Aggressively reclusive, Salinger's discomfort with the commodification of his work and person leads him, first, to shun all publicity—no interviews, no author bios — and then, in 1966, to cease publication. Still, despite his reported contempt for hippies and his support of the Vietnam War, he becomes, for the '60s counterculture, the consummate dropout. And though in subsequent years he is repeatedly caught in an unflattering light, he retains an aura of martyred integrity, which the recurring censorship of *Catcher* only intensifies.

Academia, too, presses on. Critic Alan Nadel, noting that the cold war blossomed in the period between 1946—when, for unknown reasons, Salinger withdrew from publication a ninety-page version of the book—and 1951, when it was published, interestingly sees in Holden not so much heroic nonconformity as a reflection of McCarthyism. Many features of the narrative—the obsession with control in its rhetorical patterns, as well as its preoccupation with duplicity and the compulsion to "name names"—bespeak, for Nadel, a psychic imprisonment in which the performance of truth-telling can never yield truth. And indeed, the insistence of phrases such as "I really mean it" and "to tell the truth" do finally seem to signal quicksand more than terra firma. Holden at story's end is under interrogation — more isolated than independent, more defeated than defiant. "D. B. [Holden's brother] asked me what I thought about all this stuff I just finished telling you about . . . If you want to know the truth, I don't know what I think about it," he says, touchingly. "I don't know what I think about it": Is this the author of the military-academy class hymn wondering about the act and value of writing? Has Holden, the avatar of American authenticity, become an avatar of American inauthenticity? Here Salinger's fun-house proves, once again, I think, ours.

Bibliography

Paul Alexander, *Salinger* (Los Angeles, 1999). Harold Bloom, ed., *Holden Caulfield: Modern Critical Views* (New York, 1990). Catherine Crawford, ed., *If You Really Want to Hear about It: Writers on Salinger and His Work* (New York, 2006). Warren French, *J. D. Salinger, Revisited* (Boston, 1988). Ian Hamilton, *In Search of J. D. Salinger* (New York, 1988). Joyce Maynard, *At Home in the World* (New York, 1998). Leerom Medovoi, *Rebels* (Durham, NC, 2005). Alan Nadel, *Containment Culture: American Narratives, Postmodernism, and the Atomic Age* (Durham, NC, 1995). Margaret A. Salinger, *Dream Catcher* (New York, 2000). J. D. Salinger, *The Catcher in the Rye* (1951; New York, 1989). Jack Salzman, ed., *New Essays on* The Catcher in the Rye (Cambridge, 1991). J. P. Steed, ed., The Catcher in the Rye: *New Essays* (New York, 2002).

Reading the Genre

1. *The Catcher in the Rye* has been widely read and widely discussed. How does Jen use other critics' assertions about the book to establish an overview and to support her own claims? (See "Draw on previous research," p. 208.)

2. What strategies does Jen use to integrate material from her research? What do these other voices add to her analysis? (See "Clearly identify the author and works you are analyzing," p. 218; "Follow conventions for quotations," p. 230; and Chapter 47, "Integrating Sources into Your Work," p. 497.)

3. Jen cites several flaws in J. D. Salinger's novel. What does she see as its weaknesses? How does she explain the book's enduring popularity with readers and scholars, even in spite of these problems?

4. Can you think of a fictional character who defines your generation the way Jen believes Holden Caulfield defined his? What makes this character representative of you and your peers?

5. **WRITING:** How would *Catcher in the Rye* be different if its main character used Twitter, Facebook, a blog, or Skype instead of a notebook to share his thoughts? (See Chapter 51, "Understanding Digital Media," p. 568.) Write a short analysis of the ways technology has changed how teenagers communicate — and how those changes diminish or enhance feelings of isolation.

6. **COMPOSING VISUALLY:** Jen's discussion of *The Catcher in the Rye* should give you a good sense of the novel, even if you haven't read it yourself. Based on your impressions — from Jen's analysis or your own reading — design a cover for the book.

Rhetorical Analyses: Readings

DISCOURSE ANALYSIS
Deborah Tannen, *Oh, Mom. Oh, Honey.: Why Do You Have to Say That?* 970

ANALYSIS OF AN ADVERTISEMENT
Stanley Fish, *The Other Car* 976

CULTURAL ANALYSIS
Laurie Fendrich, *The Beauty of the Platitude* 980

MEDIA ANALYSIS
John W. Jordan, *Sports Commentary and the Problem of Television Knowledge* 983

ANALYSIS OF AN ADVERTISEMENT
Caroline Leader, *Dudes Come Clean: Negotiating a Space for Men in Household Cleaner Commercials* 988

See also Chapter 8:

ANALYSIS OF AN ADVERTISEMENT
Seth Stevenson, *Ad Report Card: Can Cougars Sell Cough Drops?* 253

ANALYSIS OF AN ARGUMENT
Matthew James Nance, *A Mockery of Justice,* 264

CULTURAL ANALYSIS
J. Reagan Tankersley, *Humankind's Ouroboros,* 270

ANALYSIS OF A VISUAL TEXT
Beth Teitell, *A Jacket of the People,* 279

DISCOURSE ANALYSIS   Deborah Tannen is a professor in the linguistics department at Georgetown University, and her book *You Just Don't Understand: Women and Men in Conversation* (2001) was on best-seller lists for years. She has also written about the ways people talk at work, with friends and siblings, and in the press, politics, academics, and law. This rhetorical analysis, adapted from Tannen's book *You're Wearing That? Understanding Mothers and Daughters in Conversation* (2006), is also a sociolinguistic analysis, or discourse analysis—a study of the ways language is used and how conversation structures relationships.

Oh, Mom. Oh, Honey.: Why Do You Have to Say That?

Deborah Tannen

The five years I recently spent researching and writing a book about mothers and daughters also turned out to be the last years of my mother's life. In her late eighties and early nineties, she gradually weakened, and I spent more time with her, caring for her more intimately than I ever had before. This experience—together with her death before I finished writing—transformed my thinking about mother-daughter relationships and the book that ultimately emerged.

All along I had in mind the questions a journalist had asked during an interview about my research. "What is it about mothers and daughters?" she blurted out. "Why are our conversations so complicated, our relationships so fraught?" These questions became more urgent and more personal, as I asked myself: What had made my relationship with my mother so volatile? Why had I often ricocheted between extremes of love and anger? And what had made it possible for my love to swell and my anger to dissipate in the last years of her life?

Though much of what I discovered about mothers and daughters is also true of mothers and sons, fathers and daughters, and fathers and sons, there is a special intensity to the mother-daughter relationship because talk—particularly talk about personal topics—plays a larger and more complex role in girls' and women's social lives than in boys' and men's. For girls and women, talk is the glue that holds a relationship together—and the explosive that can blow it apart. That's why you can think you're having a perfectly amiable chat, then suddenly find yourself wounded by the shrapnel from an exploded conversation.

Daughters often object to remarks that would seem harmless to outsiders, like this one described by a student of mine, Kathryn Ann Harrison:

"Are you going to quarter those tomatoes?" her mother asked as Kathryn was preparing a salad. Stiffening, Kathryn replied, "Well, I was. Is that wrong?"

"No, no," her mother replied. "It's just that personally, I would slice them." Kathryn said tersely, "Fine." But as she sliced the tomatoes, she thought, can't I do anything without my mother letting me know she thinks I should do it some other way?

I'm willing to wager that Kathryn's mother thought she had merely asked a question about a tomato. But Kathryn bristled because she heard the implication, "You don't know what you're doing. I know better."

I'm a linguist. I study how people talk to each other, and how the ways we talk affect our relationships. My books are filled with examples of conversations that I record or recall or that others record for me or report to me. For each example, I begin by explaining the perspective that I understand immediately because I share it: in mother-daughter talk, the daughter's, because I'm a daughter but not a mother. Then I figure out the logic of the other's perspective. Writing this book forced me to look at conversations from my mother's point of view.

I interviewed dozens of women of varied geographic, racial, and cultural backgrounds, and I had informal conversations or e-mail exchanges with countless others. The complaint I heard most often from daughters was, "My mother is always criticizing me." The corresponding complaint from mothers was, "I can't open my mouth. She takes everything as criticism." Both are right, but each sees only her perspective.

One daughter said, for example, "My mother's eyesight is failing, but she can still spot a pimple from across the room." Her mother doesn't realize that her comments—and her scrutiny—make the pimple bigger.

Mothers subject their daughters to a level of scrutiny people usually reserve for themselves. A mother's gaze is like a magnifying glass held between the sun's rays and kindling. It concentrates the rays of imperfection on her daughter's yearning for approval. The result can be a conflagration—whoosh.

This I knew: Because a mother's opinion matters so much, she has enormous power. Her smallest comment—or no comment at all, just a look—can fill a daughter with hurt and consequently anger. But this I learned: Mothers, who have spent decades watching out for their children, often persist in commenting because they can't get their adult children to do what is (they believe) obviously right. Where the daughter sees power, the mother feels powerless. Daughters and mothers, I found, both overestimate the other's power—and underestimate their own.

The power that mothers and daughters hold over each other derives, in part, from their closeness. Every relationship requires a search for the right balance of closeness and distance, but the struggle is especially intense between mothers and daughters. Just about every woman I spoke to used the word *close*, as in "We're very close" or "We're not as close as I'd like (or she'd like) to be."

In addition to the closeness/distance yardstick—and inextricable from it—is a yardstick that measures sameness and difference. Mothers and daughters search for themselves in the other as if hunting for treasure, as if finding sameness affirms who they are. This can be pleasant: After her mother's death, one woman noticed that she wipes down the sink, cuts an onion, and holds a knife just as her mother used to do. She found this comforting because it meant her mother was still with her.

Sameness, however, can also make us cringe. One mother thought she was being particularly supportive when she assured her daughter, "I know what you mean," and described a matching experience of her own. But one day her daughter cut her off: "Stop saying you know because you've had the same experience. You don't know. This is my experience. The world is different now." She felt her mother was denying the uniqueness of her experience—offering too much sameness.

"I sound just like my mother" is usually said with distaste—as is the wry observation, "Mirror mirror on the wall, I am my mother after all."

When visiting my parents a few years ago, I was sitting across from my mother when she asked, "Do you like your hair long?"

I laughed, and she asked what was funny. I explained that in my research, I had come across many examples of mothers who criticize their daughters' hair. "I wasn't criticizing," she said, looking hurt. I let the matter drop. A little later, I asked, "Mom, what do you think of my hair?" Without hesitation, she said, "I think it's a little too long."

Hair is one of what I call the Big Three that mothers and daughters critique (the other two are clothing and weight). Many women I talked to, on hearing the topic of my book, immediately retrieved offending remarks that they had archived, such as, "I'm so glad you're not wearing your hair in that frumpy way anymore"; another had asked, "You did that to your hair on purpose?" Yet another told her daughter, after seeing her on television at an important presidential event, "You needed a haircut."

I would never walk up to a stranger and say, "I think you'd look better if you got your hair out of your eyes," but her mother might feel entitled, if not obligated, to say it, knowing that women are judged by appearance—and that mothers are judged by their daughters' appearance, because daughters represent their mothers to the world. Women must choose hairstyles, like styles of dress, from such a wide range of options, it's inevitable that others—mothers included—will think their choices could be improved. Ironically, mothers are more likely to notice and mention flaws, and their comments are more likely to wound.

But it works both ways. As one mother put it, "My daughters can turn my day black in a millisecond." For one thing, daughters often treat their mothers more callously than they would anyone else. For example, a daughter invited her mother to join a dinner party because a guest had bowed out. But when the guest's plans changed again at the last minute, her daughter simply uninvited her mother. To the daughter, her mother was both readily available and expendable.

There's another way that a mother can be a lightning rod in the storm of family emotions. Many mothers told me that they can sense and absorb their daughters' emotions instantly ("If she feels down, I feel down") and that their daughters can sense theirs. Most told me this to illustrate the closeness they cherish. But daughters sometimes resent the expectation that they have this sixth sense — and act on it.

For example, a woman was driving her mother to the airport following a visit, when her mother said petulantly, "I had to carry my own suitcase to the car." The daughter asked, "Why didn't you tell me your luggage was ready?" Her mother replied, "You knew I was getting ready." If closeness requires you to hear — and obey — something that wasn't even said, it's not surprising that a daughter might crave more distance.

Daughters want their mothers to see and value what they value in themselves; that's why a question that would be harmless in one context can be hurtful in another. For example, a woman said that she told her mother of a successful presentation she had made, and her mother asked, "What did you wear?" The woman exclaimed, in exasperation, "Who cares what I wore?!" In fact, the woman cared. She had given a lot of thought to selecting the right outfit. But her mother's focus on clothing — rather than the content of her talk — seemed to undercut her professional achievement.

Some mothers are ambivalent about their daughters' success because it creates distance: A daughter may take a path her mother can't follow. And mothers can envy daughters who have taken paths their mothers would have liked to take, if given the chance. On the other hand, a mother may seem to devalue her daughter's choices simply because she doesn't understand the life her daughter chose. I think that was the case with my mother and me.

My mother visited me shortly after I had taken a teaching position at Georgetown University, and I was eager to show her my new home and new life. She had disapproved of me during my rebellious youth, and had been distraught when my first marriage ended six years before. Now I was a professor; clearly I had turned out all right. I was sure she'd be proud of me — and she was. When I showed her my office with my name on the door and my publications on the shelf, she seemed pleased and approving.

Then she asked, "Do you think you would have accomplished all this if you had stayed married?" "Absolutely not," I said. "If I'd stayed married, I wouldn't have gone to grad school to get my PhD."

"Well," she replied, "if you'd stayed married you wouldn't have had to." Ouch. With her casual remark, my mother had reduced all I had accomplished to the consolation prize.

I have told this story many times, knowing I could count on listeners to gasp at this proof that my mother belittled my achievements. But now I think she was simply reflecting the world she had grown up in, where there was one and only one measure by which women were judged successful or pitiable: marriage. She probably didn't know what to make of my life, which was so different from any she could have imagined for herself. I don't think she intended to denigrate what I had done and become, but the lens through which she viewed the world could not encompass the one I had chosen. Reframing how I look at it takes the sting out of this memory.

Reframing is often key to dissipating anger. One woman found that this technique could transform holiday visits from painful to pleasurable. For example, while visiting, she showed her mother a new purchase: two pairs of socks, one black and one navy. The next day she wore one pair, and her mother asked, "Are you sure you're not wearing one of each color?" In the past, her mother's question would have set her off, as she wondered, "What kind of incompetent do you think I am?" This time she focused on the caring: Who else would worry about the color of her socks? Looked at this way, the question was touching.

If a daughter can recognize that seeming criticism truly expresses concern, a mother can acknowledge that concern truly implies criticism—and bite her tongue. A woman who told me that this worked for her gave me an example: One day her daughter announced, "I joined Weight Watchers and already lost two pounds." In the past, the mother would have said, "That's great" and added, "You have to keep it up." This time she replied, "That's great"—and stopped there.

Years ago, I was surprised when my mother told me, after I began a letter to her "Dearest Mom," that she had waited her whole life to hear me say that. I thought this peculiar to her until a young woman named Rachael sent me copies of e-mails she had received from her mother. In one, her mother responded to Rachael's effusive Mother's Day card: "Oh, Rachael!!!!! That was so WONDERFUL!!! It almost made me cry. I've waited 25 years, 3 months, and 7 days to hear something like that."

Helping to care for my mother toward the end of her life, and writing this book at the same time, I came to understand the emotion behind these parallel reactions. Caring about someone as much as you care about yourself, and the critical eye that comes with it, are two strands that cannot be separated. Both engender a passion that makes the mother-daughter relationship perilous—and precious.

Reading the Genre

1. In addition to rhetorical analysis, this essay offers a discourse analysis — a study of language use. How does Tannen present the evidence (the specific discourse) that she will analyze? How do you think she chose this evidence — these example of discourse? (See Chapter 22, "Critical Thinking," p. 372, and Chapter 44, "Annotating Sources," p. 487.)

2. Think about Tannen's categories for analysis — such as "yardsticks," "techniques," and topics like the "Big Three." How do these categories allow her to analyze what is said, how it is said, and how people deal with what is said? (See "Use classification," p. 401, and Chapter 27, "Strategies," p. 398.)

3. How does Tannen address the danger of stereotypes in this essay? How does this essay consider race, class, and gender differences? Identify parts of this essay where Tannen considers individuality. (See Chapter 36, "Inclusive and Culturally Sensitive Style," p. 440.)

4. This essay has many quotes. Closely review how Tannen handles these quotations. What kinds of signal words does she use to introduce and summarize quotes? How does her language add meaning to the quotes? (See Chapter 47, "Integrating Sources into Your Work," p. 497.)

5. **WRITING:** Do some fieldwork. Sit at a busy table in a cafeteria, restaurant, or food court, and observe what is said and how. Get permission from everyone you observe, and take detailed notes. Using your notes, make observations about how the people you observed interacted, based on what they said and how they said it. How do people talk about food? How do families interact? How do food workers relate to customers? (See Chapter 42, "Doing Field Research," p. 478.)

ANALYSIS OF AN ADVERTISEMENT   Renowned teacher and cultural critic Stanley Fish has written a number of books, most recently *How to Write a Sentence: And How to Read One* (2011). He has taught at many colleges and universities, and though famous as a literary theorist, he also teaches law. The following article first appeared in the *New York Times* blog The Opinionator in 2008.

New York Times.com

Posted: May 4, 2008, at 4:47 PM
From: Stanley Fish

The Other Car

Six years ago my wife and I traded in two cars for two new-used ones. Twice in a few weeks, one of us drove an old car up a ramp to the cavernous second floor of the dealership and just left it there. Well, not quite, for later we reported to each other the same experience. Each of us walked away, but then looked back, realizing that this familiar friend would be gone from our lives forever and, more poignantly, that we were abandoning a faithful, if increasingly troublesome, retainer.

These feelings were of course irrational. Inanimate objects do not have emotions (Stephen King's Christine and Arthur Clarke's HAL are cautionary exceptions), and it makes no sense to experience guilt at having mistreated them (can you in fact mistreat, except in a technical sense, a machine?), but I am sure that we were not unique in our self-reproaches and misgivings.

Avis Rent-a-Car certainly agrees with me, for that company is now running a series of commercials featuring older cars that are being neglected and fear being discarded in favor of the shiny new and with-it high-tech vehicles available, on demand, for around 45 dollars a day. The genius of the commercials is that they foreground the sexuality that informs the relationship between the car owner and the object of his/her affection.

It is of course a commonplace to note that sex is a staple of automobile advertising, but in most ads the idea is that a car with the right curves will attract the girl with the right curves; the piece of machinery is instrumental to the effort to attain the object of desire. But in the Avis ads, the piece of machinery *is* the object of desire (there is a hint of the human-cyborg union promised at the end of the first *Star Trek* movie), and the very act of desiring it constitutes infidelity.

In three of these ads, infidelity is not a metaphor; it is literally what is going on; and the parallels between car-adultery and husband/wife adultery are delineated with such precision, point for point, that the experience of watching is uncomfortable for anyone who has been on either the giving or receiving end in this age-old scenario.

My favorite (and a favorite on the blogosphere) is entitled "Look Back." It features, in the starring and tragic role, a battered red Saab 900 (I own a black one). The scene opens on a sparsely populated airport parking lot. A well-dressed man is getting himself together in preparation for boarding. He puts some trash on the dashboard, gets out of the car, kicks the door shut (wince!), and puts a coffee cup on the roof.

While all this is happening, the car is speaking in a mournful male voice. It/he says, "So, he's going away with Avis, again. He'll get something with the GPS so that he can find his lattes and his driving range. If that's the way he wants it, fine." But this moment of bravado-dignity doesn't last. As the philandering driver walks away, he pauses and rummages in his pocket, concerned that he may have left something in the old clunker. Hope revives, and the Saab says, "Did he just look back? I think he looked back."

The last shot is of the parking lot, empty except for the forlorn automobile sitting there with an abandoned coffee cup, which it cannot see, on its abandoned "head." Another voice — here's where the traditional commercial kicks in — chimes in cheerfully, "One more reason why Avis should be your other car."

One viewer who rates the ad on the Internet likes it, but complains that "the gender of the voice of the vehicle should be the opposite gender of the owner." No, these ads are indifferent to gender. Lust is lust and betrayal is betrayal, whether the relationship is gay or straight.

In another ad ("Three Days"), the straying partner is a woman who has just returned from a three-day vacation. As she settles into the front seat, the car, a tired-looking, sickly green thing, spots the Avis receipt in her handbag, just as a wife or husband might spy a telltale matchbook from a restaurant in a town neither of them has ever visited. The car voice-over comes on, and it is sarcastic: "Who does she think she's kidding. You know what she's been doing in Miami. You sit here staring at a cement wall, alone, and she has the gall to just show up three days later and pretend that she doesn't smell like 'new car.'" (Another gender reversal: it's usually the woman who smells perfume on the man.) The ad ends with more sarcasm: "She was with a Prius hybrid. Oh, suddenly, she's an environmentalist?"

In the third ad, "Conference," the cuckolded vehicle is a Buick, sitting, iced-over, in a parking lot. A flier for a New Mexico resort is on the seat. The Buick speaks: "He said he had to go to Santa Fe for work. Big Conference. Right! You know what's happening. He's driving around with another car. He'll say he was with a client. He was probably with that red Cadillac CTS from Avis, again." Just before the word *again* (the equivalent in this series of Poe's "nevermore") is intoned, a piece of ice, obviously a tear, falls from the Buick's tail light.

When the hucksterish voice of the company spokesperson chirps, "With dozens of the hottest cars to choose from, there's a reason Avis is your other car," the effect is jarring because the dramatization has been so affecting. We care about these people — I mean cars — and the intrusion of the profit motive is unwelcome.

Strange to say, these are not good ads precisely because they are so good. The point of a commercial is to make the viewer fall in love with the product, in this case the hot cars Avis is pimping. But the viewers of these commercials are more likely to give their affections to the product's victims, for it is from their point of view that the narrative has been presented.

While Avis's intention is, no doubt, to advance its corporate fortunes through these commercials, the image the ads project is less than flattering. Avis comes across as the supplier of temptation, the enabler of seduction, a corporate madame. Its stable of "hot cars" lures men and women to default on their responsibilities, to throw away the tried and true, to surrender to the meretricious glitter of the new. But these wiles are defeated by the sympathy we are made to feel for those who have been harmed by them.

Who would have thought that in the early years of the twenty-first century, advertising would give us a morality tale of such power?

I still wonder whenever I see a car that looks like one of those I have discarded whether it is in fact mine. Forgive me.

Reading the Genre

1. What are the rhetorical appeals that Fish identifies in the advertisements? What is the dominant rhetorical appeal of the ads? How is this appeal made, and what is the desired effect? (See "Consider its use of rhetorical appeals," p. 260.)

2. The online version of this article includes hypertext links to all three of the ads that Fish analyzes. What do these links add to the essay? Do we need to be able to see the advertisements ourselves to understand Fish's analysis? (See "Make the text accessible to readers," p. 263.)

3. **WRITING:** These ads give emotions, thoughts, and voice to inanimate objects. In this way, the advertisements' creators get to imagine an emotional world that doesn't exist—they write monologues for neglected cars. Write a similar monologue from the perspective of the rental car. How does it feel to be shiny and new? How does it feel to be used only temporarily, never committed to or owned? How might you create a monologue from the perspective of a new car that might be used, inversely, to sell used cars?

4. **WRITING:** In groups, in pairs, or on your own, write an advertisement for a new product, using a monologue written from the perspective of the old product it will replace. What would the old product say that might make you desire the new product instead of it?

CULTURAL ANALYSIS   Laurie Fendrich is an artist, an art critic, and a professor of fine arts at Hofstra University. Her articles about both art and art education have been published in the *New York Times* and *ArtNews* magazine, and her drawings and paintings have been exhibited in museums and galleries in the United States and Canada. This article originally appeared in *The Chronicle of Higher Education* in 2008.

The Beauty of the Platitude

LAURIE FENDRICH

Platitudes—hackneyed declarative sentences that assert the truth—are maligned for a reason. Ordinarily found in speech (most people know enough to avoid them in writing), platitudes assert everything—and nothing—all at once. Because they've been uttered so many times previously, and in so many trivial conversations, they tend to arrive stillborn, no more than a clump of meaningless words. Their form, stiff and unbendable by nature, permits little if any wiggle room for play. Just as greetings like "Hello" are conversation-starters, platitudes like, "Life is a process of change," or the one that's most particularly grating to me as an artist—"Art is a form of communication"—are conversation-stoppers.

For the educated, who are on call 24/7 to be as clever and quick-witted as possible, to be caught uttering a platitude is as embarrassing as being caught making a grammatical error. Once it's slipped out of the mouth (by accident, of course), the only recourse is to quickly smother the mortifying moment by piling on a few sentences making it clear the platitude was meant ironically.

Sometimes platitudes are a way for the speaker to assert his or her power over others. For example, "Education is the key"—a particularly popular platitude in today's lexicon—frequently masks a hidden agenda. It doesn't mean, "Education will make you successful in life," as much as it means, "If only you'd come around to my position, you'd be right." To say, "Education is the key" is often no more than code for the command, "Think like I do."

Then there are the platitudes that, although clearly intended on takeoff to mean well, and to comfort the suffering, can accidentally land very roughly.

One of my colleagues, a classicist who teaches courses in etymology, told me he can't stand it when people say, "Death is a part of life." Whenever he hears those words, he says, he always thinks, "No it's not. It's death. That's why it's got its own word." This little platitude is particularly fascinating because it easily can be turned on its head to become, "Life is a part of death." Since only a mortician could possibly take comfort from these words, however, this particular baby never got off the ground.

Not all platitudes are bad. Like WD-40, the handiest and most efficient grease for opening that pesky stuck drawer, some platitudes open stuck conversations. Moreover, they lend a human loveliness, if not a liveliness, to speech. They work beautifully when people can't find any way to end a bad conversation.

For example, a long tale of woe, coming from a nice but bothersome neighbor, can be abruptly and satisfactorily ended with the gentle platitude, "Well, you know, life is a process of growth and change." Repugnant and new-agey as it might seem to an intelligent soul to utter this sentence, it can be a powerful, yet delicate, deus ex machina when applied with care. The conversation instantaneously leaps from wallowing in muck to a happier plane where, not so surprisingly, it all works out for the best.

Reading the Genre

1. How many specific types of platitude does Fendrich identify? How does her identification of types of platitude lend an organization to this short essay? (See "Develop a structure," p. 262, and Chapter 37, "Vigorous, Clear, Economical Style," p. 444.)

2. Write a paragraph about education using as many platitudes as you can think of. Reread this paragraph and find one platitude that seems to say something important. What exactly does this platitude mean, and how does it help you to write about education?

3. Watch an athlete or entertainer being interviewed (online or on television), and identify the platitudes he or she uses. Why would athletes and entertainers use these platitudes? Underneath the platitudes, do you sense that the interviewee really wants to say something different? (See "Take words and images seriously," p. 252.)

4. **WRITING:** Building on question 3, rewrite an interview with a famous athlete or entertainer, replacing platitudes with the statements you believe this star would *really* like to make. Then develop a list of interview questions for this person that might lead the interviewee to give answers that aren't "conversation-stoppers."

MEDIA ANALYSIS John W. Jordan, an associate professor of communication at the University of Wisconsin–Milwaukee, has published many articles on issues concerning the media and contemporary culture. This essay, analyzing the rhetorical techniques of sports announcers and commentators, was originally posted to the cultural studies Web site FlowTV (www.flowtv.org).

FlowTV

Posted: October 27, 2007
From: John W. Jordan

Sports Commentary and the Problem of Television Knowledge

John Frankenheimer's 1998 film, *Ronin,* contains a truly sublime moment that illustrates the raw power of athleticism as an audio/visual spectacle. In one narratively insignificant scene, the camera follows a figure skater, played by former Olympic champion Katarina Witt, as she rehearses her routine. Rachmaninoff plays over the empty stadium's speakers as Witt gracefully strides and leaps across the ice. Audible above the music are the more jarring sounds of her skates grinding into the ice as she gathers energy for her next maneuver. The scene becomes a study in contrasts, and the cumulative effect is enthralling; the violent noise of Witt's skates belying the smooth grace of her movements, the sights and sounds of an exceptional athlete engaged in the perfection of her sport.

I have watched, but never really been a fan of, figure skating on television, and was surprised by my attraction to this scene. What made it so compelling compared to its television counterpart, I later realized, was the conspicuous absence of the omnipresent sports commentators. Their overly enthusiastic discourse on lutzes and Biellmanns, and their pontifications about how a particular jump was "sending a message" to the other competitors, drowned out the beauty of the skating with a flood of technical jargon. The film allowed me to experience the skater on her own terms while television insisted that I engage skating on the commentators' terms. Obviously, sports commentary is not limited to figure skating; all televised sports exhibit similar tendencies for over-discussion. For example, no quarterback can complete a pass without the audience being told what kind of a pass it was by a former quarterback-turned-commentator who then analogizes the play to one from his own playing past. Watching sports on television is less about observing the athletic spectacle of graceful competition than it is witnessing the construction of a televisual compendium of sports knowledge for which the game is merely the backdrop.

Given the ubiquity of sports commentary on television, there must be some perceived purpose behind it. But what might that purpose be? More importantly, what does it say about television sports audiences and the regard in which they are held by television networks that no sporting activity can be conveyed to the public without commentary? Why are television audiences not allowed to experience televised sports with only the natural sounds of the event? Inquiring about the role of commentating in televised sports engages how television creates knowledge and situates audiences with respect to sports. What we find is that television sports commentary turns sports from a visceral spectacle into a technical oration, and for no discernible benefit.

The most generous view of television sports commentary suggests that its purpose is to provide otherwise inaccessible information to viewers in a timely manner so as to enhance their viewing experience. And commentary can and does fulfill this function. With research staff on hand and their own well of experience, television commentators can draw out those interesting bits of history and trivia that, at the right moment in a game, can both inform and entertain their audiences with explanations of obscure rulings or contextualizations of significant plays. But commentators are not held in reserve off-camera until this information is needed; they are thrust into the foreground and seemingly required to speak even when there isn't really much to say. They are the vanguard of the over-verbalizing forces of modern television. But information dissemination is not the same as conveying understanding, and it is the difference between those two that generates the knowledge problematic for television.

Any quality assessment of information is subjective, but one needn't be a cynic to question the instructional value of much of the sports commentary on television. John Madden's teleprompter circles around and discussion of the sweat stains of defensive linemen may be amusing, but certainly stretch the consideration of what counts as sports commentary. Similarly, tennis commentator Mary Carillo's extended stories about Roger Federer's attendance at a New York fashion show, with which she regaled audiences during play at this year's U.S. Open, certainly make it fair to question the information value of such details over more pertinent information about the actual play on the court. Even those who applaud these digressions admit that the commentators are known more for their personalities than for their ability to provide quality information to audiences (e.g., Maffei, 2006). But I'm not describing only those instances when commentary moves from the trivial to the tangential; too much substantive information can also distract the viewers by asking them to give more attention to the commentator than to what is being commented on.

For those "in the know," technical jargon indeed may be neither impenetrable nor detrimental to their viewing enjoyment, much in the same way that casual fans may appreciate Madden's and Carillo's meanderings through sensibility. But television is not a democratic but a tyrannical medium — we can only observe what it gives us. When the commentary is present, we must all accept it or mute it; there can be no in-between. The coverage interpellates the viewer as someone needing this data in order to enjoy the sporting event. Familiarity is rewarded, but not knowledge — the latter is claimed as the medium's province. The audience is positioned as not being knowledgeable enough about the sport to enjoy it on its own terms or with only minimal informational assistance. Consequently, the commentary is a rhetoric of entertainment more than instruction. The unfortunate consequence of this assumption is that commentators believe that any factoid or story they convey — no matter its relation to what is taking place on the field of play — is of interest to the home viewer. Audiences have few means available for escaping or challenging their position in this dynamic. The forceful manner of the medium seldom creates an opportunity for audiences to assess this claim independent of the commentary and its self-established justification.

On a very few occasions, however, a different perspective has been available, and is helpful for situating sports commentary within the politics of the audience's relationship to television. On December 20, 1980, NBC experimented with an "announcerless" broadcast of an NFL game between the New York Jets and the Miami Dolphins. Viewers at home heard only the natural sounds of the game, similar to what the fans in the stadium heard that night. The game earned respectable ratings, but the format was not continued because network executives considered it a "one-time gimmick" (Rubinstein, 2000). A quarter of a century later, following a media lockout by the Canadian Football League, several weeks' worth of announcerless games were broadcast to fans, and their ratings were dramatically higher than games which featured commentary (King Kaufman's, 2005). Fans, it would seem, are both capable of and willing to experience sports on television without the informational assistance of commentators or their anecdotes, and while these instances may be too few to support the claim that viewers prefer announcerless broadcasts, they do warrant additional thought along these lines.

If any event on television could be broadcast without worrying about the audience's ability to understand and appreciate what they are seeing, relying on the audience's existing level of familiarity with the concept, it certainly would be a sports event. And yet, sports are the most heavily commented events on television, to the point where it is not uncommon for there to be more commentators for an event than there are actual competitors on the field. If the explanation for this circumstance is that the audience needs educating, then there are significant issues both with the quality of this education and the manner in which it is provided. Sports commentary on television, in its current form, is not simply too often distracting and trivial; its self-insistence is detrimental to fans' ability to experience the events they have tuned in to watch. The technical knowledge hurled at television sports audiences shifts them from a position of being able to appreciate the athlete's skills at the visceral level to a position where technical understanding is rewarded. Sports commentary as such is television's vestigial organ, the unnecessary remnant that points out how the medium has not completely evolved into the modern media sphere. With the Internet in particular, the mythos of the uninformed audience is challenged. This is not to say that Internet audiences are smarter or better educated about the sports that they are watching, merely that they have access to a wealth of information and are far less reliant on commentators to provide it to them, as countless fan and media sites across the Web demonstrate. The realization needed here by networks is that, when it comes to sports, television is a medium of stimulation much more than it is a medium of information. Perhaps it would be best if television sports coverage were reshaped as a medium of appreciation, where the visceral impact of sport is conveyed more cleanly and directly. In the current media age, commentating is the province of audiences eager to make their own voices heard, not to simply listen to intermediaries who drift increasingly into shouting outrages in an attempt to garner attention and justify their airtime. Television should handle the transmission of the natural sites and sounds of the games and the commentary should be left to the fans to discover and generate for themselves.

References

King Kaufman's sports daily. (2005, August 31). Retrieved September 15, 2007, from
    http://www.salon.com/news/sports/col/kaufman/2005/08/31/wednesday/
Maffei, John. (2006, June 22). These voices don't mince words. *North County Times*.
    Retrieved September 15, 2007, from http://www.nctimes.com/articles/2006/06/23/
    sports/maffei/22_00_516_22_06.txt
Rubinstein, Julian. (2000, September 3). Monday night football's hail Mary. *New York
    Times Magazine*. Retrieved September 15, 2007, from http://www.julianrubinstein
    .com/football.html

Reading the Genre

1. How does Jordan focus his essay on purpose and audience? How are the two connected? What are the purposes of commentary? How does this sports commentary give the audience what they want or need? (See Chapter 21, "Smart Reading," p. 365.)

2. Why might commentators be wrong about the purposes of what they say, and wrong about what their audiences want and need? How important is it for the audience to recognize when a speaker is getting things wrong? (See "Consider the audiences of the text," p. 259, and Chapter 35, "High, Middle, and Low Style," p. 432.)

3. Who is Jordan's audience for this essay? Is he writing for sports fans? If you are a fan, do you feel he speaks to you? If you aren't a fan, what do you think about this article?

4. Jordan ends the essay with a proposal. Does this proposal seem like a reasonable possibility? Is this essay an argument for change in sports commentary, or a critique of something that isn't likely to change? Should the main purpose of this article be to argue or to analyze? (See "Make a difference," p. 256.)

5. **WRITING:** Watch a national sporting event, and then write an analysis of the roles of the different commentators and the on-screen visual information. To prepare, list all the names of the broadcast's voices and faces, and try to define their roles or functions. Then review the commentary the viewer is given through on-screen data, visuals, and interviews; list all the "otherwise inaccessible information" that fans are given; and consider the ways that each element instructs or entertains. Use these notes to construct your short analysis of the sports commentary for this national sporting event. (See "Mine texts for evidence," p. 252.)

ANALYSIS OF AN ADVERTISEMENT   Caroline Leader is a staff writer and senior columns editor for FlowTV (www.flowtv.org). In the following analysis, she scrutinizes the ways men are depicted in advertisements aimed at women.

FlowTV

Posted: June 18, 2010
From: Caroline Leader

Dudes Come Clean: Negotiating a Space for Men in Household Cleaner Commercials

A mother walks into her kitchen, surprised to find her husband and son busy at the dishwasher. The husband explains that he set a record for the most dishes cleaned in one load, 61 dishes and a garlic press, and that the son is trying to beat it. His wife insists that 61 dishes will overcrowd the dishwasher and some dishes will not get clean, to which the husband retorts, "Got clean when I broke the record!" He continues to hover over the son, sabotaging his efforts, as the wife looks on, disgruntled.

Commercial advertising persists as one of the most contentious sites of ideological discussion in mass media. Especially in T.V. commercials, where time constraints limit the range of complex narratives, advertisers must rely on what attracts its target audience. By relying on standard narrative forms, advertisers "reduce production costs, and conform to audience expectations."[1] Some industries, like household cleaning aids, rely on traditional selling points and representations to sell their products. Household cleaner commercials—dish washing aids, laundry detergents, surface cleaners, etc.—generally target women, especially mothers, and portray women in their advertisements. They are stewards in the domestic space, concerned with the cleanliness and health of the home.

Men or male figures do feature in household cleaner ads, but generally to reinforce the woman as the active cleaner. Husbands often appear in the periphery, either separate from the action or a cleaning novice who looks to the wife to find the solution. This tradition has been challenged over time, with commercials that feature men as cleaners (usually inadequate ones[2]). More recent campaigns by prominent brands— Tide and Cascade of Procter & Gamble, and also the emerging "green" company Seventh Generation—complicate the role of the father and husband as participants in the maintenance of the home.

The female homemaker is traditionally the protagonist and often the only character in a household cleaner advertisement. Even when children or husbands are present, it is typically the singular task of the mother to clean spills, wash clothes, and generally maintain the beautiful home. Other family members represent a kind of playful chaos, which only the mother's determination and work ethic can counteract. While the product may lighten her workload, it is still her responsibility to buy, use, and enjoy the products. It is also important that the woman finds contentment in the clean home. At the conclusion of a commercial, we will often see the triumphant and serene smile on the woman's face as she surveys her domestic landscape.

The recent Cascade campaign (2009–present) parodies the traditional household cleaning narrative, upsetting the "natural order" in the home, but does not overthrow the ideologies inherent in the more traditional narrative. The Cascade commercial referred to as "World Record"—noted in the introduction of this paper—follows a traditional narrative arc of a household cleaner commercial; the dishwasher is dirty, we hear about the cleaning power of Cascade and the dishes are cleaned.[3] It is instead the dynamics between the characters that deviate from the norm. Instead of ending in bliss, the ad leaves us with a sense of disorder in the home. First, the introduction of the husband as the cleaner is jarring. Although the wife holds the traditional knowledge—that a "too full" dishwasher will never properly clean the dishes—the husband has learned that the power of Cascade can overcome a full dishwasher. However, because the commercial is comedic, we excuse these abnormal occurrences; the masculine competition in a traditionally domestic site, and more importantly, that Dad is cleaning. Because of the unreliable nature of the family narrative in this commercial, we do not see the father as a steward of the home, and the tradition of the feminine domestic sphere is not challenged.

Another commercial, Tide's "Busted," takes the man's role as cleaner a little further. In the advertisement, the father stains his wife's tablecloth while eating a Sloppy Joe, but gets it out with Tide, thereby avoiding trouble. The wife/mother is absent during the entire process, and the father and sons clean Mom's tablecloth, which provides them with a sort of bonding and learning experience.[4] In the Tide ad, the woman is visually absent and therefore independent of the domestic scene, but we still acknowledge her as the maintainer of cleanliness. It is Mom's tablecloth and she is the one who will be upset to see it ruined. The father, on the other hand, enjoys a carefree, "plate-less" meal with his sons. He may be the one who cleans it up, but he is still representative of chaos and messiness. Just as in the Cascade ad, the husband takes over the role of cleaner, but does not challenge the wife's as the primary arbiter of cleanliness.

Men also tend to appear in household cleaner commercials that do not include the act of cleaning, thereby bypassing the danger of feminization. Many advertisers focus on their brand "story" as opposed to the efficacy of the product. Often referred to as the self-congruity theory, advertisers align the personality of their brands with the perceived personality of their consumers, hoping to establish brand loyalty.[5] My first example brings us back to the Tide brand, with a commercial called "Dad." Like the earlier Tide commercial in this paper, we see another man and his son. The primary shot zooms out from the baby's face, strategically catching the father's wedding ring and eventually widening to a touching scene of the two napping on a clean set of linens. The soft female vocals in the background express a (woman's) need to be with the family, the two we see napping in the shot. The ad may feature male characters, but the ultimate audience is the absent mother, similar to the other Tide ad, "Busted."

Seventh Generation, the eco-conscious household and hygienic care company, also approaches the household cleaner commercial as a chance to express their company mission over the efficiency of the products. Known as "Protect Planet Home," the campaign supports a sustainable, environmentally friendly world.[6] The aired T.V. commercial depicts slices of life from different characters' points of view. Some are men, some are women, but the important element to note is that no one is actively cleaning. The commercial focuses on the responsibility of consumers to buy "green" products and promotes a verdant, harmonious world. For Seventh Generation, the consumer may be male or female, but the duty of cleaning is not addressed and therefore does not place the the man, or anyone, as the primary maintainer of the clean home.

Household cleaner commercials are no longer limited to the product comparison or cause-and-effect narratives that only feature women in the home. As we've seen, men have entered the domestic space as participants in maintaining a clean home. In addition, commercials have stepped outside the act of cleaning and focused more on the lifestyles of their consumer markets. Ultimately, the household cleaner commercial is about family and harmony in the home. As such, it behooves advertisers to maintain a traditional—or at least non-controversial—depiction of the family, focusing on women as the primary consumers and homemakers, and men as their helpers.

Notes

1. Fairclough, N. (2000). Critical analysis of media discourse. In P. Harris & S. Thornham (Eds.), *A media reader, second edition* (pp. 308–325). New York: New York University Press.
2. Elliot, R. et al. (1993). Re-coding gender representations: Women, cleaning products, and advertising's "New Man." *Journal of research in marketing, 10*, 311–324.
3. This video is no longer live. Original content was on the Cascade site at http://www.cascadeclean.com/en_US/video.do#.
4. The race implications of Tide's ad campaign are out of scope for this paper.
5. Mulyanegara, R.C., Tsarenko, Y., & Anderson, A. (2009). The Big Five and brand personality: Investigating the impact of consumer personality on preferences towards particular brand personality. *Journal of brand management, 16* (4), 234–247.
6. This video is no longer available for public consumption. Original content was on the Seventh Generation site at http://www.seventhgeneration.com/protecting-planet-home.

Reading the Genre

1. The first paragraph of this essay is a blow-by-blow account of a single commercial. Why is this kind of description so vitally important in a rhetorical analysis? (See "Make the text accessible to readers," p. 263.)

2. What major rhetorical appeals are evident in the commercials Leader analyzes? (See "Consider its use of rhetorical appeals," p. 260.)

3. How does Leader extend her analysis of advertisements for cleaning products into an argument about gender roles in popular culture? What is that argument? (See "Make a difference," p. 256.)

4. The purpose of a television advertisement is to sell something, not necessarily to be artistic—or intelligent. With this in mind, how is conducting a rhetorical analysis of a television commercial different from doing so with a political speech, a Web site, or an op-ed in the newspaper?

5. **WRITING:** While some television advertisements are worthy of deep analysis, others may not be. List ten commercials you have recently seen and choose one that seems deserving of study. Describe it in detail, and then jot down any inferences your description lets you make about the commercial. If the commercial still seems worthy of close examination, write a rhetorical analysis. If not, choose another commercial and start over. Repeat the process until you find a commercial worth writing about. (See "Choose a text with handles," p. 256.)

Acknowledgments

Natalie Angier. "Almost Before We Spoke, We Swore." Originally published in the *New York Times*. Copyright © 2005 by Natalie Angier. Reprinted by permission of the author.

Jane Austen. Dialogue from *Pride and Prejudice*.

Michael Barone. "The Beautiful People vs. The Dutiful People." From *Real Clear Politics*, January 16, 2006.

Lynda Barry. "Lost and Found." Copyright © 2002 by Lynda Barry. Originally published by Sasquatch Books and used courtesy of Darnansoff, Verrill, Feldman Literary Agents.

Emily Bazelon. "Hitting Bottom: Why America Should Outlaw Spanking." From *Slate*, January 25, 2007. Copyright © 2007. Reprinted by permission.

Sharon Begley. "Learning to Love Climate 'Adaptation.'" From *Newsweek*, December 22, 2007.

Sven Birkerts. "Reading in a Digital Age." From the *American Scholar*, Spring 2010. Reprinted by permission.

Adam Bradley. "Rap Poetry 101." Prologue from *Book of Rhymes: The Poetics of Hip Hop*. Copyright © 2009 Basic Books. Reprinted in the formats of Text and E-book by Copyright Clearance Center.

David R. Brower. "Let the River Run Through It." From *Sierra*, March/April 1997. Copyright © 1997. Reprinted by permission of The Estate of David R. Brower.

Carrie Brownstein. "So I Thought I Could Dance." From *NPR Monitor Mix*, September, 2008. Copyright © 2008. Reprinted by permission of the author.

Robert Bruegmann. Excerpt from "How Sprawl Got a Bad Name." From *American Enterprise*, Volume 17, Issue 5, June 16, 2006, page 6. Copyright © 2006. Reprinted by permission of the author.

Frank Bruni. "Life in the Fast Food Lane." From the *New York Times*, May 24, 2006.

Sara Buttsworth. "CinderBella: *Twilight*, Fairy Tales, and the Twenty-First-Century American Dream." From *Twilight and History* by Nancy Reagin. Copyright © 2010 John Wiley & Sons, Inc.

Nicholas Carr. "Does the Internet Make You Dumber?" From the *Wall Street Journal*, June 5, 2010.

Nicholas Carr. "Is Google Making Us Stupid?" From the *Atlantic Monthly*, July/August 2008. Reprinted by permission.

Michael Chorost. "Rebuilt: How Becoming Part Computer Made Me More Human." Copyright © 2005, Houghton Mifflin Company.

Clive Cook. "John Kenneth Galbraith, Revisited." From *National Journal*, May 15, 2006.

Calvin Coolidge. "Address at the Celebration of the 150th Anniversary of the Declaration of Independence."

Richard Corliss. "*The Last Airbender*: Worst Movie Epic Ever?" From *Time*, July 2, 2010. Reprinted by permission of Time, Inc. in the formats of Text and Other Book via Copyright Clearance Center.

Ann Coulter. "Godless: The Church of Liberalism." Copyright © 2006 Random House, Inc.

Thomas L. Friedman. "A Well of Smiths and Xias." From the *New York Times*, June 7, 2006.

James P. Gannon. "America's Quiet Anger." From the *American Spectator*, March 30, 2010. Reprinted by permission.

Bill Gates and Melinda Gates. "Educating America's Young People for the Global Economy." From *Waiting for "SUPERMAN": How We Can Save America's Failing Public Schools*, by Karl Weber. Copyright © 2010 Karl Weber, Participant Media. Reprinted by permission of Public Affairs, a member of the Perseus Books Group.

Nancy Gibbs. "Cool Running." From *Time*, January 17, 2008. Copyright © 2008. Reprinted in the formats of Text and E-book by Copyright Clearance Center.

Malcolm Gladwell. "Brain Candy." First appeared in the *New Yorker*, May 16, 2005. Copyright © 2005. Reprinted by permission of the author.

Malcolm Gladwell. "Troublemakers." First appeared in the *New Yorker*, February 6, 2005. Copyright © 2005. Reprinted by permission of the author.

Jonah Goldberg. "Global Warming and the Sun." From the *National Review Online*, September 2, 2009.

Owen Good. "*Backbreaker* Review: The Challenger Crashes." From *Kotaku*, June 2, 2010.

Samuel D. Gosling. "Of Mice and Men." From *Psychological Bulletin*, Volume 127, page 46. Copyright © 2001. Reprinted by permission of the author.

Tony Hillerman. "People of Darkness."

Ann Hulbert. "Will Boys Be Boys?" First published in *Slate*, February 1, 2006. Copyright © 2006 by Ann Hulbert. Reprinted with permission of The Wylie Agency, Inc.

John Humbert. "To *Home Design* Magazine."

Charles Isherwood. "Stomping onto Broadway with a Punk Temper Tantrum." From the *New York Times*, April 21, 2010.

Sid Jacobson and Ernie Colón. Excerpt from *The 9/11 Report: A Graphic Adaptation*. Copyright © 2006 by Castlebridge Enterprises, Inc. Reprinted by permission of Hill and Wang, a division of Farrar, Straus and Giroux, LLC.

Gish Jen. "Holden Raises Hell." Reprinted by permission of the publisher from *A New Literary History of America*, edited by Greil Marcus and Werner Sollors, pages 819–23, Cambridge, Mass: The Belknap Press of Harvard University Press. Copyright © 2009 by the President and Fellows of Harvard College.

John W. Jordan. "Sports Commentary and the Problem of Television Knowledge." From *FlowTV*, October 27, 2007. Copyright © 2007. Reprinted by permission of the author.

Michio Kaku. From *Physics of the Impossible: A Scientific Exploration into the World of Phasers, Force Fields, Teleportation and Time Travel*. Copyright © 2008 by Michio Kaku. Used by permission of Doubleday, a division of Random House, Inc.

Jon Katz. "Do Dogs Think?" From *Slate*, October 6, 2005. Copyright © 2005. Reprinted by permission of the author.

Jon Katz. "Train in Vain." From *Slate*, January 14, 2005. Copyright © 2005. Reprinted by permission of the author.

Kevin Kelly. "Reading in a Whole New Way."

John F. Kennedy. "Moon Speech."

Scott Keyes. "Stop Asking Me My Major." From the *Chronicle of Higher Education: Commentary*, January 10, 2010. Reprinted by permission.

Kyu-heong Kim. "Bending the Rules for ESL Writers."

Andrew and Judith Kleinfeld. "Go Ahead, Call Us Cowboys." From the *Wall Street Journal*, July 19, 2004. Copyright © 2004 by Dow Jones & Company, Inc. Reproduced with permission of Dow Jones & Company, Inc. in the formats Other Book and Textbook via Copyright Clearance Center.

Verlyn Klinkenborg. "Further Thoughts of a Novice E-Main Text & Reader." From *Editorial Notebook*, *New York Times*, May 29, 2010.

Wade Lamb. "Plato's *Phaedrus*."

John Lancaster. "The Global Id." From the *London Review of Books,* Volume 28, Number 2, January 2006, page 26.

Laura Layton. "Uranus's Second Ring-Moon System." From *Astronomy,* December 2007, p. 29. Reproduced by permission. Copyright © 2007 Astronomy magazine, Kalmbach Publishing Co.

Donald Lazere. "A Core Curriculum for Civic Literacy." From the *Chronicle Review*, January 31, 2010. Reprinted by permission.

Caroline Leader. "Dudes Come Clean: Negotiating a Space for Men in Household Cleaner Commercials." From *FlowTV*, June 18, 2010. Reprinted by permission of the author.

Elaine Liner. "Dumpster Diving." Copyright © 2006. Reprinted by permission of The Phantom Professor.

Nancy Linn. "Cover Letter."

"The Lost Children of Haiti." From the *New York Times*, September 5, 2006.

Kelli Marshall. "Show Musical Good, Paired Segments Better: *Glee*'s Unevenness Explained." From the academic forum of *FlowTV*, January 16, 2010. Reprinted by permission.

Eileen McDonagh and Laura Pappano. "Time to Change the Rules" in *Playing with the Boys: Why Separate Is Not Equal in Sports*. Copyright © 2008. Reprinted by permission of Oxford University Press, Inc.

Ellen McGrath. "Is Depression Contagious?" From *Psychology Today*, July/August 2003.

Kembrew McLeod. "A Modest Free Market Proposal for Education Reform." From the *Huffington Post,* June 29, 2010. Reprinted by permission of the author.

Shane McNamee. "Synthesis of Luminol."

Kathryn Miles. "Dog Is Our Copilot." From *Ecotone*, Volume 4, Issue 1 & 2, Winter 2008. Reprinted by permission of the author.

Joni Mitchell. WOODSTOCK. Words and Music by JONI MITCHELL. Copyright © 1969 (Renewed) CRAZY CROW MUSIC. All Rights Administered by SONY/ATV MUSIC PUBLISHING, 8 Music Square West, Nashville, TN 37203. All Rights Reserved.

Gabriela Montell. "Do Good Looks Equal Good Evaluations?" From the *Chronicle of Higher Education*, October 15, 2003. Copyright © 2003. Reprinted by permission of The Chronicle of Higher Education.

James Morris. "My Favorite Wasteland." From *Wilson Quarterly*, Autumn 2005. Copyright © 2005. Reprinted by permission of the author.

Tricia Rose. "Hip Hop Causes Violence." From *Hip Hop Wars*. Copyright © 2008 Basic Books. Reprinted in the formats of Text and E-book by Copyright Clearance Center.

Christina Rosen. "The Myth of Multitasking." From the *New Atlantis*, Spring 2008. Reprinted by permission.

Michael Ruse. "Science for Science Teachers." From the *Chronicle of Higher Education*, January 13, 2010.

John Ruszkiewicz. "Annual Big Bend Trip."

"Safe at Any Speed." From the *Wall Street Journal* by Editors, July 7, 2006. Copyright © 2006 by Dow Jones & Company, Inc. Reproduced with permission of Dow Jones & Company, Inc. in the formats Textbook and Other Book via copyright Clearance Center.

Terri Sagastume. "Presentation on Edenlawn Estates."

"Sanity 101." From *USA Today*, January 19, 2006. Reprinted with permission.

Marjane Satrapi. *Persepolis: The Story of a Childhood*, translated by Mattias Ripa and Blake Ferris. Translation copyright © 2003 by L'Association, Paris, France. Used by permission of Pantheon Books, a division of Random House, Inc.

Barrett Seaman. "How Bingeing Became the New College Sport." From *Time*, August 21, 2005. Copyright © 2005. Reprinted by permission of Time, Inc. in the formats of Text and Other Book via Copyright Clearance Center.

David Sedaris. "Advice on What to Write About, When I Was Teaching." From *January*, June 2000. Copyright © 2000 by David Sedaris. Reprinted by permission of Don Congdon Associates, Inc.

David Sedaris. "Me Talk Pretty One Day." From *Me Talk Pretty One Day* by David Sedaris. Copyright © 2000 by David Sedaris. By permission of Little Brown & Company and Don Congdon Associates.

Rob Sheffield. Excerpts from *Love Is a Mix Tape: Life and Loss, One Song at a Time*. Copyright © 2007 by Rob Sheffield. Used by permission of Crown Publishers, a division of Random House, Inc.

Clay Shirky. "Does the Internet Make You Smarter?" From the *Wall Street Journal*, June 4, 2010.

Peter Singer. "'One Person, One Share' of the Atmosphere." From *People and Place*, Volume 1, Issue 2. Copyright © 2009 Peter Singer. Reprinted by permission of the author.

Kelsi Stayart. "Authentic Beauty in Morrison's *The Bluest Eye*."

Bret Stevens. "Just Like Stalingrad." From the *Wall Street Journal*, June 23, 2004.

Seth Stevenson. "Ad Report Card: Can Cougars Sell Cough Drops?" From *Slate.com*. Posted: Monday, November 9, 2009.

Ben Stewart. "Muscle Car Competition." From *Popular Mechanics*, March, 23, 2009.

Peter Suderman. "Don't Fear the E-Main Text & Reader." From *Reason*, March 23, 2010. Reprinted by permission of Reason magazine and reason.com.

Ira Sukrungruang. "Chop Suey." First published in *Brevity 19*. Used by permission of the author.

Andrew Sullivan. "Society Is Dead: We Have Retreated into the iWorld." From *Times Online*, February 20, 2005. Copyright © 2005 by Andrew Sullivan. Reprinted with permission of The Wylie Agency, Inc.

Deborah Tannen. "Oh, Mom. Oh, Honey.: Why Do You Have To Say That?" From the *Washington Post*, January 22, 2006. Adapted from the book *You're Wearing That? Understanding Mothers and Daughters in Conversation*. New York: Random House, 2006; paperback Ballentine. Copyright © 2006 Deborah Tannen. Reprinted by permission of the author.

Beth Teitell. "A Jacket of the People." From the *Boston Globe*, January 28, 2010.

Tyghe Trimble. "The Running Shoe Debate: How Barefoot Runners Are Shaping the Shoe Industry." From *Popular Mechanics*, December 18, 2009.

Barbara Tuchman. Excerpt from *The First Salute: A View of the American Revolution*. Copyright © 1989 Random House, Inc.

Michael Villaverde. "Application Essay for Academic Service Partnership Foundation Internship."

Katelyn Vincent. "Technology Time-out."

Joel Waldfogel. "Short End." From *Slate*, September 1, 2006.

Peter M. Whiteley. Excerpt from "Ties that Bind: Hopi Gift Culture and Its First Encounter with the United States." From *Natural History*, November 2004. Copyright © Natural History Magazine, Inc. 2004. Reprinted by permission.

George Will. "Let Cooler Heads Prevail." From the *Washington Post*, April 2, 2006.

George Will. "An Olympic Ego Trip." From the *Washington Post Op-Ed*, October 6, 2009.

Alex Williams. "Here I Am Taking My Own Picture." From the *New York Times*, February 19, 2006.

Ian R. Williams. "Twilight of the Dorks." From *Salon.com*, October 29, 2003.

Annie Winsett. "Inner *and* Outer Beauty."

Douglas Wolk. "Something to Talk About." From *Spin*, August 2005. Copyright © 2005. Reprinted by permission of the author.

David Wolman. "The Truth about Autism: Scientists Reconsider What They *Think* They Know." From *Wired*, February 25, 2008. Reprinted by permission.

James Woods. "Acts of Devotion." From the *New York Times*, November 28, 2004.

Mike Wirth and Suzanne Cooper-Guasco. "How Our Laws Are Made."

Michael Yon. "An Army of Davids: How Markets and Technology Empower Ordinary People to Beat Big Media, Big Government, and Other Goliaths." Copyright © 2006 Nelson Current.

Cathy Young. "Duke's Sexist Sexual Misconduct Policy." From the *Boston Globe Op-Ed*, April 14, 2010.

Molly Young. "Sweatpants in Paradise." From the *Believer* magazine, September 2010. Reprinted by permission of the author.

Art credits (in order of appearance)

Page 5: Courtesy of StoryCorps.org an independent nonprofit whose mission is to record and collect stories of everyday Americans. www.storycorps.net.

Page 10: *Sun God*, 1983. Concrete structure, paint 413.4 x 177.2 x 118 inches. Stuart Collection, University of California, La Jolla Campus San Diego, California, USA.

Page 14: The Orange County Register/ZUMAPress.com.

Page 17: John J. Ruszkiewicz.

Page 20: Library of Congress, Prints & Photographs.

Page 21: Copyright © Bettmann/CORBIS.

Page 22: Courtesy Sid Darion.

Page 45: (left) The Colbert Report/Comedy Central copyright © 2011. All rights reserved. (right) Copyright © 2011 by Consumers Union of U.S., Inc. Yonkers, NY 10703-1057, a nonprofit organization. Reprinted with permission from the February 2011 issue of *Consumer Reports* for educational purposes only. No commercial use or reproduction permitted. www.ConsumerReports.org.

Pages 47–48: NASA, ESA, and M. Showalter of the SETI Institute. Images courtesy of NASA Hubble site.

Page 50: Natural History Museum/The Image Works.

Page 57: Bob Daemmrich/The Image Works.

Page 65: Hugh Herr MIT Media Lab.

Page 67: Kenneth Garrett/Getty Images.

Page 73: Copyright © Estate of Ben Shahn/Licensed by VAGA, New York, NY. Photo copyright © Smithsonian American Art Museum, Washington, D.C./Art Resource, NY.

Page 74: Utah Department of Public Safety. Creative Director/Art Director: Ryan Anderson; Creative Director/Copywriter: Gary Sume; Account Supervisor: Peggy Lander; Agency: Richter7; Client: Utah Highway Safety Office, Derek Miller.

Page 80: (top) Ghislain & Marie David de Lossy/Getty Images. (bottom) Courtesy of Dr. Susan Farrell.

Page 84: Courtesy of Dr. Susan Farrell.

Page 85: Popperfoto/Getty Images.

Page 87: Jeff Foott/Getty Images.

Page 90: Bodo Marks/dpa/Landov.

Page 94: Courtesy of the Pima County Sheriff's Department.

Page 100: Marcus Maschwitz.

Page 104: Courtesy IfItWereMyHome.com/Copyright © 2011 Google, Europa Technologies, INEGI.

Page 107: Cover Photo from *Rolling Stone*, December, 27, 2010 © Rolling Stone LLC, 2005. All Rights Reserved. Reprinted by Permission.

Page 116: John J. Ruszkiewicz.

Page 118: www.CartoonStock.com.

Page 120: Andy Singer.

Page 122: (left) Photo by: Rob Rich/Everett Collection. (right) Linda Davids/Getty Images.

Page 126: Jeff Kay.

Page 127: Sara Krulwich/NYTimes/Redux Pictures.

Page 136: Courtesy of Insurance Institute for Highway Safety, http://www.iihs.org.

Page 139: Courtesy of the Environmental Protection Agency.

Page 144: Reprinted with permission of THE ONION. Copyright © 2010, by ONION, INC. www.theonion.com.

Page 148: Everett Collection.

Page 154: Mary Evans Picture Library/Everett Collection.

Page 156: Copyright 2006. USA TODAY. Reprinted with permission.

Page 170: Bettmann/Corbis.
Page 171: John Springer Collection/Corbis.
Pages 172–73: Bettmann/Corbis.
Page 177: Courtesy of Denver Water.
Page 181: AP Photo/Israel Leal.
Page 183: By permission of Michael Ramirez and Creators Syndicate, Inc.
Page 185: David Young-Wolff/PhotoEdit.
Page 186: Copyright © Corbis.
Page 191: HKS, Inc.
Page 204: City of New York Department of Parks & Recreation and Courtesy of Plastics.com.
Page 207: Courtesy of Kayla Mohammadi. Reprinted with permission.
Page 217: (top) MIRAMAX/Kobal Collection/Jill Sabella. (bottom) HBO/Courtesy of Everett Collection.
Page 229: United Artist/Photofest.
Page 238: Copyright © 20th Century Fox/Everett Collection.
Pages 246–48: Library of Congress, Prints and Photographs Division, Washington, D.C.
Page 251: Courtesy of Joint Economic Committee.
Page 258: Used by permission of Deutsch, Inc. as agent for National Fluid Milk Processor Promotion Board.
Page 260: United States Navy (Courtesy of Navy Environmental Health Center).
Pages 271–72: Everett Collection.
Page 272: Mary Evans Picture Library/Copyright © 20th Century Fox/Everett Collection.
Page 280: Darren McCollester/Getty Images.
Page 285: Copyright © Bill Aron/PhotoEdit, Inc.
Page 286: Jim Zook/@ Images.com/Corbis.
Page 291: © George Steinmetz/Corbis.
Page 293: NSDAP/The Kobal Collection.
Page 297: Lauren Nicole/Getty Images.
Page 301: Copyright © 1993, Maggie Hopp photographer, Creative Time. Courtesy of Maira Kalman.
Page 303: (top to bottom) Will Vragovic/*St. Petersburg Times*/ ZUMA PRESS; Jackie Ricciardi/ *The Augusta Chronicle*/ ZUMA PRESS; ZUMA PRESS; Lannis Waters/ *The Palm Beach Post*/ZUMA PRESS.
Page 311: DILBERT Copyright © 2010 Scott Adams. Used By permission of UNIVERSAL UCLICK. All rights reserved.
Page 317: (left to right) ABC; Tim Graham/Getty Images; Copyright © Brigette M. Sullivan/PhotoEdit, Inc.
Page 319: Copyright © Gero Breloer/dpa/Corbis.
Page 325: Bob Daemmrich/The Image Works.
Page 327: Copyright © Hulton-Deutsch Collection/Corbis.
Page 331: Lumina Foundation.
Page 337: Copyright © Reuters/Christian Charisius/Landov.

Page 344: (left) A publication of The Council of Science Editors, www.council scienceeditors.org. (right) *The ACS Style Guide: Effective Communication of Scientific Information, Third Edition* edited by Anne M. Coghill and Lorrin R. Garson (2006). By permission of Oxford University Press, Inc.

Page 347: Copyright © Hulton-Deutsch Collection/Corbis.

Pages 350–51: Microsoft.

Page 357: Courtesy of Jacob Bøtter.

Page 358: Library of Congress, Prints and Photographs Division, Washington, D.C.

Page 359: (top to bottom) Allie Goldstein; Sid Darion; Sid Darion.

Page 360: (left) Copyright © 2011 Google. (right) N.J. Schweitzer.

Page 361: (left) http://en.wikipedia.org/wiki/CSI_effect. (right) Courtesy of National Institute of Justice, Department of Justice.

Page 362: NBC/Photofest. Copyright © Copyright NBC.

Page 363: Robert W. Ginn/Age Fotostock/Photolibrary.

Page 365: READ is a registered trademark of the American Library Association. Image courtesy of ALA Graphics, alastore.ala.org.

Page 366: Copyright © Dick Dickinson.

Page 367: Harry Ransom Center, The University of Texas at Austin.

Page 368: (top) Courtesy of Minnesota State University, Mankato. (bottom) Created by Stephen Von Worley.

Page 369: Dan Wesley.

Page 370: U.S. Geological Survey.

Page 376: Copyright © Pat Brynes/The New Yorker Collection/www.cartoonbank.com.

Page 377: Copyright © Ariel Molvig/The New Yorker Collection/www.cartoonbank.com.

Page 381: Courtesy of University of Northern Carolina.

Page 385: Dan Burn-Forti/Getty Images.

Page 386: Library of Congress, Prints and Photographs Division, Washington, D.C.

Page 387: Peter Dazeley/Getty Images.

Page 391: (top to bottom) Copyright © Paramount Pictures/Photofest; Copyright © Paramount Pictures/Everett Collection; Copyright © Universal Pictures/Everett Collection; 20th Century Fox/Photofest.

Page 401: (left) Binghamton University, State University of New York. (right) Oklahoma State University.

Page 404: Adam Zyglis, The Buffalo News (blogs.buffalonews.com/adam-zyglis/).

Page 407: Gusto/Photo Researchers, Inc.

Page 408: Courtesy of PARC, Inc., a Xerox company.

Page 411: Jonathan Alcorn/ZUMA PRESS.

Page 416: Steve Terrill/Corbis.

Page 419: Simone End/Getty Images.

Page 421: Jeffrey Coolidge/Getty Images.

Page 429: (top to bottom) Photofest; Federal Emergency Management Agency/Ready Campaign; Copyright © 2011 Merriam-Webster, Incorporated.

Page 432: (left to right) Michael Siluk/The Image Works; Andy Whale/Getty Images; UPI Photo/Landov.

Page 433: John Cole, www.politicalcartoons.com.

Page 582: Image from Airnow.gov.

Page 583: Allie Goldstein.

Page 584: Inge Druckrey.

Page 585: Source: *Education Pays.* Copyright © 2010 The College Board. www.collegeboard.org. Reproduced with permission.

Page 586: Children's Defense Fund.

Pages 587–88: National Oceanic and Atmospheric Administration and The Department of Commerce.

Page 589: Congressional Budget Office.

Page 590: U.S. Bureau of Labor Statistics.

Page 591: Linda Nakanishi.

Page 592: Science Source/Photo Researchers, Inc.

Page 593: Associated Press/Department of Defense.

Page 594: Courtesy of Anthro Corporation.

Page 595: NASA.

Page 596: Colin Harman, colinharman.com.

Page 597: The Cleveland Plain Dealer.

Page 665: Guido Bergmann/dpa/Landov.

Pages 692 and 694: Jessica Dimmock/VII Network.

Page 740: Chen Xiaowei/Xinhua/Landov.

Page 766: Kelsey S. McNeal/TM and Copyright © 20th Century Fox Film Corp. All rights reserved. Courtesy: Everett Collection.

Page 788: Everett Collection.

Page 913: *Peanuts* Copyright © United Feature Syndicate, Inc.

Page 937: (left to right) *Twilight, Eclipse,* and *Breaking Dawn,* all by Stephenie Meyer, published by Little Brown and Company.

Index

Abbreviations, in literary
    analyses, 230
Abr., APA references and, 551
Abstracts, evaluating sources by,
    482, 484
Academic degrees, capitalization
    of, 604
Academic fair use, 583
Academic reports
    description of, 44
    "Inner *and* Outer Beauty"
      (Winsett), 66–69
Academic Service Partnership Foun-
    dation, 332–34
Act
    legal, MLA works cited
      and, 533
    theatrical, MLA in-text citation
      and, 508
Active verbs, in narratives, 19
Ad hominem attacks, 376
"Ad Report Card: Can Cougars Sell
    Cough Drops?" (Stevenson),
    253–55
Advertisement analyses
    description of, 250
    "Dudes Come Clean: Negotiating
      a Space for Men in House-
      hold Cleaner Commercials"
      (Leader), 988–91
    "Other Car, The" (Fish), 976–78

Advertisements, MLA works
    cited and, 536
Advice, in evaluations, 108
African American, 441, 442
Afterword, MLA works cited
    and, 519
Agenda, for group brainstorming,
    363
Age of audience, arguments and, 84
almost, 627
"Almost Before We Spoke, We Swore"
    (Angier), 811–16
"Ambition Incarnate" (Ramon), 21
"American Gothic" (Parks), 248
American Psychological Association
    documentation. *See* APA
    documentation
"America's Quiet Anger" (Gannon),
    418
Ampersand
    APA in-text citation and,
      543–44
    APA references and, 548,
      550–51
Analogies
    faulty, 378
    in narratives, 19
and, joining independent
    clauses with, 607. *See also*
    Coordinating conjunctions
Angier, Natalie, 811–16

Anglo, 441
Annotated bibliographies
    purpose of thesis in, 396
    summaries for, 493
    understanding and writing,
      296–99
Annotating sources, 487–90
Annotating text
    in rhetorical analyses, 263
    while reading, 367–68
Anonymous authors
    APA in-text citation and, 545
    APA references and, 549
Antecedents
    pronoun/antecedent agreement
      and, 620–21
    pronoun reference and, 622–23
Anthologies
    APA references and, 550–51
    MLA in-text citation of, 507
    MLA works cited and, 515
Anthropology, documentation
    and style guide for, 502
Anthro Technology Furniture, 594
APA documentation, 540–65
    annotated bibliography and,
      297, 299
    capitalizing titles and, 603
    in-text citation and, 540–46
    page formatting in, 562–65
    purpose of, 501

APA documentation (*cont.*)
   references and, 541, 547–61.
     See also References
   verbs of attribution and, 498
Apollo: The Epic Journey to the Moon
   (Reynolds), 413–14
Apostrophes, 605–6
Appositives, pronoun case and, 626
Argument analyses
   description of, 250
   "Mockery of Justice, A" (Nance)
     264–69
Arguments, 72–105
   audience and, 82–84
   "Cool Running" (Gibbs),
     739–41
   deciding to write, 73–74
   "Don't Send in the Clones"
     (Dowd), 736–37
   examples of, 75–78, 95–104
   "Glutton Intolerance"
     (Engber), 758–62
   "Hitting Bottom: Why America
     Should Outlaw Spanking"
     (Bazelon), 743–46
   materials for, 85–87
   purpose and topic of, 79–81
   purpose of thesis in, 396
   structure of, 88–90
   style and design of, 91–94
   "Young, the Rich, and the
     Famous, The: Individualism
     as an American Cultural
     Value" (Natadecha-Sponsel),
     748–56
Arguments for change, "Hitting
   Bottom: Why America Should
   Outlaw Spanking" (Bazelon),
   743–46
Argument to advance a thesis: "Stop
   Asking Me My Major" (Keyes),
   75–78
Aristotle, 85
Army of Davids, An (Reynolds), 18
Art, MLA works cited and, 536
Articles (*a, an, the*), capitalization of
   in titles, 603

Arts reviews
   description of, 106
   "Stomping onto Broadway with a
     Punk Temper Tantrum" (Isher-
     wood), 127–30
as cited in, APA in-text citation
   and, 546
Asian American, 441, 442
"Asian Longhorned Beetles from
   Wood Pallets Invading NYC!"
   (Pallettruth.com), 204
Assertions, thesis as, 394
Assignment, beginning research for,
   466
Assumptions
   in arguments, 80–81
   critical thinking and,
     373–74
   reading to understand,
     487–88, 490
Atheist, 84
Atlases, 589
Audience
   arguments and, 82–84
   assumptions and, 374
   business letters and, 318
   causal analyses and, 147–48
   e-mail and, 312
   evaluating sources for,
     483, 486
   evaluations and, 115–16
   introduction and, 423
   literary analyses and, 218–19
   narratives and, 11–13
   oral reports and, 348
   personal statements and, 331
   proposals and, 184–86
   reports and, 51
   revising for, 453
   rhetorical analyses and, 252, 258,
     259
   writing thesis for, 396–97
Audio podcasts, elements and purpose of, 569, 572
Audio recording, MLA works cited
   and, 535
Austen, Jane, 20

"Authentic Beauty in Morrison's *The
   Bluest Eye*" (Stayart), 209–16
Authorities
   false, 375
   getting help from, 379–83
Authors
   APA in-text citation and,
     540–46
   APA references and, 548, 549–50
   dates for, 229
   ethos and, 260
   evaluating sources by, 483
   literary analyses and, 222
   MLA in-text citation and, 503,
     505–11
   MLA works cited and, 512–13
   rhetorical analyses and, 259

"*Backbreaker* Review: The Challenger
   Crashes" (Kotaku), 115
Background information,
   in introductions, 422
Ballet, MLA works cited and, 535
Bandwagon appeals, 378
Bar graphs, 586–88
Barone, Michael, 404
Barry, Lynda, 654–69
Bazelon, Emily, 743–46
"Beautiful People vs. the Dutiful
   People, The" (Barone), 404
"Beauty of the Platitude, The"
   (Fendrich), 980–81
Begley, Sharon, 687–89
"Bending the Rules for ESL
   Writers" (Kim), 157–64
Bernstein, Leonard, 386
Bias, avoiding in reports, 46, 60
Bible
   MLA in-text citation of, 508
   MLA works cited and, 518
Bibliographies
   evaluating sources by, 483
   purpose of thesis in, 396
   recording while researching, 470
   summaries for, 493
   understanding, 296–99

Biology, documentation and style guide for, 502
Birkerts, Sven, 302
Black, 441, 442
Blind copy (Bcc), email, 312
Block format for business letters, 318
Block quotations
    APA in-text citation and, 543
    MLA in-text citation and, 505
Blogs (Weblogs)
    APA references and, 555
    doing research with, 477
    elements and purpose of, 569, 570
    MLA works cited and, 524–25
Bluebook, The: A Uniform System of Citation, 533
"Blue Marble," 592
Boldface type
    proper use of, 599
    in titles, 429
Book number, MLA in-text citation and, 508
Books
    APA references and, 550–52
    doing research with, 477
    MLA works cited and, 514–19
    online, MLA works cited and, 525
Brackets
    changing grammar of quotation with, 500
    inserting material in quotation with, 499
Bradley, Adam, 899–911
"Brain Candy" (Gladwell), 155–56
Brainstorming
    for narrative topics, 10
    with others, 362–64
    for topic ideas, 356–61
Brower, David R., 184–85, 191
Brown, Jordyn, 123, 131–35
Brownstein, Carrie, 765–67
Bruegmann, Robert, 155
Bruni, Frank, 20
Burchard, Jeremy, 399–400

"Burroughs Family Cabin, Hale County, Alabama" (Evans), 247
Business and management, documentation and style guide for, 502
Business letters
    purpose of thesis in, 396
    understanding and writing, 316–23
but, joining independent clauses with, 607. *See also* Coordinating conjunctions
Buttsworth, Sara, 935–59
Byrnes, Pat, 376

Calendar
    for research, 467
    writer's block and, 385–86
Campus writing center, 379–80, 382–83
Capitalization, 602–04
Capote, Truman, 449
Captioning images, 583
Carr, Nicholas, 302–3, 800–09
Cartoon, MLA works cited and, 536
"Case against Coldplay, The" (Pareles), 413
Causal analyses, 138–75
    "Almost Before We Spoke, We Swore" (Angier), 811–16
    audience and, 147–48
    deciding to write, 139–40
    examples of, 141–43, 157–174
    "Global Warming and the Sun" (Goldberg), 141–43
    "Here I Am Taking My Own Picture" (Williams), 818–21
    "Hip Hop Causes Violence" (Rose), 829–56
    "Is Google Making Us Stupid?" (Carr), 800–09
    materials for, 149–51
    "Pop Psychology" (Postrel), 823–27
    purpose and topic of, 144–46

purpose of thesis in, 396
structure of, 152–54
style and design of, 155–56
"Causal Analysis Proposal: Awkward Atmospheres" (Eades), 471
Cause and effect. *See also* Causal analyses
    faulty, 377–78
    issues of, 139
Causes
    chain of, 154
    various kinds of, 149–51
CD-ROM, MLA works cited and, 531
Cervantes, Adriana, 575
Chain of causes, 154
Chapter number, MLA in-text citation and, 508
Character assassination, 376
Characters, in narratives, 21
Charts
    added to reports, 60
    evaluating sources by, 482
    in lab reports, 345
    MLA works cited and, 536
    reading, 369
"Check. Mate?" (Pequeno), 29–35
Chemistry, documentation and style guide for, 502
"*Cherokee Nation* Decision, The" (Deloria), 717–24
Chiu, Lauren, 305–7
"Chop Suey" (Sukrungruang), 664–66
Chorost, Michael, 19
Chronological order
    reports organized by, 54
    résumés and, 327
"CinderBella: *Twilight*, Fairy Tales, and the Twenty-First-Century American Dream" (Buttsworth), 935–59
Claims
    in causal analyses, 140
    critical thinking and, 372–73
    definition of, 79

Claims (*cont.*)
essay examinations and, 286
in literary analyses, 208, 226
paraphrasing of, 494
qualifying, 80
reading to identify, 487, 488–90
in rhetorical analyses, 252
thesis as, 394
using in arguments, 73–74
Classification
reports organized by, 56
for sorting objects or ideas,
401–02
Climax, in narratives, 16
Clip art, 580
Close reading
description of, 206
"Insanity: Two Women,"
(Sathasivan), 231–37
literary analysis and, 208
CNET Reviews, 117–18
Collection
APA references and, 550–51
MLA works cited and, 515
Collective nouns
pronoun/antecedent agreement
and, 621
subject/verb agreement and, 616
Colón, Ernie, 438–39
Colons
capitalization after, 603
for comma splices and run-ons,
611
MLA in-text citation and,
507, 508
Colors, document design and, 598
Column graphs, 586–88
"Comfort Zone, The" (Franzen),
668–84
Comic strip, MLA works cited
and, 536
Commas
for comma splices and
run-ons, 611
common errors using,
607–09
MLA works cited and, 512, 514

Comma splices, 610–12
Comparison and contrast
in evaluations, 123
outlines and, 410
reports organized by, 57–58
for showing similarities and
differences, 404–05
Compass points, capitalization
of, 604
Compatibility mode, 582
Complete sentences, thesis
as, 393
Compound verbs, commas
and, 609
Computer software
APA references and, 555
for editing digital media, 581
Concert reviews, "Live Review: Lady
Gaga at Staples Center" (Powers), 795–97
Conclusions
on essay examinations, 286
evaluating sources by, 483
understanding and writing,
425–27
Conference proceedings
APA references and, 560
MLA works cited and, 532
Connection, transitional words/
phrases for, 417
Connotative language, avoiding in
reports, 59–60
Consequences
in causal analyses, 153, 154
transitional words/phrases
for, 417
Contractions, apostrophes
in, 606
Contrast
and comparison. *See*
Comparison and contrast
transitional words/phrases
for, 417
Contributing factors, causal analyses
and, 151
"Cool Running" (Gibbs), 739–41
Cooper-Guasco, Suzanne, 70

Coordinating conjunctions
capitalization of in titles, 603
for comma splices and
run-ons, 611
joining independent clauses with,
607
"Coping with Population Aging in
the Industrialized World"
(Tran), 190
Copy (Cc)
for business letters, 319
for e-mails, 312
Copyright infringement, digital me-
dia and, 580, 583
"Core Curriculum for Civic Literacy,
A" (Lazere), 192–97
Corliss, Richard, 443
Corporate authors
APA in-text citation and, 544
APA references and, 549, 560
MLA in-text citation and, 506
MLA works cited and, 513
Correlation, transitional words/
phrases for, 417
Coulter, Ann, 91
Council of Science Editors
documentation, 501
Counterarguments
addressing, 89–90
finding, 87
Course titles, capitalization of, 604
Courtesy copy (Cc), email, 319
Cover letter, 318
"Crash Test" (Insurance Institute for
Highway Safety), 136
Creative commons, 580
Criteria in evaluations
finding and developing,
117–19
purpose of, 108
structure for, 121–22
Critical thinking, 372–78
Criticism, peer editing and,
459–60
Crook, Clive, 124–25
CSE documentation, 501
Cuban American, 441, 442

Cultural analyses
    "Almost Before We Spoke, We
        Swore" (Angier), 811–16
    "Beauty of the Platitude, The"
        (Fendrich), 980–81
    as causal analysis, 138
    example of, 170–74, 238–45,
        270–78
    "Here I Am Taking My Own
        Picture" (Williams), 818–21
    "Holden Raises Hell" (Jen),
        961–67
    "Humankind's Ouroboros"
        (Tankersley), 270–78
    identifying claim of, 226
    as literary analysis, 206
    "Politics of Pants, The" (Freund),
        170–74
    as rhetorical analysis, 250
    "Show Musical Good, Paired Seg-
        ments Better: Glee's Uneven-
        ness Explained" (Marshall),
        238–45
    "Young, the Rich, and the
        Famous, The: Individualism as
        an American Cultural Value"
        (Natadecha-Sponsel), 748–56
Culturally sensitive language, 440–43
Curriculum vitae, 324

Dahlstrom, Marissa, 58, 426, 563–65
Dangling modifiers, 627–28
Dashes
    capitalization after, 603
    for comma splices and run-ons,
        611
Data, in reports, 45–46
Databases
    "How to cite from a database
        (APA)," 558–59
    "How to cite from a database
        (MLA)," 528–29
    online, finding sources in, 472–74
Dates
    APA in-text citation and, 540–46
    APA references and, 548

for authors and literary works, 229
    MLA works cited and, 511
    of publication, evaluating sources
        by, 486
    reports organized by, 54
Days of the week, capitalization of, 604
Decorative fonts, 599
Definitions
    for clarifying meaning, 402–3
    reports organized by, 56–57
Deloria, Philip, 717–24
DeLuca, Geraldine, 914–23
Descriptions, for setting scene,
    398–400
Descriptive reports, "Sweatpants in
    Paradise" (Young), 726–33
Deshpande, Manasi, 228, 421
Design
    of arguments, 91–94
    of causal analyses, 155–56
    of documents, 592–99
    of evaluations, 124–26
    of literary analyses, 228–30
    of narratives, 18–22
    of presentation slides, 352
    of proposals, 190–91
    of reports, 59–60
    of rhetorical analyses, 263
de Vellis, Phil, 576
Developing material. See Sources
"Developmental Disorders:
    Cri Du Chat Syndrome"
    (Dahlstrom), 58, 426, 563–65
de Witt, Johannes, 55
Diagrams, reading, 370
Dialogue, in narratives, 20
Diaz, Jesus, 420
Dickinson, Emily, 231
Dictionary of American
    Biography, 475
Digital media
    elements of, 577–83
    genres in, 581–88
    in literary analyses, 320
    understanding, 568–76
Digital object identifier, APA
    references and, 554

Digital Photography Review, 116
Directions, capitalization of, 604
Disagreements, in synthesis papers,
    302, 309
Discourse analyses, "Oh, Mom. Oh,
    Honey.: Why Do You Have to
    Say That?" (Tannen), 970–74
Display fonts, 599
Dissertations
    APA references and, 560–61
    MLA works cited and, 531
"Distinguishing the Other in Two
    Works by Tolstoy" (Miller),
    538–39
Division of subject
    reports organized by, 55–56
    as strategy of writing, 400–401
.doc/.docx, 582
Doctoral dissertation, APA references
    and, 560–61
Document design, 592–99
"Do Dogs Think?" (Katz), 414–15
"Does the Internet Make You
    Dumber?" (Carr), 302–03
"Does the Internet Make You
    Smarter?" (Shirky), 304
"Dog Is Our Copilot" (Miles),
    703–15
Dogmatism, 376
"Do Good Looks Equal Good
    Evaluations?" (Montell), 422
DOI, APA references and, 554
"Don't Fear the E-Reader"
    (Suderman), 304
"Don't Send in the Clones" (Dowd),
    736–37
Doublings, avoiding, 447
Dowd, Maureen, 90, 736–37
Draft, zero, 386–87
"Dudes Come Clean: Negotiating
    a Space for Men in House-
    hold Cleaner Commercials"
    (Leader), 988–91
"Duke's Sexist Sexual Misconduct
    Policy" (Young), 101–03
DVD, MLA works cited and, 534–35
Dyer, Ezra, 11

Eades, Micah, 471
Earth sciences, documentation and style guide for, 502
Ebert, Roger, 115–16
Economic income/class of audience, arguments and, 83–84
ed. (edition)
  APA references and, 551
  MLA works cited and, 518
ed./eds. (editor)
  APA references and, 550–51
  MLA works cited and, 514, 532
Editing
  by peers, 458–63
  understanding, 453–55
Edition number
  APA references and, 551
  MLA works cited and, 518
Editorials
  "Don't Send in the Clones" (Dowd), 736–37
  MLA works cited and, 521
Editors
  APA references and, 550–51
  MLA works cited and, 514, 532
Edmundson, Mark, 7–9
"Educating America's Young People for the Global Economy" (Gates and Gates), 859–70
Ehlers, Lynn, 95–100
either . . . or, subject/verb agreement and, 616
Either/or choices, 376–77
Electronic sources
  APA in-text citation and, 546
  APA references and, 554–59
  browsing for, 360–61
  finding, 472–77
  MLA works cited and, 524–31
  reliability of, 475–76
  tracking to original sources, 52–53
Ellipsis marks
  APA references and, 549
  changing grammar of quotation with, 500
  shortening quotation with, 498–99

E-mails
  address for, 315
  APA in-text citation and, 545–46
  MLA works cited and, 530
  purpose of thesis in, 396
  understanding and writing, 310–15
Emoticons, 315
Emotional appeals
  in arguments, 87
  logical fallacies and, 377
Emotions, *pathos* and, 260–61
Encyclopedias, doing research with, 477
Engber, Daniel, 758–62
Engineering, documentation and style guide for, 502
Engoron, Nelle, 788–93
Envelopes, for business letters, 323
Epiphany, in narratives, 16
Epstein, Joseph, 19
Equivocations, 378
especially, 627
Essay examinations
  purpose of thesis in, 396
  understanding and writing, 284–89
et al.
  APA in-text citation and, 544
  APA references and, 551
  MLA in-text citation and, 506
  MLA works cited and, 512
Ethnic groups
  capitalization of, 602
  inclusive language and, 441
Ethnicity, of audience, arguments and, 83
Ethos
  in arguments, 82
  rhetorical analyses and, 260
Evaluations, 106–37
  audience and, 115–16
  deciding to write, 107–08
  examples of, 109–12, 127–36
  "Force Fields" (Kaku), 769–81
  "Live Review: Lady Gaga at Staples Center" (Powers), 795–97

materials for, 117–20
  purpose and topic of, 113–14
  purpose of thesis in, 396
  "So I Thought I Could Dance" (Brownstein), 765–67
  structure of, 121–23
  style and design of, 124–26
  "Why *Mad Men* Is Bad for Women" (Engoron), 788–93
  "You, the D.J." (Frere-Jones), 783–86
Evans, Walker, 247
Evasions of truth, 378
even, 627
"Everything Must Go" (Nance), 420
Evidence
  in arguments, 86
  in causal analyses, 140
  critical thinking and, 375
  essay examinations and, 286
  in evaluations, 108, 119–20
  in literary analyses, 208
  logos and, 260, 261
  paraphrasing of, 495
  in position papers, 292
  reading to find, 488, 489–90
  in rhetorical analyses, 252
Examinations, essay
  purpose of thesis in, 396
  understanding and writing, 284–89
Executive dysfunction, 384
Experts
  false, 375
  getting help from, 379–83
  writing evaluations for, 115
Expletives, avoiding, 442–43, 448
Exploratory arguments
  description of, 72
  "Play 'Free Bird'!" (Ehlers), 95–100
Exploratory essays
  description of, 138
  "Hip Hop Causes Violence" (Rose), 829–56
  "What's Really behind the Plunge in Teen Pregnancy?" (Mundy), 165–69

Fact-checking, for reports, 53
Fallacies, logical, 375–78
False authority, appeals to, 375
Fast Food Nation: The Dark Side of the All-American Meal (Schlosser), 366
Faulty analogies, 378
Faulty causality, 377–78
Feasibility of proposal, 178, 188
Feminine pronouns, pronoun/antecedent agreement and, 620–21
Fendrich, Laurie, 980–81
Field research, 478–81
Figures of speech, in narratives, 19
Film
    APA references and, 561
    elements and purpose of, 569, 575
    MLA works cited and, 534–35
Finding materials. *See* Sources
First person, narratives written in, 18
First Salute, The (Tuchman), 423
Fish, Stanley, 976–78
Flow, editing for, 453–54
Flowcharts
    description of, 44
    "How Our Laws Are Made" (Wirth and Cooper-Guasco), 70
    reading, 368–69
Focal point, in evaluations, 122–23
Fonts
    document design and, 598–99
    presentation slides and, 352
for, joining independent clauses with, 607. *See also* Coordinating conjunctions
"Force Fields" (Kaku), 769–81
Foreword, MLA works cited and, 519
Formal analyses, "Rap Poetry 101" (Bradley), 899–911
Formal outline, from informal to, 411
Formal proposal

"Core Curriculum for Civic Literacy, A" (Lazere), 192–97
    description of, 176
Formal style. *See* High style
Foul language, avoiding, 442–43
Fragments, 612–13
Framing source material, 497–98
Franzen, Jonathan, 668–84
Frazier, Kendrick, 58
Freewriting
    for narrative topics, 10
    for topic ideas, 358–59
Frere-Jones, Sasha, 783–86
Freund, Charles Paul, 170–74
Friedman, Thomas L., 92–93, 884–85
"From Mice to Men: What Can We Learn About Personality from Animal Research?" (Gosling), 433
"Further Thoughts of a Novice E-Reader" (Klinkenborg), 303

Gannon, James P., 418
Gates, Bill, 859–70
Gates, Melinda, 859–70
Gender
    of audience, arguments and, 83
    inclusive language and, 440–41
    pronoun/antecedent agreement and, 620–21
Generalizations, hasty, 377
Genres
    choosing, 390–92
    in digital media, 581–88
    introduction style for, 423–24
    literary analyses and, 222, 226
    rhetorical analyses and, 259–60
Geographical areas, capitalization of, 604
Gibbs, Nancy, 739–41
Gladwell, Malcolm, 91–92, 155–56
"Global Warming and the Sun" (Goldberg), 141–43

"Glutton Intolerance" (Engber), 758–62
"Go Ahead, Call Us Cowboys" (Kleinfeld and Kleinfeld), 395
Goals
    for group brainstorming, 363
    writer's block and, 385
Godless: The Church of Liberalism (Coulter), 91
God's Secretaries (Nicolson), 418
Goldberg, Jonah, 141–43
Google
    browsing for ideas with, 360
    using intelligently, 476
Google Maps, 572–74
Google Scholar, 476
Gosling, Sam D., 433
Government authors
    APA in-text citation and, 544
    APA references and, 549, 560
    MLA in-text citation and, 506
    MLA works cited and, 532
Government documents, documentation and style guide for, 502
Grammar
    editing, 455
    in e-mails, 315
    on essay examinations, 289
Grant writing, 177, 184
Graphic narratives
    description of, 4
    "Lost and Found" (Barry), 654–69
    from *Persepolis* (Satrapi), 35–42
Graphics. *See* Visual images
Graphs
    added to reports, 60
    in lab reports, 345
    reading, 369
    using to enhance design, 584–91
Greeting, of business letters, 322
Group author
    APA in-text citation and, 544
    APA references and, 549, 560

Group author (*cont.*)
    MLA in-text citation and, 506
    MLA works cited and, 512–13
Group brainstorming, 362–64

Handwriting, essay examinations
    and, 289
Harman, Colin, 596
Hasty generalizations, 377
Haupt, Alison J., 428
Headings
    document design and, 598
    evaluating sources by, 482, 484
    parallelism in, 630
    for transitions, 419
"Here I Am Taking My Own Picture"
    (Williams), 818–21
hers, apostrophes and, 606
High-resolution images, 582–83
High style
    for essay examinations, 286
    for evaluations, 124
    for literary analyses, 228
    for personal statements, 332
    for proposals, 190
    for reports, 59
    for rhetorical analyses, 263
    understanding and using, 432–39
Hillerman, Tony, 398–99
"Hip Hop Causes Violence" (Rose),
    829–56
his, apostrophes and, 606
his or her, 621
Hispanic, 441, 442
Historical analyses, "Cinder-
    Bella: *Twilight*, Fairy Tales,
    and the Twenty-First-
    Century American Dream"
    (Buttsworth), 935–59
Historical periods, capitalization
    of, 604
History, documentation and style
    guide for, 502
"Hitting Bottom: Why America
    Should Outlaw Spanking"
    (Bazelon), 743–46

"Holden Raises Hell" (Jen), 961–67
Holidays, capitalization of, 604
how, answering in introduction, 422
"How Bingeing Became the New Col-
    lege Sport" (Seaman), 179–81
"How Did the Economy Go
    Bad?" 144
"How Our Laws Are Made" (Wirth
    and Cooper-Guasco), 70
"How Sprawl Got a Bad Name"
    (Bruegmann), 155
"How Teenagers Consume Media"
    (Robson), 303
"How to browse for ideas," 360–61
"How to cite from a book (MLA),"
    516–17
"How to cite from a database (APA),"
    558–59
"How to cite from a database (MLA),"
    528–29
"How to cite from a magazine (MLA),"
    522–23
"How to cite from a Web site (APA),"
    556–57
"How to cite from a Web site (MLA),"
    526–27
"How to insert a comment in a Word
    document," 462–63
"How to insert an image into a Word
    document," 578–79
"How to revise your work," 456–57
"How to use the writing center,"
    382–83
Hulbert, Ann, 89–90
Humanities, documentation and
    style guide for, 502
"Humankind's Ouroboros"
    (Tankersley), 270–78
Humbert, John, 321
Humor, in evaluations, 125
Hunger of Memory (Rodriguez), 23
Hurston, Zora Neale, 467
Hyphens, three, in place of author's
    name, 513
Hypothesis
    introduction and, 421
    for rhetorical analyses, 262

I
    avoiding in reports, 59
    versus *me*, 625
    narratives and, 18
Ideas
    browsing for online, 360–61
    listing, for outlines, 409
"I felt a Funeral, in my Brain" (Dick-
    inson), 231
"'I felt a Funeral, in my Brain': The
    Fragile Comedy of Charles
    Schulz" (DeLuca), 914–23
IfItWereMyHome.com, 104
Illustrations. *See also* Visual images
    added to narratives, 22
    added to reports, 60
    evaluating sources by, 482
Images. *See* Visual images
Implementation of proposal,
    178, 188
Importance, order of, reports
    organized by, 54
Inclusive language, 440–43
"In Defense of Chain Stores"
    (Postrel), 500
Indefinite pronouns
    apostrophes with, 606
    pronoun/antecedent agreement
    and, 621
    subject/verb agreement and, 615,
    616
Indented format for business letters,
    319
Index
    evaluating sources by, 483
    online, finding sources in, 472
Indian, 441
Indication, transitional words/
    phrases for, 417
Infinitives, sentence fragments and,
    613
Infographics
    description of, 44
    design of, 596
    reading, 369
    using to enhance design,
    584–91

Informal outlines
      beginning with, 408
      for organization, 406–7
Informal style, 432, 437–39
Information, in reports, 45–46
Informative reports
      "Dog Is Our Copilot" (Miles),
            703–15
      "Learning to Love Climate
            'Adaptation'" (Begley),
            687–89
      "Truth about Autism, The:
            Scientists Reconsider What
            They *Think* They Know" (Wol-
            man), 691–701
"Inner *and* Outer Beauty" (Winsett),
            66–69
"Insanity: Two Women" (Sathasivan),
            231–37
Inside address, 318
Instructor, getting help from, 379
Insurance Institute for Highway
            Safety, 136
Integrating sources, 497–500
Internet
      doing research with, 477
      finding sources with, 472–77
      locating facts and information
            with, 53
Interviews
      APA in-text citation and, 545–46
      field research from, 479–80
      MLA works cited and, 534
In-text citation
      in APA documentation,
            540–46
      in MLA documentation, 503,
            504–11
Introductions
      of causal analyses, 152–53
      evaluating sources by, 482–485
      MLA works cited and, 519
      understanding and writing,
            420–24
Introductory word group, comma
            after, 607–08
Inuit, 441, 442

Investigative reports
      description of, 44
      "Running Shoe Debate, The"
            (Trimble), 61–65
"iPad Is the Future" (Diaz), 420
Irregular verbs, 618–19
"Is Depression Contagious?"
            (McGrath), 436–37
"Is Google Making Us Stupid?"
            (Carr), 800–09
Isherwood, Charles, 127–30
"Issues and Causes" (Yahoo), 79
Italicizing titles
      in APA references, 548
      correctly, 429
      in MLA works cited, 511
      of published dissertations, 532
Items in series
      commas for, 608
      parallelism and, 630
it is, avoiding, 448
its, apostrophes and, 606

"Jacket of the People, A" (Teitell),
            279–80
Jacobson, Sid, 438–39
Jen, Gish, 961–67
Job application letter, 318
"Jobless on Edge of Pea Field, Impe-
            rial Valley, California" (Lange),
            246
"John Kenneth Galbraith, Revisited"
            (Crook), 124–25
Jordan, John W., 983–86
Journal articles
      APA references and, 552–53, 554
      MLA works cited and, 520
Journalism, documentation and style
            guide for, 502
Journals
      doing research with, 477
      narratives based on, 14
Judgments based on value, in evalua-
            tions, 107
"Just Like Stalingrad" (Stephens),
            395–96

Kaku, Michio, 769–81
Kalman, Tibor, 301
Katz, Jon, 152, 414–15
Kelly, Kevin, 303
Kennedy, John F., 185–86
Keyes, Scott, 75–78
Key points. *See* Main points
Key terms/words
      close repetition of, 446–47
      defining in literary analyses, 218
      defining in position papers, 295
      evaluating sources by, 483
      in titles, 429
      topic idea searches and, 359
Kim, Kyu-heong, 157–64
King, Stephen, 366
Kleinfeld, Andrew, 395
Kleinfeld, Judith, 395
Klinkenborg, Verlyn, 303
Kotaku, 115

Lab reports
      purpose of thesis in, 396
      understanding and writing,
            336–45
Lamb, Wade, 287–88
Lange, Dorothea, 246
Languages, capitalization of, 604
Lanham, Richard, 444
"*Last Airbender, The*: Worst Movie
            Epic Ever?" (Corliss), 443
Law, documentation and style guide
            for, 502
Laws, MLA works cited and, 533
Layton, Laura, 47–48
Lazere, Donald, 192–97
Leader, Caroline, 988–91
Leader, for group brainstorming, 363
"Learning to Love Climate
            'Adaptation'" (Begley), 687–89
Lecture, MLA works cited and, 533
Legal reports, "*Cherokee Nation* Deci-
            sion, The" (Deloria), 717–24
Legal sources, MLA works cited and,
            533
"Let Cooler Heads Prevail" (Will), 93

Letters
    APA in-text citation and, 545–46
    business, 316–23
    MLA works cited and, 533
Letters to editor
    APA references and, 553
    MLA works cited and, 521
"Let the River Run Through It"
    (Brower), 184–85, 191
LexisNexis, 85
Librarians, getting help from, 380
Library
    electronic catalog of, 473
    finding sources at, 472–77
    research guides of, 473–74
Library subscription service, MLA
    works cited and, 525
"Life in the Fast-Food Lane" (Bruni), 20
Line graphs, 586
Line numbers, MLA in-text citation
    and, 508
Linn, Nancy, 320
Listing
    for narrative topics, 10
    parallelism in, 630
    while brainstorming, 357–58
Literacy narratives
    "Comfort Zone, The" (Franzen),
        668–84
    description of, 4
    Me Talk Pretty One Day (Sedaris),
        635–40
    "Strange Tools" (Rodriguez), 23–28
Literary analyses, 206–49
    audience and, 218–19
    "CinderBella: *Twilight*, Fairy Tales,
        and the Twenty-First-Century
        American Dream" (Butts-
        worth), 935–59
    deciding to write, 207–8
    examples of, 209–16, 231–48
    "Holden Raises Hell" (Jen), 961–67
    "'I felt a Funeral, in my Brain':
        The Fragile Comedy of Charles
        Schulz" (DeLuca), 914–23
    materials for, 220–25
    "Peanuts" (Schulz), 913

purpose and topic of, 217
purpose of thesis in, 396
"Rap Poetry 101" (Bradley),
    899–911
structure of, 226–27
style and design of, 228–30
"Woodstock" (Mitchell), 925–26
"Woodstock" (Paglia), 927–33
Literary interpretation
    "Authentic Beauty in Morrison's
        The Bluest Eye" (Stayart)
        209–16,
    description of, 206
Literary resources
    MLA in-text citation of, 508
    online, 225
    in print, 224
Literature review
    paraphrase for, 496
    synthesis paper as, 300
"Live from Baghdad: More Dying"
    (Dowd), 90
Live performance, MLA works cited
    and, 535
"Live Review: Lady Gaga at Staples
    Center" (Powers), 795–97
Location, reports organized by, 56
Locus, James, 429
Logic, *logos* and, 260, 261
Logical fallacies, 375–78
Logic trees, to map topic ideas, 358
Logos, 260, 261
"Looking at the iPad from Two
    Angles" (Pogue), 109–12
"Lost and Found" (Barry), 654–69
"Lost Children of Haiti, The," 434
Lovelady, Cheryl, 229
Low style
    for evaluations, 125
    narratives in, 18
    proper use of, 432, 437–39

Magazine articles
    APA references and, 553
    MLA works cited and, 520, 522–23
    online, MLA works cited and, 530

Magazines, doing research
    with, 477
Magnitude, reports organized
    by, 54
Main points
    paraphrasing of, 494
    summarizing and connecting in
        conclusion, 425–26
Manifesto
    description of, 176
    "Technology Time-out" (Vincent),
        198–203
Mapping topic ideas, 358
Maps
    elements and purpose of, 569,
        572–74
    MLA works cited and, 536
    reading, 371
    using to display information, 589,
        590
Margins, of business letters, 322
Marshall, Kelli, 228, 238–45
Masculine pronouns, pronoun/
    antecedent agreement and,
    620–21
Mashups, elements and purpose of,
    569, 575–76
Materials. *See* Sources
Mathematics, documentation and
    style guide for, 502
McDonagh, Eileen, 872–82
McGrath, Ellen, 436–37
McLeod, Kembrew, 887–90
McNamee, Shane, 339–43, 427
me, versus *I*, 625
Mechanical errors
    editing, 455
    on essay examinations, 289
Media, digital
    elements of, 577–83
    in literary analyses, 230
    understanding, 568–76
Media analyses, "Sports
    Commentary and the
    Problem of Television
    Knowledge" (Jordan), 983–86
Medium. *See* Genres

Memoirs
  "Check. Mate?" (Pequeno), 29–35
  "Chop Suey" (Sukrungruang),
    664–66
  description of, 4
  "Rumblefish" (Sheffield), 642–52
Memories, narrative topics and, 10
Memory prompts, for topic ideas, 359
Me Talk Pretty One Day (Sedaris),
    635–40
Metaphors
  in arguments, 92–93
  in narratives, 19
Metcalfe, Bob, 408
Mexican American, 441, 442
Microsoft Office, Project Gallery in,
    596
Microsoft Word
  "How to insert a comment in a
    Word document," 462–63
  "How to insert an image into a
    Word document," 578–79
Middle style
  for causal analyses, 155–56
  for essay examinations, 286
  for evaluations, 124–25
  for literary analyses, 229
  for narratives, 18
  for personal statements, 332
  proper use of, 432, 435–37
  for proposals, 190–91
  for rhetorical analyses, 263
Miles, Kathryn, 703–15
Miller, Melissa, 13, 538–39
"Mind over Mass Media" (Pinker),
    303
"Mint Snowball" (Nye), 661–62
Misplaced modifiers, 627–28
Misstatements, 378
Mitchell, Joni, 925–26
MLA documentation, 503–39
  annotated bibliography and, 297,
    299
  capitalizing titles and, 603
  in-text citation and, 503, 504–11
  page formatting in, 537–39
  purpose of, 501

verbs of attribution and, 498
works cited and, 504, 510–36. *See
    also* Works cited
*MLA Handbook for Writers of Research
    Papers*, 230, 503
"Mockery of Justice, A" (Nance),
    264–69
Modern Language Association
    documentation. *See* MLA
    documentation
"Modest Free Market Proposal
    for Education Reform, A"
    (McLeod), 887–90
Modified-block format for business
    letters, 318
Modifiers
  capitalization of, 602–03
  misplaced and dangling, 627–28
  in narratives, 20
Mohammadi, Kayla, 207
Molvig, Ariel, 377
Montell, Gabriela, 421–22
Months, capitalization of, 604
"Moon Speech" (Kennedy), 185–86
Morley, John, 73
Morris, James, 118–19
Morris, John, 120
Movies
  APA references and, 561
  elements and purpose of, 569, 575
  MLA works cited and, 534–35
Multivolume works
  APA references and, 551
  MLA in-text citation of, 507
  MLA works cited and, 515
Mundy, Liza, 165–69
"Muscle Car Competition" (Stewart),
    123
Music
  APA in-text citation and, 546
  APA references and, 561
  documentation and style guide
    for, 502
  MLA works cited and, 535
"My Favorite Wasteland" (Morris), 119
"Myth of Multitasking, The" (Rosen),
    304

n. pag., MLA works cited and, 525
Nakanishi, Linda, 591
Name-calling, 376
Nance, Matthew James, 264–69
Nance, Michael, 420
Narratives, 4–43
  audience and, 11–13
  "Chop Suey" (Sukrungruang),
    664–66
  "Comfort Zone, The" (Franzen),
    668–84
  deciding to write, 5–6
  examples of, 7–9, 23–42
  "Lost and Found" (Barry),
    654–69
  materials for, 14–15
  Me Talk Pretty One Day (Sedaris),
    635–40
  "Mint Snowball" (Nye), 661–62
  purpose and topic of, 10
  purpose of thesis in, 396
  "Rumblefish" (Sheffield), 642–52
  structure of, 16–17
  style and design of, 18–22
  synthesis paper as, 308
NASA, 447, 595
Natadecha-Sponsel, Poranee, 748–56
Nation's Report Card, 124
Native American, 441
n.d.
  APA in-text citation and, 542
  APA references and, 548
Necessary cause, 149
Negro, 441
neither . . . nor, subject/verb
    agreement and, 616
Neutrality, of reports, 46, 60
"New Horizons Spacecraft Ready for
    Flight" (NASA), 447
Newspaper articles
  APA references and, 553
  MLA works cited and, 520–21
  online, MLA works cited and, 530
Newspapers
  design of, 596, 597
  doing research with, 477
  on microfilm, 475

News reports
    description of, 44
    "Uranus's Second Ring-Moon
        System" (Layton), 47–48
New York Times, on microfilm, 475
Nicolson, Adam, 418
9/11 Report, The: A Graphic Adaptation
    (Jacobson and Colón), 439
Nonrestrictive elements, commas
    around, 608
Noonan, Peggy, 261
nor, joining independent clauses
    with, 607. *See also* Coordinat-
    ing conjunctions
"No Sex Please, We're Middle Class"
    (Paglia), 148
Note-taking, during group
    brainstorming, 364
Nouns
    avoiding wordiness with, 445–46
    pronouns related to, 418
    specific versus abstract, 444–45
Novels, MLA in-text citation of, 508
Novices, writing evaluations
    for, 116
N.p., MLA works cited and, 524
Number, pronoun/antecedent agree-
    ment and, 620–21
Nursing, documentation and style
    guide for, 502
Nye, Naomi Shihab, 661–62

Objections, critical thinking
    and, 375
Objectivity, in reports, 46, 60
Object pronouns, 624, 625
Objects, specific versus abstract,
    444–45
Observations, from field research,
    480–81
O'Connell, Christine, 428
"Oh, Mom. Oh, Honey.: Why Do You
    Have to Say That?" (Tannen),
    970–74
"Olympic Ego Trip, An" (Will), 261

"'One Person, One Share' of the
    Atmosphere" (Singer), 892–96
Online sources. *See* Electronic
    sources; Internet
only, 627
"On the Juice" (Dyer), 11
Opera, MLA works cited and, 535
or, joining independent clauses with,
    607. *See also* Coordinating
    conjunctions
Oral reports
    purpose of thesis in, 396
    understanding and writing,
        346–52
Order of importance, reports
    organized by, 54
Organization
    revising, 454
    understanding, 406–7
Original work published, APA
    references and, 552
"Other Car, The" (Fish), 976–78
ours, apostrophes and, 606
Outlines
    sketching out, 406–7
    understanding and writing,
        408–11
*Oxford Dictionary of National
    Biography*, 475

Page format
    in APA style, 562–65
    in MLA style, 537–39
Page numbers
    APA in-text citation and, 542
    APA references and, 548
    none, MLA in-text citation
        and, 509
Paglia, Camille, 147–48, 927–33
Palladino, Andrea, 327–28
Pallettruth.com, 204
Palumbi, Stephen R., 428
Pamphlets, MLA works cited
    and, 532
Pappano, Laura, 872–82

para., APA in-text citation
    and, 542
Paragraph numbers, APA in-text cita-
    tion and, 542, 546
Paragraphs, 412–15
Parallelism
    in arguments, 92–93
    common errors in, 629–30
    for connecting ideas, 417–18
Paraphrasing
    basics of, 494–96
    for synthesis papers, 301–02
Pareles, Jon, 412–13
Parentheses
    APA in-text citation and, 540–46
    MLA in-text citation and, 503,
        505–11
Parks, Gordon, 248
Participles, sentence fragments and,
    613
Passive verbs, in narratives, 19
Past participles, of irregular verbs,
    618–19
Past tense
    APA in-text citation and, 540–41
    of irregular verbs, 618–19
Pathos, 260–61
"Patriots, Then and Now" (Noonan),
    261
.pdf, 582
"Peanuts" (Schulz), 913
Peer editing, 458–63
Peer-reviewed articles, 483
Peers, feedback from, 380–81
*People of Chaco: A Canyon and Its
    Culture* (Frazier), 58
People of color, 441, 442
People of Darkness (Hillerman),
    398–99
Pequeno, Miles, 29–35
Periodicals
    APA references and, 552–53
    MLA works cited and, 520–24
    online, APA references and, 554
    online, MLA works cited
        and, 530
Persepolis (Satrapi), 35–42

Personal communication, APA in-text citation and, 545–46
Personal interviews
 APA in-text citation and, 545–46
 field research from, 479–80
 MLA works cited and, 534
Personal letters
 APA in-text citation and, 545–46
 MLA works cited and, 533
Personal narratives, 4. *See also* Narratives
Personal statements
 genre of, 390
 purpose of thesis in, 396
 understanding and writing, 330–35
Photographs
 added to narratives, 22
 added to reports, 60
 editing, 581–82
 as literary text, 206, 246–48
 narratives based on, 14
Pie charts, 588–89
Pinker, Steven, 303
"Pink Floyd Night School, The" (Edmundson), 7–9
Plagiarism, paraphrasing and, 495
"Plagiary, It's Crawling All Over Me" (Epstein), 19
Plain text format, 582
Plan, sketching out, 406–07
"Play 'Free Bird'!" (Ehlers), 95–100
Plays
 citing, 230
 MLA in-text citation of, 508
Plural nouns, forming possessive of, 606
Plural pronouns, pronoun/antecedent agreement and, 620–21
Plural subjects, subject/verb agreement and, 614–15
Podcasts
 APA references and, 555
 elements and purpose of, 569, 572
 MLA works cited and, 531

Poems, MLA in-text citation of, 508
Pogue, David, 109–12
Policy arguments, "Glutton Intolerance" (Engber), 758–62
Political groups, capitalization of, 602
Political science, documentation and style guide for, 502
"Politics of Pants, The" (Freund), 170–74
"Pop Psychology" (Postrel), 823–27
Position, reports organized by, 56
Position papers
 literary analyses as, 229
 purpose of thesis in, 396
 understanding and writing, 290–95
Possession, apostrophes for, 605–06
Possessive pronouns
 apostrophes with, 606
 pronoun case and, 624
Postings, online
 APA references and, 555
 elements and purpose of, 569, 570
 MLA works cited and, 530
Postrel, Virginia, 500, 823–27
PowerPoint, oral reports and, 350–52
Powers, Ann, 795–97
p./pp.
 APA in-text citation and, 542
 APA references and, 548
Praise, peer editing and, 460
Precipitating cause, 150
Preface, MLA works cited and, 519
Premises, critical thinking and, 373–74
Prepositional phrases, avoiding wordiness with, 446
Prepositions, capitalization of in titles, 603
Presentation software, oral reports and, 350–52
Present perfect tense, APA in-text citation and, 540–41
Present tense, literary analysis in, 229

Prezi, 352
Pride and Prejudice (Austen), 20
Primary sources, distinguishing between secondary and, 469–70
Print sources. *See* Sources
Problem, proposals for, 178, 182, 187
Proc. of, MLA works cited and, 532
Procrastination, 384
Product reviews
 description of, 106
 "Looking at the iPad from Two Angles" (Pogue), 109–12
Profiles
 "Cool Running" (Gibbs), 739–41
Project Gallery, 596
Pronoun/antecedent agreement, 620–21
Pronoun case, 624–26
Pronoun reference, 622–23
Pronouns
 inclusive language and, 440
 nouns related to, 418
Proofreading symbols, peer editing and, 460–61
Proper nouns, capitalization of, 602–3
Proposals, 176–205
 audience and, 184–86
 deciding to write, 177–78
 "Educating America's Young People for the Global Economy" (Gates and Gates), 859–70
 examples of, 179–81, 192–204
 materials for, 187–88
 "Modest Free Market Proposal for Education Reform, A" (McLeod), 887–90
 "'One Person, One Share' of the Atmosphere" (Singer), 892–96
 purpose and topic of, 182
 purpose of thesis in, 396
 "Start-Ups, Not Bailouts" (Friedman), 884–85
 structure of, 189

Proposals (*cont.*)
style and design of, 190–91
"Time to Change the Rules"
(McDonagh and Pappano),
872–82
for topic, 470–71
Proposals for change
"Educating America's Young Peo-
ple for the Global Economy"
(Gates and Gates), 859–70
"'One Person, One Share' of the
Atmosphere" (Singer), 892–96
"Start-Ups, Not Bailouts"
(Friedman), 884–85
"Time to Change the Rules"
(McDonagh and Pappano),
872–82
"Protecting What Really Matters"
(McNamee), 427
Proximate cause, 150
Psychology, documentation and style
guide for, 502
Public addresses, MLA works cited
and, 533
Publication information, in MLA
works cited, 511
*Publication Manual of the American
Psychological Association*, 540
Publication year, APA in-text citation
and, 540–46
Publisher, evaluating sources
by, 483
Punctuation
ampersand. *See* Ampersand
apostrophes, 605–6
colons. *See* Colons
commas. *See* Commas
dashes, 603, 611
ellipsis marks. *See* Ellipsis marks
hyphens, 513
parentheses. *See* Parentheses
semicolons. *See* Semicolons
Purpose
of arguments, 79–81
of causal analyses, 144–46
of evaluations, 113–14
of literary analyses, 217

of narratives, 10
of proposals, 182
of reports, 49–50
of rhetorical analyses, 256–57
of written piece, writing thesis for,
396–97

qtd. in, MLA in-text citation and, 509
Questions
for essay, 285
reports to answer, 49
thesis as, 394
Quotation marks
for titles in MLA works cited, 511
for unpublished dissertations, 531
Quotations
for arguments, 86–87
block, APA in-text citation
and, 543
block, MLA in-text citation
and, 505
brackets in, 499
changing grammar of, 500
ellipsis marks in, 498–99
in literary analyses, 230
[sic] in, 500
in synthesis papers, 309
Qur'an
MLA in-text citation of, 508
MLA works cited and, 518

Race
of audience, arguments and, 83
inclusive language and, 441
Radio program, MLA works cited
and, 534
Ramirez, Michael, 183
Ramon, Bettina, 21
"Rap Poetry 101" (Bradley), 899–911
Readers' Guide to Periodical Literature,
475
Reader's reactions, recording, 488–90
Reading, to generate ideas, 365–71
"Reading in a Digital Age" (Birkerts),
302

"Reading in a Whole New Way"
(Kelly), 303
Reasons
critical thinking and, 372–73
logos and, 260, 261
*Rebuilt: How Becoming Part Computer
Made Me More Human*
(Chorost), 19
Rebuttals, in synthesis papers,
302, 309
Reciprocal cause, 150–51
Recommendations, in proposals, 178
Red Tide—Maine (Mohammadi), 207
Refereed articles, 483
Reference books
APA references and, 552
MLA in-text citation of, 507–08
MLA works cited and, 519
References, 541, 547–61
authors and, 548, 549–50
books and, 550–52
electronic sources and, 554–59
labeling as, 297
other sources and, 560–61
periodicals and, 552–53
Reflections
description of, 4
"Mint Snowball" (Nye), 661–62
"Pink Floyd Night School, The"
(Edmundson), 7–9
Refutation arguments
description of, 72
"Duke's Sexist Sexual
Misconduct Policy" (Young),
101–03
Relationships between ideas, outlines
and, 409
Religion
of audience, arguments and, 84
inclusive language and, 441
Religious groups, capitalization of, 602
Remixes, elements and purpose of,
569, 575–76
Remote cause, 150
Repetition
avoiding, 447
for connecting ideas, 417–18

Reports, 44–71
    audience and, 51
    "*Cherokee Nation* Decision, The"
        (Deloria), 717–24
    deciding to write, 45–46
    "Dog Is Our Copilot" (Miles),
        703–15
    examples of, 47–48, 61–70
    "Learning to Love Climate
        'Adaptation'"(Begley),
        687–89
    materials for, 52–53
    purpose and topic of, 49–50
    purpose of thesis in, 396
    structure of, 54–58
    style and design of, 59–60
    "Sweatpants in Paradise" (Young),
        726–33
    "Truth about Autism, The:
        Scientists Reconsider What
        They *Think* They Know"
        (Wolman), 691–701
Republished books, MLA works cited
    and, 518
Research
    beginning, 466–71
    field, 478–81
    library guides to, 473–74
Research studies
    "Bending the Rules for ESL
        Writers" (Kim), 157–64
    description of, 138
Resources, literary
    online, 225
    in print, 224
Respect, avoiding stereotypes and,
    440–43
Restrictive elements, commas
    around, 609
Résumés
    purpose of thesis in, 396
    understanding and writing,
        324–29
Return address, 318
Rev., APA references and, 551
Rev. ed., MLA works cited
    and, 518

Rev. of, MLA works cited and, 524
Reviews
    APA references and, 553
    MLA works cited and, 524
Revising, 452–57
Reynolds, David West, 413–14
Reynolds, Glenn, 18
Rhetorical analyses, 250–81
    audience and, 252, 258, 259
    "Beauty of the Platitude, The"
        (Fendrich), 980–81
    deciding to write, 251–52
    "Dudes Come Clean: Negotiating
        a Space for Men in Household
        Cleaner Commercials"
        (Leader), 988–91
    examples of, 253–55, 264–80
    materials for, 259–61
    "Oh, Mom. Oh, Honey.: Why
        Do You Have to Say That?"
        (Tannen), 970–74
    "Other Car, The" (Fish), 976–78
    purpose and topic of, 256–57
    purpose of thesis in, 396
    "Sports Commentary and
        the Problem of Television
        Knowledge" (Jordan), 983–86
    structure of, 262
    style and design of, 263
Rhetorical appeals, 260–61
Rhetorical questions, in arguments,
    93
Rich text format, 582
Road maps, 589
Robson, Matthew, 303
Rodriguez, Richard, 23–28
Rogers, Heidi, 292–94
Rose, Tricia, 829–56
Rosen, Christine, 304
.rtf, 582
"Rumblefish" (Sheffield), 642–52
"Running Shoe Debate, The: How
        Barefoot Runners Are Shaping
        the Shoe Industry" (Trimble),
        61–65
Run-ons, 610–12
Ruse, Michael, 260

's, 605–06
Sacred works
    MLA in-text citation of, 508
    MLA works cited and, 518
"Safe at Any Speed," 147
Sagastume, Terri, 349–50
Saint Phalle, Niki de, 10
"Sanity 101"
    paraphrasing, 495, 496
    reader's reactions to, 488–90
    summarizing, 491–92
Sans serif fonts, 599
Sarcasm, in evaluations, 125
Sathasivan, Kanaka, 231–37
Satires
    description of, 106
    example of, 131–35
    low style and, 125
Satirical proposals, "Modest
        Free Market Proposal for
        Education Reform,
        A" (McLeod), 887–90
Satrapi, Marjane, 35–42
Scare tactics, 377
Scene number, MLA in-text citation
    and, 508
Schedule
    for research, 467
    writer's block and, 385–86
Schlosser, Eric, 366
Scholarly journal articles. *See* Journal
    articles
Scholarly writing, high style for, 433
Schulz, Charles, 913
"Science for Science Teachers" (Ruse),
    260
Scientific evaluations, "Force Fields"
    (Kaku), 769–81
Scientific writings
    high style for, 433
    lab reports as, 336–45
Scratch outlines
    beginning with, 408
    for organization, 406–7
Seaman, Barrett, 179–81
Searchable titles, 429
Seasons, capitalization of, 604

Secondary sources
    APA in-text citation of, 546
    distinguishing between primary
        and, 469–70
    MLA in-text citation
        of, 509
Section names, APA in-text citation
    and, 542, 546
Sedaris, David, 15, 635–40
Semicolons
    APA in-text citation and, 546
    for comma splices and
        run-ons, 611
    MLA in-text citation and,
        508, 509
Sensational language, avoiding,
    442–43
Sentence fragments, 612–13
Sentimental appeals, 377
Sequence
    of events, reports organized by, 54
    outlines and, 410
    sketching out, 406–7
    transitional words/phrases
        for, 417
Series, items in
    commas for, 608
    parallelism and, 630
Series of books, MLA works cited and,
    515
Serif fonts, 598–99
"Servant and Stranger: Nelly and
    Heathcliff in *Wuthering
    Heights*" (Deshpande), 421
Setting, in narratives, 21
Sexist pronoun usage, 621
Sexual orientation of audience, argu-
    ments and, 83
Shahn, Ben, 73
Sheffield, Rob, 642–52
Shirky, Clay, 304
"Short End" (Waldfogel), 436
"Show Musical Good, Paired
    Segments Better: *Glee*'s
    Unevenness Explained"
    (Marshall), 238–45

[sic], for errors in quotations, 500
Signaling source material, 497–98
Signal verb, 498
Signature, on e-mail, 314
Similes, in narratives, 19
Simple sequence, in narratives, 16
Singer, Peter, 892–96
Singular nouns, forming possessive
    of, 605
Singular pronouns, pronoun/
    antecedent agreement and,
    620–21
Singular subjects, subject/verb
    agreement and, 615
Slide-based presentations,
    350–52
Slippery-slope arguments, 378
Smith, Sara, 6
so, joining independent clauses with,
    607. *See also* Coordinating
    conjunctions
Social satires
    description of, 106
    low style and, 125
    "Word from My Anti-Phone Soap-
        box, A" (Brown), 131–35
"Society and Culture" (Yahoo), 79
"Society Is Dead: We Have Retreated
    into the iWorld" (Sullivan),
    426–27
Sociology, documentation and style
    guide for, 502
Software
    APA references and, 555
    for editing digital media, 581
"So I Thought I Could Dance"
    (Brownstein), 765–67
"Something to Talk About"
    (Wolk), 448
Songs
    APA in-text citation and, 546
    APA references and, 561
Sound recordings
    APA in-text citation and, 546
    APA references and, 561
    MLA works cited and, 535

Sources
    annotated bibliographies and,
        297–98
    annotating, 487–90
    APA documentation of. *See* APA
        documentation
    for arguments, 85–87
    for causal analyses, 149–51
    checking documentation
        of, 486
    documenting styles for, 501–02
    evaluating, 482–86
    for evaluations, 117–20
    finding, 472–77
    integrating into writing, 497–500
    for literary analyses, 220–25
    MLA documentation of. *See* MLA
        documentation
    for narratives, 14–15
    paraphrasing, 494–96
    primary versus secondary, 469–70
    for proposals, 187–88
    recording while researching, 470
    reliability of, 46
    for reports, 52–53
    for rhetorical analyses, 259–61
    summarizing, 491–93
    for synthesis papers, 301–02,
        308–09
Spacing, of business letters, 322
Spatial organization, of reports, 56
Speaking, oral reports and, 346–52
Speech, MLA works cited and, 533
Spelling
    business letters and, 322
    editing, 455
    essay examinations and, 289
    position papers and, 295
    résumés and, 327
Spirituality of audience, arguments
    and, 84
"Sports Commentary and the Prob-
    lem of Television Knowledge"
    (Jordan), 983–86
*Stanford Undergraduate Research Jour-
    nal*, 428–29

"Start-Ups, Not Bailouts" (Friedman), 884–85
Statistics, tables for, 585
Stayart, Kelsi, 209–16
Steinbeck, John, 21
Stephens, Bret, 395–96
Stereotypes, avoiding, 440–43
Stevenson, Seth, 253–55
Stewart, Ben, 123
Stock photography, 580
"Stomping onto Broadway with a Punk Temper Tantrum" (Isherwood), 127–30
"Stop Asking Me My Major" (Keyes), 75–78
Story, synthesis paper as, 308
Story-telling, narratives as, 5
Stowell, Scott, 301
"Strange Tools" (Rodriguez), 23–28
Strategies for writing
  versus genres, 391
  understanding and using, 398–405
Straw men arguments, 378
Structure
  of arguments, 88–90
  of causal analyses, 152–54
  of evaluations, 121–23
  of literary analyses, 226–27
  of narratives, 16–17
  of proposals, 189
  of reports, 54–58
  of rhetorical analyses, 262
Student memoirs
  description of, 4
  example of, 29–35
Style
  of arguments, 91–94
  of causal analyses, 155–56
  of evaluations, 124–26
  of literary analyses, 228–30
  of narratives, 18–22
  of proposals, 190–91
  of reports, 59–60
  of rhetorical analyses, 263
Su, Christine, 429

Subgenres, 390, 391
Subjective pronouns, 624–25
Subject line, of e-mail, 314
Subjects
  comma between verb and, 609
  specific versus abstract, 444–45
Subject/verb agreement, 614–17
Subordinating conjunctions
  for comma splices and run-ons, 611
  for sentence fragments, 612
Subordination, of ideas, outlines and, 409–10
Subtitles, evaluating sources by, 482
Suderman, Peter, 304
Sufficient cause, 149–50
Sukrungruang, Ira, 664–66
Sullivan, Andrew, 426–27
Summarizing
  of main points in conclusion, 425–26
  of sources, 491–93
  for synthesis papers, 301–02
Sun God (Saint Phalle), 10
"Sweatpants in Paradise" (Young), 726–33
Symphony, MLA works cited and, 535
Synonyms, for connecting ideas, 418–19
"Synthesis of Luminol" (McNamee), 339–43
Synthesis papers
  paraphrase for, 496
  purpose of thesis in, 396
  understanding and writing, 300–09

Table of contents, evaluating sources by, 482
Tables
  added to reports, 60
  evaluating sources by, 482
  in lab reports, 345

reading, 369
  using to enhance design, 584–91
Tankersley, J. Reagan, 270–78
Tannen, Deborah, 970–74
Teacher, getting help from, 379
Technology analyses, "Is Google Making Us Stupid?" (Carr), 800–809
Technology reviews, "You, the D.J." (Frere-Jones), 783–86
"Technology Time-out" (Vincent), 198–203
Teitell, Beth, 279–80
Television programs
  APA references and, 561
  MLA works cited and, 534
Television reviews
  "So I Thought I Could Dance" (Brownstein), 765–67
  "Why Mad Men Is Bad for Women" (Engoron), 788–93
Templates, document design and, 596
Tests, essay, 284–89
Text annotation
  in rhetorical analyses, 263
  while reading, 367–68
Textual analyses
  "'I felt a Funeral, in my Brain': The Fragile Comedy of Charles Schulz" (DeLuca), 914–23
  "Peanuts" (Schulz), 913
  "Woodstock" (Mitchell), 925–26
  "Woodstock" (Paglia), 927–33
that
  avoiding, 447
  vague reference of, 623
theirs, apostrophes and, 606
there is/there are, avoiding, 448
Thesis
  argument to advance, 72, 75–78
  for rhetorical analyses, 262
  of synthesis papers, 308
  writing, 393–97

Thesis statement
    as claim, 373
    introduction and, 421
    reports organized by, 58
Thinking critically, 372–78
Third person, reports written in, 59
this, vague reference of, 623
Three-dimensional images, reading,
    371
"Ties That Bind: Hopi Gift Culture
    and Its First Encounter with
    the United States" (Whiteley),
    499
Time management
    essay examinations and, 286
    group brainstorming and, 363
    during oral reports, 348–49
    for research, 467
Time order
    reports organized by, 54
    transitional words/phrases
    for, 417
Times New Roman font, as standard,
    599
"Time to Adapt" (Chiu), 305–7
"Time to Change the Rules" (Mc-
    Donagh and Pappano), 872–82
Titles
    APA in-text citation and, 542
    APA references and, 548
    capitalization of, 603
    evaluating sources by,
        482, 484
    MLA in-text citation and, 506,
        507, 508
    MLA works cited and, 511
    within title, MLA works cited
        and, 519
    for transitions, 419
    understanding and writing,
        428–29
Topics
    of arguments, 79–81
    brainstorming for, 356–61
    of causal analyses, 144–46
    of evaluations, 113–14
    of literary analyses, 217

manageable, finding, 467–68
    of narratives, 10
    proposal for, 470–71
    of proposals, 182
    of reports, 49–50
    of rhetorical analyses, 256–57
"Train in Vain" (Katz), 152
Tran, Thao, 190
Trans.
    APA references and, 552
    MLA works cited and, 518, 519
Transitional words/phrases
    for comma splices and
        run-ons, 611
    commas with, 608
    on essay examinations, 289
    list of common, 417
    organizing with, 407
    revising, 454
    using correctly, 417
Transitions
    understanding and using,
        416–19
    using paragraphs for, 415
Translations
    APA references and, 552
    MLA works cited and,
        518, 519
Tree diagrams, to map topic
    ideas, 358
Trial balloons
    description of, 176
    "How Bingeing Became the New
        College Sport" (Seaman),
        179–81
Trimble, Tyghe, 61–65
"Triumph of the Lens" (Rogers),
    293–94
"Troublemakers" (Gladwell),
    91–92
"Truth about Autism, The: Scientists
    Reconsider
    What They *Think* They Know"
    (Wolman), 691–701
Truth avoidance, 378
Tuchman, Barbara, 423
Tufte, Edward R., 584

Tutorials, visual. *See* Visual tutorials
Tutors, writing center, 379–80
Twain, Mark, 20
"Twilight of the Dorks?" (Williams),
    403
.txt, 582

Underlining titles
    correctly, 429
    in MLA works cited, 511
United States Department of Labor,
    589, 590
"Uranus's Second Ring-Moon
    System" (Layton), 47–48
URL, APA references and, 554–59

Value judgments, in evaluations, 107
"Velo's Crayola Color Chart,
    1903–2010" (Von Worley), 368
Verbs
    of attribution, 498
    avoiding wordiness with, 446
    comma between subject
        and, 609
    compound, commas and, 609
    irregular, 618–19
    subject/verb agreement and,
        614–17
Verse numbers, MLA in-text citation
    and, 508
Videos
    elements and purpose of,
        569, 575
    MLA works cited and, 534–35
    narratives based on, 14
Villaverde, Michael, 333–34
Vincent, Katelyn, 198–203
Visual analyses
    description of, 206
    examples of, 246–48
Visual arguments
    description of, 72
    "Visualizing the BP Oil Spill
        Disaster" (IfItWereMyHome
        .com), 104

Visual comparisons
  description of, 106
  "Crash Test" (Insurance Institute
    for Highway Safety), 136
Visual images
  added to narratives, 22
  added to reports, 60
  in arguments, 87, 94
  in causal analyses, 156
  digital, 577–83
  document design and, 592–99
  evaluations and, 125–26
  inserting in Word documents,
    578–79
  in lab reports, 345
  in literary analyses, 230
  narratives based on, 14
  for oral reports, 350–52
  in proposals, 191
  reading, 368–71
"Visualizing the BP Oil Spill Disaster"
  (IfItWereMyHome
    .com), 104
Visual narratives
  description of, 4
  example of, 35–42
Visual proposals
  "Asian Longhorned Beetles"
    (Pallettruth.com), 204
  description of, 176
Visual text analyses
  description of, 250
  "Jacket of the People, A" (Teitell),
    279–80
Visual tutorials
  "How to browse for ideas,"
    360–61
  "How to cite from a book (MLA),"
    516–17
  "How to cite from a database
    (APA)," 558–59
  "How to cite from a database
    (MLA)," 528–29
  "How to cite from a magazine
    (MLA)," 522–23
  "How to cite from a Web site
    (APA)," 556–57

  "How to cite from a Web site
    (MLA)," 526–27
  "How to insert a comment in
    a Word document,"
    462–63
  "How to insert an image into a
    Word document," 578–79
  "How to revise your work,"
    455–57
  "How to use the writing center,"
    382–83
Volume number
  MLA in-text citation and, 507
  MLA works cited and,
    515, 520
Von Worley, Stephen, 368
"Vote Different" (de Vellis), 576

Waldfogel, Joel, 436
Wall Street Journal, on microfilm, 475
Weblogs. See blogs
Web sites. See also Internet
  APA references and, 554–57
  doing research with, 477
  elements and purpose of,
    569, 570–71
  MLA works cited and, 524–27
"Well of Smiths and Xias, A"
  (Friedman), 92–93
Wells, H. G., 459
West Virginia Surf Report, 126
what, answering in introduction, 422
"What Are We Eating?" 369
What if, causal analyses and,
  144–45
"What's Really behind the Plunge in
  Teen Pregnancy?" (Mundy),
    165–69
when, answering in introduction, 422
where, answering in introduction, 422
which
  avoiding, 447
  vague reference of, 623
White, 441
Whitehead, Alfred North, 358
Whiteley, Peter M., 499

who
  avoiding, 447
  versus whom, 625
whoever, versus whomever,
  625–26
whom, versus who, 625
whomever, versus whoever, 625–26
whose, apostrophes and, 606
why
  answering in introduction, 422
  causal analyses and, 144–45
"Why Mad Men Is Bad for Women"
  (Engoron), 788–93
Wikipedia
  authority of, 486
  browsing for ideas with, 361
  collaboration with others and,
    571–72
  doing research with, 477
Wikis
  APA references and, 555
  elements and purpose of,
    569, 571–72
  MLA works cited and, 531
Will, George, 93, 261
"Will Boys Be Boys?" (Hulbert),
    89–90
Williams, Alex, 818–21
Williams, Ian R., 403
Winsett, Annie, 66–69, 580
Wirth, Mike, 70
Wolk, Douglas, 448
Wolman, David, 691–701
Wood, James, 218
"Woodstock" (Mitchell), 925–26
"Woodstock" (Paglia), 927–33
Word, Microsoft. See Microsoft Word
"Word from My Anti-Phone Soapbox,
  A" (Brown), 131–35
Wordy language, avoiding, 444–49
Work of art, MLA works cited
  and, 536
Works cited, 504, 510–36
  authors in, 512–13
  books in, 514–19
  electronic sources in, 524–31
  labeling as, 297

Works cited (*cont.*)
　other sources in, 531–36
　periodicals in, 520–24
Works consulted, labeling as, 297
Writer's block, 384–87
Writing center
　getting help from, 379–80
　learning to use, 382–83
Writing strategies
　versus genres, 391
　understanding and using,
　　398–405

Yahoo "Issues and Causes"/"Society
　and Culture," 79
yet, joining independent clauses with,
　607. *See also* Coordinating
　conjunctions
Yon, Michael, 18
you, avoiding in reports, 59
"You, the D.J." (Frere-Jones), 783–86
"You have not converted a man
　because you have silenced
　him" (Shahn), 73
Young, Cathy, 101–03

Young, Molly, 726–33
"Young, the Rich, and the Famous,
　The: Individualism as an
　American Cultural Value"
　(Natadecha-Sponsel), 748–56
"Your New Health Care System," 251
yours, apostrophes and, 606

Zero draft, 386–87
Zyglis, Adam, 404